Theory and Practice of Investment Management

Theory and Practice of Investment Management

Edited by Perry Stinson

Clanrye International
www.clanryeinternational.com

Clanrye International,
750 Third Avenue, 9th Floor,
New York, NY 10017, USA

ISBN: 978-1-63240-643-9

Cataloging-in-Publication Data

Theory and practice of investment management / edited by Perry Stinson.
p. cm.
Includes bibliographical references and index.
ISBN 978-1-63240-643-9
1. Portfolio management. 2. Investments. 3. Industrial management. I. Stinson, Perry.
HG4515 .T44 2018
332.6--dc23

For information on all Clanrye International publications
visit our website at www.clanryeinternational.com

CLANRYE INTERNATIONAL

Printed in China.

Contents

Preface

Investment management can be defined as the management of stocks, shares and securities of a company or a financial group in such a way that they achieve the fixed targets as well as the profit margins for investors. This book contains some path-breaking studies in the field of investment management. Topics included in it highlight the significant growth seen in this sector and in the field of asset management and their expertise in the efficient handling of money as well as valuation of present and future assets. Flexibility in dealing with market situations as well as the tendency of investment is a key aspect in this field. This book provides significant information of this discipline to help develop a good understanding of investment management and its related fields. It will help the readers in keeping pace with the rapid changes in this field.

The information shared in this book is based on empirical researches made by veterans in this field of study. The elaborative information provided in this book will help the readers further their scope of knowledge leading to advancements in this field.

Finally, I would like to thank my fellow researchers who gave constructive feedback and my family members who supported me at every step of my research.

Editor

Development of a Health Workforce Monitoring System in Greece

Christos Zilidis[1], Catherine Kastanioti[2], Nikos Polyzos[3, *], John Yfantopoulos[4]

[1]Department of Medical Laboratories, Technological University (TEI) of Thessaly, Larissa, Greece
[2]Department of Businesses' and Organizations' Administration, Technological University (TEI) of Peloponnese, Kalamata, Greece
[3]Department of Social Administration and Political Sciences, Democritus University of Thrace (DUTH), Komotini, Greece
[4]Department of Political Sciences and Public Administration, National (Capodestrian) University of Athens (EKPA), Athens, Greece

Email address:
npolyzos@socadm.duth.gr (N. Polyzos)

Abstract: Background: Recent Greek economic crisis has had a mayor impact on healthcare system. A complete absence of planning human resources leeds to a need for healthcare workforce management tools, among them a re-distribution at a national and regional level following international indicators. Objectives: Aim of the study was to collect data on the current and future demand for and supply of human resources in the Greek health system, to map these data and finally to propose a model for future projections or actions. Methods: Data collected from various sources mainly of Ministry of Education for the supply and Ministry of Health for the demand. These data were aggregated in order tables to be standardized for future standard collection by these Ministries and the National Statistical Authority. The proposed model constitutes a combination between a stock-and-flow model and a workforce-to-population ratio approach. Results: Greece insists to an obvious oversupply of health professionals (over 7.000 annually), while demand can not absorb over 20-25% of these staff. Due to economic crisis, there is an urgent need for reinforcing especially public sector in terms of new hires mainly of nursing and midwifery staff, and re-distribution of all. Conclusions: The main results indicate that health policy makers could reach an optimal matching between future supply of and demand for healthcare workforce by adjusting the flexible supply components. This presupposes an accurate and stable system of data collection. On the demand side, it is also important to collect demographics and other related data that are more indicative of health needs.

Keywords: Human Resources, Education, Health, Demand, Supply, Planning, Indicators, Projections

1. Introduction

Health sector is a highly labor intensive production process and it is one of the most significant sectors of the European Economy. According to Eurostat (1), in 2010, there were around 17.1 million Europeans employed in the health sector which accounted for 8% of the total labor force. During the 2000 - 2010 period the number of jobs in the health sector increased by 21% (2-5). The distribution across countries, taking the mobility into account, especially in Europe (6-8), is another special issue to be examined.

There is a growing interest in the development of methodologies for integrated approaches to planning and forecasting of health workforce, with the overall objective to develop effective interventions to better match demand and supply of health professionals (9-10). Towards that, a multispectral approach is needed in forecasting future demand and supply of human resources in the health sector, along with forecasting demographic and population's health needs in conjunction with technological changes, resource constraints and health expenditure restrictions (11).

In an economic crisis environment, there is an additional need to redefine health objectives and priorities in order to tackle the problems of health inequalities and the inefficiencies in the production and distribution of health services (12).

GIZ (German NGO) and DUTH (Democritus University of Thrace) were contracted in 2014 in order to study factors that are related to current and future demand for and supply of human resources in the Greek health system. This study finished in March 2015. Responsible for GIZ was Dr. Franz non Roenne (and colleagues) and for DUTH Prof. Nikos

Polyzos (and a scientific team). This study aims to develop a methodology to monitor workforce developments in health sector in Greece, which can be used in health manpower planning, in the frame of the restrictions coming from the long-standing economic crisis. Models from other countries and organizations were examined (13-14), especially WHO templates etc. (15-16). Data mainly from the Greek Ministries of Education and Health were collected and aggregated.

2. Methods

The study focus on finding the sources of HRH information based on "stock and flow" approach (figute 1).

Figure 1. *Process of workforce flow in the health sector.*

This research included the first attempt to systematically identify a. the national system tracking at the same time graduates of health professions education programmes, international immigration of workers with health-related skills or exits due to career change, b. the stock and distribution of health workforce in Greek NHS, through gathering and synthesizing data from different available sources and including flows into and out of the health manpower. HRH data mapping template (17, WHO, version 2.2) tool was deemed most appropriate and was primarily administered through email exchanges with the above sources. Follow-up telephone interviews were then conducted to complete the template.

To meet the aim of the study, three human resources management tools were developed:

a. A classification of health professions

b. A set of Health Manpower Indicators

c. An identification of a set of data sources needed.

Health Professions Classification. The first step in developing a health workforce monitoring system is to establish a classification of health professions. In order to ensure comparability, the classification of health professions should take into consideration internationally standardized classifications for social and economic statistics, such as (a) the ILO's *International Standard Classification of Occupations 2008 (ISCO-08)*, and (b) the United Nation's *International Standard Classification of Education 2011 (ISCED)*. The classifications were appropriately modified and adapted to meet the detailed needs of health manpower planning and to adapt them to the national specificities on health profession profiles. A Classification of Health Professions was developed (see below).

1. Physicians
1.1. General Practitioners
1.2. Specialist physicians of all other medical specialties (excluding General Practitioners)
1.3. Trainee physicians of all specialties
1.4. Physicians without specialty
1.5. Dentists
2. Nursing workforce
2.1. Qualified (registered) nurses
2.2. Qualified (registered) midwives
2.3. Assistant nurses
2.4. Ambulance crews & bearers
2.5. Other auxiliary nursing personnel
3. Public Health workforce
3.1. Health visitors and community nurses
3.2. Public Health Inspectors
3.3. Veterinarians working in health sector per
3.4. Other public health professions
4. Long-term care and rehabilitation workforce
4.1. Physiotherapists
4.2. Occupational therapists
4.3. Speech therapists
4.4. Estheticians
4.5. Assistant Physiotherapists
4.6. Other auxiliary rehabilitation personnel
4.7. Home-care personal assistants and domestic assistants
5. Other scientific health professions
5.1. Pharmacists
5.2. Biochemists
5.3. Biologists and Molecular Biologists
5.4. Dieticians
5.5. Psychologists
5.6. Assistants of 5.1 – 5.5 professions
6. Technological heath workforce
6.1. Higher education technological personnel
6.2. Medical Laboratory Technicians
6.3. X-ray Laboratory Technicians
6.4. Medical Equipment Technicians
6.5. Dental Technicians
6.6. Opticians
6.7. Medical Laboratory Technician Assistants
6.8. Craftsmen and maintenance workers
6.9. Drivers
6.10 Other technical personnel
7. Administrative workforce
7.1. Health and Welfare Units Management
7.2. Management and Economics
7.3. Health Informatics
7.4. Office Assistants and Secretaries
7.5. Housekeeping and maintenance personnel (except dieticians)
7.6. Security personnel
7.7. Other auxiliary personnel
8. Health industry workforce
8.1. Pharmaceutical production and trading industry workforce
8.2. Medical supplies production and trading industry workforce
8.3. Medical laboratory reagents production and trading industry workforce
8.4. Medical equipment production, maintenance and trading industry workforce
8.5. Health information systems production and trading

8.6. Medical tourism industry workforce
8.7. Private sector health insurance workforce
8.8. Private sector health training workforce
8.9. Other health industry workforce

Health Workforce Indicators. To map human resources in Greek health sector, a set of Health Workforce Indicators was developed. This set of indicators follows a "stock and flow" model, which can describe both inflow and outflow of the health workforce market. The set includes 5 categories of indicators: (a) Health workforce production indicators, (b) Population-based indicators, (c) Health workforce distribution indicators, (d) workforce efficiency indicators and (e) Outflow indicators.

Health workforce production indicators describe the workforce inflow to the total health system. The workforce inflow includes (i) the domestic production of health professions and (ii) the health professions inflow from other counties, both of Greek and non-Greek origin people.

Population-based indicators measure the availability of health personnel per 100,000 people. They provide: (i) a measurement of quantitative adequacy of the various categories of health workforce, (ii) a set of indices to investigate inequalities in human resources availability and distribution, as well as inequalities in health service provision and finally, (iii) a set of indicators to evaluate efficiency of human resources.

Health workforce distribution indicators describe the distribution of health workers into the health sector, in terms of proportions and ratios of health personnel in the various parts of health sector. They provide tools to examine inadequacies and inequalities in health services staffing, and help in prioritizing needs.

Workforce efficiency indicators measure the health services output in relation to personnel. They provide a measure of workforce productivity and efficiency of human resources.

Outflow indicators describe the rate of personnel withdrawals from the health sector.

Data sources. We conducted Ministry of Health and other government agencies with HRH roles (e.g. Ministry of Education, Labour, Administrative Reform and e-Government) and Hellenic Statistical Authority (EL.STAT.), supported by Ministry of Health, in order to combine different types of information scattered across different sources. Data sources identification follows the same "stock and flow" model and includes sources that provide data needed for each one category of indicators. The model was tested on mapping health workforce facts of Greece of 2013, as well as in forecasting short-term personnel needs.

3. Results

Inflow indicators. Base on data collected from the sources reported, indicators describing the dynamics of workforce inflow in each professional category were calculated.

Table 1 demonstrates the total production of healthcare professions from both Greek and foreign Universities in 2013. The greatest workforce production is related to the medical profession (10.8/100,000) closely followed by Psychologist profession (10.7/100.000). On the other hand, nurse production shows a rate of only 1.9/100,000, which is lower compared to other developed countries (18). The average annual production of Medical Doctors corresponds to 1.7% of the existing "stock" of respective workforce whereas university level nurse production reaches 6.5%, pharmacists production 3.1% and dentists 1.5%. A lack of sufficient data on existing "stock" of workforce of other professions raises obstacles in calculating the respective indicator of other health related professions. However, substitution of doctors by nurses should be examined, mainly in Primary Health Care (19), especially during this crisis (20).

Table 2 shows the proportion of health professionals' production abroad to overall inflows that reaches 20.7% in pharmacists, 15.8% in dentists, 12.7% in Medical Doctors, but only 3.9% in nurses.

Table 1. *Health professionals' production from domestic universities per 100,000 population, 2013.*

Health profession	Graduates	per 100,000 population	Number of new professionals per 100 existing
Medicine	1,165	10.8	1.7
Nursing	204	1.9	6.5
Dentistry	209	1.9	1.5
Pharmacy	352	3.3	3.1
Biology - Biotechnology	504	4.7	...
Nutrition and Dietetics	36	0.3	...
Psychology	1,153	10.7	...
Veterinary Medicine	152	1.4	...
Midwifery	132	1.2	...
Nursing	1,247	11.5	3.4
Dental Technology	65	0.6	...
Aesthetics and Cosmetology	193	1.8	...
Medical Instrument Technology	75	0.7	...
Medical Laboratories	278	2.6	...
Nutrition and Dietetics	157	1.5	...
Optics and Optometry	102	0.9	...
Physiotherapy	428	4.0	7.0
Radiology	43	0.4	...

Health profession	Graduates	per 100,000 population	Number of new professionals per 100 existing
Speech & Language Therapy	249	2.3	…
Ocupational Therapy	74	0.7	…
Public Health	132	1.2	…
Social work	340	3.1	…
Health Management	242	2.2	…
Assistant midwifery	6	0.1	…
Assistant nursing	875	8.1	12.1
Other dental care services	32	0.3	…
Assistant Physiotherapist	349	3.2	…
Medical laboratory technology	293	2.7	…
Pharmacy and Cosmetic Technology	216	2.0	…
Medical Information technology	20	0.2	…

Table 2. *Health professionals' production from Greek and foreign universities, 2013.*

Health Profession	Domestic Universities	Foreign Universities	TOTAL	Foreign Universities (%)
Medical Doctors	1,017	148	1,165	12.7%
Dentists	176	33	209	15.8%
Pharmacists	279	73	352	20.7%
Qualified nurses	196	8	204	3.9%

Table 3. *Population based indicators of selective health professions by region, 2013.*

Regions	Medical Doctors per 100,000	Dentists per 100,000	Pharmacists per 100,000	Physio- therapists per 100,000
Attiki	892.9	179.2	110.8	72.3
Sterea Ellada	311.5	88.4	92.6	43.8
Dytiki Ellada	553.8	96.4	97.4	46.9
Peloponnisos	391.2	99.5	97.6	40.8
Thessaly	480.8	111.8	110.5	42.4
Ipeiros	599.7	102.4	98.3	39.5
East Macedonia & Thraki	482.6	88.5	92.1	55.9
Central Macedonia	602.6	126.4	112.9	56.0
West Macedonia	301.7	95.5	108.6	38.8
Ionia Nisia	409.4	81.3	89.5	53.9
North Aigaio	399.0	80.3	99.9	41.7
South Aigaio	367.3	96.4	95.5	34.3
Kriti	618.2	105.1	84.6	45.9
Total	640.0	131.4	104.6	56.4

Population based indicators and regional distribution of health workforce. Table 3 reports the density of four selective health professions per 100,000 by region. Region of Attica (region of Athens) shows the largest numbers in almost all cases. In three of four professions, Attica is the only region above the national average. Regarding Pharmacists, Central and West Macedonia as well as Thessaly are also above the national average. Table 4 shows a large concentration of medical professions in the Greater Athens area.

Table 4. *Medical Doctors per 100.000 population, by medical specialty and region (2013).*

Region	Medical Doctors per 100,000	Generalist Medical Doctors per 100,000	Specialist Medical Doctors per 100,000	Doctors without a medical specialty per 100,000	Dentists per 100,000
Attiki	892.9	9.7	514.5	368.7	179.2
Sterea Ellada	311.5	28,0	208,0	75.6	88.4
Dytiki Ellada	553.8	28.5	303.8	221.5	96.4
Peloponnisos	391.2	34.6	222.1	134.6	99.5
Thessalia	480.8	24.3	302.1	154.3	111.8
Ipeiros	599.7	32.1	393.3	174.3	102.4
East Macedonia/Thrace	482.6	30.6	259.8	192.2	88.5
Central Macedonia	603.2	26.3	385.6	191.3	126.5
West Macedonia	301.7	22.9	206.1	72.6	95.5
Ionia Nisia	409.4	20.2	265.5	123.6	81.3
North Aigaio	399.0	27.6	253.5	118,0	80.3
South Aigaio	367.3	27.5	241.5	98.4	96.4
Kriti	618.2	38.7	351.8	227.7	105.1
Greece, total	640.0	21.9	380.2	237.8	131.4

Table 5. *Hospital personnel per 100 beds, by category, in public and private hospitals (2013)*

Personnel by category per 100 beds	Public	Private	Total
Medical Doctors	65.6	55.3	61.8
Nursing personnel	108.1	42.3	84.0
Administrative personnel	24.9	14.6	21.1
Other health professions	9.0	9.0	9.0
Technical and other health associate professionals	35.0	14.3	27.4
Other health associate professionals	14.7	0.0	9.3
Total	257.3	135.5	212.7

Table 5 indicates the number of Medical Doctors per 100,000 population by medical specialty and region. In average, there are only 21.9 Generalist Medical Doctors per 100,000 vs 380.2 Specialist Medical Doctors. However, the rate of Generalist Medical Doctors is much lower in the Attica region (9.7/100,000) whereas the rate of Specialist Medical Doctors is much higher (514.5/100,000). Both should be awared the policy makers, taken into account international standards (Watson et al, 2006).

Health workforce distribution. Table 6 reports the total number of hospital personnel per 100 beds, by category of personnel, in public and private hospitals (34,092 and 19,681 hospital beds respectively). Staffing in private hospitals is found to be significantly lower compared to public hospitals, in almost all categories of health personnel. Similar indicators can be calculated by region.

Table 6. *Population-based NHS workforce indicators.*

Population-based nhs workforce indicators	Health Region 1	2	3	4	5	6	7	Total
Medical doctors / physicians per 100.000	198.9	346.7	135.6	243.5	148.4	204.3	237.7	206.9
Nursing and midwifery professionals per 100.000	151.1	254.8	131.6	227.4	126.3	167.5	209.1	170.7
Other health professionals per 100.000	26.5	66.1	22.4	26.0	17.8	24.9	28.9	28.5
Medical and pharmaceutical technicians per 100.000	34.6	52.4	25.3	42.2	25.2	31.6	32.1	34.2
Nursing & midwifery assistants per 100.000	124.1	274.7	103.0	176.8	130.3	187.5	170.0	155.9
Other health associate professionals per 100.000	33.6	89.3	28.3	58.0	38.0	52.3	54.2	46.0
Personal care workers in NHS per 100.000	9.8	38.3	9.4	10.8	12.9	15.8	12.4	14.1
Administrative personnel per 100.000	67.0	153.9	51.5	77.9	63.6	84.6	89.7	78.3
Technical & other per 100.000	54.8	160.3	52.9	73.9	66.7	90.8	86.3	76.1
Health personnel not elsewhere classified	1.1	0.1	0.3	0.2	0.0	0.1	0.0	0.4
Total	701.4	1,436.4	560.5	936.7	629.2	859.3	920.4	811.1

Table 7 shows the population-based NHS personnel indicators across the seven Health Regions (DYPE) of the country. In the whole NHS, Medical Doctors constitute the largest group of professionals (206.9/100,000) followed by nursing personnel (170.7/100,000). Significant inequalities are shown across Health Regions.

Table 8 describes the distribution of NHS personnel between hospitals and PHC sector. In total, 92.2% of the whole NHS workforce is employed in hospitals and 7,8 % in PHC units. However, this proportion drops to 3, 5 % in nursing personnel and increases to 14.6% in medical personnel.

Table 9 presents NHS hospital personnel per 100 hospital beds, across Health Regions. Significant inequalities are found among Health Regions, in most categories of hospital personnel. In all Regions, qualified nurses in hospitals are less than medical doctors, and they constitute 52, 3 % of all nursing personnel (assistants included). Table 12 provides further information on the proportional distribution of NHS nurses (both hospital and PHC included) by educational level across Health Regions.

Table 7. *NHS personnel distribution in hospitals and PHC* centers.*

	N			(%)		
	Hospitals	PHC	Total	Hospitals	PHC	Total
Physicians	20,824	3,574	24,398	85.4	14.6	100
Nursing personnel	33,969	1,223	35,192	96.5	3.5	100
Administrative personnel	7,916	455	8,371	94.6	5.4	100
Other health personnel	10,309	1,385	11,694	88.2	11.8	100
Technical personnel	8,004	118	8,122	98.5	1.5	100
Personal care workers	1,344	177	1,521	88.4	11.6	100
Total	82,366	6,932	89,298	92.2	7.8	100

* Prtimary Health Care

Table 8. *NHS hospital personnel per 100 beds.*

hospital personnel indicators	health region							Total
	1	2	3	4	5	6	7	
Medical doctors per 100 beds	73.2	57.5	49.1	67.6	75.7	68.9	65.1	65.6
Nursing and midwifery professionals per 100 beds	55.6	42.2	47.7	63.1	64.4	56.5	57.3	54.1
Other health professionals per 100 beds	9.8	11.0	8.1	7.2	9.1	8.4	7.9	9.0
Medical and pharmaceutical technicians per 100 beds	12.7	8.7	9.2	11.7	12.8	10.6	8.8	10.8
Nursing & midwifery assistants per 100 beds	45.6	45.5	37.3	49.1	66.5	63.2	46.5	49.4
Total nursing personnel per 100 beds	101.2	87.8	85.0	112.1	130.9	119.7	103.8	103.6
Percentage of professional nurses in total nursing personnel	54.9	48.1	56.1	56.3	49.2	47.2	55.2	52.3
Other health associate professionals per 100 beds	12.4	14.8	10.3	16.1	19.4	17.6	14.9	14.6
Personal care workers in NHS per 100 beds	3.6	6.3	3.4	3.0	6.6	5.3	3.4	4.5
Administrative personnel per 100 beds	24.7	25.5	18.7	21.6	32.4	28.5	24.6	24.9
Technical & other per 100 beds	20.1	26.6	19.2	20.5	34.0	30.6	23.6	24.1
Health personnel not elswere classified	0.4	0.0	0.1	0.1	0.0	0.0	0.0	0.1
Total	258.0	238.2	203.0	259.9	320.9	289.8	252.1	257.3

Table 9. *Proportional (%) distribution of NHS nurses by educational level and Health Region.*

Education Level	Health Region							Total
	1st	2d	3d	4th	5th	6th	7th	
Qualified nurses	60.3	49.8	58.3	56.0	56.5	54.3	61.4	56.5
Assistant nursing personnel	39.7	50.2	41.7	44.0	43.5	45.7	38.6	43.5
Total	100.0	100.0	100.0	100.0	100.0	100.0	100.0	100.0

Workforce efficiency indicators. Table 10 surmises workforce efficiency indicators (i) average annual admissions and (ii) average hospital days per staff member, by Health Region. Data of table 14 show substantial differentiation among Regions in these indicators, in almost all categories of hospital personnel. Average annual admissions per doctor varies from 86 to 133.2 across Health Regions, while average annual hospital days per doctor ranges from 325.2 to 521.5. Similarly, average annual admissions per qualified nurse ranges from 115.3 to 137.3, while average annual hospital day per qualified nurse from 356.1 to 537.4. These findings revealed significant variation in workforce efficiency across Health Regions.

Outflow indicators. Table 11 presents personnel outflow indicators, by Health Region, per 100,000 population. Retirement with resignation constitutes the major reason for exiting the healthcare workforce. Significant variation among Regions can be observed, which mainly are due to differences in age-maturity of health personnel across the country.

Table 10. *Annual admissions and hospital days per staff member, by Health Region.*

hospital efficiency indicators	Health Region							
	1st	2d	3d	4th	5th	6th	7th	Total
Average annual admissions per physician	96.0	86.0	133.2	107.7	108.7	100.7	101.7	101.6
Average annual admissions per nurse/midwife	126.4	117.1	137.3	115.3	127.7	122.8	115.6	123.2
Average annual admissions per other health professional	720.2	451.3	808.2	1007.1	905.5	827.5	836.9	737.8
Average annual admissions per assistant nursing personnel	153.9	108.6	175.4	148.3	123.8	109.7	142.2	134.9
Average annual admissions per total nursing personnel	69.4	56.3	77.0	64.9	62.9	57.9	63.8	64.4
Average annual hospital days per physician	371.0	491.2	521.5	332.5	325.2	360.7	367.9	392.4
Average annual hospital days per nurse/midwife	488.6	468.3	537.4	356.1	382.1	440.1	418.2	475.8
Average annual hospital days per other health professional	2196.9	1907.8	2496.1	1396.6	1268.8	1410.4	1612.1	1767.0
Average annual hospital days per assistant nursing personnel	594.9	620.0	686.6	458.0	370.4	393.1	514.5	521.0
Average annual hospital days per total nursing personnel	268.3	321.6	301.4	200.3	188.1	207.6	230.7	248.7

Table 11. *Personnel outflow indicators by Health Region per 100,000 population.*

outflow indicators by health region PER 100.000 population	Health Region							
	1st	2d	3d	4th	5th	6th	7th	Total
Retirement with resignation	6.2	9.5	4.8	5.3	-	7.8	10.4	6
Compulsory retirement with age limit and 35-year service	0.4	0	0.1	0	-	0.2	0.2	0.2
Compulsory retirement with 35-year service and 67 age limit	0.1	0.1	0.1	0.3	-	0	0.2	0.1
Early retirement with 35-year service and 55 age limit	0.5	0.1	0	0.1	-	0	0	0.2
Early retirement with 35-year service and 55 age limit up to 31-12-2013	0.7	0.5	0.2	0.2	-	0	0.2	0.3
Total	7.9	10.2	5.2	5.9	-	8	11	6.7

4. Discussion

Like many other countries, in Greece, comprehensive data on human resources are not available in one single repository (21), as there is not a national system tracking data from all sources listed, like OECD referred (22-23). This means that any attempt to determine the size and core characteristics of the health workforce requires some level of analysis and synthesis of available information from multiple sources. Some of the main problems occurring in gathering appropriate data are: (i) data on health professions that, apart from the health sector, work in other sectors too, (ii) data on health professionals abroad graduated, in professions that have no obligation for a recognition of their qualifications, (iii) retirement and other reason of withdrawals from work in health sector, (iv) employment of medical doctors in private hospitals etc. A particular problem we faced is the uncertainty on health workforce availabiblity introduced of the high proportion of unemployment.

The set of Health Workforce Indicators developed follows a "stock and flow" model, based on international literature (24) and WHO methodology (7, 17, and 21). The quality and adequacy of available data led to a combination between the workforce-to-population ratio and the health needs method concerning demand projections, while supply projections were performed using the stock-and-flow model. Concerning demand projections we forecasted domestic population over the period 2015-2020 using an ARIMA (0,2,1) model. Apart from the normal forecast two extreme scenarios were developed too. The main conclusion is that demand for HRH in Greece is expected to follow an average downward trend over the examined period mainly due to the expectations of decreasing population. However the model is highly sensitive to population numbers, hence accuracy will be achieved through annual adjustment to actual population developments, as well as the total work-force (mainly the solo-practice added). The results from this modeling have already published (25) and referred in the below summary.

5. Conclusion

In fact, the above results based on specific indicators were essential in order to implement some of the core human resource management policies namely human resource planning and recruitment (26). To elaborate more, being aware of the number of employees working in health care organizations facilitates their effective allocation and distribution and it leads to the projection of workforce needs in the future (27). The main results of this phase of the study are the following:

1. Universities' system provides many doctors and psychologists (11/100,000 p.), while nurses' and others' population ratios is similar or even better only due to technological and secondary education. However, nurses' employment should be immediately increased, mainly to the NHS.
2. Work-force distribution indicates inequalities among regions mainly in favour of Attica, Salonika and Crete. This is the case among professions or medical specialties.
3. Efficiency indicators reveal discrepancies among professions and regions too.
4. Outflow indicators vary among regions (and professions) concerning work-force/population ratios. Athens' area shows the higher ratio of exits, mainly due to retirements, all-though other reasons were not available from the data.
5. The development of classification and health work-force indicators is important for Greece, thus we provide this in accordance with a set of health work-force and other indicators.

General findings of the study contract (between GIZ and DUTH) indicate the following:

A. On the supply side, every year, over 7.000 health professionals were graduated from the Greek higher education, 2.000 from secondary education, and over 230 from abroad (officially). The main problem of all those professionals is the limited offer of jobs either in public or in private sector.

B. On the demand side, 87.000 health workers employed in the NHS and at least 26.000 in private hospitals and clinics. It is estimated that still 37.000 doctors are in the private (solo practice or diagnostic) sector and approximately 20% of them are contracted with EOPYY (National Organization of Health Service Provision that is the newly established Unified Fund of Social Security Sickness Fund). Concerning doctors, pharmacists, dentists, etc. ratios, Greece has the highest numbers per population, compared to international data.

C. Thus, the education system in collaboration with the health system needs an immediate plan to match the relevant demand and supply of the future, taking into account the restrictions and limitations referred in the conclusion of the study.

In conclusion, it was infeasible to examine the health needs model, if the national statistical authority (EL.STAT.) or/and "health.map" do not record all demographics and health related data that should potentially quantify health needs. Next, more accurate data is included in the study for future projections. Finally, we developed templates to ensure intergraded, accurate and universal data collection. These templates should constitute the main business components of the relevant HRM software that has to be established immediately.

References

[1] Eurostat (2014) Disaggregated data for the healthcare sector.

[2] Alcimed (2010) *Study on Healthcare Services, Sectors and Products in Europe for the European Commission.* Final Report February 2010.

[3] European Commission (2010) *Conclusions of the 3053rd EPSCO Council meeting*. Brussels, 7 December 2010. *Investing in Europe's health workforce of tomorrow: Scope for innovation and collaboration.*

[4] European Commission (2011) *Proposal for a Health for Growth Programme 2014-2020*, COM (2011) 709 final of 9.11.2011.

[5] European Commission (2012) RN4CAST Report. *Nurse forecasting: Human resources planning in nursing.* 12 European countries (Belgium, UK, Finland, Germany, Greece, Ireland, Norway, Poland, Spain, Sweden, Switzerland and Netherlands) and also USA, China, Botswana and South Africa.

[6] Maier, CB. et al. (2011) Cross-country analysis of health professional mobility in Europe: the results. In Wismar M et al., eds. *Health professional mobility and health systems. Evidence from 17 European countries.* Copenhagen,

[7] World Health Organization (2011) Regional Office for Europe, Copenhagen: Study by M. Wismar, C. B. Maier, I. A. Glinos, G. Dussault and J. Figueras (eds., 2011), Health professional mobility and health systems. Evidence from 17 European countries, Observatory Study Series No. 23, European Observatory on Health Systems and Policies.WHO Regional Office for Europe on behalf of the European Observatory on Health Systems and Policies.

[8] Jelfs, E. (2012) Workforce issues in European Union health policy. *Health Service Management Research*, 25:48-49.

[9] O'Brian-Pallas, L., Baumann, A., Donner, G., Murphy, G., Lochhaas-Gerlach, J. and Luba, M. (2001) Forecasting models for human resources in health care. *Journal of Advanced Nursing*, 33(1):120-129.

[10] Ono, T., Lafortune, G. and Schoenstein, M. (2013) *Health workforce planning in OECD countries: a review of 26 projection models from 18 countries.* Paris, Organisation for Economic Co-operation and Development (OECD Health Working Paper 62).

[11] Stuckler, D. et al. (2011) Effects of the 2008 recession on health: a first look at European data. *Lancet,* 378:124–125.

[12] Buchan, J., O'May, F. and Dussault, G. (2013) The nursing workforce and the global economic crisis. *Journal of Nursing Scholarship*, 45(3):298-307.

[13] Joyce, C. and McNeil, J. (2006) Participation in the workforce by Australian medical graduates. *Medical Education*, 40(4):333-339.

[14] Canadian Academy of Health Sciences (2009) *Making an Impact, A Preferred Framework and Indicators to Measure Returns on Investment in Health Research.* FullReport.pdf

[15] World Health Organization (2001) *Toolkit for Planning, Training and Management. Projecting Workforce Requirements: Planning with the WHO Scenario Models.* World Health Organization: Geneva.

[16] World Health Organization (2010) Policy *Brief How to create an attractive and supportive working environment for health professionals*, Health Evidence Network and the European Observatory on Health Systems and Policies.

[17] World Health Organization (2010) *Models and tools for health workforce planning and projections.* World Health Organization: Geneva.

[18] European Federation of Nurses Associations (2012) Caring in crisis: the impact of the financial crisis on nurses and nursing. A comparative overview of 34 European countries. Brussels, European Federation of Nurses Associations.

[19] Laurant, M., Reeves, D., Hermens, R., Braspenning, J., Grol, R. and Sibbald, B. (2004) *Substitution of doctors by nurses in primary care*. John Wiley & Sons Ltd.: Chichester, UK.

[20] Staiger, D., Auerbach, D. and Buerhaus, P. (2012) Registered nurse labor supply and the recession: are we in a bubble? *New England Journal of Medicine*, 366:1463-1465.

[21] World Health Organization (2013) *The health workforce: advances in responding to shortages and migration, and in preparing for emerging needs.* Geneva, World Health Organization (Report by the Secretariat for the Sixty-sixth World Health Assembly, Provisional Agenda Item 17.4) (http://apps.who.int/gb/ebwha/pdf_files/WHA66/A66_25-en.pdf).

[22] OECD (2011) *Health at a glance 2011: OECD indicators.* Paris, Organization for Economic Co-operation and Development.

[23] OECD (2012) *Health at a glance: Europe 2012.* Paris, Organization for Economic Co-operation and Development.

[24] Sullivan, L. and Michel, I. (2004) *Core Competencies in Public Health: Literature Review.* Ontario Public Health Association, March 4, 2004. Accessed from http://www.opha.on.ca/corecompetencies/index.html June 2004.

[25] Polyzos, N., Karakolias, S., Mavridoglou, G., Gkorezis, P., Zilidis, C., (2015) Current and future insight into human resources in Greece. *Open Journal of Social Sciences*, v.3 (n.5): 5-14.

[26] Dreesch, N., Dolea, C., Dal Poz, M., Goubarev, A., Adams, O., Aregawi, M., Bergstrom, K., Fogstad, H., Sheratt, D., Linkins, J., Scherpbier, R. and Youssef-Fox, M. (2005) An approach to estimating human resource requirements to achieve the Millennium Development Goals. *Health Policy and Planning*, 20(5):267-276.

[27] World Health Organization (2004) *World Report on Knowledge for Better Health: Strengthening Health systems.* World Health Organization: Geneva.

2

Financing the Expansion of Family Businesses in Ghana: Which Way to Go, Debt or Equity

Joseph Yensu, Edmond Oppong-Peprah, Elizabeth Dwomo-Fokuo, Francis Boadu, Anthony Kusi

Institute of Entrepreneurship and Enterprise Development, Kumasi Polytechnic, Kumasi, Ghana

Email address:

Joseph.yensu@yahoo.com (J. Yensu), eddidore@yahoo.com (E. Oppong-Peprah), lizzydef@yahoo.co.uk (E. Dwomo-Fokuo), linnacus@yahoo.com (F. Boadu), Anthonykusi@hotmail.com (A. Kusi)

Abstract: Financing activities are crucial exercises in any organizational set-up. It has attracted intense debate and scholarly attention in the financial management arena over the years, whether businesses should opt for debt or equity financing to expand their businesses or not. This paper attempts to ascertain the type of finance that family business operators in Ghana use to expand their business using Ashanti Region as the study area. Questionnaires were administered to 148 family businesses in Ghana. Descriptive survey study design was adopted to achieve the envisaged aims of the study. A total of 150 questionnaires were administered but 148 family businesses responded. Generally, the study revealed that founders or owner-managers use equity financing (68.92 %) as a source of start-up capital to commence their business activities. Also, founders or owner-managers admitted that they will only allow external investors (venture capitalist and business angels) to come in, if they would be prepared to offer advice and expertise to them alone, and nothing more. To establish whether family business use debt or equity financing for their expansion activities, a total of seven variables were used to measure the level of acceptance among the family business operators. These variables were analyzed using principle component factor analysis with varimax rotation. Varimax rotation with Kaiser Normalization was done to simplify and minimize the number of factors to achieve meaningful construction. As a result, 7 crucial variables were established as the sources of development finance by family businesses, which include external equity funding (venture capital and business angel), equity (family & friends, partnership) funding, rotational savings, owner's equity, debt funding, re-invest profits earned, and government support, 4 factors are also established as sources of development finance by family businesses namely internal investment fund, mixed investment fund, external investment fund (funds from non family members) and source from anywhere. The paper seeks to establish that family business operators in Ghana utilize both debt and equity financing (mixed investment) for their business developmental activities. However, the equity financing is limited to family & friends, and partners alone and not private equity investors-venture capitalist and business angels. The study recommends that Ghana Venture Capital Trust Fund and venture capital companies should embark on massive educational and information program on venture capital support activities in order to disseminate the needed information to family business owners concerning the financing options and support services available to them.

Keywords: Family Business, Debt, Equity, Financing and Owner-Manager

1. Introduction

Family business is a business that involves two or more members of a particular family, with financial control and management of the administration, operations and strategic direction of company's destiny. Family businesses were considered as some of the engines of the post-industrial growth processes as they were credited for nurturing entrepreneurial talent across generations, a sense of loyalty to business success and long-term strategic commitment. Family businesses range from small, medium size and large companies around the world. Companies such as Wal-Mart, Marriott's, Mars, Saarland, Cardone (manufacturing), Ratner, Ford, Walgreen, Kasapreko, Joefel (catering) services, Poku Transport Children's Hospital are famous examples of family businesses (G. W. Dyer, 2006). They play a major role in economic development in every country across the globe.

Researchers view them as the backbone of the private economy, as they make a substantial contribution to national socio-economic and entrepreneurial development (G. Connolly, C. Jay, 1996; P. Poutziouris, C. Chittenden, 1996; F. Neubauer, G. A. Lank, 1998; P. Leach, T. Bogod, 1999; A. C. Romano, G. Tanewski, X. K. Smyrnios, 2000). They account for up to 80 percent of enterprises worldwide (G. W. Dyer, 2006), and contribute on average 60 percent of total formal employment in the manufacturing sector (C. Dannreuther, L. Perren, 2013; M. Ayyagari, T. Beck, A. Demirguc-Kunt, 2007). For most developed economies, the family business sector is estimated to account for over two thirds of all enterprises and about half of the GDP (E. K. Gersick, J. Davis, M. Hampton, I. Lansberg, 1996). In the United States, it is estimated that more than 90 percent of all firms are believed to be family businesses and 78 percent of the new jobs generated come from this sector (The Business Forum, 2001). The situation is not quite different from what pertains in European countries as family businesses make an important contribution to macro-economic activity, in some cases accounting for at least 85 percent of all European companies' operations (G. W. Dyer, 2006). The picture prevailing in African economies towards family business is quite good as the sector contributes huge employment opportunities and about 60 percent of the GDP of the continent as a whole.

For all these businesses to survive and continue to play a leading role towards socio-economic development across the globe, financing should be a crucial component. Financing of businesses have received extensive research in the literature. Businesses normally opt for either debt or equity financing. These are the two main sources of financing available to business operators. A World Bank study found that about 90 % of small enterprises surveyed stated that one of the main obstacles of doing business is access to finance (R. Parker, R. Riopelle, W. Steel, 1995). This affects a lot of businesses which operate in developing countries, and adversely affect the growth of the smaller and medium size family business sector than that of large companies (M. Schiffer, W. Beatrice, 2001; T. Beck, A. Demirguc-Kunt, R. Levine, 2005; T. Beck, A. Demirguc-Kunt, L. Laeven, V. Maksimovic, 2006). According to enterprise-level data collected by the World Bank (in various years), smaller and medium size family businesses in Sub-Saharan Africa are more financially constrained than in any other developing region. Only 20 percent of smaller and medium size family businesses in Sub-Saharan Africa have a line of credit from financial institutions, compared, for example, to 44 percent in Latin America and the Caribbean's. Only 9 percent of their investments are funded by banks as against 23 percent in Eastern Europe and Central Asia.

Financing challenges facing businesses as a world-wide phenomenon have never been fully addressed (W. Lili, 2003). Countries around the world have adopted many policies like fiscal subsidies, credit supplementations and policy loans. China for instance has resorted to a variety of measures, including the establishment of hundreds of agencies to help businesses. In Africa, financing of businesses is an important policy priority to both government and business captains.

In Ghana, a lot of financial reforms have taken place over the years to cater for businesses. The financial sector is regulated by the Bank of Ghana. Its core business is to give credit to business entities that may apply for debt financing as a seed or expansion capital. In 2006, the government set up Venture Capital Trust Fund to aid businesses which are in need of seed and expansion capital funds. Because of the vital role that family businesses play towards economic growth and development, in Ghana, various programs and agencies are available to support and promote the growth and expansion of family businesses. Some of these agencies are the National Board for Small-Scale Industries (NBSSI), Business Assistance Fund, Ghana Investment Fund, GRATIS Foundation, and the Rural Enterprise Project. Yet, to be specific, family businesses face the difficulty in sourcing and ascertaining the type of finance they need for capital expansion.

The aim of this study is to better understand the type of finance that family businesses in Ghana opt for when they are in need of capital for expansion. Specifically, this study endeavors to achieve the following objectives: (1) to examine the funding structure of family business operators, and (2) to identify sources of development finance available to family business operator. Our findings could enrich discussions of appropriate policy frameworks that could stimulate family business finance in Ghana.

2. Literature Review

Contemporary financing literature reveals keen focus of experts and researchers on small and medium scale business financing. Financing is a core factor for the success of business organization in the long-run (F. Boadu, G. Dwomoh, A. Sarpong, E. Dwomo-Fokuo, 2014). It plays a very crucial role in every business endeavor. It is the engine of business development and expansion and for that reason institutions all over the world take steps to run efficient and prudent financial systems. To sustain businesses or entrepreneurial activities in an economy, financial institutions or financial markets have to satisfy the business community by providing them with enough capital for business development, especially to small and medium family businesses for effective running of business activities (F. Boadu, 2008). If businesses are satisfied with the supply, productivity gets enhanced while job creation, wealth creation, business growth and expansion, as well as revenue and taxes to the government are addressed. These lead to the development of the businesses and their long-term economic growth (I. Stefanovic, P. Damnjanovic, O. Jasko, 2010). Businesses are now deeply concerned with the factors which cause financing gabs to constrain family businesses and small and medium size enterprises. Understanding the financing gabs may help in sustaining businesses and avoid the adverse effects that may results due to financing.

2.1. Financing Gap of Family Business

The gap affects both formal and informal small and medium size family businesses, with access to credit the biggest problem (IFC, 2009). Available literature is clear on the fact that small businesses mostly have problems accessing funds from financial providers to finance fixed assets and working capital for their operations (J. Tucker, and J. Lean, 2003). This gap, hampering the strategic financial development of family businesses, has been under the microscope of business researchers and enterprise policy makers for decades (E. J. Bolton, 1971; H. Wilson, 1979; Aston Business School, 1991; ESRC—Business Research Centre, 1992, 1996; Bank of England, 2001: P. Poutziouris, 2001). This finance gap is a multi dimensional barrier involving the problematic flow of development debt financing, the persistence of an equity gap which exacerbates the debt gap the short-term approach to strategic financial management and development planning of closely family firms, widening the gap as they are often skeptical about the deployment of externally generated, long-term funding. This attitude is indicative of the under capitalization of family businesses as a result of the over reliance on short-term financial options (P. Poutziouris, F. Chittenden, N. Michaelas, 1998, P. Poutziouris, 2001). But the widely held view that small businesses are the engine of economic growth and that market imperfections impede their growth have encouraged government interventions in the markets for small business finance (T. Beck, A. Demirguc-Kunt, L. Laeven, V. Maksimovic, 2006). All these gaps have prompted various governments across the globe to institute numerous measures to close the finance gap. For instance in Ghana, the government has set up Venture Capital Trust Fund, Business Assistance Fund, Ghana Investment Fund, and GRATIS Foundation to address the issues of funding towards SME projects. In the United Kingdom, the response of the government is aimed at closing the equity side of the finance gap via channeling more equity capital essential for the realization of the growth potential of entrepreneurial family and small scale enterprises. These have been achieved through orchestration of a number of schemes including the promotion of the Business Angel Network and the Business Expansion Scheme (P. Poutziouris, 2001).

2.2. Debt Financing or Equity Financing

Lack of access to finance is consistently cited in surveys as a principal constraint on the development of businesses in African countries (E. Aryeetey, A. Baah-Nuakoh, T. Duggleby, H. Hettige, F.W Steel, 1994). Family business entrepreneurs have four funds options to consider when starting or expanding their businesses. These are: by acquiring a debt, by accepting equity shares in the business, by securing funds from a mix of both above, by funding the company oneself – categorized as Private Investment.

Debt financing is a process of borrowing money from a person or institution and signing a promissory note to pay the said amount together with interest when the time is due. This source does not involve giving up part of the ownership of the business. The main sources of debt financing include family loans (loans from friends and relations, usually on very favorable terms), state support, mortgages, leasing, bank loans, trade credit, finance companies, and insurance companies. One main motive for starting a small business is to maintain greater control over the operation of the business and to internalize the benefits of personal effort and risk-taking. In this regard, then, it is understandable that many family business managers would not tolerate any dilution of this control through the introduction of outside equity. Thus, the motives of owner-managers of family business may constitute a major constraint on the range of external financing sources available to the firm (J. Tucker, J. Lean, 2003).

On the other hand, equity financing is a process of trading a percentage of the ownership of the business for money. The sources include personal savings, venture capital, funds from established companies for research cooperation, stock exchange, friends and family members, partnership, and business angels. In this regard, the concept of "risk investors, mainly Business Angels (BA) and Venture Capitalists (VC) which invest in both start-up and expansion stage expecting however, a portion of the company in return, is important to be considered. Venture Capital is a widely used form of financial intermediation that is particularly well suited to support the creation and growth of entrepreneurial companies (T. Hellman, M. Puri, 2000; J. T. Chemmanur, S. He, D. Nandy, 2011; F. Boadu, G. Dwomoh, A. Sarpong, and E. Dwomo-Fokuo, 2014). It has also been credited with stimulating job creation, innovation, and economic growth (S. Kortum, J. Lerner, 2000; Global Insight, 2007; F. Boadu, G. Dwomoh, A. Sarpong, and E. Dwomo-Fokuo, 2014). Venture Capital market has tremendous effect on family businesses. According to F. Boadu (2008), Venture Capital market which comprises both Business Angels (BA) and Venture Capitalists raises enough capital for business development especially for family businesses for effective running of business activities.

Lastly, family business founders or owner-managers can resort to finance their business activities with their own personal funds without recourse to any external funds. This helps the owners to maintain full ownership of the business.

2.3. Family Business Expansion and Source of Development Fund

Most of the governments in the world are focusing on their support programs including financing for the family business development, in order to sustain a stable national economy (S. Butler, 2008). Financial resources are of vital importance for a business to run its operations profitably. Family businesses have comparatively limited resources and greater difficulty in accessing funding for both starts up and expansion stages of the business life, due to the inward looking attitude of these businesses. These inward looking attitudes prevent them from accepting external bodies in the running and managing of their businesses. According to C. S. Myers (1984) privately held, smaller companies finance their capital needs in a hierarchical fashion, first using internally available funds, followed by debt and finally, external equity. This preference reflects the relative costs of various sources of finance, owing to the existence of information asymmetries. It could be argued that Myers assertion is particularly relevant to family businesses, as they are widely characterized by an aversion to outside capital infusions (B. Dunn, M. Hughes, 1995; A. M. Gallo, A. Vilaseca 1996; P. Poutziouris, F. Chittenden, N. Michaelas, 1998; A. C. Romano, G. Tanewski, and X. K. Smyrnios, 2000; P. Poutziouris, 2000, P. Poutziouris, 2001), and experience relatively more restrictive transactional and behavioral costs in raising external equity (R. Pettit, R. Singer, 1985).

Furthermore, the use of external equity including stock market flotation would widen the share ownership of the family business, leading to loss of control by the original founders or owner-managers or even a hostile takeover. This has scared most of family business founders or owner-managers to avoid the use of external equity finance and to rely more heavily on retained profits and short-term bank loan finance, followed by medium-term bank loans. This is not to say that family business founders or owner-managers entirely refuse external equity for expansion projects. They often consider it as a last resort to finance strategic transitions, such as market-oriented business growth, generational and management succession, widening the capital base in the context of management buy-out (MBO), and other exit options (P. Poutziouris, 1999).

In a recent empirical investigation, P. Poutziouris, F. Chittenden, N. Michaelas, (1998) established that the financial development of private companies is influenced by the state of the economy, conditions in the capital markets, internal business characteristics, and the owner-directors' attitudes toward financial independence, business risk, and family business control (P. Poutziouris, 2001).

3. Methodology

3.1. Study Area

Ashanti Region is chosen as our case study area since it is a cosmopolitan region in Ghana. The region is the third largest of 10 administrative regions in Ghana, occupying a total land surface of 24,389 square kilometers or 10.2 per cent of the total land area of Ghana. In terms of population, however, it is the most populated region with a population of 4,780,380 in 2010 population and housing census (PHC), accounting for 19.4 percent of Ghana's total population; however, its density (148.1 per square km) is lower than those of the Greater Accra (895.5/km2) and Central Region (162.2/km2) (Ghana Statistical Service, 2010). The region is centrally located in the middle belt of Ghana. It lies between longitudes 0.15W and 2.25W, and latitudes 5.50N and 7.46N. The region shares boundaries with four of the ten political regions, which are Brong- Ahafo Region in the north, Eastern Region in the east, Central Region in the south and Western Region in the south west. The region is divided into 30 districts, each headed by a district chief executive. Majority of the region's population are Ghanaians by birth (87.3%) with about five per cent naturalized Ghanaians. A smaller proportion (5.8%) of the population originates from outside Ghana, being 3.7 per cent mainly from the five English-speaking countries of ECOWAS and 2.1 per cent from other African countries. The non-African population living in the region is 1.8 per cent of the total population. Akans are the predominant ethnic group in the region, representing 77.9% of Ghanaians by birth. A high proportion (78.9%) of the Akan population is Asante. The non-Akan population in the region comprises the Mole-Dagbon (9.0%), the Ewe (3.2%), the Grusi (2.4%), the Mande-Busanga (1.8%) and the Ga-Dangme (1.4%). The other smaller ethnic groups form about 1.3 per cent of the population of the region (Wikipedia, 2015). Ashanti region is the cultural heartbeat of Ghana. It is land of the Golden stool.

3.2. Population of the Study

The population of the study is made up of all the family businesses operating in the Ashanti Region of Ghana as at 2015.

3.3. Sample Size and Procedure

The researchers used the Association of Ghana Industries' directory of the Ashanti Region of Ghana to select the elements of the study. In all, one hundred and fifty (150) family businesses were contacted for the survey, but only one hundred and forty-eight of the questionnaires were retrieved for the analysis. In each business entity, the Chief Executive Officers (C.E.O's) were given questionnaire to respond to. Purposive method was used in this study due to the number of family businesses in Ashanti Region, as well as its suitability in reaching all the respondents across the region.

3.4. Research Instrument

The researchers designed one set of questionnaire, for the Chief Executive Officers. The questionnaire for C.E.O's covered general background of the respondents, sources of start-up capital, willingness of founders or owner-managers to partner external fund providers and sources of development finance. The final open-ended questionnaire was designed to gather opinions, suggestions and comments in general with regard to the research and areas of further study. Data collected were analyzed using descriptive and inferential statistics. The questionnaire was designed to obtain a fair representation of the opinions of the 148 sample respondents using a five-point Likert type scale ranging from Strongly disagree (SD) - 5 points, Disagree (D) -4 points, Not Sure (NS) -3 points, Agree (A) -2 points, Strongly Agree (SA) - 1 point. As at May, 2015 a total of 150 questionnaires were given out, and 148 were received and used for the analysis.

3.5. Data Presentation

Data gathered were coded and the results were analyzed using an STATA computer package. The findings of the study were presented using appropriate tables to ensure easy interpretation.

4. Discussion of Results

The findings of the survey are discussed in this section. This section begins with description of the general characteristics of the respondents. It then examines the results on sources of start-up capital, and willingness of founders or owner-managers to partner external fund providers and finally, the sources of development finance to family businesses.

4.1. Characteristics of the Respondents

Table 1 shown below demonstrates the characteristics of the sample. Regarding the gender distribution of the respondents 68.92 % were male and 31.08 % female. The imbalance ratio of male to female can be accepted as normal in family business as it requires long working hours. In terms of age distribution, the result indicates that 78.38 % of the respondents were within the age group of 21-50. The mean age of the total number of respondents fell around the age of 35 years. This means that family business operators in Ghana are relatively young and can work effectively to promote family business towards economic development for a longer period. From the table, it is clear that the level of education was high among family business operators selected for the study. Approximately eighty-two percent of them were literate. The study indicates that 16.89 % of the respondents completed elementary school education. And almost 30 % completed secondary school while 54.06 % of the respondents have higher national diploma, university education and professional designation (nursing and accounting). The main reason for the high proportion of graduate was probably due to the characteristics of urban population.

The study also found that trading is the dominant type of business for 48.65 %. This is followed by service industry (37.16 %). Since trading and service industry requires little initial capital investment, it appears more suitable for most Ghanaians. Manufacturing only accounts for 14.19 %. Manufacturing is an engine of growth to every economy, the collapse of which can lead to massive unemployment. Ghanaian situation is not far from this. As the study indicates, 14.19 % of the business sector is devoted to manufacturing. This should be of much concern to developing country like Ghana.

When asked about the legal status of the businesses, 60.81 % of the respondents indicated that they run the sole proprietorship form of business. Approximately twenty-two percent have registered as private companies and 17.57 % are in partnership. None of them is a public company.

Table 1. *Sample Characteristic.*

Sample Characteristic	Items	Frequency (N= 148)	Percent of Total
Gender	Male	102	68.92
	Female	46	31.08
Respondent's Age Range	21-30 yrs	26	17.57
	31-40 yrs	40	27.03
	41-50 yrs	50	33.78
	51-60 yrs	29	19.59
	61 and above	3	2.03
Education	Elementary	25	16.89
	Secondary	43	29.05
	Polytechnic	44	29.74
	University	34	22.97
	Other	2	1.35
Legal Status of the Business	Sole Proprietorship	90	60.81
	Partnership	26	17.57
	Private Company	32	21.62
	Public Company	-	-
Sector of the Business	Manufacturing	21	14.19
	Service	55	37.16
	Trading	72	48.65

Source: Field Data, 2015

4.2. Sources of Start-Up Capital of Family Businesses

There are obvious differences in the type of financing in family businesses in Ghana. As it can be seen from Table 2, founders or owner-managers adopt equity financing for their family businesses more than the others. Equity financing in the form of Venture Capital and Business Angel has a slightly smaller percentage (4.05 %) than the overall equity financing of start-up family businesses (68.92 %) in the business economy as a whole, and a much lower percentage of both debt and equity financing (16.22 %). It is evident that equity financing usually comes from the founders or owner-managers relying on personal savings from previous engagement, money from friends or family members and other partners. This study clearly shows that family business founders in Ghana place high importance on the retention of family ownership and preservation of the business and its traditions for the next generation. As an option Venture Capital and Business Angel recorded the least figure. It is an indication that family businesses do not want to lose control of ownership to strategic investors at the initial stage of the business operation.

Table 2. *Funding Structure of Family Businesses.*

Start-Up Financing	Number	Percent of Total
Owner's equity	32	21.62
Bank debt	16	10.81
External equity funding (venture capital, business angel)	6	4.05
Equity (family & friends, partnership, etc)	70	47.30
Both debt and equity	24	16.22
Total	148	100

Source: Field Data, 2015

4.3. Active Role of Investors in Family Businesses Financed by External Investors

Preferred active role of investors in family business financed by external investors towards family businesses development in Ghana is shown in Table 3. The highest assistants expected by all founders or owner-managers were to offer their advice and expertise to them. This represents 54.10 % of the total respondents. In addition, 32.40 % of the respondents added that they would be prepared for investors to take a seat on the board and / or voting right. In totality 69.6 % of the respondents did not want external investors meddling in the affairs of the family business. One of the reasons could be that they want to hide their trade secrets and inside information from the general public.

Table 3. *Active Role of Investors in Family Business Financed by External Investors.*

Active Role of Investors in Family Business Financed by External Investors	Number	Percent of Total
Investors to take a seat on the board and / or voting right	45	32.40
Investors to offer their advice and expertise	80	54.10
Investors that are completely passive	23	15.50
Total	148	100

Source: Field Data, 2015

4.4. Sources of Development Finance in Ghana

The question on sources of development finance required the founders or owner-managers to rate the importance of each objective on a five-point scale with one (1) being "strongly agree" to five (5) being "strongly disagree". Table 4 below summarizes the reasons given by respondents for deciding on how to finance their business expansion. The analysis was carried out in accordance with the research questions. The responses to questions were scored and the mean and standard deviation determined. A mean response cut-off score of 3.00 that is (5+4+3+2+1)/5 was adopted. Based on the responses, the primary reasons concerning sources of development finance were: "Re-invest profits earned" (4.28), "Debt Funding" (4.09), "Owner's Equity" (3.27), "Government Support" (3.02), "Equity (Family & Friends, Partnership)" (3.01), and finally "External Equity funding (Venture Capitalist and Business Angels)" (2.99) receiving relatively less priority.

Table 4. *Mean Score and Standard Deviation for Sources of Development Finance in Ghana.*

	Variables	Mean	Std. Dev
1.	We are willing to consider external equity funding (venture capital, business angels) for expansion	2.99	1.22
2.	We are willing to consider equity (family & friends, partnership, etc) funding for expansion	3.01	1.33
3.	We are willing to consider rotational savings for expansion	2.84	1.19
4.	We are willing to use owner's equity for expansion	3.27	1.12
5.	We are willing to consider debt funding for expansion	4.09	0.87
6.	We are willing to re-invest profits earned for expansion	4.28	0.86
7.	We are willing to consider government support for expansion	3.02	1.22

Sources: Field Data, 2015

4.5. Factor Analysis Results

A factor analysis was conducted on the data collected on the sources of development finance of family businesses in Ghana. The factor analysis was performed on the 7-item scale to examine for dimensions in the scale. As presented in Table 5a, using eigenvalue ≥ 1, the analysis produced four factors, accounting for 76.80 % of the total variance in the 7 variables (Table 5b). Based on the weights on each of the four factors and the relative factor score of each variable, the four factors are named Internal Investment Fund, Mixed Investment Fund, External Investment Fund (funds from non family members) and sources from anywhere. As recommended by F. J. Hair, C. W. Black, B. J. Babin, (2010), a solution of about 60.0 % for social science study is considered satisfactory.

The first factor named Internal Investment Fund is loaded with "We are willing to consider equity (family & friends, partnership) funding for expansion"; "We are willing to consider rotational savings for expansion" and "We are willing to consider owner's equity". This study clearly indicates that family business operators are ever ready to source for funds within and outside the business boundaries for expansion projects.

The second factor which is named Mixed Investment Fund is loaded with "We are willing to consider debt funding for expansion" and "We are willing to re-invest profits earned and use for expansion". This result suggests that family business operators can use either debt or equity to expand their business activities. But, when using debt financing they need to be careful as the cost of capital charged by banks and investors is often so high that it impedes the business profitability and also requires huge collaterals for the acquisition and repayment of the loans (J. N. Amu, 2004). The interest rate in Ghana is too high for businesses which are aiming for expansion (K.N. Sowa, A. Baah-Nuakoh, A.K. Tutu, B. Osei, 1992; E. Aryeetey, A. Baah-Nuakoh, T. Duggleby, H. Hettige, and F.W Steel, 1994; A. Bigsten, P. Collier, S. Dercon, M. Fafchamps, B. Guthier, W. Gunning, M. Soderbom, A. Oduro, Oostendorp, C. Patillo, F. Teal and A. Zeufack, 2000; N. S. Buatsi, 2002; J. Abor and N. Biekpe, 2006). For instance, financial institutions such as standard Chartered Bank and Barclays Bank were charging an interest of 28.4 percent on loans in the year 2013-2014. Having such high interest rates on loans drives away entrepreneurs especially family business operators since they are not high risk-takers, and can eventually retard the progress and development of these businesses which are considered as the backbone of economies around the globe. On the other hand, it is good for family business operators to re-invest earned profit to expand their business activities. This always helps operators to have tremendous freedom over decision-making. However, operators need to tread cautiously in order not to create conflict between shareholders since; it may impose a heavy burden on shareholders, as the more that is re-invested in the business, the fewer dividends are distributed; and the longer it lasts, the more it will impact upon their individual ventures and standard of living.

Finally, the third factor which could be called External Investment Fund is loaded with "We are willing to consider external equity funding (venture capitalist and business angels)" and "We are willing to consider government support for expansion". From the Table 5b, it is clear that the third factor is having less than 1, which is against Kaiser Criterion suggestion, which states that factors with eigenvalues equal or higher than 1 should be retained. It is also of interest to note that factor 3 items have high uniqueness values of 76.36 % and 84.30 % respectively. This suggests that both variables are not relevant to this model and need to be discarded. The fourth factor was also dropped through analysis (Table 5b). It is clear from family business literature that finding external sources of capital to finance growth and expansion will mean diluting control, which is a situation that could impact quite emphatically on many families not to share control through sourcing funds and thereby altering their long-term vision, and this happens to be one of the key success factors of family businesses. This result is in conformity with table 3 which indicates that, family business operators in Ghana are not willing to risk their ownership control to outsiders.

The above study suggests that, family businesses in Ghana are ever ready to use equity from family and friends, owner's equity, debt financing and re-investing their profits earned for expansion purpose. Among the listed path for expansion, owner's equity and re-investing profit earned had high uniqueness value of 69.38 % and 69.33 % respectively. This result tends to support the assertion that family businesses use more internally generated funds for their development (J. Wards, 1987, G. Corbetta, 1995; P. Poutziouris, F. Chittenden, and N. Michaelas, 1998; P. Poutziouris 2001). On the contrary, it is clear that family business operators do not want any assistance from venture capitalist and business angels as well as government for their business expansion. This supports the views expressed by some researchers that family firms have a stronger antipathy towards external private equity-venture capital deals (R. D. Dreux, 1990; B. Dunn, M. Hughes, 1995; P. Westhead, M. Cowling, 1997b; A. M. Gallo, A. Vilaseca, 1996; N. Upton, W. Petty, 2000; P. Poutziouris, 2001). However, family business operators should not discard the services of external private equity providers. The researchers suggest that venture capital trust fund as well as the venture capital companies should intensify their educational programs to enlighten the family business operators about their existence and programs that they offer towards business development in Ghana.

Table 5a. *Principal Component Factor Analysis, factor loadings and unique variances for sources of development finance variables. (UNROTATED SOLUTION)*

(Obs=148)

Factor Analysis/Correlation				**Number of Obs=148**
Method: Principal Factors				**Retained Factors=4**
Rotation: (Unrotated)				**Number of Params=2**
Factor	**Eigenvalue**	**Difference**	**Proportion**	**Cumulative**
Factor 1	1.24612	0.56672	0.7841	0.7841
Factor 2	0.67940	0.39925	0.4275	1.2116
Factor 3	0.28015	0.24617	0.1763	1.3879
Factor 4	0.03398	0.14084	0.0214	1.4093
Factor 5	-0.10686	0.07764	-0.0672	1.3421
Factor 6	-0.18451	0.17459	-0.1161	1.2260
Factor 7	-0.35910		-0.2260	1.0000
LR test:	Independent vs.	Saturated:	chi2 (21) = 136.83	Pro>chi2 =0.0000

Factor loadings (pattern matrix) and unique variances

Variable	Factor 1	Factor 2	Factor 3	Factor 4	Uniqueness
1.We are willing to consider external equity funding (venture capital and business angel) for expansion	0.2669	0.2924	0.2822	-0.0057	0.7636
2. We are willing to consider equity (family & friends, partnership) funding for expansion	0.6357	-0.0145	0.0163	0.1068	0.5840
3. We are willing to consider rotational savings for expansion	0.6448	-0.1426	-0.1373	0.0259	0.5444
4. We are willing to consider owner's equity for expansion	0.5423	0.0132	0.0094	-0.1092	0.6938
5. We are willing to consider debt funding for expansion	0.1807	0.5486	-0.1565	-0.0602	0.6383
6. We are willing to re-invest profits earned and use for expansion	-0.1619	0.5211	-0.0512	0.0795	0.6933
7. We are willing to consider government support for expansion	0.0453	0.0269	0.3927	-0.0023	0.8430

Table 5b. *Principal Component Factor Analysis (Varimax Horst Blank Rotation), rotated factor loadings and unique variances for sources of development finance variables. (ROTATED SOLUTION)*

.rotate

Factor Analysis/Correlation				**Number of Obs=148**
Method: Principal Factors				**Retained Factors=4**
Rotation: Orthogonal Varimax (Kaiser on)				**Number of Params=12**
Factor	**Eigenvalue**	**Difference**	**Proportion**	**Cumulative**
Factor 1	1.22045	0.55675	0.7680	0.7680
Factor 2	0.66370	0.34440	0.4176	1.1856
Factor 3	0.31930	0.28309	0.2009	1.3865
Factor 4	0.03620		0.0228	1.4093
LR test:	Independent vs.	Saturated:	chi2 (21) = 136.83	Pro>chi2 =0.0000

Rotated Factor Loadings (Pattern Matrix) and Unique Variances

Variable	Factor 1	Factor 2	Factor 3	Factor 4	Uniqueness
1.We are willing to consider external equity funding (venture capital and business angel) for expansion			0.3728		0.7636
2. We are willing to consider equity (family & friends, partnership) funding for expansion	0.6298				0.5840
3. We are willing to consider rotational savings for expansion	0.6686				0.5444
4. We are willing to consider owner's equity for expansion	0.5270				0.6938
5. We are willing to consider debt funding for expansion		0.5781			0.6383
6. We are willing to re-invest profits earned and use for expansion		0.5105			0.6933
7. We are willing to consider government support for expansion			0.3728		0.8430

(Blanks represent abs (loading) <.3)

5. Conclusion

Finance is the lifeblood of family businesses. Many are seeking capital to fund expansion plans, yet the uniquely long-term perspective most family members have when managing their companies, together with a reluctance to relinquish control and a desire for discretion, means that finding finance that matches their requirements can be a challenge (KPMG, 2014). As a result, family businesses are casting a wide net when seeking for financing growth and expansion, using a variety of development finance sources including bank debt, retained profit, owner's equity, rotational savings, equity from friends and family, equity from venture capitalist and business angels among others. All have advantages and disadvantages, and for each option the founder or owner-manager needs to evaluate carefully the degree of control they will lose over the business, and determine just how many internal problems each financing solution might generate. The paper therefore, assessed financing family business expansion in Ghana. It explored whether family businesses use debt or equity financing as their development finance source or not. The paper has shown that family business operators in Ghana utilize both debt and equity financing for their business developmental activities. But the equity financing is limited to family & friends, and partners alone, not Private Equity Investors-Venture Capitalist and Business Angels. It also revealed that founders or owner-managers use equity financing (68.92 %) as a source of start-up capital to commence their business activities. Also, founders or owner-managers admitted that they will only allow external investors (venture capitalist and business angel) to come in, if they would be prepared to offer advice and expertise to them alone, and nothing more.

Finally, it is clear from the findings that, for a family business to propel growth and expansion, serious attention need to be paid to funding sources. Also, founders or owner-managers must evolve to accommodate changing family dynamics in order to continue the unique role of family businesses across the globe.

Recommendations

In the light of the findings and conclusion above, it is recommended that:

i. Ghana Venture Capital Trust Fund and venture capital companies embark on massive educational and information program on venture capital support activities in order to disseminate needed information to family business owners concerning the financing option and support services available to them.

ii. Family members or shareholders should be educated fully to understand the reason why the business needs to re-invest in the business to avoid any imminent conflict in the organization.

iii. Businesses that rely on re-investment as their expansion pad should set up distribution plans that will allow owners to benefit from appreciation over time.

iv. The importance that family businesses operators attach to the debt financing should be sustained by increasing the credit facilities and decreasing the interest rate. This could be possible when the prime rate charged by the central bank is minimized to allow the commercial banks to also reduce their interest rates.

v. Finally, there should be formation of family business association in Ghana. This will serve as appropriate vehicle to channel their grievances concerning interest rate, tax and other economic issues affecting their businesses.

Once these recommendations (base on the results and findings of the study) are adopted, it is hoped that ceteras paribus, the Family Business could thrive through favorable financing for fruitful and expansive outcome without any threat of undesirable external control.

References

[1] J. Abor and N. Biekpe, "Small business financing initiatives in Ghana" Problems and Perspectives in Management, Vol. 4, Issue 3. pp. 69-77,(2006).

[2] J. N. Amu,"The role of women in Ghana's economy" Accra: Federich Ebert Foundation, (2004)

[3] E. Aryeetey, A. Baah-Nuakoh, T. Duggleby, H. Hettige, and F.W Steel, "`Supply and demand for finance of small scale enterprises in Ghana"World Bank Discussion Paper No. 251, (1994)

[4] M. Ayyagari, T. Beck, and A. Demirguc-Kunt, "Small and medium size enterprises across the globe" Small Business Economics, Vol. 15 No. 1, pp 49-61, (2007).

[5] Aston Business School, "Constraints on the growth of small firms" London: Department of Trade & Industry, HMSO, (1991)

[6] Bank of England, "Finance for small firms: Eighth report. London: Bank of England" (2001)

[7] T. Beck, A. Demirguc-Kunt, L. Laeven, and V. Maksimovic, "The determinants of financing obstacles" Journal of International Money and Finance 25, 932-952, (2006)

[8] T. Beck, A. Demirguc-Kunt, and R. Levine, "SMEs, growth, and poverty: Cross-country evidence" Journal of Economic Growth, 10: 199-229, (2005).

[9] A. Bigsten, P. Collier, S. Dercon, M. Fafchamps, B. Guthier, W. Gunning, M. Soderbom, A. Oduro, Oostendorp, C. Patillo, F. Teal and A. Zeufack,"Credit Constraints in Manufacturing Enterprises in Africa" Working Paper WPS/2000. Centre for the study of African Economies, Oxford University, Oxford. (2000)

[10] F. Boadu, "Venture Capital Financing of Small and Medium Scale Enterprises in Ghana" MPhil Thesis, Kwame Nkrumah University of Science and Technology, (unpublished), (2008)

[11] F. Boadu, G. Dwomoh, A. Sarpong, and E. Dwomo-Fokuo, "Venture Capital Financing: An opportunity for Small and Medium Scale Enterprises in Ghana"Journal of Entrepreneurship and Business Innovation, 1(1), 1-15. Doi: 10.5296/jebi.v1i1.2161 http://dx.doi.org/10.5296/jebi.v1i1.2161,(2014).

[12] E. J. Bolton, "Small firms" Report of the Committee of Inquiry on Small Firms, Cmnd. 4811.) London: HMSO, (1971)

[13] N. S. Buatsi, "Financing Non-traditional Exporters in Ghana" The Journal of Business and Industrial Marketing, 17(6), pp. 501-522, (2002).

[14] J. T. Chemmanur, S. He, and D. Nandy, "The exit choices of entrepreneurial firms" Working paper. Boston College, (2011).

[15] G. Connolly, and C. Jay,"The private world of family business" Australia: Woodslane Pty. Ltd, (1996)

[16] G. Corbetta, "Patterns of development of family businesses in Italy" Family Business Review, 8 (4), 255-265, (1995).

[17] G. Corbetta, and A.C. Salvato, "Boards of directors in Italian family businesses" Family Business Review, Vol. XVII No. 2, pp. 119-34, (2004)

[18] C. Dennreuther, and L. Perren, "The political economy of small firms" Routledge, 711 Third avenue, New York, NY 10017, (2013).

[19] G. W. Dyer, "Examining the "family effect" on firm performance" Family Business Review 19, 253-273, (2006).

[20] F. deVisscher, C. Aronoff, and J. Ward, "Financing transitions: Managing capital and liquidity in the family business" Marietta, GA: Business Owner Resources, (1995).

[21] R. D. Dreux, "Financing family business: Alternatives to selling out or going public" Family Business Review, 3(3), 225-243, (1990).

[22] B. Dunn, and M. Hughes, "Family businesses in the United Kingdom" Family Business Review, 8 (4), 267-291, (1995).

[23] ESRC—Business Research Centre, "The state of British enterprise" Cambridge: University of Cambridge, (1992).

[24] ESRC—Business Research Centre, "The state of British enterprise" Cambridge: University of Cambridge, (1996).

[25] A. M. Gallo, and A. Vilaseca, "Finance in family business" Family Business Review, 9 (4), 387-402, (1996).

[26] E.K. Gersick, J. Davis, M. Hampton, and I. Lansberg, "Generation to generation: Life cycles of the family business" Boston: Harvard Business School Press, (1996).

[27] Ghana Statistical Service, "Population and housing census" (PHC), (2010).

[28] Global Insight, Venture Impact: The Economic Importance of Venture Capital Backed Companies, Fourth Edition, National Venture Capital Association, (2007).

[29] J. Hair, B. Black, R. Anderson, and R. Tatham, Multivariate data analysis, 7th ed. Upper Saddle River NJ: Prentice-Hall, (2010).

[30] T. Hellman, and M. Puri, "The Interaction Between Product Market and Financing Strategy: The Role of Venture Capital" Review of Financial Studies 13 (4), (2000).

[31] IFC, "Regional economic department, background note on micro, small and medium enterprises" Database. Washington, DC: World Bank Group, (2009).

[32] S. Kortum, and J. Lerner, "Assessing the Contribution of Venture Capital to Innovation" The Rand Journal of Economics 31 (4), (2000).

[33] KPMG,"Financing family business growth through individual investors" KPMG Enterprise, (2014).

[34] P. Leach, andT. Bogod, "The BDO—Stoy Hayward guide to the family business" London: Kogan Page, (1999).

[35] W. Lili,"Seminar on Venture Capital and Start-up Companies" Asia-Pacific Economic Cooperation, December 10-11, 2003 Beijing, China, (2003).

[36] N. Michaelas, "Financial policy and capital structure choice in UK privately held companies" Unpublished doctoral dissertation, Manchester Business School, University of Manchester, Manchester, England, (1998).

[37] S. C. Myers, "The capital structure puzzle" Journal of Finance, Vol. 39, Issue 3, pp. 575-592, (1984).

[38] F. Neubauer, and G. A. Lank,The family business, London: MacMillan Business., (1998).

[39] R. Parker, R. Riopelle, and W. Steel,"Small Enterprises Adjusting to Liberalization in Five African Countries" World Bank Discussion Paper, No. 271, African Technical Department Series, The World Bank, Washington DC, (1995).

[40] R. Pettit, andR. Singer, "Small business finance: A research agenda" Financial Management, Autumn, 47-60, (1985).

[41] P. Poutziouris, "The view of family companies on venture capital: Empirical evidence from the UK small to medium-size enterprising economy" Family Business Review, Vol. XIV, no. 3. Doi. 10.1111/j. 1741-6248.2001.00277.x (2001).

[42] P. Poutziouris, "Venture capital and small-medium size family companies: An analysis from the demand perspective" In P. Poutziouris (Ed.), Family business—Tradition or entrepreneurship in the new economy (pp. 255-282). Book proceedings: 11th Annual Family Business Network World Conference, FBN, London, (2000).

[43] P. Poutziouris, N. Michaelas, F. Chittenden, and S. Sitorious, "The financial structure, behavior and performance of SMEs: Family and private companies" Small Business and Enterprise Development Conference, Manchester, (2000).

[44] P. Poutziouris, The development of the ethnic small business venture: Lessons from breaking out strategies of the Anglo-Cypriots 21st Institute for Small Business Affairs (ISBA) National Small Firms Conference, Leeds (UK), November, (1999).

[45] P. Poutziouris, F. Chittenden and N. Michaelas, "The financial affairs of private companies" Liverpool: Tilney Fund Management, (1998).

[46] P. Poutziouris, F. Chittenden, and N. Michaelas, "The financial development of smaller private and public Ltd companies" Liverpool: Tilney Fund Management Publication, p. 34 (1998).

[47] P. Poutziouris, and C. Chittenden, "Family business or business families?" The Institute of Small Business Affairs, Research Series Monograph 2, (1996).

[48] A. C. Romano, G. Tanewski, and X. K. Smyrnios, "Capital structure decision making: A model for family business" Journal of Business Venturing, 16, 285-310, (2000).

[49] M. Schiffer, and W. Beatrice, "Firms size and the business environment: Worldwide survey Results" IFC discussion paper number 43, (2001).

[50] K.N. Sowa, A. Baah-Nuakoh, A.K. Tutu, and B. Osei,"Small Enterprise and Adjustment, The Impact of Ghana's Economic Recovery Program on Small-Scale Industrial Enterprises", ODI Research Reports, (1992).

[51] I. Stefanovic, P. Damnjanovic, and O. Jasko, "The Analysis of contemporary environment impact upon organizational operations" Serbian Journal of Management, Vol.5, No. 1, pp. 97-109, (2010).

[52] J. Tucker, and J. Lean, "Small firm finance and public policy"Journal of Small Business and Enterprise Development, 10(1), pp. 50-61, (2003).

[53] N. Upton, and W. Petty, "Venture capital and U.S. family business" Venture Capital, 2 (1), 27-39, (2000).

[54] J. Ward, "Keeping the family business healthy" San Francisco: Jossey-Bass, (1987).

[55] P. Westhead,andM. Cowling, and D. Storey, "The management and performance of unquoted family companies in the UK" Centre for Small and Medium Sized Enterprise. Warwick Business School, UK BDO—Stoy Hayward, (1997a).

[56] P. Westhead, and M. Cowling, "Performance contrasts between family and non-family unquoted companies in the UK" International Journal of Entrepreneurial Behavior and Research, 3(1), 30-52, (1997b).

[57] Wikipedia,"Map of Ashanti Region" Retrieved March 6, 2015, from http://en.wikipedia.org/wiki/Ashanti_Region, (2013).

[58] H. Wilson, "The financing of small firms" (Interim report of the Committee to Review the Functioning of Financial Institutions, Cmnd. 7503.) London: HMSO, (1979).

3

Innovation, the New Challenge of Today's Entrepreneurship

Adela Mariana Vadastreanu[1], Adrian Bot[2], Dorin Maier[3, *], Andreea Maier[3]

[1]National Institute of Research and Development for Isotopic and Molecular Technologies, Cluj Napoca, Technical University of Cluj Napoca, Romania
[2]National Institute of Research and Development for Isotopic and Molecular Technologies, Cluj Napoca, Romania
[3]Technical University of Cluj Napoca, Romania and University of Economic Studies, Bucharest, Romania

Email address:
adella.vadastreanu@itim-cj.ro (A. M. Vadastreanu), adrian.bot@itim-cj.ro (A. Bot), dorin.maier@gmail.com (D. Maier), maier_andreea@ymail.com (A. Maier)

Abstract: The aim of this article is to evaluate the importance of innovation for entrepreneurship environment in the context of current economic conditions. Throughout the last century, industry leaders learnt to master the production process to such an extent that now it no longer functions as a significant competitive advantage. Every entrepreneur is now facing a harsh and highly competitive business context in a globalized economy, and in order to resist and to be successful the new challenge is to master the innovation process, harnessing change, creating new competitive advantages by offering better products, using better processes, delivering better services or even offering entirely new solutions. Although the process of innovation is one of the most important drivers of growth and prosperity in today's global economy, it is also one of the least understood. This paper wants to bring a contribution to a better understanding of the innovation process and to identify some characteristics of the future entrepreneur. At the end of the paper are presented some recommendations that a company should be aware of in order to be more innovative and also we have identified some characteristics that an entrepreneur must have in order to be successful. This article can be also used as a base for future studies regarding the process of innovation, the management of the innovation process, the establishing of a management system of innovation and its implementation into existing management systems.

Keywords: Innovation, Entrepreneurship, Business Success

1. Introduction

In today's national and global economy, innovation, knowledge and information are the central concerns of private and state entities. In this context, innovation is an important dimension of restructuring and modernization policies within an economy based on knowledge and competitiveness. Innovation is an everyday phenomenon that progressively changes economy and society [1], [2], [3], seen as the elixir of life for enterprises, regardless of their size and profile [4], [5], [6].

Figure 1 presents the evolution of the key forces for determining the competitiveness of the industrial sector over five decades. It may be noted that, until 1970, most companies approached innovation from a very narrow perspective, focusing mainly on results only [6].

Then, in the 80s, the focus was on productivity, followed by quality and not very often by innovation. In the last twenty years, enterprises have been oriented towards quality management through processes and systems. The concept of continuous improvement helped competitive positioning strategy.

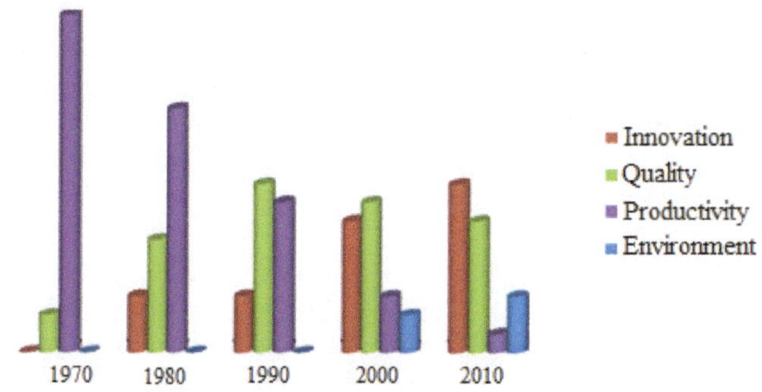

Figure 1. *The evolution of the key forces for determining the competitiveness of the industrial sector over five decades [6].*

In the 90s, competition in a global market has led enterprises to consider quality as a key driving force, without leaving out productivity from the competitiveness equation. In the 2000s, there was a change of priorities and enterprises realized that innovation is as important as quality in order to provide a competitive advantage in the market. This approach is very popular nowadays.

2. Defining the Concept of Innovation

Innovation efforts over the years have provided a wealth of innovation projects that failed. Even large companies that were once forerunners and creators of all markets have failed to remain competitive when major changes occurred, particularly technological. Organizations are accustomed to what they do (basic competencies) that they get stuck there, and when the environment changes (for example, change in customer requirements, change in regulations), they are unable to adapt quickly and easily [6].

Innovation is novelty, change, transformation, solving a technical problem or work organization problem in order to improve a performance indicator. Innovation comes from the verb to innovate, the action to innovate and its outcome, renewal, innovation. To innovate means to make a change, to introduce a novelty in a field, in a system, to renew, to introduce, adopt or disseminate innovation [7].

Innovation can be analyzed as an invention and its commercialization. However, the boundaries are not always clear, as the invention may be relevant not only for research and development, but also for optimizing or enhancing new methods and processes, and its marketing may also include significant research work [8].

Innovation is seen as the key element to obtaining sustainable competitive advantages for the success of the enterprise. The goal of innovation is mostly to survive, to grow, to make a profit, but what matters for innovation is how it affects the chances of survival, profit and growth opportunities.

3. Approaches to the Process of Innovation in Connection with Business Processes

A thorough examination of the literature on the innovation process carried out in this paper allows us to point out some important conclusions regarding the approach to the innovation process in organizations, the stages of the innovation process, as well as the outcome and benefits of the innovation process.

The innovation process is a sequence of activities carried out by the management of an enterprise to create products and services, intended for sale [11]. At the same time, the category of innovation processes also includes market expansion activities, supply improvement activities, production processes, equipment maintenance, distribution channels, service activities and, not least, administrative and management improvement activities [12]. In other words, any change made in the enterprise in order to improve its economic situation, its position on the market, staff working conditions or environmental protection, is an essential part of the innovation process [13]

The Organisation for Economic Co-operation and Development (OECD)[14] has proposed a systemic view of the innovation process (Figure 2).

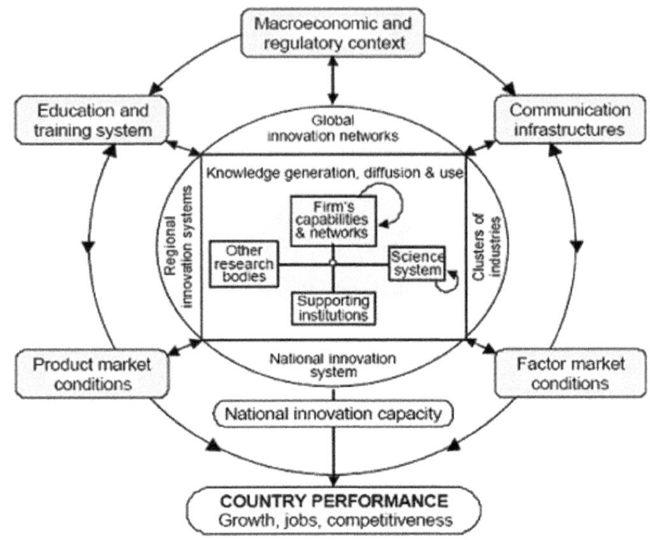

Figure 2. *Parties and relationships in an enterprise's innovation system: the OECD model [14].*

The key processes that lie at the center of the system are knowledge, dissemination and exploitation, which are shaped by the organization's capabilities and the strength of its relationships. Supporting the commercial, technological and regulatory environments where enterprises operate is another key component of the system. The result of this complex set of capabilities and the connections of the national innovation capacity is an important factor in determining economic performance. According to OECD [14], a national innovation system is a set of distinct institutions which jointly and individually contribute to the development and dissemination of new technologies and provide the framework for governments to implement policies that influence the innovation process. Therefore, it is a system of interconnected institutions that create and store the transfer of knowledge and skills that define new technologies (viewed from a wider perspective).

The model in Figure 2 also suggests that regional differences in levels of innovation activities can be substantial, and that the identification of the main characteristics and factors that promote innovation activity and the development of specific sectors at regional level can contribute to the innovation process[15].

Another important idea emerging from the pattern in Figure 2 is that enterprises do not innovate in isolation. The "journey" of innovation is a collective achievement that requires many entrepreneurs in both the public and private sector[16].

Innovation is a complex process, all innovation models comprising several stages. In its most synthetic form, there are three stages, and the most extensive model is that proposed by

Tidd and Bessant, which consists of seven stages [17].

The first stage of all models is to collect information and then generate the idea. While most authors have attributed this first step a simple name, such as idea generation, or the stage of market analysis and opportunity identification.

The next step identified by most authors is to choose the best idea, deciding and preparing to develop the idea. This step is called "selection", "idea conversion" or "innovation generation and investigation".

The next step is to obtain a tangible product, process or service from the innovative idea, followed by product testing and commercialization. For some models, these two stages are united under the name of "idea conversion", "development period".

The last stage is implementing the new product, process or service in the market, commercializing and obtaining added value from the innovative idea. Some authors show a further step, after the product, process or service is launched, in order to learn and prepare for another innovative process [18].

Innovation is the result of a process that consists of a set of activities and a sequence of events as shown in Figure 3 The innovation process typically consists of seven distinct phases, starting with an idea and ending with putting the idea into practice.

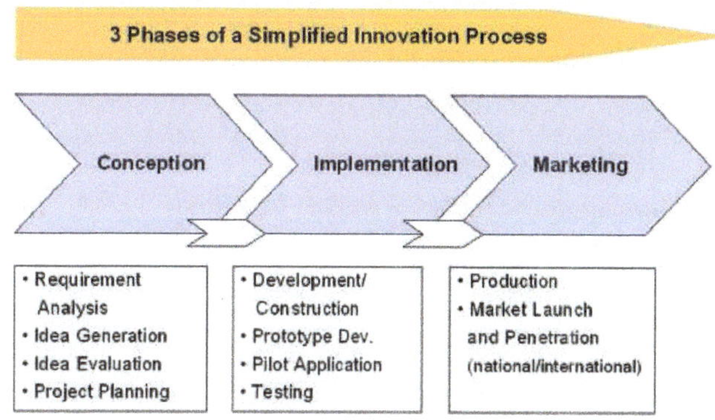

Figure 3. *Phases of the innovation process [19].*

The innovation process has influenced managers to create their innovation models within the organization. A very good model that pinpoints the factors that influence an organization's innovation process is the one found in [20], and it is shown in Figure 4.

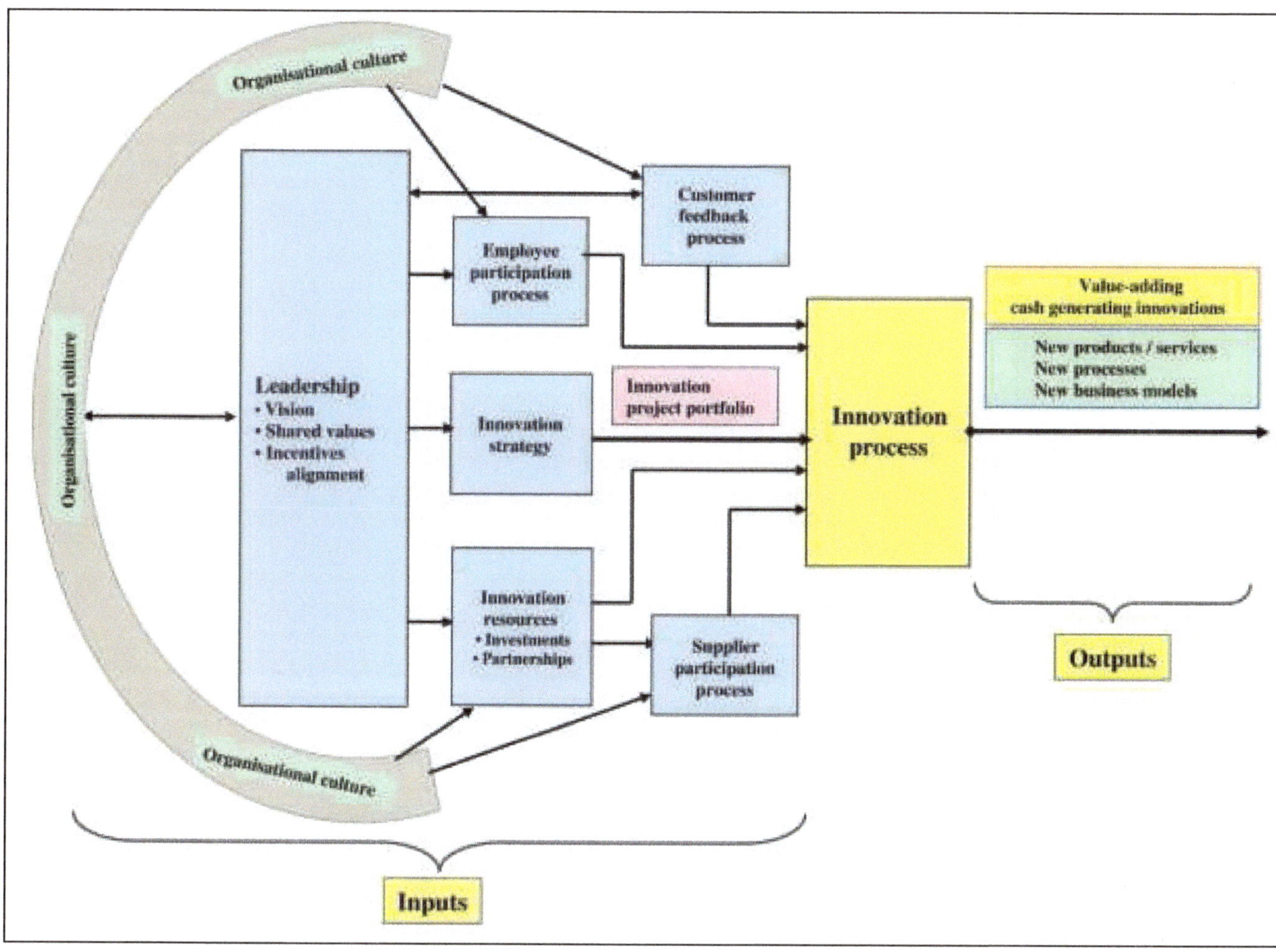

Figure 4. *Innovation process model[20].*

According to this model, the innovation process is influenced by:

- leadership, which shapes the vision, shared values and incentive alignment, both tangible and intangible, for all key stakeholders

- The organizational culture, which establishes the perfect ground for creative talent hiring. Key attributes for culture include current reliability, attitude to risk experimenting with new ideas, tolerance for failure, the degree of diversity in education and ethnicity of employees, willingness to share knowledge and cooperate, and others.
- Innovation strategy, which identifies and takes advantage of new opportunities emerging in a changing business environment. This strategy is reflected in the portfolio of innovation projects in order to balance the benefits and risks that improve products, creating new value to meet customer needs.
- Employee involvement in the process, which makes a valuable contribution and supports innovation strategy, particularly with regard to product characteristics and production process improvements.
- Innovation resources, necessary investments and external partnerships.
- Client feedback, which allows organizations to collect opinions from the market regarding product performance.
- Supplier involvement in the process, using expertise, unique skills and partner counseling in developing new products and services.

The innovation process uses all the above mentioned inputs to select the best ideas for developing new value-added products and services that can reach the market quickly and become new sources of revenue and profit (Figure 5).

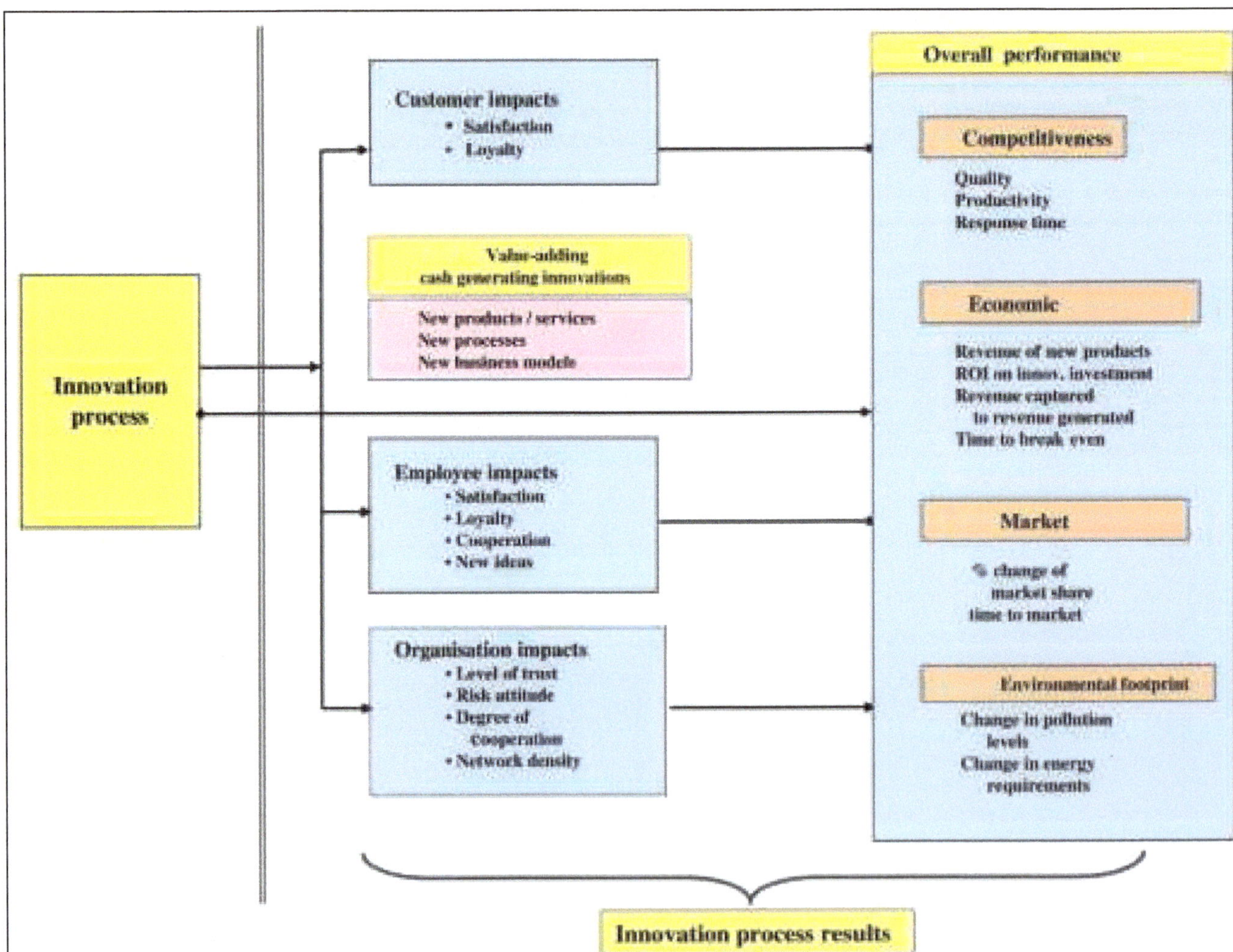

Figure 5. *Results of innovation process [20].*

This process is analyzed for each of the four added value phases: generating new ideas, selecting specific innovation projects; developing new products through prototyping and commercialization. The results and benefits of the innovation process include the following:

- the impact on customers, as customer satisfaction increased to products / services that offer greater value, together with increased loyalty towards the organization
- the impact on employees, as employee satisfaction increased loyalty and led to greater cooperation within the organization
- the impact on the organization, as the level of confidence increased, leading to a healthy attitude towards reasonable risks and a higher degree of cooperation
- overall performance improvement, measured by revenue from new products

4. Framework to Support Innovation

Supporting innovation, measuring and improving the efficiency of national innovation systems are the most important issues and priorities in Europe, especially the mechanisms and measures to support innovation, turning research into new products and services. There are many definitions of innovation support measures, but herein we will mention the most widely applied definition suggested by Reid and Peter: "an innovation policy measure can be defined as any action taken or (co-) financed by the public sector in order to influence innovation processes and capacities in enterprises"[21].

Four types of action policies can be identified within this definition:

1. Provision of financial resources directly to enterprises to support innovation processes (Modality: State aids, R&D funds, Innovation projects, Public procurement).

2. Provision of financial resources to organization functioning such as innovation-related service providers or intermediaries which support innovations in enterprises and/or connect research and business actors (Modality: knowledge and technology transfer, business incubation innovation management training, infrastructural development for new-technology based firms, entrepreneurship policies for start-ups).

3. Creating and coordinating knowledge exchange among actors in innovation system by public authorities through establishing public-private partnerships (Modality: transfer and exploitation of research results, mobility of personnel between two sectors of academia and business, information and best practice diffusion, demonstrator projects, networks and clusters).

4. Creation of new institutions, as a kind of legal framework, that indirectly affect innovation process in enterprises (Modality: Legal framework, Tax and financial incentives, support to protection of IPR, standardization & certification, administrative simplification).

A version with innovation support measures divided into 5 categories was developed:

1. Improving the management of innovation and strategic information in order to draw up policies;

2. Fostering an innovation friendly environment;

3. Encouraging the transfer of knowledge and technology to enterprises, as well as the development of innovation poles and clusters;

4. Promoting and supporting the creation and growth of innovative enterprises;

5. Strengthening entrepreneurial innovation, including intellectual property protection and commercialization.

5. Conclusions

The competition on the market is increasing and in order to be competitive an entrepreneur must adopt innovation as his weapon and thus to overcome competition.

Our research has shown some key aspect that every entrepreneur must be aware of. One of the aspect is the management support, this is the beginning of the innovative thinking for every company, but the managers must have an active support not only to approve the new innovative way of thinking but also a more active support such as employees motivation or the provision of training and development programs.

Another aspect is related to the involvement of the employs in the innovation process, and for this an environment where every employee can freely expose his ideas.

The rewarding of employees, they should be rewarded accordingly and here we do not mean just a monetary reward but also an emotional one, such as public recognition of theirs merit in the company.

The resources of the company must be intelligent allocated and the culture must be an innovative culture where it is possible to take the risk, to embrace constructive failure to obtain extraordinary results.

We can conclude that the future entrepreneur must be an innovative one, a more creative, flexible and communicative one. The future entrepreneurs must have confidence in their abilities; they must be brave to express and support innovative ideas; they must be ready and willing to make responsible decisions, in other words to be willing to take a moderate risk.

Acknowledgements

This paper benefited from financial support through the National Institute of Research and Development for Isotopic and Molecular Technologies, Cluj-Napoca, Romania.

References

[1] Brad, S., (2007), *Innovative Production and Its Implications on New Product Design*, Proceedings of the 8th International Conference MTeM 2007, pp. 79-82, 2007.

[2] Leavengood, S., (2011), Identifying Best Quality Management Practices for Achieving Quality and Innovation Performance in the Forest Products Industry, Portland State University, 2011.

[3] Hill, C., R., (2003), The performance of incumbent firms in the face of radical technological innovation, Academy of Management Review, Vol. 28, Nr. 2, pp. 257-74, 2003.

[4] Wright, R., (2005), Types of product innovations and small business performance in hostile and benign environments, Journal of Small Business Strategy, Vol. 15, Nr. 2, pp. 33-34.

[5] Tenhunen, L., (2007), *How International Collaboration Benefits Companies – Evaluation of the Scale Effects of an Expanding Innovation Environment*, InnoSteel: True Stories Made Out of Steel, pp. 109-130, Hamk University of Applied Sciences

[6] Maier, A., Fulea, M., (2012), *Integrating concepts of quality and innovation - a key to business excellence*, Calitatea- acces la success, Vol. 13, Nr. 131, p.13-19 (ro)/ 77-81(en), ISSN: 1582-2559.

[7] Maier, A., (2014) *Cercetări şi contribuţii la dezvoltarea modelelor de management al inovării*, Universitatea Tehnică Cluj – Napoca, România.

[8] *Dicționarul explicativ al limbii române* (DEX), Academia Română, Editura Univers Enciclopedic

[9] Rothwell, R., *Successful industrial innovation: critical factors for the 1990s*, R & D Management, vol. 22, nr. 3, pg. 221-39, 1992

[10] Rothwell, R., (1994) *Towards the fifth-generation innovation process*, International Marketing Review, Vol.11, Nr. 1, pp. 7

[11] Rogers, E., (1995) *Diffusion of Innovations*, New York: The Free Press

[12] Bessant, J., (2005) *Managing Innovation beyond the Steady State*, Technovation, Vol. 25, pp 1366-1376

[13] Adamides, E., Karacapilidis, N., (2006) Information technology support for the knowledge and social processes of innovation management, Technovation, Vol. 26.

[14] OECD (Organization for Economic Co-operation and Development), (2009), A Forward looking response to the crisis. Fostering an Innovation –led sustainable recovery. http://www.ioe-emp.org. Downloaded on 01.03.2011.

[15] Coccia, M., (2006) Classifications of Innovations. Survey and Future Directions, National Research Council of Italy, W.P. 2/2006.

[16] Fagerberg, J., *Innovation: A Guide to the Literature, in the Oxford Handbook of Innovations*, Oxford University Press, pp. 1-26, 2004.

[17] Tidd, J., Bessant, J., Pavitt, K., *Managing Innovation: Integrating Technological*, Market and Organizational Change, JohnWiley & Sons, Chichester, 2001.

[18] Hesmer, A., (2010) *Knowledge Exploration to Enhance the Product Develop Process*, Towards new challenges for Innovative management practices, Vol. 3, Nr. 1, European Research on Innovation and Management, Wiesbaden, Germany, pp. 67-75.

[19] http://www.global-innovation.net, accesed on 23.07.2014

[20] Dervitsiotis, K., *A framework for the assessment of an organisation's innovation excellence*, Total Quality Management, Vol. 21, Nr. 9, pp. 903–918, 2010

[21] *Ghidul Metodologic al inovării*, http://www.i3e.eu/innovation/mgi_RO.pdf.

4

Impact of Monetary Policy on Stock Price: Evidence from Bangladesh

Afrin Rifat

Department of Accounting and Finance, School of Business and Economics, North South University, Dhaka, Bangladesh

Email address:
afrin.rifat@northsouth.edu

Abstract: This study intends to explore the impact of monetary policy on the performance of stock market from the perspective of a developing country-*namely Bangladesh.* The issue of monetary policy has been a subject of debate among several financial economists since a long time. Monetary policy is basically that part of the macroeconomics, which aims to achieve a set of objectives that are, conveyed in terms of several macroeconomic variables such as inflation, real output, money supply, exchange rate etc. As a result, any change in the monetary policy will have an effect on these variables. Understanding the sensitivity of stock market with respect to these variables of monetary policy frameworks is very important, particularly to recognize the monetary policy mechanism transmission into the stock market. This paper investigates whether current economic activities or more specifically the monetary policy tools of Bangladesh can explain stock market returns by using a number of econometric models of measuring long-run and short-run relationship between monetary policy tools and stock price.

Keywords: Bangladesh, Monetary Policy, Dhaka Stock Exchange (DSE), Stock Return

1. Introduction

In the field of economics and finance, the effect of monetary policy on the real asset market has been and proceeds to be one of the most popular studied topics. Monetary policy is used in mostly by the central banks as a tool to influence the economic variables such as GDP, Industrial Production Index, Consumer Price Index, Exchange Rate or the Inflation rate. One of the most popular monetary tools applied by central bank is to alter the short term interest rate to achieve the macroeconomic goals of government. On the other hand, in modern economy; stock exchange plays a very important role. For example stock exchange can help an economy to diversify the domestic funds and channels into productive investment. Nevertheless for a stock exchange of any country, to play such role, the existence of a significant relationship between macroeconomic variables and stock market is very essential. Moreover, we all know that, modern economy is a market based economy where the capital market plays a very significant role. It is the capital market which transfers the excess money of the savers to the borrowers which is at the key of the developments of an economy. In a country economic growth and propensity cannot happen, as long as their capital market is inefficient. As a result we can say that economic growth and prosperity is possible only when capital market works efficiently [1].

According to Efficient Market Hypothesis (EMH), investors should know, all the necessary or relevant information regarding their investment and also about profit maximizing and the macroeconomics variables which might lead to a supernatural earning. This clearly indicates that stock price actually reflects the shocks from macroeconomic variable. In case of the existence of EMH in capital market, markets become efficient. Therefore we can say that stock market plays the vital role to transfer of funds from capital borrowers to capital investors which is very essential for economic growth. Therefore, in order to understand how monetary policy changes transmit to the economy and how the market responds to the changes is important for both policy makers and investors.

Poole et al. [2] tested and showed how the monetary policy changes affected the bank bill rate in different maturities using U.S. data from 1988 to 1999. According to their study, market is becoming better day by day in forecasting the monetary policy action. The research conducted by Cook and Hahn [3] was one of the first, which found a significant relationship between monetary policy and bond return by using the event study method to test the daily effect of monetary policy on asset prices. In 2001 another researcher, Kutter has further extended the study of Cook and Hahn by decomposing the interest rate changes into expected and unexpected changes and found a significant reaction on the part of stock market to surprise monetary policy changes [4]. Afterwards, Bredin et al. [5] and Gregoriou et al. [6] employed the method of Kutter to explore the effect of monetary policy on stock returns and found the similar kind of significant relationship.

2. Literature Review

Monetary policy in any country, attempts to achieve a set of objectives that are expressed in terms of macroeconomic variables such as inflation, real output, employment, money supply, exchange rate etc. Nevertheless, monetary policy actions such as changes in the central bank discount rate can have an indirect effect on these variables and considerable lags can be involved in the policy transmission mechanism [7]. For equity prices, an approach for determining stock prices is commonly assumed to be forward looking. For monetary policy, the monetary authority affects both the current and the expected future real interest rate. This in turn has an effect on decisions of household to consume and to invest, respectively, in terms of timing. To establish the relationship, changes in expected future interest rate serving as a discount rate are directly attributed to the link between monetary policy and the stock market. Preceding empirical evidences also strengthen the notion that monetary policy (restrictive or expansive) affects both contemporaneous and future stock returns. It is generally believed that restrictive monetary policy and expansionary monetary policy lead to lower stock prices and higher stock prices respectively. Moreover, according to some researchers, changes in monetary policy influence forecasts of market determined interest rates, equity cost of capital, and expectations of corporate profitability [8]. The basic idea is that an increase in interest rates due to a restrictive monetary policy will force investors to raise funds through the equity market. Besides in order to heighten the demand for stock, the price will drop to a level that will attract investors, in the short run at least. According to Bernanke and Gertler [9], apart from the interest rate, monetary policy affects the external finance premium as well, which brings the concept of credit channel of monetary transmission mechanism to focus. However, the primary focus has always been on banks as they are considered as the major conveyors of monetary policy shocks to the real sectors of the economy.

The relationship between monetary policy and stock market has been a topic for study in several parts of the world since long. In 2007, Mbutor [10] studied the lending channel of Monetary Policy Transmission in Nigeria. He has used GDP as a dependent variable on the explanatory variables which includes consumer price index as a proxy for domestic prices, treasury bill rates as a proxy for minimum rediscount rate, broad money (M2), exchange rate, total quantity of loans and maximum lending rate as a proxy for the price of loans. According to this study, increase in the minimum rediscount rate by 0.25 percentage points will leave the quantity of loans made by the banks unaffected in the first period [10]. This finding of Mbutor is consistent with the concept that loan contracts need some time to be adjusted. Nonetheless this study proves that an increase in the minimum rediscount rate (MRR) forces banks to cut down the amount of loans that they extend to their customers. Another important source of monetary policy transmission mechanism is exchange rate [11]. According to Kim [12], exchange rate is one of the major determinants of business profitability and equity prices.

Mukherjee et. al tested the relationship between stock prices and several macroeconomic variables-exchange rate, money supply, index of industrial production, inflation and interest rates- in 1995 and observed a positive relationship for all other variables except for inflation and interest rates where a miscellaneous relationship was experimented [13]. Similar to the study of Mukherjee et. al., Ibrahim has conducted a study in 2003 and tested the long run relationship and dynamic interactions between Malaysian Stock Market and various economic variables [14]. He has used real output, aggregate price level, money supply, and exchange rate as explanatory variables for the variations in stock price movements [14]. The evidences from this study showed a positive relationship between the Malaysian stock price index and economic variables such as money supply, consumer price index & industrial production. However, the study found a negative relationship between that stock price index and exchange rates.

Another study has been conducted by using the Vector Autoregressive (VAR) model to test the relationship between stock prices and macroeconomic factors (exchange rate, industrial production, money supply, and consumer prices) in Cyprus by Tsoukalas [15]. The evidences from the study showed a strong relationship between stock prices and all the macroeconomic factors.

Thorbecke [16] on the other hand used a number of alternative methodologies to study the relationship between monetary policy and stock prices in the United States. One of the methodologies that he has employed in his research is VAR model and has used macroeconomic factors such equity returns, output growth, inflation, and the federal funds rate. In his study he has found that monetary policy shocks, measured by orthogonalized innovations in the federal funds rate, have a greater impact on smaller capitalisation stocks [7], which is in line with the hypothesis that monetary policy affects firms' access to credit [9]. Another methodology that Thorbecke [16] employed in the same study is the Boschen and Mills' [17] index which he has used as an alternative measure of monetary policy conditions. The results from this methodology once again confirmed the result he got from VAR model that expansionary monetary policy exerts a large and statistically significant positive effect on monthly stock returns. Patelis [18] also examined whether shifts in the monetary policy stance is responsible for at least some portion of the observed predictability in excess stock returns in the United Ststes. He has used the long-horizon regression methodology in his study, using two sets of explanatory variables-monetary policy variables and financial variables. According to his study, monetary policy variables are significant predictors of future returns, although they cannot account fully for the observed stock return predictability [7].

In 2006, Cassola and Morana [19] employed a cointegrated VAR model including real GDP, inflation, real M3 balances, short term interest rate, bond yield, and real stock prices with an intention to inspect the transmission mechanism of monetary policy in the Euro area. Through their study they have found out that a permanent positive monetary shock has a temporary positive effect on real stock prices. The results of Cassola and Morana [19] support the findings of Jensen and Johnson [20] that monetary policy developments are indeed associated with stock returns. In their study Jensen and Johnson showed that long-term stock returns following discount rate decreases are higher and less volatile than returns following rate increases [7]. They have used discount rate as a proxy for the state monetary policy in their study because discount rate is typically regarded as a signal of monetary and possibly economic developments. According to several financial economists there are various reasons behind the effects of changes in the discount rate on stock returns. For instance, discrete policy rate changes influence forecasts of market determined interest rates and the equity cost of capital [7]. In addition, Waud [8] stated in his study that changes in the discount rate possibly affect expectations of corporate profitability. In a following study, Jensen et al. [21] extended the Fama and French [22] analysis by signifying that the monetary policy affects investors' required returns. In their study Jensen et al. [22] found that "predictable variation in stock returns depends on monetary as well as business conditions, with expected stock returns being higher in tight money periods than in easy money periods" [7].

One of the most important monetary dynamics is inflation which reflects money growth per unit of output. The poor performance of the stock market during periods of inflation is a well studied topic in financial literature [23]. In 1988, United States Presidential Task Force has conducted a study on market mechanisms for the Group of Seven Countries and found a significant negative relationship between real stock returns and inflation on four of the seven countries. 'Inflation fears' was cited as a probable contributing reason behind the stock market crash of October 1987 which led to the setting up of the task force [24]. Previously this negative relationship between stock returns and both actual and expected inflation was recognized by the studies of Nelson [25] and Fama and Schwert [26]. There were basically two lines of thoughts that have been come forward as possible explanations for this anomaly particularly for the United States stock market [27]. The first line of thought focused on 'tax effect' hypothesis which deals with "the treatment of depreciation and the valuation of inventories in periods of inflation, particularly that share prices fail to keep pace with inflation because inflation increases corporate tax liabilities and thus reduces after tax earnings" [28]. In this regard inflation can be considered as a reason behind the changes in stock prices. The second line of thought focused on the 'proxy-effect' hypothesis which is the alternative explanation of the reason behind the inverse relationship the between real stock returns and inflation. Two main assumptions are involved in this case –"one that cyclical variations in earnings and output growth are positively correlated, and the other that monetary policy is counter cyclical" [28].

According to Eugene Fama [29] the forward looking nature of individuals' money demand causes an inverse relationship between existing inflation and expected future growth in national productivity. In consequence a decrease in future output growth leads to a decline in current stock returns along with an increase in existing inflation. In a subsequent study [30] supported Fama by providing evidences against any direct relationship between stock returns and inflation. However unlike Fama, in their study Benderly and Zwick argued that the relationship runs from inflation to expected output growth [28]. On the other hand, in 1983, Geske and Roll [31] extended Fama's argument and stated that a "reverse causality" actually drives the inverse relationship between stock returns and inflation. According to their study, when deficit begins to grow as a result of a decrease in output, outstanding government debt increases. As a response to this movement when central bank decides to monetize a portion of this debt, inflation occurs. However there always exists a group of rationale individuals who are capable of anticipating such debt monetization. As a result a decline in the stock market will ultimately lead to an increase in expected future inflation [29]. Thus, according to Geske and Roll [31], stock returns are inversely correlated with expected future inflation. Later another study by Kaul [32], regarding the relationship between stock return and inflation produced the similar results. Nevertheless in contrast to Geske and Roll, this study did not pivoted on debt monetization entirely.

On the other hand, a study has been carried out to examine the relationship between inflation, output and stock prices in the Chinese economy by Zhao in 1999 [33]. Evidences from this study showed a significant but negative relationship between stock prices and inflation and a similar kind of relationship between output and stock prices. In 2001, Udegbunam and Eriki [34] conducted a similar kind of study on the Nigerian Stock Market, and observed strong evidence which strengthen the earlier proposition that inflation indeed wields a significant negative effect on stock prices. Moreover, in their study Udegbunam and Eriki provided evidences in favour of a strong relationship between stock prices and Gross Domestic Product (GDP), interest rate, money stock and financial deregulation. However unlike the preceding studies mentioned, a recent study by Omotor [23], provided evidences in favor of a significant and positive relationship between inflation and stock prices in Nigerian Stock Market.

In 2007, Ahmed et. al. [35] examined the relationship

between monetary policy and stock price in Bangladesh using the VAR model including consumer price index, industrial production index, 28-day treasury bill rate, money supply (M1) and all share price index of Dhaka Stock Exchange (DSE) as economic variables. According to this study, contractionary monetary policy shock has insignificant negative effect on the stock price index. On the other hand, Banerjee and Adhikary [36] tested the effects of interest rate and exchange rate (USD against BDT) changes on share price in the stock market of Bangladesh in 2009 by using Johansen-Juselius procedure and the Vector Error Correction Model (VECM) respectively and found that the interest rate and exchange rate changes affect for the stock market in the long-run and there is no significant influence in the short-run [37].

Rahman and Uddin [38] explored the relationship between stock prices and exchange rates by using Johansen cointegration and Granger causality test in three emerging South Asian countries - Bangladesh, India and Pakistan and found neither cointegrating relationship nor any causal relationship between stock prices and exchange rates in the countries. However, Alam & Uddin [39] studied the linear relationship between share price and monetary policy, particularly between share price and changes in interest rate on DSE. Evidences from his study showed that monetary policy has significant negative relationship with share price.

Another researcher, Quadir examined the relationship of macroeconomic variables-treasury bill interest rate and industrial production with stock returns in DSE by using Autoregressive Integrated Moving Average (ARIMA) model and observed a positive relationship between Treasury bill interest rate and industrial production with market stock returns [40]. A further research has been conducted on the relationship between monetary policy and stock price in DSE by Saidjada et. al. in 2013 [37]. Johansen cointegration approach and VEC model have been used in this study to unveil the relationship between stock price and broad money, reserve money & 91-day treasury bill rate. The study found a negative relationship between stock price and treasury bill rate but could not pin point any significant relationship between stock price and broad money & reserve money.

3. Data Description and Research Method

The monthly data employed in this article range from January, 2003 through December, 2013. Monthly data have been used because it avoids the problems of thin trading and price limits in a stock market [41]. As stock market data, the DSE all share price indices were collected. The discount rate of Bangladesh Bank has been used as a proxy for monetary policy. Consumer price Index has been used as a proxy for Inflation because inflation can directly affect stock prices and monetary policy. Therefore, in order to effectively examine the influence of monetary policy on stock returns, it is imperative to put the impact of inflation on stock returns under control. The conditioning variables for Bangladesh Bank feedback rule include the contemporaneous values of money supply and exchange rate, as well as the lagged values. As a result broad money of both Bangladesh and exchange rate of Bangladeshi Taka against U.S Dollar has been used along with central bank's discount rate.

The relationship between stock prices and monetary policy has been tested through several methods by many researchers in the past. In this research article one of the most popular methods to examine the effectiveness of monetary policy on stock price-the Vector Autoregressive (VAR) model have been used. This model has been used mainly for three reasons-there is no exogenous variable because all are considered as endogenous which can give us a better result. Furthermore, VARs allow the value of a variable to depend on more than just its own lags or combinations of white noise terms, so VARs are more flexible other than univariate models. In addition, the forecasts generated by VARs are often better than 'traditional structural' models. Now-a-days VARs are more commonly used method to measure the relationship between monetary policy instruments and stock price. Geske and Roll [31] and Kaul [32] individually studied the fundamental relationship between monetary policy and stock market returns using VARs. Recently many researchers have been used VARs approach to estimate such relationship, for instance, Thorbecke [16] and Neri [42]. The main reason behind the wide use of VARs by researchers to examine monetary policy transmission is because of their ability to recognize the effects of the policy without a complete structural model of the economy.

The motive of this research paper is to inspect that whether there will be any long-run cointegrating relationships between the stock market and monetary policy instruments. The base estimating equation to examine the relationship in log-linear form is as follows:

$$\ln SPIt = \alpha + \beta \ln DRt + \gamma \ln CPIt + \psi \ln MSt + \Omega \ln ERt + \varepsilon t \quad (1)$$

Where, SPI = stock market indices of Bangladesh, DR = Discount Rate, MS=Money Supply, CPI= Consumer Price Index and ER = exchange rate.

There are two reasons behind the conversion of the variables into natural logs. Firstly, if variables are converted into natural logs then coefficients of the cointegrating vector can be interpreted as long-term elasticities if the variables are in logs. On the other hand the second advantage is, if the variables are in logs, the first difference can be interpreted as growth rates. The error (ε) term is assumed to be iid (independently and identically distributed). On the other hand, the additional symbol t has been used for the time subscript.

To implement the empirical design, the nature of the data distribution has been studied by using a series of tests- Unit Roots, Cointegration, Vector Error Correction models (VECM) etc. However, the empirical tests have been started by using a simple descriptive analysis. The standard descriptive statistics test includes the results of- mean, median, standard deviation, skewness and kurtosis. The normality of data distribution has also been estimated by studying the Jarque-Bera test given by the descriptive statistic test.

After the analysis of descriptive statistics, this paper approaches the most important part of the its empirical studies where the following series of tests has been ran.

Unit Root Test

According to many studies, most macroeconomic time series are non-stationary with a deterministic trend [43]. There are several reasons behind the importance of the concept of non-stationarity and the essentiality of those variables non-stationary being treated differently from those that are stationary. The stationarity or non-stationarity of series can strongly influence its behavior and properties [44]. In addition, the use of non-stationary data can results in spurious regression. If one stationary series regressed on another, the t-ratio on the slope coefficient usually become insignificantly different from zero, while the value of R^2 is generally expected to be quite low. This symptom essentially indicates that the variables are not related to one another. However, even two unrelated variables would have high R^2, while trending over time. As a result, running regression with such data produces questionable, invalid and spurious outcomes. In order to eliminate such problem, a stationarity test must be performed for each variable. That is the reason behind performing an unit root test. In statistics, a unit root test examines the nonstationarity of a time series variable by using an autoregressive model. There have been a variety of proposed methods for conducting stationarity tests which include Dickey and Fuller (ADF) test, Phillips and Perron (PP) test, Kwaitkowski (KPSS) test. In this paper all three of these tests have been performed.

Augmented Dickey-Fuller Unit Root Tests

The most popular tests for unit root are the ones derived by Dickey and Fuller. According to the simplest Dickey-Fuller tests, the disturbances in a model are white noise, whereas ADF test is an extension which will allow for some serial correlation. The augment of Said and Dickey [45] regarding the basic autoregressive unit root test to accommodate general ARMA(p, q) models with unknown orders is referred to as the augmented Dickey- Fuller (ADF) test. The ADF test tests the null hypothesis that a time series has a unit root against the alternative while assuming that the dynamics in the data have an ARMA structure. In general he ADF test in the context of model can be specified as follows,

$$z_t = \mu + \beta_t + \varphi y_{t-1} + \varphi \Delta Z_{t-1} + \dots + \varphi \Delta y_{p-1} + \varepsilon_t \qquad (2)$$

Where, z indicates all the explanatory variables along with the dependent variable.

Philips Perron Test

After ADF test, the most popular test for unit roots is Phillips Perron test which was developed by Philips & Perron [46]. Phillips & Perron have developed a more comprehensive theory of unit root non-stationarity [44]. Although, this test is similar to ADF test, but it incorporate an automatic correction to the DF procedure whereby allowing for autocorrelated residuals. Generally PP tests give the same conclusion as the ADF test and also face same kind of limitations.

The KPSS Test

"Kwitkowski et.al [47] (KPSS) have formulate an alternative to the DF test for stationary of a time series". The methodology of this alternative option is a test of non-stationarity against the null hypothesis of stationary in the model. In general the regression model has the following form,

$$Z_t = \mu + \beta_t + \varphi \sum_{i=1}^{k} \eta i + \epsilon t , t = 1, , T \qquad (3)$$

With stationary η_i and i.i.d. ε_t with an expected value of 0 and variance 1. Here, z indicates all the explanatory variables along with the dependent variable.

Johansen Cointegration Method

There are two ways of testing the cointegrating relationship among variables or testing the possibility of a long-run equilibrium relationship in case of the non-stationarity of each variable - the Engle-Granger method or the Johansen-Juselius procedure- that can be used to overcome the related problem of spurious correlation and misleading inferences [36]. Cointegration analysis plays a very important part in the estimation of the error correction models (ECM). According to Engle and Granger [48], "when two variables are cointegrated, an error correction data generating mechanism exists, and vice versa." Additionally when two variables will be cointegrated, there there will be a very low chance of them drifting apart on an average [49]. This model as a result gives us an insight into the long-run relationship between the two variables while testing for the cointegration between two them. In this study, Johansen's Maximum Likelihood procedure for Cointegration has been applied to estimate the cointegration among the variables. Johansen's methodology has its beginning point in the vector autoregression (VAR) of order p generally given by,

$$Y_t = A_1 Y_{t-1} + A_2 Y_{t-2} + \dots\dots\dots + A_p Y_{t-p} + BX_t + \varepsilon_t \qquad (4)$$

Where Y_t is a k-vector of variables which are integrated for 1 or also known as I(1), X_t is a d vector of deterministic variables, and εt is a vector of innovations. We can rewrite the model as:

$$\Delta y_{t=} \Pi Z_{t-1} + \sum_{i=1}^{p-1} \Gamma i \, \Delta Y_{t-1} + BX_t + \varepsilon_t \qquad (5)$$

Where, $\Pi = \sum_{i=1}^{p} A_i - I$ and $\Gamma i = -\sum_{j=i+1}^{p} A_j$

Here Yt is represent as a vector of nonstationary variables. The Johansen test focuses on an examination of the Π matrix which can be interpreted as a long-run coefficient matrix, as in equilibrium, all the Y_{t-i} will be zero, while setting the error terms, $\varepsilon_{t\ to}$ their expected value of zero will leave $Y_{t-i} = 0$.The information regarding the coefficient matrix between the levels of the series (Π) is decomposed as $\Pi = \alpha\beta'$.On the other hand, the relevant elements of the α matrix are known as adjustment coefficients, whereas the β matrix contains the cointegrating vectors. According to Johansen and Juselius, [50] "there are two likelihood ratio test statistics to test for the number of cointegrating vector". For instance, the first likelihood ratio statistics for the null of r cointegrating vectors against the alternative of r+1 vectors is the maximum eigenvalue statistic whereas, the second statistic for the hypothesis of at most r cointegrating vectors against the alternative is the trace statistic. Critical values for both test statistics can be found in Johansen and Juselius [50]. The number of lags which is a very important part of this cointegration test can be generally determined based on the information provided by the multivariate generalization of the AIC.

Vector Error Correction (VEC) Model

After performing the Johansen cointegration test, a Vector Error Correction model (VECM) has been estimated on the evidence of cointegrating relationship, for long-run causality and short-term dynamics. A VECM can be taken as a scaled down VAR model which allow us to identify the structural coefficients. Hence we can define a vector error correction (VEC) model as a restricted VAR which involves cointegration restrictions built into the specification. These types of models are designed in a way which allows the use of cointegrated non-stationary series. The VEC specification restricts the long-run behavior of the endogenous variables to converge to their cointegrating relationships while allowing a wide range of short-run dynamics [43]. In a VECM, the cointegration term has been seen as the error correction term as here a series of partial short-run adjustments have been used to correct deviation from long-run equilibrium. The VEC model used in this research paper can be specified as follows,

$$\Delta \ln SPI_t = \alpha + \lambda e_{t-1} + \sum_{i=0}^{n} b_i \, \Delta SPIt - i + \sum_{i=0}^{m} c_i \, \Delta DR_{t-i} +$$

$$\textstyle\sum_{i=0}^{k} d_i \, \Delta MS_{t-i} + \sum_{i=0}^{j} ei\Delta INF_{t-i} + \sum_{i=0}^{1} fi\Delta ER_{t-i} + U_t \quad (6)$$

The VECM approach is generally justified under the arguments that the identification and testing for the significance of the structural coefficients which underlies the theoretical relationship is essential. Since the simple VAR models do not allow the identification of structural coefficients nor do value the relevance of unit root tests, VECM model came into picture.

Vector Autoregressive (VAR) Model

Next in the absence of the cointegrating relationship among the variables, the vector autoregressive (VAR) model has been estimated. The Vector autoregressive models (VARs) based on Gaussian (normally distributrd errors) has frequent been popular choice as a description of macro-economic time series due to its good fit to such type of data [51]. VARs were popularised in econometrics as a generalised form of univariate autoregressive models by Sims [52]. A VAR is known as a systems regression model that can be considered a kind of hybrid between the univariate time series models and the simultaneous equations models. According to Angel and Fildes, "VAR approach is beneficial to use as it collects many causal variables" [53]. The VAR model can used in this research paper can be specified as follows,

$$\Delta \ln SPT_t = \alpha + \sum_{i=1}^{n} b_i \Delta SPI_{t-1} + \sum_{I=0}^{M} C_i \, \Delta DR_{t-i} +$$

$$\textstyle\sum_{i=0}^{k} d_i \, \Delta MS_{t-i} + \sum_{i=0}^{j} ei\Delta CPI_{t-i} + \sum_{i=0}^{1} fi\Delta ER_{t-i} + U_t \quad (7)$$

The components of the vector DR_{t-i}, MS_{t-i},CPI_{t-i} and ER_{t-i} are known as exogenous variables since their values are determined outside of the VAR system. The lag length for this model is determined by using multiple information criteria, particularly the AIC criteria.

In this research article, the relationship between stock price index and the other important monetary policy instruments has been tested through a series of tests. I have used both VAR and VECM approach to measure the effectiveness of monetary policy instruments on stock price index. Since, simple VARs do not identify structural coefficients and ignore relevance of unit root tests, VECM model has been estimated here.

Empirical Studies

This section includes detailed discussion of all the empirical results and their interpretations. For the purpose of simplicity, all the empirical results presented here, has been shown up-to two decimal points.

Summary Statistics

All the tables under this category represent the summary statistics of the variables under study. At 1st I did it on the level by taking the Ln of the raw data. After that the test was performed on the return series by taking the 1st difference of the Ln series.

***Table 1.** Descriptive Statistics Test: Bangladesh (Level).*

	LSPI	LDR	LER	LMS	LCPI
Mean	7.18	1.71	4.13	7.27	4.59
Median	7.27	1.61	4.10	7.25	4.57
Maximum	8.39	1.95	4.27	8.10	4.95
Minimum	6.18	1.61	3.93	6.57	4.33
Std. Dev.	0.58	0.13	0.10	0.45	0.19
Skewness	0.08	0.86	-0.28	0.13	0.27
Kurtosis	1.71	2.13	1.80	1.82	1.73
Jarque-Bera	8.50	18.72	8.87	7.35	9.41
Probability	0.01	0.00	0.01	0.03	0.01

A study of the descriptive statistics shows approximate normality in the data distribution of each variable in terms of skewness and kurtosis. The coefficient of skewness of each variable is low and is positively skewed except for exchange rate. The figure for kurtosis in each variable is below its benchmark of 3 for a normal distribution, confirming near normality. The mean-to-median ratio of each variable is close to 1. The range of variation between maximum and minimum is reasonable. The standard deviation is also quite low compared to the mean, showing a small coefficient of variation. Although the above descriptive statistics show the normality of each variable, the Jarque-Bera test indicates non–normality of the variables. However, the problem does not seem serious.

Table 2. *Descriptive Statistics Test: Bangladesh (Return).*

	SPI	DR	ER	MS	CPI
Mean	0.02	0.00	0.00	0.01	0.01
Median	0.02	0.00	0.00	0.01	0.00
Maximum	0.26	0.00	0.06	0.06	0.04
Minimum	-0.27	-0.18	-0.03	-0.02	-0.01
Std. Dev.	0.07	0.02	0.01	0.02	0.01
Skewness	0.14	-7.60	2.55	0.72	1.01
Kurtosis	5.89	59.18	15.35	3.42	5.77
Jarque-Bera	41.71	16792.67	885.53	11.25	58.22
Probability	0	0.00	0.00	0.00	0

The study of the descriptive statistics for return (Table 2) does not show normality in the data distribution of the variables in terms of skewness and kurtosis. Apart from the coefficients for stock price & Money Supply, it is relatively high for others. The figure for kurtosis in each variable is above its benchmark of 3 for a normal distribution, confirming non-normality. Although the mean-to-median ratio of each variable is close to 1 and the range of variation between maximum and minimum is quite reasonable, the standard deviation is quite high compared to the mean, showing large coefficient of variation. In addition, the Jarque-Bera test indicates non–normality of the variables, indicating serious problem.

Test for Stationarity

The next set of tables summarizes the ADF test results for Bangladesh. The first panel of the tables present the ADF, PP and KPSS test statistics of the variables under study considering for with trend but no constant category. The 2nd panel represents the critical values at 1, 5 and 10 percent level for the test statistics. The optimal lag length the in the augmented Dickey-Fuller test, has been determined with the Schwarz criterion being the default. Schwarz's criterion has in this case chosen maximum 12 lags to perform the ADF test.

Table 3. *Unit Root & Stationarity Tests: Bangladesh.*

Variables	Null Hypothesis: Variable is Non-Stationary		Null Hypothesis: Variable is Non-Stationary		Null Hypothesis: Variable is Non-Stationary	
	Augmented Dickey-Fuller (ADF) Test statistic		Phillips Peron (PP) Test Statistic		Kwiatkowski-Phillips-Schmidt-Shin (KPSS) Test Statictic	
	Level	1st Difference	Level	1st Difference	Level	1st Difference
LnSPI	-0.10	-9.71***	-0.13	-9.67***	1.26	0.07***
Ln IR	-1.68	-10.96***	-1.68	-10.96***	1.06	1.06
LnER	-1.66	-11.54***	-1.78	-11.74***	1.24	0.53
LnMS	2.35	-2.22	3.48	-16.63***	1.31	0.53***
LnINF	0.72	-7.54***	1.61	-7.09***	1.30	0.07***
Critical Values						
1% Level	-3.49		-3.49		0.74	
5% Level	-2.89		-2.89		0.46	
10% Level	-2.58		-2.58		0.35	

*** indicates stationarity at the first differencing

The calculated ADF and PP statistics cannot reject the null hypothesis of unit root at either the 1 percent, 5 percent or 1 percent significance levels when compared with the respective critical values as it is clear from the result that the test statistic is not more negative than the critical value.The calculated KPSS statistics also clearly reject the null hypothesis of no unit root at 1 percent, 5 percent or 10 percent significance levels when compared with the corresponding critical values. In other words, the ADF, PP and KPSS tests decisively confirm the nonstationarity of each variable. The above Table shows that LnSPI, LnDR and LnER and LnMS possess I(1) behaviour. To be precise, the stationarity of all variables except money supply is restored on first differencing, showing the same order of integration. On the other hand, stationarity for the variable MS restores at the 2nd differencing.

Cointegration Results and Long-run Equilibrium Relationship

Next the cointegration procedure developed by Johansen and Johansen & Juselius is employed to test the long run equilibrium relationship between the stock price index and components of monetary policy.

The unit root test performed the section confirms that variables are all non-stationary in their levels form, which is the first step in cointegration analysis [44]. Johansen method uses likelihood ratio test to determine the number of cointegrating relationships, which may exist between the variables. If the hypothesis of no cointegration is rejected, then a stable long run relationship between stock index and related variable does exist. In Eviews we can perform the cointegration test and the subsequent estimation, under 5 assumptions. In this case, the cointegration test and the subsequent estimation is determined under the assumption of intercept with no trend in the potentially cointegrating relationship and/or the VAR. However, at firs by examining the sensitivity of the result to the type of specification has been used to determine the appropriate lag length for the test. The values of AIC[2] and SBIC[3] can be used to determine the optimal lag length. In this case AIC selects a VECM with 2 lags and SBIC a VECM with 0 lags.

Table 4. *Trace Test: Bangladesh.*

Null Hypothesis	Trace statistic	5% Critical value	Probability
r = 0	40.75	69.81	0.94
r ≤ 1	23.47	47.86	0.95
r ≤ 2	11.49	29.80	0.95
r ≤ 3	5.23	15.49	0.78
r ≤ 4	0.00	3.84	0.99

*denotes rejection of the hypothesis at the 0.05 level
Trace test indicates no cointegrating equations at the 0.05 level

Table 5. *Maximum Eigen Value: Bangladesh.*

Null Hypothesis	Max-Eigen statistic	5% Critical value	Probability
r = 0	17.27	33.88	0.91
r ≤ 1	11.98	27.58	0.93
r ≤ 2	6.27	21.13	0.98
r ≤ 3	5.23	14.26	0.71
r ≤ 4	0.00	3.84	0.10

*denotes rejection of the hypothesis at the 0.05 level
Max-eigenvalue test indicates no cointegrating equation(s) at the 5% level

Table 6. *Normalized Cointegrating Coefficients: Bangladesh.*

Variables	Coefficient	Std. Error	t-statistic
LSPI	1.00	-	-
LDR	2.78	1.75	1.59
LER	-0.37	2.68	-0.14
LMS	-5.07	1.06	-4.78
LCPI	-2.53	0.33	-8.43
Constant	1552.31	-	-

Critical value at 5% level of significance with 1 degree of freedom for the chi-square distribution: 3.841
*denotes rejection of the hypothesis at the 0.05 level

The results of Johansen Cointegration tests have been shown in a set of 3 tables. The first table shows the results for the λtrace along with their test statics and probabilities. On the other hand the 2nd table shows the λmax and their test statics and probabilities. Finally the last table in each set shows the estimation for normalized cointegration coefficient.

Table 4 (Trace Test) provides the test statistics for cointegration vectors and critical values at 5 percent significance level. The result shown in the table is obtained by considering two lags and without any trend term. The test result clearly indicates that there is no relationship between LSPI. LDR, LER. LMS and LCPI as in each case the test statistic is lower than the critical value. Furthermore, Table 5 (Maximum Eigen Value[4] Test) and Table 6 (Normalized Cointegrating Coefficients) also confirms the absence of a long-run equilibrium relationship between the variables.

Short-run Dynamic Adjustment using VECM

As mentioned earlier, the Vector Error Correction Model (VECM) allows us to make inferences on the long-run impacts of the variables in levels to those in differences [43]. The variables' responses to themselves are significant and negative which indicates positive autocorrelation. Generally, there are eight options for running a VEC model. However, in this study the VEC model has been run with no trend but with an intercept included. On the other hand, the optimal lag-interval has been determined by the values of AIC, estimated earlier by the sensitivity test which was performed in the Johansen Cointegration test under the category of summary of all assumptions. Hence, in this case AIC selected a VECM with 2 lags.

Table 7. *Vector Error Correction Estimates: Bangladesh.*

Variables	Coefficient	Std. Error	t-statistic
Error correction term (ρ)	0.00	0.00	-0.01
D(SPI(-1))	0.07	0.10	0.74
D(SPI(-2))	-0.04	0.10	-0.43
D(DR(-1))	-0.22	0.29	-0.75
D(DR(-2))	-0.51	0.29	-1.76
D(ER(-1))	0.01	0.53	0.02
D(ER(-2))	-1.51	0.54	-2.78
D(MSY(-1))	0.81	0.7	1.15
D(MSY(-2))	0.18	0.45	0.40
D(CPI(-1))	-0.11	0.8	-0.14
D(CPI(-2))	-0.76	0.78	-0.97
Constant	0.02	0.01	2.77
R-squared	0.20		
Adjusted R-squared		0.12	
Residual Sum of Squares	0.47		
F-statistic	2.37		

Critical value at 5% level of significance with 1 degree of freedom for the chi-square distribution: 3.841
*denotes rejection of the hypothesis at the 0.05 level

From Table 7 it can be seen that, the estimated coefficient (λ) of the error correction term *ρ is* negative which is expected but it is not statistically significant in terms of its associated t-value. It confirms that there is no significant long-run equilibrium relationship exists among the variables or more preciously no long term causal flow runs from changes in interest rates, exchange rate, money supply or inflation to the stock market of Bangladesh. Moreover, the value of R-Square 0.20 or Adjusted R0Squared 0.12 also shows low explanatory power of the model. The F statistics at 2.37 shows only a modest result.

The coefficients of the subsequent lagged terms of changes in the discount rate reveal a short-term net negative but very small feedback effect from interest rate to stock market, as their sum is negative. This finding seems counter-intuitive. However, the associated T-values of the coefficients of the lagged variables are insignificant which indicates a very restrained influence of the exchange rate on stock market return. Similarly, the sum of the co-efficient of the lagged changes in the exchange rate reveals a short term net negative feedback from exchange rate to stock market which lowers the adjusted rate of returns for foreign investors. However, the associated T-values of the coefficients of the lagged variables are insignificant. The same trend goes with the variables Money Supply and Inflation. Even though both of them have a negative effect bit it is insignificant.

Vector-Autoregressive Estimates

In this the estimation of VAR and its interpretation has been discussed. It is clear from the earlier estimations that the relationship between the determinants of monetary policy and Stock Market is not that significant for Bangladesh. Moreover as per the trace statistics, no cointegration prevails in the system. Whereas according to the Monte Carlo Experiments reported in Cheung and Lai [54] suggest "that the trace test shows more robustness to both skewness and excess kurtosis in the residuals than the maximum eigen value cointegration prevails in the system" [36]. In consequence, we cannot reject the null hypothesis of no cointegration. As a result VAR is estimated by following the equation which is the main model for this article. A VAR is actually estimated in order to examine whether there are lead-lag relationships for the returns to the considering variables. The first step in determining optimal lag length and this can be achieved in a variety of ways. Here in this paper, lag-length has been determined by using the multivariate information criterion. EViews presents the values of various information criteria and other methods for determining the lag order. In this case, the Schwartz and Hannan--Quinn criteria both select a zero order as optimal, while Akaike's criterion chooses a VAR(3).

Table 8. *Vector Autoregressive Estimates: Bangladesh.*

Variables	Coefficient	Std. Error	t-statistic
D(SPI(-1))	0.03	0.11	.31
D(SPI(-2))	-0.03	0.10	-.31
D(SPI(-3))	0.11	0.10	1.11
D(DR(-1))	-0.28	0.30	-0.93
D(DR(-2))	-0.48	0.29	-1.65
D(DR(-3))	0.20	0.30	0.68
D(ER(-1))	-0.07	0.54	-0.12
D(ER(-2))	-1.52	0.55	-2.76
D(ER(-3))	-0.91	0.57	-1.60
D(MSY(-1))	1.40	0.50	2.09
D(MSY(-2))	-0.47	0.51	-0.92
D(MSY(-3))	-0.25	0.48	-0.51
D(CPI(-1))	0.94	0.81	0.12
D(CPI(-2))	-0.42	0.88	0.48
D(CPI(-3))	0.47	0.87	0.54
Constant	0.02	0.02	1.06
R-squared	0.24		
Adjusted R-squared	0.12		
Residual Sum of Squares	0.44		
F-statistic	2.01		

Critical value at 5% level of significance with 1 degree of freedom for the chi-square distribution: 3.841

*denotes rejection of the hypothesis at the 0.05 level

Table 8 shows not a very significant relationship among the variables based on the evidence of F statistic 2.01. The associated t-values of the coefficient of the explanatory variables are also insignificant. This is also reflected in the numerical value of R-Square and Adjusted R-Squared which are 0.24 and 0.12 respectively. More preciously we can say that, the relationship between changes in stock market return and changes in the interest, exchange rates, changes in the money supply and changes in consumer production index is not very significant for Bangladeshi Market.

4. Findings

The main purpose of this article was to analyze the relationships dynamics between stock price index and monetary policy instruments. The key monetary policy instruments have been represented by discount rate, exchange rate, money supply and consumer price index as a representation of inflation. In this article, I have used several multivariate models to analyze the relevance such relationship between monetary policy and stock market in Bangladesh. However, unfortunately and surprisingly all the models nearly provided the same result of poor connection between stock market and monetary policy or less effectiveness of monetary policy in the a stock market The first multivariate model Johansen Cointegration found no cointegration which considers the relationship between stock market index with discount rate, exchange rate, money supply and consumer price index or inflation in the context of Bangladesh. Since there is no cointegration, it clearly indicates the non-existence of long run relationship between stock market and these fundamental monetary policy instruments. The second multivariate model that has been estimated to measure the effectiveness of monetary policy factors on stock market is the Vector Error Correction Mode. VECM generally provides the estimates short-run adjustment for the long run relationship between the stock market and monetary policy instruments. For Bangladesh, VECM found no significant long run relationship between stock price index and discount rate, exchange rate, money supply and consumer price index because of its insignificant error term. In addition to the long run relationship, there exists no strong argument in favour of the short term adjustment. It clearly indicates that, for economy of Bangladesh, VECM found no such type of adjustments, which in the absence of long run relationship, could make the stock market return converged to the long run equilibrium. This type of results indicates the high volatility of Dhaka stock exchange. In 2004, a study was conducted on the volatility of the DSE stock return by Imam and Amin [55], which also confirms that volatility of DSE return series increases over time. After that, comes the Vector Autoregressive multivariate model which has been considered as the main model for this article. Apparently in this study VAR almost provides the similar results as VECM. Even though few earlier studies claim the existence of significant relationship between stock market and monetary policy mechanism, the VAR model used here, reveals a not so very strong relationship between the stock market index and the other variables-discount rate, exchange rate, money supply and consumer price index. The poor connection has been even conformed by the very low R^2 the exchange rate to stock market with insignificant associated T-values of the coefficients and insignificant t-values of the coefficients of the explanatory variables. Ultimately even from VAR we get the similar results of no effectiveness of monetary policy on Dhaka Stock Market. It indicates that Dhaka Stock exchange and the monetary policy framework of Bangladesh are independent of each other.

5. Conclusion

This article examined the connection between stock market and monetary policy framework for the economies of Bangladesh. Through this article I have attempted to investigate whether the actions of monetary policy regulators can explain stock market return in the long run by conducting a co-integration test and in the short run by the dynamics of Vector error Correction model or Vector Autoregressive model. However after conducting the empirical studies, it is found that there is no significant relationship between monetary policy instruments and stock market for in Bangladesh. The shallow and small size market of the country can be one of the reasons behind this. Nevertheless for an efficient stock market, it is expected that policy announcements should have a significant impact on the stock market. Generally, in an efficient market, the prices react instantly to new information. According to market efficiency theory, a market riding on stale information is informationally inefficient. In case of monetary policy framework, when a market anticipates an announcement to be forthcoming, it definitely should react to the unexpected component in the monetary policy shock.

In addition, the existence of such a relationship has important implications for both stock market participants and central bankers. For instance, with respect to the former this issue relates to the broader topic of stock price determination and portfolio formation, while the latter may be interested in knowing, whether monetary policy actions are transmitted through financial market. Theoretically the implications of monetary policy framework on stock price are intense, as we all know that central bank can affect stock market profoundly by altering the central bank discount rate. Many earlier researches conducted across a variety of countries have already proved the existence of such sensitivity and also proved that how beneficial that can become for the countries. In order to get the benefits many countries have already adopted a new policy framework that can which can affect the stock market positively. For example, explicit inflation targeting practised by UK, Sweden, and Canada or implicit targeting, where no formal targets are in place by U.S.

Moreover for developing or emerging countries like Bangladesh the importance of sound development of the market cannot be undermined. In order to make the market less volatile, stock markets in the country should have more trained professionals who can monitor the monetary policy mechanism. In addition, more people from both regulatory body and stock market should have involved in doing research on the sensitivity of stock market with respect to monetary policy. The regulatory body should make decisions regarding monetary policy in a predictable way, with providing adequate explanation for the investors. They should make information relevant for securities available to the stock market participants and also make sure the transparency and accountability of audit report. Furthermore, monetary authorities should exercise restraint in the use of policy instruments indiscriminately, because it is clearly evidenced that the use of monetary policy instruments affects the performance of the stock market to a very large extent. Lastly, another policy implication for Central Bank can be to maintain inflation at a reasonably low level so that it will not erode the real value of stock gains. Given this information, now it is the responsibility of the monetary authority to calibrate the appropriate policy response to potential stock price arrangements.

References

[1] Mohammad,S.d.,Hussain, A., & Jalil, M. A.(2009). Impact of Macroeconomics Variables on Stock Prices: Emperical Evidance in Case of Kse (Karachi Stock Exchange). *European Journal of Scientific Research 38*(1), 97-102.

[2] Poole, W., Rasche, R. H., & Thornton, D. L. (2002) "Market Anticipations of Monetary Policy Actions," *Federal Reserve Bank of St. Louis Review*, *84*(4), 65-94.

[3] Cook, T., and Hahn, T. (1989). "The Effect of Changes in the Federal Funds Rate Target on Market Interest Rates in the 1970s." *Journal of Monetary Economics*, 24(9), pp. 331-51.

[4] Kuttner, K. N. (2001) "Monetary Policy Surprises and Interest Rates: Evidence from the Fed Funds Futures Market," *Journal of Monetary Economics*, *47*(3), 523-44.

[5] Bredin, D., Hyde, S., Nitzsche, D., and Reilly, G. O. (2007), 'U.K. stock returns and the impact of domestic monetary policy shocks', *Journal of Business, Finance and Accounting*, *34*, 872–888.

[6] Gregoriou, A., Kontonikas, A., MacDonald, R., and Montagnoli, A. (2009), 'Monetary policy shocks and stock returns: Evidence from the British market', *Financial Markets and Portfolio Management*, *23*, 401-410.

[7] Ioannidis, C., & Kontonikas, A. (2006). Monetary Policy and Stock Market: Some International Evidences,1-25.

[8] Waud, R., (1970), "Public Interpretation of Federal Reserve Discount Rate Changes: Evidence on the 'Announcement Effect", *Econometrica*, *38*, 231-250.

[9] Bernanke, B. S., and Gertler, M. (1995), "Inside the Black Box: The Credit Channel of Monetary Policy Transmission," *Journal of Economic Perspectives*, *9* (4); 22-48.

[10] Mbutor, M. O. (2007), "The Lending Channel of Monetary Policy Transmission in Nigeria; Vector Autoregressive (VAR) Verification," *Central Bank of Nigeria; Economic and Financial Review,* 45.

[11] Uchendu (1996), "The Transmission of Monetary Policy in Nigeria". *Central Bank of Nigeria: Economic and Financial Review*, *34*(2), 606 – 625.

[12] Kim, K (2003) "Dollar Exchange Rate and Stock Price: Evidence from Multivariate Cointegration and Error Correction Model." *Review of Financial Economics*,*12*, 301-313.

[13] Mukherjee, Tarun K. and Naka,.A(1995), "Dynamic Relations Between Macroeconomic Variables and the Japanese Stock Market: An Application of Vector Error Correction Model," *The Journal of Financial Research, 18* (2), 223-235.

[14] Ibrahim, M. H. (2003), "Macroeconomic Variables and Stock Prices in Malaysia: An Empirical Analysis," *Asian Economic Journal, 13* (2), 219 – 230.

[15] Tsoukalas, D.(2003), "Macroeconomic Factors and Stock Prices in the Emerging Cypriot Equity Market", *Managerial Finance 29*(4), 89-91.

[16] Thorbecke, W. (1997). "On Stock Market Returns and Monetary Policy". *Journal of Finance, 52*, 635-654.

[17] Boschen, J.F. and Mills, L.O. (1995). "The Relation between Money Market and Narrative Indicators of Monetary Policy," *Economic Inquiry 23*, pp. 24-45.

[18] Patelis, A., (1997). "Stock Return Predictability and the Role of Monetary Policy". *Journal of Finance, 52*, 1951-1972.

[19] Cassola, N., & Morana, C. (2006). Monetary Policy and The Stock Market in The Euro Area.*Journal of Policy Modeling 26*, 387-399.

[20] Jensen, G. R., and Johnson, R. R. (1995). "Discount Rate Changes and Security Returns in the U.S., 1962–1991." *Journal of Banking and Finance, 19*, 79–95.

[21] Jensen, G. R., Mercer, J. M., and Johnson, R. R. (1996). "Business Conditions, Monetary Policy, and Expected Security Returns", Journal *of Financial Economics 40*, 213–237.

[22] Fama, E. and French, K. (1989), "Business Conditions and Expected Returns on Stocks and Bonds", *Journal of Financial Economics, 25*, 23-49.

[23] Omotor,D. G (2010). "Relationship between Inflation and Stock Market Returns: Evidence from Nigeria". *Journal of Applied Statistics, 1*(1), 1-15.

[24] Carlson, M.(2007)."A Brief History of the 1987 Stock Market Crash with a Discussion of the Federal Reserve Response," *Finance and Economics Discussion Series 2007-13*, Washington: Board of Governors of the Federal Reserve System.

[25] Nelson, C. R. (1976) "Inflation and Rates of Return on Common Stocks," *Journal of Finance, 31*(2), 471-483.

[26] Fama, E. F. and Schwert, G. W. (1977). "Asset Returns and Inflation", *Journal of Financial Economics, 5*, 115-146.

[27] Ely, D. P., & Robinson, K. J. (1997). "Are stocks a hedge against inflation? International evidence using a long-run approach", *Journal of International Money and Finance, 16*, 141-167.

[28] Osuagwu, E. S. (2009) "The Effect of Monetary Policy on Stock Market Performance in Nigeria", *Nigerian Journal of Securities and Finance, 14*, (2).

[29] Fama, E. F. (1981), "Stock Returns, Real Activity, Inflation and Money," *American Economic Review, 71*, 545-565.

[30] Benderly, J., and Burton, Z. (1985), "Inflation, Real Balances, Output and Real Stock Returns," *American Economic Review*, 1120-1123.

[31] Geske, R, & Roll, R (1983), "The Fiscal and Monetary Linkage between Stock Returns and Inflation," *Journal of Finance, 38*, 1 – 33.

[32] Kaul, G. (1987), "Stock Returns and Inflation: The Role of the Monetary Sector," *Journal of Financial Economics, 18*, 253 – 276.

[33] Zhao, X (1999), "Stock prices, inflation and output: Evidence from China," *Applied Economics Letters, 6* (8), 510-51.

[34] Udegbunam, Ralph & P. O. Eriki (2001), "Inflation and Stock Price Behavior: Evidence from Nigerian Stock Market, *Journal of Financial Management & Analysis, 20*(14), 1-10.

[35] Ahmed, M. K., Akhtaruzzaman, M., and Barua, S. (2007). "Effects of Monetary Policy on Price Formation of Financial Assets:A Test for Bangladesh*", Working Paper Series No: WP 0703*, Policy Analysis Unit, Bangladesh Bank, Dhaka.

[36] Banerjee, P. K., & Adhikary, B. K. (2009). "Dynamic Effects of Changes in Interest Rates and Exchange Rates on the Stock Market Return in Bangladesh". *Ritsumeikan Journal of Asia Pacific Studies*, 119-133.

[37] Saidjada, K. M., Hossain, M. S. and Rahman, M. H. (2014). "Effects of monetary policy on capital markets in Bangladesh", *Bangladesh Bank Monetary Policy Review, 8*(1), 50-62.

[38] Rahman, M. L., & Uddin, J. (2009). "Dynamic Relationship between Stock Prices and Exchange Rates: Evidence from Three South Asian Countries", *International Business Research, 2*(2), 167-174.

[39] Alam, M., & Uddin, G.S.(2009). "Relationship between Interest and Stock Prices: Empirical Evidences from Developed and Developing Countries". *International Journal of Business and Management, 4*(3), 43-51.

[40] Quadir, M. M. (2012). "The Effect of Macroeconomic Variables on Stock Returns on Dhaka Stock Exchange", *International Journal of Economics and Financial Issues, 2*(4), 480-487.

[41] Shen, C. H., and Wang, L. R. (1997). "Daily Serial Correlation, Trading Volume, and Price Limit", *Pacific Basin Finance Journal, 6*, 251-274.

[42] Neri,S.(2004).Monetary Policy and Stock Price Theory & Evidence.*ournal of Economic Literature 32,*7-47.

[43] Ahmed. M. N. and Imam M. O., (2007),"Macroeconomic Factors and Bangladesh Stock Market", *International Review of Business Research Paper, 3*(5), 21-35.

[44] Brooks, C.(2008). *Modern Introductory Econometrics for Finance* (2nd.ed.), (pp.298-365). New York: Cambridge University Press.

[45] Said, S.E. and Dickey, D.(1984). "Testing for Unit Roots in Autoregressive Moving-Average Models with Unknown Order," *Biometrika, 71*, 599-607.

[46] Phillips, P. C. B., and P. Perron (1988). "Testing for Unit Roots in Time Series Regression," *Biometrika, 75*, 335-346.

[47] Kwiatkowski, D., Phillips, P.C.B., Schmidt, P., and Shin, Y. (1992). "Testing the Null Hypothesis of Stationarity Against the Alternative of a Unit Root," *Journal of Econometrics, 54*, 159-178.

[48] Engle, R. F. and C. W. J. Granger (1987), "Cointergration and Error Correction: Representation, Estimation and Testing", *Econometrica*, 55 (2), 251-276.

[49] Ahmed,S. (2008). "Aggregate Economic Variables and Stock Market in India", *International Research Journal of Finance and Economics,14*, 145-148.

[50] Johansen, S., and K. Juselius (1990), "Maximum likelihood estimation and inference on cointegration—with applications to the demand for money", *Oxford Bulletin of Economics and Statistics, 52*, 169–210.

[51] Juselius,k. (2006). "The cointegrated VAR model: Methodology and Applications", *New York: Oxford University Press*, 14-16.

[52] Sims, C. A. (1980). "Macroeconomics and reality", *Econometrica, 48*, 1-48.

[53] Rahman, T., & Moazzem K. G. (2011). "Capital market of Bangladesh: Volatility in the Dhaka Stock Exchange (DSE) and role of Regulators", *International Journal of Business and Management*, *6*(7), 86-93.

[54] Cheung, Y. W. and Lai, K. S.(1993). "Finite–Sample Sizes of Johansen's Likelihood Ratio Tests for Cointegration," *Oxford Bulletin of Economics and Statistics, 55*, 313- 28.

[55] Imam, M. O., and Amin, A. S. M. M. (2004). "Volatility in the Stock Return: Evidence from Dhaka Stock Exchange", *Journal of the Institute of Bankers Bangladesh, 51*(1), 01-08.

5

Alpine tourism as an economic development factor: A market perspective

Giuseppe Tardivo

Department of Management, University of Turin, Turin, Italy

Email address:
giuseppe.tardivo@unito.it

Abstract: Tourism trends and policies is becoming an international reference and benchmark on how effectively countries are supporting competitiveness, innovation and growth, and shed light on policies and practices associated with this. Despite the topic of attractiveness of tourist destinations is at the center of the international economic debate, there are still many areas showing important gap among potentials and performances and in most cases literature doesn't offer a suitable measure and strategic solutions for this problem. From a destination-based tourism model, the transition has been made to a model driven by motivation and the search of experience. The forces driving the change are: internet, low costs, tour operators, OTAs and the new demand for experiences from tourists, which have changed the rules of the game and, most importantly, altered the balance between supply and demand. The paper has three research goals. Firstly, a driven-based analysis will be presented, aimed at identifying the factors which condition and/or support the sector, briefly touching a legislation, governance, funding and infrastructure and cultural heritage. Subsequently the paper will focus some deficiencies of the tourist system in Italy, still organized according to an endogenous vision of the sector's development, and based on a model turned to a production perspective in which the offer is placed at the center of the system, with no added value and limited activity in term of retails, marketing and innovation and low level of professional competence. Finally the research will aim to propose a change of the tourism policy in Italy. As well as a reorganization of offer in a more innovative and experienced-based key, to be more competitive Italy needs the role of local government to be extensively reviewed: local administrations will have to take leadership of the destinations, bringing a strategic vision to the territory and becoming the main actor in conceiving and designing the offer of tourism.

Keywords: Destination Management, Governance, Tourism Development, Tourism Cultural Heritage

1. Introduction

Tourism is associated with travel and consumption which is in turn generally linked to possession of such resources as leisure time and disposable wealth. It is a large industry and the subject of considerable study and interest.

"In the OECD area, domestic tourism consumption represents a very significant share of the total tourism economy, averaging 61%, and above 80% for Chile, Germany, Japan, Mexico, the United Kingdom an the United States. Evidence shows that domestic tourism consumption, as a proportion of internal tourism consumption, is much higher for OECD member economies, than for non-member (47.5%). It is noticeable that many countries are placing greater emphasis on, and taking additional supportive measures to encourage domestic tourism, recognizing that domestic tourism is as capable of supporting employment and adding local value as international tourism. Many of the emerging tourism destination countries are enjoying significant growth in arrivals, and outperforming OECD and global average for GDP and employment. While still accounting for a relatively small proportion of global international arrivals, the potential impact of tourism on these economies is clear. Countries such as Argentina, Brazil, Egypt, India, Indonesia, and South Africa represent a significant potential as sources of growth for traditional tourism destinations. Against this background, it is unsurprising that governments increasingly regard tourism as an area for which the development and application of supportive policies are important, and an area where the potential benefit of government intervention should not be overlooked. In 2012, the dominant concern of those responsible for the development of tourism remains the international financial and economic crisis and the relatively poor outlook for many national economies. Some countries have also had to deal with the consequences of major natural disaster – such as the tsunami in Japan and the earthquake in New Zealand – or political upheaval such as that experienced in a number of Middle Eastern and Mediterranean countries." [1]

Italian touristic model is still based on the one of the '80-'90ies, characterized by the scarcity of competitors and the abundance of demand. In this case, supply dictates conditions and the client must consume a standardized and rigid product. Italian touristic system is not too flexible and it has evident weaknesses when adapting to demand trends.

"This is primarily a service industry (as contrasted to manufacturing) and generally employs a large number of people on relatively low wages (as opposed to banking and financial services). The industry according to the ECORYS Report confronts a number of what they describe as megatrends" [2]:

Tourism Megatrends

1: Globalisation

2: Demographic change

3: Access to information

4: Experience economy

5: Customisation

6: Sustainability

7: Health and wellness

This model refers to a post-fordist and industrial logic. In most cases, the Italian touristic business is characterized by its extreme simplicity: operators use and exploit resources and attractions, with no transformation and no added value in creating the supply, with poor structural investments and very poor commercial and marketing activities.

Joseph Ejarque, President and Managing Director of Four Tourism S.r.l. states: "In the Italian business model, the commercial aspect and the relation with the market are not developed. A strong relationship with clients is inexistent or poorly developed. The supply is commercialized and put into the market by third parties (i.e. tour operators and online travel agencies – OTA). Italian tourism has a passive attitude and an inadequate commercial capacity, which compromises the operative efficiency and causes a strong reduction in benefits.The national touristic supply consequently becomes excessively standardized, and loses attractiveness in comparison with the one of competitors. It is penalized by a very expensive cost structure deriving from poor innovation and the insufficient use of new product management technologies.

The change tourism is undergoing is so strong that inevitably all management and governance models for tourism policies still applied in Italy are totally obsolete and inadequate to real market demand" [3].

This change in tourism paradigm has happened because of the irruption of two factors: low cost models and the Internet as instruments to inform and advert-commercialize. Both elements have brought about a change in demand. At first, annual holydays were the most important economic investment in a year (apart from buying a house or a car) and were taken in a one and only break. Then tourism started being considered as a "commodity".

Commoditization of tourism changed. The annual and expensive demand became a cheaper demand for shorter trips and cost attention started being stronger (short-break tourism): demand for a new kind of tourism, with a huge growth in the number of journeys. Easier access to information greatly favoured and accelerated this process of change, especially thanks to the Internet. More destination supplies, shorter time to reach final destinations and strong low-cost models provoked the rise of new short and medium-range destinations perfect for short-break tourism. Together with new destinations, new forms of tourism were born, linked to specific interests that caused a further evolution, i.e. the segmentation of demand.

Post-modern society has favoured the birth of new values in tourists: hedonism, ethical value research, mental and physical health. All this gave rise to a new model of motivational touristic consumption and the search for added value deriving from touristic experience [4].

The new model of touristic demand is based on personalization (instead of standardization), on activity and experience (instead of passivity), on intensity and on multi-products (instead of simplicity). From destination tourism to tourism for destination products: present motivations for choosing a destination are not very different from those of a dozen years ago. The need for innovation and change has destroyed loyalty and the loyalty management of tourists for a specific destination. The rise of new products, the interest in health, sport and hobby has accelerated the maturity of destinations and these have not been able to renovate their attractiveness (cities full of art and history).

The new paradigm of tourism responds to a "liquid" society in continuous transformation, in which tourism is considered a direct extension of everyday life, a temporary and necessary parenthesis, with a great intrinsic value for the self. We then witness the birth and the progressive consolidation of "theme tourism". What really counts here is not just the destination but also the kind of activity and motivations that mark each destination [5].

Destinations become competitors not because of their brand but as product containers. In sum, and without entering into, analysing and justifying the totality of factors that have an impact on Italian competitiveness (i.e. the dimension of tourism businesses, their low capability to innovate and all high operational and managerial costs) we can state that Italian touristic offer is still too "solid" compared with a more and more "liquid" market.

Tourists today are profoundly diverse from the one on which the Italian touristic model was elaborated. Tourists are innovators. They are informed, unfaithful, deceived, impatient and "intoxicated", which means bombed by a lot of information daily. Especially, they are mature and evolved tourists, and often they have more expectations that touristic destinations manage to fulfil.

Tourists today must not be defined as Prosumers, but as Adprosumers: thanks to the Internet, they produce both the product they wish to consume and its relevant information. Available instruments are numerous: they can publicize, inform, share and comment. There emerges a huge lack of tourism supply: its inadequate presence in the Internet".

In some Italian regions there are few integrated strategic and touristic management marketing plans. In most cases no accurate touristic strategy exists, no functional organization to be able to design and manage a regional, competitive, attractive, efficient and effective touristic system.

Many areas have a strong touristic vocation and a high potentiality is present in many others but they never managed to emerge because of an absence of strategy, direction and management skills. The potential of land resources could activate touristic theme-based projects and offers that could be easily positioned on the market, but they don't manage to do it because of a lack of strategy in the construction of product-destination.

2. Possible Improvement Paths

The Italian touristic system must analyse two aspects. The first one is destination management to which administrations can contribute with a strategic vision of the territorial system. The second one is the organization and creation of product destinations - structuring and managing the area, taking on the strategic leadership of tourism in destinations, both at a local and at a global level [6]

Dealing with tourism from the inside of an administration today, at any level, forces people to keep updated and to be fully conscious about tourism. The time when the administrative approach and resolutions were dominating this sector is over.

"It is necessary to know the realty of this market, to understand the dynamics of this sector and of its demand and supply. One must know that the tourism of an area must be able to answer to demand trends and not to a vision and a logistic or flag-waving will. Tourism must not be taken for granted anymore but it must be organized, structured and managed.

Administrations should take on the responsibility to look in the distance and decide the leading path towards the development of the touristic system based on destinations, both at a local level and at a regional one.

"These trends present challenges for tourism and also raise questions over the relationship between sectors in the tourism industry. They key role of the public sector in tourism is well established in terms of such factors as infrastructure (roads, health care, sanitation and security for example).

The prominence of the EU as a tourism destination is implicitly linked to the fact that EU countries are considered to be safe destinations and to possess good infrastructure. The concerns following incidents of terrorism are demonstrative of this.

Conventionally the economic value chain involved in tourism has involved the private sector as provider of travel, accommodation and the majority of aspects of the value chain other than that furnished by the public sector infrastructure as described above.

The service aspects of tourism carry the implication of a purchaser and a market place. The value attached to the purchase in conventional terms is seen in economic terms – namely that usual laws of supply and demand operate and that factors such as price, economies of scale in production and a focus upon competitive forces are the determinants of outcome" [2].

It is necessary to abandon political-administrative dynamics and accept the vision that tourism is a market with its economic attraction and the tourist is the client of an area.

Renewing the supply, creating new touristic-territorial products, reorganizing tourism area management, giving more incentives to innovation, ameliorating promotions, realizing advert-commercialization and especially managing the governance of this system in the best possible way, are the fundamental objectives for a sustainable touristic policy.

Two basic strategic concepts may be useful as a possible development process. Tourism today moves because of motivations and not because of destinations. The evolution of clients in the last few years has been much faster than the one of destinations. Touristic demand has changed from a model of non-migratory and passive tourism to an active tourism made of emotions and experiences.

The growth of activities at the heart of the system (promotion, investment, innovation, etc....) and the newness and differentiation of the product will have to co-habit with differentiated products and destinations. Obviously market relations will have to be managed in a multichannel optic, directly or indirectly".

The improvement of touristic governance should have an impact on aspects such as strategic promotional coordination, re-engineering of destinations and of mature touristic products, together with an ameliorated flux management and the organization of the system, supporting the creation of networks among operators [7].

Innovation and intelligence development techniques in the market can help design new product and re-engineered destinations and mature products. Distribution, entering in new markets and market segments with adequate advert-commercialization techniques could certainly help the evolution of Italian Regions, from simple destinations in pain to new and successful realities on the new market.

From this point of view, tourism can have a fundamental role for a socio-economical area that is particularly dear to the economy of Piedmont and Cuneo: alpine tourism.

3. Alpine Tourism

Alpine tourism, magic words that transform an unknown water source dear to a shepherd and his herd in a famous thermal source whose water is sold at the price of wine, is now apparently oriented to satisfy a seasonal kind of demand.

Let's remember the case of Limone (2012): 600 beds available in hotels; 28.000 beds in holyday homes (90.000 in the whole mountain area of Cuneo); 20.000 daily occupancies in the two central weeks of August and Christmas.

During the last ten years, tourism has become an amazing tool to develop and valorise alpine economy [8] (fig.1 and tab.1).

From the high valleys, rich in trees and woods, vast meadows, natural lakes and itineraries for excursions, to the

foothill area, with its chestnut woods, thermal venues, mineral water springs, fantastic natural attractions (i.e. Bossea grottoes), the soft hills of Langhe and Astigiano, Piedmont can offer the most varied possibilities of attraction.

The explosion of agro-tourism and "equipped parks", thanks to an ever-growing demand also proves this [9].

In most cases we witness a divarication of structures. On one side, one finds great touristic locations, where big investors build huge home-buildings (Limone Piemonte is one of the many examples. Let's cite Bardonecchia too, where hotel available beds are only 6% of the total). On the other side, there are local traditional housing facilities offered by the local people. The basis of tourism – the Alps, a "wonderful landscape" or a cultural and incoming area – is not then an acquired "certainty", but it only develops in the context of the industrial revolution as a clear re-evaluation of the relation between humans and nature.

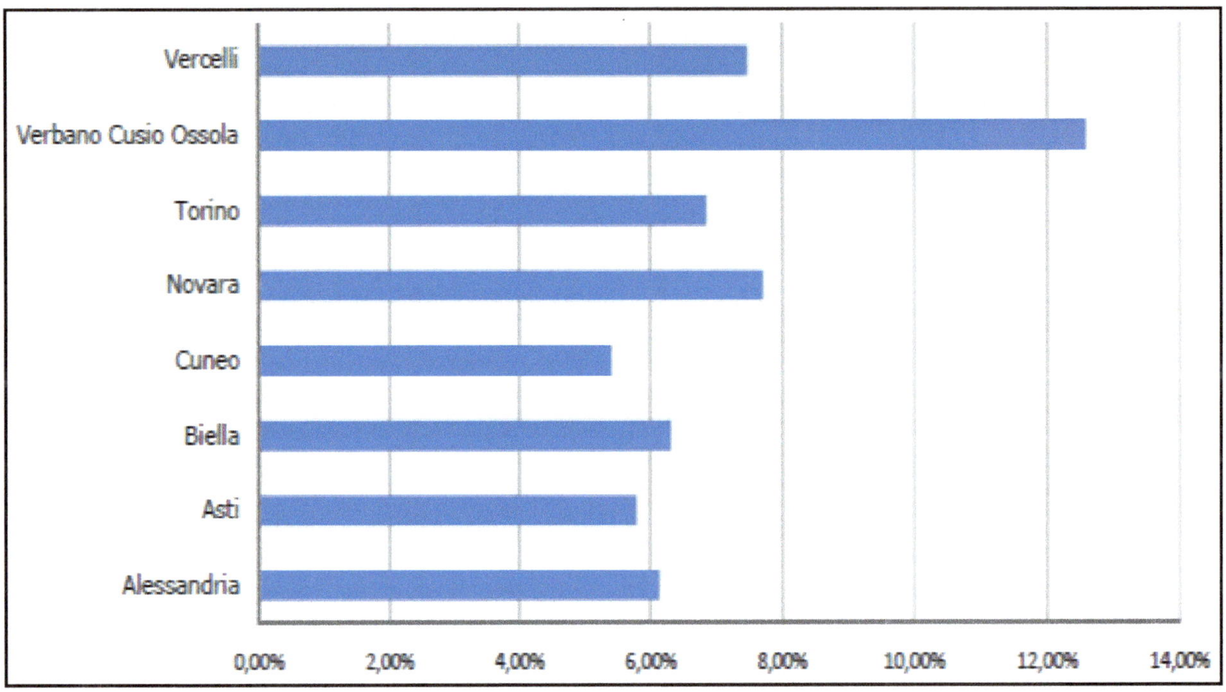

Source: Camera di Commercio di Cuneo (2014)

Figure 1. *Piedmont: touristic companies on total companies (%)*

Thousands of small craftsmanship businesses are directly linked to tourism. These are 36,6% of total local enterprises with high quality products.

In some zones, in Piedmont, (i.e. the "Via Lattea" tourist resort) there are lots of small artisanal businesses and they are very well integrated with tourism.

How can one valorise alpine tourism?

We mentioned before that the main motive for touristic travels is and will always be, for alpine areas, the landscape and the charm of mountain areas.

The second exploitable potential is wine and food attractions.

Tourism means education, culture, and respect of the landscape and of art. It also means an especially important source of wealth, which compensates in the near future many humiliating frustrations [10].

Critical situations exist. Mountains in Piedmont are also a fragile area with a certain level of irregularly distributed criticalities and risks.

First of all, the ample presence of "Les Favorites Areas", presented as a negative process going through sequential phases of demographic and economic connotation, the loss of human capital and the impoverishment of services and local infrastructures.

This problem is fundamental because on local levels, as far as development is concerned, technology plays a leading role. For example, human resources availability and qualification come from it, the social burden, the demand for services and market development opportunities too.

These factors also have important repercussions on the local society visibility, on the job market and on the all kinds of consumes and supplied services [11].

Depopulation is another problem. Young people run away from inhabitable alpine zones because they have not received the due spiritual and school preparation, suited for transmitting values.

The young people's nice-dress, trendy-model, fun-time and new-car psychosis, are not sufficient to explain this phenomenon [12].

***Table 1.** Italian tourists in accommodation establishments in the province of Cuneo by region of origin (2013)*

Region	Total Accommodation Establishments			
	Arrivals	Attendances	Incidence of arrivals on total	Average length of stay
Abruzzo	1.594	3.564	0,46%	2,24
Basilicata	913	2.785	0,26%	3,05
Bolzano	1.731	3.879	0,50%	2,24
Calabria	2.916	7.355	0,84%	2,52
Campania	5.387	13.550	1,55%	2,52
Emilia Romagna	18.642	40.542	5,37%	2,17
Friuli Venezia Giulia	3.502	7.705	1,01%	2,20
Lazio	11.587	29.482	3,33%	2,54
Liguria	58.305	212.129	16,78%	3,64
Lombardia	65.515	132.889	18,86%	2,03
Marche	2.589	5.640	0,75%	2,18
Molise	691	1.593	0,20%	2,31
Piemonte	128.374	445.525	36,95%	3,47
Puglia	3.669	10.744	1,06%	2,93
Sardegna	2.420	7.491	0,70%	3,10
Sicilia	4.919	17.308	1,42%	3,52
Toscana	10.922	22.999	3,14%	2,11
Trento	2.857	5.185	0,82%	1,81
Umbria	2.347	4.835	0,68%	2,06
Valle d'Aosta	2.122	4.671	0,61%	2,20
Veneto	16.462	35.410	4,74%	2,15
TOTAL	347.464	1.015.281	100,00%	2,92

Source: Camera di Commercio di Cuneo (2014)

It reminds us of another great person from Cuneo, an alpine passionate, Gianromolo Bignami, and of the Alpine Switzerland's young men and women who share these very same wishes and satisfy them while continuing to live in alpine centers, facing life with an aware sense of responsibility. They received a different preparation. Their State gave them what was due to them by law, no need to beg for that, and they never lost faith in the future.

In this respect IRES states (La montagna del Piemonte. Varietà e tipologie dei sistemi territoriali locali, a study): "Generally speaking, marginality is described as a cumulative process, that goes through sequential phases of demographic and economic continuation, loss of Human capital and impoverishment of the area. This is especially true for small and isolated municipalities. Demographic decrease causes the weakening of the population structure and causes a series of negative feedbacks: local residents escape, the weakening of the productive area, the collapse of local services system.

These effects generate, in return, further pushes on depopulation, creating a "perverse spiral" and a structural obstacle to the revitalization of the area. With no corrective actions, this marginality spiral forces territories towards their decline. The demographic problem, in particular, continues to be mentioned among the main causes of alpine areas critical situations, but with a decreasing importance or with, at least, different evaluation from the past. No doubt the exodus, that has long impoverished local human resources has deeply compromised this demographic structure which is very unbalanced: many more elderlies than active or qualified young people" [13] (tab.2).

***Table 2.** Number of foreign tourist by Province and area of destinations (in thousands)*

Provinces and Regions	2009	2010	2011	2012	2013
Torino	1.674	1.722	1.821	1.968	2.048
Vercelli	43	74	50	77	90
Novara	163	190	201	254	235
Cuneo	257	341	352	353	284
Asti	106	109	106	108	115
Alessandria	163	241	144	236	265
Biella	76	83	66	75	70
Verbano-Cusio-Osso	457	694	523	799	876
PIEMONTE	2.940	3.455	3.263	3.871	3.983
NORD-WEST	28.634	29.852	31.659	32.114	32.844
NORD-EAST	28.872	29.483	29.670	31.180	31.188
Center	18.088	18.506	20.179	20.014	21.236
South and Isles	7.187	6.817	7.130	7.209	7.752
Other	6.613	6.129	6.958	7.084	7.089
Italy	89.395	90.788	95.596	97.602	100.110

Source: Camera di Commercio di Cuneo (2014)

4. Results and Discussion

In conclusion, the situation of pulverized residentiality that especially hits alpine areas, generating huge socio-economic problems is a worrisome aspect.

What should we do then to help alpine mountains of Piedmont to successfully face the present challenges?

The answer is easy:

One should not consider it apart. One should insert it in the larger game of the European economic integration.

We will need to clarify that in the alpine area there is no school problem, no health problem, no agricultural problem, and no fiscal problem. There is a "mountain problem" made up of all these aspects. Alpine economy rests on the pillars of a polyhedral and delicate system. This is what Regione Piemonte is doing, creating the Fondo regionale per la Montagna and all the Euromed initiatives. UNCEM also often pressures for this reason, at various levels, to sustain the economic development of the area. In Piedmont, alpine municipalities (515 town halls mainly - 96%, in the Verbano Cusio Ossola area, vs. 59% in Provincia di Cuneo) account for a considerable quota of this area, a very large population and many resources. Many of these municipalities have demonstrated huge rally abilities.

Let's think about the XX Winter Olympic Games, which confirmed the principle that problems in many alpine areas can be faced and solved transforming them in opportunities to re-launch and develop regional economy.

Today, we should consider that local alpine systems are pictured in literature and praxis as strategic areas on which to count to create an innovative and sustainable development considering differentiation and integration among local territorial systems.

Our mountains must then be safeguarded as a whole and valorised in their different aspects, as centres of biological e cultural diversity.

5. Conclusions

In conclusion, what can an economist suggest in this respect? One could state: be local in a global context and innovate through what is presently existing. Give a look beyond horizontal and local limits and develop connecting nets or attraction poles on a qualitative basis.

In order to safeguard the mature area development, it seems necessary to move following five fundamental directions:

1. to identify production systems with a strategic value on which to concentrate an explicit local policy of development;
2. to grant support functions that the area has towards many variables (production, mobility, etc.) and to intervene on the relevant process of territorialisation, through articulated programs;
3. to create synergies augmenting the competition of the system;
4. to identify a small number of local homogeneous systems as areas of development and attraction;
5. to promulgate regional and trans-regional groupings able to emphasize and valorise local specificities.

Two main streams of thought dominate doctrine, with little influence though on political praxis: cohesion and rich development.

For the alpine area of Piedmont, these two concepts bring about, a totally diverse orientation from the traditional one used until now.

It is fundamental to promote:

1. territorial quality (areas where we live and work, wealth, services, knowledge, motivation);
2. territorial efficacy, in terms of development of natural resources, landscape, energy, attractiveness and competition;
3. territorial identity, safeguarding specificities and productive vocations, reinforcing competitive advantage.

Alpine mountains still have a say, what's more this say is of the utmost importance for Piedmont and for its populations. Much will depend on how our State and Region will interpret development instances, such as the construction or the amelioration of train rails, highways, alpine galleries, the effort of new and renovated industrial businesses, the sacrifice of farmers and the hard work of operators of different economic categories and local departments in charge of the management of an area.

This challenge is fascinating and gives us hope, but one must face it as a leading character and not as a passive actor.

References

[1] S. Arzeni, "Tourism a driver for growthand employment", Il Turismo, Fattore Economico di Sviluppo Locale, No. 1, 2012.

[2] A. Murdoch, "Synergies between tourism and the wider social economy: an underexplored territory?", Il Turismo, Fattore Economico di Sviluppo Locale, No. 1, 2012.

[3] J. Ejarque, "Competitività e attrattività turistica nel Mezzogiorno italiano, una prospettiva in ottica di mercato", Il Turismo, Fattore Economico di Sviluppo Locale, No. 1, 2012.

[4] W. Batging, Le Alpi. Torino: Bollati Boringhieri, 2005.

[5] M.G. Caroli, Il Marketing Territoriale. Strategie per la competitività sostenibile del territorio. Milano: Franco Angeli, 2006.

[6] S. Conti, "La città nel contemporaneo scenario competitivo", in Conti S. (a cura di), Torino nella competizione europea. Torino: Rosemberg e Sellier, 2002.

[7] V. Della Corte, La gestione dei sistemi locali di offerta turistica. Padova: Cedam, 2000.

[8] M. Franch, U. Martini, M.S. Barbera, and G. Parisi, "Lo sviluppo dell'eco-turismo come opportunità di riposizionamento strategico e di innovazione dell'offerta: uno studio di caso in una destinazione turistica matura", Proceedings of the 6th International Conference Marketing Trends, University of Cà Foscari – ESCP-EAP, Paris, 26th-27th January, 2007.

[9] R. Garibaldi, Economia e gestione delle imprese turistiche. Milano: Hoepli, 2008.

[10] A. Macchiavelli, Il Turismo montano tra continuità e cambiamento, Milano: Franco Angeli, 2006.

[11] G. Tardivo, and M. Viassone, "The measure of Financial Crisis Negative Impact on a regional context: the Piedmont case study", paper discussed at the 1er colloque international Atlas/ AFMI Association francophone de management international, les defies du Management International a l'aube du XXIe Siecle, Paris, 26th-27th May, 2011.

[12] A. Zucchella, and S. Denicolai, Analisi strategico-organizzativa per lo sviluppo locale. Milano: Franco Angeli, 2006.

[13] IRES, La montagna del Piemonte. Varietà e tipologie dei sistemi territoriali locali. Torino: IRES, 2010.

6

Industry Variations of Relationship Banking in Mergers and Acquisitions

Zeynep Topaloglu

Department of Banking and Finance, Bursa Orhangazi University, Bursa, Turkey

Email address:
zeynep.topaloglu@bou.edu.tr

Abstract: In this study we examine the acquirer-advisor relation in mergers and acquisitions. Among other issues we study the effect of this relation in major industry sectors. We have found that the average log abnormal return from acquirer-advisor relation is $0.5 millions. Relationship advisers are rewarding in the range of $1.5 millions to $2.5 millions in all sectors except media, consumer products and services, high technology, industrials and real estate.

Keywords: Mergers and Acquisitions, Relationship Advisers, Relationship Banking, M & A Advising

1. Introduction

The rapid pace of mergers and acquisitions in recent years stimulated extensive research on this issue. Maximizing shareholder value, increasing market power or efficiency are proposed as the main motivations behind the merger activity; the details of consequences, the role of managers, the effect of financial conditions and deregulation issues are pointed out particularly. As an ancillary to this subject matter, M&A advising emerges as another theme.

This paper focuses primarily on the advising side of mergers, mainly the bidder advising using the SDC M&A data from the beginning of 1995 to the end of 2006. The impacts of the analysts over the merger success, the motivations behind hiring an advisor, the pricing and performance issues have been investigated in prior research to understand the reasoning behind advisor choice. Beyond the issues related to advisor choice, in this study we aimed to use the M&A advising as a tool to comprehend relationship banking or more broadly relationship intermediation. Acquirer-advisor relation will be treated as a proxy to examine the effect of prior relation between two parties over future advising activities.

Relationship banking in borrowing-lending framework is most directly intended to resolve information asymmetries, which is the main subject for financial intermediation literature. We can incorporate the know-how regarding the origin and scope of relationship banking, its potential informational and contractual benefits and its primary problems like soft-budget constraint problem and the hold-up problem into M&A context with a parallel insight. The primary purpose of this paper is not to deal with the cost-benefit analysis of relationship banking but more to study the outcome of this relation in different industries.

We will start our discussion with a review of M & A advising and relationship banking literature in the following section. Then we will describe our data and methodology in the third section; and elaborate our results in the forth one. In the fifth and last section we will conclude our discussion.

2. Literature Review

2.1. The Scope of Relationship Banking

Relationship banking is present when the financial intermediary gathers confidential information beyond what is publicly available through provision of multiple financial services, which is not the case in transactions-based services. Banks can obtain this customer specific information when they involve in screening[1] or monitoring services[2] and reuse this information in multiple occasions[3].

Relationship banking has not been taken literally, it is a terminology also used for investment banks and other non-bank financial intermediaries like finance companies, as long as the financial services provided involve the propriety

1 For the analysis of screening: Allen, 1990; Ramakrishnan and Thakor, 1984
2 For banks providing monitoring services: Diamond, 1984; Winton, 1995
3 Information reusability: Chan *et al.* 1986

information and multiple interactions. While lending is the main service referred in the definition, the financial products like syndicated loans, underwriting public issues, the operations in private equity and private debt markets and other financial services like deposits, check clearing and letters of credit involve varying degrees of relationship. Degryse and Van Cayseele (2000) have argued the information obtained through the relationship in multiple services has value in lending. Likewise the lending and advising role of financial intermediaries in mergers and acquisitions are two faces of relationship banking.

2.2. Benefits and Problems of Relationship Banking

Motivations for relationship banking can be classified as informational and contractual benefits. Bhattacharya and Chiesa (1995) show the borrower may share the confidential information with its bank that it would otherwise never reveal to the market. Informational gains stemming from this interaction produce flexible contracts with more effective covenants and collaterals[4], and reducing the moral hazard and adverse selection problems provides smoother contract terms for the borrower compared to transactions-based services. The relationship established through lending activity possessing a certification role, provides credibility for the borrower in public-debt markets as shown by Hoshi *et al.* (1993).

The major costs of relationship banking are the soft-budget constraint problem and the hold-up problem. The borrower knowing that the relationship bank, which is already loaned money, would easily extend credit to recover its previous loan, would be as Bolton and Scharfstein (1996) stated, reluctant to take necessary precautions to prevent poor outcomes. On the other hand in the hold-up problem, the information monopoly of the creditor might let him make loans with non-competitive terms like higher interest rates[5].

2.3. Relationship Banking and Mergers and Acquisitions

2.3.1. The Link Between Relationship Banking and M & As

The connection between relationship banking and M&As in the literature mainly evolves around the question of whether relationship banking diminishes as a result of banking mergers. The main argument behind this debate is the larger institutions formed by M&As might prefer to offer less relationship-based credit to small borrowers because of organizational inconvenience of providing these services along with providing transactions-based services to large customers[6]. The change in the availability of services to small customers is one of the consequences of merger and acquisition activity besides the changes in the firm's market power and efficiency, payment system efficiency, and financial system safety and soundness.

On the other hand there is another link between M&A and relationship banking literature through M&A advising role held by financial intermediaries. Serving as the lender and the advisor in mergers, they hold a certification role in the merger process. Allen *et al.* (2004) found that this certification effect is positive for targets, yet neutral for acquirers. The target firm receives positive abnormal returns when its own bank is hired as the merger advisor since it certifies its value in the deal, whereas the acquirer would suffer from a similar situation, due to the concerns of the bank regarding previous and future lending activity between them.

2.3.2. Mergers and Acquisitions

As put forward by Berger *et al.* (1999) in their review, the main reason behind consolidations is to maximize shareholder value besides managers and governments' value. The value maximization would be realized by increasing market power or efficiency. Most of the literature employs abnormal returns framework using market based information to assess the results of mergers and acquisitions, yet the analysis based on financial performance are also available. The empirical evidence agreed on the positive and significant abnormal return for target firms; however the acquirer firms' return is, generally, not determined[7].

Discussions regarding diversification, M & A announcements, tender offers, payment method in mergers, and target firms' book to market value built the body of research. Firstly, focus rather than diversification is proposed in mergers[8], Berger and Ofek (1995) found a negative relationship between diversification and merger returns, supporting this proposition. Asquith *et al.*(1987) demonstrated the positive announcement effect in mergers and stock-based deals are associated with negative returns while cash payment is neutral in return. Rau and Vermaelen (1998) found that in the long-run value-oriented buyers (low book-to-market ratios) outperform glamour buyers (companies with high book-to-market value ratios) and there are positive returns to bidders in tender offers.

2.3.3. M & A Advising

The literature on M&A advising mostly deals with investment bank advising. Earlier studies were presenting higher returns for the acquirers when a high quality adviser was hired. However the recent empirical evidence suggests no positive return in hiring an advisor and no superiority of first-tier banks over lower-tier banks[9]. Allen *et al.*(2004) proposes the conflict of interest between acquirer and its bank advisor as a reason for this finding. On the other hand Hunter and Jagtiani showed that top tier acquirer advisors are more likely to complete the deals and complete them in less time compared to lower tier advisor.

4 For the analysis of collateral in long-term contracts: Boot and Thakor (1994)
5 Banks charging higher loan interest rates: Sharpe (1990) and Rajan (1992)
6 An empirical study and discussion on small business lending after M&As: Berger *et al.*(1998), Berger *et al.*(1999)

7 For a review of empirical evidence: Bruner, 2001
8 Focus increases share value: DeLong, 2001
9 Servaes and Zenner, 1996, Rau, 2000

3. Data and Methodology

3.1. Sample Construction

The sample used in this study consists of all completed and unconditional M&A transactions involving US acquirers and targets that are announced from January 1995 to December 2006. The data source is *Thomson Financials Securities Data Collection Platinum* (SDC) database. We have started identifying 46,625 transactions with the above condition and we have imposed some criteria. The first one was to drop the transactions with a value less then 50 million dollars, leaving 5612 transactions. Then, in order to compute the acquirer abnormal returns in the transactions, the deals with the missing values for acquirer's market data have been dropped. Out of 2068 transactions left, in 163 transactions the bidder company did not retain any advisor and in 281 transactions there was a prior relationship between the acquirer and advisor. To construct the second sample of 281 transactions, we have sorted all the mergers by the acquirers and advisors. Then first transaction of the same acquirer-advisor couple is assumed to be the reference point and dropped. As a result, in the remaining sample of relationship advisors, all the acquirer companies has a prior "M&A advising relationship" with his advisor.

3.2. Methodology

We have used an abnormal returns framework to determine the association between acquirer-advisor relation and the acquirer's industry sector. The definitions of the variables used in the regressions are presented in Table 1.

Table 1. *Definition of Variables Used.*

Variable Name	Variable Type	Variable Label
AAREL	Binary	Acquirer-Advisor Relation Dummy 1= Relationship acquirer advisor hired. 0= No acquirer advisor hired
VALUE	Continuous	Value of Transaction ($mil)
AMV4WP	Continuous	Acquirer Market Val 4 Weeks Prior to Announcement ($ mil)
TARMV4WP	Continuous	Tgt. Market Val 4 Weeks Prior to Announcement($ mil)
MARET	Continuous	Mean Adjusted Abnormal Return
AR	Continuous	Abnormal Return in Logs
AIND	Categorical	Acquirer Macro Code 1= Media 2= Finance 3= Consumer Products and Services (CPS) 4= High Technology 5= Health 6= Industrials 7= Telecommunications 8= Retail 9= Staples 10= Real Estate 11= Energy 12= Materials
TARIND	Categorical	Target Macro Code The same categories in acquirer Macro codes are used.
TARBVPS	Continuous	Target Book Value Per Share LTM (US$)
TARCPA	Continuous	Target Closing Price At Announcement Date ($)
P/B	Continuous	Offering Price/ Book Value
GEA	Continuous	Ratio of Total Debt to Shareholders Equity (Gearing)
TOTDF	Continuous	Total Deal Fees ($mil)
NOAA	Continuous	Number of Acquirer Advisors
NOTARA	Continuous	Number of Target Advisors
IS	Binary	Intrastate 1= Intrastate 0= In-state
DEF	Binary	Defense 1= Target used defense strategy. 0= No defense.
AIMAN	Binary	Acquirer Includes Mgmt 1= Acquirer includes management 0= Management is not involved.
OCASH	Continuous	% of Cash used in the payment.
SAMEIND	Binary	Acquirer and Target Firms in the same industry 1= Acquirer and Target in the same industry. 0= Acquirer and Target in different industries.
TTCOMP	Continuous	Days to Complete Deal
T	Ordinal	Year: 1= 1995 2= 1996 3= 1997 4= 1998 5= 1999 6= 2000 7= 2001 8= 2002 9= 2003 10= 2004 11= 2005 12= 2006
AT	Categorical	Attitude 1= Friendly 2= Hostile 3= Neutral 4= Unsolic. 5= Not Appl.

Acquirer-Advisor Relationship Model:

The first regression is a logistic regression to test the factors that effect the decision to use a relationship advisor:

AAREL $= \beta_0 + \beta_1$ TOTDF+ β_2 AMV4WP $+ \beta_3$ TARMV4WP $+ \beta_4$ MARET $+ \beta_5$ TARIND $+ \beta_6$ IS $+ \beta_7$ TTCOMP $+ \beta_8$ T $+ \beta_9$ VALUE $+ \beta_{10}$ SAMEIND $+ \beta_{11}$ OCASH $+ \beta_{12}$ AT $+ \beta_{13}$ GEA $+ \beta_{14}$ P/B $+ \beta_{15}$ TARBVPS $+ \varepsilon$

Abnormal Returns Model-1

The second regression is an OLS regression where the significance of acquirer advisor relation is tested with a dummy variable:

AR $= \beta_0 + \beta_1$ AAREL$+ \varepsilon$,

where the dummy variable gets a value of 1 when there is a prior M&A advising relation between the acquiring company and advisor, and zero otherwise. The coefficient incorporates the information regarding the absence of adviser relation.

Afterwards to show the outcome of prior relationship in different industries, the sample has been divided into twelve subgroups of acquirer major industry sectors (MIS): media, finance, consumer products and services (CPS), high technology, health, industrials, telecommunications, retail, staples, real estate, energy and materials. We have run the same regression in these groups.

To calculate the abnormal returns, first we identified the returns. Returns are defined as the return of the target company[10] in the stock market from 4 weeks prior to 4 weeks after the announcement date of the merger. Abnormal returns are the logarithm of the sample mean adjusted values of the returns defined above.

Abnormal Returns Model - 2

Lastly to test the robustness of the model, total deal fees, the value of the transaction, target closing price at announcement, offering price to book value, gearing, number of acquirer advisors, number of target advisors, intrastate, defense, managerial involvement to the bidder side, percentage of cash payment, acquirer and target being in the same industry, year and time to complete the transaction are included into the model. The regression turns out to be:

$$AR = \beta_0 + \beta_1\, TOTDF + \beta_2\, VALUE + \beta_3\, TARCPA + \beta_4\, P/B + \beta_5\, GEA + \beta_6\, NOAA + \beta_7\, NOTARA + \beta_8\, IS + \beta_9\, DEF + \beta_{10}\, AIMAN + \beta_{11}\, OCASH + \beta_{12}\, SAMEIND + \beta_{13}\, T + \beta_{14}\, TTCOMP + \beta_{15}\, TARBVPS + \varepsilon$$

We expect total deal fees and the number of acquirer and target advisors to improve the abnormal returns since they can be considered as a proxy to the contribution of advisors in the model. The value of the transaction and the target closing price at announcement date present the size and complexity of the deal and the size of the target and supposed to have significantly positive influence. Regarding the effect of financials, the coefficient of P/B ratio presumed to be positive, while the coefficient for gearing should be negative. Likewise intrastate, defense and time to complete the transaction are supposed to deteriorate returns. On the other hand the presence of management in the acquirer side, the percentage of cash payment, same industry merger and year are assumed to contribute to the regression.

4. Results

4.1. Summary Statistics

Table 2a represents the distribution of the advisors to the years in the sample. More than sixty percent of the sample is coming from the year 1997 to 2000. We have 281 transactions with acquirer-advisor relationship, which makes the 63.29 percent of the total sample. Out of these 281 mergers, 216 of them contain one relationship advisor; the remaining 65 include more than one relationship advisor. The number of advisors exceeds one after 1997. From 1998 to 2000 the number of mergers with multiple advisors was augmented by two to three fold, later it doubled again in 2005. We have 163 mergers completed without any acquirer advisors. This group lies in 1995-2001 period, with the bulk in three years from 1997 to 1999. After 2001, all transactions were completed hiring at least one relationship advisor.

Our sample shows the elevation of mergers in 1997. The companies were completing mergers with or without advisors; we can say before that the amount of deals including or excluding advisor were more or the less evenly balanced. As the number of transactions in both groups went up, the balance faded out towards exclusion of advisors, yet we also observe the use of multiple advisors with this boom. Towards the end of that merger balloon, multiple advisors became popular. In 2000 when merger balloon started to burst with a sharp drop in transactions without advisors, we witness the highest percentage of multiple advisors in total for that stage. The merger wave totally disappears in 2002 putting an end to the no-advisor mergers. Then in 2005, we observe an increase in the number of mergers and acquisitions again. It is reflected on the mergers with multiple advisors.

Table 2b and Figure 1 displays the density and distribution of mergers and acquisitions of the major industry sectors. Finance, high technology and health constitute more than sixty percent of the M&As. 154 mergers in finance industry with 34.68% in total is the top consolidated industry. It is followed by 88 deals of high technology with 19.82% in total. The third one is health with 48 transactions which makes 10.81% of total mergers and acquisitions. For the remaining industries we observe that media, consumer products and services, industrials, telecommunications and energy demonstrate higher consolidation than retail, staples and real estate industries.

Most of the industries accomplished same industry mergers, yet the percentages vary for each. Overall, 81.98% of all mergers are horizontal mergers. Except consumer products and services, staples and materials, in all industries the amount of horizontal mergers is higher than 60%. In industries like finance, retail and real estate the percentage goes up even further, more than 90% of the deals are in the same industry. Financial industry pioneering the horizontal mergers has 148 same industry mergers out of 154 total deals with a percentage of 96.1.

The amount of deals with relationship advisors lies between 50% and 70% in most of the industries. Health being the first with 89.58%, in consumer products and services, telecommunications and materials more than 70% of the deals employ relationship advisors. Unexpectedly, with 53.9% of deals using relationship advisor, finance industry seems to be indifferent to relationship advisors.

10 In his review Bruner (2001) shows the significant positive returns to target firm as a result of mergers, however the return to acquirer firms are undetermined. Since the main purpose of the paper is not to examine the results of the merger itself but the influence of the relationship advising, we have taken this information given.

Table 2a. *Distribution of Advisors.*

			Number of Transactions							
Years	Number	% of Total	Without Advisor	% of Total	With Advisor	% of Total	With One Advisor	% of Total	With More Than One Advisor	% of Total
1995	16	*3.60%*	8	*1.80%*	8	*1.80%*	8	*1.80%*		
1996	27	*6.08%*	10	*2.25%*	17	*3.83%*	17	*3.83%*		
1997	56	*12.61%*	27	*6.08%*	29	*6.53%*	26	*5.86%*	3	*0.68%*
1998	96	*21.62%*	47	*10.59%*	49	*11.04%*	41	*9.23%*	8	*1.80%*
1999	99	*22.30%*	67	*15.09%*	32	*7.21%*	23	*5.18%*	9	*2.03%*
2000	42	*9.46%*	2	*0.45%*	40	*9.01%*	29	*6.53%*	11	*2.48%*
2001	25	*5.63%*	2	*0.45%*	23	*5.18%*	17	*3.83%*	6	*1.35%*
2002	15	*3.38%*			15	*3.38%*	12	*2.70%*	3	*0.68%*
2003	16	*3.60%*			16	*3.60%*	14	*3.15%*	2	*0.45%*
2004	12	*2.70%*			12	*2.70%*	9	*2.03%*	3	*0.68%*
2005	28	*6.31%*			28	*6.31%*	13	*2.93%*	15	*3.38%*
2006	12	*2.70%*			12	*2.70%*	7	*1.58%*	5	*1.13%*
Total	444	*100.00%*	163	*36.71%*	281	*63.29%*	216	*48.65%*	65	*14.64%*

Table 2b. *Distribution of Industries.*

			Number of Transactions							
Acquirer Macro Industry	Number	% of Total	Same Industry	% of Total	% of Industry	Without Advisor	% of Total	With Advisor	% of Total	% of Industry
MEDIA	23	*5.18%*	16	*3.60%*	*69.57%*	10	*2.25%*	13	*2.93%*	56.52%
FINANCE	154	*34.68%*	148	*33.33%*	*96.10%*	71	*15.99%*	83	*18.69%*	53.90%
CPS	17	*3.83%*	6	*1.35%*	*35.29%*	5	*1.13%*	12	*2.70%*	70.59%
HT	88	*19.82%*	67	*15.09%*	*76.14%*	35	*7.88%*	53	*11.94%*	60.23%
HEALTH	48	*10.81%*	44	*9.91%*	*91.67%*	5	*1.13%*	43	*9.68%*	89.58%
IND	20	*4.50%*	17	*3.83%*	*85.00%*	8	*1.80%*	12	*2.70%*	60.00%
TELECOM	26	*5.86%*	16	*3.60%*	*61.54%*	7	*1.58%*	19	*4.28%*	73.08%
RETAIL	10	*2.25%*	9	*2.03%*	*90.00%*	3	*0.68%*	7	*1.58%*	70.00%
STAPLES	9	*2.03%*	5	*1.13%*	*55.56%*	3	*0.68%*	6	*1.35%*	66.67%
REALEST	10	*2.25%*	9	*2.03%*	*90.00%*	4	*0.90%*	6	*1.35%*	60.00%
ENERGY	27	*6.08%*	22	*4.95%*	*81.48%*	9	*2.03%*	18	*4.05%*	66.67%
MATERLS	12	*2.70%*	5	*1.13%*	*41.67%*	3	*0.68%*	9	*2.03%*	75.00%
Total	444	*100.00%*	364	*81.98%*	*81.98%*	163	*36.71%*	281	*63.29%*	63.29%

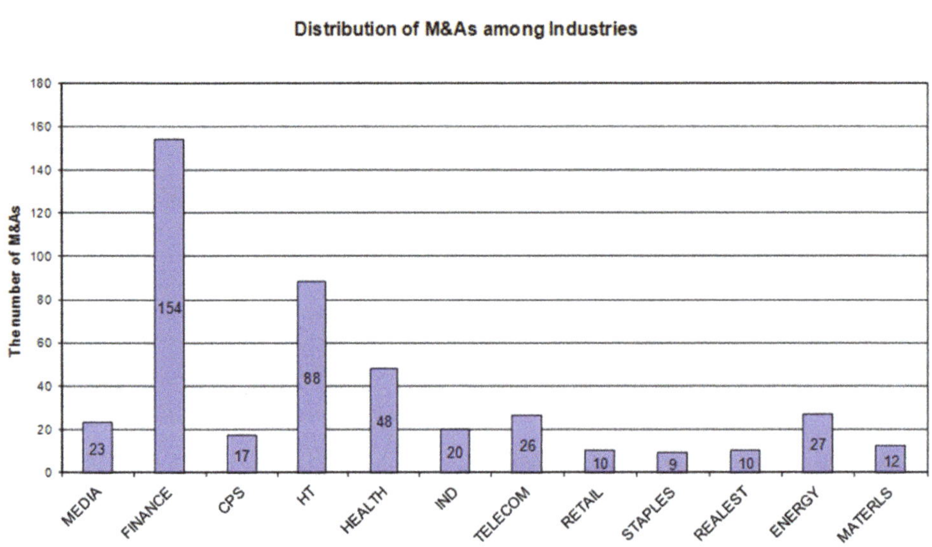

Figure 1. *Distribution of M&A'a among industries.*

Table 3a represents the descriptive statistics for two sub-samples, M & As with acquirer employing relationship advisor and M & As without acquirer advisor. The second sample works as a control group for the first one. The values in the table are mean values for each variable, below which in italics standard deviations can be found. In the table the statistics regarding returns, values, advisors, financials and deal listed in order.

Examining the return and value statistics, for the acquirer we observe the superiority of employing a relationship advisor over not employing any. Logarithm of abnormal returns in the first group is 0.57 million dollars while in the second group it is a loss of 0.94 million dollars.[11] Using a relationship advisor brings on average mean adjusted 317.5 million dollars to the acquirer. Likewise, the mean value of transaction is more than eight fold higher when there is a relationship advisor compared to a transaction without any acquirer advisor. The size of the deal can be considered as a proxy for complexity of the deal. Higher transaction value shows that the target is more complex and hard to execute. For that reason acquirers would prefer to use relationship advisors in those deals.

The statistics regarding advisors show that, the control group contains target advisors; however the mean is lower, confirming that the likelihood of not hiring a target advisor is higher when there is no acquirer advisor. As expected the mean total deal fees are excessive when both acquirer and target hire an advisor.

In the sample with acquirer advisor relationship, the target's book value per share is on average $10.53 which is higher than the control group value of $9.29. Both numbers are lower than the mean closing price for the target at announcement date, implying that the companies are on average overvalued in the market. On the other hand we can consider this difference as a positive expectation regarding target companies; in essence the market believes that target companies have more than their accounting value. Price to book ratio as well contains information regarding overvaluation. The P/B ratio for the first group is 6.90 while for the control group it is 6.17, indicating the same intuition stated above. The debt to equity ratios demonstrate that the targets are riskier in the control group compared to the sample with relationship advisors. The mean gearing of the target company is 4.51 when the acquirer hires a relationship advisor, yet it is 4.78 when acquirer hires no advisor. Therefore it can be stated that relationship advisor has a positive effect on selecting stronger targets.

Deal statistics show the deal properties of both groups. In our sample acquirer companies do not include managers, and on average they have a friendly attitude[12], in exchange of which, target companies do not follow a defense strategy. Another property of the sample that is valid for the both groups is the industry focus. About 80% of the sample is composed of consolidations in the same industry.

On the other hand, we observe that the deals without an advisor are concentrated around the year 1998[13] while the average for the other is the year 2000[14]. Hence we can conclude that there is a higher demand for relationship advising in recent years. Regarding the time to complete the deals, there is difference between two groups. It takes on average 138.69 days to complete the transaction when there is no acquirer advisor which is faster, compared to 144.6 days of the deals where there is a relationship advisor. At this point, we should note that one reason behind that longer span is the complexity of the deals in the first group. Another reason can be the payment method of the deal. Higher percentage of the cash payment in the deals without an advisor makes them to be completed faster since in cash bids acquirers do not need to engage in share registry and target shareholders would prefer the certainty of cash payment[15]. Lastly, the percentage of intrastate transactions are more or the less equal for both groups.

Table 3a. *Descriptive Statistics.*

		Sample With Relationship Advisor		Sample Without Acquirer Advisor	
	Number of Observations	281.00		163.00	
Returns					
	AR	0.57	*$mil*	-0.94	*$mil*
		1.78		*1.39*	
	MARET	317.50	*$mil*	-547.35	*$mil*
		3517.29		*376.65*	
Values					
	VALUE	4600.46	*$mil*	551.79	*$mil*
		14082.89		*1867.22*	
	AMV4WP	25679.46	*$mil*	30461.62	*$mil*
		49790.50		*71011.67*	
	TARMV4WP	3091.12	*$mil*	385.84	*$mil*
		9087.17		*1422.36*	
	TARCPA	34.08	*$*	23.85	*$*
		28.64		*22.35*	
Advisors					
	NOAA	1.30			
		0.62			
	NOTARA	1.27		1.08	
		0.57		*0.30*	
	TOTDF	12.58	*$mil*	2.82	*$mil*
		17.72		*4.50*	
Financials					
	TARBVPS	10.53	*$*	9.29	*$*
		8.77		*8.23*	
	P/B	6.90		6.17	
		25.42		*32.00*	
	GEA	4.51		4.78	
		13.06		*4.73*	
Deal					
	AIMAN	0.00		0.00	
		0.00		*0.00*	
	AT	1.04		1.02	
		0.26		*0.31*	
	DEF	0.00		0.00	
		0.00		*0.00*	
	SAMEIND	0.81		0.83	
		0.39		*0.37*	
	T	6.13		4.04	

11 It should be kept in mind that these figures are in logarithms. The actual mean abnormal return for the relationship advising sample is 317.5 million dollars.

12 Mean attitude is 1.04 where 1 stands for friendly.

13 Mean year is 4.04 where 4 stands for the year 1998.

14 Mean year is 6.1 where 6 stands for the year 2000.

15 Percentage of cash payment is higher in the no-advisor group.

	Sample With Relationship Advisor	Sample Without Acquirer Advisor
	2.99	*1.20*
TTCOMP	144.60	138.69
	105.43	*72.43*
OCASH	73.47	89.70
	31.51	*22.77*
IS	0.21	0.26
	0.41	*0.44*

Table 3b represents the descriptive statistics for the industries. The data exhibits interesting properties. The mean value for the logarithm of abnormal returns in the industries finance and consumer products and services are negative while for the rest it is positive. The highest mean value of transaction is in the telecommunications industry with 9.6 billion dollars and the highest average for the number of acquirer advisors is as well in this industry. As a result, telecommunications industry pays the highest average total deal fees of $22.49 million among other industries. Furthermore the average P/B ratio for telecommunications is 24.59, showing the amount of overvaluation in the target companies, and 13.75 debt-to-equity ratio implies that they engage in high risk transactions on average. On the other hand, the longest time to complete the transactions can be found in the energy sector with an average of 205.81 days. Regarding the percentage of cash payment, we observe that 100% of real estate mergers were paid in cash.

Table 3b. *Descriptive Statistics II.*

		Industries											
		Media	Finance	CPS	HT	Health	IND	Telecom	Retail	Staples	Realest	Energy	Materls
	Number of Observations	23.00	154.00	17.00	88.00	48.00	20.00	26.00	10.00	9.00	10.00	27.00	12.00
Returns													
	AR	0.44	-0.79	-0.15	0.23	0.40	0.38	1.47	0.21	1.48	0.40	0.48	0.29
		1.77	*1.69*	*1.33*	*1.74*	*1.72*	*1.45*	*2.12*	*1.35*	*1.58*	*1.39*	*1.67*	*1.46*
	MARET	171.95	-390.11	-433.29	380.98	255.83	-249.74	1230.26	-418.31	463.33	-267.47	-37.90	-466.63
		2540.58	*1067.25*	*570.55*	*4850.79*	*3286.21*	*668.05*	*4620.41*	*418.26*	*1388.34*	*714.45*	*1053.97*	*633.86*
Values													
	VALUE	2453.54	2169.32	1073.94	3482.88	5319.23	1493.83	9599.66	924.88	3553.53	936.25	2344.88	1559.73
		5065.14	*7058.08*	*2666.94*	*18029.79*	*15866.76*	*1880.72*	*16461.19*	*1014.01*	*5898.46*	*1401.21*	*3912.84*	*2644.98*
	AMV4WP	9410.89	17462.96	9709.05	45726.42	45176.21	11335.29	77071.34	9036.27	22914.04	4370.53	8874.54	8960.00
		11198.61	*43850.63*	*18403.97*	*89065.58*	*64277.77*	*10926.60*	*75970.52*	*7309.50*	*35234.88*	*4590.02*	*12561.64*	*10617.46*
	TARMV4WP	1457.85	1671.93	796.31	1866.69	4002.56	974.84	6375.58	582.30	2176.95	497.10	1708.74	1002.08
		2412.22	*5871.92*	*2144.85*	*9130.17*	*11701.37*	*1239.11*	*12437.77*	*528.74*	*3806.05*	*628.94*	*3065.58*	*1660.05*
	TARCPA	26.13	32.10	19.14	29.72	37.00	31.25	36.04	26.40	26.09	15.93	27.77	19.38
		22.44	*24.74*	*12.85*	*39.05*	*26.50*	*19.96*	*22.99*	*14.25*	*10.67*	*7.55*	*20.45*	*17.76*
Advisors													
	NOAA	1.46	1.18	1.08	1.23	1.28	1.42	1.68	1.14	1.50	1.50	1.61	1.22
		0.66	*0.63*	*0.29*	*0.51*	*0.59*	*0.51*	*0.75*	*0.38*	*0.55*	*0.84*	*0.92*	*0.44*
	NOTARA	1.36	1.11	1.12	1.13	1.42	1.20	1.46	1.20	1.11	1.00	1.15	1.58
		0.79	*0.32*	*0.33*	*0.33*	*0.77*	*0.41*	*0.81*	*0.42*	*0.33*	*0.00*	*0.36*	*0.79*
	TOTDF	9.93	5.74	8.12	8.92	11.02	10.95	22.49	5.93	9.93	4.41	7.21	9.80
		11.05	*10.62*	*11.56*	*17.07*	*18.80*	*13.91*	*27.70*	*8.79*	*10.89*	*4.77*	*9.50*	*11.00*
Financials													
	TARBVPS	6.16	14.56	6.23	5.73	8.02	11.10	6.67	10.19	12.21	12.79	10.23	6.82
		6.98	*9.92*	*4.19*	*4.36*	*7.75*	*7.93*	*6.88*	*7.01*	*7.71*	*7.20*	*6.19*	*8.93*
	P/B	5.16	2.77	4.10	12.39	7.10	3.57	24.59	3.50	3.11	1.59	3.14	5.03
		5.49	*1.62*	*3.09*	*44.34*	*5.62*	*1.95*	*81.59*	*2.34*	*1.21*	*0.93*	*1.83*	*4.93*
	GEA	1.26	8.26	1.17	0.83	0.95	1.29	13.75	3.29	1.10	1.93	1.65	0.79
		1.22	*4.43*	*1.63*	*2.10*	*1.94*	*1.06*	*44.81*	*5.53*	*0.80*	*2.66*	*2.59*	*0.73*
Deal													
	AIMAN	0.00	0.00	0.00	0.00	0.00	0.00	0.00	0.00	0.00	0.00	0.00	0.00
		0.00	*0.00*	*0.00*	*0.00*	*0.00*	*0.00*	*0.00*	*0.00*	*0.00*	*0.00*	*0.00*	*0.00*
	AT	1.00	1.03	1.00	1.06	1.04	1.10	1.00	1.00	1.00	1.00	1.04	1.08
		0.00	*0.32*	*0.00*	*0.38*	*0.20*	*0.31*	*0.00*	*0.00*	*0.00*	*0.00*	*0.19*	*0.29*
	DEF	0.00	0.00	0.00	0.00	0.00	0.00	0.00	0.00	0.00	0.00	0.00	0.00
		0.00	*0.00*	*0.00*	*0.00*	*0.00*	*0.00*	*0.00*	*0.00*	*0.00*	*0.00*	*0.00*	*0.00*
	SAMEIND	0.70	0.96	0.35	0.76	0.92	0.85	0.62	0.90	0.56	0.90	0.81	0.42
		0.47	*0.19*	*0.49*	*0.43*	*0.28*	*0.37*	*0.50*	*0.32*	*0.53*	*0.32*	*0.40*	*0.51*
	T	5.30	5.14	3.82	5.41	5.60	5.50	6.58	5.30	6.00	4.40	6.00	5.25
		2.58	*2.80*	*2.46*	*2.31*	*2.94*	*2.21*	*3.07*	*2.79*	*2.35*	*1.26*	*3.21*	*1.86*
	TTCOMP	149.65	161.97	98.41	101.20	114.33	160.85	180.65	125.30	160.11	113.90	205.81	123.50
		71.53	*50.76*	*37.00*	*49.96*	*75.79*	*189.37*	*140.05*	*83.18*	*99.64*	*38.04*	*208.18*	*63.67*
	OCASH	70.80	71.04	93.80	89.58	87.94	76.19	61.19	62.61	73.72	100.00	79.62	76.49
		32.91	*31.42*	*13.87*	*24.12*	*26.65*	*29.76*	*36.44*	*38.67*	*23.63*	*0.00*	*29.45*	*38.91*
	IS	0.30	0.31	0.06	0.30	0.04	0.20	0.12	0.00	0.11	0.10	0.26	0.08
		0.47	*0.46*	*0.24*	*0.46*	*0.20*	*0.41*	*0.33*	*0.00*	*0.33*	*0.32*	*0.45*	*0.29*

4.2. Models

Acquirer-Advisor Relationship Model

Table 4 displays the results of the logistic regression. Total deal fees, acquirer and target market values 4 weeks prior to transaction, time and value of the transaction are significant at the 5% level. Odds ratio shows that acquirer and target market values 4 weeks prior to transaction and the value of the transaction are equally likely in both groups. However total deal fees and time have a positive relation with the presence of acquirer advisor relation. An additional $ 1 million in total deal fees increases the odds of using relationship advisor by a factor of 2.33. Total deal fees can be considered as a proxy for the quality of the advisors and the complexity of the deals. When the deal size is significant and the target is large, advisors charge higher fees and the acquirers would prefer to employ the advisors they trust. Therefore it is reasonable to observe the positive association between the deal fees and the choice of relationship advisor. Furthermore, a rise of one year in the time of the transaction improves the odds of using relationship advisor by 3.74 times. The reason behind this finding can be the confidence and trust built up between the acquirer and advisor as time passes. If the acquirer is satisfied with the previous jobs of the advisor, it would be more inclined to work with the same company rather than a new and unknown one. This outcome satisfies the informational benefits hypothesis of relationship banking literature.

Mean adjusted return, target's industry, P/B ratio, book value per share, gearing, transaction being intrastate or in the same industry, the time to complete it, the percentage of cash payment are not significant in the decision to use a relationship advisor.

Table 4. *Acquirer-Advisor Relationship Model.*

	Coefficients	Odds Ratio
TOTDF	0.8477303*	2.334343*
	3.12	*3.12*
AMV4WP	-0.0000381*	0.9999619*
	-2.22	*-2.22*
TARMV4WP	0.0149318*	1.015044*
	2.62	*2.62*
MARET	0.0021039	1.002106
	0.67	*0.67*
TARIND	0.1930939	1.212997
	1.17	*1.17*
IS	-2.143171	0.1172824
	-1.52	*-1.52*
TTCOMP	-0.0068809	0.9931427
	-1.35	*-1.35*
T	1.320643*	3.74583*
	2.96	*2.96*
VALUE	-0.0108832*	0.9891758*
	-2.57	*-2.57*
SAMEIND	-0.9380254	0.3913999
	-1.01	*-1.01*
OCASH	-0.0361571	0.9644888
	-1.85	*-1.85*
AT	-0.7137831	0.4897878
	-0.92	*-0.92*
GEA	0.3709398	1.449096
	1.8	*1.8*
P/B	0.1592554	1.172637
	0.93	*0.93*
TARBVPS	0.1303441	1.13922
	1.79	*1.79*
CONS	-4.420985	
	-1.16	
Pseudo R2	0.634	0.634

* Significant at the 5 % level.

The acquirer-advisor relationship model 'Acquirer-Advisor Relation= $\beta 0$ + $\beta 1$ total deal fees+ $\beta 2$ acquirer market value 4 weeks prior to announcement + $\beta 3$ target market value 4 weeks prior to announcement + $\beta 4$ mean adjusted abnormal return + $\beta 5$ target macro code + $\beta 6$ intrastate + $\beta 7$ time to complete the deal + $\beta 8$ year + $\beta 9$ value of the transaction + $\beta 10$ same industry + $\beta 11$ percent of cash + $\beta 12$ attitude + $\beta 13$ gearing + $\beta 14$ P/B ratio + $\beta 15$ target book value per share + ε' is estimated using logistic regression. The numbers in italics are the z-statistics for the variable above.

Abnormal Returns Model -1

The results of the model are presented in the Table 5. The coefficient for the acquirer-advisor relationship is significantly positive for the whole sample. Advisor relationship increases log of abnormal returns by $1.5 million.

Table 5. *Abnormal Returns Model-1.*

	Total	Media	Finance	Cps	Ht	Health	Ind	Telecom	Retail	Staples	Realest	Energy	Materls
No. of Obs.	400	20	142	15	77	45	18	22	9	8	9	24	11
Constant	-0.9437*	-0.3609	-1.5750	-0.9451	-0.2282	-1.4088	-0.1334	-0.2322	-0.8892	-0.0784	0.0434	-0.7706	-1.4311*
	-7.02	*-0.65*	*-8.37*	*-1.7*	*-0.74*	*-1.96*	*-0.25*	*-0.3*	*-1.35*	*-0.14*	*0.06*	*-1.52*	*-2.46*
AAREL	1.5108*	1.4481	1.4582*	1.1982	0.7617	2.0296*	0.8358	2.3472*	1.6456*	2.4881*	0.6429	1.8759*	2.3701*
	8.89	*1.95*	*5.67*	*1.76*	*1.91*	*2.66*	*1.21*	*2.61*	*2.04*	*3.46*	*0.67*	*3.02*	*3.47*
R-squared	0.1657	0.1737	0.1866	0.1929	0.0466	0.1411	0.0839	0.2540	0.3720	0.6666	0.0597	0.2925	0.5720

* Significant at the 5 % level.

The abnormal returns model 'Log(Abnormal Returns)= β_0 + β_1 acquirer-advisor relationship + ε' is estimated using an OLS regression. The dependent variable in all cases is the logarithm of the abnormal returns. The numbers in italics are the t-statistics for the variable above.

Relationship advisor is not significant in media, consumer products and services, high technology, industrials and real estate industries. The presence of relationship advisor in a transaction increases the log abnormal returns by $1.46 million in Finance, $2.03 million in Health, $2.35 million in Telecommunications, $1.64 million in Retail, $2.49 million in Staples, $1.87 million in Energy, and $2.37 million in Materials.

Figure 2a and 2b demonstrates the distribution of abnormal returns to the industries in two cases. In the first graph, there is relationship advising, while in the second one there is no advisor.

Abnormal Returns Model-2

Table 6 represents the outcome for the second abnormal returns model. The number of acquirer and target advisors, intrastate, the percentage of cash payment, same industry acquisition, year and time to complete the transaction are not significant. On the other hand total deal fees, value of the transaction, target closing price at the announcement and P/B ratio have significantly positive impact on the abnormal returns, while debt-to equity ratio has a negative impact.

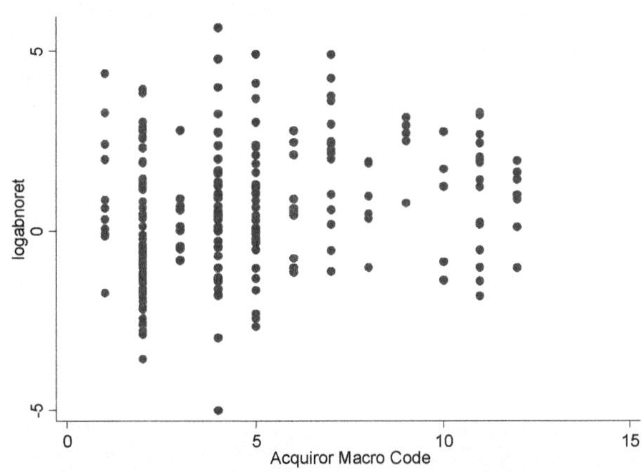

*Mean value is 0.57 million dollars.

Figure 2a. *Sample with Relationship between Acquirer and Advisor.*

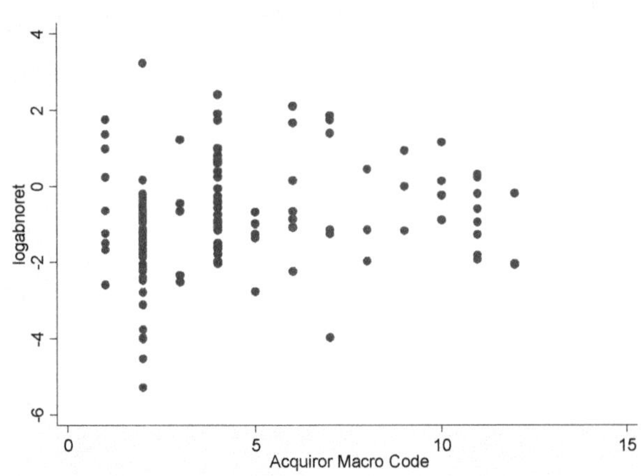

*Mean value is -0.94 million dollars.

Figure 2b. *Sample Without Acquirer Advisor.*

Table 6. *Abnormal Returns Model-2.*

	Coefficients
TOTDF	0.043518*
	2.38
VALUE	0.0000733*
	2.01
TARCPA	0.0229557*
	2.15
P/B	0.0753676*
	2.81
GEA	-0.0865124*
	-2.34
NOAA	0.3109213
	0.79
NOTARA	0.2364301
	0.81
IS	0.5156145
	0.99
OCASH	-0.0069311
	-0.94
SAMEIND	0.2412365
	0.64
T	-0.0649156
	-0.97
TTCOMP	-0.0007589
	-0.45
CONS	-0.7772764
	-0.72
R-squared	0.6955
* Significant at the 5 % level.	

The abnormal returns model 'Log (Abnormal Returns)= $\beta_0 + \beta_1$ total deal fees+ β_2 value of the transaction+ β_3 target closing price at announcement + β_4 P/B ratio + β_5 gearing + β_6 number of acquirer advisors+ β_7 number of target advisors+ β_8 intrastate+ β_9 percent of cash+ β_{10} same industry+ β_{11} year+ β_{12} time to complete the transaction+ ε' is estimated using an OLS regression. The numbers in italics are the t-statistics for the variable above.

5. Conclusion

In this paper we examine the role of M&A advising in major industry sectors. We used a sample of 444 completed US transactions from Thomson Financial SDC Platinum Database. We have started our analysis by examining the motivations behind the choice of acquirer-advisor relationship. Deal fees and the time realized to be the most important motivations. When the deals are large and complex, the acquirers choose the advisors they rely on. In addition, as time passes as the confidence and trust between the two parties improve, there is a tendency in acquirers to use relationship-advisors.

Furthermore, we have found the positive effect of relationship advising over abnormal returns. Macro industries Finance, Health, Telecommunications, Retail, Staples, Energy and Materials observe this positive influence, yet Media, Consumer Products and Services, High Technology, Industrials and Real Estate do not receive any contribution from relationship advising.

Finally, we checked the robustness of our model and get

the results for fees, deal size, target closing price, P/B ratio and gearing that we anticipated. This study tries to fulfill the need for the expansion of relationship advising literature into industry specification. The reasons and consequences of the findings regarding the industry differences of relationship advising need further research to be done.

References

[1] Allen, F. (1990). The market for information and the origin of financial intermediation, *J. Finan. Intermed.* 1, 3–30.

[2] Allen, L., J. Jagtiani, S. Preistiani, and A. Saunders. (2004). The role of commercial bank advisors in mergers and acquisitions, *Journal of Money, Credit, and Banking*, 36, No. 2.

[3] Berger, A. (1999). The 'Big Picture' of relationship finance, *in* "Business Access to Capital and Credit" (J. L. Blanton, A. Williams, and S. L. Rhine, Eds.), pp. 390–400. A Federal Reserve System Research Conference.

[4] Berger, A. N., R. S. Demsetz, and P. E. Strahan. (1999) "The Consolidation of the Financial Services Industry: Causes, Consequences, and Implications for the Future," *Journal of Banking and Finance*. 23, 135-194.

[5] Berger, A., Saunders, A., Scalise, J. M., and G. F. Udell (1998). The effects of bank mergers and acquisitions on small business lending, *J. Finan. Econ.* 50, 187–230.

[6] Berger, P. G., and E. Ofek. (1995) "Diversification's Effect on Firm Value," *J. Finan. Econ.* 37, 39-65.

[7] Bhattacharaya, S., and Chiesa, G. (1995). Proprietary information, financial intermediation, and research incentives, *J. Finan. Intermed.* 4, 328–357.

[8] Bolton, P., and Scharfstein, D. S. (1996). Optimal debt structure and the number of creditors, *J. Polit. Econ.* 104, 1–25.

[9] Boot, Arnoud W. (2000) "Relationship Banking: What Do We Know?" *J. Finan. Intermed.* 9, 7-25.

[10] Boot, A. W. A., and Thakor, A. V. (1994). Moral hazard and secured lending in an infinitely repeated credit market game, *Int. Econ. Rev.* 35, 899–920.

[11] Bruner, R. (2002) Does M & A pay? A survey of evidence for the decision-maker, *Journal of Applied Finance*. Vol. 12, pp. 48–68.

[12] Chan, Y., Greenbaum, S. I., and Thakor, A. V. (1986). Information reusability, competition and bank asset quality, *J. Banking Finance* 10, 255–276.

[13] Chang, X., Shekhar, C., Tam, L., & Zhu, A. (2010). Prior relationship, industry expertise, information leakage, and the choice of M & A advisor. *SSRN Working Paper Series*.

[14] Francis, B. B., Hasan, I., & Sun, X. (2014). Does relationship matter? The choice of financial advisors. *Journal of Economics and Business*, *73*, 22-47.

[15] Degryse, H., and van Cayseele, P. (2000). Relationship lending within a bank-based system: Evidence from European small business data, *J. Finan. Intermed.* 9, 90–109.

[16] DeLong, Gayle (2001), "Stockholder Gains from Focusing versus Diversifying Bank Mergers." Journal of Financial Economics 59: 2 (February), 221-252.

[17] Diamond, D. (1984). Financial intermediation and delegated monitoring, *Rev. Econ. Stud.* 51, 393–414.

[18] Hoshi, T., Kashyap, A., and Scharfstein, D. (1993). "The Choice between Public and Private Debt: An Analysis of Post-deregulation Corporate Financing in Japan," NBER Working Paper, 4421.

[19] Ismail, A. (2010). Are good financial advisors really good? The performance of investment banks in the M & A market. *Review of Quantitative Finance and Accounting*, *35*(4), 411-429.

[20] Kisgen, D. J., & Song, W. (2009). Are fairness opinions fair? The case of mergers and acquisitions. *Journal of Financial Economics*, *91*(2), 179-207.

[21] Kolasinski, A. C., & Kothari, S. P. (2008). Investment banking and analyst objectivity: Evidence from analysts affiliated with mergers and acquisitions advisors. *Journal of Financial and Quantitative Analysis*, *43*(04), 817-842.

[22] Rajan, R. (1992). Insiders and outsiders: The choice between relationship and arms length debt, *J. Finance* 47, 1367–1400.

[23] Ramakrishnan, R. T. S., and Thakor, A. V. (1984). Information reliability and a theory of financial intermediation, *Rev. Econ. Stud.* 51, 415–432.

[24] Rau, P. R. (2000) Investment bank market share, contingent fee payments, and the performance of acquiring firms, *Journal of Financial Economics* 56, 293-324.

[25] Rau, R. P., and T. Vermaelen. (1998) Glamour, value and the post-acquisition performance of acquiring firms, *Journal of Financial Economics* 49, 223-253.

[26] Sharpe, S. (1990). Asymmetric information, bank lending and implicit contracts: A stylized model of customer relationships, *J. Finance* 45, 1069–1087.

[27] Song, W., Wei, J. D., & Zhou, L. (2013). The value of "boutique" financial advisors in mergers and acquisitions. *Journal of Corporate Finance*, *20*, 94-114.

[28] Winton, A. (1995). Delegated monitoring and bank structure in a finite economy, *J. Finan. Intermed.* 4, 158–187.

7

Financial Market Development and Capital Inflows in Nigeria: The Role of Stock Market Development

Nwosa Philip Ifeakachukwu

Department of Economics, Accounting and Finance College of Management Sciences, Bells University of Technology, Ota, Ogun State, Nigeria

Email address:
nwosaphilip@yahoo.com

Abstract: This study investigated the relationship between capital inflows and stock market development in Nigeria for the period spanning 1986 to 2013. Capital inflow was proxied by foreign direct investment and foreign portfolio investment while stock market development was proxied by market capitalization, turnover ratio and value traded ratio. The study employed error correction modelling techniques. From the regression estimate, it was shown that only market capitalization and value traded ratio had significant influence on foreign portfolio investment while none of the measures of stock market development significantly influenced foreign direct investment in the long run in Nigeria. The short run estimate showed that among the three measures of stock market development only market capitalization influenced both foreign direct investment and foreign portfolio investment while value traded ratio only had significant influenced on foreign direct investment in the short run. The study concluded that stock market development had not significantly promoted the inflows of foreign capital inflow in Nigeria.

Keywords: Market Capitalization, Turnover Ratio, Value Traded Ratio, Foreign Direct Investment, Foreign Portfolio Investment, ECM, Nigeria

1. Introduction

Over the years, the stock market has emerged as a vital aspect of the capital market in emerging economies due to the underdeveloped nature of the banking system in providing long term finance for real sector growth and also as an alternative source for long term finance (Blackburn, Bose & Capasso, 2005; Boyd & Prescott 1986; Oyejide, 2002; Nnana, 2002; Sanusi, 2002; Boyd & Smith, 1998). The stock market enhances investment opportunities of the investors by providing avenues for the sale of securities when the need for cash/liquidity arises and enables investors to alter their choice of asset portfolio. For the business firm, the stock market provides access to long term finance at a reduced cost (Dailami & Aktin, 1990; Kohli, 2003) and enable firms in the undertaking certain very-long term investments which seldom occur due to savers unwillingness to tie-up their investment for a long time (Adenuga, 2011; Greenwood & Smith, 1996).

The existence of a well organized and liquid stock market is a potent incentive to foreign investors which facilitates inflows of foreign capital (Stiglitz, 1985; WIDER, 1990). The high performance of the capital market in terms of increased volume of market capitalization, turn over ratio and all share price index equally serve as factors capable of pulling capital flows into the capital market of an economy (Otker-Robe et al., 2007). In spite of the potential of the stock market in attracting capital inflows, the underdeveloped nature of the Nigerian stock market in terms of opportunities for portfolio diversification and weak regulatory infrastructures have acted as strong militating factors to the inflows of foreign capital into the Nigeria economy (Ndikumana, 2003; Levine & Zervos, 1998). Despite this constraint, the Nigerian stock market has experienced notable and unprecedented growth over the years. The annual all share index grew from 127.3 in 1986 to 8,111.0 in 2000 and further to 57,990.2 in 2007 before declining to 20,730.5 in 2011 owing to the aftermath of the 2007/2008 global financial crisis. In a similar fashion, the annual market capitalization grew from ₦6.6 billion in 1985 to ₦472.3 billion in 2000 and further to ₦13,294.6 billion in 2007 before declining to ₦9,672 in 2011 owing also to the global financial crisis.

This phenomenal growth experienced in the Nigerian stock market has raised keen concern on the contribution of the stock market on capital inflows in Nigeria, given the gross inadequate domestic savings that have constraint economic growth in the Nigerian economy. Therefore, understanding the role of the stock market in attracting foreign capital is a topic that warrants cautious enquiry. The perusal of literature showed that little attention has been paid on the relationship between stock market development and capital inflows. The very few studies in this regard include Adam and Tweneboah (2008) in Ghana, Al Nasser and Soydemir (2010) on Latin American countries, and Otchere, et al. (2011). Within the Nigerian economy, plethora of studies has only focused on the relationship between stock market development and economic growth (see Adenuga, 2011; Solarin, 2011; Osinubi & Amaghionyeodiwe, 2003; Nyong, 1997). Despite the substantial quantum of research on stock market separately and capital inflows separately as discussed above, little attention have been paid on the nexus between stock market development and capital inflows.

Apart from the above, this study considered three measures of stock market development (which include market capitalization; turnover ratio and value traded ratio) and two measures of capital inflows (foreign direct investment and foreign portfolio investment[1]). To the author's knowledge, no existing study has examined the relationship between stock market development and capital inflows, taking into cognizance the above mentioned measures of the variables. It is against the above background that this study seeks to examine the relationship between stock market development and capital inflows in Nigeria for the period 1986 to 2013.

2. Literature Review

As noted above, the concern on the relationship between stock market development and capital inflows has been a leading issue in the financial literature owing largely to the importance of both investments in the growth of an economy. Some of the literatures that have examined this issue are reviewed herein. In India, Chauhan (2013) examined the impacts of foreign capital inflows on stock market development for the period 2000:1 to 2011:12. Specifically, the study analysed the impacts of Foreign Direct investment (FDI), Foreign Institutional Investment (FII), and Foreign Portfolio investment (FPI) inflows on the movement of Bombay Stock Exchange (BSE) and National Stock Exchange (NSE). The study employed Ordinary Least Square, Karl Pearson's correlation and Analysis of Variance techniques. The findings of the study showed that FDI had the greatest effect on both Bombay and National stock exchanges up to 61 per cent and 86 per cent respectively. The Karl Pearson's coefficient of correlation showed that foreign direct investment was highly and positively associated with both the markets with a score of 0.78 and 0.92 respectively. Further, the study observed that FPI had a very low impact on Bombay stock market and a comparative high impact on the National stock exchange while FII had the least impact on both markets.

Lamouchi and Zouari (2013) examined the role played by the financial development in the influencing capital flows on real effective exchange rates for thirty-eight developed and developing countries for the period 1989 to 2011. Using a dynamic panel co-integration technique, the study observed that in the long run financial development weaken the appreciation effect of capital flows on real effective exchange rates. Through the calculation of the threshold value, the study concluded that from a certain threshold of financial development, capital flows can have a real depreciation effect on exchange rates.

In Pakistan, Zafar (2013) examined the relationship between foreign direct investment and stock market development for the period 1988 to 2008. The study observed a strong positive relationship between the two variables. Also in Pakistan, Syed et al. (2013) examined the impacts of foreign capital inflows and economic growth on stock market capitalization for the period of 1976 to 2011. Employing an ARDL bound testing co-integration approach the study observed that foreign direct investment, workers' remittances and economic growth have significant positive relationship with the stock market capitalization both in long run and the short run. Using of variance decomposition test, the study also observe bidirectional causal relationship of foreign direct investment and economic growth with stock market capitalization while unidirectional causal relationship was observed from workers' remittances to stock market capitalization.

Nyang`oro (2013) examined the relationship between foreign portfolio flows and stock market performance in Kenya. The study observed that foreign portfolio flows had a significant and positive effect on domestic stock market return and that stock market return is affected by lagged unexpected foreign portfolio flows and not by its contemporaneous value. Oke (2012) examined the relationship between foreign direct investment and stock market capitalization for the period 1981 to 2010. Employing co-integration and error correction modelling techniques, the study observed a positive relationship between foreign direct investment and stock market capitalization in short run while in the long run the study failed to establish any relationship between foreign direct investment and stock market development in Nigerian.

Vagias and van Dijk (2011) examined the nexus between international capital flows and local market liquidity for a group of forty-six countries in six regions for the period 1995:1 to 2008:12. Utilizing a vector auto-regressive technique, the study observed that international capital flows to developed Europe and Asia/Pacific positively responded to local market liquidity, while U.S. market liquidity positively predicted international capital flows to developed and emerging Europe and emerging Asia.

Kaleem and Shahbaz (2009) examined the impact of foreign direct investment on stock market capitalization in Pakistan for the period 1971 to 2006. Employing an Error Correction Modelling (ECM) technique and an Auto

1 In recent times, foreign portfolio investments have become highly visible and often dominant components of foreign capital inflows with the rise of foreign institutional investors (FIIs) and sovereign wealth funds on the horizon that seeks to make quick returns through short term speculative activities abroad (Kumar, 2010; Kohli, 2003).

regressive distributed lag (ARDL) bound testing approach, the study observed a positive and significant impact of foreign direct investment on stock market capitalization both in the long and short run. Kim and Yang (2008) investigated the impacts of capital inflows on asset prices by employing a panel VAR model. The study observed that capital inflows contributed to asset price appreciation while shocks to capital inflow only explained a relatively small part of asset price fluctuations.

Hau and Rey (2006) examined the relationship among exchange rates, equity prices and capital inflows for seventeen OECD countries. The study developed an equilibrium model in which exchange rates, stock prices, and capital flows were jointly determined under an incomplete foreign exchange (forex) risk trading. The study noted that incomplete hedging of forex risk, documented for U.S. global mutual funds, induces equity price and capital flow dynamics: Higher returns in the home equity market relative to the foreign equity market were associated with indigenous currency depreciation. Further, net equity flows into the foreign market were positively correlated with a foreign currency appreciation. The study also observed that correlation was strongest after 1990 especially for countries with higher equity market capitalization relative to GDP, suggesting that the observed exchange rate dynamics is indeed related to equity market development.

Kohli (2003) conducted a preliminary analysis of the impact of capital flows on domestic financial sector in India. The study observed that foreign capital inflows had significant impact on domestic money supply and stock market growth. However, the banking sector remained relatively insulated to foreign capital inflows due to policy responses of the central bank and barriers to direct capital inflows into the banking system. Singh and Weisse (1998) examined the relationship between stock market development, capital flows and long term economic growth in emerging economies. The study concluded that stock market development and portfolio capital inflows in the era of financial liberalization are unlikely to assist developing and emerging economies in achieving speedier industrialization and faster long term economic growth. The study recommended that developing and emerging market economies should promote bank based systems, influence the scale and composition of capital inflows and prevent a market for corporate control from emerging.

From the above reviewed literature, it was apparent that most studies dominate on the impact of capital inflows (with particular focus on foreign direct investment) on stock market development (with particular reference to market capitalization) while only a few examine the role of stock market development in attracting capital inflows. Furthermore, previous studies paid little attention on other types of capital inflows (such as foreign portfolio investment) and equally paid little attention to other measures of stock market development (such as turnover ratio and value traded ratio) which measure the liquidity of the stock market (Levine & Zevros, 1998)

3. Research Methodology

3.1. Model Specification

To examine the relationship between capital inflows and stock market development, this study specifies a simple model with suggested explanatory variables from the literature influencing capital inflows in a developing economy like Nigeria. This model is given as:

$$FCI_t = \alpha_0 + \alpha_1(STK)_{it} + \alpha_2(WIR)_t + \alpha_3(EG)_t + \alpha_4(OPEN)_t + \alpha_5(IRT)_t + \alpha_6(EXT)_t + \varepsilon_t \qquad (1)$$

World interest rate (*WIR*) is included in the model to account for changes in global macroeconomic conditions. A fall in the world interest rate can spur cross-country capital flows as foreign investors from developed countries can borrow at low cost in their home currency and invest in riskier and high yielding assets abroad (Vagias & van Dijk, 2011). Economic growth *(EG)* has been identified by studies as an important pull factor of capital inflows into an economy (see Obida & Abu, 2010; Ewe-ghee, 2001). Domestic interest rate also plays an important role in influencing the capital inflows. Higher domestic interest in a domestic economy acts as pull incentive for foreign investors seeking higher return on their investment (De Paula, Ferrari & Gomes, 2012). Finally, Walsh and Yu (2010) and Blonigen (2005) identified exchange rate as an important factor influencing the inflow of foreign capital into a domestic economy.

3.2. Variable Measurement and Sources

In line with the focus of this study, capital inflow *(FCI)* is proxied by (i) foreign direct investment (FDI) measured by the ratio of FDI to GDP; and (ii) foreign portfolio investment (FPI) measured by the ratio of FPI to GDP. Stock market development *(STK)* is proxied by (i) Market capitalisation *(CAP)* measured by the ratio of capital market capitalization to GDP; (ii) turnover ratio *(TUR)* measured by the ratio of trading volume to market capitalization; and (iii) value traded ratio *(VTR)* measured by trading volume to GDP (Brasoveanu et al., 2008; Levine & Zevros, 1998). World interest rate *(WIR)* is measured by the US effective federal fund rate; economic growth *(EG)* is measured the real gross domestic product; and domestic interest rate *(IRT)* is measured by monetary policy rate.

Data on foreign capital inflow, stock market development indicators, real gross domestic product, trade openness and domestic interest rate are sourced from Central Bank of Nigeria (CBN) statistical bulletin 2013 edition while data on world interest rate is sourced from the Federal Reserve Bank of st. Louis statistical bulletin.

4. Empirical Analysis

This study commenced its empirical analysis by providing information on characteristics of variables used in the regression. The descriptive statistics of the variables is provided in table 1 below. From the table, the averages (means) of the variables are 0.55, 0.26, 4.33, 0.06 and 0.38 for foreign direct investment (*FDI*), foreign portfolio investment (*FPI*), market capitalization (*MCAP*), turnover ratio (*TUR*) and value traded ratio (*VTR*) respectively while the averages of the remaining variables: world interest rate (*WIR*), economic growth (*EG*), domestic interest rate (*IRT*), and exchange rate (*EXT*) are 4.14, 12.86, 13.81 and 73.74 respectively. The standard deviation showed that exchange rate (60.29) was the most volatile variable in the time series while turnover ratio (0.04) was the least volatile variable.

The skewness statistic from table below revealed that with exception to world interest rate *(WIR)* which was negatively skewed, the other remaining variables were positively skewed. The kurtosis statistics showed that foreign direct investment *(FDI)*, world interest rate *(WIR)*, economic growth *(EG)* and exchange rate *(EXT)* were platykurtic, suggesting that their distributions were flat relative to normal distribution. Conversely, foreign portfolio investment *(FPI)*, market capitalization *(MCAP)*, turnover ratio *(TUR)*, value traded ratio *(VTR)* and domestic interest rate *(IRT)* are leptokurtic, suggesting that their distributions are peaked relative to normal distribution. Lastly, the Jarque-Bera statistic rejected the null hypothesis of normal distribution for foreign portfolio investment *(FPI)*, market capitalization *(MCAP)* and value traded ratio *(VTR)* at five per cent critical value while the null hypothesis of normal distribution for the other variables were accepted at the same critical value.

Table 1. *Descriptive Statistics.*

Variables	FDI	FPI	MCAP	TUR	VTR	WIR	EG	IRT	EXT
Mean	0.551	0.259	4.328	0.061	0.383	4.137	12.858	13.812	73.741
Median	0.366	0.045	0.973	0.060	0.046	4.960	12.651	13.500	92.693
Maximum	1.772	3.023	20.961	0.176	2.498	9.220	13.698	26.000	157.499
Minimum	0.004	-0.041	0.033	0.010	0.001	0.100	12.230	6.130	2.020
Std.Dev.	0.558	0.608	6.025	0.038	0.610	2.611	0.462	4.128	60.289
Skewness	0.835	3.720	1.383	0.740	2.013	-0.081	0.428	0.678	0.046
Kurtosis	2.323	17.173	3.700	4.053	6.812	2.067	1.802	4.265	1.210
Jarque-Bera	3.657	288.275	9.162	3.710	34.585	1.008	2.440	3.866	3.616
Probability	0.161	0.000	0.010	0.156	0.000	0.604	0.295	0.145	0.164
Sum	14.871	7.005	116.856	1.652	10.350	111.690	347.159	372.940	1991.02
Sum Sq. Dev.	8.094	9.607	943.865	0.038	9.683	177.365	5.542	442.969	94502.5

4.1. Unit Root and Lag Selection Criteria

To avoid spurious regression estimates, the unit root or stationarity tests on the variables were carried out using the Phillip-Perron (PP) and the results are presented on table 2 below. From the table it was observed that all the variables were integrated of order one, suggesting that the variables were I(1) series. Sequel to the unit root test and before estimating of the co-integration estimates, the maximum numbers of lags (for the two models to be estimated) was determined using the Akaike criterion (AIC), Schwartz Bayesian Criterion (BIC) and Hannan-Quinn Criterion (HQC). The result of the lag selection criteria was presented in table 3 below. From the table, a unanimous number lags which is two (2) was reported by the three lag selection criteria.

Table 2. *Unit Root.*

Variables	Phillips Perron Test			
	Level	1st Diff	2nd Diff	Status
FDI	-0.9398	-8.5517*	-	I(1)
FPI	3.1588	-5.3534*	-	I(1)
MCAP	-0.1615	-5.8197*	-	I(1)
TUR	-1.9628	-7.1815*	-	I(1)
VRO	-1.1467	-5.3885*	-	I(1)
WIR	-1.1467	-3.0489**	-	I(1)
EG	1.0834	-3.4254**	-	I(1)
IRT	-2.7644	-10.6579*	-	I(1)
EXT	-0.4032	-4.8447*	-	I(1)

Note: * and ** denotes 1% and 5% respectively.

Table 3. *Lag Selection Criteria.*

Lags	loglik	p(LR)	AIC	BIC	HQC
FDI, MCAP, TUR, VRO, WIR, EG, IRT and EXT					
1	16.5252		-06841	-0.2378	-0.5710
2	23.0408	0.0003	-1.1855*	-0.6896*	-1.0687*
FPI, MCAP, TUR, VRO, WIR, EG, IRT and EXT					
1	15.3740		-0.5795	-0.1331	-0.4743
2	18.1822	0.0178	-0.7438*	-0.2479*	-0.6270*

Source: Author, 2014.
Note: The asterisks below indicate the best (that is, minimized) values of the respective information criteria. AIC is Akaike criterion; BIC is Schwartz Bayesian Criterion and HQC is Hannan-Quinn Criterion.

4.2. Co-integration Estimate

Sequel to the above preliminary tests and given that the model to be estimated is multivariate, this study employed the Johansen co-integration test owing to the possibility of having more than one co-integration vector. The results of the Trace and Maximum Eigen tests presented on table 4 below clearly showed the presence of co-integration among the variables. For the FDI model, the trace test rejected the null hypothesis of no co-integration for $r=0$ to $r\leq5$ at five percent critical values while the null hypothesis of no co-integration for $r\leq6$ at five percent critical value could not be rejected. This is because the statistic value at $r\leq6$ was less than the critical value at five percent. The Maximum Eigen test for the FDI model also rejected the null hypothesis of no co-integration for $r=0$ to $r\leq2$ at five percent critical values while the null hypothesis of no co-integration for r≤3 at five percent critical value could not be rejected. While respect to the FPI model, the trace test rejected the null hypothesis of no co-integration for r=0 to r≤5 at five percent critical values while the null hypothesis of no co-integration for r≤6 at five percent critical value could not be rejected. The Maximum Eigen test for the FPI model also rejected the null hypothesis of no co-integration for r=0 to r≤4 at five percent critical values while the null hypothesis of no co-integration for r≤5 at five percent critical value could not be rejected. The above co-integration estimates suggest that the linear combination of the variables in equation (1) were stationary and there exists a long run relationship among the variables in both models.

Table 4. *Summary of the Co-integration Estimate.*

Trace Test				**Maximum Eigen value Test**			
Null	**alternative**	**Stat. Value**	**95% critical values**	**Null**	**alternative**	**Stat. Value**	**95% critical values**
MODEL FOR FDI							
r=0	r≥1	442.24	159.53	r=0	r=1	175.74	52.36
r≤1	r≥2	266.51	125.62	r≤1	r=2	124.68	46.23
r≤2	r≥3	141.83	95.75	r≤2	r=3	55.67	40.08
r≤3	r≥4	86.17	69.82	r≤3	r=4	32.11	33.88
r≤4	r≥5	54.06	47.86	r≤4	r=5	22.20	27.58
r≤5	r≥6	31.86	29.80	r≤5	r=6	18.60	21.13
r≤6	r≥7	13.26	15.49	r≤6	r=7	13.20	14.26
MODEL FOR FPI							
r=0	r≥1	499.34	159.53	r=0	r=1	178.24	52.36
r≤1	r≥2	321.11	125.62	r≤1	r=2	126.90	46.23
r≤2	r≥3	194.21	95.75	r≤2	r=3	74.78	40.08
r≤3	r≥4	119.43	69.82	r≤3	r=4	43.85	33.88
r≤4	r≥5	75.58	47.86	r≤4	r=5	42.40	27.58
r≤5	r≥6	33.17	29.80	r≤5	r=6	18.05	21.13
r≤6	r≥7	15.12	15.49	r≤6	r=7	11.98	14.26

Source: Authors' computation, 2013.

4.3. Long Run and Short Run Estimates

The long run estimate on the relationship between foreign direct investment and stock market development with other explanatory variables (see table 5) showed that market capitalization (MCAP), turnover ratio (TUR), domestic interest rate (IRT) and exchange rate (EXT) had negative and insignificant effect on the inflow of foreign direct investment in Nigeria. In contrast value traded ratio (VRO) and world interest rate (WIR) had positive but insignificant effect on the inflow of foreign direct investment while only economic growth (EG) had positive and significant effect of foreign direct investment. Specifically, a unit increase in real economic growth will promote the inflow of foreign direct investment in Nigeria by 3.14 per cent. The insignificant effect of the three measure of stock market development (that is MCAP, TUR, and VRO) on the inflow of foreign direct investment clearly showed that despite the impressive performance of the Nigerian stock market over the years, the stock market had not played a noteworthy role in attracting foreign direct investment in the Nigerian in the long run. This finding is in contrast to the findings of Zafar (2013) and Syed et al. (2013).

Table 5. *Long Run Estimate of the Impact of Stock Market Development on Capital Inflows in Nigeria.*

	EXPLANATORY VARIABLES						
FDI MODEL	MCAP	TUR	VRO	WIR	EG	IRT	EXT
Coefficient	-0.0206	-0.5707	0.2321	0.0152	1.2042	-0.023	-0.0007
t-value	-0.8814	-0.2626	1.0817	0.5624	3.1324*	-1.9318	-0.2924
R-Squared = 0.92; F-Stat. = 31.94 (p<0.05); D-W Stat. = 2.81							
FPI MODEL	MCAP	TUR	VRO	WIR	EG	IRT	EXT
Coefficient	0.1653	3.2017	-1.2064	-0.0292	0.5692	0.0248	-0.0048
t-value	3.1347*	0.6515	-2.4867**	-0.4778	0.6548	0.9220	-0.9491
R-Squared = 0.66; F-Stat. = 5.33 (p<0.05); D-W Stat. = 1.86							

Note: * and ** implies 1% and 5% respectively.

With respect to the foreign portfolio investment model, evidence from table 5 showed that world interest rate (WIR) and exchange rate (EXT) had negative and insignificant effect on the inflow of foreign portfolio investment in Nigeria while value traded ratio also had negative but significant effect on the inflow of foreign investment in Nigeria. Contrarily, turnover ratio (TUR), economic growth (EG), and domestic interest rate (IRT) had positive but insignificant effect on the inflow of foreign portfolio investment while market capitalization had positive and significant effect on the inflow of portfolio investment in Nigeria. The import of the above analysis on the relationship between foreign portfolio investment and stock market development showed that different measures of stock market development had differential impact on foreign portfolio investment. While stock market capitalization exerted a positive effect on foreign portfolio investment, value traded ratio had negative influence on the inflow of foreign portfolio investment in Nigeria in the long run. This finding is in contrast to the one obtained by Nyang'oro (2013).

In addition to the long run regression estimate, the short run estimate on the relationship between foreign direct investment and stock market development is presented in table 6 below. From the table, the coefficient of the error correction term was correctly negatively signed (-1.03) and statistically significant. The coefficient estimate of the error correction term implied that the model corrects its short run disequilibrium by more than 100 per cent speed of adjustment in order to return to the long run equilibrium. Also, the negative sign of the error correction term indicated a backward movement towards equilibrium. The coefficient of the current value of domestic interest rate was negative and insignificant while the coefficient of value traded ratio was negative but significant in the short run. In contrast, the coefficient of current values of market capitalization (0.047) and world interest rate (0.037) were both positive and statistically significant.

Table 6. *Short Run Estimate of the Impact of Stock Market Development on Foreign Direct Investment in Nigeria.*

	EXPLANATORY VARIABLES				
FDI MODEL	ECM_{t-1}	ΔIRT	ΔMCAP(-1)	ΔVRO	ΔWIR
Coefficient	-1.0275	-0.0088	0.0466	-0.3330	0.0366
t-value	-6.4236*	-1.5753	3.8758*	-3.7656*	2.2394**
R-Squared = 0.85; F-Stat. = 22.06 (p<0.05); D-W Stat. = 2.18					

Note: * and ** implies 1% and 5% respectively.

Table 7 below presents the short run estimate on the relationship between foreign portfolio investment inflows and stock market development. From the table, the coefficient of the error correction term was correctly negatively signed (-2.23) and statistically significant. The coefficient estimate of the error correction term implied that the model corrects its short run disequilibrium by more than 100 per cent speed of adjustment in order to return to the long run equilibrium. The first lagged value of foreign portfolio investment had a positive and significant effect on current foreign portfolio investment in the short run while domestic interest rate and the first lagged value of value traded ratio had positive but insignificant effect on current foreign portfolio investment. The first lagged value of market capitalization had negative but statistically significant effect on current foreign portfolio investment while current value of exchange rate had negative insignificant effect on foreign portfolio investment in the short run.

Table 7. *Short Run Estimate of the Impact of Stock Market Development on Foreign Portfolio Investment in Nigeria.*

	EXPLANATORY VARIABLES					
FPI MODEL	ECM_{t-1}	ΔFPI(-1)	ΔEXT	ΔIRT	ΔMCAP	ΔVRO(-1)
Coefficient	-2.2393	1.8294	-0.0082	0.0329	-0.3775	1.0611
t-value	-2.9816**	2.7525**	-1.2566	1.2797	-2.9134**	1.8699
R-Squared = 0.58; D-W Stat. = 1.59						

Note: * and ** implies 1% and 5% respectively.

5. Conclusion and Policy Recommendation

This study investigated the relationship between capital inflows (foreign direct investment and foreign portfolio investment) and stock market development in Nigeria for the period 1986 to 2013. Capital inflow was proxied by foreign direct investment and foreign portfolio investment while stock market development was proxied by market capitalization, turnover ratio and value traded ratio. From the regression estimate, it was shown that only market capitalization and value traded ratio had significant influence on foreign portfolio investment while none of the proxies for stock market development significantly influenced foreign direct investment in the long run in Nigeria. The short run estimate showed that among the three measures of stock market development only market capitalization influenced both foreign direct investment and foreign portfolio investment while value traded ratio only had significant influenced on foreign direct investment in the short run. Drawing from the findings of the study, it was concluded that stock market development have not significantly promoted the inflow of capital inflow in Nigeria. Thus, there is the need government to do more in terms of financial market regulation (with particular reference to stock market development) that will guarantee and ensure increased inflow of foreign capital into the Nigeria economy.

References

[1] Adam, A. M., & Tweneboah, G. (2008). Foreign direct investment (FDI) and stock market development: Ghana evidence. MPRA Paper No.11985.

[2] Adenuga, A. O. (2011). Stock market development and economic growth in Nigeria: a vector error-correction approach. *West African Journal of Monetary and Economic Integration*, 11(1), pp.95-124.

[3] Al Nasser, O. M., & Soydemir, G. (2010). Domestic and international determinants of foreign direct investment in Latin America. FMA Annual Meeting, New York, USA.

[4] Blackburn, K., Bose, N., & Capasso, S. (2005).Financial development, financing choice and economic growth. *Review of Development Economics*, 9(2), 135-149.

[5] Blonigen, B. (2005). A Review of the Empirical Literature on FDI Determinants, *NBER Working Paper* No. 11299.

[6] Boyd, J., & Prescott, E. C. (1986). Financial Intermediary Coalitions. *Journal of Economic Theory*, 38, pp. 211-232.

[7] Boyd, J., & Smith, B. (1998). The Co-evolution of the Real and Financial Sectors in the Growth Process. *The World Bank Economic Review,* Vol. 10 No.2, 371-396.

[8] Brasoveanu, L. O., Dragota, V., Catarama, D., & Semenescu, A. (2008). Correlations between Capital Market Development and Economic Growth. The Case of Romania. *Journal of Applied Quantitative Methods.* 3(1), pp. 64-75.

[9] Chauhan, S. (2013). Impact of Foreign Capital Inflows on Indian Stock Market, *TRANS Asian Journal of Marketing & Management Research*, 2(3-4), pp.79-90.

[10] Dailami, M., & Aktin, M. (1990). "Stock markets in developing countries: key issues and a research agenda". Policy Research and External Affairs Working Papers Series, No. 515. Financial Policy Systems, the World Bank.

[11] De-Paula, L. F., Ferrari-Filho, F., & Gomes, A. M. (2012). Capital flows, international imbalances and economic policies in Latin America, Retrieved on January 13, 2013 from http://www.ufrgs.br/PPGE/pcientifica/2012_12.pdf.

[12] Ewe-Ghee, L. (2001). Determinants of and the relation between, foreign direct investment and growth: a summary of the recent literature, *IMF Working paper,* WP/01/175.

[13] Greenwood, J., & Smith, B. (1996). Financial markets in development and the development of financial markets. *Journal of Economic Dynamics and Control*, 21, 145-181.

[14] Hau, H., & Rey, H. (2006). Exchange Rates, Equity Prices and Capital Flows, *The Review of Financial Studies*, 19(1), pp. 273-317.

[15] Kaleem, R., & Shahbaz, M. (2009). Impact of Foreign Direct Investment on Stock Market Development: The Case of Pakistan. *9th Global Conference on Business and Economics, Cambridge University*, Uk.

[16] Kim, S., &Yang, D. Y. (2008). The Impact of Capital Inflows on Asset Prices in Emerging Asian Economies: Is Too Much Money Chasing Too Little Good? *Working Paper Series On Regional Economic Integration* Asian Development Bank (ADB) No. 15.

[17] Kumar, N. (2010). Capital flows and development: lessons from South Asian experiences, Macroeconomic Policy and Development Division (MPDD) Working Paper Series, WP/10/11.

[18] Kohli, R. (2003). Capital Flows and Domestic Financial Sector in India, *Economic and Political Weekly*, February 22, pp. 761-767.

[19] Lamouchi, A., & Zouari, E. (2013). Financial Development and Capital Inflows: The effect on the real exchange rate, *Global Journal of Management and Business Research Finance*, 13(3), pp. 30-42.

[20] Levine, R., & Zervos, S. (1998). Stock Market, Bank and Economic growth: *American Economic Review 88(3),* 537-558.

[21] Ndikumana, L. (2003). Capital Flows, Capital Account Regimes, and Foreign Exchange Rate Regimes in Africa. *Working Paper Series* No. 55, Political Economy Research Institute (PERI), University of Massachusetts Amherst.

[22] Nnanna J. O. (2002). Monetary Policy and Exchange rate Stability: A general overview: Proceedings of Nigeria Economic Society's One-day seminar held Lagos.

[23] Nyang`oro, O. (2013). Foreign Portfolio Flows and Stock Market Performance in Kenya: Case of Nairobi Securities Exchange, *An extracted from my thesis submitted to the University of Nairobi,* Kenya.

[24] Nyong, M. O. (1997). Capital market development and long-run economic growth: theory, evidence and analysis. *First Bank Review,* December, pp.13-38.

[25] Obida, G. W., & Abu, N. (2010). Determinants of foreign direct investment in Nigeria: an empirical analysis, *Global Journal of Human Social Sciences*, 10(1), 26-34.

[26] Oke, M. O. (2012). Foreign Direct Investment and the Nigerian Financial Sector Growth, *Asian Economic and Financial Review*, 2(2), pp.262-275.

[27] Osinubi, T. S., & Amaghionyeodiwe, L. A. (2003). Stock Market Development and Long-run Growth in Nigeria, *Journal of African Business*, 4(3): 103-129.

[28] Otchere, I., Soumare, I., &Yourougou, P. (2011). "FID and financial market development in Africa" [On line] Available at: http://www.uneca.org/sites/default/files/page_attachments/soumare_and_otcherel-fdi_and_financial_market_development_in_africa_0.pdf [Retrieved September 28, 2013].

[29] Ötker-Robe, İ., Polański, Z., Topf, B., & Vávra, D. (2007). Coping with Capital Inflows: Experiences of Selected European Countries, IMF Working Paper, WP/07/190.

[30] Oyejide T. A. (2002). Monetary Policy and its Effects on the Nigerian Economy*: Proceedings of Nigeria Economic Society's One-day seminar held Lagos.*

[31] Sanusi J. O. (2002). "Central Bank and the Macroeconomics' Environment in Nigeria". A Lecture Delivered at *Senior Executive course No 24 Institute for Policy and Strategy Studies.*

[32] Solarin, S. A. (2011). "Financial development and economic growth: the role of stock markets and banking sector in Nigeria". *Journal of Sustainable Development in Africa*, 13(7), pp. 96-113.

[33] Singh, A., & Weisse, B. A. (1998). Emerging Stock Markets, Portfolio Capital Flows and Long-term Economic Growth: Micro and Macroeconomic Perspectives, *World Development* Vol. 26(4), pp.607-622.

[34] Stiglitz, J. E. (1985). Credit Markets and the Control of Capital, *Journal of Money, Credit and Banking*, 71, pp.324-376.

[35] Syed, A. R., Syed, T. J., & Sahar, A. (2013) Is Stock Market Sensitive to Foreign Capital Inflows and Economic Growth? Evidence from Pakistan, *MPRA* paper No. 48399.

[36] Vagias, D., & van Dijk, M. A. (2011). International Capital Flows and Liquidity. [Online] Available at: http://ssrn.com/abstract=1571858 [Retrieved September 28, 2013].

[37] Walsh, J. P., & Yu, J. (2010). Determinants of Foreign Direct Investment: A Sectoral and Institutional Approach, *IMF Working Paper,* Asia Pacific Department, WP/10/187.

[38] WIDER (1990). *Foreign Portfolio investment in Emerging Equity Markets.* Study Group Series, No. 5, WIDER. Helsinki.

[39] Zafar, M. (2013). Determinants of Stock Market Performance in Pakistan, *Interdisciplinary Journal of Contemporary Research in Business*, 4(9), pp.1017-1026.

Research on the Risk Factors of Power Coal Supply in China's Shanxi Province Based on ISM

Jun Dong, Huijuan Huo*

School of Economics and Management, North China Electric Power University, Beijing, China

Email address:
315159099@qq.com (Huijuan Huo)

Abstract: The stability of power coal supply is of great significance for coal base construction and the focus of thermal power enterprise investment in Shanxi province. This paper analyzes the risk factors of power coal supply chain, builds up the power coal supply risk identification model based on ISM and identifies the major power coal supply risks. It is found that the key power coal supply risks for Shanxi's thermal power enterprise are coal enterprises business risk, the coal price fluctuation, coal supply contract risk etc. And then put forward the risk prevention measures.

Keywords: Power Coal Supply Risk, Interpretative Structural Modeling (ISM), Thermal Power Enterprise, Risk Prevention

1. Introduction

Shanxi province is rich in coal resources, and coal-fired electric industry is suitable for large-scale development. According to China's 12th five-year, Shanxi will be built three million kilowatts modern large-scale coal bases in northern, central and southern. Many power generation companies will invest in Shanxi province to build power plants and expand scale. Therefore, maintain long-term stability of coal supply is essential for the sustained and healthy development of Shanxi coal and electricity base. Aimed at the actual situation of Shanxi's coal resources and coal-fired electric enterprise development, we will use the interpretation structure model (ISM) to analyze the risk factors for a stable power coal supply, recognize the key risk factors and provide certain reference for Shanxi's power coal supply chain risk management.

This paper is organized as follows: Section 2 analyzes the risk factors from coal supply for electricity generation in Shanxi province. Section 3 establishes the Interpretative Structural Modeling(ISM) to determine the relationship between risk factors. Section 4 identifies the key risk factors from coal supply for electricity generation based on the risk conduction mechanism. Section 5 puts forward risk prevention and control measures. Section 6 concludes this paper.

2. Risk Factors Analysis

For Shanxi's power coal supply uncertainty in the production, sales, transportation and other areas, we believe that the power coal supply risks affecting the stability are divided into four aspects: external environment risk, production risk, transportation risk, and coal enterprise risk.

External environment risk mainly includes natural environment risk, policy environment risk and economic environment risk. Natural environment risk mainly comes from the natural disasters. Shanxi province, located in the Loess Plateau of northern China, is one of the Chinese disaster areas, and earthquakes, landslides, landslides, hail, frost and other natural disasters occur usually. Policy environment risk mainly refers to the risk factors from the national and local policies change related to power coal supply. Economic environment risk includes macroeconomic operation risk, international market risk, etc. As China's important energy base, Shanxi's coal supply is closely related to Chinese economic growth trend. When the economy is in a high-speed development stage, the coal-fired power plant and other energy-intensive enterprises will increase coal consumption, which will give the power coal supply of coal some risks.

Production risk comes from the mine production, which includes a substantial fluctuation of coal quality, production equipment failure or maintenance, mine safety accidents. In the process of coal mining, mining area changes, mining coal tectonic fault can cause the variety and quality of coal changes. When mining process changes, equipment troubleshooting or mine safety accidents may occur, the mining area of coal production will decline, leading to the shortage of coal supply.

The coal transportation relies on the highway and railway in

Shanxi. The transportation risks include transportation equipment malfunction, transportation safety accidents, shortage of transport capacity and transportation costs rise, etc. In railway transportation, Chinese railway transport capacity constraints, the train wagons are difficult to fully meet the power coal transportation. Coal railway facilities are aging, which causes transportation accidents. As the railway transportation equipment upgrade, the transportation costs rise year by year. In road transport, the transport capacity is limited, traffic accidents frequently occur, and transportation costs are also increasing.

Coal enterprise risks include the coal-fired power plants profit risk, coal price fluctuation, coal supply contract risk, peer competition risk and business risk. The profitability of power generation enterprises can significantly affect the bearing capacity of the coal price. Coal prices can significantly affect the coal supply and demand, and then influence the stability of power coal supply. In order to ensure a reliable power coal supply, thermal power enterprises usually sign the power coal supply contracts with the coal suppliers. Due to market coal price fluctuations, coal suppliers maybe break the contracts for seeking maximum benefits, thus the normal operation of thermal power enterprises will be at risk. Numerous coal enterprises in Shanxi Province maybe cause the peer competition risks. Unfair competition within the power coal industry will damage the lawful rights and interests of the most coal enterprises and thermal power enterprises, and influence the stability of power coal supply. Business risk refers to investment risk, financial risk and operational management risk from the coal enterprise interior.

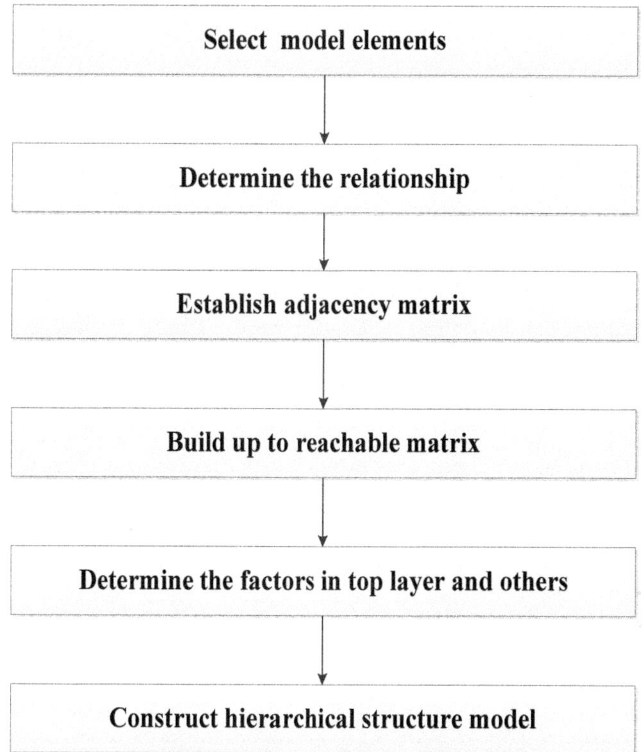

Figure 1. *ISM model analysis processing.*

Table 1. *Power coal supply risks and their relationship in Shanxi.*

risk sources	risk factors	name	factor relationship
External environment risk	Natural environment risk	S_1	$S_5,S_6,S_7,S_8,S_9,S_{13},S_{14},S_{16}$
	Policy environment risk	S_2	S_{13},S_{15},S_{16}
	Economic environment risk	S_3	$S_{11},S_{12},S_{13},S_{14},S_{15},S_{16}$
Production risk	Mining process change	S_4	S_5,S_{13},S_{14}
	Substantial fluctuations of coal quality	S_5	S_{13},S_{14}
	Production equipment failure or maintenance	S_6	S_4,S_5,S_{13},S_{14}
	Mine safety accidents	S_7	$S_4,S_5,S_6,S_{13},S_{14}$
Transportation risk	Transportation equipment failure	S_8	S_9,S_{10}
	Transportation safety accidents	S_9	S_8,S_{10}
	Shortage of transport capacity	S_{10}	$S_{13},S_{14},S_{15},S_{16}$
	Transportation costs rise	S_{11}	$S_{12},S_{13},S_{14},S_{15},S_{16}$
Coal enterprise risk	Coal-fired power plants profit risk	S_{12}	-
	Coal price fluctuation	S_{13}	$S_{12},S_{14},S_{15},S_{16}$
	Power coal supply contract risk	S_{14}	S_{12},S_{15},S_{16}
	Peer competition risk	S_{15}	S_{12},S_{13},S_{16}
	Business risk	S_{16}	S_{12},S_{14},S_{15}

3. ISM Establishment

Interpretative Structural Modeling (ISM) is a qualitative analysis model, mainly used to analyze the relationships between the various entities in economic society. The modeling steps include selecting model elements, determining the relationship between each other, establishing adjacency matrix, building up to reachable matrix and constructing hierarchical structure model. According to the hierarchical structure model, the levels of the risk factors can be determined. ISM model analysis process is shown in Figure 1. There is certain relevance between each risk. We construct the power coal supply risk identification model based on ISM, in order to find the main risks.

3.1. To Determine the Risks and Their Correlation

According to the power coal supply risks analysis, we select the 16 risks as the model elements and determine the interaction relation, as shown in Table 1.

3.2. To Establish the Adjacency Matrix

According to Table 1, we establish the adjacency matrix of power coal supply risks, $A=(a_{ij})_{16\times16}$, and $a_{ij}=\begin{cases}1 & \text{There is relationship between } s_i \text{ and } s_j\\ 0 & \text{There is no relationship between } s_i \text{ and } s_j\end{cases}$. The adjacency matrix A is shown in Table 2.

3.3. To Build up to the Reachable Matrix

We construct the A+I matrix, where I is the unit matrix, and use the Matlab7.14 to build up the reachable matrix T about power coal supply risk in accordance with the Boolean algebra, as is shown in eq (1)

$$(\mathrm{A+I})^4=(\mathrm{A+I})^3\neq(\mathrm{A+I})^2\neq(\mathrm{A+I}) \tag{1}$$

Then

$$T=(\mathrm{A+I})^3 \tag{2}$$

The reachable matrix T is shown in eq (3).

$$T=\begin{bmatrix}1&0&0&1&1&1&1&1&1&1&0&1&1&1&1&1\\0&1&0&0&0&0&0&0&0&0&0&1&1&1&1&1\\0&0&1&0&0&0&0&0&0&0&1&1&1&1&1&1\\0&0&0&1&1&0&0&0&0&0&0&1&1&1&1&1\\0&0&0&0&1&0&0&0&0&0&0&1&1&1&1&1\\0&0&0&1&1&1&0&0&0&0&0&1&1&1&1&1\\0&0&0&1&1&1&1&0&0&0&0&1&1&1&1&1\\0&0&0&0&0&0&0&1&1&1&0&1&1&1&1&1\\0&0&0&0&0&0&0&1&1&1&0&1&1&1&1&1\\0&0&0&0&0&0&0&0&0&1&0&1&1&1&1&1\\0&0&0&0&0&0&0&0&0&0&1&1&1&1&1&1\\0&0&0&0&0&0&0&0&0&0&0&1&0&0&0&0\\0&0&0&0&0&0&0&0&0&0&0&1&1&1&1&1\\0&0&0&0&0&0&0&0&0&0&0&1&1&1&1&1\\0&0&0&0&0&0&0&0&0&0&0&1&1&1&1&1\\0&0&0&0&0&0&0&0&0&0&0&1&1&1&1&1\end{bmatrix} \tag{3}$$

3.4. To Determine the Risk Levels

For reasonable risk control, we will divide the power coal supply risks into different levels by the reachability matrix. We need a clear concept of the reachable set and antecedent set. Element s_i reachable set is a collection of the reachable matrix column elements that the elements corresponding to line s_i are 1, R (s_i). Element s_j antecedent set is a collection of the line elements that the elements corresponding to column s_j are 1, P (s_j). As shown in Table 3.

Table 2. *The adjacency matrix A.*

	s_1	s_2	s_3	s_4	s_5	s_6	s_7	s_8	s_9	s_{10}	s_{11}	s_{12}	s_{13}	s_{14}	s_{15}	s_{16}
s_1	0	0	0	0	1	1	1	1	1	0	0	0	1	1	0	1
s_2	0	0	0	0	0	0	0	0	0	0	0	0	1	0	1	1
s_3	0	0	0	0	0	0	0	0	0	0	1	1	1	1	1	1
s_4	0	0	0	0	1	0	0	0	0	0	0	0	1	1	0	0
s_5	0	0	0	0	0	0	0	0	0	0	0	0	1	1	0	0
s_6	0	0	0	1	1	0	0	0	0	0	0	0	1	1	0	0
s_7	0	0	0	1	1	1	0	0	0	0	0	0	1	1	0	0
s_8	0	0	0	0	0	0	0	0	1	1	0	0	0	0	0	0
s_9	0	0	0	0	0	0	0	1	0	1	0	0	0	0	0	0
s_{10}	0	0	0	0	0	0	0	0	0	0	0	0	1	1	1	1
s_{11}	0	0	0	0	0	0	0	0	0	0	0	1	1	1	1	1
s_{12}	0	0	0	0	0	0	0	0	0	0	0	0	0	0	0	0
s_{13}	0	0	0	0	0	0	0	0	0	0	0	1	0	1	1	1
s_{14}	0	0	0	0	0	0	0	0	0	0	0	1	0	0	1	1
s_{15}	0	0	0	0	0	0	0	0	0	0	0	1	1	0	0	1
s_{16}	0	0	0	0	0	0	0	0	0	0	0	1	1	0	1	0

Table 3. *R(s_i)、P(s_i) and R(s_i)∩P(s_i).*

s_i	The reachable set R(s_i)	The antecedent set P(s_i)	R(s_i)∩P(s_i)
s_1	1、4、5、6、7、8、9、10、12、13、14、15、16	1	1
s_2	2、12、13、14、15、16	2	2
s_3	3、11、12、13、14、15、16	3	3
s_4	4、5、12、13、14、15、16	1、4、6、7、	4
s_5	5、12、13、14、15、16	1、4、5、6、7、	5
s_6	4、5、6、12、13、14、15、16	1、6、7	6
s_7	4、5、6、7、12、13、14、15、16	1、7	7
s_8	8、9、10、12、13、14、15、16	1、8、9	8、9
s_9	8、9、10、12、13、14、15、16	1、8、9	8、9
s_{10}	10、12、13、14、15、16	1、8、9、10	10
s_{11}	11、12、13、14、15、16	3、11	11
s_{12}	12	1、2、3、4、5、6、7、8、9、10、11、12、13、14、15、16	12
s_{13}	12、13、14、15、16	1、2、3、4、5、6、7、8、9、10、11、13、14、15、16	13、14、15、16
s_{14}	12、13、14、15、16	1、2、3、4、5、6、7、8、9、10、11、13、14、15、16	13、14、15、16
s_{15}	12、13、14、15、16	1、2、3、4、5、6、7、8、9、10、11、13、14、15、16	13、14、15、16
s_{16}	12、13、14、15、16	1、2、3、4、5、6、7、8、9、10、11、13、14、15、16	13、14、15、16

We divide the risk factors into different levels according to Table 3.

If s_i satisfies the condition (eq (4)), it is the highest element set.

$$R(s_i)\bigcap P(s_i) = R(s_i) \quad (4)$$

So the first level system is $L_1 = \{s_{12}\}$ .Then we remove the row and column corresponding to the element of L_1 in the reachable matrix, and get the new reachable matrix T. According to the above steps, we can obtain the second level system $L_2 = \{s_{13}, s_{14}, s_{15}, s_{16}\}$, the third layer system $L_3 = \{s_2, s_5, s_{10}, s_{11}\}$, the fourth layer system $L_4 = \{s_3, s_4, s_8, s_9\}$, the fifth layer system $L_5 = \{s_6\}$, the sixth layer system $L_6 = \{s_7\}$ and the seventh layer system $L_7 = \{s_1\}$.

3.5. To Construct Hierarchical Structure Model

Based on the above layer systems of power coal risk, we can get a multi-level hierarchical structure model, as is shown in Figure 2.

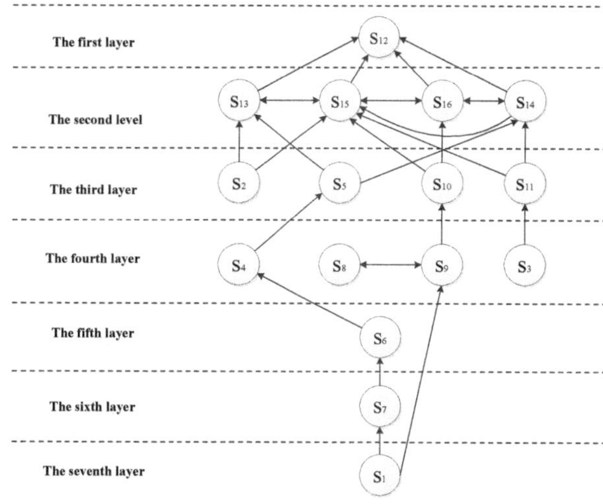

Figure 2. *Hierarchical directed structure.*

4. Power Coal Risks Identification

According to the Figure 2, we can get the relationship between each risk and the transmission mechanism. There are five risk transmission paths.

Path 1 Natural environment risk→ Mine safety accidents→ Production equipment failure or maintenance→ Mining process change→ A substantial fluctuation of coal quality→ Coal price fluctuation→

$$\begin{cases} \text{Coal} - \text{fired power plants profit risk} \\ \text{Business risk} \to \text{Coal} - \text{fired power plants profit risk} \\ \text{Peer competition risk} \to \text{Business risk} \to \text{Power coal supply contract risk} \to \text{Coal} - \text{fired power plants profit risk} \end{cases}$$

Path 2 Natural environment risk→ Transportation safety accidents→ Shortage of transport capacity→ Business risk →

$$\begin{cases} \textit{Coal} - \textit{fired power plants profit risk} \\ \textit{Power coal supply contract risk} \to \textit{Coal} - \textit{fired power plants profit risk} \\ \textit{Peer competition risk} \to \textit{Coal price fluctuation} \to \textit{Coal} - \textit{fired power plants profit risk} \end{cases}$$

Path 3 Economic environment risk→ Transportation costs rise→ Power coal supply contract risk→

$$\begin{cases} \textit{Coal} - \textit{fired power plants profit risk} \\ \textit{Business risk} \to \textit{Coal} - \textit{fired power plants profit risk} \\ \textit{Peer competition risk} \to \textit{Coal price fluctuation} \to \textit{Coal-fired power plants profit risk} \end{cases}$$

Path 4 Transportation equipment failure→ Transportation safety accidents→ Shortage of transport capacity→ Business risk→

$$\begin{cases} \text{Coal} - \text{fired power plants profit risk} \\ \text{Power coal supply contract risk} \to \text{Coal} - \text{fired power plants profit risk} \\ \text{Peer competition risk} \to \text{Coal price fluctuation} \to \text{Coal-fired power plants profit risk} \end{cases}$$

Path 5 Policy environment risk→ Coal price fluctuation →

$$\begin{cases} \text{Coal} - \text{fired power plants profit risk} \\ \text{Business risk} \to \text{Coa-fired power plants profit risk} \\ \text{Peer competition risk} \to \text{Business risk} \to \text{Power coal supply contract risk} \to \text{Coal-fired power plants profit risk} \end{cases}$$

Business risk, coal price fluctuation, peer competition risk and power coal supply contract risk in the second layer form a loop. There is a mutual influence relationship between the transportation equipment failure and transportation safety accidents.

According to the transmission mechanism of power coal supply risks, we can get the following conclusion.

(1) Natural environment risk, policy environment risk and economic environment risk as the external indexes are the essential factors affecting the power coal supply, without control. They are the priority in the power coal supply risk management.

(2) Business risk, coal price fluctuation, peer competition risk and power coal supply contract risk has a strong correlation and are related to coal-fired power plants profit. They are the key in the power coal supply risk management.

(3) Mine safety accidents, transportation safety accidents, transportation equipment failure and transportation costs rise maybe induce business risk, coal price fluctuation and peer competition risk through risk transmission mechanism. They affect the stability of power coal supply and need to be paid attention by investors.

5. Risk Prevention Measures

5.1. External Environment Risk Prevention Measures

Natural environment risk, policy environment risk and economic environment risk as the external environment risks aren't controllable. Investors should undertake risk prediction based on past experiences and data, and prepare the response plant for ensuring the power coal supply and the coal-fired power plants normal operation in Shanxi.

5.2. Production Risk Prevention Measures

Mine safety accidents as the important production risk should be paid attention by investors. Coal enterprises should monitor the coal quality fluctuation and the change of coal seams structure, timely repair equipment, update the technology and strengthen the mine safety awareness to prevent accidents.

5.3. Coal Enterprise Risk Prevention Measures

Business risk, coal price fluctuation, peer competition risk and power coal supply contract risk as the important coal enterprise risk have certain relevance with coal-fired power plants profit risk. Business risk, power coal supply contract risk and coal-fired power plants profit risk are controllable to a certain extent. Coal enterprises and coal-fired power plants should pay attention to enterprise management status, and guard against business risk. Investors should pay close attention to the power coal supply contracts performance and formulate corresponding measures to prevent the economic loss caused by the contract breach. Investors should also control costs and other measures to improve coal-fired power plants profit and enhance the coal price affordability.

6. Conclusions

There are a variety of power coal supply risks in the process of coal production, transportation, use, storage, etc. The thermal power enterprises need to control the main risk factors in the investment. This paper analyzed Shanxi's power coal supply risks, including external environment risk, production risk, transportation risk, and coal enterprise risk. It studied the relationship among the risks based on the ISM and obtained the hierarchical interpretative structure model. We identified the key risks that affect the stable power coal supply through risk transmission mechanism, including natural environment risk, policy environment risk, economic environment risk, business risk, coal price fluctuation etc. What's more, some suggestions are put forward to control the key risks.

References

[1] DOU Xun, LI Yang, GAO Ciwei, SONG Hongkun, RUAN Wenjun. A Coal Supply Security Early Warning System Based on Fuzzy Comprehensive Evaluation Method [J]. Automation of Electric Power Systems, 2011, 01: 29-33+76.

[2] YAN Bing. Study on the Coordination Mechanism about the Sustainable Supply Chain of Power-coal [D].North China Electric University (Beijing), 2010.

[3] Jian Zhiguo. Research on Risk Analysis and Control of Power Coal Supply Chain [D]. North China Electric University, 2014.

[4] Han Yuzhong. Analysis of Guohua Power Coal Supply Chain Risk [D]. Dalian Maritime University, 2013.

[5] YU Zuo, KONG Xian-li. The Formation Mechanism of Tense Atmosphere in Coal-electricity Relationships in the Policies Conflict Aspects [J]. China Industrial Economics, 2010, 04:46-57.

[6] ZHENG Jiaxi. WANG Jiao. Analysis on the risk factors of the FUZZY-ISM structure model of government farmland water conservancy construction project [J]. Journal of Agrotechnical Economics, 2013, 12: 110-117.

[7] WANG Hui, QIAO Jie. Clustering and testing the influence factors of cost management based on ISM [J].Statistics & Decision, 2014, 22: 174-176.

[8] SUN Xue-jun. On the influential factors of low carbonization of coal supply chain based on the interpretative structural model [J]. Journal of Safety and Environment, 2014, 05: 270-274.

[9] HAO Yun-jian, HU Xing-qiiu, WANG Hong-liang. An Analysis of Hydropower Investment Risks in Southeast Asia of China's Hydropower Enterprises Based on ISM [J]. China Rural Water and Hydropower, 2014, 01: 157-160.

[10] Yokabed Beikkhakhiana, Mohammad Javanmardib, Mahdi Karbasianb, Bijan Khayambashib. The application of ISM model in evaluating agile suppliers selection criteria and ranking suppliers using fuzzy TOPSIS-AHP methods [J]. Expert Systems with Applications, 2015, 42: 6224-6236.

[11] Li Haobo, Sun Qiubai, Jiang Xin, Chen, Xuebo. Impact Factor Analysis of Undergraduate Innovative Thinking Based on ISM Model [A]. In: International Conference on Management and Engineering[C]. Destech Publications: 2014.

[12] Ansari, Md. Fahim; Kharb, Ravinder Kumar; Luthra, Sunil. Analysis of barriers to implement solar power installations in India using interpretive structural modeling technique [J]. Renewable and Sustainable Energy Reviews, 2013, 27: 163-174.

9

Evaluating performance in the hotel industry: An empirical analysis of Piedmont

Gabriele Santoro

Department of Management, University of Turin, Turin, Italy

Email address:
gabriele.santoro@unito.it

Abstract: The hotel industry is a key sector in the tourism industry because it is essential for the supplying of all other tourism services and it is the first service demanded by tourists who reach the destination. To assess hotel's performance appears a hard task, because of the presence of many factors to consider, economic but also less tangible. The aim of the research is to verify the correlation between performance and its determinants in the context of the Piedmont hotel industry, through valuating a sample of 112 hotels of Piedmont. More in particular, the study in vestigates whether variables as stars rating, dimension and added services provided are correlated to performance, measured by Rev Par (revenue per available room), a performance metric typical of the hotel industry. To reach these goals, the research starts with a literature review, on hotel industry in general and on performance evaluation methods more used in hotel industry. Subsequently, it will be explained the methodology and the assumptions. Finally, it will be provided results discussed on a managerial perspective, useless for management to improve quality and performance.

Keywords: Tourism, Hotels, Performance, Strategy, Piedmont

1. Introduction

The increasing share of the service sector all over the world has raised competition and created new models of competitive advantage sustainability through the provision of high quality services, allowing the development and growth of a territory ([1]; [2]).

In last decades, tourism demand has evolved, creating a whole new generation of tourists, which highlight new specific needs. To satisfy these needs, the areas have to adapt themself and provide the customer a high level of quality.

Tourism services is a very high value for many countries, becoming more important in the actual scenario, where multinational enterprises are competing to reach competitive advantages quickly ([3]; [4]; [5]).

The World Economic Impact Report by the World Travel and Tourism Council [6] shows that tourism industry continues to grow in spite of continuing economic competitiveness.

The direct contribution of tourism industry to GDP in 2013 was USD 2,155.4bn (2.9% of GDP). This is forecast to rise by 4.3% to USD 2,248.2bn in 2014. Data reflects the economic activity generated by industries such as hotels, travel agents, airlines and other passenger transportation services (excluding commuter services). It also includes the activities of the restaurant and leisure industries directly supported by tourists. The direct contribution of tourism industry to GDP is expected to grow by 4.2% pa to USD 3,379.3bn (3.1% of GDP) by 2024.

The total contribution of tourism industry to GDP (including wider effects from investment, the supply chain and induced income impacts, see page 2) was USD 6,990.3bn in 2013 (9.5% of GDP) and is expected to grow by 4.3% to USD 7,289.1bn (9.6% of GDP) in 2014. It is forecast to rise by 4.2% pa to USD 10,965.1bn by 2024 (10.3% of GDP).

Tourism industry generated 100,894,000 jobs directly in 2013 (3.4% of total employment) and this is forecast to grow by 2.2% in 2014 to 103,069,000 (3.4% of total employment). This includes employment by hotels, travel agents, airlines and other passenger transportation services (excluding commuter services). It also includes the activities of the restaurant and leisure industries directly supported by tourists.

By 2024, tourism industry will account for 126,257,000 jobs directly, an increase of 2.0% pa over the next ten years.

The total contribution of tourism industry to employment (including wider effects from investment, the supply chain and induced income impacts, see page 2) was 265,855,000 jobs in 2013 (8.9% of total employment). This is forecast to rise by 2.5% in 2014 to 272,417,000 jobs (9.0% of total employment).

By 2024, tourism industry is forecast to support 346,901,000 jobs (10.2% of total employment), an increase of 2.4% pa over the period.

The hotel industry assumes an important value in the tourism industry because it is essential for the provision of all other tourism services and it is the first service demanded by tourists who reach the destination [7]. Furthermore, it carries a high weight in the totality of tourist expenditure.

For these reasons, this paper focuses on the hotel industry within the tourism sector. More particularly, the aim of the research is to verify the correlation between performance and its determinants in the context of the Piedmont hotel industry.

The remainder of the paper is structured as follows. Section 2 discusses the theoretical framework; Section 3 describes the contributions in literature on the determinants of performance in the hotel industry; Section 4 analyzes data about Piedmont tourism; Section 5 explains the research methodology; Section 6 shows the formulation of hypotheses and findings; finally, Section 7 offers conclusions and discussion on a managerial perspective.

2. Theoretical Framework

The growth of touristic services demand and the subsequent request for higher standards by the guests has enforced the competition among hospitality suppliers and emphasized how the attractiveness of the touristic destination is influenced by the services provided by the local hotels.

In a such scenario, providing high quality services is the key to improving hotel performance and profitability [8].

Hospitality industry is traditionally more focused on the physical product, but a new customer class is rising, demanding consistent delivery of the brand promise and the experiential dimension.

Hotel is a part of hospitality industry, which counts a wide range of service industries including restaurants, casinos, private clubs, managed food service, event planning, tourism related businesses, and travel providers, and refers to the relationship process between a guest and a host.

Generally speaking, a hotel can be defined as a place where tourist stops being the traveler and becomes a guest.

Technically, a hotel is an establishment that provides lodging paid on a short-term basis and facilities which can range from a basic bed and storage for clothing, to luxury features, so even for the hotels it is important collaborating with firms [9].In many cases, attributes such as price, location, cleanliness, reputation, personal service, and appealing image are decisive by travelers to evaluate the quality of the hotel [10].

It is now known that tourist destinations compete with each other in a competitive arena. In recent years, competition within hospitality industry has increased, as well as that between hotels within a territory.

Consequently, over the years, many hotels started to increase the number of services offered, including suites, public dining, banquet facilities, lounges and entertainment facilities; this has increased the difficulty of the activities management, sometimes moving away from the hotel core competencies [11]. From this point of view, outsourcing is an effective way to manage these difficulties [12].

Therefore, the hotel's management passes through the identification of variables and drivers that increase the results and performance.

3. Evaluating Performance in the Hotel Industry

Performance measurement is a basic element of business management to understand the source of sector's competitiveness and support the implementation of strategies.

In general, firm's performance relates to both external and internal factors: external, because firms compete in sectors and markets which influence strategy and results; internal, because firms have to choose strategies to be adopted and, in general, to decide the correct way to operate, to allocate resources in order to manage business functions and reach goals [13].

In recent years, the parameters of performance measurement have changed significantly [14], becoming necessary to join the classics financial indicators with non-financial indicators creating an integrated system of evaluation.

To stay abreast of competition, firms have to consider non-financial and operational aspects [15], such as quality, flexibility and the implementation of new technologies. The limitations in using only financial indicators of performance are that "they are lagged indicators which are the result of management action and organizational performance and not the cause of it"[16].

Literature provided us many studies on performance indicators, based primarily on firm's financial indicators. Many authors ([17]; [18]) emphasized the empirical contribution on the industrial sector and, subsequently, on service sector. Some features of high intangibility make the hotel industry performance so difficult to analyze, but fascinating at the same time. In fact, there are fewer contributions on hotel management issues ([19]; [20]; [21]).

For the service sector, more than the others, evaluating performance is not just a matter of balance sheet and financial data [22], but is also necessary to consider human resources, quality, brand awareness, image and other non-tangible factors [23].

In the hotel industry, in particular, competition is based on the "total value" offered with the services, so it is necessary to evaluate the various dimension of the value.

Hence, hotel industry performance can be measured using occupancy performance, such as average occupancy rate [24], operating revenues, average production value per employee and others indicators.

Several studies have investigated the topic through different interpretations. A first stream of studies have looked for a correlation between performance and external factors. Tang and Jang [25] analyzed the relationship between the performance of four industries linked to tourism (casinos, restaurants, hotels, airlines) and GDP in the U.S. finding no correlation between industry performance and economic growth. Conversely, it is possible to assume that tourism drives economic growth and development [26].

Other research tried to find a correlation between performance and internal factors through using the Balanced Scorecard, which highlights the importance of some internal factors to reach performance [20] and emphasized the importance of internal function like strategy, marketing, production and organization ([27]; [28]).

Among all of the indicators and method listed by now, the research focuses on RevPAR([29]; [30]), a performance metric in the hotel industry, which is calculated by dividing a hotel's total guestroom revenue by the room count and the number of days in the period being measured.

The formula of RevPar is:

$$\frac{\text{Total Room Revenue in a Given Period, Net of Discounts, Sales Tax, and Meals}}{\text{number of Available Rooms in Same Period}}$$

It provides insight into how well a hotel is utilizing its room inventory, and it is very helpful in trying to price your guest rooms properly.

Furthermore, RevPar is useless to compare performance of the same period (months or year), and to compare performance of different hotels of the same category.

4. Piedmont Tourism

The Piedmont region offers a great variety of morphological aspects and natural resources useful to implement processes of local and regional development.

In fact, Piedmont can boasts wonderful territory such as Langhe, Roero and Monferra to Hills, with their sweet landscapes shaped by the combined action of nature and man, which are now UNESCO World Heritage Site. This prove the decision of the Piedmont region to develop a series of initiatives aimed to enhancing tourism, adapting by improving hospitality offering. Actions aimed at strengthening trade capacity and competitiveness of tourism enterprises and actions in support of the overall qualification of the tourist offer.

These policies should and could lead to positive results in the near future, in terms of increase of tourists in Piedmont, Italian and foreign.

Analyzing the situation of the last 10 years, in terms of attendance and arrivals in the region, there has been a substantial increase. More specifically, an increasing of 35.85% of attendance and 48.92% of arrivals [31], but at the same time, there is a delay in comparison to some Italian regions.

During the lasts ten years, the peaks have been recorded particularly in July and August, to prove that, even not being a seaside territory, summer tourism in Piedmont has a high potential value.

Even the number of accommodation establishments have increased over the last 10 years (+60.54%). These results are mainly due to the XX Olympic Winter Games of 2006, a significant opportunity for the development of the tourism industry in the whole region.

The Piedmont region, in particular, counts nearly eight hundred hotels, of which six hundred of stars rating between three and five, but very few hotels with a rating of five stars.

However, Piedmont suffers competition from other Italian regions also with regard to the social aspect, measured by how many "like" on different social network pages, the frequency of "talk about this" and by the general engagement. From this point of view, the Piedmont is located at the bottom of the ranking, showing not to be in step with current trends and with the entrance of technology even in the tourism sector.

Social networks, and technology in general, are useful for creating community around a territory, and at the same time creating new business within the tourism offer. In this way, even the hotel may enjoy benefits from creating synergies between the territory and enterprises.

5. Methodology

The data used in the analysis are taken from the "World Economic Impact Report" by the World Travel and Tourism Council (WTTC, 2014) integrated with data collected on web platforms such as Booking, Expedia, etc. The research was conducted selecting 112 hotels of Piedmont, which have a star rating of three or more (on a rising scale of one to five).

Several studies use RevPar as indicator of the hotel performance due to the fact that it is not an economic variable and it catches the importance of competitive/strategic indicators. RevPAR or revenue per available room, indeed, is a performance metric in the hotel industry, which is calculated by dividing a hotel's total guestroom revenue by the room count and the number of days in the period being measured.

Hence, the purpose of the paper is to verify a correlation between the RevPar and the following variables:

1. Dim = number of available rooms;
2. Category = number of stars of the hotel;
3. Serv P = binary variable which detects the presence of meeting rooms and congress spaces (1 = yes; 2 = no);

Based on the survey research, data on size, category, and services provided were collected. To better understand the nature of enterprises Table 1 presents the characteristics of the hotels in the sample.

***Table 1.** hotels*

Variables		
Size/Dimension (Dim)	**Hotels number**	**%**
<50 rooms	66	58.9%
50-79 rooms	29	25.9%
>79 rooms	17	15.2%
Total	**112**	**100.0%**
Category (Stars)		
5 stars	5	4.5%
4 stars	27	24.1%
3 stars	80	71.4%
Total	**112**	**100.0%**
Services provided (ServP)		
yes	61	54.5%
no	51	45.5%
Total	**112**	**100.0%**

Source: primary research results

6. Hypotheses development

It is possible to divide the different stream of the literature to verify possible correlations between factors that provide value to hotel offering (category, size, service provided, and location).

Some studies analyzed the relation between size and performance, proving the presence of economies of scale in the industry ([32]; [33]; [34]; [35]; [36]). According to these studies, it is possible to formulate the following hypothesis:

Hp1: there is a positive correlation between hotel dimension and performance.

Other studies found a positive correlation between the category/rating (number of stars) and performance ([37]; [38]; [39]). Considering this authors it is possible to formulate the following hypothesis:

Hp2: there is a positive correlation between the stars-rating (and therefore quality) and performance.

Alternative studies use the presence of facilities like meeting rooms and congress spaces as additional measures of performance, trying to find a correlation between the alternative services provided and performance [40]. Subsequently it is possible to formulate the following hypothesis:

Hp3: there is a positive correlation between the service provided (facilities) and performance.

Table 2 allows us to analyze the possible correlation between the RevPar and the three variables listed above.

***Table 2.** correlation matrix*

		RevPar	Category	Dim	ServP
	Pearson Correlation	1	,919**	,472**	,225**
RevPar	Sig. (1-tailed)		,000	,000	,000
	N	112	112	112	112

**. Correlation is significant at the 0.01 level (1-tailed).
Source: research analysis

7. Findings and Conclusions

According to Claver-Cortez [35], who has conducted research on the performance of Spanish hotels, hotel's performance improvement should pass through the following strategies:

- increasing the size, because in bigger hotel stands a better chance of generating economies of scale (more rooms to sell) and economies of scope (possibility to offer a wider variety of services in the same establishment);
- belonging to a chain, the affiliation to a chain brings the hotel numerous advantages, for example to greater commercialization capacity, better chances to deliver higher service quality level, the possibility to offer the guest services or more a greater financial capacity to face investment projects;
- increasing category (stars rating) offering more quality

Considering these contributions and comparing it with the collected data, it is possible to draw the following conclusions. As it can be seen from the results, all of the variables affect the performance, measured by the RevPar index, but in a different way. In fact, there is a significant correlation between the performance and the category (stars) (0,919), evidence that quality is the first driver of performance in the hotels industry.

There is a significant correlation too between hotel dimension and performance (Hp1) and between services provided and performance (Hp3), but is weaker correlation (respectively 0,472 and 0,225)

In a managerial perspective, appear clear that quality is the key factor for hotel's performance improvement. Not quality perceived by customers, but quality measured through the national system of assigning stars (category).

Therefore, from the perspective of competitiveness, the hotel management should consider the idea of increasing the size, monitoring the effect and impact of this strategy on the quality provided and then on the stars obtained (category).

Another suggestion for management is to implement TQM in hotel industry having a market-oriented approach. This implies the study of customer's perception and needs, strategies of competitors and policies of training to employees. Market orientation can help hotel design and offer a service mix that customers perceive as superior quality, in turn enhancing hotel performance ([41];[42]).

In conclusion, results seem to confirm the fact that, within the current worldwide scenario, characterized by high competition and rapid erosion of market shares, competition between tourist destinations is affected by quality offered by the hotels in the area. From a managerial perspective, therefore, it appears necessary to provide quality services and pay particular attention to the needs and customer satisfaction. This adds value to the hotel and consequently to the territory.

From a performance evaluation perspective, results confirm the need to take more account of less tangible and qualitative nature indicators.

Acknowledgements

I would like to express my sincere thanks to Prof. Giuseppe Tardivo for his patience and kindness, who kindly gave me his time helping and encouraging me. Without him, this paper would not have been possible.

References

[1] G. Tardivo, S. Bresciani, and M. Cugno, "Sviluppo economico ed infrastrutture: un'analisi empirica delle Province italiane," Sinergie rivista di studi e ricerche (2013).

[2] A. Shani, N. Uriely, A. Reichel, and L. Ginsburg, "Emotional labor in the hospitality industry: The influence of contextual factors." International Journal of Hospitality Management, vol. 37, 2014, pp. 150-158.

[3] G.M. Golinelli, L'approccio sistemico al governo dell'impresa, vol. III, Padova: Cedam, 2008.

[4] G. Tardivo, "L'evoluzione degli studi sul Knowledge Management", Sinergie, no. 76, 2008, pp. 21-42.

[5] S. Bresciani, and A. Ferraris, Imprese Multinazionali: Innovazione e Scelte Localizzative, Santarcangelo di Romagna (RN): Maggioli, 2012.

[6] World Travel and Tourism Council (2014), World Economic Impact Report, World Travel and Tourism Council http://www.wttc.org/.

[7] F. Orfila-Sintesa, R. Crespi-Cladera, and E. Martinez-Ros, "Innovation activity in the hotel industry: Evidence from Balearic Islands", Tourism Management, vol. 26, no. 6, 2005, pp. 851–865.

[8] M. Oppermann, "Destination Threshold Potential and the Law of Repeat Visitation", Journal of Travel Research, vol. 37, no. 2, 1998, pp. 131-137.

[9] M. Arnaboldi, and N. Spiller,"Actor-network theory and stakeholder collaboration: The case of Cultural Districts," Tourism Management, vol. 32, no. 3, 2011, pp. 641-654.

[10] J. Barsky, and R. Labagh, "A strategy for customer satisfaction," The Cornell Hotel and Restaurant Administration Quarterly, vol. 35, no. 3, 1992, pp. 32–40.

[11] N. Hemmington, and C. King, "Key dimensions of outsourcing hotel food and beverage services," International Journal of Contemporary Hospitality Management, vol. 12, no. 4, 2000, pp. 256–261.

[12] G. Gonzalez-Rivera, "Outsourcing: three long run predictions," Global Business and Economics Review, vol. 7, no. 2/3, 2005, pp. 226 – 233.

[13] S. Bresciani, A. Thrassou, and D. Vrontis, "Human Resource Management – Practices, Performance and Strategy in the Italian Hotel Industry," World Review of Entrepreneurship, Management and Sustainable Development, vol. 8, no. 4, 2012, pp. 405-423.

[14] A. Neely, and M. Bourne, "Why measurement initiatives fail," Measuring Business Excellence, vol. 5, no. 2, 2000, pp. 6–13.

[15] B.A. Hu, and A.C. Cai, "Hotel labor productivity assessment: a data envelopment analysis," Journal of Travel and Tourism Marketing, vol. 16, 2004, pp. 27-38.

[16] S. Brignall, and J. Ballantine, "Performance Measurement in Service Businessess Revisited," International Journal of Service Industry Management, vol. 7, no. 1, 1996,pp. 6-31.

[17] N. Evans, "A resource-based view of outsourcing and its implications for organizational performance in the hotel sector," Tourism Management, vol. 26, no. 5, 2005, pp. 707-21.

[18] K.H. Kang, S. Lee, and C. Huh, "Impacts of positive and negative corporate social responsibility activities on company performance in the hospitality industry," «International Journal of Hospitality Management», vol. 29, no. 1, 2010, pp. 72-82.

[19] R. Chenhall, "Theorizing contingencies in management control systems research," in Handbook of Management Accounting Research, C. Chapman, A. Hopwood, and M. Shields, Eds. Amsterdam: Elsevier, 2007.

[20] R. Sainaghi, "Hotel performance: state of the art," International Journal of Contemporary Hospitality Management, vol. 22, no. 7, 2010, pp. 920-952.

[21] R. Sainaghi, and R. Baggio. "Structural social capital and hotel performance: Is there a link?." International Journal of Hospitality Management, vol. 37, 2014, pp. 99-110.

[22] A. Ghalayini, and J. Noble, "The changing basis of performance measurement," International Journal of Operations and Production Management, vol. 16, no. 8, 1996, pp. 63–80.

[23] A. Thrassou, and D. Vrontis, "A New Consumer Relationship Model: The Marketing Communications Application," Journal of Promotion Management, vol. 15, Issue 4, 2009, pp. 499-521.

[24] S. Sun, and W. Lu, "Evaluating the performance of the Taiwanese hotel industry using a weight slacks-based measure," Asia-Pacific Journal of Operational Research, vol. 22, no. 4, 2005, pp. 487–512.

[25] C.H. Tang, and S.C. Jang, "The tourism-economy causality in the United States: A sub-industry level examination," Tourism Management, vol. 30, no. 4, 2009, pp. 553-558.

[26] J.G. Brida, J.S. Pereyra, M.J. Such, and M. Pulina, "Causality between tourism and long-term economic growth: a critical review of the econometric literature," MPRA Paper No. 37332, April 2011.

[27] H.B. Kim, and W.G. Kim, "The relationship between brand equity and firms' performance in luxury hotels and chain restaurants," Tourism Management, vol. 26, no. 4, 2005, pp. 549-560.

[28] T. Øgaard, E. Marnburg, and S. Larsen, "Perceptions of organizational structure in the hospitality industry: consequences for commitment, job satisfaction and perceived performance," Tourism Management, vol. 29, no. 4, 2008, pp. 661-671.

[29] K. Namasivayam, L. Miao, and X. Zhao, "An investigation of the relationships between compensation practices and firm performance in the US hotel industry," International Journal of Hospitality Management, vol. 26, no. 3, 2007, pp. 574-587.

[30] A. Campos Blanco, A. Oehmichen, A. and S. Frood, "European hotel development – Focus on budget hotels," Journal of Retail & Leisure Property, vol. 9, no. 5, 2011, pp. 373–379.

[31] Dati statistici del turismo in Piemonte-anno 2013. http://www.regione.piemonte.it/

[32] A.A. Israeli, "Star rating and corporate affiliation: their influence on room price and performance of hotels in Israel," International Journal of Hospitality Management, vol. 21, no. 4, 2002, pp. 405-424.

[33] C.P. Barros, "A stochastic cost frontier in the Portuguese hotel industry," Tourism Economics, vol. 10, no. 2, 2004, pp. 177-192.

[34] R. Pine, and P.A. Phillips, "Performance comparisons of hotels in China," International Journal of Hospitality Management, vol. 24, no. 1, 2005, pp. 57-73.

[35] E. Claver-Cortés, J.F. Molina-Azorìn, and J. Pereira, J. "The impact of strategic behaviours on hotel performance," International Journal of Contemporary Hospitality Management, vol. 19, no. 1, 2007, pp. 6-20.

[36] A. Assaf, and L.K. Cvelbar, "The performance of the Slovenian hotel industry: evaluation post-privatisation," International Journal of Tourism Research, vol. 12, no. 5, 2010, pp. 462–471.

[37] P. Ingram, and P.W. Roberts, "Friendships among Competitors in the Sydney Hotel Industry," American Journal of Sociology, vol. 106, no. 2, 2000, pp. 387–423.

[38] S. Danziger, A. Israeli, and M. Bekerman, "The relative role of strategic assets in determining customer perceptions of hotel room price," International Journal of Hospitality Management, vol. 25, no. 1, 2006, pp. 129-145.

[39] J.J. Tarí, E. Claver-Cortés, J. Pereira-Moliner, J., and J.F. Molina-Azorín, "Levels of quality and environmental management in the hotel industry: Their joint influence on firm performance," International Journal of Hospitality Management, vol. 29, no. 3, 2010, pp. 500–510.

[40] A. Urtasun, and I. Gutíerrez, "Hotel location in tourism cities. Madrid 1936-1998," Annals of Tourism Research, Vol. 33, No. 2, 2006, pp. 382-402.

[41] R.C.M. Yam, A.Y.K. Tam, E.P.Y. Tang, C.K. Mok, "TQM: a change management model or market orientation," Total Quality Management & Business Excellence, vol. 16, no. 4, 2005, pp. 439–461.

[42] C.H. Wang, K.Y. Chen, and S.C. Chen, "Total quality management, market orientation and hotel performance: the moderating effects of external environmental factors," International Journal of Hospitality Management, vol. 31, no. 1, 2012, pp. 119-129.

10

Ethical food as a differentiation factor for tourist destinations: The case of "Slow Food"

Milena Viassone[1, *], Martin Grimmer[2]

[1]Department of Management, University of Turin, Turin, Italy
[2]Tasmanian School of Business and Economics, University of Tasmania, Hobart, Australia

Email address:
milena.viassone@unito.it (M. Viassone), martin.grimmer@utas.edu.au (M. Grimmer)

Abstract: In recent years, the topic of ethical food has assumed increasing importance in international academic debate. Despite there being some studies carried out on this topic, there is limited literature on the role ethical food plays in the tourism sector and, specifically, in tourist destination attractiveness. This paper explores how ethical food can be a driver of destination attractiveness and how it is possible to take advantage of this issue for particular tourist destinations. In this paper, ethical food as a destination attraction is explained through the case of Slow Food. Results show that ethical food has a very important role to play in the future of destination attractiveness thanks to special events and projects concerning ethical food, which also contribute to the sustainability of a destination. Finally, strategies to exploit the potential of this ethical food so as to develop tourist destination attractiveness are drawn.

Keywords: Ethical Food, Tourist Destination, Slow Food, Tourist Strategies, Sustainability

1. Introduction

The theme of ethical food has received increasing attention in recent years and it is more and more at the center of the international economic debate. At the same time, food tourism has grown considerably, becoming one of the most dynamic and creative segments of tourism. Food is considered an important factor to diversify tourism and to stimulate tourist destination development. However, food tourism must also consider ethical and sustainability values based on the culture and specific local products of the regions in question [1].

Consumers in general understand that ethical food choices are good not just for society, but for themselves and their families [2]. The growing awareness of consumers has provoked an increase of the demand for ethical foods, resulting in demand in the organic and fair-trade market. In particular, the sector is estimated to account 5%-10% of the total food and beverage trade globally [3]. The UK, Western Europe, the USA and Canada have dominated the ethical food market for the last decade, accounting for 97% of organic and fair-trade sales. In emerging markets such as India and China, the growth of ethical food and drink sales is predicted to increase in the next few years [4].

This growth in interest in ethical food also positively affects ethical tourism and ethical tourism products. Indeed, the behavior of tourists has changed such that they often opt for new kinds of destinations with food and beverages playing an important role in tourist attractiveness. In this way, food and drink are now considered part of the character and culture of a destination [5]. This is particularly important in the Italian context where food plays a significant role in attracting tourists.

While the topic of ethical food has attracted interest in and of itself, there is a lack of work on the role it plays in the tourism industry. This paper aims at emphasizing how ethical food can be a driver of destination attractiveness and how it is possible to take advantage of this issue for particular tourist destinations. To achieve this objective, an example of how ethical food results in attracting tourists to specific regions is offered through the case of Slow Food. This paper provides the first examination of literature on supply and consumption barriers regarding ethical food and its link with the tourism industry. Slow Food, as the exemplar case of the tourism link, is one of the most famous ethical food organizations in the world. Its origin, projects and events which attract tourists are analyzed using existing Slow Food documents, relevant databases and extant literature on the organization. Finally, several strategies are proposed for the exploitation of ethical food for the development of tourist destination attractiveness.

2. Literature Review

2.1. Ethical Food: Supply and Consumption

The importance of the food industry has increased in different economies around the world. Food distribution is about more than moving products from one place to another; lifestyles, diets and health are of course influenced by the rise of the ready meal, the pre-packed sandwich and the exotic fruits that the chill-chain makes possible [6]. In a 2006 speech, the European Commissioner for Agriculture, Marian Fischer Boel, suggested that ethical foods could play a significant role in re-orienting Europe's food system for the 21st century [7]. Consumers are more and more aware of their consumption choices and their impact, and this awareness is particularly seen in food consumption where ethical considerations apply to product, brand and channel choices [8] [9].

On the demand side, ethical stances are able to shift consumers away from specific market offerings and moderate behaviors to be more responsive to ethical requirements [8]. Ethical consumption does not have a shared definition. Muncy and Vitell [10] consider it as "the moral principles and standards that guide [the] behavior of individuals or groups as they obtain, use and dispose of goods and services". For Crane and Matten [11], the main essence of this concept is "the conscious and deliberate decision to make certain consumption choices due to personal moral beliefs and values". Discussion on ethical food and green consumption investigates whether or not people have a moral obligation to act ethically in order to achieve sustainable development or are individually overburdened by taking on a responsibility they cannot shoulder [12]. Szmigin and Carrigan [13] conceptualize ethical consumption by positioning it within Holt's (1995) typology of consumption practices. Holt analyzes ethical consumption as an integration process, that is, the "methods used by consumers to enhance perception that a valued consumption object is a constitutive element of their identity" [14]. He identifies four possible dimensions of ethical consumption: as a distinction process, as hedonistic pleasure, as a sign of love and as engaging an aesthetic response.

On the supply side, firms are engaging more and more in Corporate Social Responsibility (CSR) activities and making efforts to communicate their CSR purposes [15, 16]. The ethical food sector currently accounts for 5% - 10% of the total food and beverage market, and there is an awareness that agriculture's future objective consists of feeding the globe in volume and quality terms but doing so on a sustainable basis [17]. It is important here to distinguish the different responsibilities of companies versus government: the first are responsible for food organizing and production while the second for the grant of safety of the food and for fair access to food supply for everyone. Various supply sources of ethical food and their related capacity are discussed as follows.

Many firms have developed an offer of organic and natural food without genetic modification, that is, without the use of chemical pesticides, artificial fertilizers or sewage sludge with reference to crops; or with reference to animals, raised without use of antibiotics or hormones. In 2009, the number of organic producers worldwide was 1.8 million, with 40% in Asia, 28% in Africa and 16% in Latin America [18]. The UK, Western Europe, the US and Canada have meaningful domestic supply bases of organic food, and Australia and New Zealand have substantial production, Yet, there is a worldwide undersupply of organic produce, particularly with reference to fruit and vegetables, meat and dairy [4]. Local organic food supply chains are complex and mainly composed of SMEs that are engaged in shortening the distances between themselves and the final customers. These producers often sell their products through alternative food purchasing venues (e.g., farmers' markets) [19]. These types of products have developed more and more in the food and beverage sector in response to the increasing needs of customers to know more information on the sources and operations related to their products.

An example of this particular model is offered by Starbucks which buy fair-trade certified coffee from importers who have purchased it from farmers for a price higher than that of the market [20]. Fair-trade in 2009 counted 827 producer organizations spread over 60 countries. Increases have been registered in fair-trade sugar, fruit juices, herbs and spices. In particular, in 2009, bananas fair-trade sales volume rose by 311,465 metric tonnes, coffee by 73,781, fruit juices by 45,582, fresh fruit by 20,091, cocoa by 13,898, wine by 11,908, tea by 11,524, rice by 5,052, honey by 2,065, nuts and oilseeds by 859, herbs and spices by 578, dried fruit by 541 [4]. But in this case, fair-trade product supply is higher than demand, by a considerable margin.

Free Range (i.e., animals raised for consumption living a more natural life) and Animal Welfare Friendly labelling have also become more prominent. Starting in the 1970's, agricultural animal production has been affected by several changes, showing a higher level of specialization of farms, a high number of animals per farm and an increase in mechanization, all resulting in more industrialized animal production. This often meant focusing price, supply and competition more on quantity than on quality, which has also affected perceptions of animal farm production and conditions [21].

In conjunction, the topic of animal welfare increased in importance in the economic debate, especially after swine fever and avian influenza. Methods identified by Welfare Quality to improve animal welfare in Europe consist of defining innovative, knowledge-based, practical species-specific strategies that can be applied directly on the farm or in primary production (i.e., breeding companies). The development of a standardized welfare monitoring system and improved EU regulations concerning animal welfare (ensuring better conditions of housing, transport, etc) have also been mooted, in addition to making animal husbandry practices more transparent thus allowing consumers to be more informed in their purchases. [22].

Ethical food has also been associated with environmentally responsible and sustainable production systems. The main elements of the sustainability of ethical food concern sustainable production (the creation of goods/services using economically, safe and non-polluting processes, being able to conserve energy and natural resources, and providing socially rewarding for the working people). Local production is also favored (due to freshness of the produce, its nutritional content, and the lower carbon emissions as a result of reduced transport miles), as well as seasonality (seasonal food also generally doesn't travel great distances). Waste reduction and reduced packaging similarly are advantages of ethical food (e.g., purchasing loose fruits and vegetables, avoiding small bottles, purchasing only what is necessary) [4].

As a consequence of the importance of these aspects of ethical food, there is increasing international economic debate on the impact of different food product styles (e.g., fast versus slow food, international cuisine, health food). Of particular interest is the relationship between consumers, supply chains and the state. This relationship invokes more than just branding [23, 24] in that ethical food is supported by state-sanctioned certification systems, resulting in important social relationships between customers and food [25]. Generally speaking, demand and supply of ethical food interact dialectically, and there is a tension that exists between ethical stances that occur on the demand side and corporate initiatives for market growth that occur on the supply side. An exception is represented by the case of "Eataly" – the Italian food emporium founded in Torino – which is based on a collaboration between a private company and the Slow Food social movement with the purpose of creating a new business model. In this particular case, customers purchase Eataly's products while Slow Food acts as supporter of the initiative [8]. Another well-known model is Infinity Foods, a workers' co-operative that produces only organic, fair-trade, vegetarian and locally grown products, owned and managed entirely by its staff of nearly 100 people. It operates like a normal place of business but distinguishes itself by its selection of fair-trade and organic herbal teas available on its warehousemen's tea trolley [26].

With reference to the supply channel, in Western Europe, retail sales of food represents about 80 per cent of total food sales. This includes two different circuits:

1. Modern retailing, representing approximately 70% of total food and drinks sales in Western Europe and constituted by supermarkets and hypermarkets mainly operating in groupings of various types, and

2. Secondary retailing, covering approximately 30% of total food and drinks sales in Western Europe and consisting of traditional independent grocers, specialists (i.e., bakers, fishmongers, greengrocers,), CTN (confectionery, tobacconists, newsagents, with some food sales), petrol filling stations with specialist shops and kiosks, drinks stores, convenience stores, and so forth [17].

Notwithstanding the general interest in ethical food, as stated earlier, it constitutes only 5-10% of the total food and beverage market and there are limited ethical food alternatives. In many cases it is expensive and consumption is affected by availability and price [27, 28].

2.2. Ethical Food as a Driver of Tourist Destination Attractiveness

According to Sánchez Taylor [29] tourism is considered to be potentially exploitative and capable of perpetuating inequity and exclusion [30-32]. Indeed, while tourism is driver of growth of tourist destinations, it can provoke damaging effects associated with mass tourism (e.g., due to increased traffic, crowds, urban sprawl) [33, 34]. Thus, the sustainability of some tourist destinations can be compromised. In contrast, there is a trend that pushes tourism towards ethical behaviors: terms such as sustainable tourism, eco-tourism, and ethical tourism are more and more diffused in the literature [35].

The increasing number of tourists underlines the need for an ethical approach to travel and tourism. This point is also relevant with regard to food when it is considered as a "cultural product" [36]. There are important links between food and tourism and in the use of food as an expression of identity and culture [1]. Food can be "used as a means of differentiation for a destination in an increasingly competitive global marketplace" [37]. The promotion of traditional cuisine evokes nostalgia for "dishes of the past" and differentiates a destination from others, as is the case with Eataly in Torino. According to Vengesayi [38], an important driver of destination attractiveness concerns support facilities such as transport, accommodation, health and shopping, and food. Trunfio et al. [39] emphasize the increasing role of food tourism in the immersion of tourists in the culture of the destination [40].

Tourists look for concrete learning experiences, and in this field, gastronomic experience plays an increasingly prominent part. Hall and Sharples [41] consider food tourism as an experiential trip to a gastronomic destination, related to a particular lifestyle that includes experimentation, learning from other cultures, and the acquisition of knowledge about the characteristics of specific tourism products. These experiences constitute the main motivations that push tourists towards gastronomic destinations [1] and thus food becomes a real driver of destination attractiveness.

Wine and food tourism is a niche area of tourism studies that has grown rapidly in recent years [42]. Food tourism must include in its discourse ethical and sustainability values based on the territory, the landscape, the local culture and its products. As supported by FAO [43], a more equitable, ethically-based food and agriculture system must incorporate concern for three widely accepted global goals: improved well-being, protection of the environment and improved public health. In addition, biological efficiency and agro-biological diversity must be reconciled with economic efficiency. This means allowing the production of goods with fewer resources and limiting the pressure on the environment.

Research carried out by Birch [42] shows how consumers

consider ethics as important in making buying decisions, and that buying local ethical foods results in stronger attachment to a local region. In this way, ethical identity can be a driver of the consumption of local food and beverages [43], and can be encouraged by the adoption of promotional messages and labeling by a particular destination [44]. Indeed, given that cuisine and culture affects tourist decisions, producers and associations of ethical food can link with tourism providers to develop tourist attractiveness around existing agricultural products in a region [46] [47]. In this regard, ethical food satisfies both the need for sustainability and for the differentiation of a destination.

2.3. Barriers from the Supply and the Demand Side

Despite efforts by government and business for the improvement of food distribution, and accepting the demand from consumers, sustainable development goals in food production still seem far away. Ethical food is affected by several barriers in terms of supply:

- the inability of government and business initiatives to promote sustainable food distribution as a response to geopolitical and cultural change [6];
- the high level of vulnerability to various kinds of contamination in supply chains due to longer connections and rapid fragmentation of ingredient sourcing (e.g., herbs from Kenya, conservation packages from Canada, soy sauce from India) [48];
- poor collaboration and information sharing among local organic food supply chain partners [49] that make their supply chains complex to design and manage;
- the limited availability of ethical products in supermarkets: the problem of "food miles" and the complicated logistics required to provide a wide choice to consumers in developed countries [50];
- rapid progress in the technologies applied to food production and conservation [25] that results in insufficient information to consumers;
- lack of knowledge of these products by consumers;
- high costs due to various factors including higher animal welfare standards and the internalization of costs normally externalized by conventional foods [51], and
- the "productionist paradigm" applied to food production practices during the last sixty years which actively militates against the producer taking heed of ethical concerns [52].

Żakowska-Biemans [53], referring to a specific country (Poland), argues that the main barriers to the consumption of ethical food from the demand side are: a lack of information and its absence in local or most frequently visited shops, limited availability, high prices, and the lack of confidence in the reliability of information on organic products. The Queensland Government in Australia [44] considers the main barriers to the consumption of ethical food to be: inadequate marketing and distribution with products not clearly branded; the perception that this type of food is expansive, and the inconvenience of these products. The same barriers are provided by Young et al. [54] who add also lack of time for research, decision-making and purchasing by the consumer. Other miscellaneous barriers include brand loyalty, culture, demographic and personality characteristics, habit, lifestyle, and the trading off between different ethical issues [55].

As ethical food can constitute an important driver for tourist destination attractiveness, it is necessary to develop strategies to overcome these constraints.

3. The Impact of Ethical Food on Tourist Attractiveness: the Slow Food Movement

3.1. The Origin and Principles of Slow Food

One of the most well-known ethical food organizations in the world is Slow Food. Now a global phenomenon, Slow Food was born from the passion for food (and politics) by the inhabitants of a small town in Italy (Bra) [56] as a type of opposition to fast food culture and also to establish a relationship between nature, pleasure and tradition. Slow Food had its genesis in the creation in 1986 of the association called "Arcigola" which formed in reaction to the methanol crisis of that year and the perceived diffusion of fast foods in Italy. Its main promoter, the journalist Carlo Petrini, wanted to advance Italian quality wines and local simple dishes which he saw as being under threat. Petrini created two important food guides: "Osterie d'Italia" and "Vini d'Italia". The Slow Food organization was officially created in Paris in 1989.

The Slow Food philosophy is encapsulated in the words "good, clean, fair" - "good" because food must stimulate the pleasure of eating; "clean" because food must be produced respecting the environment, animal welfare and people's heath, and "fair" because farmers, dealers and craftsmen must be adequately paid [57]. In this regard, Slow Food advocates the payment of the "right" price to a producer so as to reduce the risk of exploitation and increase the chance of food/product preservation. The Slow Food Manifesto states:

"We are enslaved by speed and have all succumbed to the same insidious virus: Fast Life, which disrupts our habits, pervades the privacy of our homes and forces us to eat Fast Foods. In the name of productivity, Fast Life has changed our way of being and threatens our environment and our landscapes. So Slow Food is now the only truly progressive answer".

Today, Slow Food has over 100,000 members joined in 1,500 "Convivia" or chapters, as well as a network of 2,000 food communities who practice small-scale and sustainable production of quality foods (Slow Food International Website). Slow Food is articulated in four different administrative units: Arcigola Slow Food Promotion Srl, responsible for the big initiatives, such as "Salone del Gusto"; Arcigola Slow Food Editore Srl, in charge of the editorial program of the association; Arcigola Slow Food Association, in charge of recruitment and associates activities in Italy, and Slow Food International, in charge of recruitment and associated activities abroad [58].

3.2. How Slow Food Attract Tourist through Ethical Food: Results and Discussion

Given that tourism is an important economic activity in Italy, it is important that traditional tourist activities - and in particular those focused on food tourism - develop the sensitivity to protect and integrate with the natural and cultural resources available in a particular region [59].

Slow food tourism can be considered as an important part of the cultural tourism market, attracting tourists who seek unique experiences and the consumption of local food and beverages. For this same reason several rural communities use food festivals and farmers' markets to promote local products, thus enhancing the image of the destination [60].

Using the principles mentioned in the previous subsection as a basis, many food tourism oriented practical projects have been developed by Slow Food:

- Taste education, organized in order to educate consumers to recognize and appreciate seasonal foods. In order to achieve these results several initiatives are organized by Slow Food: the "Salone del Gusto", an event which began in 1996 and organized every two years in Turin, where producers and farmers from around the world showcase their products; courses and workshops organized by Slow Food, and the creation of the first "Università del Gusto" in Pollenzo (close to Bra), and in Colorno (close to Parma) that brings together experts and promoters of food from around the world.
- Foundation Slow Food, created to promote biodiversity and preserve the diversity of tastes in respect of the environment.
- The "Ark of Taste", an international project created in 1996 in Turin aimed at saving from extinction local and regional foods and supporting their producers.
- Slow Food "Presidia", which are considered the executive level of the "Ark of Taste" project (explained in more detail below).

The Slow Food Presidia project was founded to safeguard typical and traditional food production through the identification and public recognition of foods, linked to territorial identities, that are in danger of extinction [61]. Initially focused on Italian destinations, Slow Food now counts more than 400 Presidia across more than 50 countries aiming at protecting good, clean and fair products. The process of selection of these products is structured on several criteria: taste (as the product must be of high quality); history/culture/relationship with the territory (as the product must be linked to the memory and identity of a particular group or region); production scale (as the product must be realized in low quantities and from small firms); real or potential extinction risk, and the environmental and social sustainability of the product. Of the more than 400 Presidia, 269 are in Europe with 224 in Italy; each of the Presidia collects from three to 70 producers. Each Presidia focusses on particular topics such as agriculture and farming. Within each Presidia, a central role is played by the chefs who create the cuisines (and who have a specific network named "Alleanza tra i cuochi italiani con i Presidi Slow Food"). European Presidia are classified by typology in Table 1 and territorial distribution in Table 2 [60].

Table 1. *Slow Food "Presidia" classified for typology*

Typology	N. of "presidia"
Coffee, cacao	1
Cereals and flours	8
Fruits and derivates	27
Milk and cheeses	59
Legumes	20
Honey	1
Oil	1
Vegetables and vegetable conserves	34
Pain, Sweets and oven products	14
Fish	17
Animal races and farmer	39
Salt	2
Salamis and derivates	35
Spices, herbs and spontaneous products	4
Wine and alcoholic drinks	7
Total	269

Source: Peano and Sottile, 2012.

Table 2. *Slow Food "Presidia" classified for territorial distribution*

Country	N. of presidia"	Country	N. of presidia
Armenia	1	Macedonia	2
Austria	5	Italia	201
Bosnia Herzegovina	2	Netherlands	8
Belorussia	1	Poland	2
Bulgaria	3	Portugal	1
Cyprus	1	United Kingdom	5
Croatia	1	Romania	2
France	15	Spain	9
Georgia	1	Switzerland	3
Germany	4	Hungary	1
Ireland	1	Total	269

Source: Peano and Sottile, 2012.

Research conducted by Slow Food in 2012 shows how, on the basis of a sample of 46 Presidia, the level of sustainability measured on three scales (socio-cultural, food and economic) has improved in every case from their inception. With reference to the socio-cultural dimension, their research showed the importance of the relationships developed within the Presidia that became like virtuous circles of different people aimed at protecting and improving their products. Slow Food, in this regard, plays a very important role in connecting different people with each other. A meaningful element in the success of Presidia is also the presence of a local leader who develops a local project, as well as the presence of young people in the local Slow Food organization. Slow Food Presidia represent an alternative model of traditional production by small producers that anchor quality food products to their region and culture of origin [62].

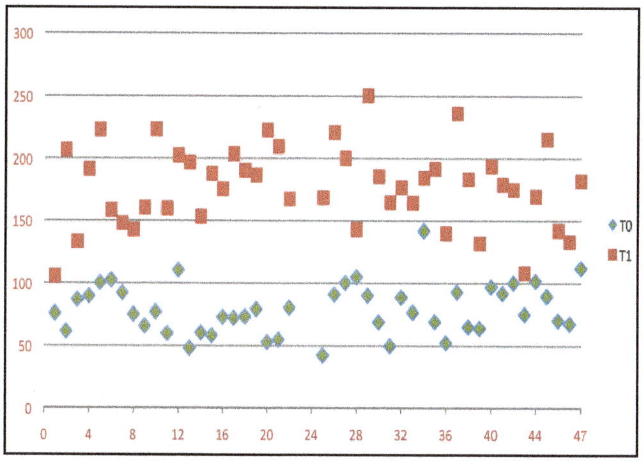

Source: Peano and Sottile, 2012.

Fig. 1. Sustainability analysis of 47 Slow Food "Presidia

In addition to the Presidia, as stated earlier, Slow Food is organized into approximately 1,500 chapters or "Convivia" across the globe. Each Convivia organizes a number of events each year. Even if the Convivia, and the related Cittaslow movements (developed in conjunction with Slow Food to ease the pace of urban life), are not directly aimed at tourism, they do influence local tourism by contributing to destination development. In addition, the Slow Food brand attached to Convivia events adds a layer of quality to the reputation of the event.

The "slow philosophy" has also led to the concept of Slow Tourism which encompasses travel and tourism activities that follow two essential principles: taking time, and attachment to a particular place. Slow Tourism emphasizes an engagement with place, encouraging tourists to establish local routines, try local food and appreciate local culture. Thus, Slow Tourism promotes "slow" lifestyle practices connected to the overall social movement.

The Slow Tourism label is able to attract tourists [63] towards international events (Slow Food website) including:

- "AsiO Gusto", the biennial celebration of the food traditions of Asia and Oceania.
- "Cheese", dedicated to milk in all its forms and cheese, held every two years in Bra, Italy.
- "Eurogusto", a celebration of European food and culture, held every two years in Tours, France.
- "Indigenous Terra Madre", a meeting of representatives of indigenous communities and food producers from around the world, held in Sweden in 2011.
- "Salone del Gusto" and "Terra Madre", the global meeting of the Slow Food and the Terra Madre network held in Turin, Italy.
- "Slow Fish", an event dedicated to sustainable and artisanal fishing, held every two years in Genoa, Italy.
- "Terra Madre Day", a celebration of local food held every year on 10 December [64]. The Terra Madre network also organizes many local and regional meetings.

In general terms, destinations have for some time utilized their local cuisine and gastronomic products as a source of tourist attraction [65]. But these specific events listed above are attractors for slow tourists. Salone del Gusto attracts over 150,000 visitors to Turin every two years, while Cheese attracts over 100,000 in a the small town of Bra [66]. Terra Madre involves about 5,000 persons representing different food communities. Indeed, the 2010 offering of Terra Madre and Salone del Gusto attracted more than 200,000 people and over 5,000 representatives of the global network from 160 countries [67], celebrating the crucial role played by local communities in fostering sustainable methods of food production and consumption [68, 69].

In this manner, the Slow Food movement participates in international markets and fairs to promote regional products at a global level, but also to promote traditional food in its own country. The development of gastronomic tourism represents one of the existing possibilities for rural areas to transition successfully to the new reality of a market-based economy [70]. This has the effect of increasing tourist arrivals to a region because of the specific products for which it becomes known [71]. The risk of this movement is that it may be an attractor of only a niche class while in reality it needs to find a way to attract a wider consumer base [72].

Slow Food can be considered a lifestyle reinvention approach which at the same time, due to its ethical food credentials, is an important attractor for tourists. This may occur through its influence on destination development. In addition, its brand equity may increase the perception of the quality of a region [63].

4. Concluding Remarks

Integrating ideas from ethical behavior, destination management and strategies for tourism development, this paper emphasizes the important role that ethical food could have in the future in destination attractiveness, contributing as well to the sustainability of a destination. The case of Slow Food shows that the association of a common philosophy and ethical background with the concept of eco-tourism can lead to tourism development, especially when linked to rural areas. With the development of gastronomic tourism, the value of the tourism product could be raised [70]. As maintained by Redl [5], local food and beverages are considered an important part of the travel experience and an important part of a country's culture. At the same time, gastronomic tourism allows for the preservation of local production, and advances the attractiveness and sustainability of the destination. As demonstrated by the case of Slow Food, building on cultural heritage through gastronomy can be a very important part of tourism development [6].

Given the limited number of studies on the impact of ethical food on tourism, there are significant gaps in the literature with respect to this field of study. This paper is an initial attempt to illustrate, through a real case study, the importance of ethical food in the attractiveness of destinations, and in tourism development. This study is conceptual only, and further empirical analysis is necessary to confirm the assertions made. Further, a comparison between different successful and unsuccessful ethical food tourism case studies may bring important results.

Another limitation of the paper is its focus specifically on an Italian case study. While Slow Food has obvious affiliates in other countries, some caution should be exercised in how far the conclusions can be extended. Further research might extend this paper's findings through an empirical analysis of the effect of ethical food destination image on tourist destination attractiveness.

Finally, a qualitative analysis based on interviews of stakeholders in this sector could result in important developments for ethical food marketing and ethical food tourism.

Given the impact that ethical food could have on the tourist industry, several strategies could be developed by different stakeholders for further development and growth.

Governments and local bodies should support the consumption and production of ethical food, thus driving prices down as consumption increases. At the same time, it is important to remember the need for appropriate pricing, to ensure animal welfare, environmental respect, and a salary sufficient to provide a living wage for the producer [52].

Further, it is only through education in ethical values that it may be possible to achieve long term behavior change; this can be realized by a structured educational program, including the development of research, information interpretation and decision making skills [73].

Producers could also diversify their product range in order to respect and accommodate the cultural diversity of food choices. It is consequently important to improve the level of transparency for the customer so that they can understand the provenance of the products they are buying. In addition, there is a need for marketers to create alternative ways of presenting value and costs, changing the way businesses define value in the economic exchange system [74]. Efforts could also be made in terms of promotion of various attributes of ethical food and in building trust in this food category; this could ensure the increased development of the ethical food market. FAO in 2001 outlined several important objectives to pursue in this direction: the creation of suitable mechanisms to balance competing market interests and solve conflicts; the promotion of the use of science and technology for a more equitable food system; the development of ethical codes of conduct able to guide food production systems where they don't exist; the encouragement of broad stakeholder participation in food policies, programs and projects; the promotion of transparency and public scrutiny in decision-making procedures in international food policy, and the periodic review of ethical commitments [75].

Food and logistics industries should also aim at a higher level of "sustainable distribution" so as to cover more than carbon emissions. In particular, businesses could supply an explanation of the way their distribution models contribute to addressing the social and cultural concerns expressed through the notion of food miles. This may be done by promoting local distinctiveness and diversity through the sharing of services and overheads with local operators [6].

In 2011, the Food Ethics Council stressed the importance of working with smallholders, who remain the majority of farmers worldwide, in order to gain the volumes they require to develop new forms of supply chain [76]. In this regard, a further strategy could consist of creating a sustainable supply chain able to align the incentives of all supply chain players. This would require open and cooperative relationships among the players [77, 78].

In addition to the previous proposals, it is necessary to achieve a higher level of flexibility in policy implementation when it comes to the effect of agriculture on the environment as well as the impact of rural development on upstream and downstream industries [17]. Furthermore, some form of taxation on unhealthy food stuffs (such as saturated fats, sugar and salt) could be an important step toward the diffusion of ethical food.

Finally, new solutions could be developed for the packaging of ethical food. The development of active packaging that provides recyclable, lightweight and biodegradable products should be encouraged. Technology may be harnessed for a more sustainable food supply chain, able to eliminate wasted space, increase shipping capacity, and reduce inbound shipping costs and greenhouse gas emission during transport and production (CDF Corporation).

Overcoming all these limitations would constitute an important step for ethical food tourism and allow, at the same time, a particular destination to be more attractive for a wide range of tourists.

References

[1] UNWTO, Global Report On Food Tourism. Madrid, Spain: UNWTO, 2012.

[2] Context Marketing, Ethical Food. Context Marketing, 2010.

[3] P. Sarkar (2014) Ethicurean- A Study on ethical Food Trends, Opportunities and Risks, in Advances in Hotel, Travel and Tourism Research: A Global Perspective, Babarasidas Chandiwala Institute of Hotel Management and Catering Technology, New Delhi, pp. 93-102.

[4] M. Clarke, Ethical Foods. International Situation Assessment, Opportunities and Threats. Barton: RIRDC, 2012

[5] S. Redl, Culinary Tourism for Young Adult Travellers and its connection to Destination Management, Bachelor Thesis, Vienna: Modul Vienna University, 2013.

[6] Food Ethics Council, Food Distribution. An Ethical Agenda. Brighton, UK: Food Ethics Council, 2008.

[7] M. Fischer Boel, "'Just desserts': Ethics, Quality and Traceability in EU Agricultural and Food Policy" in Ethical Traceability and Communicating Food, C. Coff, D. Barling, M. Korthals, T. Nielsen, Eds. Dordrecht NL: Springer, 2008, pp. 260-263

[8] R. Sebastiani, F. Montagnini, and D. Dalli, "Ethical consumption and new business models in the food industry, evidence from the Eataly case",. Journal of Business Ethics, Vol. 14, No. 3, 2012, pp. 473-488

[9] B. Huybrechts, and D. Reed, "Introduction: Fair trade in different national contexts", Journal of Business Ethics, Vol. 92, No. 2, 147–150.

[10] J.A. Muncy, and S.J. Vitell "Consumer ethics: An empirical investigation of the ethical beliefs of the final consumer", Journal of Business Research, Vol. 24, No.1, 1992, pp. 297-312.

[11] A. Crane, and D. Matten, Business Ethics. Oxford: OUP, 2004.

[12] W. Sinnott-Armstrong, "It's Not My Fault", in Advances in the economics of environmental resources: Vol. 5. Perspectives on Climate Change. Science, Economics, Politics, Ethics, W. Sinnott, Armstrong, and R. B. Howarth, Eds. Amsterdam, Elsevier, 2005, pp. 285–307.

[13] I. Szmigin, and M. Carrigan, "Exploring the dimensions of ethical consumption", European Advances in Consumer Research, Vol. 7, 2006, pp.608-613.

[14] D. B. Holt, "How consumers Consume: A Typology of consumption practices", Journal of Consumer Research, Vol. 22, No. June, 1995, pp. 1-16.

[15] J. Snider, R.H. Paul, and D. Martin, "Corporate social responsibility in the 21st century: A view from the world's most successful firms", Journal of Business Ethics, Vol. 48, No. 2, 2003, pp. 175–187.

[16] M. Grimmer, and T. Bingham "Company environmental performance and consumer purchase intentions", Journal of Business Research, Vol. 66, 2013, pp. 1945-1953.

[17] OECD, The Future of Food. Long-term Prospects for the Agro-food Sector. Paris: OECD, 1998.

[18] H. Willer, and L. Kilcher, The World of Organic Agriculture Statistics and Emerging Trends 2011, FIBL-IFOAM Report, Bonn, Germany: IFOAM, 2011.

[19] E. Tavella, and C.N. Hjortso, "Design and manage local organic food supply chains: benefits of using soft systems methodology", 2011, Online available from http://journals.isss.org/index.php/proceedings55th/article/view File/1629/603 (Accessed 18 November 2014).

[20] S. Balu, N. Garg, P. Majumder, J. Park, R. Sawani, and D. Sharma, "Ethical food consumption: a discussion on the environmental and social impacts of "green foods"", MBA White Paper, UNC Kenan-Flagler Business School, W06-021, 2006, pp. 1-6.

[21] H. Buller, and C. Morris, Farm animal welfare aspects of the CAP. London: RSPCA, 2002.

[22] Welfare Quality, "Science and society improving animal welfare", Welfare Quality conference proceedings, Brussels, Belgium, pp. 1-8, 2005.

[23] H. Buller, and C. Morris, "Farm animal welfare: a new repertoire of nature-society relations or modernisms re-embedded?", Sociologia Ruralis, Vol. 43, No. 3, 2003, pp. 216-237

[24] D.E. Goodman, "Agro-Food Studies in the 'Age of Ecology': Nature, corporeality, bio-politics", Sociologia Ruralis, Vol 39, No. 1, 1999, pp. 17-38.

[25] L. Busch, "The moral economy of grades and standards", Journal of Rural Studies, Vol. 16, No. 3, 2000, pp. 273-283.

[26] http://www.ft.com/cms/s/0/236d978c-bbac-11e1-9436-00144feabdc0.html#axzz25Col1UXR

[27] E. Papaoikonomou, G. Ryan, and M. Ginieis, "Towards a holistic approach of the attitude behaviour gap in ethical consumer behaviours: empirical evidence from Spain", Int. Adv. Econ. Res., Vol. 17, No. 1, 2011, pp.77–88.

[28] IGD, Ethical Shopping in Europe, Radlett, Herts: IGD, 2008.

[29] J. Sánchez-Taylor, J., "Sex tourism and inequalities" in Tourism and Inequality: Problems and Prospects, S. Cole, and N. Morgan, Eds. Wallingford, Oxfordshire: CAB International, 2010, pp. 49–66.

[30] S. Carlisle, "Access and Marginalization in a Beach Enclave Resort" in Tourism and Inequality: Problems and Prospects, S. Cole, and N. Morgan, Eds. Wallingford, Oxfordshire: CAB International, 2010, pp. 67–84.

[31] S. Cole, and N. Morgan, Tourism and Inequality: Problems and Prospects. Wallingford, Oxfordshire: CAB International, 2010.

[32] C.M. Hall, "Equal access for all? regulative mechanisms, inequality and tourism mobility", in Tourism and Inequality: Problems and Prospects, S. Cole, and N. Morgan, Eds. Wallingford, Oxfordshire: CAB International, 2010, pp. 34-48.

[33] K.L. Andereck, M.V. Karin, R.C. Knopf, and C.A. Vogt, "Residents' perceptions of community tourism impacts", Annals of Tourism Research, Vol. 32, No. 4, 2005, pp. 1056-1076.

[34] C. Choi, and I. Murray, "Resident attitudes toward sustainable community tourism", Journal of Sustainable Tourism, Vol. 18, No. 4, 2010, pp. 575-594.

[35] M. Grimmer, M. Cugno, and M. Viassone, "Vecchie e nuove prospettive di sviluppo del turismo in Italia", Rassegna Economica, Vol. 1, 2012, pp. 45-73.

[36] C. Bender, "Thinking globally, acting locally, discussing online: The slow food movement quickens with new media", Communication Theses. Paper 86, 2012.

[37] C.M. Hall, L. Sharple, R. Mitchell, and N. Macionis, Food Tourism around the World. Development, Management and Markets. Abingdon, Oxon: Butterworth-Heinemann, 2003.

[38] S. Vengesayi S, "Destination attractiveness: Are there relationships with destination attributes", The Business Review, Cambridge, Vol. 10, No. 2, pp. 289-294.

[39] M. Trunfio, L. Petruzzellis, and C. Nigro, "Tour operators and alternative tourism in Italy: Exploiting niche markets to increase international competitiveness", International Journal of Contemporary Hospitality Management, Vol. 18, No. 5, 2006, pp. 426-438.

[40] D. Alexander, "The geography of Italian pasta", The Professional Geographer, Vol. 52, No. 3, 2000, pp. 553-566.

[41] C.M. Hall, and L. Sharples, "The consumption of experiences or the experiences of consumption? An introduction to the tourism of taste", in Food Tourism Around the World: Development, Management and Markets, C. M. Hall, E. Sharples, R. Mitchell, N. Macionis, and B. Cambourne, Eds. Oxford: Butterworth-Heinemann, 2003, pp. 1-24.

[42] C.M. Hall, E. Sharples,R. Mitchell, B. Cambourne, and N. Macionis, Food Tourism Around the World: Development, Management and Markets. Oxford: Butterworth-Heinemann, 2003.

[43] FAO, Ethical Issues in Food and Agriculture. Rome: FAO.

[44] D. Birch, Understanding Drivers and Barriers to Consumption of South East Queensland Local and Regional Foods. Maroochydore: Queensland Government, 2012.

[45] SERIO, Research & Innovation. 2008. Understanding of Consumer Attitudes and Actual Purchasing Behaviour, with Reference to Local and Regional Foods, Plymouth, Devon: University of Plymouth, Drake Circus, 2008.

[46] J. Sweney, "Slow Food. Enriching the Tourism experience through agricultural diversity", Tourism and Hospitality Research in Ireland. Concepts, Issues and challenges, THRC Waterford Institute of Technology. School of Humanities publications, 2007.

[47] Almatourism, Food between Tourism and Life Quality, https://blogeirest.files.wordpress.com/2014/01/almatourism-call.pdf

[48] T. Lang, "From 'value-for-money' to 'values-for-money'? Ethical food and policy in Europe", Environment and Planning A, Vol. 42, No. 8, pp. 1814–1832.

[49] C. Strauch, and B. Schaer, Netzwerke für Kommunikation und Kooperation in den Produktmärkten Bio-Fleisch und Bio-Getreide, Freising: Ecozept GbR, 2005.

[50] http://ec.europa.eu/research/participants/data/ref/fp7/89847/research-food_en.pdf

[51] J.N. Pretty, A.S. Ball, T. Lang,. and J.I.L. Morison, "Farm costs and food miles: An assessment of the full cost of the UK weekly food basket", Food Policy, Vol. 30, No. 1, 2005, pp. 1-19.

[52] http://www.wordwendang.com/en/word_economy/0617/49537_2.html

[53] S. Żakowska-Biemans, "Factors underlying consumption of organic food in the opinion of Polish consumers", Agronomy Research, Vol. 7, Special issue II, 2009, pp. 768–774.

[54] W. Young, K. Hwang, S., McDonald,. and C.J. Oates, "Sustainable consumption: green consumer behaviour when purchasing products", Sustainable Development, Vol. 18, No. 1, 2010, pp. 20–31.

[55] http://www.ethicalconsumer.org/commentanalysis/consumerism/thepriceofethics.aspx

[56] C. Petrini, and G. Padovani, Slow Food Revolution. Milano: Rizzoli, 2005.

[57] C. Petrini, Buono, Pulito e Giusto. Turin: Einaudi, 2005.

[58] M. Fonte, "Slow Food's presidia: what do small producers do with big retailers?", in Between the Local and the Global (Research in Rural Sociology and Development, Volume 12) T. Marsden, and J. Murdoch, Eds. Bingley, UK: Emerald Group Publishing Limited, 2006, pp.203 - 240

[59] S. Buiatti, "Food and tourism: the role of the 'Slow Food' Association'", in Food Agri-culture and Tourism, K. Sidali, A. Spiller, and B. Schulze, Eds. 2011, Heidelberg, Springer.

[60] http://www.academia.edu/896364/SLOW_FOOD_Enriching_the_Tourism_experience_through_agricultural_diversity

[61] E. Lorenzini, "Origin labelled products, territorial marks and their contribution to rural development. Evidence from Italy and France", Working Paper SIEP, No. 649, 2010.

[62] C. Peano, and F. Sottile, Slow Food Presidia in Europe: A Model of Sustainability. Bra, Slow Food Foundation for Biodiversity, Accessible on: http://www.slowfood.com/sloweurope/wp-content/uploads/Ricerca-presidi-Europa-ENG.pdf .

[63] H.R. Yurtseven, and O. Kaya, "Slow tourists: a comparative research based on cittaslow principles", American International Journal of Contemporary Research, Vol.1, No. 2, 2011, pp. 91-98.

[64] http://www.slowfood.com/international/21/our-events

[65] A. H.N. Mak, M. L., and A. Eves, Globalisation and food consumption in tourism, Annals of Tourism Research, Vol. 29, No.1, 2012, pp. 171-196.

[66] S. Fullagar, K. Markwell, and E. Wilson, Slow Tourism: Experiences andMobilities. Bristo: Channel View, 2012.

[67] Salone Internazionale del Gusto (2011). http://www.salonedelgusto.com/. Accessed December 14, 2011.

[68] Terra Madre (2011), http://www.terramadre.info/pagine/welcome.lasso?n=en&-session=terramadre:6D711C1E02a9e20041uXV32A86DC. Accessed December 14, 2011.

[69] A. Tencati, and L. Tsolnai, "Collaborative enterprise and sustainability: the case of Slow Food", Journal of Business Ethics, Vol. 110, No. 3, 2012, pp. 345-354.

[70] M. Bratec, "Sustaining through Gastronomy: The Case of Slow Food Movement in Slovenia, its Impacts on Socio-cultural Environments and Tourism Development", BEST Education Network Think Tank VIII Sustaining Quality of Life through Tourism, 2008.

[71] M.C. Muntean, C. Nistor, R. Nistor, D. Sarpe, "OENO-Gourmet Tourism – A new way of Romanian tourism boost", Latest Trends on Cultural Heritage and Tourism, 2010, 241-246.

[72] C. Petrini, B. Watson, and D. Madison, Slow Food: Collected Thoughts on Taste, Tradition, and the Honest Pleasures of Food. Bra: Slow Food Editore, 2001.

[73] A. Dobson, "Environmental citizenship: towards sustainable development", Sustainable Development, Vol. 15, No. 5, 2007, pp.276–285.

[74] M.J. Polonsky, "Transformative green marketing: Impediments and opportunities", Journal of Business Research, Vol. 64, No. 12, 2011, pp. 1311-1319.

[75] FAO, Report of the Panel of Eminent Experts on Ethics in Food and Agriculture. Rome: Editorial Group FAO Information Division, 2001.

[76] Food Ethics Council, The Future of Food. Foresight and beyond. Brighton: Food Ethics Council, 2011.

[77] N. Dolšak, and E. Ostrom, The Commons in the New Millennium: Challenges and Adaptation. Cambridge, MA: MIT Press, 2003.

[78] Sustainability Institute, Commodity System Challenges: Moving Sustainability into the Mainstream of Natural Resource Economies. Hartland: Sustainability Institute, 2003.

Quality, Environment and Health Integrated Management Systems

Adela Mariana Vadastreanu[1], Adrian Bot[2], Dorin Maier[3, *], Andreea Maier[3]

[1]National Institute of Research and Development for Isotopic and Molecular Technologies, Technical University of Cluj Napoca, Cluj Napoca, Romania
[2]National Institute of Research and Development for Isotopic and Molecular Technologies, Cluj Napoca, Romania
[3]Technical University of Cluj Napoca, Romania and University of Economic Studies, Bucharest, Romania

Email address:
adella.vadastreanu@itim-cj.ro (A. M. Vadastreanu), adrian.bot@itim-cj.ro (A. Bot), dorin.maier@gmail.com (D. Maier), maier_andreea@ymail.com (A. Maier)

Abstract: The context of the research made in this article is the harsh economic environment where in order to stay on the market organizations need to reduce production cost to make more profit but also to meet the quality, environment, and health and safety requirements. The implementation of the standards in the organization involve an allocation of resources both human and financial and all this are time consuming, the necessity of implementing two or more standards make this allocation of resources to increase, in this conditions applying an integrated standards model is shown to be a more effective way then applying the standards independently. The problem that arises is that in order to adopt the integrated version of standards there have to be made some changes at the organizational level. This article analyzes the principal models of integration management systems found in the literature, highlights the benefits of the three standards. This article can be also used as a base for future studies regarding the integrated management systems and future implementation of other management systems like the management system of innovation.

Keywords: Integrated Management Systems, Quality Management System, Environmental Management System, Occupational Health, Safety Management System

1. Introduction

A management system is the framework of processes and procedures used to ensure that an organization can fulfill all tasks required to achieve its objectives [1]. A management system is a tool that aids the organization, being used to communicate the interdependence between people and processes, allowing decision making as provided by fair analysis, which will make it possible to increase profits [2].

The management system is the interconnection of components in order to achieve a given objective. These components include the organization, resources and processes. Therefore, people, equipment and culture are part of the system as well as the documented policies and practices [3].

A management system consists of four main elements [2]:

- management policy and objectives, acting as a guide to the organization;
- management responsibilities, defined so that each person involved should know what are the needs and requirements of their job;
- define the processes, thus establishing the connection between people and organizational objectives;
- data distribution and analysis (documents and records), so as to ensure an improved organizational performance.

2. Characteristics of Current Management Systems

2.1. The Main Characteristics of Quality Management Systems

Quality is one of the most important factors for most organizations and the requirements of global competitiveness. The main objective of quality is customer satisfaction, which together with employee satisfaction represents the key performance indicator of an enterprise and an important indicator of business effectiveness [4].

According to Santos and Escanciano (2002), the quality management system is "a set of managerial structures or planned systematic work methods considered by the organizations as effective ways to bridge customer satisfaction".

Concerns about quality management systems led to the development of international standards of quality management, the most popular being the ISO 9000 family of standards. According to these standards, quality management system is that management system that focuses on and keeps an enterprise under control in terms of quality. The actual design and implementation of such a system depends on business-specific objectives, products, processes and activities [5].

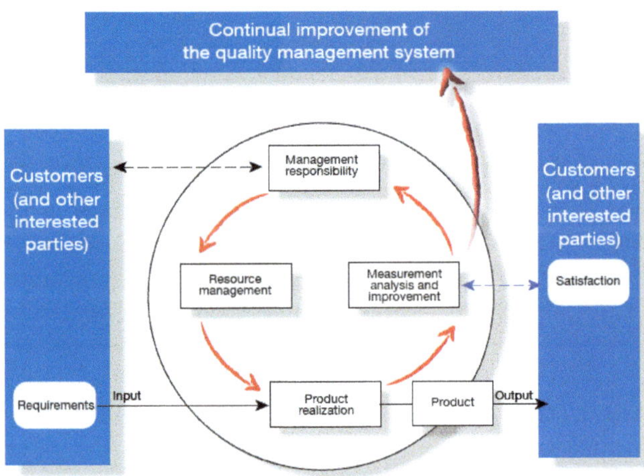

Figure 1. The process approach to quality management system (the author's proposal).

ISO 9001 standard proposes a model of process approach to quality management (Figure 1). The model considers that, in defining requirements and data entry, the customer plays an important role. Therefore, the graphical representation includes customers at both the beginning and end of the quality improvement cycle. This cycle is based on the PDCA (Plan-Do-Check-Act) mechanism proposed by Edwards Deming and known as the Shewhart-Deming Cycle.

The last stage is implementing the new product, process or service in the market, commercializing and obtaining added value from the innovative idea. Some authors show a further step, after the product, process or service is launched, in order to learn and prepare for another innovative process [6].

In order to show the ability to provide products that meet requirements, the enterprise must identify and conduct many associated processes. A process is any activity that uses resources and turns input data into output data. As stated in ISO 9001 standard, "the process approach is defined as the identification and systematic management of processes applied within the enterprise, as well as the interactions between these processes."

The ISO 9000 international standards were developed primarily to facilitate trade relations, especially at regional and international level, and to give customers more confidence on the ability of a particular tradesman to consistently satisfy requirements related to product and service quality offered. They are general standards, including requirements regarding the enterprise's quality management system and recommendations to improve performance [7].

The implementation of a quality management system has positive implications for all the components of the organizations' management system (informational, organizational, decision-making, human and methodological-managerial). Most users get benefits from the process of implementing the ISO 9001 standard requirements within the organization. Generally, initial advantages relate to improved organization and communication. The advantages become significant through effective internal auditing and by analyzing the performance of the quality management system performed by the management.

Following the third review from 2008, the ISO 9000 family of standards includes four basic standards (Table 1), accompanied by a number of technical reports.

Table 1. Basic standards of the ISO 9000 family of international standards [8].

No.	Name	Application domain
1	ISO 9000:2005 Quality management systems – Fundamentals and vocabulary	Describes basic principles of quality management and specifies terminology related to those systems.
2	ISO 9001:2008 Quality management systems - Requirements	Specifies requirements for a quality management system where an organization needs to demonstrate its ability to consistently provide product that meets customer and applicable statutory and regulatory requirements, and aims to enhance customer satisfaction through the effective application of the system.
3	ISO 9004:2000 Quality management systems - Guidelines for improving performance	Provides advice on quality management systems, applicable to improve enterprise performance, so as to better meet customer requirements and the requirements of other stakeholders.
4	ISO 19011:2002 Guidelines for quality and/or environmental management systems auditing	Provides guidance on the principles of auditing, managing audit programs, conducting quality management system audits and environmental management system audits, as well as guidance on the competence of quality and environmental management system auditors.

This structure was meant as a simplification of the ISO 9000 family of standards (whose 1994 edition has expanded greatly, reaching about 20 standards, assigned to specific areas), ensuring a better adaptation to the needs of different categories of users, so that standards become an effective tool that can increase enterprise competitiveness [8].

The most important advantage of the implementation and certification of quality management systems is internal, meaning that a certified system demonstrates that the development of enterprise processes, from market research to the supervision of products in use, meets the reference standard. But overall, the main advantages for businesses also involves external aspects (increased customer confidence, improved image, improved market position, etc.).

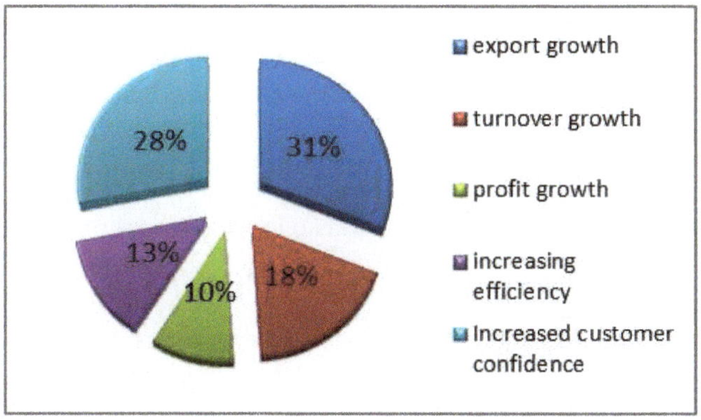

Figure 2. *The advantages obtained after quality management system certification (the author's proposal).*

All the advantages mentioned above provide the prerequisites for improving the economic and financial results of enterprises: increase sales, market share and profit. According to the main interests of businesses, the most important results obtained by enterprises after quality management system certification in accordance with ISO 9001, are shown in Figure 2.

After certification, compliance with the requirements of the established referential must be ensured, which requires continuous efforts to improve all processes within the enterprise, avoiding the appearance of any kind of deficiencies throughout the entire trajectory of the product.

2.2. The Main Features of the Environmental Management System

The current economic context, marked by globalization, has led in recent years to the awareness of the interdependence between the environment and development, as well as the increasing demands from society regarding environmental protection, requirements embodied in regulations that are becoming more stringent. Production processes have an important impact on the environment. To promote the reduction of pollution, national, regional and international models of environmental management have been developed to facilitate the control of all environmental aspects related to businesses [9].

The implementation of an environmental management system enables the development of activities in a planned and systematic manner, finding ways to improve the environmental performance of companies [10]. The role of this system is to facilitate the control of all processes throughout the whole product development process, so as to minimize their negative impact on the environment [11].

Similarly to the ISO 9000 family of standards, the International Organization for Standardization has developed the ISO 14000 family of standards for environmental management systems [12]. This family of standards is presented in Table 2.

Table 2. *The ISO 14000 family of standards for environmental management systems.*

Nr. Crt.	ISO Standards	Standard name
1	SR EN ISO 14001:2005	Environmental management systems. Requirements with guidance for use.
2	SR EN ISO 14001:2005/C91:2005	Environmental management systems. Requirements with guidance for use
3	SR ISO/TS 14048:2005	Environmental management systems. Live cycle assessment. Data documentation format
4	SR EN ISO 14040:2007	Environmental management systems. Live cycle assessment. Requirements and guidelines
5	SR EN ISO 14040:2007	Environmental management systems. Live cycle assessment. Principles and framework
6	SR ISO/TR 14062:2008	Environmental management systems. Integrating environmental aspects into product design and development
7	SR EN ISO 14001:2005/AC: 2009	Environmental management systems. Requirements with guidance for use.
8	SR EN ISO 14004:2010	Environmental management systems. General guidelines on principles, systems and support techniques
9	SR EN ISO 14015:2010	Environmental management systems. Environmental assessment of sites and organizations
10	SR EN ISO 14050:2010	Environmental management systems. Vocabulary
11	SR EN ISO 14063:2010	Environmental management systems. Environmental performance evaluation. Guidelines and exemples
12	SR EN ISO 14013:2014	Environmental management systems. Environmental performance evaluation. Guidelines

Supporting innovation, measuring and improving the efficiency of national innovation systems are the most important issues and priorities in Europe, especially the mechanisms and measures to support innovation, turning research into new products and services.

These environmental standards are an extension of the series of ISO 9000 quality standards by turning products and processes into greener versions. An environmental management system frames, implements and reviews environmental policies, all of which are intended to help companies minimize their impact on the environment.

The ISO 14001 standard is applicable to all types of businesses, including industry and all trade and services sectors. It has similarities with the principles of the quality management system defined by ISO 9001, which facilitates the integration of management systems. The ISO 14001 standard describes the following key elements needed for certification, but does not include specific environmental performance criteria:

- environmental policy statement

- planning, including establishing procedures regarding the identification of environmental aspects and legal requirements
- environmental management system implementation, identifying responsibilities, training and emergency procedures
- checking and undertaking corrective action, including monitoring

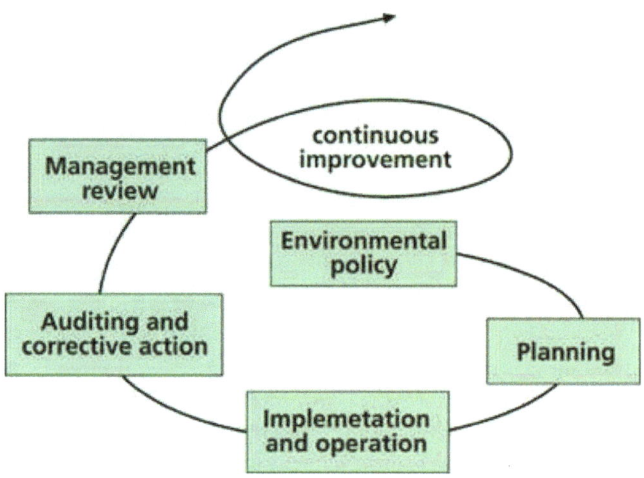

Figure 3. *The environmental management system according to ISO 14001 (the author's proposal).*

The ISO 14001 model (Figure 3) follows the same PDCA improvement cycle used by the ISO 9001 quality management standard, to ensure that environmental issues are identified, controlled and monitored systematically. This approach actually seeks to improve the environmental management system over time.

The environmental management system will be different depending on the type, nature, size and complexity of the enterprise's activities, products and services. According to the ISO 14001 standard, the elements of the environmental management system are those shown in Table 3 [13].

Accordingly, the overall objective of the ISO 14001 standard is to achieve optimum environmental performance for the enterprise. On the other hand, the actual means for the implementation of the standard depends on a number of factors, including the environmental policy of the enterprise, the nature of its business, the specific conditions under which it operates. The successful implementation of an environmental management system is subject to the commitment of all levels of leadership, especially the top management that is responsible for implementing an environmental management system so as to meet the requirements of ISO 14001 [14].

Table 3. *The elements of environmental management systems as defined by ISO 14001.*

No.	EMS elements	ISO 14001 requirements
1	Environmental policy statement	• in writing, expressing the commitment of top management to ensure compliance with environmental legislation and pursue the continuous improvement of environmental performance, thus ensuring not only the responsibility for the implementation of the environmental policy, but also its necessary support
2	Environmental management system planning	• the enterprise identifies the environmental aspects of its activities, which can be controlled and influenced, in order to determine those which have or can have a significant impact on the environment • in determining and analysing its objectives, the enterprise considers the legal prerequisites and other types of requirements, significant environmental issues and the views of the parties involved • to achieve the general and specific environmental objectives, the enterprise must establish and maintain one or more programs to achieve them
3	Environmental management system implementation and operation	• enterprise management must provide the necessary resources for environmental management system implementation and control • training needs should be identified and the entire staff whose work may have a significant impact on the environment must be adequately trained • the enterprise must consider the external communication process on significant environmental aspects and keep its decisions • to describe the essential elements of the environmental management system and their interaction, the enterprise must draw up documentation regarding the environment and also to establish and maintain procedures to control all documents • the enterprise must identify those operations and activities that are associated with significant environmental aspects, appropriate to its policy, general and specific objectives • the enterprise must establish and maintain procedures to identify potential accidents and emergency situations and respond to such situations and prevent and reduce the environmental impact that may be associated with them
4	Checking and corrective and preventive action	• periodically, the compliance with environmental regulations and laws in force must be assessed • any preventive or corrective action taken to eliminate the existing or potential causes of non-compliance must be adapted to the importance of problems and must be proportional to the impact on the environment • the enterprise must establish and maintain one or more programs and procedures to conduct periodic environmental management system audits
5	Analysis of the environmental management system conducted by the management	• the enterprise management must analyse the environmental management system at predetermined time intervals to ensure its continuing suitability, adequacy and effectiveness

The benefits of implementing the environmental management system. The environmental management system is a "part of the overall management system which includes organizational structure, planning activities, responsibilities, practices, procedures, processes, and resources for developing, implementing, achieving, reviewing, and maintaining the environmental policy"[15]. Although at first glance the only thing that distinguishes an environmental management system from other management systems is that it focuses on the performance of environmental protection, small and medium enterprises that have adopted environmental management systems managed to achieve an important objective, namely to gain a higher market share.

The benefits of implementing the environmental management system can be experienced by significantly improving enterprise organization, reducing pollution and reducing costs. In the medium term, organizations will improve relations with the authorities by ensuring compliance with environmental legislation. An advantage resulting from the implementation of an environmental management system, which in the current context has a growing importance, is linked to the improvement in the enterprise's image, thus leading to market advantages, as the public wants a clean environment and products that have no negative impact on the environment.

Environmental management systems provide a tool to identify and solve specific environmental problems that can be implemented in an enterprise in different ways and according to specific conditions [14]. Cheremisinoff and Bendavid-Val support the idea according to which the implementation of an environmental management system reduces production costs, increases product quality and improves control over the production process. The ISO14001 standard was designed so that environmental protection improvements would be felt in every aspect of the enterprise's operations, with a complex and dynamic relationship between profitability and environmental concerns [16].

2.3. Occupational Safety and Health Management Systems

Occupational safety and health management has the same importance as the management of other functions of an enterprise, such as financial, commercial, human resources, production, quality, etc. As part of an integrated management system, in addition to social and legal obligations of enterprises, it involves major economic issues, raising profits by reducing downtime, absenteeism, lack of material losses due to accidents and damages, savings for medical leave, etc [17].

The occupational safety and health management system constitutes the tool for the design, organization and creation of procedures and mechanisms within the enterprise, to meet all health and safety requirements for the employees and to comply with relevant legislation. It includes self-monitoring and self-assessment components that allow detection of deficiencies in the organization and implementation of measures to improve the system [18].

Different studies have shown that accidents at work and occupational diseases are very often associated with deficient management. Good management involves the best use of available resources and this requires a safe workplace that protects the health and safety of employees, which improves their motivation and mood, promotes quality production and therefore increases productivity [19].

There is no occupational safety and health management system that is universally applicable to all businesses regardless of size, sector and specific risks [20]. The basic conditions for an occupational safety and health management system to be effective are shown in Table 4.

Table 4. *Conditions for the effectiveness of the occupational safety and health management system.*

No.	Conditions for effectiveness
1	It must be applied voluntarily.
2	It must take into account the special characteristics of enterprises.
3	Evaluation procedures must be provided for the required mandatory external audits.
4	Its objectives must not be linked to certification.
5	It must be economically justified.
6	It must determine better enforcement of legal provisions on occupational safety and health.
7	It must encourage cooperation with the authorities that issue provisions in this domain.
8	It must maintain the role played in labour relationships by employee involvement mechanisms.

The BS OHSAS 18001 standard and the OHSAS 18002 implementation guidelines (including the OHSAS 18001 implementation guidelines) have been developed to meet the demand of those interested in the recognition of a standard occupational safety and health management system, which can help assess and certify an occupational safety and health management system [21].

The basic elements of an occupational safety and health management system are as follows:

a) Input data on occupational safety and health

Inputs include:

- management commitment and resources made available, including organizational structures, to support the development and implementation of a program on occupational safety and health;
- legal and regulatory compliance;
- responsibility, duties and authority;
- employee involvement, either direct, individually, or indirect, through representative entities, such as a committee on health and safety at work.

b) Documentation and implementation of the occupational safety and health management system

The main requirements for occupational safety and health management system documentation are:

- objectives related to occupational safety and health;
- performance measurement criteria;
- basic assessment and risk/hazard assessment;
- system planning and development;
- occupational safety and health management system manual and procedures.

System implementation requires the following elements:
- training, particularly in terms of technical skills and staff qualifications;
- a system for controlling risks, including contingency plans, to reduce or eliminate risks at work;
- preventive and corrective systems to protect personnel in the event of any problems that might occur;
- purchase goods and services that are compliant with enterprise security standards.

c) Output data on occupational safety and health

The measures that ensure the effectiveness of an occupational safety and health management system have to be quantifiable and must have a practical purpose. There are various options available:
- success in achieving the objectives relating to occupational safety and health;
- frequency of illnesses and injuries, possibly by comparison to other enterprises within the same sector;
- general health and wellbeing of the workforce;
- changes in the enterprise's efficiency, measured for example by improving productivity;
- overall performance of the enterprise.

d) Assessment
- a communication system for drafting, updating and dissemination of information related to occupational safety and health within the enterprise;
- an assessment system for auditing the occupational safety and health management system, investigating and analyzing the main causes that gave rise to accidents and ensuring medical surveillance of health.

e) Continuous improvement and integration
- processes to ensure continuous improvement, including regular assessments and procedures for evaluating incidents;
- periodic assessment of the leadership to assess the effectiveness of occupational safety and health management and to ensure compliance with legal and regulatory provisions;
- integration of the occupational safety and health management throughout the enterprise.

2.4. The Benefits of Implementing the Occupational Safety and Health Management System

An effective occupational safety and health management system ensures the optimum use of resources available: protects the health of the workforce and the local community, increases staff motivation to have a healthy and conscious behavior, increases staff and enterprise performance and creates safe jobs. Although the introduction of an occupational safety and health management system requires material investments, it leads to the direct and significant reduction of additional costs and to medium-term optimization of production processes.

In terms of occupational safety and health, the ability to determine the level of performance over time is essential in order to verify continuity regarding progress on eliminating occupational injuries and illnesses.

3. The Current State of Knowledge Regarding the Integration of Quality - Environment - Occupational Safety and Health Management Systems

3.1. Specific Requirements for the Integration of Management Systems in the Current Business Environment

There have been growing numbers of new challenges for successful business management in the new millennium. Success can only be achieved if there is a systematic approach to processes. A successful integration of management systems essentially depends on good planning and effective implementation. An integrated management system is a logical and systematic management approach allowing optimal strategic and operational decisions that take into account all the key aspects that lead to the effective functioning of an organization, in terms of both quality and environment on the one hand, and safety or food hygiene on the other hand, etc [22].

The perspective of integrated management systems will require the orientation of managers of various organizations towards reformulating strategies and redefining the mission by changing vision. The relevance of integrated management systems is becoming much better defined by the increasing number of organizations that implement their “special” quality, environmental protection and health and safety management systems.

The academics interest in this topic, expert opinions and market development indicate that “integrated management systems” are seen as “management systems of the future”, outlining the idea of transforming themselves into organizational concepts.

From an operational perspective, the integration of management systems lies in the combination and alignment of all internal management practices into a single system. Independent management systems may become part of the organization's integrated management system if strong connections develop between them beyond process borders [23].

The main objective of integrated quality - environmental - occupational safety and health management systems is to optimize an enterprise’s efforts to meet customer needs and expectations of all stakeholders in terms of economic competitiveness.

According to the opinions expressed in the literature, the main condition for ensuring business success is the implementation of an integrated quality - environmental - occupational safety and health management system, which is a prerequisite for the development of enterprises in Romania [24].

Integration means assembling individual elements to form a whole (Figure 4). In practice, this means assembling and coordinating individual management systems and eliminating inconsistencies and duplication. Due to the overall vision, the result is more than the pure sum of the management system components that are integrated. Essentially, all of these management systems consist of the same elements, although the structure of current reference documents regarding these management systems differs. The idea, and therefore the main advantage of an integrated management system, is to use existing elements, identify similarities between the elements and reference documents.

Figure 4. *The integration of management systems.*

An important similarity between the three reference documents is the consideration of customer needs and requirements and the needs and expectations of all stakeholders. Each organization has several stakeholders, which all have their own requirements, needs and expectations. Each stakeholder expects to derive some benefits from the enterprise. Top management must earn and maintain stakeholder trust and must communicate the needs of these stakeholders within the enterprise.

There are many similarities between the three standards and for this reason, there are fewer and fewer enterprises that choose completely separate quality, environmental and occupational safety and health management systems. The most important commonalities in terms of the actual approach to the design, implementation and operation of quality, environmental and occupational safety and health management systems are presented below:

- all three reference documents take into account the concept of continuous improvement;
- all three reference documents take into account the concept of prevention;
- all three reference documents put the human factor at the centre of the processes linked to the design, implementation and operation of management systems.

In order to establish the correlation between the requirements of the three management systems, we must first define the product, stakeholders, requirements and non-compliance aspects for each of the three systems[15], [21], [25] (Table 5). The ISO 9001 standard aims at creating the product, while ISO 14001 and BS OHSAS 18001 standards specify the steps required in order not to unintentionally create the product.

Table 5. *Common elements of the three quality - environmental - occupational safety and health management systems.*

Element	Reference document		
	ISO 9001	**ISO 14001**	**OHSAS 18001**
Product	Intentionally designed product, intended for a client	Unintentionally designed product, environmental performance (environmental impact)	Unintentionally designed product, accident, occupational disease (risks)
Product cause	Processes	Environmental issues	Risk factors
Stakeholder (direct)	Clients, owners, employees	Community, government, owners, neighbours, insurance companies, investors, suppliers, customers, etc.	Employees / unions, employers / owners, government
Requirements	Client, legal, regulatory, own, others	Legal, regulatory, own	Legal, regulatory, own
Non-compliance (deviation from requirements)	System / product	System / environmental performance	System / occupational safety and health performance

3.2. Models of Achieving Integrated Management Systems

Integration is the complete harmony and alignment of an organization's strategy and operations. This means that different departments and levels speak the same language and are tuned to the same wavelength. Most studies on the integration of management systems in the literature aimed at merging the quality management system, environmental management system, occupational safety and health management system and information security management system [26].

Indeed, to survive and thrive in a period of increasing global competition, organizations must consider every aspect of the processes, including cost reduction, employee welfare, work environment and the impact of the organization's operations on their neighbors and the local community [27], [28].

Figure 5. *The integration of management systems. (author processing after [29]).*

Moreover, companies need to address these issues while continuing to provide quality products and services, the concept of integrated management systems arising from this necessity.

Effective integration of various management systems can be achieved in three different ways, depending on the specific situation that exists in the organization at a certain point:

- by conversion: from a management system that is already implemented in the organization, adding further processes according to the requirements of the standards underlying the management systems desired to be introduced, thus developing specific practices and procedures; management systems based on internationally recognized referential have some common processes (Figure 5), which facilitates the application of this integration model.

The drawback of this model is the strong dependence of the successful implementation of an IMS on the existing management system that has been previously implemented in the organization – which represents the starting point [29].

- by merging: if there are more independent management systems that work in parallel within the organization, they can merge and even add other systems, formalizing practices; even if the documentation of different systems will be combined, we can only talk about an IMS when the practices that meet the purpose of each system will aim at achieving the IMS purpose.
- by technical design: even if the organization has implemented an operational management system, a completely new IMS will be developed through a unitary effort, which will aim at achieving a specific purpose; as part of this approach, the integrated management system shall be designed taking into account the recommendations of the standards, but it is strongly connected to business (restricted to the strategy, mission, distinctive competences).

4. Conclusions

In the literature, we can find several models for integrating different management systems, the most used are quality, environmental and health and safety management systems. The requirements of the organizations related to standards are to enable it to control those key management functions with maximum effectiveness and minimum bureaucracy.

In addition, the researches identify the advantages and the disadvantages of the integrated management system. We can consider as the main advantages the coordinated decisions, coherence in the organization's activity and in the end the efficiency with lower costs. If we focus on the disadvantages, the difficulty of implementation and the reduction of flexibility are the main ones. However, by analyzing all the advantages and disadvantages we can conclude that in order increase the performance in business a necessary step is implementation of integrated management systems.

Acknowledgements

This paper benefited from financial support through the National Institute of Research and Development for Isotopic and Molecular Technologies, Cluj-Napoca, Romania.

References

[1] Maier, D., Vadastreanu, M., Keppler, T., Eidenmüller, T. şi Maier, A., Innovation as a part of an existing integrated management system, 4th World Conference on Business, Economics and Management, WCBEM, 2015, Turkey

[2] Sisteme de management - Consultanţă, http://www.manager.ro/articole/management/sisteme-de-management-412.html, accesat în Decembrie 2012

[3] Cadar, D., Sisteme de Management Integrate, Universitatea Tehnică, Cluj - Napoca, 2005

[4] El Sakka, S., The Impact of Applying Quality Management System and Environment Standard on Organization Performance an Application on SME'S in Egypt European, Journal of Business and Management, www.iiste.org, ISSN 2222-1905 (Paper) ISSN 2222-2839 (Online), Vol.5, No.19, 2013

[5] Paris, C., The complete guide to understanding and implementing ISO 9001's process management requirements, Oxebridge Quality Resources Inc., Florida, 2003

[6] Maier, A., (2014) Cercetări şi contribuţii la dezvoltarea modelelor de management al inovării, Teza de doctorat, Universitatea Tehnică Cluj – Napoca, România

[7] Thwani, S., Challenges of implementing ISO 9001:2000, Adnoc Distribution, Abu Dhabi, 2001

[8] Olaru, M., Fundamentele ştiinţei mărfurilor, ediţia a 2-a rev., Ed. Economică, Bucureşti, 2005

[9] Olaru, M., Managementul calităţii, ediţia a II-a revizuită şi adăugită, Editura Economică, Bucureşti, 1999

[10] Rojanschi, V., Bran, F., Diaconu, G., Grigore, F., Elemente de economia şi managementul mediului, Editura Economică, Bucureşti, 2004 şi Rojanschi, V., Bran, F., Diaconu, G., Grigore, F., Evaluarea impactului ecologic şi auditul de mediu, Editura ASE, Bucureşti, 2004

[11] Olaru, M., Implementarea unui sistem de management de mediu, potrivit standardului ISO 14001, în relaţie cu standardele ISO 9000, în „Orientări actuale în managementul calităţii", vol. 1, Editura ASE, Bucureşti, 1998

[12] http://www.asro.ro, accesat în mai 2013

[13] Standardul SR EN ISO 14001:2005, Sisteme de management de mediu. Cerinţe cu ghid de utilizare

[14] Whitelaw, K., ISO 14001 environmental systems handbook, edition 2, Butterworth-Heinemann, Oxford, 2004

[15] SR EN ISO 14001:2005, Sisteme de management de mediu. Cerinţe cu ghid de utilizare

[16] Edwards, A., J., ISO 14001 environmental certification step-by-step, Butterworth-Heinemann, Oxford, 2001.

[17] Dăscălescu, A., Costul accidentelor de muncă, Editura Atlas Press, Bucureşti, 2003

[18] Alli, O., B., Fundamental principles of occupational health and safety, International Labour Office, Geneva, 2001

[19] Pece, Ş., Dăscălescu, A., Securitatea şi sănătatea în muncă inclusă în managementul general al firmei, în „Obiectiv", nr. 1/2003

[20] The use of occupational safety and health management systems in the member states of the European Union, European Agency for Safety and Health at Work, Bilbao, 2002, http://agency.osha.eu.int

[21] Standardul SR OHSAS 18001:2008, Sisteme de management al sănătăţii şi securităţii ocupaţionale. Specificaţie

[22] www.srac.ro, accesat în mai 2014

[23] Matias, H., C, Coelho, D., A., Innovation in the Organisation of Management Systems as a Means of Survival and Growth of SMEs, 2006

[24] Oprean, C., Kifor, C. V., Suciu, O., Managementul integrat al calităţii, Editura Universităţii "Lucian Blaga", Sibiu, 2005

[25] Standardul SR EN ISO 9001:2000, Sisteme de management al calităţii. Cerinţe

[26] Asif, M., Process Embedded Design of Integrated Management Systems, POMS 19th Annual Conference, La Jolla, California, U.S.A., 2008

[27] Tang, J., Corporate Culture and Integrated Management Systems: A case study of the UK Construction Industry, University of East Anglia.Vinten, 2003

[28] Jorgensen, T. H., Dolores Mellado, M., Remmen, A., Integrated Management Systems, 2004

[29] Renfrew, D., Muir, G., Quenching the thirst for integration, Quality World, 24, pp.10-13, 2000.

12

Creative resources for attractive seaside resorts: The French turn

Anne Gombault[1], Ludovic Falaix[2], Emeline Hatt[3], Jérôme Piriou[4]

[1]Research Cluster for Creative Industries, KEDGE Business School, Bordeaux-Marseille, France
[2]Laboratoire ACTé EA 4281, Blaise Pascal University, Clermont-Ferrand France
[3]Laboratoire interdisciplinaire en urbanisme – EA 889, Aix Marseille Univeristy, Aix Marseille, France
[4]Tourism Management Institute, La Rochelle Business School, La Rochelle, France

Email address:
Anne.gombault@kedgebs.com (A. Gombault), Ludovic.falaix@yahoo.fr (L. Falaix), emeline.hatt@univ-amu.fr (E. Hatt), piriouj@esc-larochelle.fr (J. Piriou)

Abstract: This article presents a qualitative analysis of the specific strategies used by coastal resorts in the South of France to valorise their creative regional resources. These strategies emerge from factors of change in the trajectories of the resorts: change in the relationship between man and nature, environmental turning point and the need for sustainability, emergence of creative tourism centred on recreation, sport and culture. The research is supported by three case studies, Biarritz, Lacanau and Martigues, and assesses the constraints that arise in terms of design and management of coastal resorts and tourist areas, against a background of numerous conflicting requirements, including attractiveness and sustainability. The effects of these strategies can call into question the choice of resources selected, associated forms of governance, as well as conflicts in use that may emerge.

Keywords: Seaside Resorts, Regional Resources, Nature, Heritage, Surf, Creative Tourism, Attractiveness, Governance

1. Introduction

The French coast is today the country's foremost tourist destination in terms of overnight stays, and has been the subject of substantial affective and symbolic investment since the 18th century, as it is the embodiment of a role of pleasure and renewal based on a desire for the shore and for "the seaside" [1]. Although the challenges of coastal tourism are now clearly evident, we must nevertheless consider the dynamics of change that have affected these areas and the ways in which their tourist value is enhanced. Coastal resorts have developed mainly as urban units, whose inhabitants are temporary (tourists, visitors). However, more and more they are also becoming home to a permanent population who have expectations and needs in terms of housing, public services, jobs and quality of living environment. These areas are faced with a triple process of change (societal, economic and environmental) which challenges the frameworks and traditional points of reference of public action, and calls for fresh thinking on the conditions and issues surrounding sustainability and governance[1]. It is in this context that coastal areas were chosen as an ideal subject for the current research programme on *"Trajectories of tourist areas and resorts in South-West France since the 19th century: the dynamics of innovation, development of tensions and future issues"* (Tratso project – 2012/2015[2]). This article questions the way in which institutions redefine their public policy guidelines, i.e. *"the area of meaning that* [...] *puts limits around the values, standards and causal relations required to form a cognitive and normative framework for the actors involved"* [2]., by mobilising what they consider as *"regional resources"* [3] specific to the spatial structure and sociocultural atmosphere of seaside resorts. Here we are keen to show that as society's expectations have changed, especially the growth of creative tourism in general [4] and more specifically the hybridisation of recreational practices

1 Source : D.G.U.H.C. (2006). *Planifier l'aménagement, la protection et la mise en valeur du littoral*, Paris : MEDAD et ministère des transports, de l'équipement du tourisme et de la mer.
2 See Tratso website: http://uranus.msha.fr/tratso.

with the focus of attention on the environment, this has resulted in an ever-growing awareness of regional resources [5]. An insight is gained into the conditions necessary for this movement of regional "re-registration" to succeed by identifying the levers that managers have developed and their role in the construction and evolution of identity, image and attractiveness of coastal areas. Thus the way in which elected representatives view socio-environmental change is analysed to find out whether, and if so how, they plan to take into account on the one hand, the risks associated with climate change and on the other hand, the hypermodern [6] or even transmodern [7] nature of creative practices (cultural and sports) in the resorts' strategies to restore tourist enthusiasm. The research is supported by three case studies, covering Biarritz, Lacanau and Martigues, and assesses constraints in terms of management and governance of coastal tourist resorts and areas, against a background of many conflicting requirements, including attractiveness, sustainability and risk awareness (natural and industrial). The data production method of this empirical study is based on a field survey consisting of semi-structured interviews with about thirty local actors on three main themes: the historic character of the place and its urban development; the role of the actors and the method of governance; creativity and the different ways these resorts have introduced innovation. Lastly, the effects of promoting regional resources are analysed by considering the choice of resources that were selected and highlighted, the forms of governance put in place, and any conflicts of use that may have emerged as a result.

2. Strategies of Seaside Resorts: Change Factors

The coast as an area put to use by Man can tell us a lot about changes in society and Man's place in relation to Nature. First, the "domestication" of this environment happened as a result of man's need to find a specific activity here, one that was different from his daily occupation, moving from a therapeutic approach to a recreational approach. Second, the regulations applied to the coast required man's occupation of this environment to be channelled and adapted in the interests of conservation, even though difficulties linked with socio-economic activity remained. Third, creativity reflects the continuity and permanence of coastal practices, giving the coastal area a hypermodern and ideally a transmodern outlook, which explains in part its residential orientation.

2.1. Man/Nature Relationship at the Heart of the Arrival of Tourism in Coastal Areas

When sea bathing first became popular in the 19th century, visitors began to see the coast differently, having previously feared it or considered it as a domain reserved for men who worked at sea [8]. A "*désir de rivage*" a desire for the shore was born in western populations once interest in the curative aspect had waned. This discovery gave rise to a fascination for landscapes and a desire for experience, man challenging the harsh climate. This resulted in the appropriation of these areas and the invention of coastal tourism, from the first half of the 19th century. Sea bathing as therapy developed along the coastline of the Manche department and the North Sea, then down the Atlantic coastline as villages became occupied by tourists. Publicity and improved accessibility contributed to the growth of burgeoning seaside resorts, again first on the coasts of the Manche department and the North Sea then gradually spreading down the Atlantic coast. The arrival of the railway accelerated the development of tourism on the French coastline, from the second half of the 19th century for the coast of Aquitaine and the Mediterranean. All over the world, accessibility did contribute to the arrival of tourists in the resorts, the urban facilities that were developed were also crucial [9]. The presence of shops, a casino, cafés all contribute to urban life. During the Belle-Epoque beach fashion and bathing now complemented the original therapeutic functions. There were also sporting activities, introduced by the English and French "high society", such as golf in the South-West or tennis in Brittany. When sea bathing started to occupy only a short time of the bather's day, it became necessary to " *provide other activities to meet the needs of these temporary residents. Golf courses, tennis courts, beach clubs were created in the most exclusive resorts.* [...] *Different forms of sociability like cafés, hotels, as in the spa resorts, casinos, that were both gaming rooms and entertainment facilities became the marker for this tourist urbanization which developed through privatisation of communal resources.*". During the second half of the 20th century, the coast finally became the subject of large-scale State-led urban development along the coasts of Languedoc and Aquitaine, contributing to a tourist-driven economic boom [10].

Thus the development of seaside tourist resorts is reflected in a renewal, of sports activities and urban representations and concepts, where nature plays a key role. While the attention currently paid to nature and to the environment in general has resulted in a renewed approach to sensitive areas, the man/nature relationship lies at the very heart of the development of tourist practices, even though the widespread growth of tourism in the middle of the 20th century sometimes tends to gloss over this fact. In fact, the valorisation of the environment has never been absent from tourist issues; it even created an "*alternative model for bringing order*" [11]. In parallel with the massive development of tourist sites in the 1960s-1970s, the State put in place measures targeting landscape conservation. Different tools were devised to ensure that this protection would be implemented (nature reserves, biotope protection orders, biosphere reserves, etc.), the most powerful and symptomatic being the National Parks[3] and the Regional Nature Parks[4]. Also the action of the MIACA (Interministerial Mission for

3 Law no. 60-708 of 22 July 1960 on the creation of the National Parks (J.O. of 23 July 1960).

4 Decree no. 67-158 of 1 March 1967 which fixed the objectives and the methods for setting up the Regional Nature Parks (J.O. of 2 March 1967).

Developing the Aquitaine Coast), started towards the end of the 1960s, included this question of "nature" in its principles. The determined aim was to integrate man into nature and his environment, based on protecting the natural environment and restoring architectural heritage [12]. In terms of regional development this policy resulted in the joint introduction of priority development units (new resorts) and natural balance sectors[5].

2.2. From an Environmental Turning Point to Requirement for Sustainability

The 1970s marked a turning point, in that collective environmental awareness (together with the 1980s real estate crisis) led the State to put global protection measures in place. Here we are moving away from the productivist and sectorial reasoning of the first six plans on creating resorts (where the main concern was to produce areas for building), and entering a phase of managing them, where heritage protection (especially natural heritage) was now seen as much more important. The first oil crisis and the world economic crisis drew world attention to the excesses of industrialisation and the harm that was being done to the environment. They helped to open a window of opportunity [13] and to put the environmental question at the top of the international and national political agenda6. The conditions finally came together for a radical change in coastal development policy. The French "Mountain" and "Coastal area" laws were the high points in the institutionalisation of this change.

Law no. 86-2, on the development, protection and promotion of the coastline, known as the "coastal law", was adopted unanimously by Parliament on 3 January 1986. It represented a turning point in terms of integrated planning and sustainable development of coastal areas. Questions on habitat and housing, mobility and accessibility, environmental and heritage values in the coastal area were asked with some urgency in relation to new occupants and new activities. For example, the proportion of coastline that has been denatured increased from 39% in 1960 to 61% in the 1990s, and between 2000 and 2006, this denaturation was 2.7 times greater in the coastal municipalities than in the rest of France (MEDDE, 2012; Atout France, 2014), despite the protection targets set by legislation. Coping with these changes is a challenge that faces the political framework of tourist management and development [14]. Along with the profound change in coastal areas, the institutional framework for applying the development and spatial planning policies for these areas has evolved, introducing new forms of regional governance that must be analysed. In this respect, the concept of Integrated Coastal Zone Management (ICZM), promoted by the European Union, seems to have opened up interesting prospects in terms of consultation, sharing of a common vision and governance of coastal areas. However, reconciling tourist development and environmental protection seems to be a delicate matter for those involved in tourism for reasons of commitment, both political and financial [15]. For example, we observe a degree of reticence and misunderstanding surrounding ICZM, where initiatives and measures also vary considerably, where sometimes the environmental approach predominates, to the detriment of a human and social approach. It is for all these reasons that management methods, conflicts of use and tourist trajectories of coastal areas must be challenged.

2.3. Emergence of a Creative Tourism

In the margins of the changes brought about by institutional actors and the arrival of the sustainability paradigm in the list of operational goals in the field of tourist development, the emergence of creative tourism is another significant change that can also disrupt the socio-spatial organisation of coastal areas and resorts.

This new approach, defined in UK has gradually become established in all regions, urban and rural [16]. Destinations in nature, on the coast and in the mountains are no exception, and France is only just beginning to learn this. Tourism has always benefited from its interdependence with identity and regional cultural practices, including sport and nature. And vice versa. Cultural tourism, at one and the same time cause and consequence of the growth of mass tourism, despite being difficult to assess and judged by the World Tourism Organisation to make up about one third of world tourism, continues to grow. Today this tourism has taken on a new, more creative form. After a mass tourism that focused on *having holidays*, then cultural and elitist tourism which consisted of *must see sights*, consumers next wanted creative tourist experiences. This "creative tourism" is defined as tourism that offers visitors the opportunity to develop their creative potential on the basis of heritage resources (including nature), and also cultural and creative resources, via active participation in characteristic experiences offered by the tourist destination, experiences that aim to transform [17]. It is implied, through this participation, that the tourist becomes an inhabitant of the region he is visiting, that he becomes part of the community, co-creating with it and that the local inhabitant becomes a tourist in his own region, revisiting it through creation. The emergence of creative tourism is firmly rooted both in "new consumer behaviour" (disillusioned, distressed and defiant individualist, with many identities and allegiances, constantly seeking experiences, hedonistic, an aesthete, eclectic, reflective, a hyper- or *alter*-consumer but always an active participant in his own

5 However, it should not be forgotten that the success of this protection policy was due largely, not to this relative environmental awareness, but rather to the upheaval in the economic climate since the second oil crisis (Prefecture of the Aquitaine Region, Aquitaine coastline mission and General Council of Aquitaine, 2002).

6 The creation of the United Nations Environment Programme at the UN conference in Stockholm from 5 to 16 June 1972, testifies to this change. There were also many more initiatives at national level. In France, the Ministry for the Protection of Nature and the environment was created in 1971. Five years later it was the instigator of the law on the Protection of Nature, law no. 76-629 of 10 July 1976, which stated in article 1: "*it is the duty of every individual to ensure the safeguarding of the natural heritage in which he lives. Any public or private development, equipment and production activities must conform to the same requirements*" (http://www.legifrance.gouv.fr).

consumption) and in the "new strategic and organisational behaviour of tourism actors", tending to make tourism disappear, blending into daily life, culture and consumption, no longer differentiated from domestic and leisure activities, decompartmentalised in itself and mixing genres, global and local all at the same time, presenteeist (overexploiting signs of the present and overexploring symbols of the past), providing a hyperchoice of hyperreal offers that can provide countless diverse experiences, focusing on sensoriality, product-service design, invented authenticity, emerging from objects and from the self, immediacy, accessibility, technology, communication, images….

At the heart of this trend is the "nature sports" resource, which for a long time was the privilege of just a few social elites with considerable social and cultural capital, and whose sports aesthetic and ethic consisted of adopting a *fun culture* [17]. However, these sports have now become popularised. Factors such as the sacred right to free time, individualisation in tourism practices, the many ways in which we socialise [18], the appeal of wide open natural spaces presented as a response to the standardisation of the territories of everyday life [19], the place of leisure in the social distinction process and also the commodification of recreational sports [20], all contribute to the democratisation of nature sports. However, this democratisation raises a number of issues, an important one of which is the preservation of natural environments, the medium in which these sports and recreational practices take place, and managing the territoriality of those who practice their sport freely. In any event, in 2010, more than 4.4 million French people said that they went mountain-biking for fun [7]. However, by democratising nature sports and structuring sports in this way, a number of issues are raised that are sports-related, social, economic, environmental and in particular space-related and which precipitate the emergence of an awareness of the dynamics specific to nature sport and recreation within sectoral public policies on tourism.

Another differentiation strategy used for coastal resorts that want to become more creative is the mobilisation of the "heritage" resource which has intensified, sometimes becoming the main factor in the destination [21] and responding to authenticity quest of demand [22]. From a standpoint of economic and urban regeneration, the post-modern combining heritage and creation, "*future heritage*" to use Fairclough's expression, [23], several resorts have developed their own "*industrial archaeology worthy of being preserved and displayed*" [24] from non-traditional heritage artefacts linked with their recent past: natural resources, built environments and intangible heritage, of course (Deauville, Saint-Jean-de Luz or Collioure in France…), but also the industrial heritage of these resorts linked with specific socio-economics conditions (Bilbao, Blackpool, Brighton…) and sometimes all of these forms of heritage combined (Arcachon Basin, Brest, Toulon…).

7 Source : Ministry of sports. *Les chiffres clés du sport en France*, December 2010.

3. Valorisation of Specific Creative Regional Resources: Nature, Surfing, Heritage

In this context of an emerging creative tourism and the requirement for sustainable development, the key issue for development strategies is to seize upon the essential identity of the region in order to mobilise it more directly. The generic resources on which the attractiveness of coastal destinations are based (the *sea, sand* and *sun* triptych of mass tourism, Turner and Ash, 1975) are exploited in ways that are no longer sufficient to ensure successful tourist development. Furthermore, it is necessary to reveal *regional resources* within the meaning given by the economists Peyrache-Gradeau and Pecqueur [25]. This phenomenon of "revealing" specific resources is a key factor, especially as the resource is always relative, with its use value dependent on its socialisation and its appropriation by the actors involved. These specific resources are the key to transforming resorts into creative areas, in the sense of cultural districts [26]: first of all they are resources of regional identity through which the district can be developed via land use planning strategies focused on innovation and creative integration in an urban context. Sacco [27] insists that these districts must have the necessary governance ability if they are to be developed and maintained.

Having opted for a differentiated analysis, it was decided to use resorts with different forms and created in a variety of ways: an "old" resort (Biarritz, created in the 18th century during the first phase of tourist development in the coastal areas), a contemporary resort (Lacanau-Océan developed from an older town, with the sea front created *ex nihilo* and the forest planted during the "Thirty Glorious Years" post-world war two, using a Fordist design model) and a "new" resort (Martigues, industrial town on the Berre lagoon, approved as a seaside tourist resort for the first time in 2008). In these three resorts, regional resources are mobilised in unusual ways: nature in Lacanau, surfing in Biarritz and heritage in Martigues. Nevertheless they show that the political decision-makers have appropriated new dogmatic viewpoints that structure the neo-paradigm of public policies on tourism based on trying to find a suitable level of habitability in these regions, both for tourists and residents.

3.1. Nature as a Resource for the Development of Lacanau-Océan

The development of Lacanau as a tourist resort grew out of a desire in the 19th century to tame the dunes and to have access to the sea. The first recreational activities took place in the winter town of Le Moutchic, close to Lacanau lake, before access to the coast was provided at the start of the last century by extending the railway line from the town and building properties [28]. Equipped with basic infrastructure for seaside activities (beaches, hotels, restaurants), the resort of Lacanau-Océan next experienced a considerable impetus to its urban development through the MIACA

(Interministerial Mission for Developing the Aquitaine Coast) (1967-1984). Thus the state incorporated Lacanau-Océan into its measures to create main development units. Planning for tourism began in 1974, after agreements had been reached between the municipalities and the National Office of Forests regarding the development conditions, which were then approved by the State (Augustin, 2007). Two sites were selected in the framework of this development, which revealed the role that natural resources were to play: the seafront (creation of accommodation); the forest, with Artilouse as a designated zone for development, intended mainly for sports activities (golf course, tennis courts, gyms and playing fields). Spatial development and urbanisation also resulted in demographic growth in the municipality as the population of Lacanau increased from 1,306 inhabitants in 1906 to 4,426 in 2010 with the population in the summer ranging between 80,000 and 100,00 visitors. Also, given that the resort underwent a rapid planned development over forty years, it now faces questions in relation to sustainable development. Consideration has to be given to the risk of erosion and the retreating coastline, issues that are now a catalyst for change in public policies in this region, where nature is a key resource (especially the dunes, the sea and the forests). In fact, dune management was a major concern in the development model for the resort produced in the 1960s. The dunes continue to be eroded, especially during severe weather conditions and storms. Pierre Barrère measured an annual displacement of 25 m^3 of sand per linear metre to the north of Lacanau in 1997 (Clus-Auby, 2003). Problems related to the retreating coastline in Lacanau were the subject of studies organised by the regional consultation unit, the Public Interest Group Littoral Aquitain (GIP Littoral Aquitain). First, jointly with the Lacanau municipality, they organised the first discussion forum on "Coastal retreat and erosion of the beaches" on 20 June 2009. Next, Lacanau was chosen as an experimental test site for various possible coastal development scenarios.

In addition to the environmental risks linked with erosion in particular and hence with the retreat of the dune and the weakening of the built infrastructure, the design of the entire resort is called into question since tourism is the main economic resource if not the only resource. Actors interviewed between December 2013 and March 2014 dealt with the question of regional dynamics through the prism of the resort's urban function which has evolved and which needs to be taken into account, but also with regard to the state of relations between populations and the co-presence that this creates. In the end a "redefinition" of the resort of Lacanau was decided on rather than a "withdrawal" since some types of infrastructure are linked exclusively with coastal activity and cannot be considered in any other spatial context. Indeed, several of those interviewed hoped that the future development of the resort would focus on a long-term solution, given the phenomenon of the erosion of the dune, looking also at managing the co-presence of tourists, residents, day-trippers in the hopes of ultimately achieving an integrated management of the resort, modelled on a coastal town where the seasonal effect is reduced. Redefining the resort involved studying the tourist accommodation available in large apartment buildings. Today these aging facilities do not properly meet current expectations and practices, and they are very much affected by the shorter tourist stays and the wide diversity in coastal activities that operate throughout the year. With regard to this subject, Cécile Ha, head of press promotion with the Regional Tourist Committee of Aquitaine[8], stressed this problem of the aesthetics of the housing stock, *"several resorts along the coast are faced with this problem of aging, but the long beaches and the ocean compensate somewhat. Nevertheless, the seasonal effect is too strong, in any case the fact that everything is operating at full capacity for only a short period would seem prejudicial to the future of the economic model envisaged for these resorts since the 1960s which differ from the coastal towns that operate all year round."* The challenge is for the municipality of Lacanau to adapt a socio-spatial organisation that will meet the needs of both the permanent residents and the temporary residents.

3.2. Surfing as a Symbolic Sports Resource of Biarritz

Surfing is the second example of a resource mobilised by the coastal resorts. It now contributes to the sociospatial organisation of coastal areas in tourist resorts along the Aquitaine coast [29]. It even appears in pride of place in regional management and planning measures. The Aquitaine coastline sustainable development plan for 2007-2020, run by GIP Littoral, includes surfing as one of the aspects that should be promoted in the framework of the list of operational goals for tourist development. A prospective study on tourism in Aquitaine, piloted by the Aquitaine Regional Council and GIP Littoral, established that *"surfing has helped to reinvent sea bathing and is a reference point for inventing new and imaginary uses"*[9]. Confronted with these forms of renewal of *"beach sociabilities"* [1], the study recommends *"restoring enthusiasm for the Aquitaine coast, complementing it and telling a new story"* by mobilising surfing, given that this sport has this *"ability to deseasonalise the numbers of tourists visiting the area* [given the fact that] *these different activities are spread evenly across the entire region"*. Political discourse leaves little room for ambiguity as far as local development goals are concerned. The surfer, before being seen as a gifted practician of a notable recreational, sporting intentionality is first of all seen as a *"client"*. This study also highlights the fact that these surfer tourists contribute about 1.5% of tourist spending in Aquitaine and that almost 46 million euros are generated through organising stays based on the surfing theme. In this context, it really is the case that the standardisation, the institutionalisation and the merchandising of surfing must be strengthened. Surfing is clearly a product of tourist marketing,

8 Interview in Bordeaux, on 27 November 2013.

9 Howarth Htl – Kanopée Consultants, *Etude prospective relative au tourisme en Aquitaine. Document phase 3 – Orientations stratégiques et actions prioritaires*, 2012.

it is included in public policies and participates in spatial innovation and local tourist systems. Tourism in this segment has to be promoted, the safety of participants must be guaranteed, the image of Aquitaine as the land of surfing must be strengthened and regional development encouraged through the promotion of surfing.

In this context, we propose to analyse the case of Biarritz in more detail, a town described as the birthplace of surfing in Europe. Here we analyse the role of surfing in the socioterritorial organisation of this unusual seaside resort and the way in which this sport influenced the management and uses of public space. *Surf spots*, i.e. those areas in the sea where surf devotees congregate, crystallise surfers' sporting aspirations and give rise to new social demands in terms of recreational facilities. Local politicians are aware of the challenges involved in developing surfing in their tourist resort. Guy Lafitte, deputy to the Mayor, even stated that surfing was, *"a key feature of Biarritz's identity*[10]*"*. Michel Veunac, who was at that time deputy to the Mayor believes that, *"surfing is in the town's DNA; it is one of the elements of blue growth"* and that they must *"valorise the role of surfing in the town's cultural, economic, and sports culture*[11]*"*. In addition to this discourse on valorising the history of surfing in the municipality, the sport is also firmly rooted in space and thus contributes to the emergence of a spatial organisation at odds with the definition and the urban and seaside resort that structure the town of Biarritz. Choices made in the context of urban operations and appropriation of public space by tourists and residents bring about a transformation in the coastal landscapes and urban atmospheres where exchanges and meetings can take place. The emergence of areas that are appropriated by the surfers can lead to conflicts in spatial planning [30]. The beach and the *spots*, which are the spaces where surfing is practised, are subject to special scrutiny in terms of management by the local political powers. In fact, the municipality makes by-laws which clearly define the limits of the areas allocated to each group of users of the maritime space. Surfing therefore has its own institutional legitimacy in the public area. This legal recognition also includes recognition in terms of spatial area in that the well-defined zones are dedicated exclusively to this sport. The municipality's desire for development now extends beyond simple discourse. The construction of the *Cité de l'Océan et du Surf* ensures that the roots of surfing are a little more firmly planted in the town despite attendance figures failing to match up to initial expectations

Surfing is therefore an essential product of tourism marketing. The value of the surfing culture is enhanced and used as a support when organising sports events and festive events, with *Roxy Jam* undeniably the most emblematic of all of these. These cultural and sports events give structure to new forms of social link at the heart of the public space. They represent time to meet others, time for exchanges that shape the rhythm of leisure time of both tourists and residents in the summer. Surfing is incorporated into the framework of sectoral public policies on economic development, on tourism, on sport, on culture… and is becoming a major player in regional development in the town of Biarritz not like in the third world's surf zones [31] [32].

3.3. Nature, Industry and Urban Heritage as a Resource in Martigues

The last example is the municipality of Martigues, a historic industrial town at the edge of the Berre lagoon, which took the decision in the 2000s to showcase their tourist resources, as can be seen from their classification as a seaside and tourist resort in 2008.

In the case of Martigues, it is clear that the request for the town to be ranked as a seaside and tourist resort can be explained in part by the will of the former mayor to consider the possibility of opening of a casino; it was also made possible by the change in mentalities in this industrial area. Urban and nature heritage were gradually considered as resources that could be exploited. The gradual (although fairly measured) opening of this town to tourist development follows on from the promotion of the beauty of the landscapes and local heritage begun in the 1980s, at the same time as the industrial sector was experiencing difficulties. As highlighted by the director of the department of town planning[12], *"a change occurred with the arrival of the notion of heritage at the time of the RHI [measure to remove substandard housing, introduced from 1985-1990]. Something changed in the minds of the town councillors, the town was no longer simply an oil town, but we also considered the question of its heritage.* [...] *MP2013 helped promote this, but a turning point was reached in the 1990s which resulted in a period of redefining.*" And so the town gradually became aware of its assets and the quality of its landscapes, which have earned it the name of the "Venice of Provence". The "Martigues en couleur" operation, started at the end of the 1980s, is one of the urban promotion measures initially put in place. Finally, in Martigues, "*we put the town project and the tourist project in place at the same time. We wanted to create a project for residents and new residents, which is also favourable for our temporary residents, the tourists"* (the words of the town's Chief Architect[13]). After urban heritage, it was nature heritage that was the second resource mobilised by the local authority. Martigues was an exceptional case on the Côte Bleue (compared with Sausset and Carry for example) in setting up a real regional protection, in parallel with the industrial development that intensified after the 1960s. A proactive land acquisition policy enabled them to limit urbanisation of the coastline in favour of an urbanisation in limited sectors and in more depth along the coast. Tourist development in fact was introduced

10 Statement taken in a pilot committee organised on 12 April 2013 on the preparation of the *"Surfing white paper"* devised by the municipal team as a surfing development strategy planning tool which required contributions from those in the surfing world, from the sports movement, from private enterprise, from the French Surfing Federation, and associations.

11 Statement taken on 12 April 2013.

12 Interview with Didier Pagès, 28 January 2013.

13 Interview with Sophie Bertran de Balanda, 13 December 2013.

around three urban sites, with natural breaks being kept between them. The paradox, if there is one, is that ultimately it is the industrial development that has promoted both the protection of nature and the development of local leisure facilities, and then tourism.

Finally, the Martigues region became a tourist region and little by little has laid claim to this identity. This has happened over the last thirty years, along with the municipal policy in favour of valorising urban and natural heritage for the residents – and indirectly for potential visitors. In the mid-1990s the municipality therefore acquired a tourism and entertainment department responsible for promoting tourism in this region as it undergoes renewal. Today, there is a new phase in this evolution, the regional heritage promotion policy also resulted in obtaining the quality Label for Town of Art and History in 2012. While the worries of the past seemed to worsen, translating a need to be firmly rooted in a diversified and complex world, overloaded with information, the heritage argument emerges as the evidence of overinvestment in the local. Heritage holds a central place, since it gives meaning to places and participates in regional legitimisation. To meet the changing needs and activities of tourists, regions now exploit their heritage, seen as a resource for tourist development. Whereas the industrial crisis resulted in company relocations, the development of tourism, by exploiting regional resources that cannot be relocated, seems to be a great asset, which can guarantee local jobs, and this can be a reason for changing people's mentalities on the subject. As well as the process of revealing heritage resources, the town has also been able to communicate about this change and has "claimed" these resources as its own. According to the director of the local public company for tourism and events management[14], although it may be true that "*it could have seemed a little presumptuous at first to claim that we were a tourist town, perhaps even crazy or unrealistic. But that too is a voluntary, voluntarist discourse, which is also included in a strategy, I think, to develop other activities*". In the 1990s, it was a case of diversifying economic activities in the area, by proposing perhaps not an alternative, but at least a supplement to historic industrial development through tourist development. What we see is a change in the system of representation initiated by local actors: "*there is potential that has been recognised. There is an image of self, an image of the town with a self-representation that has been built up gradually, and that didn't exist in the years 1960-1970.*"[15] As the head of tourism recalled [16], the town first developed infrastructure and improved the quality of the living environment for its inhabitants before valorising this move outwards by embarking on a process to obtain a ranking as a seaside and tourist resort.

14 Interview on 27 May 2014 with Nicole Girard, resident of Martigues, former municipal representative in Martigues and teacher-researcher in geography.

15 Interview on 27 May 2014 with Nicole Girard.

16 Interview on 27 May 2014 with Alain Salducci in charge of tourism, events, agriculture, fishing, hunting and commemoration.

4. Discussion about the Resource Selection Process: Governance and Issues of Rhetoric

These three case studies have shown the phenomena of regional resource valorisation currently underway in coastal resorts. Strategies are differentiated and closely dependent on identifying resources specific to the identity of the areas and to the rationales of governance within which the arbitrages demonstrate a political direction. We therefore question this phenomenon of "*re-definition*", applied to specific resources that reflect the various processes by which a local society is organised and reconsider the collective value attributed to this resource.

4.1. Interactions between Players, Modes of Governance

Analysis of the processes for valorising regional resources has highlighted interactions between actors and potential conflicts of use and governance associated with these processes. In particular, the place reserved for this region within its tourist area is called into question.

At Lacanau-Océan, the rapid growth of the resort, sometimes considered too hasty and with a lack of long-term planning, especially in the framework of creating main development units, came up against problems of governance. Lacanau's transitional situation, from a large rural village to a small coastal town in forty years, and the resulting growth in population required local representatives to consider what actions to carry out: should they continue their growth or slow down development? There was indeed a paradox between the need to provide urban facilities to cope with tourist numbers and the low average population present across the year. However, even though the town's population had increased by more than 3,000 inhabitants in a century, and it was trying to continue its demographic growth, it nevertheless wanted to escape the periurbanisation of the Bordeaux urban area and the risk of becoming just a dormitory suburb on the coast. This situation, in parallel with the change in the role of the actors present, characterises a new governance, which remains fairly complex, and which makes it difficult to prepare a vision for development in the medium or the long term. However, the organisational structuring around an inter-municipality tourist office makes it possible right away to create a situation with a central pole, with more links between those involved and a clarity in what is on offer around a brand going out to multipole and complementary destinations, "Médoc-Océan". However, tourist practices are not limited to this area. The key issue for Lacanau lies both in an intensification of its urban function but also in an increase in its command force as the pole of a vast tourist area.

In the case of Biarritz, the valorisation of this historic heritage that is the establishment of surfing requires the public authorities to be vigilant inasmuch as they are the guarantors of accessibility for all to the *surf spots*. This is currently threatened, however, by appropriation rationales caused by overcrowding in the waves during the summer. This is doubtless the reason why Michel Veunac, mayor of the town since the last elections, believes it is time to *"give to surfing what surfing has given the town"*. Pragmatically speaking, the surfing General Assembly in Biarritz, recognised as a tool serving a participative democracy, is due to be held on 17 October 2014 so that the actors can construct their surfing development strategies jointly and include a prospective dimension. For without a *terra incognita* conducive to surfing at the scale of the town of Biarritz, it is clear that new regulations must be established concerning the development of surfing so that in future, the history of surfing in Biarritz can perpetuate the values of tolerance and communion with nature in which the myth of the surfing culture is immersed.

4.2. A risk of Narrative Reduction

After analysis of the conflicts inherent in the methods used to select and valorise regional resources, we ultimately question the limitations of this process or at least the queries that it has raised.

In the case of Martigues, while the municipality has taken the decision to exploit its heritage resources in order to promote its attractiveness, the question still remains as to the resources selected and staged as internal conflicts that were revealed with reference to the choices made. The choice fell to the joint valorisation of the seaside town and the historic town, over the industrial town, according to a process of narrative reduction which was to the regret of some members. However, as the head of engineering at Bouches-du-Rhône Tourism17 recalls, *"this is part of the strong identity of this area, it's an area of contrasts, oxymoron. It's a gentle violence"*. To this end, several local actors seem to identify a contradiction in policies between the tourism and the culture departments which appear to be in confrontation, whereas they could more easily act to their mutual advantage. This opposition amongst actors around the image portrayed of Martigues, between seaside tourism and industry, seems to have crystallised around the MP2013 event, when a "night of industry" was organised in Martigues. For some this was a tremendous success, testimony to this new challenge, for others it was mildly successful, revealing a lack of image, and there was no consensus for the event as a whole within the local authority departments. For the person responsible for tourism[18], who admitted he was not in agreement on this point with the head of culture, *"Industry remains part of the heritage of Martigues, we can't sweep industry away, but from there to making it the spearhead of the tourist industry, for me that's a mistake"*.

In Biarritz too, one might wonder if this transformation of the public space imposed by surfing and its iconographic planned staging by local actors from the municipality is not plunging the town into a valorisation dynamic for one aspect of sports tourism while running the risk that tourists may create a caricatural representation of this tourist resort where surfing is in fact only one asset among so many others.

The process for selecting the regional resources ultimately appears to be a determining and non-consensual issue in tourist development policies. To what extent does the rhetoric of creative regional resources prevail over reality in a unifying myth, instrumentalised by public policies (Belfiore, X).

5. Conclusion

Analysis of the processes for valorising creative regional resources in the resorts of Biarritz, Lacanau and Martigues has highlighted several observations. First, geographic and environmental location is of paramount importance when reflecting on a framework of permanence for places and their tourist trajectories. In the case of resorts such as Biarritz or Lacanau, which have experienced urban sprawl and spatial densification associated with their coastal activities (related especially to the beach and sports), the current situation of urban expansion and the co-presence of various populations makes us wonder what will remain from creating these places. Furthermore, changes in activities tend to give a different outlook on development. We note that in Biarritz, the image of surfing has encouraged the resort to define a marketing strategy for the destination which leads to focus on a practice that is localising and localised, the definition of an urbanised region; in Lacanau, however, the reverse is the case, and although surfing has helped to boost the resort's image, the aims of urban development predominate over the reality of this sporting activity. Nevertheless, in both these resorts it is definitely tourism that has enabled urbanisation to occur. In the case of Lacanau, however, State intervention in the form of rapid concentrated development in the 1970s has frozen the valorisation of regional resources, so that now there is a situation of duality in governance between taking urban change into account and measuring environmental risks. In Martigues, the trajectory is quite different, as the municipality only recently decided to become oriented towards new practices by opening up to tourism. In this case, creative tourism practices have become an integral part of the valorisation of regional resources, where transformation into heritage is one of the processes co-constructed by the actors involved.

This multi-case study presents several limitations that are important to take into account in order to define further options in the research agenda. First of all, it would be relevant to study more cases on the French Coast in order to enrich the observation sample and its validity, especially regarding implementation and governance of creative regional resources. Next, there are two issues related to the spatial dimension: first, is the transformation of the resorts limited to the resort itself, or does it cover the entire coastline? Second, the mobilisation of creative resources is restricted as the space has become confused by political issues between municipalities, and the different governmental levels which interfere with the application of European directives. Finally,

17 Interview with Valérie Carbonne, on 10 July 2013.

18 Interview on 27 May 2014 with Alain Salducci in charge of tourism, events, agriculture, fishing, hunting and commemoration.

this research does not cover enough questions on resistance and on conflicts arising from the tourist development choices made in the 3 case studies; these aspects were noted in the survey and can be dealt with at a later stage.

References

[1] J-D. Urbain, *Sur la plage : mœurs et coutumes balnéaires (XIXè-XXè siècles)*, Paris : Editions Payot & Rivages (3rd edition), 2002.

[2] P. Muller, *Les politiques publiques*, Paris : PUF, 1990, 2003.

[3] H. Gumuchian, and B. Pecqueur (ed.), *La ressource territoriale*, Paris : Anthropos, 2007.

[4] G. Richards and J. Wilson, "Developing creativity in tourist experiences: a solution to the serial reproduction of culture?", Tourism Management, vol. 27., 2006.

[5] L. Falaix, « Les sports de nature dans le département des Landes : du développement maîtrisé à la mobilisation d'une ressource territoriale », *Annales de Géographie*, n°686, 2012, pp. 410-432.

[6] N. Perry, *Hyperreality and Global Culture*, Routledge, 1998.

[7] J. Corneloup (2011). « La forme transmoderne des pratiques récréatives de nature », *Développement durable et territoires*, [On line], Vol. 2, 3, Décembre 2011.

[8] A. Corbin, *Le territoire du vide : l'Occident et le désir de rivage (1750-1840)*. Paris: Flammarion, 1988.

[9] S. Agarwal, "The resort cycle and seaside tourism: an assessment of its applicability and validity", *Tourism Management,* vol. 18, Issue 2, March 1997, pp. 65-73.

[10] M. Noailles. « La construction d'une économie touristique sur la côte Aquitaine sous la Ve République (1958-1988), *Sud-Ouest Européen*, n°29, 2010, pp. 37-42.

[11] P. Duhamel and P. Violier, *Tourisme et littoral : un enjeu du monde*. Paris : Editions Belin, 2009.

[12] J. Kingdon, *Agendas, Alternatives, and Public policies*, New York: Longman (2nd ed.), 1995.

[13] A. Haulot, R. H. Charlier, "Tourism and coastal environment", *The Tourist Review,* vol. 33, issue 1, pp. 10-12.

[14] S. Jennings, "Coastal tourism and shoreline management", *Annals of Tourism Research,* vol. 31, issue 4, October 2004, pp. 899-922.

[15] M.-N Rimaud M.-N. and Piriou J. (2013). « La GIZC et le développement touristique : enjeux d'un principe organisateur pour la durabilité des stations littorales atlantiques », *VertigO* - la revue électronique en sciences de l'environnement [En ligne], Hors-série 18 | mis en ligne le 12 décembre 2013, consulté le 25 décembre 2013. URL : http://vertigo.revues.org/14285.

[16] G. Richards, 2011, "Creativity and tourism. The state of the art", *Annals of Tourism Research*, Vol. 38, n°. 4, 2011.

[17] G. Richards and L. Marques, "Exploring Creative Tourism: Editors Introduction", *Journal of Tourism Consumption and Practice,* Volume 4 No.2, 2012.

[18] E. Hirschman and M. Holbrook, "The experiential aspects of consumption: consumer fantasies, feelings and fun", *Journal of Consumer Research*, 9, n°2, 1982.

[19] J. Urry and J. Larsen, *The tourist gaze 3.0,* London: Sage, 2011.

[20] P. Bourdeau, J. Corneloup, P. Mao, "Outdoor Sports and Tourism in French Mountains: towards a Sustainable Development?" In Ritchie, B.W. & Adair, D. (eds). Sport Tourism: Interrelationships, Impacts and Issues. Clevedon: Channel View Publications, 2004, pp. 101-116.

[21] L. Moore, "Sport and Commodification A Reflection on Key Concepts", *Journal of Sport and Social Issues*, May 2007 vol. 31 no. 2, pp. 128-142.

[22] B. Weaver, "Contemporary Tourism Heritage as Heritage Tourism, Evidence from Las Vegas and Gold Coast", *Annals of Tourism Research*, Vol. 38, No. 1, 2011, p. 249–267.

[23] G. Sedmak and T. Mihalič, "Authenticity in mature seaside resorts", *Annals of Tourism Research*, Vol. 35, Issue 4, October 2008, pp. 1007–1031.

[24] G. Fairclough, "New heritage, an introductory essay – People, landscape and change", In G. Fairclough, R. Harrison, J. Jameson, & J. Schofield (Eds.), *The heritage reader*, New York: Routledge, pp. 297- 312.

[25] J. Walton and J. Wood, "Reputation and regeneration: History and the heritage of the recent past in the re-making of Blackpool", In L. Gibson & J. Pendlebury (Eds.), *Valuing historic environments* Aldershot: Ashgate, 2009, pp. 115–138.

[26] Peyrache-Gadeau and Pecqueur B. (2004), « Les ressources patrimoniales : valorisation par les milieux innovateurs », in R.Camagni, D. Maillat and A. Matteaccioli, *Ressources naturelles et culturelles, milieux et développement local.* Neuchâtel : EDEA, coll GREMI, pp.71-89.

[27] W. Santagata, *Cultural District and Economic Development.* Mimeo, EBLA Center, Univ. di Torino et WP, 2004.

[28] P. L. Sacco, *Il disttretto culturale evoluto : competenze per l'innovazionne, la crescita e l'occupazione*, Bologna : goodwill, 2006.

[29] J.-P. Augustin, « L'attractivité plurielle d'une station océane : Lacanau-Océan dans le sud-ouest de la France », *Téoros*, n° 26-2, pp. 39-45.

[30] L. Falaix and M. Favory, « Les stations du surf sur la côte basque ». *Sud-Ouest Européen,* 13, 2002, pp. 51-61.

[31] J. Anderson, "Cathedrals of the surf zone: regulating access to a space of spirituality", *Social & Cultural Geography*, Vol. 14, Issue 8, 2013, pp. 954-972.

[32] J. Ponting, M. McDonald, "Performance, agency and change in surfing tourist space", *Annals of Tourism Research*, Vol. 43, October 2013, pp. 415-434.

[33] J. Ponting, D. O'Brien, "Liberalizing Nirvana : an analysis of the consequences of common pool resource deregulation for the sustainability of Fiji's surf tourism industry", *Journal of Sustainable Tourism*, Vol. 22, Issue 3, 2013, pp. 384-402.

13

Perceptioning as a tool for Destination Branding: The case of Liguria as Wikidestination

Kamel Ben Youssef[1], Martha Friel[2], Thomas Leicht[3], Lidia Marongiu[4]

[1]Department of Management, Université Paris Ouest Nanterre La Défense, Paris, France
[2]Department of Economics and Law, IULM University, Milan, Italy
[3]Department of Philosophy, Information/Communication, Language, Literature/Arts, Université Paris Ouest Nanterre La Défense, Paris, France
[4]Studio Giaccardi & Associati – Consulenti di Direzione, Ravenna, Italy

Email addresses:
kamel.benyoussef@u-paris10.fr (Kamel B. Y.), martha.friel@css-ebla.it (Martha F.), thomas_leicht@gmx.de (Thomas L.), l.marongiu@giaccardiassociati.it (Lidia M.)

Abstract: The perceptioning model developed by Bassani et al. (2002, 2007, and 2011) permits to design, launch and develop a strong brand in B2B and B2C markets. In recent years, it has also been used to build wikibrands (Moffit and Dover, 2010) and successful products relying on the high involvement of consumers' communities in value creation processes. The paper explores how the perceptioning model as a tool for destination branding could also find successful application in other fields such as the tourism sector. After a literature review on place branding and perceptioning, the paper applies this model at a territorial scale by analyzing the case of the region of Liguria in Northwest Italy as a prototype of wikidestination. By relying on a qualitative research design based on interviews and discourse analysis, this paper provides evidence that perceptioning is also a suitable approach for territorial marketing, especially in the case of wikidestinations that are constructed collectively.

Keywords: Brand identity, C-to-C online marketing, Perceptioning, Territorial marketing, Wikibrand, Wikidestination

1. Introduction

In a world of disorientation, territorial marketing is reinventing itself by adopting codes of influence in the image of the whole society. The empowerment of customers, employees, suppliers and citizens also disrupts our living places, notably with a holistic approach, to the attractiveness of regions [1].

According to Lewi [2], choosing a travel *destination* or a location for a future implementation depends on four parameters: Risk aversion (considering elements such as infrastructure or security), interest (including considerations on currency, taxation, etc.), hospitality (i.e. climate, empathy, etc.) and the discovery of new potential (commercial, cultural, sociological, etc.). The first three criteria result from the analysis of past and present experience while the fourth comes from a desired future. Finally, consumers and policymakers will ultimately determine where they certainly do not want to go or run their business.

This is why territorial marketing is a subtle blend of several comparative marketing dimensions: Economic, political, social and cultural. After a literature review on place marketing, branding theory and the concept of wikibrands, this paper discusses the use of social media in destination branding processes in particular by focusing on the case of the Italian region of Liguria. The paper then analyzes the construction of Liguria as wikidestination by using the perceptioning approach [3] and gives evidence that this tool is particularly helpful for identifying brand elements that are crucial for the success of a strong territorial brand.

2. Literature review

2.1. Place Marketing and Branding

Similarly to products, territories must now compete on an increasingly large and diversified market. This led in the last 30 years to the development of place marketing.

Place marketing is a new branch of broader marketing studies [4, 5, 6] which has witnessed the development of a wide literature which, in recent times, has primarily focused on place branding [7, 8, 9, 10, 11].

As pointed out by Kavaratzis [9], the application of marketing techniques to places comes from two different trends: The development of marketing for non-business and non-profit organizations and the need for many places to find an economic and image repositioning following the industrial decline. Still, Ashworth and Voogd [7] point out that the development of place marketing is initially linked to the development of marketing for non-profit organizations, Social Marketing and Image Marketing.

In this context, place branding has emerged as a tool to create or strengthen the positioning of countries, regions and cities, with the aim of attracting tourists, customers and investments. At the theoretical level, the question of place branding has been approached with very different points of view. It is now widely recognized that place branding is a multi- and cross-disciplinary field [12] and that places increasingly need to consider branding in a wide range of contexts and for a wide range of stakeholders [13].

Among these approaches, five are particularly relevant [9]: Place and origin branding that involves "branding" a product using the image of its territory of origin (and qualities underlying this); Nation branding is used for tourist purposes and for attracting investments to a country; Culture/entertainment branding, linked to the use of cultural events and branding to create economic and social effects especially in urban areas and phenomena such as the spread of buildings-landmark designed by so-called "superstars"; Destination branding, perhaps the area far more investigated, linked to the branding of tourist destinations [14, 15, 16]; and, finally, Place/city branding.

In Italy too place branding is receiving increasing attention, although with some delay compared to other nations [17, 18, 19, 20, 21]. This has been due mainly to the loss of competitiveness experienced by Italy on the international tourism market and to the need to think of new ways for promoting and innovating the Italian tourist products.

In general, even in such a diverse theoretical context, there is an increasing awareness at a local level on at least three points that have been emerging from the empirical results of place branding strategies in the last years.

The first is that if place branding is intended as a strategic scheme to improve a place's image [22], place image should be considered as an integrated part of place identity and not something juxtaposed to it [23]. In other words, integrated place branding should be considering the complex ways in which place identity is produced and negotiated.

The second one regards the fact that, as noted by Anholt, "*communications are no substitute for policies, and that altering the image of a country or city may require something a little more substantial than graphic design, advertising or PR campaigns. A robust and productive coalition between government, business and civil society, as well as the creation of new institutions and structures to achieve and maintain this behaviour, is necessary for achieving this harmonisation of goals, themes, communications and behaviours in the long term.*" [24].

The third point, which is confirmed in the first two, is the central role not only of local stakeholders but also of larger communities that today, thanks to the development of technology and Web 2.0 are fully involved in the life and development of the territories.

2.2. Defining Wikibrands

According to Moffitt and Dover [25], wikibrands are defined as "a progressive set of organizations, products, services, ideas and causes that tap into the powers of customer participation, social influence and collaboration to drive business value".

This means a shift in companies' behavior from broadcasting directly to their target audience to engaging their customers in a more collaborative interaction in order to add value to the services provided by their organization.

In general, organizations should recognize the following for creating a wikibrand:

- Customers are at the epicenter of the organization, as they are essential in assisting and supporting innovation, experience, insight, support, brand evangelism and exposure.
- Authenticity and transparency are essential organizational tenders of sustainable enterprises. The reason for existence and authenticity of organizations carry more weight than is often assumed.
- Only by standing out from the crowd, people will notice the organization and talk about it – most efforts, no matter how good they are, tend to be ignored both online and offline simply because they are not deemed to be unique enough, dynamic enough or visionary enough. The aim should be to become the 1% of efforts that do get recognized.
- "Strength is determined by the power of the company's network" and organizations should connect profoundly in order to transform their "business culture and operating models for the future." [25]
- Things that are deemed fresh and exciting today are considered out-of-date tomorrow. Paradigm changes are happening at break neck speeds and in order to keep up and accommodate the customer's needs, it is important to think about and to develop the business processes.

2.3. From Wikibrand to Wikidestination

According to the Italian consultancy agency Studio Giaccardi & Associati – Consulenti di Direzione: "With the neologism wikidestination, we mean a territory, city or country that, in order to position itself in the imagination of the people as a tourist destination, uses the collective intelligence to build a plural narrative capable of restoring, combining different points of view, the identity of the competitive territory".

As already underlined, competition between territories and tourist destinations is nowadays very tough and the need to stand out and to be appreciated by consumers-tourists does not only depend on massive advertising budgets invested on big media. Instead it depends more and more on the ability to enhance the message through word-of-mouth approaches, in which the tourist receives stimuli and information on the brand directly from its networks of horizontal relationship.

Technology and social networks then become tools for transforming happy travelers in advocate narrators and spokespersons of the brand, able to influence the choices of other travelers via C-to-C (consumer-to-consumer) online marketing.

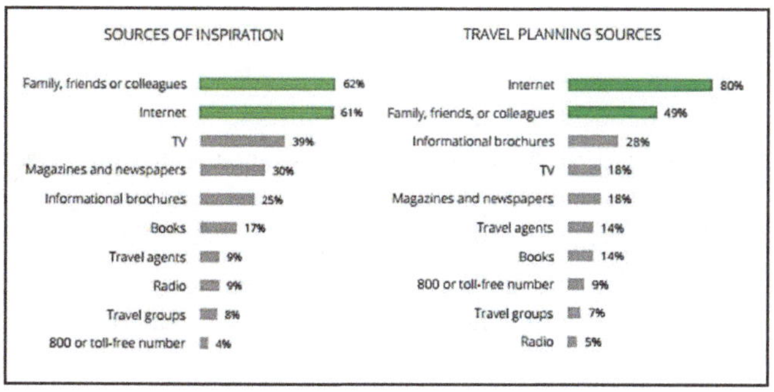

Figure 1. *The source of inspiration in the choice of a trip – Google Search Traveler 2013*

The wikidestionation model allows for setting a strategy for tourism place marketing in which the main influencers are the tourists themselves. Particularly in the field of tourism, there is evidence on the power of C-to-C online marketing influence and Internet in purchase decisions of holiday destinations.

According to Google Search Traveler 2013 [26] (Fig. 1), suggestions from friends, family and colleagues are the first source of inspiration in the choice of a trip and the second most influential source in planning the vacation.

2.4. Developing a Wikidestination with Perceptioning

According to Bassani et al. (2011, p. 108-121) [3], perceptioning is a technique for developing a brand. It is based on the assumption that the brand is the result of the perception of consumers. The perceptioning approach (Fig. 2) analyzes the basic elements constituting a brand and is therefore a guide to develop the consistency of all its components - functional product qualities, product design, brand identity, communication and genetic code - in order to strengthen and reinforce the brand perception.

The perceptioning model is composed of seven different analysis steps:

1. Positioning and definition of the perception of a brand (including context and customer analysis)
2. Decomposition of the perception of a brand according to its (three) basic elements
3. Development of the perception of a brand in terms of functional product qualities
4. Development of the perception of a brand in terms of product design
5. Development of the perception of a brand in terms of communication
6. Development of the perception of a brand in terms of brand identity
7. Definition of the genetic code of a brand.

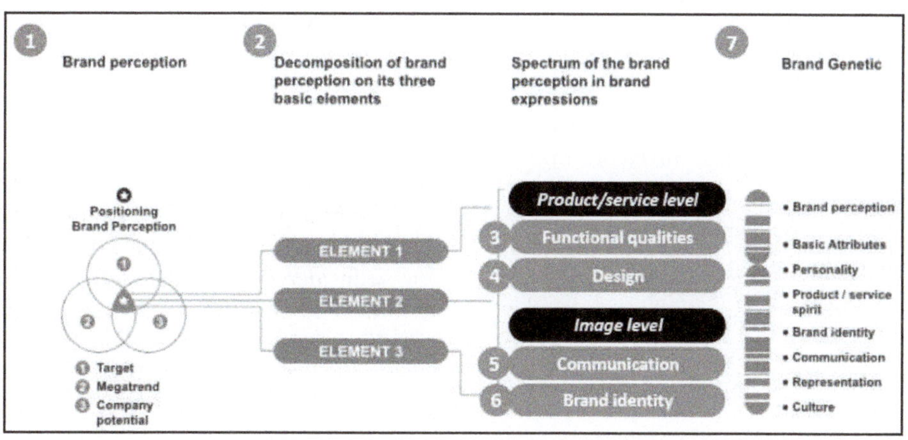

Figure 2. *The Perceptioning Model (Based on Bassani et al. (2011, p. 108-121) and (www.laurentpollefoort.com/capabilities.html)*

3. Analysis of Liguria as Wikidestination

3.1. Methodology and Analysis

The analysis is based on a qualitative research approach and the case study method was chosen as the paper investigates a contemporary phenomenon within its real-life context [27, 28]. Case studies are often more appropriate when the researcher is seeking answers for "how" and "why" questions and has little control over events [27].

This applies to our research question, which is primarily based on written sources, as well as an interview with Giuseppe Giaccardi, CEO of Studio Giaccardi & Associati – Consulenti di Direzione, which actively contributed to implement Liguria's wikibrand. After collecting some data through literature, observation and web browsing, we try to analyze both Liguria's blog and its Facebook page, dedicated to the wikidestination, to observe how the community was involved in the project *"Building and maintaining a Liguria wikibrand"*.

The place marketing strategy of Liguria has been defined in the tourism marketing plan "A Wikibrand for a

Wikidestination". The project Liguria Tourism Bottom Up, created by Studio Giaccardi & Associati – Consulenti di Direzione on behalf of the Liguria Tourism Board, outlines how to plan the development of tourism in the region. The project had the objective to define a three-year tourism plan for the region with the active involvement of all stakeholders in Liguria. The work realized in Liguria is the first Italian example of designing tourism development and was conducted with a bottom-up methodology in which objectives, actions, resources and indicators for monitoring results were identified through intensive listening and dialogue activities with all the people directly or indirectly involved in the tourism sector of the region: Tourism operators, associations, government agencies, citizens and tourists themselves.

This important work of design and listening was based on:

- Listening to tour operators' experiences, needs and expectations of development
- Analysis of online researches of tourists interested on a vacation in Liguria
- Analysis of perceptions and opinions about the brand "Liguria" and stakeholders' place brand.

The analysis has been taken as instructions to define the three-year tourism plan approved by the governing bodies of the region in December 2012. This plan has become crucial for defining the consequent promotion strategies and marketing plan.

3.2. A new Marketing Strategy for Liguria

With 3.8 million tourist arrivals and 13.5 million overnight stays, Liguria represents about 3.9% of tourism in Italy. Despite these relatively low numbers that are due to the reduced territorial extension of the region, tourism is a strategic economic sector for Liguria. It contributes to approximately 10.2% of its GDP, a number that is above the national average, and which generated revenues of 5,158 million € in 2011.

Liguria is a region that is characterized by a strong importance of seaside tourism throughout the region, with subsequent problems for the diversification of the main regional products and with respect to the seasonality of tourism. However, the offer of the region is potentially rich and ranges from wine and food tourism to adventure and nature tourism.

The tourism marketing plan of Liguria, implemented in 2012 and in force until the end of 2015, applies the wikibrand theory on the construction of the Liguria tourist brand. In other words, the marketing plan is designed to promote the tourist destination Liguria relying on the collective intelligence of prosumers, word-of-mouth influence, C-to-C online marketing, viral marketing on social media and the active involvement of tourists and citizens in creating a storytelling of the territory in which the points of view of those who live, visit and know the region are valued.

The strategy assumes that it is difficult to define Liguria with a unique description or with a characteristic that dominates the others. Liguria is known for its seaside but it is also appreciated in the international market for its cultural aspects, entertainment, gastronomic heritage and the opportunities for sports and outdoor life. The same Liguria tour operators interviewed for the research have shown different connotations and competitive factors of the tourist offer of Liguria depending on the location they were from or their specific work. Many of them, especially among tour operators, identified in the definition "Riviera dei Fiori" (Flowers' Riviera), the strongest brand of Liguria and the name by which, according to them, Liguria is known especially in the foreign market.

Actually, by checking online researches of potential tourists (using the tool Google Trends) we found that the brand "Riviera dei Fiori" is far less known and googled than the place brand "Cinque Terre" and "Liguria" itself. The same is valid for the German translation "Blumen Riviera".

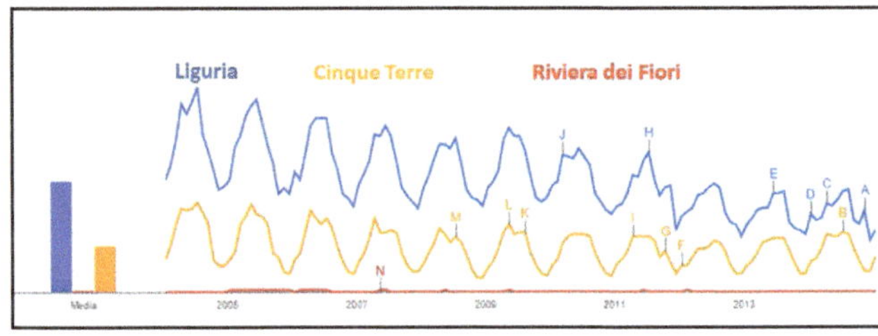

Figure 3. *Brand awareness on Google of the terms: Liguria, Riviera dei Fiori and Cinque Terre (Google Trends Analysis)*

[Caption: The numbers on the graph reflect how many searches have been done for a particular term, relative to the total number of searches done on Google over time. They don't represent absolute search volume numbers, because the data is normalized and presented on a scale from 0 to 100. Each point on the graph is divided by the highest point and multiplied by 100. When not enough data was available, the graph equals 0]

Even the definition Italian Riviera indicated by operators as "synonymous with Liguria" for foreign tourists is not confirmed by the analysis of online researches made by travelers on Google.

Different audiences who experience different places or attractions develop a set of plural perceptions and opinions that can hardly emerge without giving voice to the very protagonists of the holiday experience. Today's digital technology and social media allow the implementation of marketing campaigns in which people can amplify the story of all those involved in the experience of the destination by transforming comments, photos and articles in content that can influence the decisions of other tourists.

To do so, a space is needed to bring together the stories and where people involved with the brand can interact with the brand on horizontal flows of relationship able to promote and boost the visibility of the brand through the exponential power of social networks.

In the tourist marketing plan of Liguria "A Wikibrand for a Wikidestination", two tools have been identified to support the creation and development of communities involved and interested in having a dialogue with the brand "Liguria": the Facebook page "Liguria", registered in the category "tourist attraction", and the blog "Liguria tells".

The Facebook page and the blog played a central role in the

marketing strategy as:

- Spaces for creation and expansion of a community of people passionate about Liguria
- Place for direct interaction with the brand
- Place for storytelling and narrative of the tourist destination from the traveler's point of view
- Test and analysis of the topics of greatest interest and appreciation by the readers.

3.3. The Tools of the Marketing Plan for Making Liguria a Wikidestination

The blog "Liguria tells" gives voice to citizens and tourists who want to tell and share "their Liguria", the one they saw, lived and filtered with their eyes, memories and emotions. The result is a collection of short authentic stories, rich in nuances, points of view and possible interpretations that can motivate and influence the choices of new tourists. In about two years more than 200 articles were published on the blog, an average of 100 per year. The blog allowed for involving more than 80 bloggers who have contributed with articles full of photographs and personal views on a variety of topics. The blog generates a large number of interactions in the community:

- Over 287 comments to posts
- Several thousand likes and shares on social networks
- Repins and retweets of posts on Pinterest and Twitter.

The blog is now filled with content written by the editorial board of the Agency Liguria (planned according to an editorial plan consistent with the promotion of tourism and territorial initiatives) and content written by tourists, bloggers and citizens. The topics covered are diverse, always accompanied by a large number of images. Among the most welcomed are those dedicated to traditional culture (festivals, typical products), stories of childhoods spent in Ligurian towns that now become major tourist attractions (tales of memory), and thematic itineraries (outdoor, hiking, villages, etc.). It is important to highlight that the most successful content is the most intimate and personal, as shows the post "Cogoleto and the tale of the ugly duckling", that got more than 1,000 likes and shares on Facebook.

The Facebook page of Liguria is the place of greater dialogue and aggregation of the community of people passionate about Liguria. Updated on a daily basis, it has reached more than 90,000 clicks on "talking about this", which can be considered as a suitable indicator for measuring the number of people who interact with the content of the page. On a national ranking, the Facebook account of Liguria maintains a high position and is the sixth out of 20 regions in terms of likes and the fourth in terms of "talking about this".

Facebook posts that engage the most are:

- Sunset, sea and cities' pictures
- Food and wine traditions and recipes
- Events and spectacles.

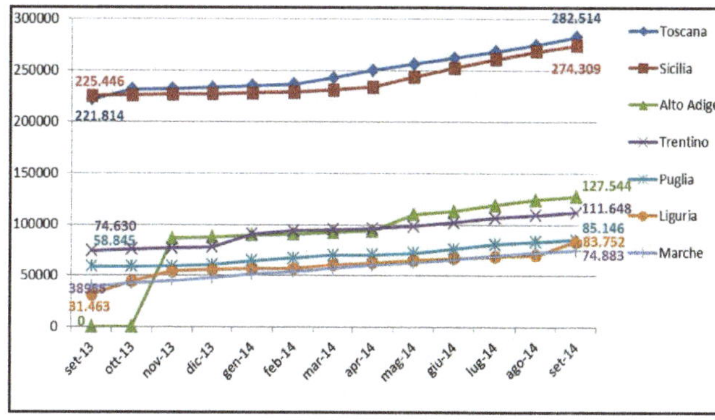

Figure 4. *Facebook like Trend 2013- 2014 – Ranking of Italian Region*

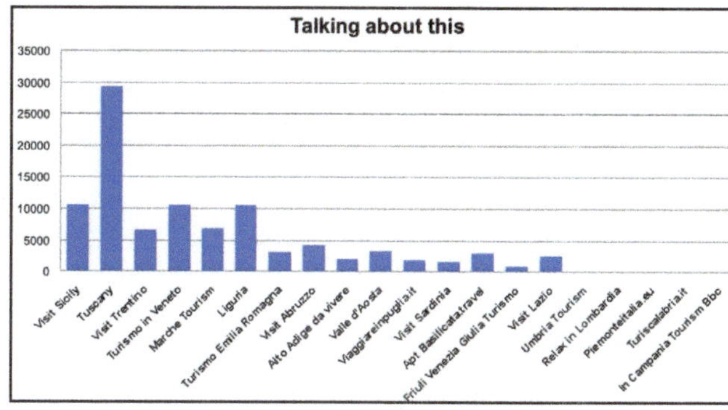

Figure 5. *Talking about this – Ranking of Italian Region 2014*

The following tools and actions are also part of the tourism marketing plan:

- Social media strategy for Twitter
- Digital Diary Liguria, a format of the company Can't Forget Italy consisting in a race with 5/6 videomakers from around the world who lived and filmed for a few days in Liguria and who tell their experience with a short video
- Social media strategy for visual social networks like Instagram and Pinterest
- Video and photo contest for tourists and citizens
- Myliguria140, a platform that creates tourist guides based on Twitter and made of tweets produced by users
- Specific initiatives for trade
- Vacation and campaign planning on online and offline media.

The whole marketing plan had the goal of making the brand "Liguria" able to communicate, engage, excite, stimulate and produce content and values for increasing its ability to attract tourists especially from foreign markets.

4. The Application of the Perceptioning Model

4.1. Positioning and Contextualization of Liguria

Contextualizing Liguria with respect to other destinations and its "prosumers" is crucial for defining a first hypothesis that serves as a guide for design choices for Liguria as a brand.

4.1.1. Target Audience

Based on general online research and observations, it turns out that couples that are between 50 and 60 years old ("Baby boomers") are part of the typical target audience of tourism destinations such as Liguria. They come to Liguria because they are great amateurs of the seaside and because they are interested in sailing activities. They eventually possess a yacht. At least one person of the couple is (still) actively working and often holds a management position, which means that they come from an upper socio-cultural background. The couple can however also be retired. They own at least one real estate, and are thinking about their personal future. They are willing to spend money because they are attracted by exclusive products that provide a permanent service (anticipated needs). They enjoy delicious food and regional dishes from Liguria. Furthermore, they are concerned about security and want to live serenely their passion for traveling. Recreational activities play an important role, as they are looking for moments of tranquility and calmness.

The second type of typical customers are seaside and landscape amateurs that go to Liguria only for doing outdoor activities. Among such tourists are groups of people and individuals, mainly between 25 and 50 years old. They often know each other and have more restricted financial resources than the first target audience. They are concerned with responsible consumption and eco-friendly behavior because they love nature. Therefore, they also do camping or stay in tents during their hiking trips. The contact with nature is thus very important for them, as they enjoy going outdoors for discovering the diverse landscapes of Liguria.

Last but not least, families that love the seaside and mountains are also a target audience of Liguria. The parents of these families are mainly between 30 and 50 years old and have relatively young children. They are actively working and belong to a middle income group. They want to enjoy nice beaches, landscape and food, as they are willing to spend money especially in the gastronomic sector. Maybe they rent a car for discovering the coastal roads, as contact with nature is essential for their journey in Liguria. They enjoy going outdoors for discovering landscapes, but they are also seeking for recreational activities for relaxing during their vacation.

4.1.2. Liguria in the Context of Italy as Tourism Destination

The consumer perceptions of tourism in Liguria and of other Italian tourism destinations are important for seizing the latent opportunities of the sector. In general, it can be observed that Italy is often considered as top-of-mind for food and gastronomy. Italy is surrounded by the Mediterranean, which represents a travel motivation for many tourists. Many Italian regions benefit thus from a strong international reputation as tourism destinations (Toscana, etc.). With regards to Liguria, the geographic proximity to France, which is a leading destination for the demands of the typical customer profiles mentioned above, could create positive synergies in terms of place image. The increase in exports (French port saturation) could also contribute to a rise of importance of Liguria as region.

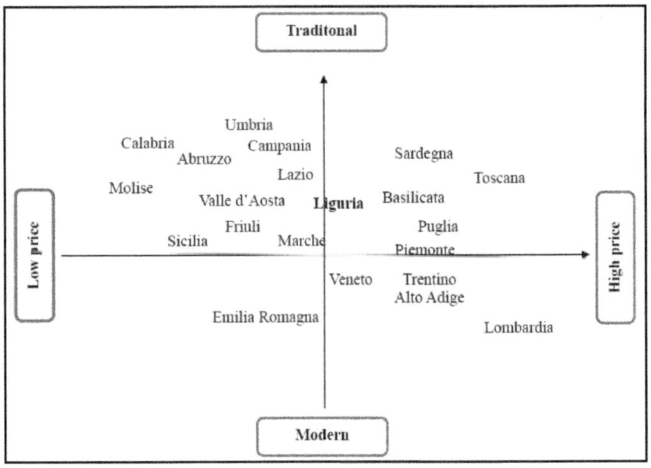

Figure 6. *Perceptional map of Italian tourism destinations*

4.1.3. Megatrend

Respecting current megatrends is essential for developing the brand perception according to the underlying macro-social tendencies. It can be observed that a demand for permanently accessible services is on the rise worldwide. The reputation of a brand or territory becomes more and more global, as globalization processes involve distinct geographic locations within international networks of immaterial and material exchange. In the contemporary world, it is thus important to stay connected. Recently, increases in the importance of recreational activities can be observed in many industrialized countries. Furthermore, there is evidence on a successive democratization of tourism prices and costs of tourism activities (guided tours, etc.). This led to a growth of the demand of activities such as sailing or hiking. The protection of cultural heritage and environment is globally also on the rise, whereas individual well-being, efficient leisure time utilization and personal pleasure and fun are one of the key values that drive customer decisions.

4.1.4. Liguria's Perception as a Brand

Observations and online research give evidence that Liguria is perceived as a tourist destination for families and couples, especially related to seaside tourism but also to sports tourism for trekking lovers, nature and outdoor sports. Thanks to its mild climate, Liguria is attractive in many months of the year both on the Riviera or the cliffs from which it is almost always possible to enjoy the view across the ocean. Liguria is perceived as a relatively expensive destination, with tourism offerings very varied. It can be distinguished between locations of strong international appeal (e.g. Cinque Terre) and some very exclusive locations such as Portofino.

Also Genoa, the capital of the region, welcomes many tourists thanks to its historical and artistic heritage such as the Strade Nuove and the Palazzi dei Rolli which are inscribed in UNESCO's WHL and attractions such as the Aquarium (1.3 million visitors every year) and the museum Galata Museo del Mare, which are of great interest especially for families.

4.2. Breaking Down the Brand into its Basic Elements

For providing a framework for the construction of the brand

perception, the perceptioning approach seeks to break down the brand perception into three basic elements (Fig. 7) by relying on online research, questionnaires (appendix 1) and other information sources such as literature.

The territorial settings of Liguria (steep, plane, steep, with the seaside and the Alps) also define its character and perception: Liguria is maritime, rocky, and full of colors.

It can be claimed to be Mediterranean, but also diverse, given that there are many suburban and urban roads with narrow streets, where traditions, culture and gastronomy are concentrated.

It is colorful because there are villages such as Vernazza, that offer views across the sea and that create a kaleidoscope of colors with picturesque sceneries, unique to walk in and explore by bicycle.

Furthermore, Liguria has a lot of mountains and littoral coastlines, what creates a harmonious alternation of mountains and ocean for a journey full of discoveries, outdoor activities and cultural experiences. The weather in Liguria is also suitable for people looking for only one activity during their holiday (e.g. relaxing, doing seaside activities, getting to know the Italian culture). The offer of the region also meets the demands of those who prefer more varied holidays.

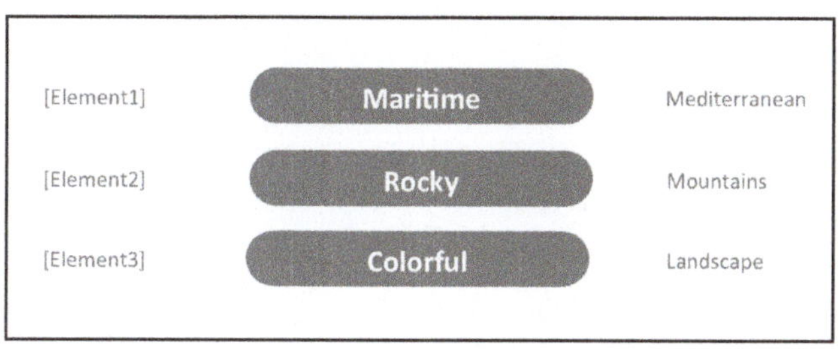

Figure 7. Basic brand elements of the brand "Liguria"

4.3. The Products and Services of the Brand "Liguria"

In this step of the perceptioning approach, the main attributes and design of the products and services of a brand are analyzed (Fig. 8). It turns out that in the case of a territory such as Liguria, many different products and services need to be considered. Liguria is a geographic region, but also a wikibrand, which makes it necessary to consider the ensemble of products and services that constitute the identity of this region. To establish the most adequate perception of the characteristics of the products and services of Liguria, three basic elements of the brand perception need to be considered:

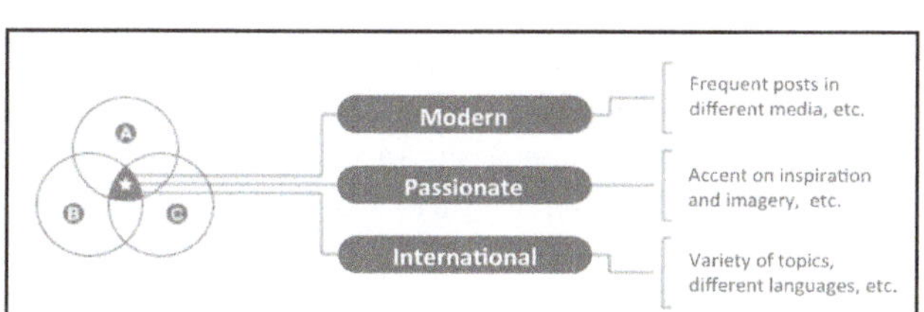

Figure 8. Characteristics of Liguria's products and services

Liguria provides especially cultural products and possesses natural resources (landscape, etc.). The richness of its environmental diversity, constituted by the seaside and the Mediterranean, littoral cliffs, romantic villages and towns, mountains and rocky landscapes can be assumed to be the main aspect differentiating Liguria from other Italian regions.

4.4 The brand communication

Nowadays, Liguria possesses different online and offline communication channels (Fig. 9), which play an essential role in its territorial marketing strategy (chapter 3). Its Facebook, Twitter, Pinterest, Instagram accounts, as well as several websites and blogs on which experiences with the region are shared, create an ensemble of online media representations that promote Liguria as tourism destination. On these platforms, the landscape of Liguria is often represented. Nonetheless, Liguria communicates also offline and via its cultural festivals.

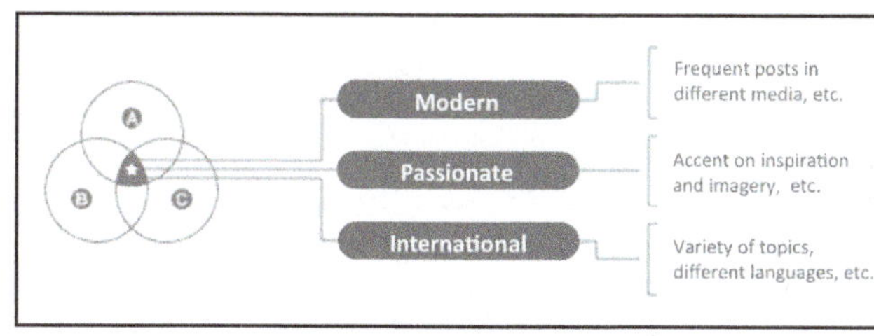

Figure 9. Liguria's communication

4.5. The Identity of the Brand

The logo of the region (Fig. 10) is used by the regional tourism promotion agency for making Liguria a brand (appendix 2).

The blue color reflects the color of the sea, whereas orange is the color of the sun shining for most of the year with temperatures above the average of other regions in northern Italy. The wave recalls the arched shape of the region that is from east to west characterized by the sea.

The logo was designed in 2006 and since then accompanies the entire institutional tourism communication of Liguria.

LIGURIA

Figure 10. Liguria's brand identity

4.6. The Genetic Code of Liguria

The genetic code of a brand aims to summarize the identified characteristics of the brand and is composed of eight different aspects described by attributes.

The representation of Liguria can thus be claimed to be natural, whereas the personality of the region is Mediterranean. The perception of the brand Liguria is beautiful and the brand identity is outdoor-oriented. Its culture is Italian, and its communication is technologically connected. The spirit of its products is eco-friendly, and the basic attributes of Liguria are maritime, rocky, and colorful.

4.7. Using Perceptioning for Wikidestination Branding

In the case of wikidestinations that are constructed collectively by the aims of online networks, further evidence on the pertinence of the results of the perceptioning approach [3] is given by a discourse analysis of these networks. A discourse analysis serves as methodology for studying the languagc uscd for talking or writing about the region of Liguria. This enables to identify how Liguria is perceived and connoted.

For this reason, blog articles on Liguria's community blog "Liguria tells", as well as publications on the Facebook page of Liguria have been analyzed. These two online platforms and their importance for the creation of the wikidestination "Liguria" have been presented in chapter 3.

It is thus referred to five blog entries (appendix 3) written in Italian that were used as sample:

- "Viaggio di una toscana nei caruggi di Genova" (by Valentina Vettori on December 29th 2014)
- "Genova: la città, le sue strade e il Natale" (by Eleonora Caldari on December 12th 2014)
- "I paesi rosa del Levante, Fiascherino e Tellaro" (by Chiara Repetto on November 21st 2014)
- "Omaggi a Chiavari" (by Daniele Pipitone on November 11th 2014)
- "I colori di Liguria-Riviera di Ponente" (by Manuela Della Corte on November 7th 2014)

Furthermore, the contents of the posts on Liguria's Facebook page have been analyzed over several weeks with respect to thematic content, visualizations and used language. The objective of this communication analysis was to identify which basic elements of the region are used to promote Liguria online in terms of C-to-C marketing in online forums.

5. Findings

In the last two years, the wikidestination strategy for Liguria has generated important results:

- Growth of the community of people involved by the brand "Liguria"
- Facebook page: More than 62,000 likes in 24 months
- Twitter: More than 6,000 followers in 24 months
- Blog: 127,000 page views and 45,000 unique visitors in 24 months
- Myliguria140: More than 400 downloaded guides, 1,330 people involved and over 8,000 tweets collected from the platform
- Involvement of tour operators in the tourism marketing strategy
- Concentration on the name of Liguria of all the tourist offer of the region making it a representative brand
- Increase in two positions (from the tenth to the eighth position) in the ranking of most sold by foreign tour operators in Italian regions
- Extension of the wikidestination strategy on the new regional tourism portal which will be online in January 2015
- Increase in international tourist arrivals and journeys
- 2009-2013: +35.6% arrivals, + 24.7% journeys.

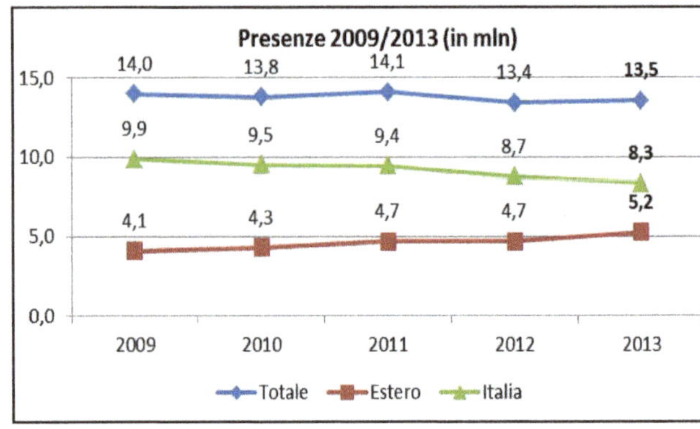

Figure 11. *Tourist arrivals –Trend 2009-2013 Source Istat, Tourism Observatory of Liguria's Region and Studio Giaccardi & Associati*

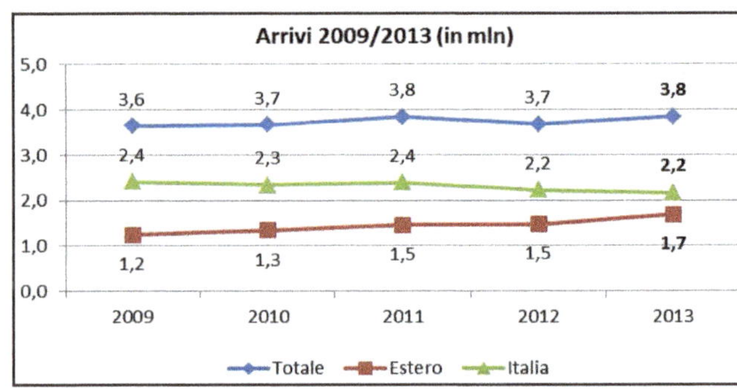

Figure 12. *Tourist day presences – Trend 2009-2013- Source Istat, Tourism Observatory of Liguria's Region and Studio Giaccardi & Associati*

The region of Liguria has thus witnessed a significant increase in meaning as tourism destination in Italy. There is evidence that its marketing strategy, which relies on online networks, shared experiences and C-to-C online marketing, found resonance in the mind of consumers. It was found that the online communication channels of the marketing concept of Liguria represent probably one of the most important ways for promoting and developing the region's identity and reputation. The striking advantage of the wikibrand concept is thereby that consumers develop the brand collectively.

In this paper, it turned out that the perceptioning model proposed by Bassani et al. (2002, 2007, and 2011) [3] provides in this context an efficient tool for crystallizing the basic components of the collective wikibrand "Liguria". It was shown that a discourse analysis of the tools used for creating the wikibrand (blog "Liguria tells" and Facebook posts) can be used for enhancing the overall findings of the perceptioning model based on observations and online research with shared experiences and C-to-C marketing in social networks.

By referring to the blog "Liguria tells", it was verified that especially the landscape and nature, the contrasts of places and towns, as well as the cultural diversity of Liguria are crucial elements for its wikibrand. "Unique", "rare", "beautiful", "colorful", "panoramic", "emotional", "natural", and "tasty" are examples for adjectives that are frequently associated with the region on the blog "Liguria tells".

The perception of the region was relatively coherent also

with other blog entries, whereas only articles by Italian people that currently live in Liguria or that already lived there have been analyzed. It can be assumed that mainly people that have positive associations with Liguria write articles on the blog. It is therefore appropriate to apply the perceptioning model, as this model has the intrinsic idea to focus on positive brand connotations, as only positive attributes are useful for developing a brand. Furthermore, different regions (not only the seaside, but also cities) of Liguria were described in the articles, so geographically representative results can be assumed.

The content of the posts on Facebook that were published over the last weeks give evidence on the same associations:

- Geographical associations (touristic sites and destinations, presentation of places, etc.)
- Natural associations (landscape, cliffs, mountains, seaside, beaches, sunset, plants, etc.)
- Cultural associations (local dishes, gastronomic highlights, cultural festivals, architecture, art, etc.)

The publications on Facebook have in common that they tend to evoke strong colorful contrasts, with an emphasis on tradition and inspiration. The posts are published in different languages (mostly in Italian, but also in English and German), what alludes to the international character as tourism destination. The frequency of the publications of sometimes more than three times per day gives a dynamic impression. The posts are published by private organizations, but comments from tourists and habitants give evidence that these elements are of principal interest for the interaction with the brand.

In general, it turns out that in the case of wikibrands such as Liguria, the shared perceptions of the region on social networks (blog, Facebook, etc.) can either be used as input for the perceptioning approach or for enhancing an already proposed perceptioning model that is based on general observations and other information sources outside from C-to-C marketing in social media. In terms of input for the perceptioning model, the perceptioning approach can serve for crystallizing the most essential features for the wikibrand "Liguria" that are mentioned in social networks. Especially in the case of wikidestinations that are created by the aims of shared experiences, C-to-C online marketing and viral marketing, perceptioning provides a helpful tool for focusing on the main elements through which a brand can be developed further. On the other side, evidence was found that an already proposed perceptioning model based on observations and online research can be further enhanced by referring to a discourse analysis of the main networks that constitute the wikibrand "Liguria": Its blog and its Facebook page. Especially the analysis of the used language in these networks serves to back-up and reinforce the proposed perceptioning model [3] in chapter 4.

All in all, there is thus evidence that in the case of wikibrands, virtually shared experiences, viral marketing and C-to-C marketing in social networks can be used for making the perceptioning approach even more empirically representative. Nevertheless, it also turned out that when applying the perceptioning model on a territory, the steps 3 and 4 of the analysis (functional product characteristics and design) need to synthetize and regroup the attributes of a variety of different products and services with different designs and characteristics, as they all belong to the wikibrand "Liguria".

6. Conclusions

The perceptioning model [3] can be used for analyzing and developing the perception of a territory as a brand. The example of Liguria shows that the perception of the region plays a key role in terms of word-of-mouth influence, shared experiences, C-to-C online marketing and viral marketing that incite consumer-tourists to spend a journey there. In this context, this paper has shown that the perceptioning model aims to develop the identity of a territory especially when considering these marketing concepts. There is evidence that especially communication and marketing strategies for creating wikibeands via social media can provide suitable input for the perceptioning model and serve to back-up its different analyses. On the other side, a perceptioning approach for wikibrands initially based on observations and online research can be enhanced with discourse analysis of social media.

Nowadays, it is important to evoke that a territory can be considered as a brand that needs to be promoted for remaining competitive in an increasingly challenging tourism market. The number of tourism destinations is globally on the rise, as many countries are more and more developed in terms of infrastructure. The global market for tourism becomes therefore increasingly competitive and can be compared with other conventional product markets that also underlie the need for remaining competitive in a globalized economy.

In the end, the contribution of the destination image is strategic for the tourism sector, and can bear significant potential for job creation, particularly in times of economic crisis. A strong territorial brand can therefore contribute to the beneficial development of a geographic region.

Acknowledgements

The authors would like to thank Giuseppe Giaccardi, CEO Studio Giaccardi & Associati – Consulenti di Direzione (www.giaccardiassociati.it) for his cooperation, Saverio Sbalchiero, Design & Marketing Strategist from Sbalchiero & Partners (www.sbalchieropartners.com), Vicenza, Italy for graphic illustration and tow anonymous reviewers provided valuable feedback and comments.

Appendix

Appendix 1: The Liguria from your Point of View

The questionnaire is part of a tourism development project of Liguria. This project aims to give voice first of all to young citizens. In order to participate you must be aged between 18 and 65 years old and live or have lived in Liguria, enough to handle it say what are your favorite places.

If I say "Liguria" what is the first thing you think of?

What are the three adjectives that you think best describe the region of Liguria?

Tell us three things that only a real inhabitant of Liguria knows (habits, places, and ways of saying ...)

Three colors to describe Liguria?

Where are the most characteristic views of Liguria?

Appendix 2: How to Create a Logo?

What is the history of this logo?

What were the previous logos?

Why today there are two logos? (Liguria region and tourism in Liguria)

What is the purpose of this logo compared with the other?

Regarding the visual of the logo:

- Why these colors (blue, orange, black (shadow of the wave)?
- Why the wave?
- Why the shadow?

Appendix 3: Results of the Discourse Analysis on the Blog "Liguria Tells"

Viaggio di una toscana nei caruggi di Genova (by Valentina Vettori on December 29th 2014)

Online via:

http://www.laliguriaracconta.it/2014/12/29/viaggio-di-una-toscana-nei-caruggi-di-genova/ on January 17th 2015

Main connotations: Reserved and decadent soul ("animo reservato e decadente"), magnificence of its ancient splendor ("magnificenza del suo antico splendore"), rare beauty ("rara belleza"), mysterious and full of contrasts ("mistero e contrasti"), world heritage of the UNESCO ("patrimonio dellumanità Unesco"), Kaleidoscope of shops ("caleidoscopio di negozi"), otherwise unobtainable ("altrimenti introvabili"), Genova is a city to be savored from below upwards ("Genova e una città da assaporare dal basso verso l'alto"), atmosphere of rare individuality ("un'atmosfera di rara unicità"), distant elements that come together in a unique reality ("Elementi distanti che si fondono in un'unica realtà"), gracious ("graziosa"), unattended ("inaspettata"), easy-going atmosphere ("l'atmosfera si fa chiassosa e allegra"), taste the diverse types of Focaccia that the culinarian tradition of Liguria offers ("assaporare i diversi tipi di focaccia che la tradizione culinaria ligure offre"), marvelous opposite ("meravigliatevi difronte"), shopping for all tastes ("negozi per tutti il gusti"), distinct smell ("odore inebriante"), large and luminous ("larga e luminosa"), and again another surprise ("a noi di nuovo sorpresa"), proving that art and beauty are all at your fingerprints, just look up ("A riprova che larte e la bellezza sono a portata di tutti, basta alzare lo sguardo"), hidden beauty ("bellezze più nascote")

Genova: la città, le sue strade e il Natale (by Eleonora Caldari on December 12th 2014)

Online via:

http://www.laliguriaracconta.it/2014/12/12/genova-la-citta-le-sue-strade-e-il-natale/ on January 17th 2015

Main connotations: I adore my city ("adoro la mia città"), contradictions ("contraddizioni"), Genova has many faces, many places and many different angles ("Genova ha tante facce, tanti luoghi e tanti angoli"), particularly lively ("particolarmente vivace"), makes me feel part of a big whole ("mi fanno sentire parte di un tutto più grande"), enthusiastic people ("raggazi entusiasti")

I paesi rosa del Levante, Fiascherino e Tellaro (by Chiara Repetto on November 21th 2014)

Online via:

http://www.laliguriaracconta.it/2014/11/21/i-paesi-rosa-del-levante-fiascherino-e-tellaro/ on January 17th 2015

Main connotations: Beautiful things remain often hidden in Liguria ("Le cose belle si tengono, si tengono strette, si tengono care, e in Liguria, troppo spesso, si tengono nascoste"), the golf of poetry, where the ancient remains of early paradise have been found ("golfo dei poeti, dove sono state rinvenute antichissime trace del paradiso terrestre"), absolute beauty ("bellezza assoluta"), most beautiful coast of the whole Mediterranean ("costa più bella di tutto il Mediterraneo"), seems like a wild paradise island ("Sembra un'isola selvaggia, il paradiso"), brilliant green of the Mediterranean pines ("verde brillante dei pini marittimi"), the blue sea, the smell of salt air, and the language of white sand ("il turchese del mare e gli scogli, il profumo della salsedine, la lingua di sabbia bianchissima"), chic establishments ("stabilimenti più chic"), panoramic road ("strada panoramica"), grace and simplicity, sophistication and mystery, seduction ("Grazia e semplicità, raffinatezza e mistero, seduzione"), elegance ("eleganza"), silence of noon ("silenza del mezzogiorno"), unique emotion ("emozione unica"), you wouldn't want to go away ("Non vorresti andare mai via"),

Ommagio a Chiavari (by Daniele Pipitone on November 11th 2014)

Online via:

http://www.laliguriaracconta.it/2014/11/11/omaggio-a-chiavari/ on January 17th 2015

Main connotations: Liguria is a little bit my land of adoption, a part of my family ("La Liguria è un po'una mia terra di adozione: parte della mia famiglia"), it is really unique ("è veramente unica"), painted with the green of the nature, the red and orange color of the houses, and the intensive blue color of the ocean ("dipinta con il verde della natura, i colori rossi e aranciati delle case, il blu intenso del mare"), Genova, a somewhat chaotic city ("Genova, città un po' caotica"), unmistakeable views ("inconfondibile affaccio"), Chiavari allows to breath fresh air and refresh your mind from a week full of work ("Chiavari permette di respirare un'aria più pulita e rinfrescare la mente dai pensieri della settimana lavorativa"), can offer so much more than swimming ("può offrire tanto oltre alla balneazione"), an example for Ligurian baroque architecture rich of golden decoration ("esempio di archittetura barocca ligure ricca di decorazioni dorate"), nice balcony over the ocean ("bella terrazza sul mare"), rich of different plants, ponds and monumental greenhouses ("ricco di piante diverse e laghetti, serre monumentali"), a little angle of paradise ("un piccolo angolo di paradiso"), beautiful sunsets ("bellissime tramonti")

I colori di Liguria-Riviera di Ponente (by Manuela Della Corte on November 7th 2014)

Online via:

http://www.laliguriaracconta.it/2014/11/07/i-colori-di-liguria-riviera-di-ponente/ on January 17th 2015

Main connotations: The Kaleidoscope of houses, the pastel shades of the churches, and the green of the hills ("caleidoscopio delle case, le tinte acquerellate delle chiese, il verde delle coline"), breathe the art and history of this landstripe ("respire l'arte e la storia di questa striscia di terra"), people that have the ocean in front of them, but never loose contact to the hinterland ("gente che ha tutto il mare devanti, ma che da siempre si aggrappa con amore e con forza al suo entroterra"), rigor of medieval villages ("il rigore medievale dei borghi"), each village is a natural art gallery ("Ogni borgo à una pinacoteca naturale"), the villages are always classical and have a sweet made of little things ("riportano indietro nel tempo con una dolcezza fatta di piccolo cose"), Liguria is a land with no plains, in which mountains plunge into the ocean ("La Liguria è una terra senza pianure, in cui i monti si gettano nel mare").

References

[1] J. Gayet, Place Marketing Trend 2014, Corps et Ame Editions, 2015.

[2] G. Lewi, E-branding: Stratégies de marque sur Internet, Pearson Education France, 2013.

[3] M. Bassani, S. Sbalchiero, K. Ben Youssef and S. Magne, Brand Design: construire la personnalité d'une marque gagnante, éditions De Boeck, 2011.

[4] J. R. Gold and S. V. Ward, Place promotion: the use of publicity and marketing to sell towns and regions. John Wiley & Sons Ltd, 1994.

[5] P. Kotler, D. Haider and I. Rein, Marketing Places: Attracting investment, industry and tourism to cities, states and nations, New York: The Free Press, 1993.

[6] S.V. Ward, Selling places: the marketing and promotion of towns and cities, Vol. 23, 1998, pp. 1850-2000.

[7] G. J. Ashworth and H. Voogd, Selling the city: marketing approaches in public sector urban planning, Belhaven Press, 1990.

[8] S. Anholt, "Competitive identity: the new brand management for nations, cities and regions" in Journal of Brand Management, 14(6), 2007, pp. 474-5.

[9] M. Kavaratzis, "Place Branding: A Review of Trends and Conceptual Models" in The Marketing Review, Volume 5, Number 4, 2005, pp. 329-342.

[10] M. Kavaratzis "City Marketing: the past, the present, and some unresolved issues" in Geography Compass, Vol.1, No.3, 2007, pp.695-712.

[11] A. Lucarelli, and P.O. "City branding: a state-of-the-art review of the research domain" in Journal of place management and development, 4(1), 2011, pp. 9-27.

[12] G. Hankinson, "Place Branding Theory: A Cross-domain Literature Review from a Marketing Perspective", in G. J. Ashworth and M. Kavaratzis (eds) Towards Effective Place Brand Management: Branding European Cities and Regions, 2010, pp. 15–35. Cheltenham, UK and Northampton, MA: Edward Elgar.

[13] S. Hanna and J. Rowley, "Towards a strategic place brand-management model" in Journal of Marketing Management, 27(5-6), 2011, pp. 458-476.

[14] L.A. Cai,. "Cooperative branding for rural destinations" in Annals of tourism research 29, no. 3, 2002, pp.720-742.

[15] E. Laws, Tourism marketing: service and quality management perspectives, Stanley Thornes (Publishers) Ltd., 1991.

[16] B. Baker, Destination branding for small cities: The essentials for successful place branding. Destination Branding Book, 2007

[17] E. Valdani and F. Ancarani., Strategie di marketing del territorio, Milamo: Egea, 2000.

[18] E. Candelo, Destination Branding, Torino: Giappichelli, 2009.

[19] C. Pasquinelli, "The limits of place branding for local development: the case of tuscany and the arnovalley brand" in Local Economy, 25, no. 7, 2010, pp.558-572.

[20] V. Calzati, E. Lorenzini and P. Giudici, "Territorial brands for tourism development: a statystical analysis on the Marche Region" in Annals of Tourism Research, 38(2), 2011, pp. 540-560.

[21] M. Giovanardi, "Producing and consuming the painter Raphael's birthplace" in Journal of Place Management and Development, 4(1), 2011, pp. 53-66.

[22] A. Kalandides "The problem with spatial identity: revisiting the "sense of place""in Journal of Place Management and Development, 4(1), 2011, pp. 28-39.

[23] A. Kalandides "Place Branding and Place Identity. An integrated approach" in Tafter Journal, 2012.

[24] S. Anholt "Place branding: Is it marketing, or isn't it?." Place Branding and Public Diplomacy 4, no. 1, 2008, pp. 1-6.

[25] S. Moffitt and M. Dover, Wikibrands: reinventing your company in a customer-driven marketplace, McGraw-Hill, 2011.

[26] Google (2013), The 2013 Traveler, disponibile a http://www.google.com/think/research-studies/2013-traveler.html

[27] R.K. Yin, Case study research: Design and methods, London: Sage, 2014.

[28] R. K. Yin, Applications of case study research, London: Sage, 2011.

14

Culinary tourism: Made in Italy food and real estate finance for the creation of a culinary theme park

Carlo Felice Maggi[1], **Michela Avataneo**[2]

[1]Dept. of Management, University of Turin, Turin, Italy
[2]Graduate in "Economia e Direzione Delle Imprese", University of Turin, Turin, Italy

Email address:
Carlofelice.maggi@unito.it (C. F. Maggi), michela.avataneo@gmail.com (M. Avataneo)

Abstract: There are numerous studies and research on tourism as well as specifically on culinary tourism, all aimed at understanding their characteristics and how to develop them into a source of growth for the country. The special features of the new culinary theme park (F.I.C.O.) render it innovative. It is not only a project that has never been seen before, but one that was able to profit by the many competitive advantages offered by the country, such as general tourism, Made in Italy food, and the driving force of a prosperous agribusiness sector. Managed by Eataly, a globally established enterprise, F.I.C.O., aims to become the largest centre in the world for the celebration of Italian agribusiness. Innovation is even found in the way that the project is organised and how it obtains its necessary funds, which are collected through a Real Estate Finance project. Its attractiveness is lastly tested through a random sample of interviews that allowed for feedback by the use of a statistical method, a practical and concrete result of a previous general analysis as well as a statistical summary of the typical behaviour of consumers and travellers.

Keywords: Tourism, Culinary, Real Estate Finance, Attractiveness and Competitiveness

1. Introduction

A topic of discussion and revolution, the tourism market is constantly growing.

Partly because of the change in the distribution of income and the increase in leisure time, in many countries tourism has become one of the most important sectors, as well as a driving force for growth.

According to the World Travel and Tourism Council [1], the total contribution of tourism to the Italian economy in 2013 amounted to €159.6 billion, the equivalent of 10.3% of the GDP., A slight decrease has been recorded compared to 2012 (-1.6%), but the forecasts for 2014 indicate continued growth, with an increase of 2.1%, bringing the sector's economic value to €163 billion.

The main factors that differentiate one destination from another one are its attractiveness and competitiveness. There are several factors that make a country more or less competitive than others when it comes to tourism. These main factors are mainly seen as price, strategy, history and culture and services [2]. The great competitive advantage of Italy, considered one of the most popular tourist destinations in the world, is its ability to bring history and culture together, offering what one would consider to be a "real" vacation thanks to its immense historical and artistic heritage and some of the most beautiful coastal and mountain regions in Europe.

The National Observatory on Italian tourism performs a statistical analysis on tourism in Italy on an annual basis, and in analysing the best-selling products, highlights the "Cities of Art" and the "beach tourism" as products with the biggest appeal both on the international and Italian markets. Following are lakes, mountains and archaeological sites, and coming in closely in sixth and seventh place are culinary tourism (11% Italy, 13% internationally) and business tourism (9% Italy, 10% internationally) [3].

Based on these analyses, Italian tourism policies seek to focus on the latter two aspects, considering that the previous positions were occupied by pre-existing destinations in the country, due to simple historical and geomorphological facts.

By using F.I.C.O. as a case study, this paper demonstrates how Italy's competitive advantages can be used as it offers innovative features as well as the diversity in its management and implementation compared to other projects.

In the following section, literary references on the topic will be discussed, in particular those regarding the country's attraction and competitiveness, followed by the method and approach used in this specific analysis.

The paper concludes with an analysis of the case and the related relevant factors in order to confirm the conclusion that it represents a competitive advantage.

2. Literature

2.1. The Attractiveness and Competitiveness of Tourist Destinations

Starting from a more general point of view, on a European level, many researchers have tried to show the continent's strengths and weaknesses in order to make it one of the most desired destinations in the world. One of the most interesting articles shows that the qualitative governance of the location increases the competitiveness of the country; "governance" means the policies, strategies employed and the selection of human resources [4]. Many researchers have tried to not only identify the most popular destinations, but also determine why they were considered such. In order to do this, we must first consider the reasons for the visit, because, depending on the needs of the traveller, several factors can influence this choice. For example, if the reason for travel is for summer holidays, statistical comparisons have been made on various regions in southern Italy [5].

In principle, it is definitely important to understand which factors generally affect the choice. These factors include the services and the site features compared with the wishes of trip, the ability of the location to meet the needs of travellers and the influence of the comments from people who have already been there [6].

These studies and many more are carried out on this topic, as tourism offers a wide range of benefits.

The most visible is that of the employment created by accommodations, restaurants, businesses and transport. A second advantage relates to support industries and professions, and the third is the multiplier effect, such as tourist money that is recycled through the local economy. The fourth advantage is at the state and local level, derived from multiple taxes on tourism. Last but not least is an additional benefit: tourism stimulates the exports of local products. The estimate of tourist expenditures on gifts, clothes and souvenirs ranges from 15 to 20% of the total [7].

To summarize and provide a complete picture, we must also point out the other side of the coin: while on one hand, tourism is an opportunity for progress based on the enhancement of the environment as a condition for new opportunities, innovation, better quality of work and an adjustment of competitiveness and quality of enterprises; on the other hand it has also been -and still is - an excuse to pave over the coastlines, hills, and delicate and fragile areas in order to privatize the beaches, ransack internal areas and apply excessive pressure on special and delicate places [8].

2.2. The Tradition of Italian Food, a Special Made in Italy Product

The widespread use of our country's culinary traditions abroad, and especially the global fame of certain products have paved the way for Italian culinary tourism. This is why public interest is very high, particularly in literature..

This specific type of tourism has grown over the years, becoming specialised and known for its dynamic nature and great potential. Italy welcomes at least 30 million Italian tourists and 20 million foreigners [9]. There are multiple definitions, considering the countless material available, but one of the most representative comes from Ignatov and Smith [10]: culinary tourism is a "trip during which the purchase or consumption of regional food (including beverage), or the observation and study of food production (from agriculture to cooking school), represents a significant motivation or activity".

Culinary art is considered an essential part of a trip to Italy, and it can be not only a reason to select a tourist destination but also a factor that can attract foreigners, somewhat like a famous monument [11]. A study on the economic impact of tourism performed by Unioncamere and Isnart in 2013 [12] reveals that about one third of the money spent during holidays in Italy by Italian and foreign tourists is on Made in Italy food.

For these and other reasons, such as the great capillarity of culinary art, as seen by a large number of agricultural companies and top internationally known brands[13], or the natural compliance with the environment, there are a large number of events, festivals and fairs in Italy to promote culinary arts (from Vinitaly, Cantineaperte Cibus, Cheese and BITEG to Eurochocolate) [14]. Just consider that the theme of Expo 2015, which will be held in Milan, is "feeding the world" [15] and will be therefore celebrating Made in Italy food.

Events can be an important tool for local marketing [16], and they can be particularly relevant to promote different areas [17].

Underlying this is the fact that tourism is funded by public bodies, as there are agencies established to deal with the various sectors and services needed [18]. The most innovative financial instrument was found in project financing [19], the "financing of a particular economic unit in which the lenders consider, from the beginning, the cash flow and earnings of the economic unit as the source of funds which will allow the repayment of the loan and the activities of the economic unit as collateral of the loan"[20].

3. Research Methodology

This study reports on an innovative case of relaunching tourism in terms of attractiveness and competitiveness, with the additional use of an unusual method for managing assets and raising funds. In order to understand how this case differs from others adopted.

The case was first assessed, starting from an analysis of

literature to both see if there were other similar cases and determine what the public opinion was regarding the project considered herein. This was made possible by a study based on theoretical knowledge on every part, in order to understand what we were talking about and have a clear idea about the factors that characterized and differentiated the analysis.

In detail, it has been essential to contact and cooperate with the companies involved in the project, Eataly and Prelios SGR, which are behind the implementation of a new idea of culinary tourism.

Lastly, all of the information found with differing and varied sources has been concretised by the application of an online survey submitted to a random sample. Data collected has then been analysed specifically through the application of measures and statistical methods with the aim of having explanations and feedback on the project, as well as to understand what kind of effect and impact it will have on the Italian and international population.

4. Prelios and Eataly, a Real Estate Fund for the Creation of an Idea for Italian Tourism: A Culinary Theme Park

4.1. The Birth of the Idea for F.I.CO.

On the basis of these premises, it is natural to see , a great potential for economic recovery as well as Italy's image in tourism and perhaps especially in wine tourism.

In 2013, an innovative and revolutionary idea came about in order to exploit these intrinsic benefits and stimulate regrowth.

When the CAAB, Centro Agro Alimentare di Bologna, realized that the area of the fruit and vegetable market (that it owns and manages) was oversized compared to its actual use - and therefore under-valued, it looked for an alternative in order to use it more efficiently.

The CAAB is a commercial logistics platform, and centre of advanced services dedicated to the Food & Beverages sector. It steams from the Middle Ages, with the aim of promoting the wholesale trade of food products and related logistics services. Being one of the most significant landmarks in the food industry both at national and European level [21], as well as being located in the city of Emilia Romagna, which stands as the region of excellence under the specific point of view for food and wine production, the CAAB planned to combine the great potential of a tourist attraction associated with Italy with the concept of Made in Italy food, in order to create a double competitive advantage.

Thus was born the idea for F.I.C.O., the Fabbrica Italiana Contadina, the largest culinary park in the world. F.I.C.O aims to become the largest centre in the world for the absolute celebration of Italian food as well as a landmark for its museum, tastings, educational purposes and "food shopping" for a wide audience, both national and international. The name, Fabbrica Italiana Contadina, looks to recall several meanings that were specifically chosen because they are all in the expression of the new culinary theme park.

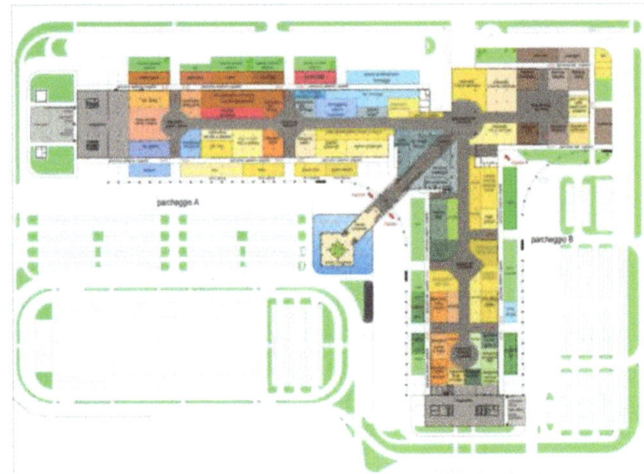

Figure 1. F.I.CO. – Eataly World Floor Plan. Source: CAAB.

Together with the City of Bologna, the CAAB has clearly identified not only the great potential of two sectors like tourism and Italian food and wine, but it also knew how to determine the right brand to be used in this project, one that is well known globally and represents excellence in these sectors: Eataly.

Thus, the agreement with Oscar Farinetti came to be, and the management of the culinary theme park was given to Eataly. The park was then called F.I.CO. - Eataly World.

4.2. F.I.CO. - Eataly World: A Sustainable Project

The project involves an area of 80,000 square metres where 50,000 are allocated to Eataly's core business with 8 assigned zones divided into different areas, while the remaining 30,000 are intended for support functions.

In order to give a further boost to advertising as well as for obvious energy efficiency reasons, a much-discussed topic, the project was designed to be "sustainable" and "green".

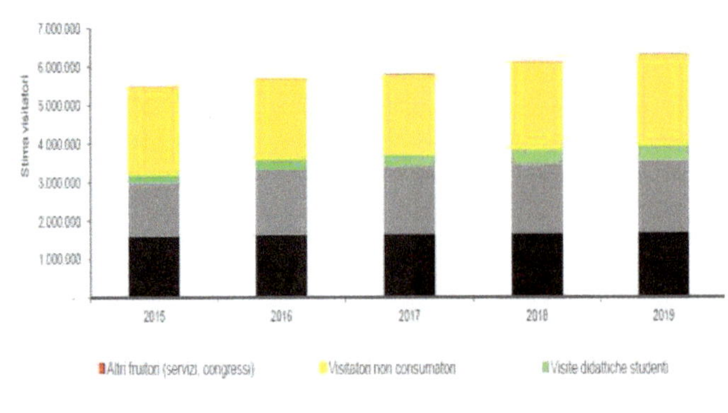

Figure 2. Estimate of visitors expected. Source: CAAB.

CAAB has the largest photovoltaic plant in Europe on the building [22], which will provide –all of the energy needed for the entire park in-house, and the panels themselves will power the last mile logistics. Other initiatives are in progress, including the recovery of rainwater washing the entire system, including the solar panels, and the last minute market.

The investment is quite significant both in terms of numbers and the country's image. Data collected by companies tasked estimate that there will be 6 million visitors a year [23] for the first 12 months and an increase of 5 percent for the following years.

4.3. F.I.CO. - Eataly World: A Real Estate Finance Project

The F.I.CO. project is innovative from many perspectives, as well as from its financial and legal structuring. The project's participants have identified the Real Estate Investment Fund of a closed type reserved for qualified operators to be the most suitable instrument for the park's creation. There are various reasons that led to this choice, including the number of investors, its low risk, favourable tax treatment, an external and private company that manages the fund, the supervision of the Banca d'Italia and - in regulatory rigour - lean operating procedures. The public private partnership is a virtuous example of cooperation between heterogeneous entities with one common goal: to create value with tourism. The CAAB and the City are public entities, Eataly is a private company, and the Investment Management Company (SGR in Italian) for the development of the PAI Real Estate Fund is also private.

SGR (Prelios Sgr, a leading company in Italy in the field of asset management [23]) has been selected by a public tender, on the basis on the fund's regulations as decided upon previously and put to tender. The Real Estate Fund had to be reserved and provide an amount between 95 million euro (minimum amount to be reached within the first subscription period) and 400 million (maximum value).

The initial funds are made up of 55% of the value of the property transferred by CAAB, whereas the remaining 45% will be collected through the subscription of shares. The nominal value of the shares was set at 250 thousand euro, and the fund is particularly long, with a duration of 40 years. The minimum initial investment was set at 1 million euro, i.e. at least four shares, with a lock-up period of three years. This was added in order to support F.I.C.O.'s start-up phase, after which the shares may be transferred in any capacity, as long as it is to qualified investors.

4.4. The PAI Fund

Once the PAI Fund was established, SGR identified the initial investors in order to raise the 40 million, needed to start the initial works. The fund's participants include relevant national investors, including leading financial institutions and operative institutions in the sector as well as major social security institutions.

A group of international investors in "*The Link Real Estate Investment Trust*", the top real estate fund in Hong-Kong, the largest in Asia and the fourth in the world in terms of market capitalisation, has already visited Bologna. They came specifically from Hong Kong due to their interest in the FICO project.

Construction will begin shortly, which is scheduled to conclude at the end of next year.

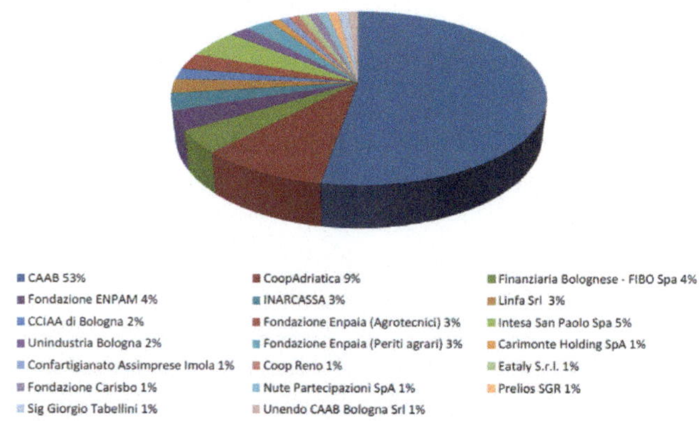

Figure 3. *Percentage of fund per investor. Source: Prelios SGR*

4.5. The Culinary Theme Park: Statistical Analyses

In order to understand if the project would be successful both in terms of interest from the Italian population and a potential boost to Italian tourism revolution and the Italian image abroad, a questionnaire was compiled by a significant sample group comprised of 170 individuals.

The questions were divided into three sections: Eataly, FICO and touristic habits and general information.

The results are interesting both from a general point of view, such as the knowledge of the brand and the project, and from a statistical point of view, as if millions of visitors were predicted, it is important to check on an average sample an "upstream" feedback.

The 19 questions were asked by means of an online questionnaire entitled World Eataly. The interviewees varied in age, gender and education, and are from different parts of Italy (mainly Piedmont). The tests revealed interesting results.

First and foremost, 95% of all interviewees know of Eataly, but almost the same percentage (94%) do not know about the FICO - Eataly World project.

The companies involved have highly accelerated the processes of organisation, considering that the idea was created at the end of 2013 and will be completed at the end of 2015; this is done in order to take full advantage of Expo 2015, considering its thematic and motivational relevance.

In the first section, it is immediately evident how CAAB has been able to identify the most suitable company to manage the park. Effectively, Eataly is known worldwide and well integrated in Italy. Considering the questions about the frequency of purchases at Eataly and the values they represent, it is clear that the consumer mentality and behaviour is changing. New consumers are much more susceptible to the specific values of Eataly and Slow Food, which include sustainability, organic, environmental protection, showing that "food shopping" is no longer a consequence of the need to eat, but rather choice of which kinds of food eat and where to buy it.

The results and final considerations of the first part are

also found in the second, but with another point of view. The answers show that the frequency of visiting an Eataly shop is very high, and 97% of those interviewed showed a keen interest in visiting a culinary theme park.

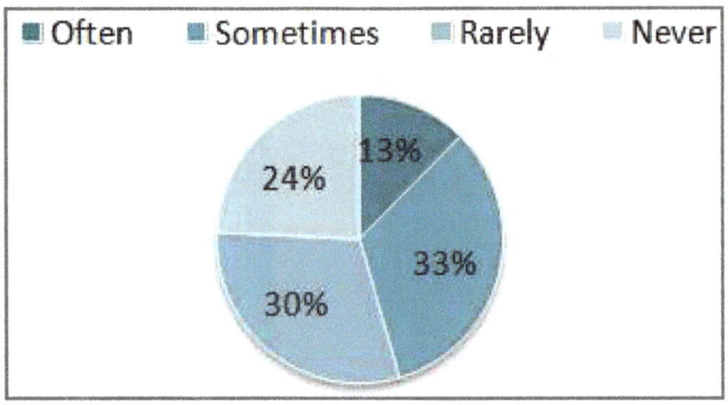

Figure 4. *Answers to the question: "Have you visited an Eataly shop in 2014?" Source: questionnaire.*

The main positive feedback is that, when answering the question "Please indicate the level of agreement or disagreement with these reasons to visit FICO - Eataly World: I would like to visit a significant Italian tourist destination, I believe a person must visit a culinary theme park for Italian food, I would like to know more about what I eat, I would like to go to a grocery store, I would like to support this project because it promotes sustainability, I might go but the park will be too far away." The higher percentage of agreement is obtained by the answer about the desire to have knowledge of what we eat and how it is produced. Consumer behaviour has changed and created the possibility to take advantage of a new opportunity, which Eataly was able to provide with its values. The reasons that follow in the percentage ranking are intrinsically linked to the considerations made thus far: I would like to visit a significant Italian tourist destination and I would like to support this project because it promotes sustainability.

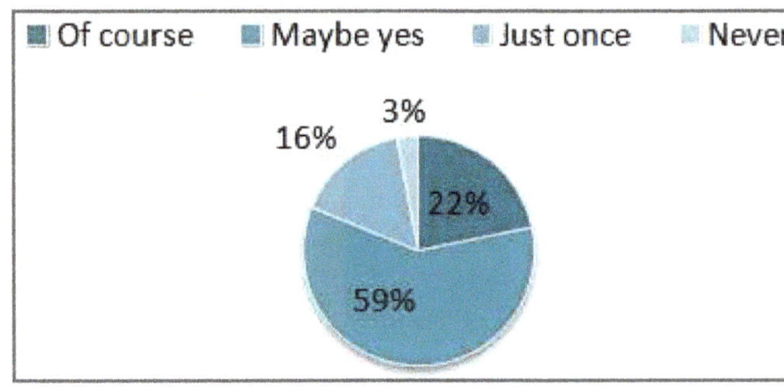

Figure 5. *Answers to the question: "Would you be interested in visiting a theme park for the celebration of Italian agribusiness that is linked with Eataly's values?" Source: questionnaire*

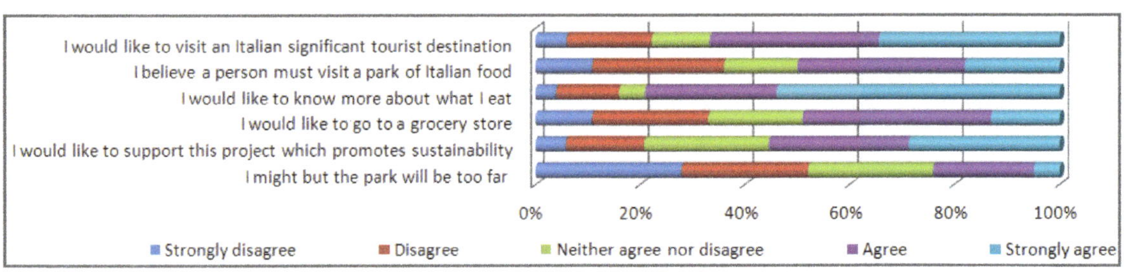

Figure 6. *Answers to the question about reasons to visit. Source: questionnaire.*

Table 1. *Differences between the average and answers to the questions "Please indicate the level of influence that these values have when making a purchase at Eataly" and that regarding the reasons to visit. Source: auto-processing.*

	I would like to visit an Italian significant tourist destination	**I believe a person must visit a Park of Italian food**	**I would like to know more about what I eat**	**I would like to go to a grocery shop**	**I would like to support this project which promotes sustainability**	**I might but the park will be too far**	
Environmental defense	2,69	-1,14	-1,25	-4,82	3,54	0,98	96
Sustainability	-4,51	0,95	3,18	-1,17	0	1,55	78
Respect	-0,61	-0,05	-3,16	2,88	1,74	-0,8	121
Generosity	-0,33	2,69	0,53	1,21	-4,12	0,02	63
Altruism	0,9	-0,99	-0,34	-0,95	0,73	0,65	43
Loyalty	1,27	-0,34	0,59	-1,23	1,16	-1,45	46
Honesty	0,28	-0,17	-0,18	-0,26	2,81	-2,48	79
Ethics	-1,18	1,22	-0,9	-0,16	0,13	0,89	67
Responsibility	0,59	-3,10	1,97	0,01	-0,73	1,26	87
Justice	0,25	-0,55	0,81	1,03	-1,5	-0,04	65
Curiosity	0,65	1,48	-1,25	3,46	-3,76	-0,58	82
	175	96	295	76	159	26	827

In order to come to a conclusion and make the questionnaire more sizable, the answers were cross-checked in order to find any connection of influence among them. It is for this reason that statistical models were used, especially the chi-square test.

In this case, the test results are also perfectly consistent with the general trend of the study and analysis.

Three cases were examined.

Firstly, a connection between Eataly's current customers and those who are interested in visiting the future culinary park was revealed by calculating the chi-square and the rejection of the null hypothesis. The result may seem obvious, but, on the contrary, it highlights how Eataly promotes values that have become such a large part of the population's mentality such as influence not only purchasing decisions but also behaviour.

The second case provided a slightly less significant result, namely a non-connection between the desire to visit FICO - Eataly World and some general characteristics, such as age, marital status and level of education.

In this case, however, both the chi-square test and two other variables have been applied, namely the quadratic coefficient of contingency and the basic coefficient of contingency. These variables are used to calculate the intensity of a potential possible connection.

Even though the dependence hypothesis has been rejected, the variables do not equal zero simply because a strong enough connection does not exist in order to make the chi-square value immune to any kind of error margin. So even though the chi-square test measures a non-connection, there would be some links between the two answers. For example, logically, the older a person is, the less likely he or she is to visit. The same result occurs with other personal information.

Finally, the more complicated case is reported, which is the study of interdependence between the values that best represent the interviewee and the reasons why people will visit that culinary park. The calculation was complicated because the sample group had to give numerical preferences to both questions, so the final number of answers was high. Considering that there were a total of 827 units, it was not possible to apply the chi-square test, because the result would vary significantly from that actual, affected by a much bigger number of interviewees than the actual sample group.

The peculiarity shown by the application of statistical models is the existence of coherence in the people's way of thinking. By going in order, it is possible to see that every reason to visit is mirrored by a value that consistent with it:

- "I would like to visit a significant Italian tourist destination" is the main reason for those who care about the environment, potentially in a perspective of those who love the environment and therefore also tourism. Conversely, ethical people are those who are less likely to support this reason to visit because they do not trust in the park's sustainability and do not believe it will create advantages for the country.
- "I believe that it is essential to visit a culinary park for Italian food" is instead created mainly by curiosity, ethics and generosity. Obviously,

if everybody is going to visit, curiosity will increase. Responsibility is the maximum negative value, whereas the reason to visit is neither rational nor logical.

- "I would like to know more about what I eat" has very specific feedback because it shows that this is not due to a so-called superficial point of view of sheer curiosity in seeing a live animal, for example, but rather a true responsibility to understand the environment, and treat and use it as best as possible. It is because of these reasons that ecosustainability and greater values of positive connection are seen, as well as curiosity as scoring lower.
- "I would like to go to a grocery store" is the most commercial. In this reason, the action to visit is out of curiosity. The basic reason is just for fun and hedonistic, and therefore clashes with the environment.
- "I would like to support a project that promotes sustainability" is the reason that is mostly connected, considering the perfect combination at the base of interest in F.ICO - Eataly World as well as the large interdependence with protecting and respecting the environment. The differences of a negative nature are noteworthy, potentially overlooked for values that incited more interest.
- Finally, "I might but the park will be too far" is less significant. On one hand, the few answers just highlights that the geographic location do not influence the number of visitors, and on the other hand, the data about the values are so few that it is impossible to glean sharp conclusions.

5. Result and Discussion

The final result of the questionnaire is more than positive. Firstly, it provided a comparison of data, different opinions and new information. Furthermore, it also made it possible to analyse numerical data with a human and psychological point of view.

The result from the sample group reflects the result of a broader project analysis. F.I.CO.'s values, competitive strategies such as the use of a well-known brand and Real Estate Finance, the aims that is promoted to reach and the time frame in which this has all been designed has created a mix of competitive factors that led to a project with infinite potential. This is not only for how Italian tourism is spread, which is also thanks to Italian food, many companies and investors are focusing on agribusiness, but also because a financial and national event of this size marks the economy and international and national image of Italy.

6. Conclusion

For the first time, a tourism project was implemented, based on the concept of an agribusiness park, through a complex use of Real Estate Finance.

The set of international and elite brands offered by Eataly, with the Real Estate competence of Prelios, has demonstrated through statistical analysis in the field that projects created in order to relaunch the economy through new concepts of tourism, are possible.

In this period of profound economic crisis, the F.I.CO. project was studied with great skill in order to use the resources that are currently available (large unused buildings) and those functioning (culinary tourism) as best as possible, making them rotate around one sole sector: culinary tourism, which has suffered the economic slowdown much less than others. The interviewed sample group, which is significant from a statistical point of view, confirmed the theories and assumptions on which the project was presented and implemented.

References

[1] World Travel & Tourism Council, Travel & Tourism, Economic Impact 2014, Italy, p.1-2.

[2] Larry D., Chulwon K., *Destination Competitiveness: A Model and Determinants*.

[3] National Touristic Researches Isitute, *Indagine sul Turismo Organizzato Internazionale*, June 2013, p. 27-29.

[4] Frank M.G., Govers R., *Integrated quality management for tourist destinations: a European perspective on achieving competitiveness*, 2013.

[5] Cracolicia M.F.,Nijkampb P., *The attractiveness and competitiveness of tourist destinations: A study of Southern Italian region*, 2012.

[6] Yangzhou Hu, J.R. Brent Ritchie, *Measuring Destination Attractiveness: A Contextual Approach*, 2013.

[7] Muliere A.,*l'importanza del turismo per l'economia di una destinazione*, part ofMarketing of tourism.

[8] *L'importanza del settore turistico nell'economia italiana*, 28th November 2003 article by Legambiente.

[9] Workshops and Conferences, *Il turismo internazionale in Italia: dati e risultati*, Bank of Italy, March 2013, p-30-35.

[10] Ignatov e Smith, *"Demand-side patterns" refers to studies of various aspects of visitor behaviour*, 2006, p.238.

[11] Pistore C., *Promuovere i prodotti locali: un modello strutturale per interpretare il behavioral intention*, 2010, p. 9-15.

[12] Oberservatory of tourism, *Indagine sui comportamenti turistici degli italiani*, 2013.

[13] Razaq Raj,Kevin Griffin,Nigel D. Morpeth, *Cultural Tourism*, CABI, 2013.

[14] Regional Observatory of Tourism, *L'enogastronomia come fattore di sviluppo turistico in Emilia Romagna*, Programma 2011, p. 4-8.

[15] www.expo2015.org

[16] Pistore C., *Promuovere i prodotti locali: un modello strutturale per intrepretare il behavioral intention*, 2010, p. 9-15.

[17] Mason M. C., Paggiaro A., *L'importanza del festivalscape: il caso degli eventi enogastronomici*, Proceedings of 8th International Conference Marketing Trends, PARIGI, 2008.

[18] Falzea A.,Grossi P.,Cheli E., Costi R.,*Enciclopedia del diritto. Annali, Volume 2.*

[19] *Il project financing per la realizzazione di opere pubbliche*, made by the project ANCI-POSTIT with the collaboration of CRESME Ricerche S.p.A.; ImmoConsulting SpA – Gruppo Aareal Bank AG; Università Bocconi.

[20] P.K.Nevitt, *Project Financing*, 2013.

[21] www.caab.it

[22] May 2013, *inaugurazione più grande impianto fotovoltaico su tetto d'Europa*, 43.750 solar panels in total for a surface of 100.000 square meters and 22,5 million in investments.

[23] Online company profile: www.preliossgr.com.

15

The widespread hotel: New hotel model for business tourist

Filippo Monge[1], Daniele Cattaneo[2], Angela Scilla[2]

[1]Department of Economia e Statistica "Cognetti de Martis", University of Turin, Turin, Italy
[2]Department of Management, University of Turin, Turin, Italy

Email address:
filippo.monge@unito.it (F. Monge), daniele.cattaneo@unito.it (D. Cattaneo), angela.scilla@unito.it (A. Scilla)

Abstract: The territories are in competition among them for attract human, economic and financial resources. The attractiveness has become the target of recent urban policies. In fact, the constant appeals to events, be they even simple events or events lasting more days, or real places built for the occasion and adaptable to multiple uses, all linked to recreational activities, are a proof. In the tourism field this situation is particularly intense. The local areas can lose the competitive play against the great areas. They must think of diversification of their supply. Therefore, in the dynamic environment of business tourism, the requirements of customers about service quality and location landscape are getting harder than in the past. The widespread hotel model represents one of the possible solution to that needs and recently it is increasing its importance. The model is able to stimulate economic and social value development through the management of several critical success factors. The analysis of a case study "Hotel Chateau Le Cagnard" permits to underline the key factors of success of the widespread hotel for business tourism.

Keywords: Territorial Competitiveness, Widespread Hotel, Business Tourist

1. Introduction

Tourism is one of the sectors that has the ability to improve the competitiveness between the territories, to promote territorial innovation [1] and thus enhance the attractiveness of the destinations [2], [3].

This is most important in small tourist areas and especially in rural ones, where need to tools and initiatives to increase income and employment, through the enhancement of local resources [4].

Thanks the implementation of tourism policy, an area can get a set of benefits. It should, however, consider that tourism is a driver that can determine strong impact, even negative, on the land and on the local community [5], [6].

Therefore, it is essential to bear in mind the definition of services and activities that improve the tourism sector, the extent of the impacts that these determine in the development of the local area, to avoid that there is a crisis.

It is therefore necessary to combine the needs of local development with the preservation of culture and local specificities.

All this must also be reconciled with the needs of the leisure or business tourist. In fact, in the tourism industry, most of economic value is represented by experiences [7]. The tourism demand is experiencing, in fact, in recent years, a particular evolution process, which causes the increase of the degree of variety (always more marked segmentation processes) and variability in time and in space. The enterprises and tourism system, in fact, should guide their strategic and marketing choices to the differentiated and personalized solutions, respecting the criteria of economy and efficiency of management decisions. To supply experiences seems to be a way for makers to survive in the ever more competitive future [8].

The hotel model known as widespread hotel seems to offer an answer to all these problems. In fact it has a network of "local flavor" houses, uninhabited and pre-existing, that are able to operate as a hotel; a network of public and private entities that start a process of collaboration. Those involved in the network are often dining and commercial facilities pre-existing or caused to be born within a project for the hospitality widespread, in order to diversify the proposal and to make the life of the village more animated or charming.

It also provides tourists a unique experience of living in an old town or a village citizen.

Thus, this paper is divided in two parts. The first part

propones a survey of the most recent contributions on:

- the competitiveness and attractiveness of territories and tourist destinations;
- the behavioral of tourist;
- the widespread hotel as a tool to promote the preservation of local culture and specificities of the small areas, the tourism development and leisure and business tourists satisfaction.

In the second part, the results of case study "Hotel Chateau Le Cagnard" are presented and commented on, highlighting the main classes of critical success factors and their features.

2. Theoretical Background

2.1. Attractiveness and Competitiveness of Tourist Destination and Local Territory

Is established that the attractiveness has become the target of recent urban policies. In fact, the constant appeals to events, be they even simple events or events lasting more days, or real places built for the occasion and adaptable to multiple uses, all linked to recreational activities, are a proof. [9].

The concept of competitiveness, initially referred only to businesses, has seen extend its meaning also to the territories even if this application is more complex. A territory can be defined competitive when it is able to compete in the market by ensuring, at the same time, an environmental, economic, social and cultural sustainability, based on inter-territorial network [10], [11], [12], [13], [14], [15], [16].

The competitiveness of a territory is the result of a virtuous circle in which three elements influence each other: territory, economic actors and resources. The territory makes available to economic actors a several factors and resources, tangible and intangible, essential to the achieve of competitive advantage. Economic actors move a substantial portion of the value created for the benefit of their territory, in this way they promote the progressive strengthening of its attractiveness and support its local development.

The competitive strategy of a territory is the acquisition of useful resources to ensure that the territory will become the context better than others to carry out economic activities more functional for its sustainable development.

The word "competitiveness", linked to a geographical area, is a concept widening used but its meaning is still unclear.

Among the most widely accepted definition of competitiveness, the OECD in 1992 offer the better one: "Competitiveness is the degree to which a nation can, in free and fair market conditions, produce goods and services that meet international competition, maintaining and expanding the real incomes of its people over the long term".

Competitiveness delves into the concept attractiveness in base on two perspectives. On the one hand the territories come into competition not only for economic gains, but also to attract flows through the quality of their physical structure and the enhancing of their image.

On the other hand, the concept of competitiveness is bound to attract enterprises which enrich and enhance their territory.

Caroli [17] identifies four determinants of territorial attractiveness: (1) physical characteristics, which include the topography, climatic and geographic conditions; (2) material capital, which includes infrastructures, the supply of means of production, the local production; (3) intangible capital, relations and trust shared, manufacturing expertise spread, vocation and image consolidated; (4) policies regarding the regulatory framework and control, management of public goods and services and the management of the factors of the public nature of the material and immaterial capital.

The territory can thus become a bulwark place to defend the specific production, the traditions, the culture of the place.

Today, it may be noted, in this regard, a growing sensitivity to the preservation of the "local", meaning the combination of supply harmonic that a territory can offer in terms of synthesis of its products, not only tangible but also intangible.

The concept of territory, therefore, is not considered in reality if not as a unitary and indivisible.

It is possible to look to the territory under three different meanings [18], which are actually present together and whole-people: (1) the territory as a destination, (2) the territory as a setting and (3) the territory as a network.

In the widespread hotel field the first and second concepts are very important.

The territory as a destination refers to the field of tourism.

The territory becomes a tourist product intended as a combination of elements to create a unique experience for the user, from the town, to the business set up in the area. Thus, from the point of view of the Destination Management, the offer that is proposed to the public includes the special features of a certain area, the activities and initiatives working on it. In short, the destination is not so much a place, but a set of activities and factors of attraction located in a defined space (location, site, area) that are able to propose an extensive and integrated proposal, that represent a specific and distinctive system of tourist hospitality that values the resources and local culture [19]

The concept of territory as a setting refers to a territory as environment, background, place of action on which it is established the culture of a people. In fact, the characteristics that affect the local identity and uniqueness become progressively of the key factors on which the development strategies of the territory are based to create differentiation and thus gain a competitive advantage [18].

This is how the area is open to the frontier of tourism oriented to the discovery, or rediscovery, of certain geographical areas.

So the offer must be organized as a real life experience in the area and not limited to an aggregate of resources; this logic experiential [20] is only possible due to the attitude of the territory to tell its tales, to drive interpretation, to give the tourist a unique and unforgettable memories, personal, non-replicable in other places.

The human element is the key for potential enhancement of an area [18]

2.2. Tourist Behavioral

The tourism demand is experiencing in these recent years, a particular evolution process, which causes the increase of the degree of variety (always more marked segmentation processes) and variability in time and in space.

The enterprises and tourism system, in fact, should guide their strategic and marketing choices to the differentiated and personalized solutions for the tourists, respecting the criteria of economy and efficiency of management decisions. To supply experiences seems to be a way for makers to survive in the ever more competitive future [8].

Behind every act of buying lies a complex system of social and individual decisions and influences. Their understanding is a prerequisite both for a correct interpretation of tourist market both for a more effective selection of the levers of appropriate marketing mix for characteristics of the target segments.

This is due to the growing complexity related both for tourism demand, with the continuous emergence of new ways of enjoying of the tourist product and of new consumer segments, both for the competitive scenario characterized by the aggressive competition of new tourist destinations highly differentiated and highly competitive in terms of price/value.

These features are due to the complexity of the tourist product, which includes an extremely wide range of heterogeneous resources, activities and services, the existence of a time gap between the time of purchase and the time of consumption, and "experiential" nature of the process of exploitation, which is characterized by the high consumer involvement and includes sensory, affective and emotional perspectives.

2.3. The Widespread Hotel

The widespread hotel is a model of hotel designed to provide an experience of authentic life in a rural village.

The features of the model are developed by Dall'Ara [21], [22]. The widespread hotel as such indicates "a special type of hotel designed to provide guests with a unique experience of life in the historic center of a town or a village. This offers guests all the amenities of a traditional hotel that is hospitality, service, common areas and restaurants, although the rooms are spread in the town center, in an approximate radius of 200 meters from the central location of principal hotel in which they are located reception, common areas and restaurant. The rooms and/or apartments are located within existing buildings, recovered in respect of local tradition or designed so as to create the feeling of being in the host resident" [23]. It is an integral part of the sector of Hospitality Widespread, along with the country-hotel, the Diffuse Residence or Borgo Hotel which is united by nature "horizontal" proposal and the type of context, more often rural, in which it operates.

Widespread hotel has proven capable of holding the depopulation of villages. The same, however, requires the presence of support services targeted by the territorial organizations, interested in encouraging the emergence of these proposals in the areas of competence. This support was formalized in an ad-hoc intervention model for the development of widespread hotel [24], [25].

The models of hospitality and intervention have been recognized as innovative by the United Nations and the European network of business incubators (EBN) through the first prize awarded to the CEO for the international competition "Helping to Grow New Talents" held in 2008 in Budapest.

However, the widespread hotel model presents some obstacles difficult to overcome. Among them, the deviation between the large number of registered projects and the number of those actually operating in the area seems to indicate the presence of problems in the design and implementation steps of the proposals. From a regulatory point of view, significant differences emerge between the range of minimum quality requirements necessary to configure a widespread hotel based on the national model, and those recognized by some regional normative, more elastic and therefore more ambiguous [26].

A widespread hotel develops in with, not height and is therefore superimposed on the geography of the village. In this context, a line of research has addressed the issue of the acquisition and development of resource type urban-architectural, important for the process of value creation for the guest and thus can play a decisive role in the generation of income necessary to the support of accommodation widespread hospitality. It is an example of enterprise resource for widespread hotel the urban architecture or the skyline of the village.

3. A New Accommodation Model for the Business Tourist: The Widespread Hotel

3.1. The Business Tourism in the French Riviera and the Cannes MIPIM Fair

The French Riviera, originally only known as an holiday destination, has gradually become one of the major centers of international business tourism. Since 1950, with the construction of the Nice Exhibition Centre, the major hotels have equipped themselves and then created the dedicated structures. In 1978, Monaco (Monte-Carlo) inaugurated the auditorium and in 1982 in the convention center of Cannes replaced the former Palais des Festivals, in 1984 Nice inaugurated its Acropolis complex, completely renovated in 2011. Monaco opened the Grimaldi Forum in 2000 and his new palace Antibes in 2013.

At the same time, specialized agencies have supported the logistics of events. The palaces of Nice, Cannes and Monaco have auditoriums of more than 1,800 seats, there are nearly 500 hotels meeting rooms over 30 "event venues".

According to the French Riviera Tourism Observatory overall, in 2013 tourism flows generated by business purposes exceeded 2.000.000 annually distributed in: 46%

meetings or business appointments (down in recent years), 31% for conferences, seminars, symposia (recovery since 2010 after a decline since 2005), 10% for fairs, expos (up from 98 when they represented only 0.4% and a peak of 16.9% in 2007, up from 2012-13), 3% studies, training, training. Only 0.5% of visitors for business indicate "incentive" as a reason for living, but the "other professionals "increased sharply (9.5%).

One of this important event is MIPIM [27] the world's leading property market that brings together the most influential players from all international property sectors (office, residential, retail, healthcare, sport, logistics and industrial, offering unrivalled access to the greatest number of development projects and sources of capital worldwide).

The event is held annually in Cannes. Last year, during the 4 days of exhibition, participants were 21000 coming from 93 different countries [28].

In the following part of the paper will be presented the results of a survey carried out on a sample of a delegation that took part to this event in March 2014.

3.2. Case Study: Hotel Chateau Le Cagnard

Built in the 13th century, Le Cagnard [29] is a stone dwelling integrated in the city wall of the medieval village of Haut-de-Cagnes. Its history is closely tied to that of the Château Grimaldi, which dates back to the 14th century.

The propriety has had different owners. In 2011, it was sold and proprietors decided to focus on hospitality and to develop an hotel according to the "widespread hotel" standards. So after undergoing a complete renovation (included the frescoes and antique furniture restoration), the hotel started focusing on both leisure and business segment.

A brief analysis of the main characteristics will follow:

Location:

The Hotel is located in Haut-de-Cagnes. It is a small hilltop village in the centre of the French Riviera and has successfully preserved its medieval character. The village is built on a top of hill and surrounds the Château Grimaldi, which is now a museum. The view of Cagnes-sur-Mer envisages both the sea and the rising hills of the backcountry. This village has been considered a privileged meeting point for artists, which led to its being named the "Montmartre of the French Riviera"

Accessibility:

The hotel is ideally connected and located in particular:

- by car: it provides quick access to the A8 highway (French Riviera Motorway);
- by train : the Cagnes-sur-Mer SNCF train station is close to the hotel;
- by bus: the central bus station, located in downtown Cagnes-sur-Mer connects with all the main cities along the French Riviera with regular service;
- by plane: the hotel is only 10 minutes (by car) far from the Nice French Riviera International Airport (connected as well with Monaco helicopter airport);
- there is a free shuttle service available for moving from the City of Cagnes-sur-Mer to the village of Haut-de-Cagnes which is useful for connecting the city with the parking placed at the edge of the village.

From the village of Haute-de-Cagne is easy to reach business and leisure destination like:

- Cannes (Congress Centre): 35 minutes
- Monaco (Principality): 45 minutes
- Ventimiglia (Italy): 55 minutes
- Saint-Tropez: 1 h and 15 minutes

Rooms:

The hotel has 28 rooms of which:

- 18 single and double room;
- 10 junior suites;
- 3 suites;

Every rooms offers air conditioning and free wi-fi.

Restaurant:

The restaurant offers Provencal cuisine with local and seasonal products.

It has specific formula for particular situations like Christmas a New Years' Eve.

It also organizes corporate Christmas Dinner.

Services:

The hotel provides high-level services for both business and leisure customers like:

- babysitting;
- cultural holidays: French classes, painting and drawing courses in the village and surrounding -area, perfume making, culinary courses, wine tasting;
- desk services: photocopies, fax, scanning, postal services, translations, etc.
- free Wi-Fi throughout the hotel;
- health, well-being and relaxation: massage, hairdresser, manicure and pedicure, nutritional advice, personal trainer, personal shopping assistant (which can be exclusively provided in the rooms)
- public transportation information: bus, train or boat;
- reservations: limousine, taxi, car or helicopter rentals, private excursions, local attractions and events, etc.

Services for business meeting:

The hotel facilities can be used as well to organize business meetings. Three rooms are available for seminars, conferences, assemblies and meetings.

For these occasions daily packages are offered, half-day with lunch and/or dinner as well as accommodation in single and or double rooms within the hotel.

The restaurant can prepare business meals, buffets or snacks during the meetings. Furthermore discretion and quietness is guaranteed by complimentary lounge (apart the main room) that can accommodate 2-15 guests.

All the meeting rooms are equipped with Wi-Fi, screen, video projector, flip chart. On request is always possible to get camcorder and sound equipment

In particular:

- -Piano Lounge can accommodate (depending on the configuration) from 10 to 25 businessmen
- -Suite Picasso (15 to 30 guests)
- -Guard Room (12 to 40 guests)

The main features will be summarized in the following table 1.

Table 1. Main Features of the hotel Le Cagnard.

Characteristics	Description
Year Hotel Established	2011
Year Village Established	13th Century
Importance of the village	Medieval settlement, artist meeting point ("The Montmartre of the French Riviera")
Presence of Unitary Management	Yes
Business services offered	-3 meeting rooms -free Wi-Fi area - desk service (photocopies, fax) -translation - limousine, car, helicopter rental - private lounge for business meals - organization of corporate event - organization of corporate business dinner (or lunch) -accessibility to Nice Airport (10 min) - accessibility to Cannes Congress Center (35 min).
Services (both business and leisure)	- restaurant - air conditioning - babysitting - massage - hairdresser - manicure - pedicure - nutritional advise - personal trainer - personal shopper
Activity (the activities are tailor-made and for organizational reason have to be booked in advance by the customer)	- French classes, - painting and drawing courses in the village and surrounding -area, - perfume making, - culinary courses, - wine tasting

Source: our elaboration on primary data

4. Discussion and Results

In relation to the literature review the following research question has been identified:

"Can the hotel developed according to the "widespread hotel" model meet and satisfy the needs of the business tourist?"

To answer to this question it has been carried out a survey (based on both quantitative and qualitative data) on a sample of 48 businessmen that can be considered representative because:

- they are all top managers of Italian associations and organization,
- their professional profile (businessmen, manager, entrepreneur) has allowed them to travel extensively
- in the role of event organizers must sometimes choose the location to host their guests.

As shown in table 3, the questionnaire is divided into three main parts:

- in the first part the respondents were asked to rate the hotel (on a scale from 1 to 10) and to tell the main points of strength of the hotel
- the second part is more focalized on the relevance of the choice of the hotel in relation to the business trip and on the analysis of the main reasons.
- in the third part it has been asked to the panel whether the "widespread hotel" could be successfully adopted in the Piedmont Region (Italian region from whom the majority of the businessman came from).

In particular questions 2,4,6,8 were open ended questions, instead questions 1,3,5,7 were close-ended (most of them were single choice answers, only the question 2 was multiple choice).

Table 2. The questionnaire.

Nr.	Question
1	How do you rate from 1 to 10 the hotel in which you stayed during your last business trip to Cannes?
2	Can you tell us the 3 points of strength of the hotel?
3	Do you think that the choice of the hotel was relevant to enjoy the business event that you have attended?
4	Can you tell us the main reasons?
5	Do you think that the "widespread hotel" model could be adopted in the Piedmont region with the same success?
6	In which area?
7	Do you think the success of the model needs some particular conditions?
8	If you answered "yes" to question 7 can you tell the most important condition in your opinion?

Source: our elaboration on primary data

The main results of the survey are shown below.

In the first question, about the overall evaluation of the structure "Le Cagnard", the respondent had to express on a scale from 1 to 10 (where 1 stands for very bad and 10 stands for excellent).

The average value attributed was of 9.24. The standard deviation of 1.02 shows that the variability from the mean value is not so high.

Table 3. How do you rate from 1 to 10 the hotel in which you stayed during your last business trip to Cannes?

Mean	St.Dev	Min	Max
9,24	1,02	6	10

Source: our elaboration on primary data

Subsequently, each respondent was asked to list the main strengths (maximum 3 items) of the facility where he had stayed.

The responses indicate that the item most significant for the sample were:

- the proximity to the convention center;
- the quality of services offered within the structure (see table 1)
- the excellence of the landscape (and the experiential aspect related to the medieval village). The presence of this element was assumed given the historic-cultural context within the structures operate, which represent the starting point for the creation of natural value [29]

Less relevant appear to be the quality of the restaurant and the high standard of the rooms (aspect that can be explained by the fact that the sample, consisting of experienced business traveler, tends to take for granted these elements).

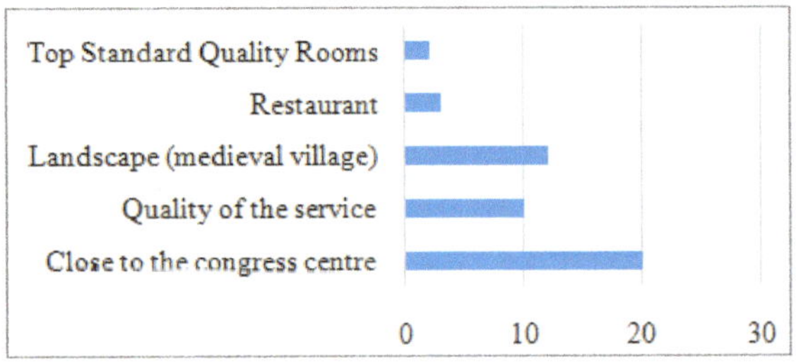

Source: our elaboration on primary data

Figure 1. *Can you tell us the 3 points of strength of the hotel?*

In question 3 was asked whether the choice of the specific structure has been considered relevant in order to enjoy the event in the best way. As a result 98% of the sample states that the choice was important and allowed them to enjoy the exhibition at the best.

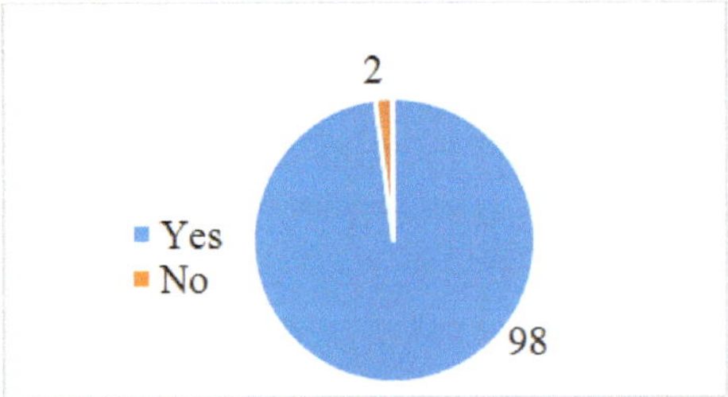

Source: our elaboration on primary data

Figure 2. *Do you think that the choice of the hotel was relevant to enjoy the business event that you have attended.*

The reasons (figure 3) have been given in detail in the answer to question 3. The most significant was that the "widespread hotel" offers at the meantime comfort and quick access to the cities of Nice and Cannes

Other answers were that:

- It facilitates, through the structure and business services (in particular the three meeting rooms) the activities of the team (such as teambuilding)
- The intimate atmosphere allowed the businessmen to relax at the end of the day's work.

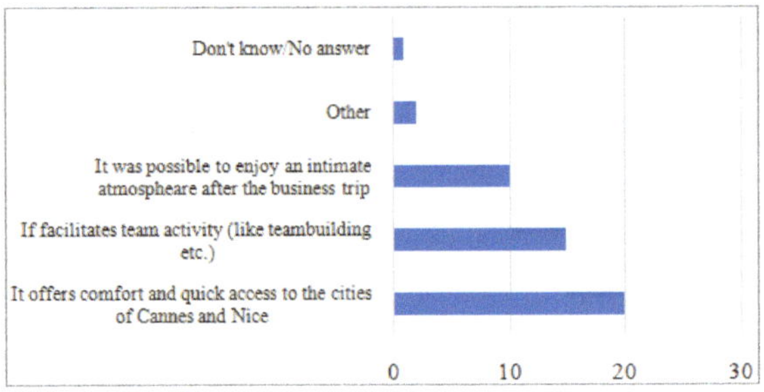

Source: our elaboration on primary data

Figure 3. *Can you tell us the main reasons?*

It has been finally asked the sample if in their opinion the "widespread hotel" model could also be adopted in the Piedmont Region with the same success. 95% of them answered positively.

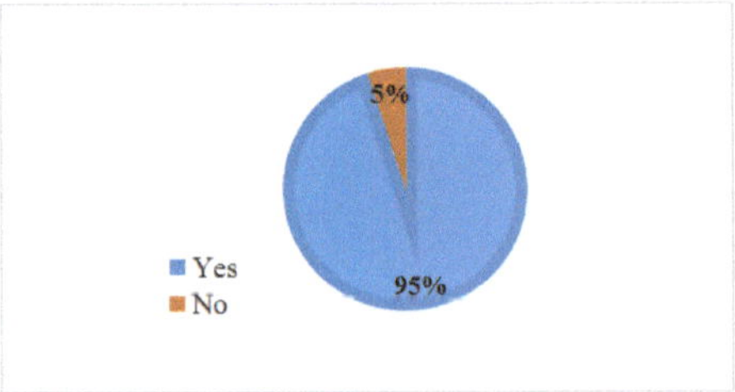

Source: our elaboration on primary data

Figure 4. *Do you think that the "widespread hotel" model could be adopted in the Piedmont region with the same success?*

About the area in which the model could be more successful, it prevails a clear majority for the mountain area, followed by the system from the lakes and hills.

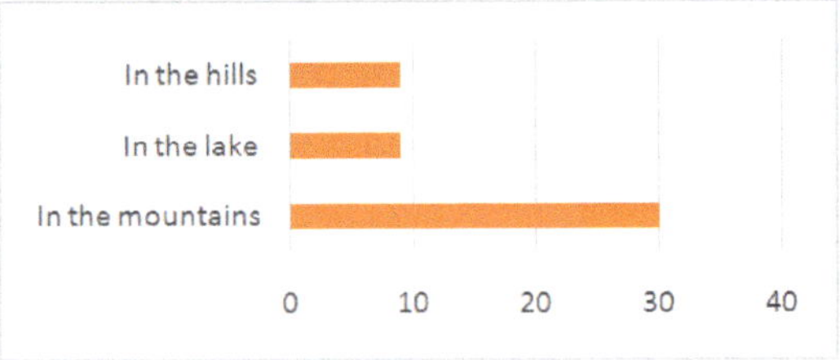

Source: our elaboration on primary data

Figure 5. *In which area?*

It was finally asked to respondents if the success of the application of the model were due to special reasons. 93% of the sample responded affirmatively.

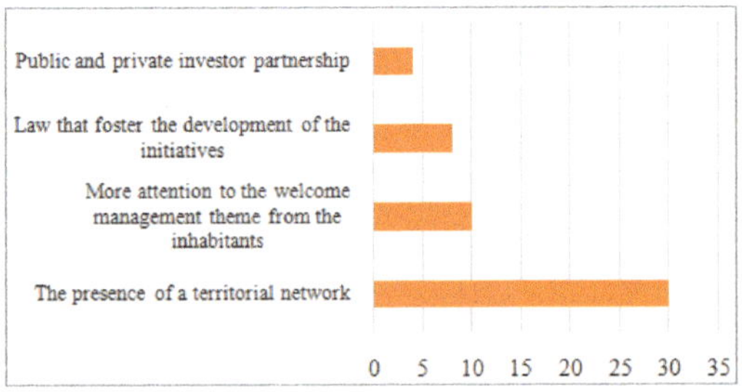

Source: our elaboration on primary data

Figure 6. *Do you think the success of the model needs some particular conditions?*

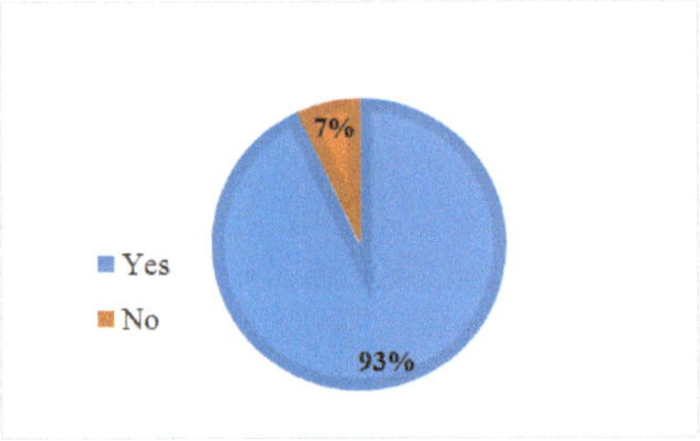

Source: our elaboration on primary data

Figure 7. *If you answered "yes" to question 7 can you tell the most important condition in your opinion?*

In particular, confirming the theories of Caroli [17] the main reasons considered were:

- the importance of the presence of a territorial network with whom the structure can establish relationships;
- the increased attention to the issues of welcome management for residents;
- the presence of laws that foster the development of these initiatives;
- the activation of positive synergies through the public-private partnership.

5. Conclusions

The "widespread hotel" can be an important player for the tourism market, while promoting at the same time sustainable economic development in the territory where it operates [31].

Critical success factors are made up by those variables that management can control, and those variables that management must consider as constraints to ensure the enterprise's survival. Following the theories of Orlandini [32].*et al,* only by operating in this way, can the enterprise be a generator of economic and social value.

The most important classes of critical success factors for the "widespread hotel" are:

- the characteristics of the environment;
- the characteristics related to the market or to the market segment;
- the strategies implemented by the economic actor.

Regarding the characteristics of the environment the most significant are:

- the territorial ties;
- the influence of the local community on the structure.

According to Pine and Gilmore observations [20], the analyzed data showed that the "widespread hotel", combining experiential aspects and elements of service excellence, might represent the optimal solution for the business tourist.

In order for this to happen, however, must be some basic determinants of territorial attractiveness which have been identified by Caroli [17] such as:

- the presence of a territorial network with whom the structure can activate relations;
- the sensitivity of the population to welcome management theme;
- a legislation that allows the development of these initiatives.

The model of the widespread hotel can be a solution to enhance the value of certain territories.

In fact, according to Giuseppe Provvisiero [34]: "I think that, if placed in the proper context, the "widespread hotel" can be an efficient model of hospitality based on the driver of sustainability and innovation".

However, the hotel does not have to remain isolated; otherwise, the limited complementary offer (of cultural events, sports, entertainment etc.) can cause a loss of appeal.

In this regard, Provvisiero[34], according to Ingallina [9]: "The first vital element is the presence of a range of infrastructure, facilities and tourist accommodation with whom the "widespread hotel" can activate synergies and virtuous processes.

The presence of a conference center and the easy accessibility to the city center are an important amplifier.

In this regard, the strength of the structure analyzed corresponds to its ability to interrelate with the eco-system generated by the congress tourism and activating synergies with it. The many personalized services for business (such as the presence of some meetings room, the possibility of having an interpreter or booking a shuttle or limousine to reach the location and venues) make it an optimal solution for this target, and an efficient opportunity for value creation for both the territory and its stakeholders.

Acknowledgements

Although this paper is based on a combined effort, Prof. Filippo Monge is to take credit for paragraphs 4 and 5; Daniele Cattaneo is to take credit for paragraph 3; while Angela Scilla for paragraphs 1 and 2.

References

[1] R. Gemmiti and L. Salvati, "Turismo e competitività territoriale. Un contributo geografico-economico", XXXI Italian Conference of Regional Science, 20-22 september 2010

[2] D.B. Weaver, Sustainable Tourism, New York: Routledge 2006.

[3] R. Scheyvens and J.H. Momsen, "Tourism and Poverty Reduction: Issues for Small Island States," in. Tourism Geographies: An International Journal of Tourism Space, Place and Environment, vol 10 n.1, 2008, pp. 22-41.

[4] (Quein, Sansbury, Le Bruto, 1998)

[5] M. Mowforth and I. Munt, Tourism and Sustainability. Development, Globalisation and New Tourism in the Third World. London: Routledge, 2008.

[6] S.F. McCool, R.N. Moisey and N.P. Nickerson, "What Should Tourism Sustain? The Disconnect with Industry Perceptions of Useful Indicators" in Journal of Travel Research, vol 40 n.2, 2001, pp. 124-131.

[7] S. Tsaur, Y. Chiu, and C. Wang, "The visitors' behavioural consequences of experiential marketing,"in Journal of Travel & Tourism Marketing, vol. 21 n. 1, 2007, pp. 47-64.

[8] E. Binkhorst and D.D. Teun, „Agenda for Co-Creation Tourism Experience Research," in Journal of Hospitality Marketing & Management, vol. 18 n.2-3, 2009, pp. 311-327.

[9] P. Ingallina, "Nuovi scenari per l'attrattività delle città e dei territori. Dibattiti, progetti e strategie in contesti metropolitani mondiali", FrancoAngeli,Milano, 2010.

[10] D.G. Pearce, "Competitive Destination Analysis in Southeast Asia," in Journal of Travel Research, vol. 36 n.1, 1997, pp. 16-24.

[11] S.S. Hassan, "Determinants of Market Competitiveness in an Environmentally Sustainable Tourism Industry," in Journal of Travel Research, vol. 38 n.3, 2000, pp. 239-245.

[12] J.R.B. Ritchie and G.I. Crouch, "The Competitive Destination. A Sustainable Tourism Perspective", Wallingford, Cabi International, 2003.

[13] M.J. Enright and J. Newton, "Determinants of Tourism Destination Competitiveness in Asia Pacific: Comprehensiveness and Universality," in Journal of Travel Research, vol. 43 n.1, 2005, pp. 339-350.

[14] W.C. Hong, "Global Competitiveness Measurement for the Tourism Sector" in Current Issues in Tourism, vol. 12 n. 2, 2009, pp. 105-132.

[15] M. Franch, U. Martini and F. Buffa, "Profili hard-path e soft-path dei turisti 4L in Italia: risultati di un'indagine sui viaggiatori del Cts", Disa Working Paper, (2), 2010, pp.1-61.

[16] G. Tardivo, M. Viassone and A. Scilla, "How to become a benchmark sustainable tourist destination? A descriptive model," Business Systems Review, vol. 3 issue 2., 2014, pp. 207-230.

[17] M. Caroli, "Il marketing territoriale: idee ed esperienze nelle regioni italiane" Franco Angeli, Milano, 2010

[18] L. Gavinelli, "Territoio, networking e management come dimensioni di analisi per le decisioni degli ecomusei italiani", Cedam, Padova, 2012.

[19] M. Rispoli and M. Tamma, "Risposte strategiche alla complessità: le forme di offerta dei prodotti alberghieri", Giappichelli, Torino, 1995.

[20] B. Pine and H. Gilmore, H., "L'economia delle esperienze. Oltre il servizio", Etas, Milano, 2000.

[21] G. Dall'Ara, "Realizzare un Albergo Diffuso: dai principi teorici alle esperienze concrete", in: L'albergo Diffuso come strumento innovativo per la valorizzazione del potenziale turistico, quaderni BICNotes, n. 4, dicembre 2007, Business Innovation Center - BIC del Lazio, Roma, 2007

[22] G. Dall'Ara, "Manuale dell'Albergo Diffuso, l'idea, la gestione, il marketing dell'ospitalità diffusa, Franco Angeli, Milano, 2010.

[23] UNDP-EBN (2008), brochure: "Albergo Diffuso: Developing Tourism Through Innovation and Tradition', IDEASS Programme, Italy, Innovation for Development and South-South Cooperation: http://www.ideassonline.org/public/pdf/br_47_01.pdf.

[24] G. Dichter, L'approccio metodologico BIC Lazio alla creazione di alberghi diffusi", in L'Albergo Diffuso come strumento innovativo per la valorizzazione del potenziale turistico, quaderni BICNotes, n. 4, dicembre 2007, BIC Lazio, Roma, pp. 74-81.

[25] M. Droli, "Tuscia romana, area Monti Ausoni: individuazione delle località più adatte ai fini della creazione di un Albergo Diffuso", in L'Albergo Diffuso come strumento innovativo per la valorizzazione del potenziale turistico, quaderni BICNotes, n. 4, dicembre 2007, BIC Lazio, Roma, pp. 49-72.

[26] M. Droli and G. Dall'Ara, "Ripartire dalla Bellezza. Gestione e marketing delle Opportunità d'Innovazione nell'Albergo Diffuso, nei Centri Storici e nelle Aree Rurali", CLEUP, Padova, 2012.

[27] www.mipim.com

[28] www.cotedazur-touriscope.com/pdf/fiches/8/normal.pdf

[29] ww.lecagnard.com

[30] G.M. Golinelli and M. Gatti, "L'impresa sistema vitale. Il governo dei rapporti intersistemici" in Symphonya. Emerging Issues in Management, ISTEI, Milano, University of Milan-Bicocca, 2002, pp. 53-81.

[31] G.Tardivo, G. Quaglia, "La creazione di valore, Vol I, La creazione di valore per l'impresa", Franco Angeli, Milano, 2013, p. 72.

[32] . Orlandini, C.Vallone, A. De Toni, R. Cecchetti, (2012). Total quality research of tourism services. Special case: "Spread hotel". In: 15th International Conference on Quality Service Sciences, Rishon Lezion, Israel, 3-5 September 2012, pp. 4-5.

[33] G. Dall'Ara, Manuale dell'Albergo diffuso; l'idea, la gestione, il marketing dell'ospitalità, Franco Angeli, Milano, 2010, p. 15

[34] President of ANCE Piemonte and Valle d'Aosta and vice president of Confindustria Piemonte (insights in F. Monge, G. Provvisiero, Il settore delle costruzioni in Piemonte e Valle d'Aosta, mercati, dinamiche, strutture, Egea, Milano, 2014).

An Impact of Banking Activities of Private Commercial Islamic Bank to Economic Development in Bangladesh: A Case Study on First Security Islami Bank Limited (FSIBL)

Md. Nazirul Islam Sarker[1], Md. Harun Or Rashid[2]

[1]School of Business, Bangladesh Open University, Gazipur, Bangladesh
[2]Department of Management, University of Dhaka, Dhaka, Bangladesh

Email address:
nazirul2012@gmail.com (Md. N. I.Sarker)

Abstract: Banks are the most important parts of the financial system of any country. Specially, developing country like Bangladesh, proper banking system is very important and essential to play a vital role, because capital market system in Bangladesh is not advanced like other country's capital market. The study analyses published texts, articles, websites and annual report of this bank through a content analysis. Key findings of this study manifest the contribution of this bank in different areas of economic development in Bangladesh like generating employment, earning foreign remittance, strengthening rural economy, promoting ecology and green banking, boosting industrialization, developing the SMEs, assisting in foreign trade (import-export) and developing the housing sector etc. This study also identifies FSIBL's significant contribution to the national exchequer. This paper contributes to the field of economic development of Bangladesh and the role of FSIBL behind it and fills the gap of literature in this specific area. The study suggests that Islamic banking has a great impact on the economic development in Bangladesh.

Keywords: Islamic Banking, Shariah, Bangladesh, Economic Development

1. Background of the Study

Banking sector of the world is contributed in the present global economy. To establish a strong banking sector it is required to have good study in banking operations. Today's Economic policy is concerned to obtain the optimum economic condition in a country's economy. Banking sector and banking activities are playing a vital and important role to achieve that optimum goal of the economy. The successful running of banking business depends upon effective banks. As a new commercial bank FSIBL has a huge responsibility to ensure efficient and effective banking operation all over the Bangladesh in a sound manner with other Banks as a competitor.

Banking sector is indispensable in a modern age and modern society.It always plays a vital role to the economic development of a country. In modern age of science and technology the banking sector all over the world has been undergoing a lot of changes due to deregulation, technological innovation and globalization. But Bangladeshi banking sector is lagging to keep pace with the other countries to adapt the changes. Basically bank take deposits from the customers against some interest payments and lend the money to the borrowers with a different interest rate and time period. To ensure safety of the depositors fund there are various types of credit facility. Also bank must hold adequate fund to meet the daily needs of the clients. The First Security Islami Bank Ltd (FSIBL) is a 3rd (Third) generation is doing its business with a view to serve the best to the customers and clients all over the country.

Kosmidou and Zopounidis (2008) evaluated and rated the performance and efficiency of the commercial and cooperative banks in Greece for the period 2003-2004. They found in this study that commercial banks are becoming more competitive and maximizing their profits by increasing their accounts, attracting more customers and improving their financial indices. But in case of the cooperative banks, it has been found that, some are enjoying considerably increased profits and market shares while financial indices have been found to be deteriorating for others.

Moreover, the services of private commercial banks in this country are now better than before. As a result, the clients are rushing to the private banks. Consequently, the private commercial banks are constantly growing in different branches, creating employment opportunities, increasing deposit, loan disbursement, net income and earnings per share over a period of time. As competition is rising in the banking industry due to the emergence of new banks in the market, it has become important to evaluate the performance of every private commercial bank. (Chowdhury and Islam, 2007).

Islamic banks are facing immense national and global challenges, when it is making financial transactions, trading or as a working partner. However, if appropriate laws and regulations persist in a society or at the global level, Islamic banks can manifest its performance appropriately. Two prolific writers of Islamic finance, Ahmad and Hassan remark that Islamic banks in Bangladesh came into existence with certain objectives, in line with the philosophy of Islamic economics that imply a direct and specific responsibility on their part to play an effective role in the socioeconomic development of the country. (Ahman, auf. and hassan, k.,2001)

It has been found that these depositors and entrepreneurs have got the opportunity to practice *Shariah*based banking and fulfil their religious obligation. Alam describes the reasons behind the success of IBBL and narrated that in addition of *Shariah*compliance, senior officials of the bank also keep a regular contact with customers and bank managers frequently visit them in their places of business. Referring to the chief of the Investment Department of the IBBL, Alam commented that though this bank initially faced some challenges, the situation is getting better than before. (Alam, M.N., 2000)

Referring to the existence of Islamic banking amid conventional banking system and economy, Sarkar expresses that Islamic banking system can provide efficient banking services if they are supported with appropriate banking laws, and regulations (Sarker, A.A.,1999)

Hassan views that the successful launching and operation of Islamic banks in Bangladesh has established that banking without interest is feasible. He also observes that Islamic banks have brought together many new depositors and entrepreneurs under the banking system. (Hasan, K., 1999).

Though there are a number of definitions exist, it is generally understood that economic development refers to the standard of living of the citizens improved through alleviating poverty and increased productivity. Also Kifle, Olukoshi, Wohlgemuth support this idea that there is a strong relationship between poverty alleviation and economic development. (Kifle, H., Olukoshi, A., Wohlgemuth, l., 1997)

Banks and financial institutions are contributing in the economic development of Bangladesh through exploring different lucrative economic segments in the form of investment and lending. Banks of our country play roles from conventional and Islamic perspective. Islamic Banks are operating based on Islamic sariah& principles that does not support interest based banking where as conventional banks are in favor of interest and conventional rules & regulation. So, it is necessary to determine how much extent of impact of Islamic Banking activities of a commercial bank on economic development in Bangladesh.

2. Objective of the Study

- To determine the extent of impact of Islamic Banking Activities of FSIBLon economic development in Bangladesh.
- To determine the major problems in banking sector.
- To recommend for the better and more efficient strategy to solve the problems in banking sector.

3. Methodology

Both the primary and secondary sources have been used. We have used some quantitative or factual information too. Simply, the information sources from which we have collected the information that are needed in the report can be divided into two categories. These are

Primary sources&Secondary sources.

*Primary Sources:*Face to face conversation and Personal interview.

*Secondary Sources:*Annual Reports and Web Sites of FSIBL.

For determining the extent of Impact of Islamic banking on economic development of Bangladesh, we have used data in successive five years from 2005 to 2009.

4. Findings

Growth& Development of the First Security Islami Bank Limited:

The growth & development ofthe First Security Islami Bankcan be observed by the following indicators which are included capital, paid up capital, branches, statutory reserve, employees, import, export, remittance, assets, investment & advances, profit before and after tax and deposit etc. and these are described below

Physical Indicators:

Table 1.*The Capital of FSIBL for successive five years from 2005 to 2009.*

	Tk. in Million
Year	**Total Capital**
2005	911.94
2006	1,147.28
2007	1,347.91
2008	2,862.19
2009	3,379.03

Source: Annual Report of FSIBL-2009

In the year 2005, the capital of the First Security Islami Bank Ltd was Tk. 911.94 million and in 2006, it was Tk.1147.28 million, thus by increasing their capital it stands Tk.1347.91 million, Tk. 2862.19 million and Tk.

3379.03 millionin respectively for the year of 2007, 2008 and 2009. So, it reflects the First Security Islami Bank as one of the growing company in the banking industry of Bangladesh and this situation is graphically discovered in below;

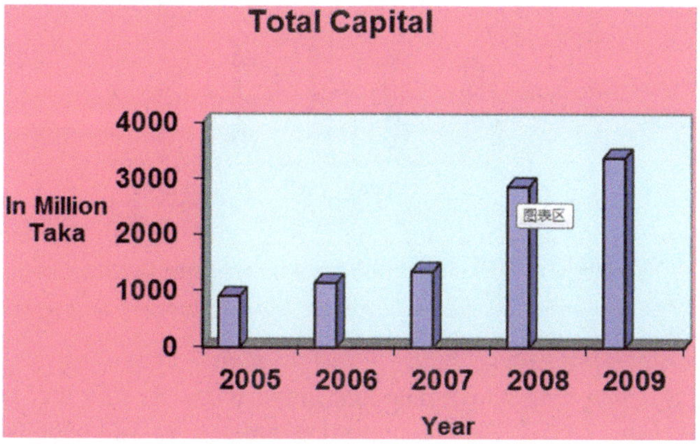

Source: Annual Report of FSIBL-2009

Figure 1. *Showing the capital of FSIBL from 2005 to 2009.*

Table 2. *The Paid Up Capital of FSIBL for successive five years from 2005 to 2009.*

	Tk. In Million
Year	**Paid Up Capital**
2005	600
2006	900
2007	1000
2008	2300
2009	2300

Source: Annual Report of FSIBL-2009

In the year 2005, the paid-up capital of the First Security Islami Bank Ltd was Tk. 600 million and in 2006, it was Tk.900 million, thus by increasing their capital it stands Tk.1000 million, Tk. 2300 million and Tk. 2300 millionin respectively for the year of 2007, 2008 and 2009. So, it reflects the First Security Islami Bank as one of the growing company in the banking industry of Bangladesh although the increasing rate of paid-up capital remain same in 2008 & 2009 and this situation is graphically discovered in below.

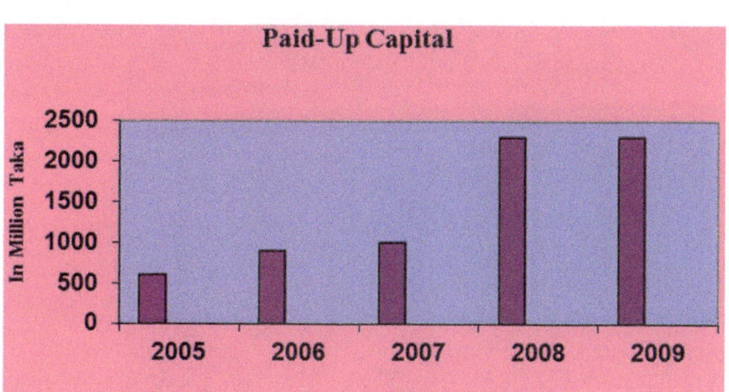

Source: Annual Report of FSIBL-2009

Figure 2. *Showing the Paid Up Capital of FSIBL from 2005 to 2009.*

Table 3. *The Number of Branches of FSIBL for successive five years from 2005 to 2009.*

Year	Branches
2005	12
2006	15
2007	20
2008	29
2009	52

Source: Annual Report of FSIBL-2009

The number of branches of the First Security Islami Bank is increasing by time. It is observed that in the year of 2005, the number ofbranches was only 12, but in 2007 it became as 20 and thus FSIBL increased the branches to 52 till 31stDecember, 2009. So that, now the number of branches is 59 and two new branches are going to open as soon as possible. This situation is graphically discovered in below

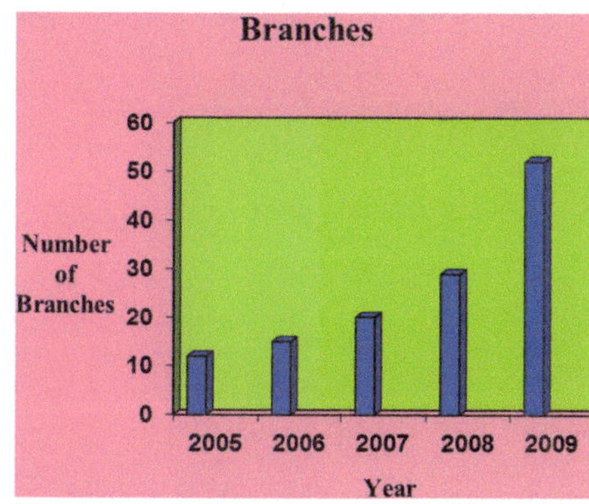

Source: Annual Report of FSIBL-2009

Figure 3. *Showing the number of branches of FSIBL from 2005 to 2009.*

Table 4. *The growth of Statutory Reserve of FSIBL for successive five years from 2005 to 2009.*

	Tk. in Million
Year	**Statutory Reserve**
2005	84.45
2006	84.45
2007	96.16
2008	134.08
2009	263.44

Source: Annual Report of FSIBL-2009

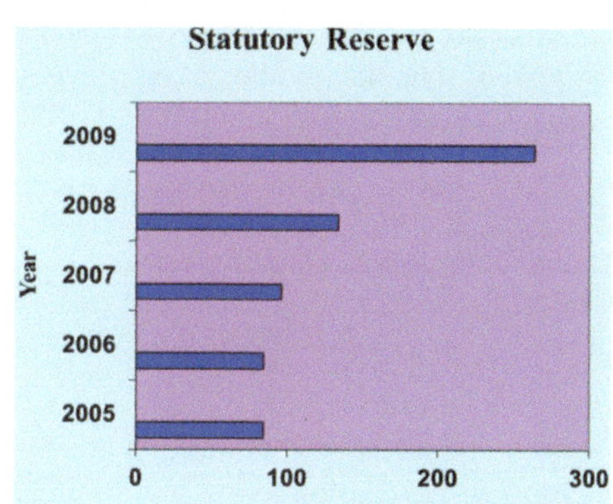

Source: Annual Report of FSIBL-2009

Figure 4. *Showing the growth of Statutory Reserve of FSIBL from 2005 to 2009.*

The statutory reserve of the First Security Islami Bank was Tk.84.45 milliomin 2005and it remained same figure in theyear of 2006, it increased in 2007 as well as 2008 in succession Tk.96.16 million and Tk. 134.08 million. Thus, statutory reserve of FSIBL became Tk. 263.44 million in the year 2009 with a positive situation and it is showed below with a graph

Table 5. *The growth of employment generation of FSIBL for successive five years from 2005 to 2009.*

Year	Employees
2005	423
2006	318
2007	412
2008	483
2009	775

Source: Annual Report of FSIBL-2009

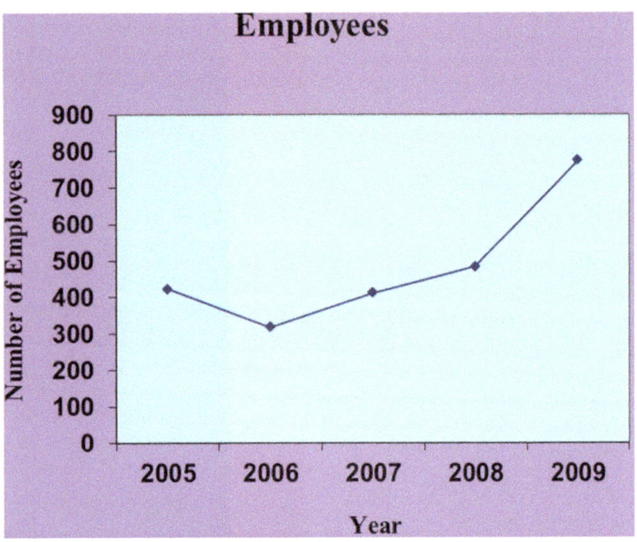

Source: Annual Report of FSIBL-2009

Figure 5. *Showing the growth of employment generation of FSIBL from 2005 to 2009.*

By observing above data and graph it can be said that in the year 2005 the number of employees in FSIBL was 423, but it decreased its employees in 2006 so it became 318 in number. Again, in 2007 FSIBL started to take employees so that the number of employees became at 412 and in the year 2008 it became 483, thus the number of employees in FSIBL was 775 which confirmed in the annual report of 2009.

Table 6. *The growth of FSIBL in case of Import Business for successive five years from 2005 to 2009.*

	Tk. in Million
Year	**Import**
2005	6605.4
2006	7153
2007	14344.44
2008	9287
2009	16101.17

Source: Annual Report of FSIBL-2009

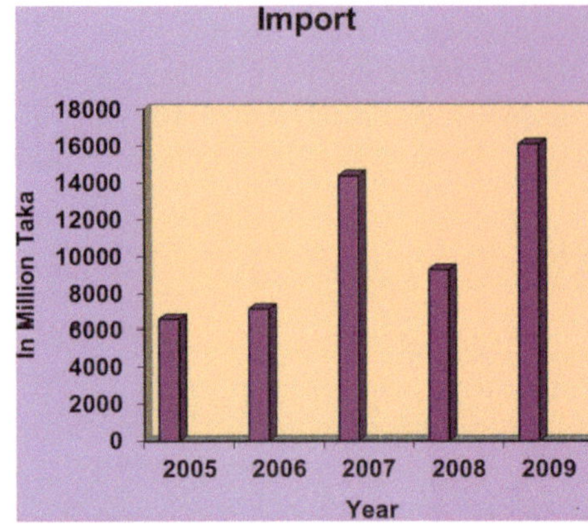

Source: Annual Report of FSIBL-2009

Figure 6. *Showing the growth in case of Import Businessof FSIBL from 2005 to 2009.*

By observing above data and graph it can be said that in the year 2005, FSIBL's importing amount is Tk. 6605.04 million as financial figure, Tk.7153 million in 2006 and Tk. 14344.44 million in 2007. But in the year of 2008 it decreased and downed at the figure Tk. 9287 million. In 2009, the financial figure of import became at Tk. 16101.17 million.

Table 7. *The growth of FSIBL in case of Export Business for successive five years from 2005 to 2009.*

	Tk. in Million
Year	**Export**
2005	2,856.40
2006	2,960.00
2007	3,648.40
2008	4,145.00
2009	3,549.00

Source: Annual Report of FSIBL-2009

By analyzing above data, we can say that, from the year 2005 to 2008, the export situation of First Security Islami Bank is good enough though in the year 2009 it decreased slightly. It increased to Tk. 4,145.00 million from Tk. 2,856.40 million. The financial figure of export of FSIBL is Tk. 3,549.00 million confirmed in the annual report of 2009.

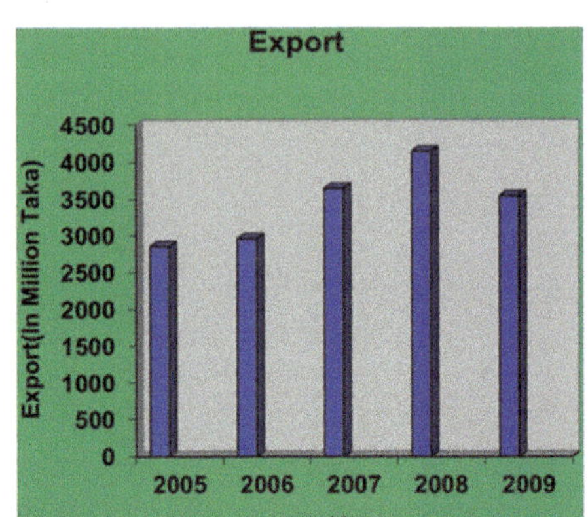

Source: Annual Report of FSIBL-2009

Figure 7. *Showing the growth of Export Business of FSIBL from 2005 to 2009.*

Table 8. *The growth of FSIBL in case of Foreign Remittance for successive five years from 2005 to 2009.*

	Tk. in Million
Year	**Remittance**
2005	62.21
2006	48.44
2007	330
2008	558.84
2009	558.75

Source: Annual Report of FSIBL-2009

By analyzing above data, we can say that, from the year 2005 to 2008, the situation of remittance was improved from the year 2005 to 2008. In 2005 the financial figure of remittance was Tk. 62.21 million which became Tk. 558.84 million in the year of 2008. In 2009, the financial figure of remittance remained same figure as Tk. 558.75 million according to the annual report-2009 of FSIBL.

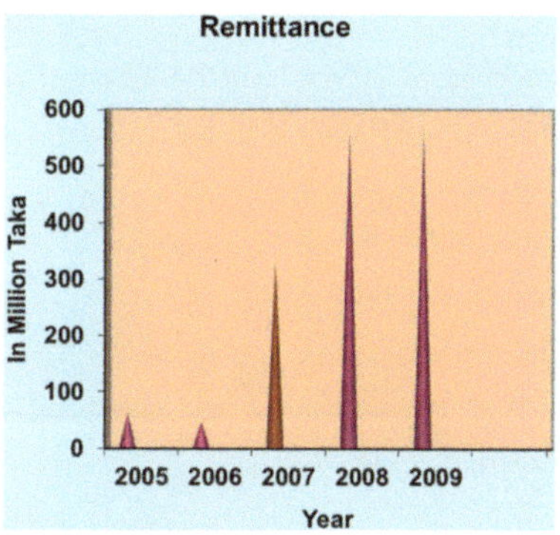

Source: Annual Report of FSIBL-2009

Figure 8. *Showing the growth of FSIBLin case of Foreign Remittance from 2005 to 2009.*

Table 9. *The growth of FSIBL in case of Asset for successive five years from 2005 to 2009.*

	Tk. in Million
Year	**Assets**
2005	20,260.33
2006	20,448.66
2007	26,942.00
2008	31,239.00
2009	47,978.55

Source: Annual Report of FSIBL-2009

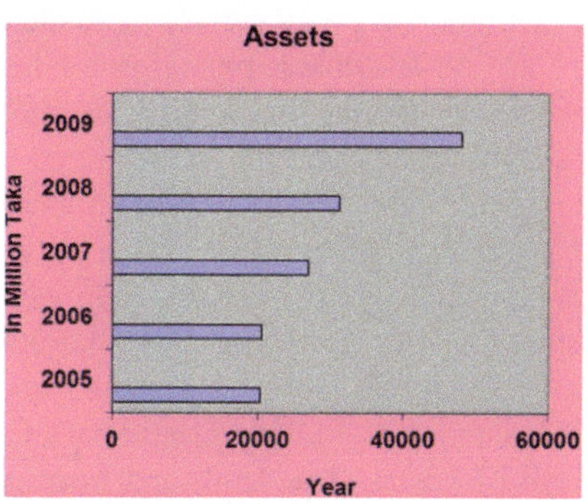

Source: Annual Report of FSIBL-2009

Figure 9. *Showing the growth in case of Foreign Remittance of FSIBL from 2005 to 2009.*

The asset of the First Security Islami Bank was Tk. 20,260.33 milliomin 2005andin theyear of 2006, it increased to Tk. 20,4448.66 million, it increased in 2007 also. In 2008, it became Tk. 31,239 million. Thus, asset of FSIBL became at Tk. 47,978.55 millionin 2009 with a positive situation and it is showed below with a graph.

Table 10. *The growth of FSIBL in case of Investments & Advances for successive five years from 2005 to 2009.*

	Tk. in Million
Year	**Investments & Advances**
2005	10722.32
2006	13646.38
2007	18616.22
2008	25094.65
2009	38725.87

Source: Annual Report of FSIBL-2009

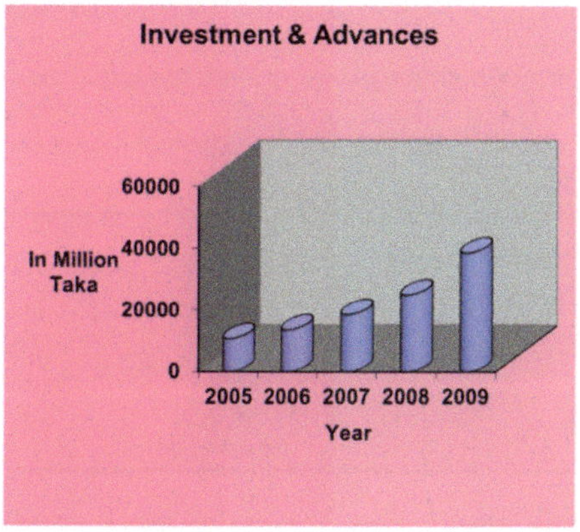

Source: Annual Report of FSIBL-2009

Figure 10. *Showing the growth in case of Investments & Advances of FSIBL from 2005 to 2009.*

By observing above data and graph it can be said that in the year 2005, FSIBL's investments & advances amount is Tk. 10722.32 million as financial figure, Tk13646.38 million in 2006 and Tk. 18616.22 million in 2007, Tk.25094.65million in the year of 2008. In 2009, the financial figure of import became at Tk. 38725.87 million. So we can include the FSIBL as one of the growing company in the banking industry of Bangladesh.

Table 11. *The growth of FSIBL in case of Profit for successive five years from 2005 to 2009.*

	Tk. in Million	Tk. in Million
Year	**Profit Before Tax**	**Profit After Tax**
2005	17.98	9.88
2006	-132.22	-117.24
2007	58.53	30.63
2008	189.6	104.28
2009	650.83	330.83

Source: Annual Report of FSIBL-2009

From the above data we can conclude that, profit before tax and after tax of the FSIBLare in respectively Tk. 17.98 million and Tk. 9.88 million in 2005. But in the year 2006, this amount is in off situation. Again, in 2007, 2008 it increased as Tk. 58.53 million & Tk. 90.63 million. At last, in the year 2009, profit before tax of the FSIBL is Tk.650.83 million and after tax is Tk. 330.83 million.

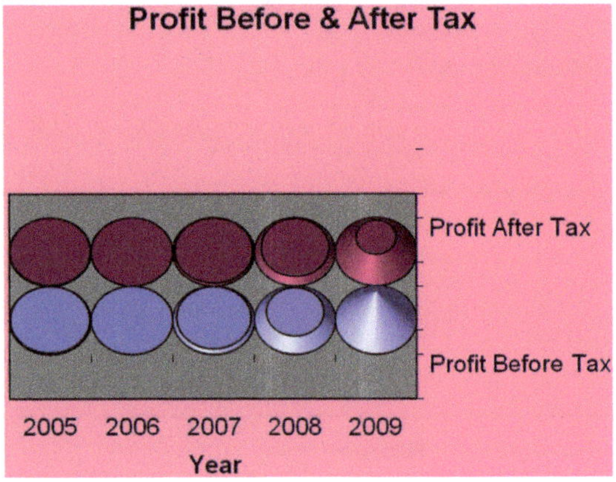

Source: Annual Report of FSIBL-2009

Figure 11. *Showing the growth in case of Profit of FSIBL from 2005 to 2009.*

Table 12. *The growth of FSIBL in case of Deposit for successive five years from 2005 to 2009.*

	Tk. in Million
Year	**Deposit**
2005	14012.17
2006	17592
2007	23504.04
2008	25854.54
2009	42423.09

Source: Annual Report of FSIBL-2009

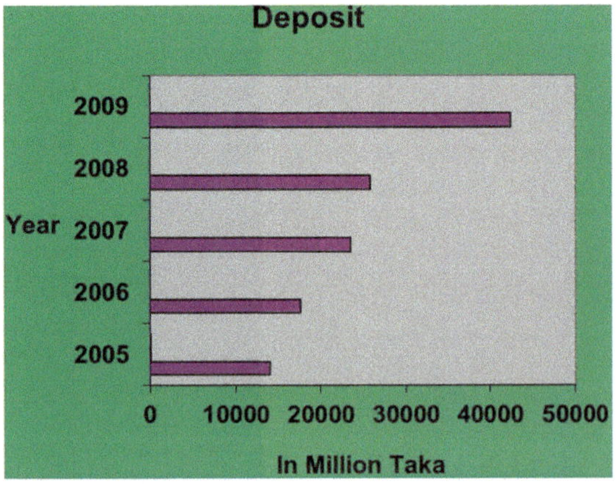

Source: Annual Report of FSIBL-2009

Figure 12. *Showing the growth in case of Deposit of FSIBL from 2005 to 2009.*

From the above data and graph of the FSIBL, we can see, the deposit amount of FSIBL in 2005 was Tk.14012.17 million, in 2006 the amount of deposit was Tk. 17592 million as financial situation of deposit increased in2007 also and it reached at Tk.23504.04 million. Thus the deposit of FSIBL increased day by day and as a result it reached at the amount of Tk. 42423.09 million. So, as a growing company in the banking industry of Bangladesh is in better performance.

Table 13. *Financial Highlights of First Security Islami Bank Limited.*

	In Taka	
Particulars	**2009**	**2008**
Paid-up Capital	2,300,000,000	2,300,000,000
Total Capital Fund	3379.03	2,862,198,083
Capital Surplus / (Deficit	267,692,742	1126,543,146
Total Assets	47,978,552,952	31,239,393,418
Total Deposits	42,423,092,722	25,854,541,500
Total Investment	38,725,874,774	25,094,658,077
Total Contingent Liabilities and Commitments	5,971,673,066	4,611,289,577
Investment Deposit Ratio (in %)	91.28%	96.39%
Percentage of Classified Loans Against Total Loans and Advances (in %)	2.14%	4.20%
Profit Before Tax and Provision	750,837,749	189,603,753
Amount of Classified Investment	830,515,000	1,053,412,705
Provision Kept Against Classified Investment	507,694,000	597,694,000
Provision Surplus / (Deficit)	53,834,571	31,818,406
Cost of Fund	9.28%	11.37%
Profit Earning Assets	41,371,529,125	28,529,063,421
Non-Profitt Earning Assets	6,607,023,827	2,710,329,997
Return On Investment in Shares & Securities (ROI)(in %)	2.79%	15.18%
Return on Assets (ROA) (in %)	1.56%	0.61%
Income From Investment in Shares & Securities	53,510,527	202,345,834
Earning Per Share	14.21.	7.35
Net Income Per Share	14.21	7.35
Price Earning Ratio	15.39	23.74

Sources: Annual Report of FSIBL-2009

5. Principles of Islamic Banking

Islamic banking has the same purpose as conventional banking except that it operates in accordance with the rules of Shariah, known as Fiqh al-Muamalat. The basic principle of Islamic banking is the sharing of profit and loss and the prohibition of riba. Amongst the common Islamic concepts used in Islamic banking are profit sharing (Mudharabah), safekeeping (Wadiah), joint venture (Musharakah), cost plus (Murabahah).

In an Islamic mortgage transaction, instead of loaning the buyer money to purchase the item, a bank might buy the item itself from the seller, and re-sell it to the buyer at a profit, while allowing the buyer to pay the bank in installments. However, the fact that it is profit cannot be made explicit and therefore there are no additional penalties for late payment. In order to protect itself against default, the bank asks for strict collateral. The goods or land is registered to the name of the buyer from the start of the transaction. This arrangement is called Murabaha. Another approach is EljarawaElqtina, which is similar to real estate leasing. Islamic banks handle loans for vehicles in a similar way.

An innovative approach applied by some banks for home loans, called Musharaka al-Mutanaqisa, allows for a floating rate in the form of rental. The bank and borrower forms a partnership entity, both providing capital at an agreed percentage to purchase the property. The partnership entity then rent out the property to the borrower and charges rent.

The bank and the borrower will then share the proceed from this rent based on the current equity share of the partnership. At the same time, the borrower in the partnership entity also buys the bank's share on the property at agreed installments until the full equity is transferred to the borrower and the partnership is ended. If default occurs, both the bank and the borrower receive the proceeds from an auction based on the current equity. This method allows for floating rates according to current market rate such as the BLR (base lending rate), especially in a dual-banking system like in Malaysia.

There are several other approaches used in business deals. Islamic banks lend their money to companies by issuing floating rate interest loans.

The floating rate of interest is pegged to the company's individual rate of return. Thus the bank's profit on the loan is equal to a certain percentage of the company's profits. Once the principal amount of the loan is repaid, the profit-sharing arrangement is concluded. This practice is called Musharaka. Further, Mudaraba is venture capital funding of an entrepreneur who provides labor while financing is provided by the bank so that both profit and risk are shared. Such participatory arrangements between capital and labor reflect the Islamic view that the borrower must not bear all the risk/cost of a failure, resulting in a balanced distribution of income and not allowing lender to monopolize the economy. And finally, Islamic banking is restricted to Islamically acceptable deals, which exclude those involving alcohol, pork, gambling, etc. Thus ethical investing is the only acceptable form of investment, and moral purchasing is encouraged. In theory, Islamic banking is an example of full-reserve banking, with banks achieving a 100% reserve ratio.

However, in practice, this is not the case, and no examples of 100 per cent reserve banking are observed. Islamic banks have grown recently in the Muslim world but are a very small share of the global banking system. Micro-lending institutions founded by Muslims, notably Grameen Bank, use conventional lending practices and are popular in some Muslim nations, especially Bangladesh, but some do not consider them true Islamic banking. However, Muhammad Yunus, the founder of Grameen Bank and microfinance banking, and other supporters of microfinance, argue that the lack of collateral and lack of excessive interest in micro-lending is consistent with the Islamic prohibition of usury.

6. ImpactIslamic Banking on Economic Development of Bangladesh

Due to global economic recession, time is very much challenging and uncertain. Specially, this calamity become acute with eventual collapse of some major banking institution and massive dips in stock market indices across the globe. As a result, developing economy like Bangladesh economy deteriorated rapidly.

Bangladesh represents a underdeveloped financial system which leads a slow economic growth. According to the international monetary fund, Bangladesh ranked as the 48th largest economy in the world in 2009, with a GDP of US$256 billion. Although Bangladeshi economy is based on agriculture, more than half of the GDP is belongs to the service sector such as transport, financial institution, real estate education, public administration, health, social and personal service. From the financial institution, banking industry is the most essential.

The banking industry of Bangladesh is now highly competitive and challenging sector rather than previous period of time. Basically banking sector is involved with financial system. To have a healthy and vibrant economy it needs a financial system that moves funds from people who save people who have strong productive investment opportunities. And we know that, a country's economic development means development the economy of a country which concern with trade, industry and wealth of the country.

Despite sluggish economic senario, the FSIBL passed successfully with the help of their efficient and prudent workforce. Thus FSIBL has been able to close the balance sheet with an enormous pre-tax profit of Tk.750 million with an excellent growth rate of 300% while the whole financial sector faced a slowdown. Banking institution can create an impacton the economy through its general activities like deposit collection, giving loan, invest in different economic sector such as agriculture, garments, house building etc. export and remittance business.

There is a link between financial system and economy. Without financial sector an economic system can not draw its growth. Banks are the most financial intermediaries and FSIBL is not different from them. General banking activities are like the flow of bloods of any bank which are practiced and operated to keep a bank alive.

So, FSIBL is also having its own general activities like other banks. A/C opening, closing, loan and investment, ATM banking, locker service, SMSbanking etc.

In the society there live different people and they have different demands and needs. FSIBL is ready to serve them as their choice by offering various types of A/C such as Al-wadiah A/C, Mudarabah Special Notice A/C, Mudarabah Savings A/C, Mudarabah Monthly Savings Scheme. FSIBL offers different types loan and opportunity to invest and shares risk with the customers.

Although, at first FSIBL was started as usual commercial bank in 1999, but after several yearit was changed to a Islamic Bank and its principles developed based on Islamic Shariah. There are 90% muslim people in Bangladesh, they have islamic mind and culture. So that, FSIBL is giving opportunity the people to invest thus by collecting deposit from them and investing from different sector such as invest in industry developing and thus bank earn profits and share with it's customer and shareholders, if failed then also be shared between them.

ATM banking of FSIBL is not fully independent. It does an agreement with Dutch Bangla Bank Limited. So thus the customer of FSIBL who want to hold ATM card they have to give service charge yearly Tk.300 and it also a way of earning and adding in GDP of the country.

Table 14. *Economic Sector wise Investments.*

	Amount in Tk.	
	31.12.2009	31.12.2008
Agriculture:		
Fishing	92400000	90453000
Tea	-	-
Others	145700000	72825000
Textiles and Readymade Garments:		
Garments	356500000	223124000
Readymade Garments- Export	413000000	379514000
Textile and Textile Products- Import	1198600000	345914000
Others-Export	455000000	348426000
Others-Import	2877300000	1227259000
Medicine-Import	83300000	56874000
Chemical-Import	15500000	10431000
Contractor Finance	2353200000	2057744000
Transport	79600000	31394000
Bricks	10100000	16890000
Cold Storage	69800000	43473000
Steel & Engineering	55000000	50748000
Internal Trade Finance:		
Whole Sale Trading	5943300000	4581529000
Retail Trading	4886700000	1367004000
Others	4559000000	4723643000
House Building:		
Commercial	2925300000	387069000
Staff	61100000	53025000
Special Program:		
Consumer Finance & Hire Purchase Scheme	67000000	54475000
Others	12078474774	8972844077

Source: Annual Report of FSIBL-2009

Like other successful bank FSIBL also has SMS banking so that customer can know about the status of their A/C and make their transaction, as always other types of services of the bank. So that, it is saving more time consuming and is able to serve many customers in a little time and get opportunity to concentrate in other objectives.

FSIBL is one of the 3rd generation bank. Despite of this it increases it's branches within a short period of time. That's why at present FSIBL have 62 branches. Along with this, it recruits skilled and experienced people as employee and arrange training program for them who are not skilled enough. Thus it decreases the unemployment problem of the country which is helping indirectly to enlarging the growth rate of GDP. FSIBL is giving services through Ahsania Mission to the root level people in easier way and low cost. It also keeps valuable products in safe by providing locker service. In this service, people are getting safety. On the other hand, bank earns profits by making service charge from the customers and obviously by giving better service.

FSIBL is one of the Islamicbank of Bangladesh, which is playing an important role in banking sector of Bangladesh through its different activities. Like other different banks, FSIBL also invest in different economic sector such as agriculture, textile & readymade garments, house building and other such special programs having great impact on the economy. It is observed through the following data comparing with the previous period which revealed in the last annual report 2009. That is presenting a positive situation is given below.

On the other side, we can relate import and export of a country with its economical consideration. So, thus, it is observed the import, export and remittance business of the FSIBL is improved.

6.1. Import Business

Import trade finance by FSIBL rose to Tk. 1610.17 crore in reporting year compared with Tk. 928.70 crore in 2008. Large LCs are opened mainly for importing rice, wheat, edible oil, fertilizer, capital machinery, fabrics and accessories.

6.2. Export Business

FSIBL successfully handled export documents of Tk. 3549 million during the reporting year compared with Tk. 4145 million in the year 2008. Readymade garments, frozen foods, fish, tanned leather, handicraft etc.

6.3. Remittance Services

From the last report we know that, foreign remittance of the bank stood at Tk. 558.7 million as of December 31,2009 as against Tk. 585.8 milllion in 2008. So thatthrough the Foreign Exchange service of FSIBLthe people of Bangladesh can well served the bank has taken initiatives to make remittance arrangements with some leading exchange houses at abroad.

More people of Bangladesh who are working out of country, for them, FSIBL has attached with 501 branches of 8 banks through ELDORADO. This bank has its own exchange house in Canada.

7. Corporate Social Responsibilities

Although FSIBL is a corporate citizen of Bangladesh, it has also some social responsibilities. Thus First Security Islami Bank is aware of its corporate social responsibilities it supports to the development of community through promotion of culture, sports, educational program and disaster and treatment aid of the distressed people. The bank actively participates for promotion of the sports, religious events and cultural activities. Recently bank has donated Tk. 25 lacs to the Aila fund, Tk. 28 lacs to the Bangladesh Association of Banks for BDR carnage and Tk. 50 lacs to the Port City League (PCL). The FSIBL is also introducing FSIBL foundation very soon.

Overall the other activities FSIBL has different contribution also such as

- FSIBL donated Tk 50, 00,000/- for Liberation War Museum
- FSIBL donated Tk 30, 00,000/- to Prime Minister's Relief & Welfare Fund
- Tk.2000000/- is given as assistance for family members of the martyred Army Officers killed in BDR

carnage by FSIBL

- To mitigate the sufferings of Aila victims, First Security Islami Bank Limited has donated Tk 10,00,000/- only to Prime Minister's Relief Fund.
- First Security Islami Bank Limited with the assistance of Bankers Forum organized an eye camp for the orphans of DhakaCity.
- As a part of Corporate Social Responsibility, First Security Islami Bank Limited has donated an ambulance to BaitusSharaf ShahJabberiaHospital.

By considering the above information we can make a conclusion that FSIBL is one of the first growing bank which has a impact on developing the economic condition of Bangladesh so it is doing well in foreign exchange service, export & import Business, economic sector wise investments as well as having corporate social responsibilities.

8. Conclusion

FSIBL is one of the fastest growing and best performing banks in Bangladesh. Because of its excellent teamwork among the top management, staff, borrowers, depositors and other stakeholders as well as outstanding banking performance, this bank has secured a very strong position in Bangladesh banking sector. FSIBL has invested in a wide range of areas that not only reduced the risk of investment, but also providing services to a large number of Bangladeshis in home and abroad. This study has portrayed clear a picture of FSIBL's role in the economic development of Bangladesh. If this trend remains continued, FSIBL's contribution will make significant impact on the social and environmental issues in the near future in addition to the economic betterment of the country.

Islamic Economy is required to executed real Islamic banking practice; Bangladesh economy does not cover real practice of Islamic banking although 90% people of Bangladesh are Muslim in religious status.

Profit Loss Sharing based Banking does not have the chance to bankruptcy of one party but it must be compiled properly.

Investment system of First Security Islami Bank Limited has highly time consuming from the borrower perspective to hamper their operation. There is no proper use of media & other means.

Recommendations

- The need for regulation and uniform supervisory of Islamic Banks.
- Issues of risk management and guidelines on risk weight of assets.
- Capital adequacy, liquidity management and issues of controlling of the asset side of Islamic banks.
- Issues in profitability and good governance.
- The necessitate of adoption of new financial methods to Islamic banks.

References

[1] Ahman, Auf. and K. Hassan, (2001), 'Regulation and Performance of Islamic Banking in Bangladesh', Thunderbird International Business Review, vol. 49, no. 2, pp. 251- 277.

[2] Alam, M.N. 2000. 'Islamic Banking in Bangladesh: A Case Study of IBBL; *International Journal of Islamic Financial Services*, vol. 1, no. 4.

[3] Chowdhury, H.A. and M.S. Islam. 2007. "Interest Rate Sensitivity of Loans and Advances: A Comparative Study between Nationalized Commercial Banks and specialized Banks,"*ASA University Review*, vol. 1, pp. 86-97.

[4] Hasan, K. 1999. Islamic Banking in Theory and Practice: The Experience of Bangladesh, Managerial Finance, vol. 25, no. pp. 60-113.

[5] Kifle, H., Olukoshi, A. and L. Wohlgemuth.1997. A New Partnership for African Development: Issues and Parameters, Stockholm: Gotab.

[6] Kosmidou, K.and C. Zopounidis. 2008. "Measurement of Bank Performance in Greece," *South-Eastern Europe Journal of Economics*, vol. 1, pp. 79-95,.

[7] Sarkar, A.A. (1999), 'Islamic Banking in Bangladesh: Performance, Problems & Prospects', *International Journal of Islamic Financial Services*, vol.1, no. 3.

17

The Impact of Regulatory Environment on the Effectiveness of Small and Medium Scale Enterprises: A Study of Selected Small and Medium Scale Enterprise in Owerri

Chikwe Goddey Chukwudi[1], Joel Augustus-Daddie[2], Achiole Emmanuel Ayozie[3]

[1]Department of Business Management, Imo State University, Owerri, Imo State Nigeria
[2]Department of Business Administration and Management, River State Polytechnic, Bori, River State, Nigeria
[3]Department of Business Management, Imo State University, Owerri, Imo State Nigeria

Email address:
chikwas4god@yahoo.com (Chikwe Goddey Chukwudi), joelad2009@yahoo.com (Joel Augustus-Daddie), emma4mgt@yahoo.com (Achiole Emmanuel Ayozie)

Abstract: This paper examines the impact of regulatory environment on the effectiveness of small and medium scale enterprises. The study employed a survey approach and used the questionnaire as its major source of data collection. In order to guide the study, two research questions and hypotheses that are consistent with the objectives of the study were raised. The population of study consists of 105 staff of selected five small and medium scale enterprises in Owerri. The researchers used purposive sampling technique to select 89 members of staff as the sampled unit. The mean score $\overline{X}$ was the tool for data analysis, and from the findings, the researchers concludes that regulatory environment has significant impact on business competitiveness and innovativeness which were used to proxy effectiveness of small and medium scale enterprises. Based on the findings also, the researchers among others recommended that consultation between SME regulators and operators of SMEs can help address some of the harsh consequences of the regulatory environment.

Keywords: Regulatory Environment, Organizational Effectiveness, Competitiveness, Innovativeness

1. Introduction

The modern business manager operates in a highly dynamic environment. The change in the environment has been rapid and unpredictable. Economic variables have been complex both in form and impact on the practice of business in Nigeria. Consumers and clients have been showing complex behaviors both in local and international markets. The most dramatic change has been that exhibited by competitive pressures. Competitors have been applying one strategy or the other to adapt to the dynamic and unpredictable nature of the business environment.The most single significant influence on organizational policy and strategy is the environment outside and inside the organization (Grant, 1999). Currently, business environment is perceived to havecomplexity, turbulence and speed in change, all Nigerian organizations (large or small) must pay greater attention than ever before to their environments when formulating and implementing policies and strategies in order to survive and grow (Otokiti & Awodun, 2003).

Discussing the relevance of understanding the regulatory environment in contemporary business practice, Agulanna and Chris (2003) opined that business and industries operate in a large web of regulatory environment. They come into existence through the web, operate within the web and go out of existence passing through the same web. They went further to posit that business managers must comply with the federal, state, and local government laws as well as court orders. According to Dickson, Gates, Kapur, Seabury and Tally, (2007) regulatory environment has been identified as a controlling element for business to legally and freely function. In this paper, we shall take the business regulatory environment as legislation, political and administrative factors that have an influence on businesses. In the 1980s, organizational effectiveness became more prominent and switched to being a concept from the status of a construct (Henry, 2011). This concept is related to issues such as the ability of an organization to access and absorb resources and consequently achieve its aims (Federman, 2006). Cameron (1978) pointed out that organizational effectiveness is the proficiency of the organization at having access to the essential resources. However, McCann (2004) noted it as the criterion of the organization's successful fulfillment of their purposes through core strategies.

According to definition of Yankey& McClellan (2003) "OE is the extent to which an organization has met its stated goals and objectives, and how well it performed in the process. Scott et al (2008) opined that the term organizational effectiveness is usually deployed to contrast with development effectiveness. It focuses on the direct results of an agency's interventions, for which it can be held accountable, in contrast with development outcomes, which are the effect of many agencies interventions. The term OE usually focuses on the internal systems that are geared towards producing development outputs and outcomes. In this sense, it is synonymous with results based management and managing for development results.Drawing upon the work of Kushner and Poole (2002), the performance of an organization may be modeled along four components: resource acquisitions, efficiency, goal attainment, and client satisfaction. Brooks (2003) believes that ignoring any of these dimensions is to possess an incomplete understanding of the organization's performance. Obviously, the feedback loop between these components is more far-reaching than the definition of each component. The researchers focused on competitiveness and innovativeness as the measures of organizational effectiveness.

Statement of the Problem

In contemporary Nigerian business environment, low-sales, high cost of production, low capital utilization, lack of foreign exchange to source needed inputs, poor power supply, and low quality of goods and services, among others have become recurring decimals in business reports. These issues have led to lack of proper integration and coordination of various corporate subsystems in Nigerian organizations, resulting in the failure to achieve the stated goals and objectives. Enterprises are subsumed in the environment with which they interact by importing inputs and exporting outputs. Thus, the vagaries and the extremities of the environment affect the fortunes of organizations (kennerly& Nelly, 2003).In order to improve the business climates and encourage the growth of SMEs, government at different times legal frameworks and policies. While these policies are made with the best of intentions, the process of their implementations most times falls short of operational environment realities. The problem of this paper therefore is to examine the impact of regulatory environment on the effectiveness of SMEs.

Objectives of the Study

The general purpose of this study is to examine the impact of regulatory environment variable on organizational effectiveness. However, the following specific objectives shall be examined;

i. To examine the impact of regulatory environment on organizational competitiveness
ii. To examine the impact of regulatory environment on the organizational innovativeness
iii. *Research Questions*
iv. The following research questions shall serve as a guide to this study;
v. What are the impacts of regulatory environment on organizational competitiveness?
vi. What are the impacts of regulatory environment on the organizational innovativeness?

Hypotheses

The following tentative assertions are made for this study

HO1: regulatory environment does not have significant impact on organizational competitiveness

HO2: regulatory environment does not have significant impact on organizational innovativeness

2. Literature Review

In this section, the researchers x-rayed the contributions of different authorities in this line of knowledge

Organizational Effectiveness

According to Hardesty (2003), organizational effectiveness is defined in many different ways depending on the organizations goals and objectives in today's market and also is dependent on the industry. In today's market, organizational effectiveness is dependent on seven to ten attributes/characteristics, dependent on the theorist.Hardesty (2003) says there are ten characteristics those highly effective organizations exhibits. They are, "clarity of the organization's mission, the power of leadership vision, adherence to shared values throughout the organization, cohesive, balanced team of leaders, clear and measurable goals and objectives, mechanisms for external feedback and input, a desire to learn continuously, pursuit of excellence, competent planning and decision-making processes, periodic celebrations of nobility of the work and collective accomplishments". Fitz-Enz (1997) concluded there are eight practices of highly effective organizations. They entail balanced values, commitment, culture, communication, partnering, collaboration, innovation and risk, and competitive passion. Stating what an organization is supposed to look like and how it should function is easy. The hard part is how to get there and practicing the characteristics of an effective organization. Most organizations know the success of an organization is dependent on the people in place that produce the product or service. It starts with the leadership who tries to instill values throughout the organization.

Edward Deming, a renowned organizational effectiveness theorist, discussed 14 points that management needs to practice to operate as an effective organization. Deming's 14 points are:

(1) Create constancy of purpose toward improvement of

product and service, with the aim to become competitive and to stay in business, and to provide jobs; (2) Adopt the new philosophy. We are in a new economic age. Western management must awaken to the challenge, must learn their responsibilities, and take on leadership for change; (3) Cease dependence on inspection to achieve quality. Eliminate the need for inspection on a mass basis by building quality into the product in the first placc; (4) End the practice of awarding business on the basis of price tag. Instead, minimize total cost. Move toward a single supplier for anyone item, on a long-term relationship of loyalty and trust; (5) Improve constantly and forever the system of production and service, to improve quality and productivity, and thus constantly decrease costs; (6) Institute training on the job; (7) Institute leadership. The aim of supervision should be to help people and machines and gadgets to do a better job. Supervision of management is in need of overhaul, as well as supervision of production workers; (8) drive out fear, so that everyone may work effectively for the company; (9) Break down barriers between departments. People in research, design, sales, and production must work as a team, to foresee problems ofproduction and in use that may be encountered with the product or service; (10) Eliminate slogans, exhortations, and targets for the work force asking for zero defects and new levels of productivity. Such exhortations only create adversarial relationships, as the bulk ofthe causes oflow quality and low productivity belong to the system and thus lie beyond the power of the work force; 0 (11) Eliminate work standards (quotas) on the factory floor. Substitute leadership and eliminate management by objective. Eliminate management by numbers, numerical goals. Substitute leadership; (12) Remove barriers that rob the hourly worker of his right to pride of workmanship. The responsibility of supervisors must be changed from sheer numbers to quality. Remove barriers that rob people in management and in engineering oftheir right to pride of workmanship. This means, inter alia, abolishment of the annual or merit rating and of management by objective; (13) Institute a vigorous program of education and self-improvement; (14) put everybody in the company to work to accomplish the transformation. The transformation is everybody's job (The Edwards Deming Institute, n.d.).

Senge (1990) states that learning organizations are Organizations where people continually expand their capacity to create the results they truly desire, where new and expansive patterns ofthinking are nurtured, where collective aspiration is set free, and where people are continually learning to see the whole together. For an individual to practice real learning one must find what they truly desire and what they believe in their heart. This is true in organizations as well. For real learning to occur in organizations, the organization as a whole and the individual units ofthe organization need to understand their purpose and mission they are trying to achieve, before they can engage in learning.He identified five dimensions that distinguish a learning organization from a traditional organization; which are: (1) systems thinking, (2) personal mastery, (3) mental models, (4) building shared vision, and (5) team learning.

Systems thinking is about looking at all of the units, processes, techniques, and branches within an organization and viewing them as a whole instead of individually. It is necessary for learning organizations to think about how a decision will impact the future. Many times the complete consequence of a decision is not seen because it is a long-term consequence. Learning organizations look beyond the quick fix to a resolution that works both short-term and long-term. Learning organizations have constant feedback systems in place to continually check the progression or regression of the decision. The second discipline, personal mastery, is defined as the following: People with a high level of personal mastery live in a continual learning mode. They never 'arrive'. Sometimes, language such as the term 'personal mastery' creates a misleading sense of definiteness, of black and white. But personal mastery is not something you possess. It is a process. It is a lifelong discipline. People with a high level of personal mastery are acutely aware of their ignorance, their incompetence, their growth areas. And they are deeply self-confident. Personal mastery is not about competence and skills; it is about the vision the organization has and recognizing where the organization has a weakness and being truthful to those weaknesses. The third discipline is mental models, which refers to looking at the assumptions that a given organization has and to realize how these assumptions impact behavior or performance. Specifically: The discipline of mental models starts with turning the mirror inward; learning to unearth our internal pictures of the world, to bring them to the surface and hold them rigorously to scrutiny. It also includes the ability to carryon 'meaningful' conversations that balance inquiry and advocacy, where people expose their own thinking effectively and make that thinking open to the influence of others. (Senge, 1990) So often organizations try to implement a new process or go after a new market that initially might be unsuccessful. The unsuccessful attempt is often remembered and carried over through generations ofthe company without the process or attempt being fully analyzed to conclude that it was a weak process or market. The fourth discipline, building shared vision, is defined as, the capacity to hold a shared picture of the future we seek to create. This discipline creates the ability for an organization to become innovative.

The fifth and final dimension of learning organizations is team learning, which is viewed as, "the process of aligning and developing the capacities of a team to create the results its members truly desire. If the organization does not operate as a team, they will struggle to succeed in their endeavors. When an organization operates as a team they openly discuss and scrutinize assumptions and "discover results and insights not attainable individually. Effective organizations do not contain individuals that focus on themselves individually, instead they work for what the entire organization is trying to achieve.

Ken Wright, an organizational effectiveness consultant, combined previous research from Covey, Senge, and Deming to develop his own definition and way to measure organizational effectiveness. Wright (1997) calls it "organizational wellness" and defines it as an, "organization that is well as one which is self-renewing and continuously improving, a true collaborative community of learners". Organizational effectiveness is developed through culture, processes, and professional growth. The culture of the organization defines the context of information, processes, people, values, beliefs, and techniques. The culture is how things get accomplished, recognized, discussed, changed, put into place; it defines how the organization operates, reacts, and implements new ideas or change. The processes of an organization are independent and interdependent. They can operate solely without one another, however, each process within an organization make up the entirety of the organization. Therefore, if one of the processes breaks down, it is likely it will affect the entire organization. Process, decision-making, and communication are the main processes that need to be flawlessly operating for an organization to have effective processes. Professional growth is related to the opportunities that exist in an organization for employees to grow. Effective organizations continuously offer their employees professional growth opportunities. Maturation is instilled and expected in effective organizations. Organizations that can excel in these three areas will become an effective organization (Wright, 1997).

Factors Affecting Organizational Effectiveness

According to Malik et al (2011) factors that may affect the organizational effectiveness are: performance,motivation, organizational environment, managerial expertise, creative synergy, multi-ethnic and racialbackground. In the following lines performance, motivation, organizational environment, and managerialexpertise will be focused for explanation.

a) Performance

An Anonymous writer has defined "performance" as all the activity of a given participant on a given occasion, which serves to influence in any way any of the other participants. Performance is usually considered to be a broader term than effectiveness and includes efficiency and behavior. However, in practice, these terms are often used interchangeably Scott et al (2008). According to Malik et al (2011) employee performance basically depends on many factors like performance appraisals, employee motivation, Employee satisfaction, compensation, Training and development, job security, Organizational structure and other. Performance may also depend on some factors such as: pay rises, flexible time system, personal satisfaction, and so on.

b) Motivation

According to Kamery, (2004) of Nova Southeastern University employees may be motivated on the job by many things, such as a sense of achievement, recognition, enjoyment of the job, promotion opportunities, responsibility, and the chance for personal growth. Employee motivation and performance are tied directly to the style of management that is applied and to principles of positive or negative reinforcement. Kamery, (2004) further elaborated that the key to motivating employees is remembering that not all employees are the same. Something different makes each employee tick. In order to achieve motivation, managers must know each employee. Managers must have a wide range of motivational techniques available. Each employee has a different set of values and personal experiences that brought them to where they are today. Employees are motivated by learning and should likewise be motivated to learn. Workers should be offered regular opportunities to attend conferences in their field, seminars, or in-house training programs. A supervisor can provide the environment in which employees are willing to motivate themselves. The purpose of a motivating environment is to encourage every member of an organization to motivate himself to contribute his best effort to the job at all times. A motivating environment is not a permissive environment, but one where the expectations of each employee are for their best work within their capability. A motivating environment is not necessarily one in which all employees are happy all of the time. A motivating environment may produce satisfied employees, which in turn may make many employees happy. A motivating environment exists with conditions of high standards, clear objectives, adequate training, effective leadership, rewards that employees value, and adequate working conditions.

c) Organizational Environment

According to Malik et al (2011) organizational environment reflects from the culture composition, rules and regulations, freedom of work etc. Malik et al (2011) explained organizational environment (Robbins, 2008) that the forces that can make an impact. Forces made upopportunities and threats. Organizational environment determines the manner and extent to which roles,power, and responsibilities are delegated, controlled, and coordinated, and how information flows betweenlevels of management. This structure depends entirely on the organization's objectives and the strategychosen to achieve them. Malik et al (2011) narrated quoting Lusthaus, Anderson and Murphy thatenvironment is made up of the administrative, technological, political, economic, socio-cultural, andstakeholder factors. Each organization is set in a particular environment to which it is inextricably linked. This environment provides multiple contexts that affect the organization and its performance, what it produces, and how it operates.

d) Managerial Expertise

Malik et al (2011) expressed that managerial expertise includes training, check and balance, opportunity ofcondensed workweek etc.According to a report of "Vernon Roche Hodgson Inc through the use of surveys, interviews andempirical research, results conclusively indicate that leadership, or how leaders behave, has a directrelationship to overall perceptions of organizational effectiveness, or how organizations will perform. This issignificant for leaders to understand, since they may be unaware of how their behaviors impact theiremployees.According to a study of Lee & Tseng (2005) (study adopted the listed, over the counter (OTC) andemerging electronic companies only operating in Taiwan as the research objects) organizational culture hasinfluence over organizational effectiveness. This study defined the eight dimensions of organizational culture as: (1) tolerant / staff-oriented; (2) achievement-oriented; (3) innovative; (4) analytical; (5) social relationships ;(6) rewarding staff; (7) stable work environment; (8) demanding. These eight dimensions of organizationalculture showed generally sufficient characteristic. This study also suggested three dimensions of organizationaleffectiveness: (1) structural flexibility/ control; (2) focus Internal /external (3) strategy means/ends. Thesethree dimensions of organizational effectiveness presented the mainly ample characteristic (Lee and Tseng, 2005)

e) Organizational Culture

Organizational culture is closely related to organizational effectiveness (Trefry 2006), because culture and subculture mould employees' values and values influence employees' perceptions and decisions (Mariappanadar, 2005). Obinna and Farkas (2011) asserted that the success and failure of atypical organization is the culture itapprehends and its conflicts management style. It is imperative that employees live and work within the fourwalls of culture be it individual, group or corporate cultures; we are bounded and breathe in cultures. Cultureaffects all people, leaders and those led, and it affects the way they organize. The management of culturaldiversity is becoming a significant issue for companies of all sizes, not just multinationals. According to a studyof Lee & Tseng (2005) (study adopted the listed, over the counter (OTC) and emerging electronic companiesonly operating in Taiwan as the research objects) organizational culture has influence over organizationaleffectiveness. This study defined the eight dimensions of organizational culture as: (1) tolerant / staff-oriented ;(2) achievement-oriented; (3) innovative; (4) analytical; (5) social relationships; (6) rewarding staff; (7) stablework environment; (8) demanding. These eight dimensions of organizational culture showed generallysufficient characteristic. This study also suggested three dimensions of organizational effectiveness: (1)structural flexibility/ control; (2) focus Internal /external (3) strategy means/ends. These three dimensions oforganizational effectiveness presented the mainly ample characteristic.Çiçek and Özer (2011) expressed that organizational culture can enhance organizational performance by energizing and motivating employees,unifying people around shared goals, and shaping and guiding employee behaviors. Some researchers asserted that organizational culture could provide a source of sustained competitive advantage for firms, particularlywhen it is seen as a firm-level resource that is valuable, rare, and difficult to imitate. An organization's culturalnorms strongly affect all who are involved in the organization. Organizational culture with a development andinnovation orientation had a direct effect on a firm's innovation performance.

Regulatory Environment

In the literatures, there had been divergent views about the concept of environment through contributions of different authors and scholars. Okoh and Munene (1986) posited two views of perceived environment in the literature. The first is inter-organizational view, which considers the environment as a collection of person, groups and other organizations that provides inputs to, or receives outputs from a local organization. The second consideration is that environment is a set of general, social, economic and technological conditions. Obasan (2001) says environment is the sum total of the physical and social forces and institutions that are relevant to the organizational goal setting and goal attainment which are taken directly into consideration by members of the organization when making business decisions and plans. According to Osuagwu (2001) environment has been seen as the totality of the factors that affect, influence, or determine the operations or performance of a business. The environment determines what is possible for the organization to achieve.

In the view of Adeoye (2013), Legal/public Policy Environment consist of the laws, regulations and procedures of acountry which business enterprises are anticipated tocomply with in the course of their operations. These lawsmay facilitate successful business conduct as well asconstitute major handicaps to successful performance.Furthermore, in carrying out their business operations, business enterprises are required by law to pay taxes, value added tax, capital gains tax, education tax, import duties, excise duties, etc. There are also labour laws that synchronize the contract of employment specifically the relationship between employers and the unions, the minimum age a person must attain before he/she can be lawfully employed, employee compensation, etc.

Regulation is a governmental tool to attain desirable public policy goals (OECD 1997).Mahon and Murray (1980) define regulation as an administrative and legal processdesigned to insure that the public interest is represented and served by means other thanmarket forces. Theyfurther differentiated between social andeconomic regulations. The main purpose of social regulation is to regulate non-economicactivities, like health and safety, whereas economic regulation targets economic activitiesin a specific industry. Primary reasons for regulation are to limit excessive competition (Vietor 1989) and to promote stability within an industry (Kim and Prescott 2005). To thisend, researchers highlight the importance of regulatory agencies or regulatory programmesto control the market (e.g. Mahon and Murray 1980). Such control takes the form ofmarket entry/exit control and price control (Vietor 1989; 1991; 1994; Viscusi, Vernon andHarrington 1995).

Theoretical Framework

According to Balduck and Buelens (2008), the issue of effectiveness in organizations revolves round four main approaches: the system resource approach, the goal approach, the strategic constituency approach and the internal process approach.

The Goal Approach: The first extensively used approach in organizational effectiveness is the goal approach. Its focus is on theoutput to figure out the essential operating objectives like profit, innovation and finally product quality (Schermerhorn, Hunt, R. N. Osborn, & R. Osborn, 2004).

There are some basic assumptions for the goal approach.

The System Resource Approach: The second approach is named the system resource approach which pays attention to the input of the figure. It explains the effectiveness from the point of view of the ability to obtain necessary resources from the environmentsoutside the organization (Schermerhorn*et. al.*, 2004).

The Process Approach: The third approach is known as the process approach which pays attention to the transformation process and isdedicated to seeing to what extent the resources are officially used to give services or produce goods (Schermerhorn*et. al.*, 2004). By effectiveness, it is meant that the organization is internally healthy and efficient and the internalprocesses and procedures in that place are quite well-oiled. In an effective organization, there is no trace of stressand strain. The members are completely part of the system and the system itself works smoothly.

The Strategic Constituency Approach: The fourth approach is the strategic constituency approach. It deals with the effect of the organization on the mainstakeholders and their interests (Schermerhorn*et. al.*, 2004). Based on this approach, effectiveness refers to theminimal satisfaction of all of the strategic constituencies of the organization. Strategic constituency involves all thepeople that are somehow connected to the organization. These people may have different roles such as the users ofthe services or products of the organization, the resource providers, the facilitators of the organization's output, themain supporters and the dependents of the organization (Cameron, 1981).

3. Methods

Aham (2000) defined data analysis as the conversion of raw data into usable information. The statistical tool used for data analysis and test of hypotheses in this paper is the men score.The data gathered were ranked as follows: SA= 5, A = 4,U = 3, D = 2, SD = 1. The mean score is mathematically expressed as:

$$\overline{X} = \frac{\sum_{i=1}^{n} X_i}{N}$$

Where $\overline{X}$ = the mean, $\sum_{i=1}^{n}$ = summation, X = the scores and N= number of scores. The decision rule is to accept results with a mean score of 2.5 and above while rejecting those with a mean score below 2.5

4. Data Presentation and Analysis

In this section of this paper, the researchers presented the data gathered. The data was later analyzed using the mean score.

Key

SA = Strongly Agree, A = Agree, U = Undecided, D = Disagree, SD = Strongly Disagree

***Table 1.** Responds on the Relationship between Regulatory Environment and SME's Effectiveness.*

S/N	Competitiveness factors	Options							
		SA	A	U	D	Sd	Fx	$\overline{X}$	Remark
1	Regulatory environment increases market share	14	36	23	13	3	257	2.89	ACCEPT
2.	Regulatory environment impacts significantly on customer's satisfaction	6	20	18	30	15	239	2.68	ACCEPT
3.	Regulatory environment impacts positively on cost efficiency	11	27	21	17	4	263	2.96	ACCEPT
4.	Regulatory environment have increased our economy of scale	14	30	13	22	10	284	3.19	ACCEPT
5.	Our employees working condition have been affected by regulation of the industry	4	9	15	38	23	175	1.97	REJECT
	Innovativeness factors								
6	Regulatory environment enhances market innovativeness	10	19	27	18	15	257	2.89	ACCEPT
7	Product innovation can be enhanced by regulatory environment	8	24	30	22	9	279	3.13	ACCEPT
8	Innovation in business processes can be affected by regulation of the business environment	12	29	29	19	-	338	3.8	ACCEPT
9	Regulatory environment has influenced our innovation in research and development	5	11	17	25	31	200	2.25	REJECT
10	Regulatory environment has led to the adoption of new technology in business processes	6	9	13	30	31	196	2.2	REJECT

5. Results and Discussions

The overall finding in this study shows that regulatory environment has significant impact on the effectiveness of small and medium scale enterprises in Nigeria. In research question one; the researchers concluded that competitiveness of SMEs in Nigeria is largely influenced by the regulatory environment. This can be seen in the response pattern as the mean score in questionnaire item 1-4 was higher than the decision point (i.e 2.89, 2.68, 2.96, and 3.19 > 2.5 respectively). However, the response of questionnaire item 5 in research question one shows that regulatory environment does not have significant impact on the working condition of employees in SMEs in Nigeria. In research question two, the mean of questionnaire 6, 7, and 8, were positive i.e their mean were higher than the 2.5 decision point. This suggests that regulatory environment impacts significantly on market, product and process innovation in Nigerian SMEs. But in questionnaire item 9 and 10, the result shows that regulatory environment has no significant impact on SME's research and development programmes as well as technological adoption. A closer review of the study shows that while regulatory environment has impacted on the market and financial dimensions of SMEs effectiveness in Nigeria, it has failed to address the issues of ethics and social concerns.

6. Conclusion and Recommendations

Sequel to the findings above, the researchers concludes that regulatory environment impacts on SMEs effectiveness in Nigeria significantly based on the dimensions of SME effectiveness covered in this study. Moreover, whereas there are laws guiding working conditions, the impact of its implementation is minimal. Therefore, the regulatory environment cannot be said to have contributed satisfactorily to the improvement of the working condition of SME employees in Nigeria. Based on the findings, the researchers further conclude that the contribution of the regulatory environment in the promotion of research and development and ICT adoption in SMEs is minimal. The researchers recommend that;

- In making regulations and policies guiding SMEs in Nigeria, standards for ethics and social concern should be given strategic attention.
- Regular consultations between business regulators and SME operators are needed if the harsh consequences of the regulatory environment must be mitigated effectively.

References

[1] Adeoye M (2013), The impact of business environment on Enterpreneurship performance in Nigeria. Computing, Information Systems, Development Informatics & Allied Research Vol. 4 No. 4

[2] Agulanna E.C and Chris M (2003),Business Policy Book 1. The Face of Strategic Management.Oweeri: Joe Mankpa Publishers

[3] Aham A. (2000), Research Methodology in Business and Social Science. Owerri; Cannum Publisher Ltd.

[4] Algbuo C.C (2005), A Practical Guide to Project Writing:Owerri Credo Publications.

[5] Balduck, A. L., &Buelens, M. (2008).A two-level competing values approach to measure nonprofit organizational effectiveness. Working Papers of Faculty of Economics and Business Administration, Ghent University, Belgium

[6] Brooks, I. (2003) Organisational Behaviour, 2nd Ed., Pearson Education, Harlow, England.

[7] Cameron K.S (1981), Domains of Organizational Effectiveness in Colleges and Universities. Academy of Management Journal, 24:25-47

[8] Çiçek, Işık and Özer, Bilal (2011), The Effect of Outsourcing Human Resource on Organizational Performance: The Role of Organizational Culture.International Journal of Business and Management Studies, Vol. 3, No 2

[9] Fitz-Enz, I. (1997). The 8 Practices of Exceptional Companies: How great Organizations make the most oftheir Human Resources. New York, NY: AMACON.

[10] Grant, R.M. (1999), Contemporary Strategy Analysis. 2nd ed. Oxford: Blackwell Publishers.

[11] Hardesty, D. C. (2003). Ten Characteristics of a Highly Effective Organization. The State Journal. Retrieved from http://www.nis.wvu.edu/wvu/guest_commentary ten_characteristics.htm

[12] Henri, Jean-François (2011), Performance Measurement and Organizational Effectiveness: Bridging The Gap. PhD Dissertation Submitted to School of Accounting Université Laval Québec City, Canada G1K 7P4(Unpublished)

[13] Kamery, Rob H. (2004), Employee Motivation as it Relates to Effectiveness, Efficiency, Productivity, and Performance, Allied Academies International Conference, Proceedings of the Academy of Legal, Ethical and Regulatory Issues, Volume 8, Number 2 Maui

[14] Kennerley M and Nelly A (2003), Measuring Performance In Changing Business Environment. International Journal of Operations and Production, 23(2),213-229

[15] Kim, B., J. E. Prescott. (2005), Deregulatory forms, variations in the speed of governance adaptation, and firm performance. Academy of Management Review, 30(2): 414-425

[16] Kushner, R.J., and Poole, P.P. (2002), Exploring Structure-Effectiveness Relationships in Nonprofit Arts Organizations, Nonprofit Management and Leadership, 7 (2), 119-136.

[17] Lee Tzai-Zang and Tseng, Ya-Fen (2005), A Study of the Relationship between Organizational Culture and Organizational Effectiveness of the Electronic Industries in Taiwan.A Chinese named Journal of Taiwan, Vol. 1461, pp. 161-178

[18] Malik M.E Ghafoor, M.M and Naseer, S (2011), Organizational Effectiveness: A Case Study of Telecommunication and Banking Sector of Pakistan. FarEast Journal of Psychology and Business, Vol. 2 No 1

[19] Mahon, J. F. and E. A. Murray. (1980), Deregulation and Strategic Transformation. Journal of Contemporary Business 9: 123-138.

[20] Mariappanadar, S. (2005), An Emic Approach to Understand Culturally Indigenous and Alien Human Resource Management Practices in Global Companies, Research and Practice in HumanResource Management, Vol.13, No. 2, pp. 31-48

[21] McMahon, A.M. (2006). Responses to diversity: Approaches and initiatives.

[22] Obasan, K. (2001), Small Business Management: An Entrepreneurial Approach.Higher Education Books Publishers, Lagos

[23] Obinna, A.K and Farkas, M.F (2011), Cultural Conflict Management Program for Firms and Organizations.International Journal of Business and Management Studies, Vol. 3, No 2,

[24] OECD (1997), Regulatory Impact Analysis: Best practices in OECD countries. http://www.oecd.org/gov/regulatory-policy/35258828.pdf

[25] Osuagwu, L. (2001), Small Business and Entrepreneurship Management. Grey Resources Limited, Lagos.

[26] Otokiti, S.O. and M.O., Awodun, (2003), The Master Strategist: Management with style in a Turbulent Business Environment.Pumark Nigeria Limited, Lagos.

[27] Schermerhorn, J. R., Hunt, J. G., Osborn, R. N., & Osborn, R. (2004), Core concepts of organizational behavior:John Wiley & Sons Inc.

[28] Scott A, Simon B., Nick H., and Karina W (2008), Assessing Multilteral Organization Effectiveness, Evaluation Study 2008/3. from Danida's evaluation department-development cooperation, ministry of foreign affairs, Denmark

[29] Senge, P. (1990). The fifth discipline: The art and practice of the leaning organization. New York, NY: Doubleday.

[30] Trefry, Mary G. (2006), A Double-Edged Sword: Organizational Culture in Multicultural Organizations.International Journal of Management Vol. 23, No. 3, Part 2,

[31] Vietor R.H.K (1989), Strategic management in the regulatory environment : case and industry notes.Englewood Cliffs (N.J.) by Prentice-Hall

[32] Wright, K. (1997),Organizational Wellness.Unpublished manuscript

[33] Yankey J.A and McCllen A (2003), The Non-Profit Boards Role in Planning And Evaluation. Book Seven of The Board Source Governance Series. Quoted in Non-profit Organizational Effectiveness.kronkosky charitable foundation.

Effect of Mortgage Market Risk on Mortgage Uptake: A Case Study of Mortgage Lenders in Kenya

Grace Melissa Akenga, Margaret Akinyi Olang, Nebat Mugenda Galo

Department of Business Administration, Chuka University, Chuka, Kenya

Email address:
akengamgrace@gmail.com (G. M. Akenga), Margaretolang087@gmail.com (M. A. Olang)

Abstract: Mortgage market is a financial system that provides opportunity for originating and trading mortgage loans. A mortgage loan is used for financing real estate investments. Although there has been a remarkable increase in demand for real estate investments in Kenya the amount of mortgage uptake is still low. Studies reveal risks as important macroeconomic variables in the mortgage market. However the effect of these risks on mortgage uptake in Kenya is inconclusive. The purpose of this study was to evaluate the effect of mortgage market risk on mortgage uptake. The objectives of the study were to determine the effect of credit risk, interest rate risk, price risk and liquidity risk on mortgage uptake in mortgage lending institutions in Kenya. Causal research design was used to establish the effect of mortgage market risk on mortgage uptake. Purposive sampling was used to select a sample size of 27 out of 37 mortgage lenders that had been involved in mortgage lending since 2008 to 2013. Secondary data was obtained from Central Bank of Kenya reports and mortgage special reports for the period under study. The assumptions that form a basis for use of the regression model were tested using homoscedasticity and autocorrelation. Ordinary Least Square method was used to determine the cause effect relationship among variables while hypotheses were tested at 5% significance level. The overall model was found to be significant with F=13.474 and p-value (0.00 < 0.05). The findings revealed that risks faced by lenders affect mortgage uptake such that if the risk involved in lending is high lenders limit the amount of mortgage lending. The study recommended that lenders should ensure risks are well managed so as to increase mortgage uptake. The findings would form a basis for lenders to formulate risk management strategies that would help to mitigate risks and increase mortgage uptake. The study also forms a basis for further research and adds to the existing body of knowledge.

Keywords: Credit Risk, Interest Rate Risk, Liquidity Risk, Mortgage, Price Risk, Real Property, Mortgage Lending Institutions

1. Introduction

Mortgage financing is an important means of financing investment in real estate (Brueggeman & Fisher, 2008). Investing in real estate requires large amount of capital to be mobilized which the investors may not raise on their own (Central Bank of Kenya, 2012). This would result to investors borrowing funds from lenders secured in real estate with a mortgage. A mortgage is a loan secured by collateral of some specified real estate property that the borrower is obliged to pay back with predetermined set of installments (Biernert & Brunauer, 2007). According to Giddings (2007) it is a source of long term finance for the development of more new housing, urban infrastructure and a major driver for the deepening of capital markets.

In developed countries mortgage financing is more available and has gained recognition as opposed to developing countries (Hahm, 2004). According to Hassler, Chiquer and Lea (2004) the development of mortgage markets in most African countries is still at infancy. Most financial institutions are limited by high interest rates and the mismatch between the short term nature of deposits and the long term nature of mortgage lending. Vuyisani (2003) noted that mortgage finance system in Africa is faced with major challenges such as default rates, lack of long term funds required to match the duration of mortgage loans and high interest rates. In an effort to resolve the situation financial institutions have been established but find the market too risky. According to World Bank (2011) the Kenyan mortgage market is underdeveloped as mortgage financing is unaffordable, inaccessible and unpopular. Although there has been a remarkable increase in demand for real estate investment in Kenya mortgage uptake is low(Arvantis, 2013).

According to Kariuki (2013) urgent attention needs to be given to increase the accessibility and eligibility of mortgages, if home ownership is to be increased to a wider band of Kenyans. The size of the mortgage portfolio is low with only a few lenders holding more than 70% in their portfolio, with a total mortgage value of Ksh 61.4 billion and 13803 mortgage accounts. This is far below expectation of bridging the housing gap of 156,000 units per annum (World Bank, 2011). The average mortgage amount is Ksh 6.6 million and requires a repayment of Ksh 90,000 per month for over 20 years at 12% interest rate, thus it is affordable only to those earning over Sh100,000 per month (Arvantis, 2013). This is way beyond what an average professional earns which means they cannot qualify even for the most basic mortgage product. This eventually has an impact on the number of people who take up mortgages and in turn the volume of the mortgage market. Initially lenders were restricted to 25% mortgage lending but the limit was increased to 40% with an intention of enhancing the growth of mortgage market (Njuguna 2011). The amount of mortgage lending in Kenya still is considered low by the international standard and with a 2.5% contribution to GDP as compared to South Africa whose contribution is at 26.4% (Central Bank; World Bank, 2013)

In a survey done by Central Bank of Kenya (2012) lenders pointed out several constraints on the further growth of the mortgage market. Most notably is long term access to funds, deficiencies in property valuation, credit risk and high interest rates. According to World Bank (2011) some mortgage lenders are liquidity constrained as a result of mismatch between short term deposits and the long term mortgage loans. Lenders also face the risk of default as credit bureaus do not offer comprehensive credit histories and the value of collateral can be affected during foreclosure and valuation process. Furthermore they face the risk that changes in interest rate will affect the net interest margin made on mortgage loans. Hass Consult Survey (2013) noted that the property market is characterized by constantly changing prices that are set arbitrarily thus affecting repayment and value of loans. Eventually, the inability of lenders to understand and manage these risks means that they charge a high risk premium making mortgages to be costly. Hassler *et al.* (2004) noted that mortgage lending is often rationed, relatively expensive and depository based when lenders remain vulnerable to credit, liquidity and interest rate risks. Therefore lenders are exposed to risks when lending but the effect of these risks on the amount of mortgage loans made is inconclusive in Kenya. Therefore this study aims to determine the effect of mortgage market risk on mortgage uptake among mortgage lending institutions.

Mortgage finance is important in increasing supply of residential property and development of urban infrastructure to support the growing population and urbanization. However according to a World Bank report, Kenya is experiencing a housing supply deficit of 156,000 units per year and mortgage finance is costly and inaccessible. Only 2.4% of the total population and 11% percent of the urban population could afford a mortgage, and assuming everyone who could afford a mortgage takes one. This would translate to just over 249,260 loan accounts, and a potential mortgage loan value of Kshs 800 billion, but the current mortgage loan value is 61.4 billion with13,803 loan accounts which is considerably smaller than the expected level of lending. In 2010 the mortgage lending limit imposed on lenders was increased from 25% to 40% and lenders were allowed to issue bonds to raise funds, this was intended to strengthen the mortgage market and increase mortgage lending. Despite of these measures, the number and total amount of mortgage loans is still low resulting to low level of housing supply and poor urban infrastructure. In a survey done in 2012 by Central Bank lenders pointed out credit risk, interest rate risk, liquidity risk and price risk as important macroeconomic variables in the mortgage market. However the effect of these risks on mortgage uptake in Kenya is inconclusive. Therefore this study aimed at determining the effect of mortgage market risk on mortgage uptake in mortgage lending institutions in Kenya. The study was guided by the following Specific objectives:

i. To determine the effect of credit risk on mortgage uptake in mortgage lending institutions
ii. To establish the effect of interest rate risk on mortgage uptake in mortgage lending institutions
iii. To establish the effect of price risk on mortgage uptake in mortgage lending institutions
iv. To determine the effect of liquidity risk on mortgage uptake in mortgage lending institutions.

2. Literature Review

2.1. Theoretical Framework

This study is premised on the loanable funds theory, it is a classical theory developed by Wicksell Robertson in 1934. This theory states that the quantity of a financial security supplied changes at every given interest rate in response to a change in another factor besides the interest rate. One of these factors is the risk of a financial security, which causes a shift in the supply curve of loanable funds. Holding all other factors constant, as the risk of financial security decreases it becomes more attractive to suppliers of fund, hence the supply of funds increases. Conversely, as the risk of financial security increases it becomes less attractive to suppliers of funds hence the supply of funds decreases (Saunders & Marcia, 2001). This theory proposes that supply of loans will decrease if the mortgage loan is considered to be risky. Brueggeman and Fisher (2008) noted that, when lenders are supplying funds to the mortgage market they consider the returns and the associated risks in lending.

In title theory, the property-law doctrine states that a mortgage transfers title to a property to the mortgagee, who holds it until the mortgage has been paid off, at which time title passes to the mortgagor. In title theory, the banks retain the title since the mortgage is said to hold a title interest, they have the right to possession under this theory. Some banks apply a lien theory. This theory only gives the mortgagee a lien interest in the property. In a title theory, the mortgage is treated as having transferred title to the mortgagee, subject to the mortgagee's duty to recovery if payment is made. The title is said to remain in the mortgagee until the mortgage has been satisfied and foreclosed. Although the mortgagee has the right of possession to the property, there is generally an express agreement giving the right of possession to the mortgagor. The mortgagee is said to hold the title for security purposes only. The mortgagor is given the right of possession.

Lien theory provides that a mortgagee of property holds only a lien, not title, to the property until such time as the mortgage is fully paid, at which time the lien is removed. In a lien theory bank, the mortgagor retains legal and equitable title to the property, but conveys an interest that the mortgagee can only foreclose upon to satisfy the obligation of the mortgagor. This is equivalent to a future interest in the property which allows the mortgagee to use the process of foreclosure. The interest is a security interest or mortgage, which forms a lien on the property. In this theory the right to possession arises upon a default. The mortgagor has a right to sue the mortgagee for any interference with his right of possession.

2.2. Mortgage Loan

According to Brueggeman and Fisher (2008) a mortgage is created in a transaction whereby one party pledges real property to another party as security for an obligation owed to that party. A mortgage can also be defined as a long term debt instrument backed by real property that is already owned or will be purchased by the borrower (Jacobus, 1999). It involves the potential buyer borrowing funds from a lender and then using these funds to purchase residential or commercial property.

In Kenya mortgage products are offered by commercial banks, microfinance institutions and housing finance company. An average mortgage loan is Sh6.6 million, and demands a monthly repayment of about Sh90, 000 for a period of 20 years (World Bank, 2011). The average interest rate charged on mortgages is 18% and ranges between 11%-25%, with most of the financial institutions charging variable interest rate other than fixed interest rate (Central Bank of Kenya, 2012). In 2013 about 97.4% of mortgage loans were on variable interest rates basis compared to 85.6% in 2012 (Central Bank of Kenya, 2013). The most common fees payable for mortgages are legal fees, valuation fees, arrangement fees, stamp duty and mortgage protection policy premium. These fees are charged to ensure the lender is compensated for the risk of lending. Although, Central Bank (2012) noted since 2006, the average mortgage loan size has been growing steadily, in December 2011 the size of the mortgage was 61.4 billion in 2012 it grew to 122.2 billion. Also the numbers of mortgage accounts grew from 16,029 in 2011 to 19,177 in 2012 but still the level of lending is low.

2.3. Mortgage Lenders in Kenya

Mortgage lenders are those institutions that have mortgage securities in their portfolio, they include commercial banks, insurance companies, savings institutions, finance companies and mortgage banks (Rose, 2003). Institutions play a crucial role in the financing of real estate through mortgage financing. They lend for the purchase of land, development of existing buildings, finance construction projects and lend to non-financial firms based on real estate collateral (Davis & Zhu, 2004). Mortgage credit is positively related to profitability because it creates a long term source or revenue for the bank offering mortgage credit (Sharpele, 2000). Lenders in the mortgage market pursue a variety of income sources; they may retain new mortgage loans in their asset portfolio and receive the borrower's interest and principal payments, while other lenders may quickly sell any loans they make and instead pursue loan servicing, securitization and other fee generating services because of more predictable liquidity demands and lower capital requirements involved with supporting services (Rose, 2003). Each of these possible cash flows sources from a mortgage loan has its own advantages and disadvantages in terms of sensitivity to default, interest rate, liquidity risk and changes in sizes of cash flow expected to be received.

According to World Bank (2011) there are two types of lenders which can be authorized by the Central Bank of Kenya. These are ordinary banks and mortgage companies which include Commercial Banks and Housing Finance Company of Kenya (HFCK). HFCK was established at the beginning of 1966 to stimulate the private sector, by the Government in collaboration with Commonwealth Development Corporation. The main objective of HFCK was to promote a savings culture and make loan funds available to people wishing to acquire their own homes. Today Housing Finance provides integrated financial solutions and focuses on both commercial and residential property. In the first quarter of 2013, the amount of loans and advances to customers made by HFCK was 37.4 Billion (Central Bank; World Bank, 2013). Commercial Banks under the Banking Act of Kenya are authorized to conduct mortgage business for the purpose of financing house purchase, construction and refinancing purposes. Banks offer mortgages to their staff members or special customers and have just one or two loans on their books while other banks are much larger players who see mortgages as a major business center. (Central Bank; World bank, 2012). A survey done in 2012 by Central Bank revealed that about 70% of lending to mortgage market was by 5 institutions, that is, one medium sized bank (25.5%) and four banks from the large banks peer group (44.6%). Although a limit was placed on institutions not to lend more than 25% of their total deposit liabilities it was raised to 40% and mortgage finance companies were allowed to open current accounts for their customers, Pension funds and insurance companies can also be involved in lending as they represent a potentially huge source of longer term funds, but for the most part, their investment in housing finance has been very limited.

2.4. Kenyan Mortgage Market

Mortgage market is defined as a market in which mortgage loans, backed by real property are originated and sometimes trade (Melicher & Norton, 2003). According to Fabozzi, Modigliani and Jones (2007) mortgage market is a collection of markets that include a primary market and secondary market where mortgages trade. Mortgages are originated by financial institutions in the primary market and can be packaged as securities to be sold in secondary market. The Kenyan mortgage market remains primary with little activity in the secondary market (Central Bank; World bank, 2012). This limits the funding base of lender market as they become liquidity constrained. According to World Bank (2011) if Kenya is to expand, it may need to emulate countries such as Colombia and South Africa, both of which have developed secondary mortgage markets. This would allow it to safely go beyond the current credit/ deposit levels and engage in longer term lending. The secondary market is established in order to free up capital by packaging mortgages and selling them as assets to institutional investors.

2.5. Importance of Mortgage Financing

According to Lea and Chiquier (2007) mortgage finance improves the operation of the property market by increasing the number of housing and commercial units. It also affects the economy directly by facilitating transactions and by improving the environment in which transactions take place. Kibirige (2006) asserts that the mortgage finance sector creates employment directly to the construction industry and indirectly to other sectors. According to Giddings (2007) construction is a driver of economic growth, a multiplier of 1.0 is generated by housing construction meaning that for every dollar spent on housing, another dollar is spent in other sectors. In industrialized countries, mortgage financing is a major driver for deepening of capital markets which then serve as sources for long term financing. As the mortgage markets deepen, the supply of housing and urban infrastructure also increases. According to Erbas (2005) availability of residential mortgages has favorable impact on poverty alleviation, quality of housing, infrastructure, and urbanization. Kibirige (2006) noted a more formalized housing market that is subject to real estate taxes and utility charges, can serve as an important source of revenue for financially strapped local governments. In South Africa, more than 95% of local government revenue is derived from local sources including real estate taxes and surcharges on water and power. This results to a more financially viable local government. Therefore mortgage finance is not only important in increasing the asset portfolio of lenders and creating access to finance for borrowers but it is also important for social, economic and civic development.

2.6. Mortgage Market Risk

Risk is the possibility of a loss or the uncertainty associated with future events. According to Nyandemo and Sigh (2003) uncertainty is a situation when decision makers do not have full knowledge about the future of a product, demand, factor costs and other relevant variables. Financial institutions will try as much as possible to avoid the risk associated with loss in order to minimize negative consequences. The risk surrounding potential losses creates significant economic burdens for financial institutions. On the other hand the investment principle says that the largest potential returns are associated with the riskiest ventures (Trieschmann, Hoyt, & Sommer, 2005). Financial Institutions have an objective to increase returns for its owners, this often comes at the cost of increased risk. These risks affect the profitability and performance of institutions as a result it is important to understand and manage risks to which an institution in a given market is exposed to.

In a study done by Renaud and Jaffe (1996) they noted several factors that hinder development of mortgage markets in developing economies and proposed a strategy to expedite that development. They noted that lenders in developing economies are reluctant to make mortgage loans because of the risks in mortgage lending (credit, liquidity, interest and price). Together with required improvements in the primary market, a secondary market is likely to help solve the problem.

In mortgage financing, there are different customers from different backgrounds, and this exposes a lot of risk to both the borrower and the lender (Scanlon & Whitehead, 2004). Lewis and Neave (2008) noted that the major risks include credit risk to the lender, that the borrower will default on loan obligations and investment risk on the owner-occupier that the value of the home will fall, and with it the value of the owner-occupier's equity will also fall. Further there is interest-rate risk to either party to a loan that the interest rate will move against them and finally prepayment risk to the lender that the borrower will repay a loan (particularly a fixed-rate loan) before the end of its term (Agada, Murumba, & Besigiroha, 2009). According to World Bank (2011) some Kenyan lenders are liquidity constrained as the market is characterized by relatively liquid banking sector as a result of mismatch between short term deposits and the long term mortgage loans. Also, credit bureaus do not yet offer comprehensive credit histories on loan applicants and the value of collateral is tampered by deficiencies in the foreclosure process.

In spite of these risks the advent of institutional investors has given rise to skills necessary to manage the complex risks associated with housing finance. The creation of mortgage related securities provide the multiple instruments by which housing lenders can access these important sources of funds and better manage and allocate part of their risks (Central Bank; World Bank, 2013). In Kenya, measures to strengthen the mortgage market were put in place such as the limit placed on institutions not to lend more than 25% of their total deposit liabilities was raised to 40%, mortgage finance companies were allowed to open current accounts for their customers to increase their term deposits and lenders were allowed to issue bonds to raise funds for mortgage lending (Njuguna, 2011). These measures were put in place to mitigate risks, increase the level of mortgage lending and facilitate growth of the mortgage market.

2.7. Credit Risk

Credit risk is one of the oldest forms of risk faced by financial institutions (Broll, Pausch & Welzel, 2002).Credit risk arises because of the possibility that promised cash flow on financial claims held by financial institutions such as loans and bonds will not be paid in full. If the principal on all financial claims held by financial institutions were paid in full on maturity and interest payments were made on their promised dates, financial institutions would always receive back their original principal plus interest-that is they would not face credit risk (Saunders & Marcia, 2001). Credit risk carries the potential of wiping out enough of a financiers capital and forcing it into bankruptcy, thus managing this kind of risk has always been one of the predominant challenges in running a financial institution (Broll *et a.l* 2002). The potential loss a firm can experience from lending suggests that institutions need to collect information about borrowers whose assets are in their portfolio and to monitor those borrowers overtime. Thus managerial efficiency and credit risk management strategies directly affect the risk and returns of the portfolio (Saunders & Marcia, 2001). Credit risk in mortgages involves the risk that the interest and principal amount will not be paid when due. According to Lea (1990) it is risk brought about when the market value of the property falls below the market value of the mortgage.

Saunders and Marcia (2001) asserts that residential mortgages are the most important loan assets to banks and saving institutions, hence these applications are the most standardized of all credit applications. Two considerations dominate a financial institutions' decision as to whether to approve a mortgage loan application or not:-First the applicants ability and willingness to make timely interest and principal repayments. This is established by application of qualitative and quantitative models such as credit scoring model. The loan officer must also establish whether the applicant has sufficient income. Secondly, the borrower's collateral is considered after determining the creditworthiness of the borrower. The lender should make sure that the collateral that secures the loan is free and clear from other claims. Some institutions require a borrower to make a down payment of the property before issuing the loan to prevent the borrower from defaulting.

2.8. Interest Rate Risk

According to Coong (1995) interest rate risk is the exposure of a financial institution's current or future earnings and capital to interest rate change. Most financial Institutions suffer losses in profits or asset value when the general level of interest rates rises. According to Kolbe, Gaylon and Rudner (2003) a financial institution potentially exposes itself to interest rate risk in mismatching the maturity of its assets and liabilities. The lender is exposed to interest rate risk if interest rate on assets and liabilities is adjusted at different times or its subject to different contractual maturities (Bangkok Bank, 2008). Interest rate is a major factor that determines the lenders interest income on assets and interest expense on liabilities thus affecting the net interest income of the lender. Also changes in interest rate affects the refinancing and reinvestment decision of a borrower. In addition, a financial institution faces economic or present value uncertainty as well when interest rates change.

The fair market value of an asset or liability is conceptually equal to the present value of the current and future cash flows on that asset and liability. Therefore rising interest rates increases the discount rate on future asset cash flows and reduce the market price or present value of that asset or liability. Moreover, mismatching maturities by holding long term assets than liabilities means that when interest rates rise, the present value of the financial institution's assets fall by a larger amount than its liabilities (Fabozzi *et al.* 2007). This exposes the financial institution to the risk of economic loss and potentially to the risk of insolvency.

The increased globalization of financial markets flows has made the measurement and management of interest rate risk a prominent concern facing many modern financial institution managers (Saunders & Marcia, 2001). In a low interest rate volatility environment, the risk exposure to financial institution from mismatching the maturity of its assets and liabilities tends to be small. On the other hand high volatility of interest rates increases the risk exposure of a financial institution. Kenya being susceptible to inflationary pressure both internally and externally generated it is vulnerable to highly volatile interest rate changes (World Bank, 2011). The movement of interest rates affects lenders cost of funds and return on assets exposing it to interest rate risk. Lenders protect themselves against this risk by matching the maturity of their assets and liabilities. However matching is not consistent with an active transformation function for institutions. Although it does reduce the interest rate risk exposure it reduces the financial institution's profitability.

2.9. Price Risk

Prices are determined by macroeconomic and credit market conditions and by the behavior of the individuals buying and selling properties. In the property market there is risk of sharp fall or increase in housing prices. This is a major concern not only to the owner of the property but also to lending institutions and to investors of structured products backed by residential mortgage loan (Brueggeman & Fisher, 2008).

The average change in prices is related to changes in fundamentals such as national and local macroeconomic variables, or market wide bubbles but not all properties in a market are affected at the same rate (Glower, Donal, & Hendersholt, 1998). Multiple studies have found that the relationship between a home's original value and the rate of appreciation varies over time according to the prevailing economic climate for example, lower-priced houses are more likely to appreciate as interest rates fall while income and employment rise. On the contrary increase in taxes would have a negative effect on prices (Li & Resenblatt, 2005). If the cost of rental housing should increase relative to house prices demand for owning should increase this is because individuals would prefer to take a loan and own if it is cheaper to own than rent and also if there is price appreciation of real estate property.

At the time the loan is originated, the lender will ensure that the appraised value of the property is greater than the amount of the loan (Claurietie & Sirmans, 2006). Lenders want assurance concerning the price of the property because it will be serving as security for repayment of the mortgage debt and over time it must remain sufficiently high to repay the outstanding loan balance in the event of default. Lenders usually require that an estimate value be made by an independent fee appraiser (Brueggeman & Fisher, 2008). Lenders give out loans based on a ratio known as loan to value ratio, this ratio enables the lender to be cushioned from the high risk involved in the longer payback period. The loan value ratio is presented in Table 1.

Table 1. *Loan Value Ratio.*

Bank Segment	Average Loan to Value	Minimum Loan to Value	Maximum Loan to Value
Large Banks	85%	60%	100%
Medium Banks	77%	60%	90%
Small Banks	79%	65%	90%
Average		82%	

Source: Central Bank of Kenya Survey, 2010

Table 2 shows that the loan to value ratio in 2010 for Kenyan banks was approximately 82% of the property value, with larger institutions offering much higher loan to value ratios (85%) than medium (77%) and smaller banks (79%).A loan to value ratio that is greater than 100% implies that loan amount is greater than the value of property which is risky. Lenders require a higher spread for a higher loan to value ratio given that the higher LTV represents a higher risk (Wang & Hongfei, 2007). In Kenya lenders offer on average a LTV that is less than 100% which means the value of property is greater than loan amount hence they are cushioned against risks of lending as they are guaranteed of the full recovery of loan in case of default as a result of fall in prices of property.

Bianco (2008) noted in the U.S there was a financial crisis in 2008 that started in the late 1990s. The house prices grew rapidly in response to low mortgage rates offered by lenders which attracted many borrowers to take up mortgages. The increased lending lead to increased demand that helped fuel the rise of housing prices and consumer spending, creating an unheard of increase in home values of 124 percent between 1997 and 2006. Some homeowners took advantage of the increased property values of their home to refinance their homes with lower interest rates and take out second mortgages against the added value to use for consumer spending. The number of loans rose as rising real estate values rose this led to lenders not considering higher-risk borrowers for loans. In turn, U.S. household debt as a percentage of income rose to 130 percent in 2007, 30 percent higher than the average amount earlier in the decade. It became difficult for borrowers to repay the loan and default rate increased; also it was difficult for lenders to recover the value of the loan as property prices declined drastically. This led to bankruptcy of some of the institutions. However, in the case where mortgage rates are high this causes loans to be expensive and therefore the demand for purchasing a house declines therefore the prices of properties decline.

In Kenya the analysis of property prices is based on the Hass Property Price Index. The index has some methodological shortcomings which are inevitable in a developing market, but it represents a very useful tool which will grow in importance as the market develops (Central Bank of Kenya, 2012).The main drawback on the reliability of property valuations is lack of comparative data as the property market is still relatively thin and not all transactions will be accurately captured, especially at the lower end of the market (World Bank, 2011). Although Coong (1995) argues that if changes in market prices are predictable, then changes in prices cannot be perceived as risky. The property price index can be used in determining the prices of property and if it is possible to forecast prices then lending backed by property is not risky. On the contrary Hass Consult Survey (2013) noted that the property market is characterized by sky-rocketing prices that affect mortgage uptake. On the other hand lenders prefer to issue mortgages when the property prices are high because this guarantees the recovery of loan in case of default and prevents refinancing. Otherwise, for borrowers when the property prices fall it becomes favorable to undertake mortgages, refinance and invest in purchase of property with the expectation that the property price will rise and they will benefit.

2.10. Liquidity Risk

Loans are the major items on a bank's balance sheet and generate the largest flow of revenue income. However loans are also the least liquid asset item and the major source of credit and liquidity risk for most banks (Saunders & Marcia, 2001). With the instability of poor households' incomes, high foreclosure costs, and liquidity risk of longer term loans, in Kenya and many developing countries, causes lenders to prefer shorter-term loans which are often less risky than long-term loans (Oriaro, 2000). Mortgage loans tend to be rather illiquid because they are large and indivisible. Although Rose (2003) asserts that a liquid financial asset is readily marketable. In addition it is reversible meaning the holder of the asset can usually recover her funds upon resale with little risk of loss. Hence liquid assets carry lower interest rates than illiquid assets. Therefore investors strongly interested in maximum profitably try to minimize their holding of liquid assets. Lenders face the liquidity problem because loans being a long term asset are financed largely by depository institutions that obtain their funds through deposits that are primarily if not entirely of short term nature. These institutions engage inevitably in a higher speculative activity: borrowing short and lending long; that is, they mismatch the maturity of assets (mortgages) and the liabilities raised to fund these assets. A depository institution's balance sheet typically has a large amount of short term liabilities, such as demand deposits and other transaction accounts which fund relatively long-term, illiquid assets such as mortgages (Saunders &

Marcia, 2001). Speculation of this sort provides a losing proposition if interest rates rise as is bound to happen in the presence of significant inflation. The institution may be earning the contractual rate but to attract the deposits needed to finance the loan it must pay the current higher market rate (Brueggeman & Fisher, 2008). On the other hand Marshall (2009) argues that lenders originating mortgage loans by the use of deposits and holding them, has the great merit that solvent lenders have strong incentives both to underwrite mortgages carefully and, if necessary, to modify them.

In Kenya asset and liability mismatch is a serious problem that lenders face. Managing this risk remains a great task for managers of institutions. In order to deal with this problem institution must maintain a high level of credibility and public confidence in their activities, particularly to attract small long term conservative savers (Mutero, 2010). The secondary mortgage market does not exist, thus mortgage lenders have to source for funds in order to issue out mortgage loans because they are mostly long term hence illiquid. However one of the aims of Kenya Vision 2030 is to establish a secondary mortgage market that will help boost the primary mortgage market. The institution which is most constrained is Housing Finance Company of Kenya which has more housing loans than deposits. This means it is dipping into its equity to fund itself together with the use of bank lines of credit. This is an expensive form of funding, and would not be sustainable over the longer term. To resolve this situation HFCK entered into the bond market to raise Ksh 10 billion to acquire finance for lending. Since the government allowed the holding of current accounts by customers of HFCK, It is actively promoting term savings products which will help extend the maturity of its retail deposit liabilities. KCB is also under pressure as it has a mortgage loan portfolio in excess of 10 percent of its deposit base. Whilst it still has room to grow, it sought to address its funding situation by doing a rights issue for Ksh 15 billion. This is in part to fund its regional growth in East Africa but also to allow it to expand its mortgage lending business. In addition, it is also entering into arrangements with International Finance Corporation for a credit facility to help expand its mortgage business (World Bank, 2011). In 2009, Co-operative Bank issued an initial public offering and was able to raise capital to support its entry into mortgage lending, also Barclays Bank ventured into the bond market to support its mortgage business (Mutero, 2010). These measures taken by lending institutions are meant to increase the amount of lending as they reduce overreliance on deposit funding.

Kenya has a large investor base made up of individual investors, pension funds, insurance companies and banks themselves. Together these institutions have substantial funds which in many cases are seeking long term investments to match the long term liabilities which are generated by the pension or insurance businesses. In the finance bill 2010 it was proposed pension funds should be used to guarantee members mortgages. This will increase mortgage uptake and eventually enhance growth of the mortgage market. The total pension assets are close to Ksh 400 billion when National Social Security Funds are also included, insurance assets are around Ksh 180 billion and the Unit Trust market as at end of 2010 was worth Ksh 28 billion. Overall funds of institutional investors, excluding the banking sector amount to over Ksh 600 billion, almost 10 times the current size of the mortgage market (Central Bank; World bank, 2013) According to Njuguna (2011) the use of pension funds to undertake mortgages is undergoing but at a slow pace. Otherwise these institutions can use their large funding base to fund mortgage loans, act as institutional investors in the secondary mortgage market and facilitate the establishment of a liquidity facility. Liquidity risk was measured by determining the loan to deposits ratio. This is computed as the total amount of mortgage loan issued divided by the total amount of deposits. Also it can be measured by the ratio of borrowed funds to total loan assets. This is computed as the total borrowed funds to finance the mortgage loans divided by the total value of mortgage loans. If the ratio of loan to deposits and borrowed funds to total assets is high it means that the lender relies heavily on short term funds to fund loans (Saunders & Marcia, 2001).

2.11. Empirical Review of Literature

According to Claurietie and Sirmans (2006) one major concern of the lender is the risk that borrowers will default on their obligations to repay the principal and interest. This is the default risk and it varies with the nature of land and credit worthiness of the individual borrower. Default risk relates to the likelihood that the borrower's income may fall after the loan is made, thereby jeopardizing the receipt of future mortgage payments. Similarly should the market value of a property fall below the outstanding loan balance the borrower will lose the motivation to repay the mortgage leading to default. The possibility that a default may occur means that lenders charge a premium or higher interest rates to offset possible loan losses. Dolde (2006) indicated that some mortgage loan defaults were believed to have a significant relationship with the characteristics of both mortgages and borrowers at the time of loan origination. He also noted that it is important that an objective analytical technique be applied to the analysis of the causes and prediction of mortgage default risk.

Mortgage Lenders advance mortgage loan on a maximum of 90% of the purchase price which as well should not exceed three times of the total annual income of the borrower, with the intent of minimizing uncertainty fall in property prices (Kolbe, Gaylon, & Rudner, 2003). At the time the loan is originated, the lender will ensure that the appraised value of the property is greater than the amount of the loan (Claurietie & Sirmans, 2006). Lenders want assurance concerning the price of the property because it will be serving as security for repayment of the mortgage debt and over time it must remain sufficiently high to repay the outstanding loan balance in the event of default. As defined by Coong (1995) interest rate risk is the exposure of a financial institution's current or future earnings and capital to interest rate change. Most financial Institutions suffer losses in profits or asset value when the general level of interest rates rises. Real estate tends to be highly levered and thus the rate of return earned by equity investors tends to be affected by changes in interest rate. The goal is to control interest rate risk to an acceptable level. Interest rates chargeable on mortgages influence the mortgage quality in that the higher the interest the more expensive the mortgage product becomes, and the more susceptible to defaults due to high repayment costs. Low interest rates on the other hand encourage compliance and prompt repayment thus guaranteeing quality products (Mutero, 2010). According to Dolde (2006) liquidity risk occurs when a continuous market with many buyers and sellers and frequent transactions are not available. The more difficult an investment is to liquidate, the greater the risk that a price concession may have to be given to a buyer should the seller have to dispose off the investment quickly. Real estate has relatively high degree of liquidity risk. It can take 6-12 months to sell real estate income properties especially during periods of weak demand. A depository institution's balance sheet typically has a large amount of short term liabilities, such as demand deposits and other transaction accounts which fund relatively long-term, illiquid assets such as mortgages (Saunders & Marcia, 2001). Marshall (2009) argues that lenders originating mortgage loans by the use of deposits and holding them, has the great merit that solvent lenders have strong incentives both to underwrite mortgages carefully and, if necessary, to modify them.

3. Methodology

3.1. Research Design

The study employed causal research design, because the purpose of this study was to determine the effect of mortgage market risks on mortgage uptake. The aim of the study was to determine the cause effect relationship between the independent variables and the dependent variable. According to Copper and Schindler (2006) this design is used to explain how the independent variable produces change in the dependent variable therefore determining the cause effect relationship that exists among variables. Thus the design was appropriate in determining the effect of mortgage market risk on mortgage uptake.

3.2. Location and Population of the Study

The study was carried out in Kenya among mortgage lenders. These lenders were commercial banks and housing Finance Company, these institutions are distributed all over the country and offer the same services in their branches. The target population for this study was mortgage lending institutions. According to banking supervision report 2013 there were 37 institutions involved in mortgage lending in Kenya.

3.3. Sampling Procedures and Sample Size

Sampling is the process of selecting a suitable sample, or representative part of a population for the purpose of determining parameters or characteristics of the whole population (Kombo & Tromp, 2006). In selecting a sample the researcher used purposive sampling. It is a non-probabilistic sampling technique that uses cases that have required information with respect to the objectives of the study (Mugenda & Mugenda, 2003). It was applied because the information concerning the lenders that have mortgage in their portfolio for the period required for study was in the Banking Supervision Reports from the year 2008 to 2013. The sampling technique was used to select 27 financial institutions that have been involved in mortgage lending between the year 2008 and 2012.

3.4. Data Collection Procedures

The study employed secondary data; the data was collected from central bank website, and financial statements of mortgage lending institutions. The data was quantitative and was collected from 27 mortgages lenders during the period 2008 to 2012. During the period under study there have been significant changes in real estate investments, level of mortgage lending, population and urbanization. Therefore this period was convenient for the collection of relevant and reliable data. This study utilized longitudinal data as it involved the collection of data for 5 years from the same subjects only once. The measurement scale applied was ratio scale; this is because when variables are measured at the ratio scale, powerful statistical procedures can be applied. This improves the quality of findings obtained from such studies and generalizations can be made to a wider population (Mugenda & Mugenda, 2003). The variables were determined by interest rate changes, ratio of nonperforming loans to new loans, changes in price of properties and ratio of loans to deposits as a measure of interest rate risk, credit risk, price risk and liquidity risk respectively.

3.5. Data Analysis

The study employed descriptive and inferential statistics in the analysis of data. Data was tested for normality, linearity, homoscedasticity, multi-collinearity and autocorrelation. This was done to determine whether the assumptions of regression model are present. Hypotheses were tested at 5% level of significance using inferential statistics such as student's t-test, and F-test in order to support the statistical hypotheses. Multiple linear regressions were used to determine the degree and magnitude of the relationship that exists between the variables; this statistical tool took in combination several independent variables that affect a dependent variable. The variables in the study were related using a stochastic multiple linear regression model of the form:

$$Y_{i,t} = \beta_{\circ} + \beta_1 CR_{i,t} + \beta_2 IR_t + \beta_3 PR_{i,t} + \beta_4 LR_{i,t} + \mu_{i,t}$$

Where Y=Loan uptake; i= Mortgage Lenders; t=Years; $\beta_{\circ}$, =fixed individual effect'; $\beta_1, \beta_2, \beta_3, \beta_4$ = Predictor Variable Coefficients; $CR_{i,t}$= Credit Risk for Lender i in year t; $IR_{i,t}$ = Interest rate risk in year t; $PR_{i,t}$ = Price risk in year t; $LR_{i,t}$= Liquidity risk for Lender i in year t; $\mu_{i,t}$= error term.

4. Empirical Results and Discussions

4.1. Descriptive Analysis

Descriptive statistics were used to test for normality of data. Normality test was used to determine the normal distribution of the sampled data in order to make accurate and reliable conclusions. The mean which is a measure of central tendency was used in generalization of findings while standard deviation was used as a measure of dispersion from the mean. The summary of descriptive statistics is shown in Table 2.

Table 2. *Descriptive Statistics.*

Variables	Minimum	Maximum	Mean	Standard Deviation
Loan	-623764600	4266600000	2404828410	15500228
Interest Rate Risk	-0.7526	0.8727	-0.092765	0.056033
Credit Risk	-0.4406	0.4952	-0.009837	0.0462099
Price Risk	-0.1861	0.1622	-0.126964	0.0716494
Liquidity Risk	0.0006	0.7108	0.164930	0.2366261

n=27

In Table 2 the mean is a summary of the average for all the variables, while as standard deviation summarizes the concentration of data around the mean, loans had a mean of 2,404,828,410 which represents the mean amount of mortgage originated by all mortgage lenders in Kenya. Interest rate risk had a mean of -0.0927 which represents the average changes in interest rates in the period under study. Credit risk had a mean of -0.009837 which indicates the mean changes in credit risk for the period under study for all lenders. Price risk had a mean of -0.127 which indicates the average changes in prices of property for the period under study. Liquidity risk had a mean of 0.1649 which indicates changes in liquidity risk for all the lenders in the period under study. The standard deviation for credit risk was 0.0462099, price risk had 0.0716494, liquidity risk had 0.2366261 while interest rate risk had 0.0560333. The standard deviations for the variables are closer to zero which implies that the values are concentrated around the mean. Liquidity risk had the highest deviation from its mean this could imply that it would have a higher effect on the dependent variable.

4.2. Homoscedasticity

Homoscedasticity was used to determine whether the variance of the error term is constant and the same for all observations. Violation of homoscedasticity makes standard errors of estimators biased and inconsistent. Therefore tests of hypothesis are no longer valid and standard errors are incorrect (Andrean, 2007). Homoscedasticity can be detected by use of scatter plot as shown in figure 1.

The residuals are plotted in the y-axis and predicted values are plotted on the x axis. If the width of the residuals either increases or decreases as the predicted values increases or are not concentrated around the centre then the assumption of constant variance is not met and the problem of heteroskedasticity exists, thus ordinary least square method should not be used rather generalized least squares method should be used in estimating the regression (Aczel & Sounderpandian, 2002). In Figure 1, as the predictive values are increasing the residuals are neither increasing nor decreasing, they are fairly clustered around the line of total fit and are concentrated around the centre. This shows existence of homoscedasticity which implies the standard errors are correct and have equal variances thus the results were used for hypothesis testing and the ordinary least square method was used.

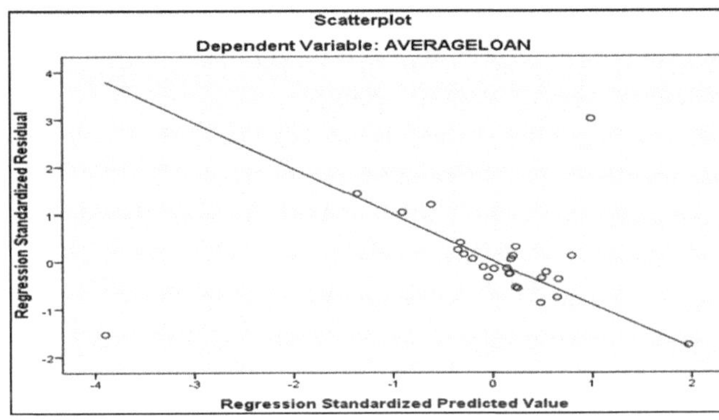

Figure 1. *Test for Homoscedasticity.*

4.3. Multicollinearity

Multicollinearity was used to test correlation between the independent variables. The presence of multicollinearity makes it difficult to isolate the impact of each independent variable on the dependent variables and also standard errors for each independent variable become inflated (Landau & Everitt, 2004). Multicollinearity can be corrected by excluding one or more of the correlated independent variable from the regression model (Lind, Marchal, & Wathen, 2008). To check for multicollinearity Variance Inflation Factor and Tolerance level were used. A VIF of less than 10 or a tolerance level of greater than 0.1 is acceptable. A summary of multicollinearity statistics is shown in Table 3

Table 3. *Collinearity Statistics.*

Independent Variables	Tolerance	VIF
Interest rate risk	0.380	2.628
Credit risk	0.580	1.724
Price risk	0.654	1.529
Liquidity risk	0.401	2.491

In Table 3 interest rate risk had the lowest tolerance level of 0.38 and price risk had the highest tolerance level of 0.654. The tolerance level for all the independent variables was greater than 0.1 which suggests the absence of multi-collinearity problem. Interest rate risk had the highest VIF of 2.628 and price risk had the lowest VIF of 1.529, the VIF for all the variables was less than 10 hence this suggests there is no multi-collinearity among the independent variables. Multicollinearity was also tested using eigen values and the condition index. The condition index is computed as square root of the ratio of the largest eigen value to each successive eigen value. A condition index is of less than 10 implies there is no existence of multicollinearity. A summary of eigen values, condition index, and variance proportions is provided in Table 4.

Table 4. *Collinearity Diagnostics.*

Dimension	Eigen Value	Condition Index	Variance proportions				
			Constant	Interest rate risk	Credit risk	Price risk	Liquidity risk
1	2.378	1.000	0.02	0.00	0.01	0.02	0.03
2	1.603	1.218	0.01	0.12	0.10	0.00	0.02
3	0.796	1.728	0.00	0.06	0.46	0.01	0.05
4	0.148	4.006	0.03	0.79	0.10	0.18	0.78
5	0.075	5.634	0.75	0.03	0.33	0.68	0.11

In Table 4 liquidity risk had the highest condition index of 5.634 while interest rate risk had the lowest condition index of 1.218. The condition index for all the independent variables was less than 10 which implies the absence of multicollinearity. Variation in the independent variables that can be explained by other independent variables was highest for price risk at 68% and lowest for interest rate risk at 3% but they were all less than 70%.This also implies there is no multicollinearity between the independent variables hence it was possible to isolate the impact of each independent variable on the dependent variable.

4.4. Pair Wise Correlations

Pearson correlation coefficient (r) was used to determine the degree or strength of linear relationship among the variables. Linearity increases the predictive power of the model and the validity of the estimated coefficients. A correlation of $r > \pm 0.7$ implies that the variables are strongly related either positively or negatively. The study sought to determine the correlation between the variables in order to determine the strength of the relationship at 5% significance level. A summary of the correlation coefficients and significance level for all the variables is shown in Table 5.

Table 5. *Correlation Coefficients.*

	Loan	Interest rate risk	Credit risk	Price risk	Liquidity risk
Loan	1.000	-0.72	-0.567	0.09	-0.670
Interest rate risk	-0.72	1.000	0.345	-0.055	0.570
Credit risk	-0.567	0.345	1.000	-0.564	0.314
Price risk	0.090	-0.055	-0.564	1.000	-0.115
Liquidity risk	-0.607	0.570	0.314	-0.114	1.000

4.4.1. Correlation Between Loan and Credit Risk

Pearson correlation was used to determine the relationship between credit risk and loan. The correlation coefficient was -0.567 with p-value (0.001) which was found to be significant at 5% significance level suggesting the existence of a moderate negative relationship between credit risk and loan amount in that the higher the ratio of non-performing loans to new loans the higher the credit risk and this results to lenders rationing the lending of mortgages.

4.4.2. Correlation Between Loan and Interest Rate Risk

Pearson correlation was used to determine the relationship between interest rate risk and loan. The correlation coefficient was -0.72 with P value (0.000) which was found to be significant at 5% significance level which implies a strong negative relationship between interest rate risk and loan amount. The more frequent there are adverse changes in interest rates such that the cost of funds is higher than the return on assets then the higher the interest rate risk and the lesser the amount of mortgages originated.

4.4.3. Correlation Between Loan and Price Risk

Pearson correlation was used to determine the relationship between price risk and loan. The correlation coefficient was -0.09 with p value (0.803) which was found not to be significant at 5% significance level. This implies that the relationship between price risk and loan is not significant. This may be attributed to lenders giving loans that have a low loan to value ratio therefore in case of fall in property prices the lenders are still able to recover the amount of mortgage lent.

4.4.4. Correlation Between Loan and Liquidity Risk

Pearson correlation was used to determine the relationship between liquidity risk and loan. The correlation coefficient was -0.607 with p value (0.01) which was found to be significant at 5% significance level. This implies there is a moderate negative relationship between liquidity risk and loan amount. The higher the amount of loans as compared to deposits the higher the liquidity risk involved in lending thus a lender may ration the amount of lending because they are liquidity constrained.

4.5. Econometric Model

Table 6. *Significance of the Model.*

R	R Square	Adjusted R Square	Std. Error of the Estimate	Durbin-Watson
0.843[a]	0.710	0.657	907236708.471	2.154

Table 7. *Analysis of Variance.*

Model	Sum of Squares	df	Mean square	F	Sig
Regression	4435911695435	4	1108977923858	13.474	0.000
Residual	1810772579432	22	8230784451966		
Total	6246684274868	26			

n=27, k=5

The multiple correlation coefficient (R) indicates the

correlation between dependent variable and the independent variables jointly predicted by the model. The multiple coefficient of determination (R^2) determines the changes or variation in dependent variable as explained by independent variables jointly. A coefficient of $R^2 \geq 0.7$ is preferred as it implies more than 70% of the variation in dependent variable is explained by the independent variables and the existence of a strong correlation between the variables. The significance of the model is presented in Table 6 and Table 7.

In Table 6 multiple coefficient of correlation (R) was 0.843 which implies that the degree of association between mortgage uptake and credit risk, liquidity risk, price risk and interest rate is strong and positive. The (R^2) was 71% which implies that 71% of the variations in mortgage uptake are explained by the credit risk, price risk, liquidity risk and interest rate risk jointly in the model, while 29% of variation in mortgage uptake is explained by random error or other factors. Anova was used to determine the usefulness of the independent variables in explaining variation in the dependent variable. It was used to test the significance of the regression relationship between mortgage uptake and credit risk, liquidity risk, price risk and interest rate risk. It provided an F test for the null hypothesis that all the slope coefficients in the regression are simultaneously equal to zero at 5% level of significance. In Table 7, the F value 13.474 and p-value (0.000) means that the smallest level of significance at which the null hypothesis can be rejected is practically zero. In this case the null hypothesis was rejected at 5% significance level so as to conclude that at least one of the slope coefficients in the model does not equal to zero hence the explanatory variables credit risk, price risk, liquidity risk, and interest rate risk significantly explain variations in mortgage uptake. Durbin Watson test (d) statistic was used to test for autocorrelation which occurs when regression errors are correlated across observations. The presence of autocorrelation may result to a multiple coefficient of determination that is overestimated or t-values that are inflated resulting to a type 1 error (Lind, Marchal, & Wathen, 2008).Autocorrelation is not present when the Durbin Watson statistic takes values between 0 and 4. From Table 9, the calculated Durbin Watson statistic was 2.154 at 5% significance level which implies the absence of autocorrelation problem in the regression model thus the multiple coefficient of determination was well estimated and the t values are correct in testing the hypotheses.

Table 8. *Coeffecients of Variables.*

Model	Unstandardized Coefficients		Standard coefficients		
	B	Std error	Beta	T	sig
Constant	-0.9949	0.4810		-1.972	0.061
Interest rate risk	-2.2529	0.8101	-0.517	-2.781	0.011
Credit risk	-6.0733	0.5977	-0.573	-3.801	0.001
Price risk	-7.4875	0.7082	-0.573	-2.438	0.023
Liquidity risk	-0.1829	0.1186	-0.028	-0.154	0.879

4.6. Test of Significance of Regression Coefficients

In determining the cause effect relationship between the dependent variable and the explanatory variables the regression coefficients were tested at the 5% level of significance using t-test. The regression is presented in Table 8.

4.6.1. The Effect of Credit Risk on Mortgage Uptake

The study sought to find out the effect of credit risk on mortgage uptake. In Table 8, the coefficient obtained from regression was -6.0733 with (p-value $0.001 < 0.05$) thus the null hypothesis that credit risk has no significant effect on mortgage uptake was rejected which leads to the conclusion that there is a statistically significant relationship between credit risk and mortgage uptake. In this case credit risk has an effect on mortgage uptake such that a unit increase in credit risk will result to a decrease in mortgage uptake by 6.0733 units. This may be attributed to the increase in the ratio of non performing loans to new loans which may result to lenders restricting loan origination and advancing loans only to credit worthy customers. This finding is consistent with finding of a study by Lewis and Neave (2008) who noted that one of the major risks faced by mortgage lenders is credit risk. The finding conflict that of Njiru and Moronge (2013) that found out that credit risk has a lesser effect on mortgage uptake in Kenya.

4.6.2. The Effect of Interest Rate Risk on Mortgage Uptake

This study aimed at determining the effect of interest rate risk on mortgage uptake. The coefficient obtained from regression was -2.529, (p value $0.011 < 0.05$). The null hypothesis that interest rate risk has no significant effect on mortgage uptake was rejected which leads to the conclusion that there is a statistically significant relationship between interest rate risk and mortgage uptake Hence interest rate risk has an effect on mortgage uptake such that a unit increase in interest rate risk will result to a decrease in mortgage uptake by 2.2529 units. Interest rate affects the cost of borrowing funds such that high interest rates will affect the cost of funds and hence resulting to high cost of borrowing as a result borrowers would find mortgage loans expensive and inaccessible. The findings support a report by Hassler *et al.* (2004) who noted that lenders remain vulnerable to significant interest rate risk when they are involved in mortgage lending. Also according to Vuyisani (2003) mortgage finance is faced with major challenges such as changes in interest rates which may result to restrictive lending.

4.6.3. The Effect of Price Risk on Mortgage Uptake

This study aimed at finding out the effect of price risk on mortgage uptake. The coefficient obtained from regression was -7.4875, (p-value $0.023 < 0.05$). Therefore the null hypothesis that price risk has no significant effect on mortgage uptake was rejected which led to the conclusion that there is a statistically significant relationship between price risk and mortgage uptake. In this case price risk has an effect on mortgage uptake such that a unit increase in price risk will result to a decrease in mortgage uptake by 7.4875 units. This may be attributed to risk of fall in property values below the mortgage value resulting to default by borrowers or the risk that the lenders may not recover the full amount from the sale thus lenders may restrict lending until when prices of property are favorable or they impose a low loan to value ratio to protect themselves from price risk. The finding is consistent with the report of Hass Consult Survey (2013) which associated property prices with mortgage uptake in Kenya. The difficulty in property valuations and changes in prices of property is a limitation to mortgage lending World Bank (2011).

4.6.4. The Effect of Liquidity Risk on Mortgage Uptake

This study sought to find out the effect of liquidity risk on mortgage uptake. The coefficient obtained was -0.1829 with (p-value 0.879 >0.05).Thus the null hypothesis that liquidity risk has no significant effect on mortgage uptake was not rejected which led to the conclusion that there is no statistically significant relationship between liquidity risk and mortgage uptake. Hence liquidity risk does not affect mortgage uptake. The findings may be as a result of high deposit amount both long term and short term that is more than the amount of mortgages advanced or lenders sourcing for funds to improve on their liquidity in order to originate mortgages. The findings of this study conflicts the results of Hassler *et al.* (2004) who noted that as lenders remain vulnerable to significant liquidity risk they often ration the amount of mortgage lending. Also according to World Bank, liquidity constraint is one of the major obstacles to mortgage lending. On the other hand the findings are consistent with Marshall (2009) who argues that originating mortgage loans by use of deposits has the merit that solvent lenders have strong incentives to underwrite mortgages.

4.7. Regression Equation

Ordinary least square regression equation

$$Y = -0.9949 - 6.0733\text{CR} - 2.2529\text{IR} - 7.4875\text{PR} - 0.1829\text{LR} + \mu_{i,t}$$

According to the equation holding credit risk, price risk, liquidity risk and interest rate risk constant would result to Kshs 0.9949 billion drop in mortgage uptake. A 1 unit increase in credit risk would lead to decrease in mortgage uptake by 6.7033 units, a 1 unit increase in interest rate risk would lead to a decrease in mortgage uptake by 2.2529 units, a 1 unit increase in price risk would lead to a decrease in mortgage uptake by 7.4875 units and a 1unit increase in liquidity risk would lead to decrease in mortgage uptake by 0.1829 units. Credit risk, interest rate risk and price risk had p- value less than 0.05 which means that these risks are significant in predicting changes in mortgage uptake. The p-values for the constant and liquidity risk were however greater than 0.05 hence they were insignificant and do not have a significant effect on mortgage uptake. After running the regression the expected value of the error term becomes zero hence the error term is not included in the model.

5. Conclusions and Recommendations

5.1. Conclusions

The study found out that credit risk has a significant negative effect on mortgage uptake. If the risk of default increases the amount of mortgages lent decreases. Loan amount is adjusted for the perceived credit risk and loans are extended only to credit worthy customers because of the significant effect the risk has on the cash flows and solvency of the lender. Price risk has a significant negative effect on mortgage uptake such that increases in price risk result to a decrease in the amount of mortgages originated. When property prices are unfavorable mortgage lenders restrict the amount of lending. The study found a significant negative relationship between interest rate risk and mortgage uptake. Increase in interest rate risk results to a decrease in amount of mortgage lent by mortgage lenders. Changes in interest rates result to mismatch between the cost of funds and return on assets this affects the net interest margin hence the profitability of lenders. Thus lenders charge a high risk premium that protects them from the risk of loss as a result of changes in interest rates. The effect of liquidity risk on mortgage uptake was found to be insignificant. Thus changes in the amount of deposits does not affect amount of mortgages originated. The level of deposits is able to fund the loans, alternatively lenders acquire funds to improve on their liquidity and this enables them to originate mortgages.

5.2. Recommendations

Based on the findings of the study the following recommendations are made:

i. Lenders should improve on their risk management strategies because risks affect the amount of lending. The inability of lenders to manage these risks means that they charge high risk premiums making mortgages to be costly or lenders restrict the amount of lending.
ii. Lending involves borrowers that have different capacity hence lenders should diversify their mortgage portfolio and develop different mortgage products that are able to suit their different customers as a strategy to reduce rate of default.
iii. Lenders should set mortgage rates that are sensitive and respond to changes in the macroeconomic environment and should not charge high interest margins that lead to increase in the costs of borrowing.
iv. A secondary mortgage market should be developed to help in reducing risks faced by mortgage lenders as well as provide a mechanism for packaging of mortgages into securities that are sold to institutional investors. Institutional investors such as pension funds and insurance companies should be encouraged to invest in the purchase of mortgages securities and also guarantee members mortgages as they have substantial funds to invest for long term this would lead to continued increase in liquidity hence increase mortgage uptake and eventually growth of mortgage market.

Acknowledgement

I acknowledge the Lord God almighty for His Grace and favour has been sufficient throughout the entire research process. I sincerely appreciate my supervisors, Nebat M. Galo and Henry M. Kimathi for their professional guidance, input and availability in the preparation of this paper. My appreciation also goes to Andrew T. Muguna and Justo Simiyu for their assistance and encouragement. Finally I wish to thank my colleagues at Chuka University for their great moral support.

References

[1] Aczel, A. & Sounderpandian, J. (2002). *Business Statistics* (5th ed.). Irwin: Mc-Graw Hill.

[2] Andrean, T. (2007). *Econometrics.* New York: Ventus Publishing.

[3] Arvantis, Y. (2013). *African Housing Dynamics:Lessons from the Kenyan Market.* African Development Bank.

[4] Bangkok Bank. (2008). *Annual Report.* Bangkok: Bangkok Bank.

[5] Bianco, K. (2008). *The Subprime Lending Crisis; Causes and Effects of the Mortgage Meltdown.* CCH Mortgage Compliance Guide and Bank Digest.

[6] Biernert, L. & Brauner, E. (2007). The Mortgage Lendin Value: Prospect for Development within Europe. *Journal of Property Investment & Finance, 25*(6).

[7] Brueggeman, W. & Fisher, J. (2008). *Real Estate Finance and Investments.* Irwin: Mc-Graw Hill.

[8] Kariuki, C. (2013). *Mortgage Special Report.* Kenya: The Mortgage Company.

[9] Central Bank of Kenya. (2007). *Banking Supervision Annual Report.* Nairobi: Central Bank.

[10] Central Bank. (2008). *Banking Supervision Annual Report.* Nairobi: Central Bank.

[11] Central Bank. (2009). *Banking Annual Supervision Report.* Nairobi: Central Bank.

[12] Central Bank. (2010). *Banking Supervision Annual Report.* Nairobi: Central Bank.

[13] Central Bank. (2011). *Banking Annual Supervision Report.* Naairobi: Central Bank.

[14] Central Bank. (2011). *Banking Supervision Annual Report.* Nairobi: Central Bank.

[15] Central Bank (2012). *Bank Supervision Annual Report.* Nairobi: Central Bank.

[16] Central Bank. (2013). *Banking Annual Supervision Report.* Nairobi: Central Bank.

[17] Central Bank; World Bank. (2013). *Mortgage Finance in Kenya: Survey Analysis.* Nairobi.

[18] Claurietie, T. M. & Sirmans, S. G. (2006). *Real Estate Finance: Theory and Practice* (5th ed.). South Western: Thomson Publishers.

[19] Cooper, D. R. & Schindler, P. S. (2006). *Business Research Methods.* Irwin: Mc-Graw Hill.

[20] Davis, P. E. & Zhu, H. F. (2004). *Bank Lending and Commercial Property Cycles.* Switzerland: Bank for International Settlements.

[21] Dolde, M. (2006). Sources of Funds for Mortgage Finance. *Journal of Housing Research*, Vol 7, 259-281.

[22] Erbas, V. W. (2005). Demand for Rural Finance Services. A Journal on *Information Finance Markets Vol. 2, 78-92*

[23] Fabozzi, F. J.; Modigliani, F. & Jones, F. J. (2007). *Capital Markets Institutions and Instuments* (3rd ed.). New Delhi: Prentice Hall.

[24] Giddings, S. (2007). *Housing Challenges & Opportunities in Sub- Saharan Africa.* Washington. D.C: International Housing Coalition.

[25] Glower, M.; Donal, R. & Hendersholt, P. (1998). Selling Price & Selling Time: The Impact of Seller Motivation. *Real Estate Economics*, Vol 5, 719-740.

[26] Guajarati, D. N. (1998). *Basic Econometrics.* New York: Mc Graw Hill.

[27] Hahm, H. (2004). *Financial Firm Production of Monetary Services. A Generalised Systemic Barnnet Profit Function Approach.* New York: McGraw Hill

[28] Hass Consult Survey. (2013). *Kenyan Property Market.* Nairobi: Hass Consult.

[29] Hassler, O.; Chiquer, L. & Lea, M. (2004). *Mortgage Securities in Emerging Markets.* Wasington.D.C: Financial Sector Operations & Policy Department.

[30] Jacobus, C. J. (1999). *Real Estate Principles* (8th ed.). New Jersey: Prentice Hall.

[31] Kibirige, M. (2006). Mortgage Financing; How it Works in Uganda. *The Journal of Capital Markets Industry, Uganda, Vol 1, 10-14.*

[32] Kolbe, P. T.; Gaylon, G. E. & Rudner, H. G. (2003). *Real Estate Finance* (1st ed.). Chicago: Dearborn Financial Publishing.

[33] Kothari, C. (2004). *Research Methodolgy: Methods and Techniques* (2nd ed.). New Delhi: New Age International (P) Ltd.

[34] Landau, S., & Everitt, B. S. (2004). *A Handbook on Statistical Analysis Using SPSS.* New York: Chapman & Hall Publishers.

[35] Lea, M. & Chiquier, L. (1999). *Providing Long Term Finnacing for Housing. The Role of Secondary Markets.* California: Office of Departmental Studies, Bureau for Development Policy United Nations Development Programme.

[36] Li, Y. & Resenblatt, E. (2005). Can Urban Indicators Predict House Price Appreciation. *Real Estate Economics, Vol 5, 85-101.*

[37] Lind, D. A.; Marchal, W. G., & Wathen, S. A. (2008). *Statistical Techniques in Business and Economics.* New Delhi: Mc Graw Hill.

[38] Marshall, J. (2009). *The Financial Crisis in the U.S : Key Events Causes and Responses.* U.K: Library House of Commons.

[39] Mugenda, O. M. & Mugenda, A. G. (2003). *Research Methods: Quantitative and Qualitative Approaches.* Nairobi: Acts Press.

[40] Mutero, J. (2010). *Mobilising Pension Assets for Housing Finance Needs in Africa.* East Africa: Centre for Affordable Housing Finance in Africa.

[41] Njiru, M. & Moronge, M. (2013). Factors Affecting Growth of Mortgage Indusries in Kenya. A Case Study of National Housing Corporation. *International Journal of social sciences and Entrepreneurship, 1*(7), 26-35.

[42] Njuguna, N. (2011). *Sterngthening the Mortgage Market.* Nairobi: Government Printer.

[43] Nyandemo, S. N. & Sigh, D. (2003). *Managerial Economics Theory and Practice.* New Delhi: Paul Sigh.

[44] Oriaro, M. (2000). *Bridging the Finance Gap in Housing and Infrastruture in Kenya. A Case study of NACHU.* Nairobi: University of Nairobi Press.

[45] Robertson, W. H. (1934). Industrial Fluctuations & the Natural Rate of Interest. *The Economic Journal, Vol 4, 650-656.*

[46] Rose, P. S. (2003). *Money and Capital Markets* (8th ed.). Irwin: Mc-Graw Hill.

[47] Saunders, A. & Marcia, C. (2001). *Financial Markets and Institutions.* New York: Mc-Graw Hill.

[48] Scanlon, A. & Whitehead, B. (2004). *International Trends in Housing Tenure and Mortgage Finance.* London: London School of Economics.

[49] Sharpele, D. (2000). Apartments and Rent, Homes for Sale and Foreclosure. *Census Rent Information Vol 5, 165-178.*.

[50] Trieschmann, J. S.; Hoyt, R. E., & Sommer, D. W. (2005). *Risk Management & Insurance.* South Western: Thomson.

[51] Vuyisani, M. (2003). *Preview of Housing Finance Systems in Four Different African Countries: South Africa, Ghana, Tanzania and Nigeria.* Washington D.C: International Finance Corporation

[52] Wang, X. & Hongfei, C. (2007). *Does Property Market Risks Matter in Commercial Loan Pricing: An Inquiry into the Determinants of Commercial Mortgage Loan Spread.* Massachusettes: Department of Urban Studies and Planning.

[53] World Bank. (2011). *Developing Kenya's Mortgage Market.* Wasington, DC: Office of the Publisher.

An Analysis of Work Motivation and Teacher Job Satisfaction in Public Secondary Schools in Rarieda Sub-County, Kenya

Fredrick Omondi Ogonda[1], Bula Hannah Orwa[2], Wambua Philip Peter[2], Muli Vika Jedida[2]

[1]Master of Business Administration Graduate, School of Business, Kenyatta University, Nairobi City, Kenya
[2]Human Resource Management, Department of Business Administration, School of Business, Kenyatta University, Nairobi City, Kenya

Email address:
bula.oh@yahoo.com (B. H. Orwa)

Abstract: In the public secondary education sub-sector, issues about job satisfaction are glaring as industrial unrest and labour turnover are almost a daily phenomenon. The fundamental question that one would ask is why does there exist this reality. Could it because teachers in the public secondary schools are not satisfied with their jobs .This study seeks to analyze work motivation and teacher job satisfaction in public secondary schools in Rarieda sub-county, Kenya. The specific objectives of this study sought to establish how remuneration, recognition, working conditions and training influence teacher job satisfaction in public secondary schools in Rarieda sub-county. A descriptive research design was employed during the study, with a sample of 205 teachers from a population of 440 being used. Primary data collection was utilized. Quantitative and qualitative data was collected and self-administered questionnaires were preferred, while the validity of the questionnaires was ensured through pre-testing. Quantitative data was analyzed using the Statistical Package for the Social Sciences. Subsequently, the analyzed data was presented using frequency tables, percentages, measures of central tendencies and measures of dispersion. From the analysis, the study concluded that motivation factors such as remuneration, working conditions, recognition and training influence teacher job satisfaction. The study makes a number of recommendations: that similar studies be conducted in other regions in order to corroborate the study or establish new findings; A study to find out whether there exist other factors influencing teacher job satisfaction; studies to establish why majority of teachers were satisfied with training yet the same teachers were not satisfied with their jobs.

Keywords: Work Motivation, Job Satisfaction, Recognition, Training, Rarieda Sub-County, Kenya, Teachers, Public Schools

1. Background to the Study

Work motivation is the process that arouses, energizes, directs, and sustains behavior and performance among employees, (Slocum, & Hellriegel, 2009). Work motivation encourages employees internally towards the actions which help them to perform the preferred tasks and employ effectiveness is a way that inspires them to do their work and have commitment towards their jobs. According to Slocum, & Hellriegel, (2009), intrinsic work motivation is the motivation to perform an activity in order to experience the pleasure and satisfaction inherent in the activity. Slocum, & Hellriegel, (2009), espouse that work motivation involves employee compensation, working conditions, training, recognition and appreciation.

According to Byars, & Rue, (2008), compensation refers to all the extrinsic rewards employees receive in exchange for their work. Usually, compensation is composed of the base wage or salary, incentives or bonuses and benefits. According to Muathe, (2008), Compensation is payment to an employee in return for their contribution to the organization, that is, for doing their job. Muathe, (2008) continues that the most common forms of compensation are wages, salaries and tips. In today's competitive business environment, organizations strive to gain competitive advantage by offering their employees highly competitive rewards. Compensation is not only a tool for gaining competitive advantage but also a strategy for attracting, motivating and retaining top talents within the organization, (Werner, & Dismore (2009).

Employee training is the process of providing employees with the knowledge and skills needed to do a particular task or job, Werner, & Dismore, (2009). They espouse that normally, a new employee's manager has the primary responsibility for his/her training. The new employee's training can have a significant influence on the new employee's productivity and favorable attitude towards his/her job, (Byars, & Rue, 2008). Today, employers have got no other choice but to ensure the training and development of their employees while they remain valued assets in the organization.

Recognition can occur both in verbal, promotion, and in tangible reward. While citing Okumbe, (1998), Njoroge, (2011), refers to promotion as the advancement of a worker to a better job in terms of more skills, responsibilities, status and remuneration. When an employee is promoted to more challenging and more demanding job, they feel trusted and their contributions valued in the organization. Such an employee is more likely to give his/her all to the organization.

Working conditions play a very central role in influencing job satisfaction of any employee. Kyongo, (2006), asserts that employees would feel satisfied in their jobs if they are working in a clear and orderly work place, with adequate tools and equipment, acceptable levels of environmental quality, temperature, humidity and noise. The surrounding in which people work should not be that which pose a threat to the workers lives; when that is the case then the employer should ensure that there are safety measures in place to ensure that the hostile conditions are tamed.

2. Statement of the Problem

Teacher absenteeism, lateness, low productivity, turnover, demonstrations and rampant strikes witnessed in public secondary schools are a serious indication that teachers in public secondary schools are not satisfied with their job. Castillo, & Cano, (2004) on a study at an agricultural college at a large university by using the Herzberg's theory studied job Satisfaction in the Wood Faculty to explore the motivational factors that affect job satisfaction. Their findings showed that the work itself was the most important factor that contributed to job satisfaction, with working conditions being the least important. Carrying out his study in USA, Ambrose *et al.*, (2005) conducted a qualitative study to investigate the influences of motivation on faculty job satisfaction and retention. The study focused on Carnegie Mellon University of Pittsburgh over a period of two years in the USA. Findings suggested work motivation causes of job satisfaction such as salaries, collegiality, mentoring, and the reappointment, promotion, and tenure process of departmental heads.

Brady, (2007) reported that leadership, recognition, working conditions, salary, interpersonal relations and professional achievement and growth affect job satisfaction in the nursing faculty in baccalaureate- and graduate degree nursing programs in the USA, and that they also influence retention in nursing faculty in associate-degree nursing programs as well. Reporting on the effects of teacher absenteeism on quality teaching and learning in Ghana, Al-hassan, (2009), established that Poor remuneration is the leading reason for most teachers to indulge in absenteeism, late coming to school and early departure from school, making up 70% of the respondents. In Kenya, Akali, (2010) concluded that factors that affect teacher job satisfaction included pay, promotion, compulsory transfer, recognition and work conditions. She further found out that among the diploma teacher trainers in Kenya, promotion played a bigger role as far as job satisfaction is concerned.

It is therefore clear that teacher job satisfaction remains a mirage in public secondary schools. It is therefore imperative that more studies be conducted to determine the extent to which the work motivation variables influence teacher job satisfaction in public secondary schools. This study therefore sought to investigate the influence of work motivation on teacher job satisfaction in public secondary schools in Rarieda sub-county.

3. Specific Objectives

i. To establish the influence of remuneration on teacher job satisfaction in public secondary schools in Rarieda sub-county.
ii. To determine the influence of working conditions on teacher job satisfaction in public secondary schools in Rarieda sub-county.
iii. To examine the influence of recognition on teacher job satisfaction in public secondary schools in Rarieda sub-county.
iv. To assess the influence of training on teacher job satisfaction in public secondary schools in Rarieda sub-county.

4. Research Questions

i. What is the influence of compensation on teacher job satisfaction in public secondary schools in Rarieda sub-county?

ii. What in the influence of working conditions on teacher job satisfaction in public secondary schools in Rarieda sub-county?

iii. What is the influence of recognition on teacher job satisfaction in public secondary schools in Rarieda sub-county?

iv. What is the influence of training on teacher job satisfaction in public secondary schools in Rarieda sub-county?

5. Scope of the Study

The study focused on finding out the influence of work motivation on teacher job satisfaction in public secondary schools in Rarieda sub-county, Siaya County in the Lake

Region. Subsequently, the study covered Teachers Service Commission(TSC) employed teachers working in Rarieda sub-county.

6. Theoretical Review

Although there are many theories of motivation, three have emerged as most popular: Maslow need hierarchy theory, Herzberg's two-factor theory, and Vroom's expectancy theory, (Kreitner 2007). However, this study was anchored on: Maslow's needs theory, Herzberg's two factor theory, McClelland's need theory and Douglas McGregor's theory X and theory Y.

7. Maslow's Need Theory

Van Der Merwe, (2008), cites Muchinsky (2006) who defines Maslow's Need Theory as a "theory of motivation based on a sequential ordering of human needs that individuals seek to fulfill in a serial progression, starting with physiological needs and culminating in the need for self actualization". Van Der Merwe, (2008) refers to Kreitner, (2004) who notes that Maslow (1943) believed that the source of motivation resided in the fulfillment of these needs. He defined these needs as Physiological needs, Safety needs, Love needs, Esteem needs and Self-Actualization needs.

Figure 1. *Maslow's Need Hierarchy Source: Kreitner, (2007).*

Maslow's theory has been heavily criticized by other behavioral scientists. Even the hierarchical arrangement of the five needs has been questioned. According to Van Der Merwe (2008) there exists practical evidence that suggests that a two-level rather than five-level hierarchy should be used. Despite Maslow's model's failure to stand up to practical testing, it still teaches that a fulfilled need does not motivate an individual anymore, (Kreitner, 1983). A good leader or effective manager will therefore anticipate their employees' unique personal need profiles and then provide opportunities to fulfill emerging needs. Once the employee reaches the level of enhanced self-esteem needs a worthwhile job and meaningful recognition could provide effective means and opportunities to motivate better job performance. Job performance refers to the ability and extend to which an employee performs in their job, (Van Der Merwe, 2008).

8. Two-Factor Theory

Herzberg (1968) conducted a series of research surveys where 200 accountants and engineers were asked to describe specific situations where they felt exceptionally bad about their jobs, and later asked the same group of accountants and engineers to describe situations where they felt exceptionally good about their jobs. Van Der Merwe, (2008) notes that Herzberg (1968) developed a theory of employee motivation based on satisfaction which implied that satisfied employees would be more motivated from within to work harder than employees who would be dissatisfied and hence would not be self-motivated.

According to Kreitner, (2007), Herzberg (1968) found that dissatisfaction generally tended to be associated with complaints about the job context or factors in the immediate work environment, while feelings of satisfaction originated from the nature of the task itself, for example the opportunity to experience achievement, receive recognition, work on an interesting job, take responsibility, and experience advancement and growth. These factors were called motivators.

The factors that lead to dissatisfaction are factors, such as company policy and its administration, supervision, working conditions, relations with others, status, and job security and called to be responsible for hygiene (Kreitner, 2007). According to this study, these realizations led Herzberg (1968) to insist that satisfaction is not necessarily the opposite of dissatisfaction. The study posits that an employee can be motivated by job context or factors in the employee's work environment such as pay, status, or working conditions, to a level of merely not being dissatisfied, but not to a level of true motivation. The theory argues that, money would be, a weak motivational tool since, at best, it could only eliminate dissatisfaction (Van Der Merwe, 2008). The study agrees with Herzberg's view on motivation that it cannot be achieved by simply eliminating dissatisfaction and that to effectively satisfy and motivate employees, an additional element is required: meaningful, interesting, and challenging work. Herzberg concluded that enriched jobs were the key to self-motivation. Meaning that, the work itself, rather than pay, supervision, or other environmental factors, was the key to satisfaction and hence motivation (Kreitner, 2007)

Herzberg's theory has been criticized especially for its practicability. Merwe (2008) refers to Beck (2000) who says that Herzberg (1968) repeatedly claimed that external incentives are not motivators, with the important distinction between external rewards and intrinsic motivation. He realizes that this distinction cannot be seen as unimportant, but criticizes Herzberg for the fact that he did not make it clear, resulting in his ideas sometimes seem very unusual. Despite Herzberg's slightly controversial views, his theory has a clear message for managers in trying to motivate employees, the first step should be to eliminate dissatisfaction by ensuring that pay, working conditions, company policies are reasonable. But pay and those other improvements will not lead to motivation, so the next step would be for managers to enhance motivation by improving factors that cause satisfaction. So managers should ensure that there are opportunities for advancement, achievement, authority, status and recognition. (Kreitner, 2007).

9. McClelland's Need Theory

McClelland's (1961) theory was based on the individual's need for achievement, affiliation and power. The achievement dimension of this need translates into an individual's desire to complete a task or accomplish a goal more effectively than before, while the need for affiliation speaks of the need for human companionship and social interaction, (Kreitner & Kinicki 2007). Van Der Merwe (2008) refers to Poisat (2006) who while referring to Kreitner (2004) states that the need for power lies in the desire to control resources or influence, coach and manipulate others. That there exists a strong correlation between the levels of achievement need and level of engagement of an employee. The strong correlation between engagement and motivation implies that the need for achievement will also relate strongly to the level of motivation as experienced by an individual.

The need for achievement: As far as Creitner & Kinicki (2007) are concerned, when an individual displays a high need for achievement, they tend to set relatively difficult goals and take relatively risky decisions. The opposite is also true, where a low need for achievement is present in individuals who are inclined to set easily achievable goals with minimum risk.

Van Der Merwe (2008), argues that people with a high need for achievement need to receive immediate, specific feedback on performance. High-need achievers become frustrated with incomplete projects, are constantly pre-occupied with their work and continuously think about it, whether at work or not. Individuals with a high need for achievement prefer to take personal responsibility for the job and are often found to take on more than is required. This gives such persons a sense of accomplishment, hence the deduction that the job itself becomes their source of motivation. Opposed to popular believe, individuals with a high need for achievement often do not succeed at making senior managerial positions since their traits seem to conflict with the requirements of higher-level positions. The study posits that the nature of higher level positions requires the incumbent to delegate more, take either more or less risky decisions, and in addition, feedback is often not immediate, if at all individuals with a high need for affiliation are dependent on others' reassurance and approval. They are normally genuinely concerned about others' feelings. The study further asserts that people with a high need for affiliation would more easily conform to their thinking and actions to that of others. People with a high need for affiliation will find professions that include high levels of interpersonal contact and substantial amounts of helping others appealing.

Poisat (2006) believes that the characteristics of high-need achievers are closely resembled by those associated with engaged employees, and it is axiomatic that organizations would prefer to recruit and appoint as many such employees as possible. The need for affiliation is another level of need. Kreitner & Kinicki (2007) report that people with a high need for affiliation will prefer to spend their time nurturing relationships and because of this, might have a problem taking unpopular decisions. However this trait might cause such people to be less effective as managers. The need for power: The need for power reflects an individual's desire to influence, coach, teach, or encourage others to achieve. The two report that if individuals need for power is positive, they focus on accomplishing group goals and helping employees attain the feeling of competence. However, if individuals need for power is negative, then they become selfish and take credit for all the group achievements. According to McClelland, top managers should have a high need for power together with a low need for affiliation. Achievement, affiliation and power need to be considered during employee selection for better placement.

10. Theory X and Theory Y

McGregor (1957) is perhaps the most well-known scholar to develop Maslow's needs hierarchy into a cogent articulation of the basic assumptions of the organizational behavior perspective‖ (Van Der Merwe, 2008). McGregor outlined two theories of how managers view and hence treat employees. Each theory is a managerial assumption regarding employees. McGregor main point seem to be that depending on the accepted assumption, those beliefs tend to be a self-fulfilling prophesy.

Theory X holds that workers are viewed as lazy, self-interested and gullible thus, predicating the assumption that they need to be guided and controlled. Managers who have these assumptions believe that it is their job to structure their subordinates work. These assumptions can lead to mistrust and eventually cause diseconomies of scale. This theory is well aligned with the works of Taylor and Simon (1997) as they focus on organizations as purely rational systems. Theory Y holds that employees are capable, self-controlled, and self-directed. They accept and desire responsibility and are receptive to change and organizational and self-improvement. Managers under the Theory Y assumption believe that good work itself is motivating. Managers are also more likely to develop positive interpersonal relationships with their workers (Van Der Merwe, 2008).

11. Empirical Literature Review

Job satisfaction as a variable deals directly with employees who are essentially the most important assets any organization have, (Slocum & Hellriegel, 2009). It is the employees who keep the organization running and ensure that the organizational objectives and goals are achieved. To this end, workers attitude and feelings towards their job should be of utmost concern to any management. A lot of empirical researches agree that employee job satisfaction is a function of employees' work motivation element such as compensation, training, working conditions, and training.

12. Compensation

Compensation refers to all the extrinsic rewards employees receive in exchange for their work, (Byars, & Rue, 2008). Usually, compensation is composed of the base wage or salary, incentives or bonuses and benefits. According to Byars, & Rue, (2008), Compensation is payment to an employee in return for their contribution to the organization, that is, for doing their job. He continues that the most common forms of compensation are wages, salaries and tips. In today's competitive business environment, organizations strive to gain competitive advantage by offering their employees highly competitive rewards. Compensation is not only a tool for gaining competitive advantage but also a strategy for attracting, motivating and retaining top talents within the organization. When employees feel that they are well compensated for the services they offer to the organization, they are likely to work harder, beat deadlines and targets, and work overtime. On the contrary, when employees feel under remunerated, then lateness, absenteeism, strikes, go-slows, may characterize employee behaviour. "The main purpose of a reward system is to motivate the employees to work in a direction that corresponds with the company's predefined goals. To make the employees work in a desired direction it is important that companies use rewards, which stimulate the desirable behaviour", Muathe, (2008).

The equity theory basically holds that employees have a strong need to maintain a balance between what they perceive as their inputs to their jobs and what they receive from the jobs in the form of rewards. For instance, if an employee believes that he/she is underpaid, they are likely to reduce expended effort by working more slowly, taking off early or being absent. Similarly, if an employee believes that he/she is being overpaid, they are likely to work harder or for longer hours

Empirical researches report inequity in pay, high rate of labor turnover, absenteeism, strikes and go-slows, poor performance among secondary school teachers. These reports beg for questions concerning whether teachers in public secondary schools are well compensated, and to what extent does compensation influence job satisfaction among the teachers.

Njoroge (2011), reporting on factors influencing job satisfaction among primary school teachers in Mombasa municipality, noted that though 53% of the teachers were satisfied with their jobs, 77% of them were not satisfied with their pay. The study further revealed that more than 56% of the respondents agreed that compensation, affect job satisfaction. The study recommends for further studies to be done in order to find out reasons why 53% of the teachers were satisfied with their jobs, yet 77% were not satisfied with the compensation they received. However her study only limited to primary teachers in Mombasa municipality.

Ondieki (2005), reported that remuneration ranked top as a factor influencing job satisfaction among teachers in south Kissi district. The study indicated that 65% of respondents were not happy with the salary they were paid for their services; other factors such as promotion, recognition, and leadership style had relatively less influence on job satisfaction among diploma teacher trainers.

Akali (2010), concluded that factors that affect teachers' job satisfaction and performance included pay, promotion, compulsory transfer, recognition and work conditions. The further found out that among the diploma teacher trainers in Kenya, promotion played a bigger role as far as job satisfaction is concerned. However from the research, it is not clear whether compensation also influence diploma teacher trainers' job satisfaction in Kenya.

13. Working Conditions

Working conditions play a very central role in influencing job satisfaction of any employee. Kyongo (2006), asserts that employees would feel satisfied in their jobs if they are working in a clear and orderly work place, with adequate tools and equipment, acceptable levels of environmental quality, temperature, humidity and noise. The surrounding in which people work should not be that which pose a threat to the workers lives; when that is the case then the employer should ensure that there are safety measures in place to ensure that the hostile conditions are tamed. According to Herzberg (1968), if working conditions are not conducive, hardworking employees who can find work elsewhere leave, while mediocre employees would remain and this compromises the success of the organization.

Castillo and Cano (2004) conducted a study at an agricultural college at a university using the Herzberg's theory to explore the factors that influence job satisfaction. The findings showed that the work itself was the most important factor that contributed to job satisfaction, with working conditions being the least important. However, they did report that all of the factors of the Herzberg's theory were moderately related to job satisfaction.

Kyongo (2006), indicates that among the public health employees of local authorities in Kenya, 62% were satisfied with the office facilities and the working space. The study concluded that, promotion and remuneration are the factors that greatly influence job satisfaction among public health employees of the city council of Nairobi. The study however was limited in scope to public health employees of local authorities in Kenya.

A study by Ndungu (2013), reveals that working conditions, compensation, and leadership style influence job satisfaction and organizational performance of Kenya Medical Training College (KMTC) workers in Kenya. The study recommends that management should improve working conditions, salary and that various leadership styles should be applied by the management for positive influence on employee satisfaction and performance. The study though, failed to establish the extent to which working conditions influence job satisfaction.

In the teaching fraternity, issues about working conditions have been raised. The nature of the geographical location of the school; the climatic conditions, the school's relations with the local community, availability of well-equipped classrooms to facilitate teaching and learning, availability of a well-equipped library, proper housing and sanitary facilities, water and electricity, and security are matters of great concern to the teachers. In the recent years, the media has reported about very deplorable conditions that teachers have to contend with in their line of duty. Njoroge, (2011) cites Prasaad, (2004) who says that the society has many expectations from the teacher, the teacher in overburdened as the teacher is expected to teach six or seven lessons out of eight daily. With the introduction of F.P.E by the NARK regime in the year 2002, teachers' working conditions have degenerated from bad to worse as teachers have to handle overpopulated classrooms like never before. In some areas, especially the northern parts of the country, teachers have to brave militia attacks, under tree classes, poor housing, poor sanitation, poor transport, and inadequate water.

14. Recognition

Recognition at the work place has to do with appreciating employee's effort. It is acknowledging of employee's accomplishment. Recognition can occur both in verbal, promotion, and in tangible reward. While citing Okumbe, (1998), Njoroge, (2011), refers to promotion as the advancement of a worker to a better job in terms of more skills, responsibilities, status and remuneration. When an employee is recognized through promoted to more challenging and more demanding job, they feel trusted and their contributions valued in the organization. Such an employee is more likely to give his/her all to the organization. Kyongo, (2006) cites Herzberg (1968), who explains that individuals at all levels of organization want to be recognized for their achievements on the job. That their success do not have to be monumental before they deserve recognition. It is just natural that peoples' effort is recognized for them to feel part of the system.

Akali, (2010) found out that factors that affect teachers' job satisfaction and performance included pay, promotion, compulsory transfer, recognition and work conditions. Her study revealed that among the diploma teacher trainers in Kenya, promotion played a bigger role as far as job satisfaction is concerned. Njoroge (2011), indicated that compensation, recognition, supervision, promotion, work conditions and training affect job satisfaction among primary teachers in Mombasa municipality, the research nevertheless does not indicate how much promotion influences job satisfaction.

15. Training

Training is the process of providing employees with the knowledge and skills needed to do a particular task or job (Werner & Dismore, 2009). Normally, a new employee's manager has the primary responsibility for his/her training. The new employee's training can have a significant influence on the new employee's productivity and attitude towards his/her job, (Byars, & Rue, 2008). Today, employers have got no other choice but to ensure the training and development of their employees while they remain valued assets in the organization. Training is a major facet of talent and knowledge management which is crucial for the future of human resources of any organization. (Muathe, 2008) explains that training is a learning process that involves the acquisition of knowledge, sharpening of skills, concepts, rules, or changing of attitudes and behaviors to enhance the performance of employees. Training is activity leading to skilled behavior. `Njoroge, (2011) indicated that compensation, recognition, supervision, promotion, work conditions and training affect job satisfaction. Among primary teachers in Mombasa municipality the research revealed that only 11% of the respondents agreed that training affect job satisfaction.

16. Job Satisfaction

Job satisfaction is a topic that attracts wide interest from both the workers who work in the organizations and scholars who study the subject. It is an often studied variable in organizational behaviour research, and also a core variable in both research and theory of organizational phenomena ranging from job design to supervision (Kreitner & Kinicki, 1989).The traditional model of job satisfaction focuses on all the feelings that an individual has about his/her job. However, what makes a job satisfying or dissatisfying might not only depend on the nature of the job, but also on the expectations that individuals have of what their job should provide (Kreitner & Kinicki, 1989). A satisfied employee is inclined to be more industrious, inspired, and dedicated to their work (Slocum, & Hellriegel, 2009).

Job satisfaction has been conceptualized in many ways. In fact job satisfaction is too complex to measure, Njoroge, (2011). Satisfied employees will commit to their jobs, come to work early, work overtime, beat deadlines, and achieve highly work goals, (Kreitner & Kinicki, 2007). On the contrary, dissatisfied employees are characterized with lateness, absenteeism, low morale, and low productivity at work. However, empirical studies seem to agree on work motivation measures that can be taken by the management to ensure employees are satisfied with their jobs. Job satisfaction results from work motivation factors such as compensation, training, recognition and working conditions, (Slocum, & Hellriegel, 2009).

Reporting on factors influencing job satisfaction among public primary school teachers in Mombasa municipality, Njoroge (2011), found out that 13% of the respondents were dissatisfied with their jobs, and that 34% were neutral. Her study revealed that despite 53% of the teachers saying that they were satisfied with their jobs, 77% were not satisfied with the compensation they received. In the study, more than 56% of the respondents agreed that compensation, recognition, supervision, promotion, work conditions and training affect job satisfaction.

Akali (2010), concluded that factors that affect teachers' motivation and performance included pay, promotion, compulsory transfer, recognition and work conditions. She further found out that among the diploma teacher trainers in Kenya, promotion played a bigger role as far as job satisfaction is concerned. Ondieki (2005), reported that remuneration ranked top as a factor influencing job satisfaction among teachers in south Kissi district. With 65% saying that they were not happy with the salary they were paid for their services.

Among the health workers, the same trends have been reported. For example, Kyongo (2006), indicates that among the public health employees of local authorities in Kenya, 57% were saying they were not satisfied with their salary. However, 62% were satisfied with the office facilities and the working space. The study concluded that, promotion and remuneration are the factors that greatly influence job satisfaction among public health employees of the city council of Nairobi.

A study by Ndungu (2013), reveals that working conditions, compensation, leadership style influence organizational performance of KMTC workers in Kenya. The study recommends that management should improve working conditions, salary and that various leadership styles should be applied by the management for positive influence on employee performance. In the teaching profession therefore, work motivation and job satisfaction issues are raised. Often stakeholders in the education industry are locked up in boardrooms discussing strategies to ensure that teachers remain contented within the service. Of course such meetings especially come during industrial unrest involving strikes that usually completely paralyze or threaten to paralyze the functions of the sector. It is interesting however to note that issues surrounding work motivation and job satisfaction in the education sector continue to elicit controversy whenever the teachers unions and their employers (TSC) seek or attempt to address them.

The education sector contributes immensely to the social and economic development of our country. The former South African head of state, Nelson Mandela noted that education is the single most powerful tool which can be used to change the society. To this end, since 1963 the subsequent post-independent governments in Kenya undertook reforms through the various commissions set up in the education sector aimed at improving quality of education in the country. According to the recommendations by the Ominde Commission (1964), Kenya as a young nation then, would only travel the path of development when the education path the country would walk promoted equality among all the races in the nation.

Since Kenya's independence, the government has worked to promote quality in terms of the scope and the depth of the content offered at secondary school level, improvement of school teaching and learning facilities such as better and adequate classrooms and laboratories, improved working conditions for teachers such as house allowance, medical allowance and commuter allowance. Besides, public secondary school teachers have been offered maternity leave and education leave. In terms of compensation, there have been improvements as a result of collective bargaining by the two teachers unions: Kenya National Union Of Teachers-KNUT and Kenya Union of Post Primary Education and Technical institutions (KUPPET).

Despite this enormous effort by the government regimes both in the past and present, the public secondary education sub-sector continues to witness unprecedented labor unrest and labor turnover which have threatened to paralyze or sometime completely bring down the public education sector across the nation.

17. Research Gaps

Various studies discussed show that job satisfaction has been studied with relevance to leadership style, supervisor behavior, pay and promotion, job environment, training and other work related factors. In almost all the studies the employees were not satisfied with their job for one reason or the other. Dominating studies in job satisfaction are available medicine, college trainers, and teaching profession. However, the studies are not consistent in their findings. Furthermore, none has been done with a focus on Rarieda sub-county public secondary schools.

For instance, Reporting on factors influencing job satisfaction among public primary school teachers in Mombasa municipality, Njoroge(2011), found out that 13% of the respondents were dissatisfied with their jobs, and that 34% were neutral. Her study revealed that despite 53% of the teachers saying that they were satisfied with their jobs, 77% were not satisfied with the compensation they received. In the study, more than 56% of the respondents agreed that compensation, recognition, supervision, promotion, work conditions and training affect job satisfaction. She recommends for further studies to be done in order to find out reasons why 53% of the teachers were satisfied with their jobs, yet 77% were not satisfied with the compensation they received. However her study only limited to primary teachers in Mombasa municipality.

Akali (2010), concluded that factors that affect teachers' motivation and performance included pay, promotion, compulsory transfer, recognition and work conditions. The study also found that among the diploma teacher trainers in Kenya, promotion played a bigger role as far as job satisfaction is concerned. However from her research, it is not clear whether supervision and compensation also influence diploma teacher trainers' job satisfaction in Kenya.

Ondieki (2005), reported that remuneration ranked top as a factor influencing job satisfaction among teachers in south

Kisii district. The results of the study indicated that 65% of respondents were not happy with the salary they were paid for their services. Further the findings indicated other factors such as promotion, recognition, and leadership style had relatively less influence on job satisfaction among diploma teacher trainers.

Among the health workers, conflicting trends have been reported. For example, Kyongo, (2006) indicates that among the public health employees of local authorities in Kenya, 57% were saying they were not satisfied with their salary. However, 62% were satisfied with the office facilities and the working space. His study concluded that, promotion and remuneration are the factors that greatly influence job satisfaction among public health employees of the city council of Nairobi.

A study by Ndungu (2013), revealed that working conditions, compensation, and leadership style influence satisfaction and organizational performance of KMTC workers in Kenya. The study recommended that management should improve working conditions, salary and that various leadership styles should be applied by the management for positive influence on employee satisfaction and performance.

It is this glaring contextual gap that this study on Analysis of motivation and job satisfaction of teachers at Rarieda sub-county, Kenya sought to help fill.

18. Conceptual Framework

Job satisfaction is a function of work motivation factors such as compensation, recognition, working conditions, and training. The presence of these motivational factors leads to job satisfaction among employees. Teachers Service Commission (TSC) and the Board of Management (BOM) therefore need to carefully design the school policies and align them with secondary school teacher needs since the absence of these factors can cause job dissatisfaction. According to Riley (2012), these factors called motivator factors are based on an individual's need for personal growth. Riley espouses that when they exist, motivator factors actively create job satisfaction. If they are effective, then they can motivate an individual to achieve above-average performance and effort. Figure 2 below shows the conceptual framework.

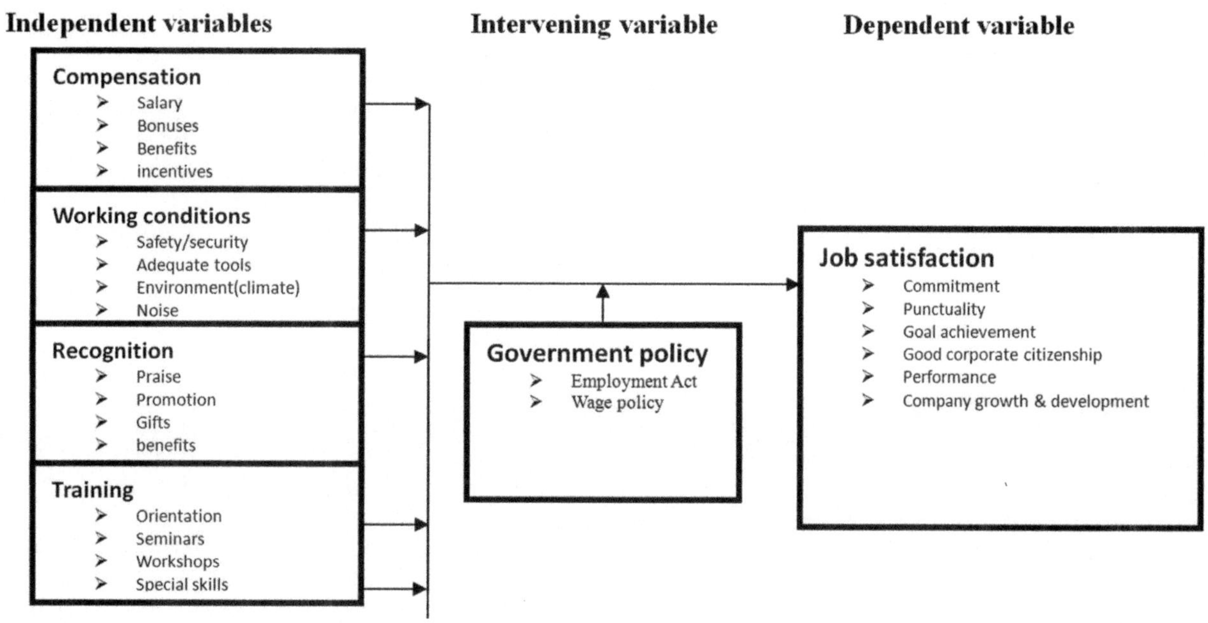

Figure 2. *Conceptual Framework Source: Author, 2015.*

An independent variable is one that a researcher manipulates in order to determine its effects on another variable, (Mugenda, & Mugenda, 2003). In the above figure, independent variables include; remuneration, recognition, supervision, working conditions and training. An intervening variable is used to explain the relationship between observed variables, such as independent and dependent variables, in empirical research. An intervening variable is recognized as being caused by the independent variable and as being a determinant of the dependent variable, (Orodho, 2004). In the conceptual framework, government policy is the intervening variable. Mugenda & Mugenda (2003), explains that dependent variable is one that varies as a function of the independent variable.

19. Research Methodology

19.1. Research Design

The research employed descriptive research design. Descriptive research studies are those studies which are concerned with describing the characteristics of a particular individual or a group of individuals, (Kothari, 2004). This design was adopted because it gives room for an in depth responses resulting in a better and a wider understanding of the phenomenon under investigation. According to Orodho, (2004), this approach should be used when the researcher intends to carry out a detailed analysis of a phenomenon. Therefore to analyze work motivation factors that influence job satisfaction among public secondary school teachers in Rarieda sub-county, this design was the best fit as it enabled the researcher to collect in depth information and carry out detailed analysis.

19.2. Target Population

A population size included TSC employed teachers working in public secondary schools in Rarieda sub-county. Out of a total population of 440 teachers according to available statistics, a sample size of 205 was used. The sample was derived using the formula, (nf=n÷1+n÷N), where n=384, (Mugenda, 2003).

19.3. Sampling Design

A sample is the portion of the population targeted for the purpose of collecting information to infer something about the target group, (Zikmund, 2003). Zikmund, (2003) notes that sampling is useful for cutting down costs, labour intensity and time constraints. Systematic random sampling method will be used as statistical sample of research since it is simple to design, easy to use, easy to determine sampling distribution of the mean and it is less expensive compared to simple random sampling. From a population of 440, a sample size of 205 was selected using the formula (nf=n÷1+n÷N), Mugenda, (2003). According to Mugenda, & Mugenda, (2003), 10% of the total population is just enough. Under systematic random sampling, the items or individuals of the population are arranged in some manner. A random starting point is selected and then every k^{th} member of the population is selected for the sample, Kothari, (2004).

Table 1. *Sample Size.*

Research Location	Total Population	Sample Population
Rarieda sub-County	440	205
Total	440	205

Source: Compiled Rarieda Sub-County Records, 2015

19.4. Data Collection Tools and Techniques

Primary data collection tools were employed. Self-administered questionnaires were used for data collection, and were divided into five sections; the first section comprised questions touching on personal data. The second section comprised of questions on job satisfaction. The third section asked questions touching on the four work motivation factors influencing job satisfaction. Section four comprised of questions on government policy. Section five involved ranking of the four work motivation factors. A Likert five choices Scale with intervals (highly satisfied, slightly satisfied, satisfied, not satisfied, and neutral) were be used.

19.5. Validity

Content validity of the study was upheld by ensuring that the questionnaires elicited the intended response from the respondents. Furthermore, the researcher ensured validity of the research results by engaging the supervisors, in addition, seeking of expert opinion.

19.6. Reliability

According to Orodho, (2012), reliability is the extent to which a questionnaire, test, observation or any other measurement produce the same results on repeated trials. Reliability of the study was ensured through test-re-test; where the questionnaires were pre-tested before the actual data collection, this was to ensure that the questionnaires elicited the relevant information from the respondents.

19.7. Data Analysis and Presentation

Data analysis consisted of examining, categorizing, tabulating, or recombining the evidence to address the initial propositions of the study, (Yin, 1994). Jorgensen, (1989) explains that the main aim of data analysis is to assemble and reconstruct data in a meaningful or comprehensible fashion. For the purposes of this study, data was collected, coded and analyzed. Computer software such (SPSS) will be employed to analyze the coded data. For descriptive statistics, measures of central tendency (mean) and measures of variability (standard deviation) were employed, in order to simplify, speed up and to enhance accuracy and validity of the analysis process. For qualitative statistics, inferential measures (correlation coefficient) were employed in order to determine and show the correlation relationship between work motivation and job satisfaction, Karl Pearson's coefficient formula: $r = \frac{\sum XY - n\overline{X}\overline{Y}}{\sqrt{\sum X^2 - n\overline{X}^2}\sqrt{\sum Y^2 - n\overline{Y}^2}}$ was operationalized.

Eventually, the analyzed data was presented using frequency tables, percentages since the techniques are easy to construct, simple and clear in understanding findings.

19.8. Ethical Considerations

The researcher upheld the research study ethics during and after the research period. Confidentiality and anonymity of the research respondents' was guaranteed. Respondents did not reveal their names as the research was conducted anonymously.

19.9. Response Rate

Questionnaires with both quantitative and qualitative questions were administered to the sampled public secondary schools in Rarieda sub-county. Table 2 below summarizes the response rate.

Table 2. *Response Rate.*

Respondents	Administered	Returned	Return rate
Teachers	205	200	98%

Source: Field Data (2015)

From Table 2, a total of 205 (100%) were administered. However, 200 (98%) respondents responded to the questionnaires and returned. According to Mugenda and Mugenda (2003) a response rate of 70 % is just adequate. The 98% return rate was achieved because the researcher self-administered the questionnaires, which helped elicit cooperation by the respondents.

19.10. Demographic Characteristics of Respondents

The respondents' demographic characteristics were categorized in terms of their gender, age, qualification, positions they hold at work place, and work experience.

19.11. Distribution of Respondents by Gender

The gender of the respondents was of concern to the study as it assisted the researcher to identify the dominant gender among the teachers in the sub-county. Table 3 shows the respondents gender distribution.

Table 3. *Distribution of the Respondents by Gender.*

Gender	Frequency	Percentage
Male	122	61%
Female	78	39%
Total	200	100%

Source: Field Data (2015)

Table 3 reveals that out of the 200 respondents, 122 making 61% of the total respondent population were male, with the female respondents being 78 a 39% of the total respondents' population. This finding therefore establishes that in public secondary schools in Rarieda sub-county the male gender is a dominant 61% of the total teacher population in the sub-county.

19.12. Distribution of Respondents by Age

The age of the respondents was very pivotal as it assisted the researcher to identify the majority age of teachers in public secondary schools in the sub-county. Table 4 illustrates the respondents' distribution by age.

Table 4. *Respondents' Distribution by Age.*

Age	Frequency	Percentage
25-34	70	35%
35-44	54	27%
45-54	66	33%
55-60	10	5%
Total	200	100%

Source: Field Data (2015)

Table 4 shows that the respondents' age distribution between (25-34) years was 70 in number, making 35% of the total respondent population. Those whose ages ranged between (35-44) years were 54, making 27% of the total respondent population. Those whose ages ranged between (45-54) were revealed to be 66, translating into 33% of the entire respondent population. The respondents who were between the ages of (55-60) were 10 in number, making into 5% of the total population of the respondents. According to the above findings, most teachers in the region are of entry age (25-34) years, at 35% of the entire respondent population. On the other hand, those in the (55-60) year's age bracket are the least represented, at 5% according to this revelation. This means therefore that most teachers in the region are of active age. By implication, the workforce therefore should be energetic, innovative, creative, and productive.

19.13. Distribution of Respondents by Qualification

This was important to the study as it revealed the education levels of the respondents thereby shading light on the abilities of the respondents to carry out their responsibilities as class teachers, heads of departments, deputies and principals. Table 5 illustrates respondents' distribution by qualification.

Table 5. *Distribution of Respondents by Qualification.*

Qualification	Frequency	Percentage
Diploma	40	20%
Bachelors	136	68%
Masters	24	12%
Total	200	100%

Source: Field Data (2015)

Table 5 reveals that a whopping 136 respondents, making 68% of the total respondents are bachelors' degree holders. Diploma holders are 40 of the entire respondents, representing 20% of the teaching workforce in the region. Those with a master degree are revealed to be 24 in number, which translates to 12% out of 100%. The majority of teachers in the sub-county are therefore well qualified as teachers as is illustrated by the table. It is therefore expected that with these sterling qualifications, teacher performance, productivity, and drive for excellence should be tenable.

19.14. Distribution of Respondents by Position

This distribution revealed the positions of the respondents, which made clear their responsibilities and duties. It was important for the researcher to understand the tasks performed by the respondents as the study sought to establish teachers' satisfaction in relation to their jobs. Table 6 illustrates distribution of respondents by their positions.

Table 6. *Distribution of Respondents by their Positions.*

Position	Frequency	Percentage
Class teacher	98	49%
HOD	58	29%
Deputy Principal	22	11%
Principal	22	11%
Total	200	100%

Source: Field Data (2015)

Table 6 reveals that among teachers in the region, 98 are class teachers, making up 49% of the total respondent population. The heads of departments amount to 58, representing 29% of the entire population. Both the deputy principals and the principals tie at 22 in number, an 11% a piece of the total respondents' population. This data reveals that the majority of teachers in the region are actually class teachers, which is the lowest in the hierarchy. The numbers diminish up the hierarchy. These findings mean that the majority of teachers occupy the lesser responsibility positions.

19.15. Distribution of Respondents by Work Experience

Finding out the respondents' work experience was fundamental to the study as their experience would relate to whether they are job satisfied or not. Table 7 illustrates distribution of respondents by work experience.

Table 7. *Distribution of Respondents by Work Experience.*

Experience	Frequency	Percentage
Less than 5	40	20%
5-10	64	32%
11-15	28	14%
16-20	30	15%
21-25	26	13%
Over 25	12	06%
Total	200	100%

Source: Field Data (2015)

Table 7 shows that teachers with less than 5 years' experience amount to 40 in number, representing 20% of the total respondents' population. Those with (5-10) experience are the leading majority of 64, a 32% of the entire respondents. Those with (16-20) experience are 28 (14%) of the entire respondents population. Those with (21-25) experience are 26 (13%) of the total respondent population. Those with experience of 25 years are 12 (6%) of the entire respondents' population. As can be gathered from the table, teachers in the region are therefore experienced enough to understand work details which is necessary to respond to the questionnaires accordingly. This finding should impact on the teacher job satisfaction as the levels of experience vary among the teacher.

19.16. Job Satisfaction

The study sought to find out whether the respondents were satisfied with their jobs or otherwise. This was crucial to the researcher as the responses here laid important milestone to the very heart and advancement of the study objectives of. Table 8 shows job satisfaction responses.

Table 8. *Job Satisfaction.*

Satisfaction	Frequency	Percentage
Yes	62	31%
No	138	69%
Total	200	100%

Source: Field data (2015)

Table 8 illustrates that out of the 200 study respondents 138, representing (69%) of entire respondent population are not satisfied with their jobs; with a paltry 62 making (31%) of the total population indicating that they are satisfied with their jobs. This finding clearly indicates that majority teachers in public secondary schools in Rarieda sub-county are not satisfied with their jobs. This finding provided a strong premise to the study general objective that is to establish the influence of work motivation on teacher job satisfaction in public schools in Rarieda sub-county.

19.17. Extent of Job Satisfaction

Respondents were asked to reveal the extent to which they were satisfied with their jobs. This helped the researcher understand the degree to which the respondents were satisfied with their jobs. Table 4.8 illustrates the extent to which the respondents are satisfied with their jobs.

Table 9. *Extent of Job Satisfaction.*

Extent of Satisfaction	Frequency	Percentage
Highly satisfied	6	3%
Satisfied	48	24%
Slightly satisfied	8	4%
Not Satisfied	138	69%
Total	200	100%

Source: Field Data (2015)

Table 9 shows that among the 62 respondents satisfied with their jobs, 6 which make 3% of the total respondent population were highly satisfied with their jobs, 8 which translates to 4% of the entire respondent population said they were slightly satisfied with their jobs. This reveals the complex nature of measuring employee job satisfaction. However, 138 (69%) were not satisfied with their jobs. This implies that many teachers in the region studied are not satisfied with their jobs.

19.18. Salary/Remuneration Influence on Job Satisfaction

The first specific objective of the study sought to determine how remuneration influence teacher job satisfaction in public secondary schools in Rarieda sub-county. Research findings reveal that the respondents agreed 100% that salary/remuneration influence teacher job satisfaction in public secondary schools in Rarieda sub-county. This finding was fundamental to the study as it clearly reveals the significant motivational role played by remuneration. To ensure teacher motivation therefore, teachers should be remunerated well.

19.19. Extent of Salary/Remuneration Satisfaction

Table 10. *Extent of Satisfaction with Remuneration.*

Extent	Frequency	Percentage
Highly satisfied	10	5%
Satisfied	40	20%
Slightly satisfied	56	28%
Not satisfied	94	47%
Total	200	100%

Source: Field Data (2015)

The researcher sought to know the extent to which respondents were satisfied with their remuneration. Their responses revealed the variability existing in terms of salary satisfaction among the teachers in the region. Table 10 shows the respondents extent of satisfaction with remuneration.

Table 10 shows that 10 of the total respondents', making up 5% were highly satisfied with their remuneration. Furthermore, 40 (20%) were satisfied with their salary, while 56 (28%) were slightly satisfied with their salaries. But 94 (47%) of the entire respondents population were not satisfied with their remuneration. These findings indicate that almost a half of teachers, population in public secondary schools in Rarieda sub-county are not satisfied with their jobs. In addition, some of those who feel satisfied with their salary only feel so slightly. This sheds further light on the need to improve teacher pay.

19.20. Job Satisfaction and Salary/Remuneration Relationships

Respondents who were both satisfied and not satisfied with their jobs were asked to state the extent to which they were satisfied with their salary. It was in the interest of the researcher to find out whether remuneration has any significant influence on job satisfaction. Table 11 shows extent of job satisfaction to extent to which satisfied with salary/remuneration.

Table 11. *Extent of Job Satisfaction * Extent to which Satisfied with Salary/Remuneration.*

		Extent to which satisfied with salary/remuneration				Total
		Highly satisfied	Satisfied	Slightly satisfied	Not satisfied	
Extent of job satisfaction	Highly satisfied	4	2	0	0	6
	Satisfied	4	32	10	2	48
	Slightly satisfied	0	2	6	0	8
	Not Satisfied	2	4	40	92	138
Total		10	40	56	94	200

Source: Field Data (2015)

From Table 11, among those respondents satisfied with their jobs, 58 out of 60 are satisfied with their remuneration while 2 of them are not satisfied. However, among those respondents not satisfied with their jobs, 46 out of 138 are satisfied with their salary, while a larger 92 are also not satisfied with their salary. It is therefore clear from these revelations that salary/remuneration influence teacher job satisfaction.

20. Remuneration and Job Satisfaction Correlation

The researcher sought to determine whether there exists significant correlation relationship between remuneration and job satisfaction. Table 12 illustrates the correlation.

Table 12. *Correlation between Remuneration and Job Satisfaction.*

		Are you satisfied with the job?	Extent to which satisfied with salary/remuneration
Are you satisfied with the job?	Pearson Correlation	1	.714**
	Sig. (1-tailed)		.000
	N	200	200
Extent to which satisfied with salary/remuneration	Pearson Correlation	.714**	1
	Sig. (1-tailed)	.000	
	N	200	200

**. Correlation is significant at the 0.01 level (1-tailed).

Source: Field data (2015)

From Table 12, using Pearson's correlation at significant level 0.01, the coefficient correlation between job satisfaction and remuneration is 0.714 which signifies that remuneration and job satisfaction are positively correlated. This finding therefore means that remuneration is a major work motivation factor since the correlation coefficient 0.714 is very close to 1. This implies that better pay leads to improved job satisfaction.

21. Working Conditions Influence on Job Satisfaction

The second specific study objective sought to determine the influence of working conditions on teacher job satisfaction in public secondary schools in Rarieda sub-county. This was intended to reveal whether or not there was any significant relationship between working conditions and teacher job satisfaction. Table 13 illustrates the correlation using Pearson's correlation coefficient of 0.01, coefficient correlation between working conditions and job satisfaction was 0.641. This implies that working conditions and job satisfaction are positively correlated. This finding therefore means that improved working conditions would lead to improved job satisfaction.

Table 13. *Correlation between Working Conditions and Job Satisfaction.*

		Are you satisfied with the job?	Extent to which satisfied with working conditions
Are you satisfied with the job?	Pearson Correlation	1	.641**
	Sig. (1-tailed)		.000
	N	200	200
Extent to which satisfied with working conditions	Pearson Correlation	.641**	1
	Sig. (1-tailed)	.000	
	N	200	200
**. Correlation is significant at the 0.01 level (1-tailed).			

Source: Field Data (2015)

22. Recognition Influence on Job Satisfaction

The third study objective sought to establish the influence of recognition on job satisfaction in public secondary schools in Rarieda sub-county. The respondents were therefore asked to state whether they had been recognized as a result of their work achievements or not. Findings indicate that 99% of the total respondent population agreed that recognition influence job satisfaction. However 2 respondents who make 1% of the population dis-agreed that recognition influence job satisfaction. Results indicate that recognition influences teacher job satisfaction.

23. Correlation Between Training and Job Satisfaction

The research sought to find out whether there exists correlation relationship between training and job satisfaction. Table 14 illustrates the correlation relationship.

Table 14. *Correlation between Training and Job Satisfaction.*

		Are you satisfied with the job?	Extent to which satisfied with training attended
Are you satisfied with the job?	Pearson Correlation	1	.150*
	Sig. (2-tailed)		.034
	N	200	200
Extent to which satisfied with training attended	Pearson Correlation	.150*	1
	Sig. (2-tailed)	.034	
	N	200	200
*. Correlation is significant at the 0.05 level (2-tailed).			

Source: Field Data (2015)

From Table 14 using Pearson's correlation of significant level 0.05, correlation coefficient between training and job satisfaction was 0.150. This signifies that training and job satisfaction are correlated, however slightly positively correlated. This means improved training will lead to slight improvement on teacher job satisfaction.

24. Conclusions

The purpose of this study was to determine the influence of work motivation on teacher job satisfaction in public secondary schools in Rarieda sub-county. The study established that work motivation factors such as remuneration, working conditions, recognition, and training influence teacher job satisfaction in public secondary schools in Rarieda Sub-county.

The first specific objective of the study sought to establish the influence of remuneration on teacher job satisfaction in public secondary schools in Rarieda sub-county. The study concluded that nature of remuneration influence to a greater extent teacher job satisfaction in public secondary schools in Rarieda sub-county. This included both the basic pay and the subsequent allowances. This was deduced from the fact that the study respondents felt that remuneration ranks top of the other variables.

The second specific objective of the study was to examine the influence of working conditions on teacher job satisfaction in public secondary schools in Rarieda sub-county. The study concluded that working conditions influence teacher job satisfaction in public secondary schools in Rarieda sub-county. According to the study findings, working conditions ranked third among the work motivation factors studied, with the study findings further indicating that the staffroom environment, classroom environment, health and sanitation being the most crucial subsets.

The third specific objective of the study was to evaluate

the influence of recognition on teacher job satisfaction in public secondary schools in Rarieda sub-county. The study concluded that recognition influence teacher job satisfaction in public secondary schools in Rarieda sub-county. However the study revealed that recognition influence less compared to the other variables.

The fourth objective of the study was to determine the influence of training on teacher job satisfaction in public secondary schools in Rarieda sub-county. The study concluded that training influence teacher job satisfaction in public secondary schools in Rarieda sub-county.

25. Recommendations for Further Studies

This study makes the following recommendations: that a more in depth study be conducted in other regions order to establish if the factors investigated in this study influence job satisfaction so as to validate the findings of this study or to establish new findings; further study be done to find out whether there exists other factors influencing teacher job satisfaction; more studies are recommended in order to establish why majority of teachers were satisfied with training yet the same teachers were not satisfied with their jobs.

References

[1] Akali S, (2010), An Analysis of the Factors Affecting Motivation and Performance of Diploma Teacher Trainers in Kenya, MBA Project, Kenyatta University.

[2] Al-Hassan S, (2009), Effects of Teacher Absenteeism on Quality Teaching and Learning in Public Schools in Ghana, MA Thesis, University of Acra.

[3] Ambrose S, Huston T, Norman M, (2007) Qualitative Method of Assessing Faculty Satisfaction, *Journal of Research in Higher Education* (7) 803-830), Pirtsburgh, Kluwer Academic Publishers-Human Science Press, Carnegie Mellon University.

[4] Armstrong, M (2006) Handbook of Human Resource Management Practice, London, Kogan Page Limited.

[5] Brady, L (2007) Motivation Factors Affecting Nursing Faculty, *Journal of Nursing Education* (2); 65-69), Albuquerque, University of New Mexico.

[6] Byars, & Rue, et al (2008) Human Resource Management, New York, McGraw-Hill.

[7] Castillo J, & Cano (2004) Job Satisfaction of Ohio Agricultural Education Teachers, *Journal of Agricultural Education* 45(2) Pg19-25.

[8] Costen, W "Job Satisfaction" in the Encyclopedia of Human Resource Management. Ed. Prescott, K Vol. 1.Wiley, San-Francisco, 2012, Print.

[9] Jorgensen, D (1989), Participant Observation, a Methodology of Human Studies, Sage Publication.

[10] Kothari, C, (2004), Research Methodology, Methods and Techniques 2nd Edition, New Age International, India.

[11] Kreitner, & Kinicki, (2007), Organizational Behaviour, New York, McGraw-Hill.

[12] Kreitner, R (1983) Management, Boston, Houghton, Miffin.

[13] Kreitner, R (2007) Management, Boston, Houghton, Miffin.

[14] Kretner, & Kinicki, (1989), Organizational Behaviour, Boston, Irwin.

[15] Kyongo, J, (2006) Factors Influencing Job Satisfaction among Public Health Employees of Local Authorities in Kenya, City Council of Nairobi, MBA Project, Kenyatta University.

[16] Merwe, V, (2008) A Critical Analysis of Factors that Influence Employee Work Performance, MBA Project.

[17] Muathe, S, (2008) Employee Compensation and Reward Systems, Kenyatta University.

[18] Mugenda & Mugenda, (2003), Research Methods, Quantitative and Qualitative Approaches, Acts Press.

[19] Mullins, L, (2007) Management and Organizational Behaviour, London, Prentice Hall.

[20] Ndungu, A, (2013) Effects of Job Satisfaction on Organizational Performance, the Case of Kenya Medical Training College, MBA Project, Kenyatta University.

[21] New Age International.

[22] Njoroge, A (2011), Factors Influencing Job Satisfaction among Primary School Teachers in Mombasa Municipality, MBA Project, Kenyatta University.

[23] Njuguna, K, (2011) Investigation on the Effects of Organizational Reforms on Employee Job Satisfaction.

[24] Ondieki, J, (2005) Factors Contributing to Job Satisfaction among Secondary School Teachers in Nyamarambe Division, South Kisii District, Implication for Counseling, MBA Project, Kenyatta University.

[25] Orodho, A. (2004), Techniques of Writing Research Proposals and Reports in Education and Social Sciences, Nairobi, Masola Publishers.

[26] Slocum, & Hellriegel, (2009) Principles of Organizational Behaviour, Canada, Cengage Learning.

[27] Werner, J, & Dismore, R, (2009) Human Resource Development, Mason, Natorp.

[28] Yin, R (1994), Case Study Research: Design and Methods, Thousand Oaks, CA, Sage Publishers.

[29] Zukmund, W, (2003), Business Research Methods 7th Edition, South Western Australia, Thomson.

20

Management Versus Science: Peer-Reviewers do not Know the Subject They Have to Analyse

Fausto Galetto

Industrial Quality Management, Politecnico Di Torino, Turin, Italy

Email address:
fausto.galetto@gmail.com

Abstract: The purpose of this paper is to show the ideas to overcome the deep ignorance on Reliability Theory of some authors and Referees (mainly professors). We analyzed some very few cases, taken from some published documents found on the web: Montgomery, Rade, M. A. El-Damcese [paper 41], M. A. El-Damcese, A. N. Salem, and N. S. Temraz [paper 42], and others (Wang, Pham, Xie, Peretto); two cases are from the Montgomery book, a very WWU (World Wide Used) Book; other cases are from books: we show that high scores on documents do not prove the Quality of those documents. This paper is especially written to settle the matter for the researchers who want to learn Reliability and Availability. Researchers must be alert in order to do a good job.... Many others cases should be shown: the paper should be 10 times longer The methods used are the Logic and the Scientific Theory (Mathematics, Probability, Statistics, Physics...). Several Professors do not practice them.

Keywords: Reliability, Availability, Integral Theory, Quality Methods, Scientific Approach, Intellectual Honesty

1. Introduction: "The Problem Outline"

The problem was originated at least 40 years ago, when the author was working in big Corporations [General Electric, Siemens] and continued in [Fiat (now FCA, Fiat Chrysler Automobiles), Philco, IVECO)] and at the Politecnico of Turin (Italy): many and many "false Scholars" were writing wrong papers that defeated the readers (managers, researchers and students) of their right of getting good ideas. UNFORTUNATELY the Peer-Reviewers were worse than the authors: very few of the readers took care of this big problem!

Fausto Galetto was ever fond of Scientific Management and tried to make the managers, professor, researchers, and students aware of their need of learning Scientific Ideas... He had little success: ignorance increased constantly.

If the reader acted sometime as a Peer-Reviewer he must admit that very few Journals asked him to evaluate the SCIENTIFIC content of the articles. The Journals prefer the "literature review of the problem" as though that is a symptom of Quality....

We do not present a literature review of the problem, because it will need at least hundreds of pages to be settled, both for Quality, Reliability, Statistics, Confidence Intervals and for Design of Experiments that are subjects very little known by managers and professors; we list here only few docs in the references [1-6,12-16,19-23,29,31-38, 44-54].

Few weeks ago I came across to some papers on reliability [41, 42]: it is a good example of Peer-Reviewers incompetence. Do not think, please, that only the "Italian" authors have problems in their papers. Other documents [44-54] show errors. At international Conferences F. Galetto met many people who did not properly know the subjects they were presenting.

The author is aware that these statements are risky (because his paper will be Peer-Reviewed)! UNFORTUNATELY the Peer-Reviewers many times, to F. Galetto experience, were worse than the authors and very few of the readers took care of this big problem!

In the paper [41] very recent, M. A. El-Damcese "Reliability Equivalence Analysis of a Parallel-Series System Subject to Degradation Facility." *Science Journal of Applied Mathematics and Statistics*. Vol. 3, No. 3, 2015, pp. 160-164. doi: 10.11648/j.sjams.20150303.19, we find (Excerpt 1)

«Following Rade (1989-1), the reliability function of each component improved by a cold via perfect switch can be given by: $R_{stb}(t)=\{1+\ln[1/R(t)]\}R(t)...$».

Excerpt 1. From the paper [41]

Citing Rade, El-Damcese improves the indexes of Rade!!! Citing Rade and El-Damcese, Fausto Galetto, WHO found them WRONG, improves the indexes of Rade and El-Damcese! WHERE is the Quality?

In the paper [42] M. A. El-Damcese, A. N. Salem, and N. S. Temraz "Semi-Markov Model of a Series-Parallel System Subject to Preventive Maintenance", J. Stat. Appl. Pro. 2, No. 3, 307-318 (2013) we find (Excerpt 2)

«Case (ii) As a special case, let us consider that the failure, repair, and maintenance times are exponentially distributed as follows [exponential distribution].... We obtain the availability function by substituting in relation (1) and using MAPLE program. The results for the availability function versus the time and the effect of preventive maintenance are shown in [the following graph, named by F. Galetto "Figure 0", *Comparison of the availability... with and without PM ...*]».---

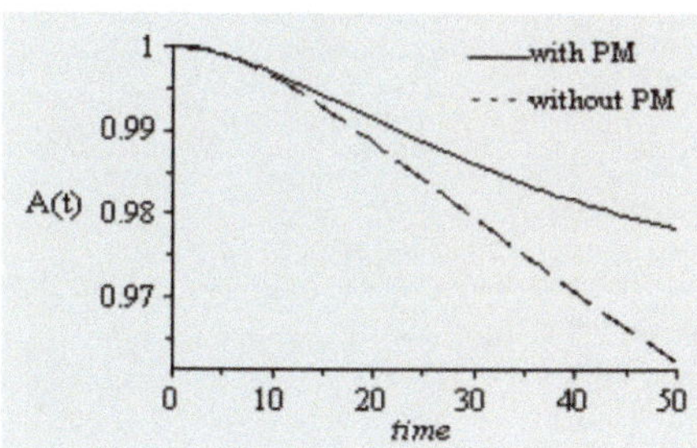

Figure 0. *Comparison of the availability function for the system with and without PM versus the time (case ii) named by F. Galetto "Figure 0"]*

Excerpt 2. From the paper [42]

Citing El-Damcese and his co-authors, Fausto Galetto, WHO found them WRONG, improves the indexes of El-Damcese! WHERE is the Quality?

AS ANY STUDENT knows the exponential distribution has the "*memoryless property*", so that the Preventive Maintenance is USELESS! HOW can the availability A(t) be better with the Preventive Maintenance?

LET'S HOPE that all those incompetent professors will consider their duty to teach scientifically, in order to satisfy the learning need of their students and of the whole society. See Deming, Gell-Mann, Galetto Fausto (figure 1)...

Actually anybody can see [44-54] that professors teach wrong ideas to the readers; we highlight some points here for the reliability field. They all say the following idea, while teaching the concept of *failure rate* or *hazard rate*. [with symbols h(t) or λ(t)]: «*the h(t)Δt [λ(t)Δt]: represents the probability that a device with age t will fail in the small interval (t, t+Δt] for small Δt>0.*» All those authors do not realise that "a device with age *t* does not mean that it never failed before the age *t*" [see Figure 5 (of this paper)], for a device where various up and down times happen till the age *t*! The failure rate is a "reliability characteristic" related to a device that NEVER failed before t. Actually the quantity $h(t)\Delta t \approx \Pr\{t < T \leq t+\Delta t | T > t\}$ represents the probability that a device will fail in an interval (*t, t+Δt*], GIVEN that the "random variable Time To Failure" is bigger than t [the duration of the interval 0---t], which means that the 1st failure will happen after t (as one can see in [17])! Putting H(t), the integral form 0 to t of h(x), it is known that [17] the Reliability is R(t)=exp[-H(t)], and, obviously, R(t)≠exp[-h(t)t], (except for the case h(x)=λ=constant).

Only Deming, Gell-Mann, Einstein and F. Galetto seem to have taken care of the "Quality in the published papers"; I would like to know somebody else who did that!

It is not surprising that professors, researcher, managers and students learn wrong ideas, in the Quality field, IF we have a very widespread book with many wrong concepts [D. C. Montgomery falls in *contradiction*!] (see figure 1)

Let's see; D.C. Montgomery says:

We prefer a **modern** definition of quality:

Definition

Quality is inversely proportional to variability.

Note that this definition implies that if variability[1] in the important characteristics of a product decreases, the quality of the product increases.

Excerpt 3. (Quality definition from the 6th edition of the Montgomery book, found in the Politecnico Library, and commented by F. Galetto)

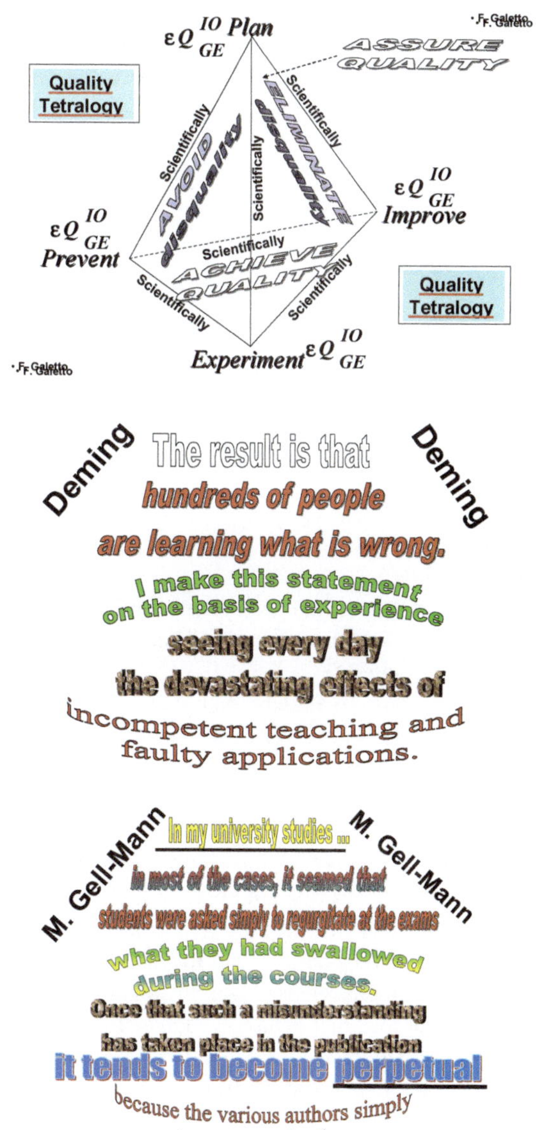

Figure 1. *Statements from Deming, Gell-Mann, Galetto ideas.*

Montgomery himself does not realize that he is in contradiction when he says:

Definition

The Weibull distribution is

$$f(x)=\frac{\beta}{\theta}\left(\frac{x}{\theta}\right)^{\beta-1}\exp\left[-\left(\frac{x}{\theta}\right)^{\beta}\right] \quad x\geq 0 \quad (3.41)$$

where $\theta > 0$ is the scale parameter, and $\beta > 0$ is the shape parameter. The mean and variance of the Weibull distribution are

$$\mu=\theta\Gamma\left(1+\frac{1}{\beta}\right) \quad (3.42)$$

and

$$\sigma^2=\theta^2\left[\Gamma\left(1+\frac{2}{\beta}\right)-\left\{\Gamma\left(1+\frac{1}{\beta}\right)\right\}^2\right] \quad (3.43)$$

respectively.

Excerpt 4. (Weibull distribution from the 6th edition of the Montgomery book, found in the Politecnico Library, and commented by F. Galetto, excerpt 5)

IF the Mean Time To Failure, MTTF (μ in the excerpt 4) increases, hence the product has both better reliability, AND higher variance; therefore a product that fails less has "Montgomery quality WORSE!!!!". *Montgomery himself does not realize that he is in contradiction!*

Moreover see the following stand-by system (Excerpt 6)

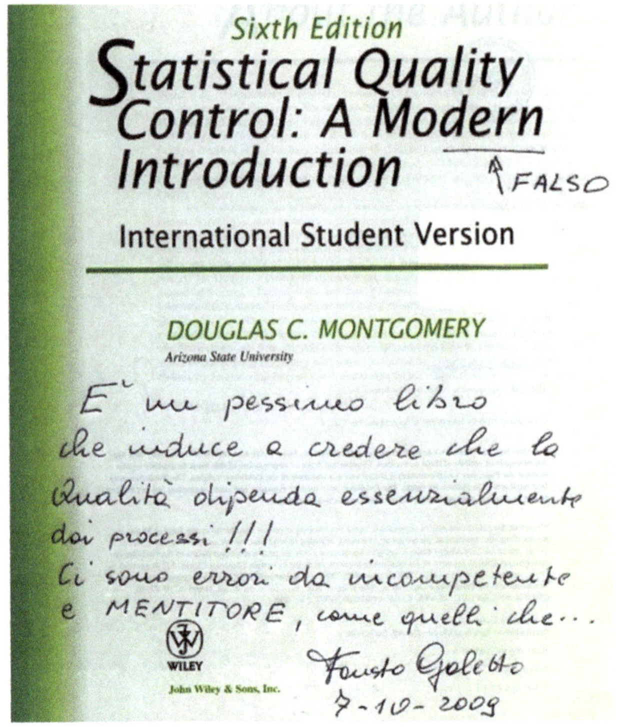

Excerpt 5. (front page from the 6th edition of the Montgomery book, found in the Politecnico Library, and commented by F. Galetto)

EXAMPLE 3.11 A Standby Redundant System

Consider the system shown in Fig. 3.24. This is called a **standby redundant system,** because while component 1 is on, component 2 is off, and when component 1 fails, the switch automatically turns component 2 on. If each component has a life described by an exponential distribution with $\lambda = 10^{-4}$/h, say, then the system life is gamma distributed with parameters $r = 2$ and $\lambda = 10^{-4}$. Thus, the mean time to failure is $\mu = r/\lambda = 2/10^{-4} = 2 \times 10^4$ h.

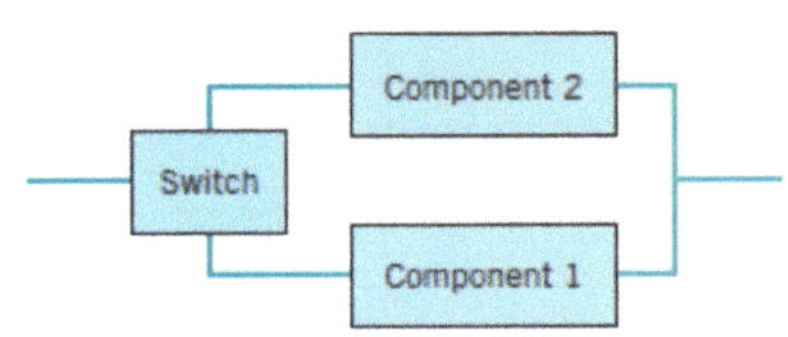

FIGURE 3.24 The standby redundant system for Example 3.11.

Excerpt 6. (Stand-by redundant system from the 6th edition of the Montgomery book, found in the Politecnico Library, and commented by F. Galetto)

IF the Mean Time To Failure, MTTF (μ in the excerpt 6) increases, hence the product has both better reliability, AND higher variance; therefore a product that fails less has "Montgomery quality WORSE!!!!". *Montgomery himself does not realize that he is in contradiction!!!!*

Any Manager needs data to take decisions, suitable to the case he has to solve. But it is not enough: he needs to analyze the data and transform them into VALID information. To get this he NEEDS methods: better it is if they are SCIENTIFIC. In my working life as Lecturer, Manager, Professor, … I have been seeing a huge number of Lecturers, Managers, Professors, … taking wrong decisions BECAUSE they used wrong methods, NOT APPLICABLE to the problems they wanted to solve! This is my long experience in the Quality field, as teacher, Manager, professor, papers writer, …When arguing on Scientific matters, everybody MUST act SCIENTIFICALLY.

2. Reliability of the Stand-By System

We consider now a *cold standby system* made of two units A and B [we assume that the "switch" S that recognize the failure of the unit A is perfect, i.e. with reliability 1 (as in the Excerpt 6)]; we know that any unit can perform the intended function of the system; the unit A start at time 0 (B stay in stand-by) and if it fails before t, at time s say, then the other unit B start working from s to t; $R_{stb}=P\{T_A+T_B>t\}$, where T_A and T_B are the random variables (RV) *"time to failure of the units A and B"*. Any student knows that the variance of two independent RVs is $Var(T_A+T_B)=Var(T_A)+Var(T_B)$: so the stand-by system which is more reliable than any of its units has "Montgomery quality WORSE!!!!". The general formula of the reliability of the stand-by system is

$$R_{Stb}(t)=R_A(t)+\int_0^t f_A(s)R_B(t-s)ds$$

If the reliability of the units is *Exponential*, then $T_A \sim Exp(\lambda_A)$

and $T_B \sim Exp(\lambda_B)$: $R_A(t)=exp(-\lambda_A t)$ and $R_B(t)=exp(-\lambda_B t)$. The cold STAND-BY system reliability is, IF the units failures are INDEPENDENT, [as in the excerpt 6!] we have the formula

$$R_{Stb}(t) = e^{-\lambda_A t} + \int_0^t \lambda_A e^{-\lambda_A s} e^{-\lambda_B (t-s)} ds =$$
$$= \frac{\lambda_A}{\lambda_A - \lambda_B} e^{-\lambda_B t} + \frac{\lambda_B}{\lambda_B - \lambda_A} e^{-\lambda_A t}$$

The failure rate $h_{stb}(t)$ has to be computed by the formula $f_{stb}(t)/R_{stb}(t)$ and is NO longer CONSTANT! NOTICE that here t is the age of the stand-by system AND not the age of the units, comprising the system. The $MTTF_{stb} = 1/\lambda_A+1/\lambda_B = MTTF_A+MTTF_B$. If the two units are identical then $\lambda_A=\lambda_B$ the previous formula cannot be used and one has (*see excerpt 6!, which proves the incompetence of Montgomery!!!* about the definition of "Quality"!!!) to use

$$R_{Stb}(t) = e^{-\lambda t} + \int_0^t \lambda e^{-\lambda s} e^{-\lambda (t-s)} ds =$$
$$= e^{-\lambda t}[1+\lambda t]$$

This formula, valid only when $h(t)=\lambda$ for both the units, originated the big and stupid error of RADE and EL-DAMCESE in his paper «Reliability Equivalence Analysis of a Parallel-Series System Subject to Degradation Facility. *Science Journal of Applied Mathematics and Statistics*. Vol. 3, No. 3, 2015, pp. 160-164. doi: 10.11648/j.sjams.20150303.19»:

$$R_{Stb}(t) = 1+\ln[1/R(t)]\, R(t)$$

Citing Rade, El-Damcese improves the indexes of Rade!!! Citing Rade and El-Damcese Fausto Galetto, WHO found them WRONG, improves the indexes of Rade and El-Damcese!!!!!! WHERE is the Quality?

This formula for a Cold Standby is true ONLY IF $R(t)=exp(-\lambda t)$ for the units!!! It is false for any other pdf!

If the RVs "time to failure" of the two units are *Weibull*, $T_A \sim Wei(\eta_A,\beta_A)$ and $T_B \sim Wei(\eta_B,\beta_B)$, then

$$R_A(t,\eta_A,\beta_A) = \exp[-(t/\eta_A)^{\beta_A}],\ R_B(t,\eta_B,\beta_B) = \exp[-(t/\eta_B)^{\beta_B}]$$

IF the failures of the of the two units are independent then the cold STAND-BY system reliability is given by the general formula

$$R_{Stb}(t) = R_A(t) + \int_0^t f_A(s) R_B(t-s) ds$$

BE CAREFUL the reliability of the system is NO longer a Weibull function!!! The failure rate $h_{stb}(t)$ has to be computed by the formula $f_{stb}(t)/R_{stb}(t)$. The $MTTF_{stb}=MTTF_A+MTTF_B$.=area under $R_{stb}(t)$.

Let's see again a *cold stand-by System, non-repairable [two identical units with non-constant failure rate h(t) and a switch with R=1]*

We can depict the *cold stand-by* system as a 3-states one, where in the state 0 one unit works while the other is in stand-by [not working and assumed that it cannot fail], in the state 1 the stand-by unit works (the other is failed) and finally in the state 2 both units are failed.

Let be H(t)=integral of h(x) in the interval 0¯¯¯t, then for each unit R(t)=exp[-H(t)]. The RV "time to failure of the SYSTEM" is the sum of two identical RVs, as one see in the diagram; we get the important formula that proves Rade and El-Damcese WRONG,

$$R_{stb}(t) = \mathbf{exp}[-H(t)] + \int_0^t \mathbf{exp}[-H(s)]h(s)\,\mathbf{exp}[-H(t-s)]ds$$

If $h(t)=\lambda$ then $H(t)=\lambda t$ and $R_{stb}(t)=exp(-\lambda t)[1+\lambda t]$, the probability of a Poisson Process (with failures=1).

One cannot derive $R_{stb}(t)=exp[-H(t)]\,[1+H(t)]$ from

$$R_{stb}(t) = \mathbf{exp}[-H(t)] + \int_0^t \mathbf{exp}[-H(s)]h(s)\,\mathbf{exp}[-H(t-s)]ds$$

The REFEREES (Peer Reviewers) of the paper were incompetent: they did not find the ERRORS. To make things easier, we assume $\lambda_1=\lambda_2=\lambda$, so that $R(t)_{orig}=2exp(-\lambda t)-exp(-2\lambda t)$; the error between the Egyptian guy and Galetto is -37%! (see fig. 2)

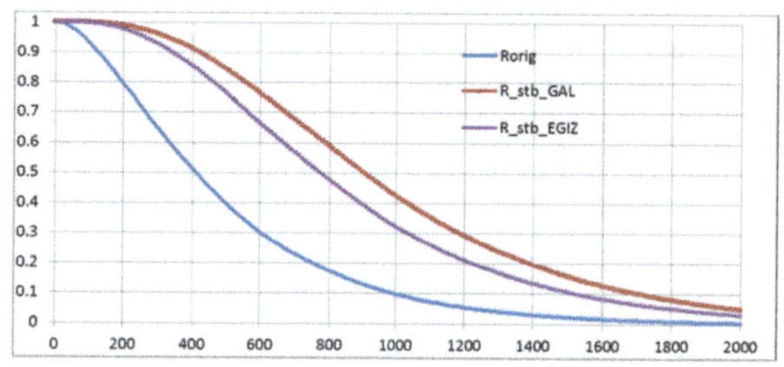

Figure 2. *Reliability of a Stand-by system with Rorig=reliability of a parallel (el-damcese vs Galetto ideas).*

So we see that using «the various indexes one cannot measure the Quality of the paper»; ONLY Logic and Probability/Reliability Theories are useful to make sound investigations. Unfortunately many "bad" managers (named by me "monagers") do not use Logic.

Let's make another example: we put in stand-by two units whose reliability is $R(t)_{orig}=exp(-\lambda t)[1+\lambda t]$; it obvious that the reliability of the stand-by system (using the formula above) is $R_{stb}(t)=exp(-\lambda t)[1+\lambda t+(\lambda t)^2/2+(\lambda t)^3/6]$. The error between the Egyptian guy and Galetto can be as big as -89 %! (see fig. 3)

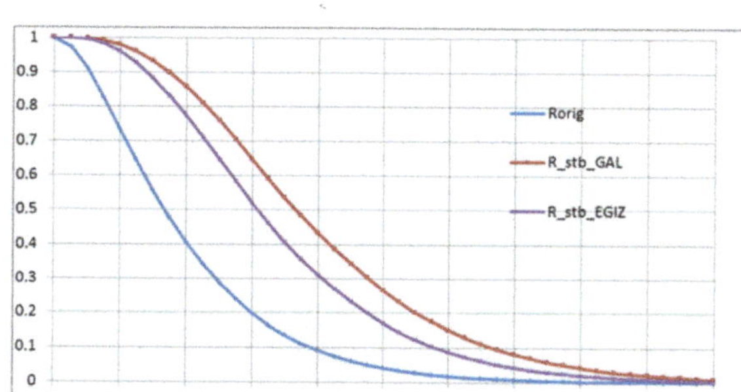

Figure 3. *Reliability of a Stand-by system with Rorig=reliability of a "stand-by" (el-damcese vs Galetto ideas).*

If the Peer-Reviewers had known the basics of probability they could have found the errors, we showed before …

Therefore we see that Managers, Researchers and Students must be alert and use the methods of Science (Logic, Mathematics, Physics, Probability, Statistics, ….) in order to avoid to be cheated by incompetents.

3. Reliability of a Parallel System with Preventive Maintenance

We consider now the paper [42] M. A. El-Damcese, A. N. Salem, and N. S. Temraz "*Semi-Markov Model of a Series-Parallel System Subject to Preventive Maintenance*", J. Stat. Appl. Pro. 2, No. 3, 307-318 (2013).

The three authors made a big mess of the reliability methods and concepts: see excerpt 2, with the figure 0. We use their own words to see how much they were in error: any logical person could find some of them. They say:

(1) The system consists of two subsystems A and B connected in parallel. Subsystem A consists of n_1 identical units connected in series and subsystem B consists of n_2 identical units connected in series.
(2) At time t = 0, the system is up and it fails when the two subsystems fail at the same time.
(3) Each subsystem fails when one unit of the subsystem is down and each failed unit is repaired.
(4) There is a preventive maintenance provided to each unit in the subsystem before it fails.
(5) There are a single repair facility and a single maintenance facility available,(i.e., in the same time one bad unit only belong to any subsystem under repair or maintenance).
(6) All distributions of the time for repair, maintenance, and time to failure are general.
(7) The model has nine states. All possible states and transitions between them are shown in ""Excerpt 7"".

Let's remind the definition of reliability: reliability of a system is the ability of a) performing its purpose adequately (i.e. either with no failures, or with no down-state of any type) b) for the period of time intended 0—t, and c) under stated operating and environmental conditions. When anybody deals with reliability he MUST consider and specify all the three points above. [17]

Let's now analyse the point (2) «At time t = 0, the system is up and it fails when the two subsystems fail at the same time.» Let's suppose that your system is made of two cars A and B; tomorrow you have to go to work (your mission!). You decide to use the car A and you realize that A is "under Preventive Maintenance, PM"; to go to work you then revert to use the car B: unfortunately you realize that B, as well, is "under Preventive Maintenance, PM"; can you go to work? NO! Your system of the two cars is not available, i.e. it is DOWN, in spite of the fact that both the cars are not failed! LOGIC!

THEREFORE the statement «All possible states of the model are given by Up states : S1(A Up, B Up), S2(A PM, B Up), S3(A Up, B PM), S4(A Down, B Up),S5(A Up, B Down), S6(A PM, B PM),S7(A PM, B Down), S8(A Down, B PM), Down state : S9(A Down, B Down).» is not suitable for describing the probabilistic system behaviour. [excerpt 7!]

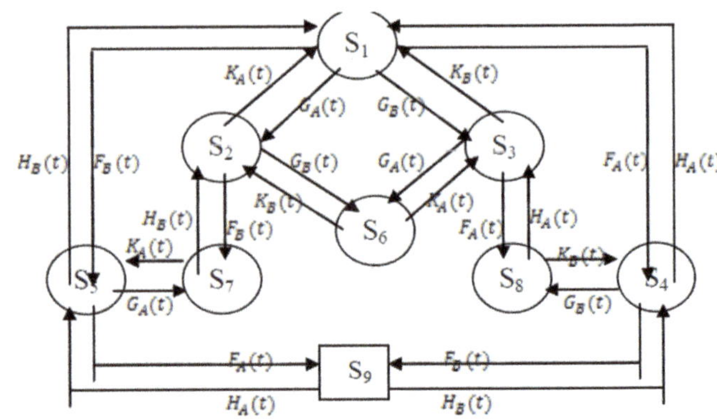

Excerpt 7. Parallel redundant system with PM, from [42]

Actually the system has 4 downstates (in the yellow oval, fig. 4): B (where both A and B are failed, and under repair), A (where both B and A are failed, and under repair), B* (where B is failed and under repair, and A, indicated as A', is under PM), A* (where A is failed and under repair, and B, indicated as B', is under PM); *we assume* that the PM is made intelligently and only one of the two items A or B can be under PM!

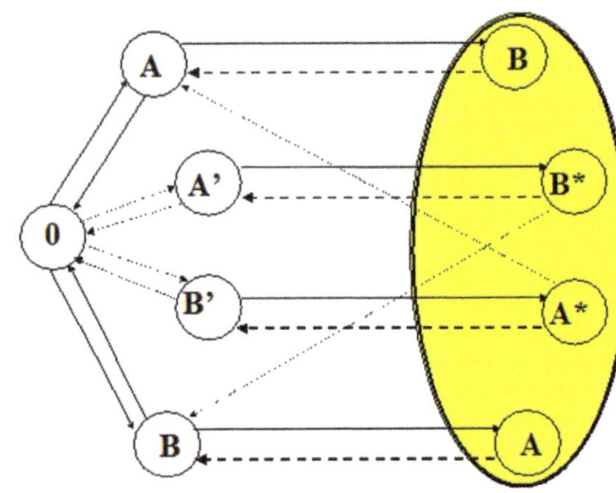

Figure 4. *Reliability of a parallel system with PM (Galetto ideas).*

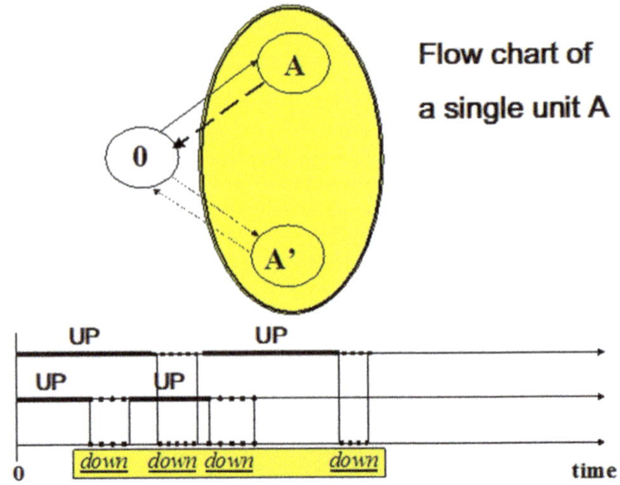

Figure 5. *Reliability of a single unit with PM (Galetto ideas).*

To make the reader understanding easy, we use first the probabilistic behaviour of a single unit A, with PM (Preventive Maintenance); as one can see in the following fig. 5, any time a failure happens the unit makes the transition from the state 0 to the state A [with a downtime due to repair], while any time a PM happens the unit makes the transition from the state 0 to the state A' [with a downtime due to PM]; since the transition depends on independent distributions the two types of downtimes add together (3rd arrow in the bottom figure). It is clear that the reliability $R_A(t)$ is the probability that the unit A stays in the up-state 0 for the whole interval 0----t. The availability A(t), on the contrary, is the probability that the unit A is in the up-state 0 at the time instant t.

In any case, it is clear that the PM reduces both the R(t) and the A(t): there is no need to make any calculation!!! ONLY Logic is needed! Letting T_A, $T_{A'}$ the RVs "time to the downstates", the RV $T=\max(T_A, T_{A'})$ does not comply with excerpt 7.

Let's go back to Excerpt 2 taken form the paper [42]; the authors of the paper [42] M. A. El-Damcese, A. N. Salem, and N. S. Temraz "Semi-Markov Model of a Series-Parallel System Subject to Preventive Maintenance", J. Stat. Appl. Pro. 2, No. 3, 307-318 (2013), use the Semi-Markov Stochastic Processes Theory to make their analysis.

We apply our considerations to the single unit A, using the Semi-Markov Stochastic Processes Theory: since there are 3 states, 0 the up state, 1 [state A, in fig. 5] and 2 [state A', in fig. 5] the down states, for the single unit A we have, according the Integral Theory of Availability [17], 3 availabilities $A_0(t)$, $A_1(t)$, $A_2(t)$; the transition rates are constant λ (for the failures), λ' (for the system going under the PM), and μ (for the repairs), and μ' (for the system coming back from the PM). We write the system of integral equations

$$A_0(t)=\exp[-(\lambda+\lambda')t]+\int_0^t \lambda\exp[-(\lambda+\lambda')r]A_1(t-r)dr$$

$$+\int_0^t \lambda'\exp[-(\lambda+\lambda')r]A_2(t-r)dr$$

$$A_2(t)=\int_0^t \mu\exp(-\mu r)A_0(t-r)dr$$

$$A_2(t)=\int_0^t \mu'\exp(-\mu' r)A_0(t-r)dr$$

The 3 availabilities [17] tend to the same value A_{SS}, the steady state availability, as $t\to\infty$. We have

$$A_{SS,\ single\ unit}=1/[1+\lambda/\mu+\lambda'/\mu']$$

It is clear that IF $\lambda'=0$ (NO Preventive Maintenance) THEN A_{SS} is better, for a single unit; the same is for $\mu'\to\infty$ (0 time for PM=immediate PM!).

It is *self-evident* that PM is useless for exponential reliability (constant failure rate), since the exponential distribution has the "*memoryless property*": at any instant t a unit with exponential reliability (constant failure rate) is GAN [as *Good As New*!] : see excerpt 2, with the silly figure 0.

For a parallel system of two units A and B, *assuming* a repair crew for A and another repair crew for B, we have

$$A_{SS}=1\ [1+\lambda_A/\mu_A+\lambda'_A/\mu'_A]+1/[1+\lambda_B/\mu_B+\lambda'_B/\mu'_B]$$
$$-1/\{[1+\lambda_A/\mu_A+\lambda'_A/\mu'_A]\ [1+\lambda_B/\mu_B+\lambda'_B/\mu'_B]\}$$

The data used by El-Damcese, Salem, and Temraz for this case are in the excerpt 8

γ_1	γ_2	γ_3	γ_4	γ_5	γ_6	γ_7	γ_8
0.001	0.002	0.003	0.004	0.008	0.009	0.005	0.006

Excerpt 8. Data for the Case (ii) with PM, from [42]

where γ_1 and γ_2 are the constant failure rates of the units comprising the serial systems A and B, γ_3 and γ_4 are the constant PM rates of the units comprising the serial systems A and B, γ_5 and γ_6 are the constant repair rates of the serial systems A and B, γ_7 and γ_8 are the constant restoring rates for PM of the serial systems A and B; El-Damcese, Salem, and Temraz for this case find the steady state availability

$$A=0.9769$$

Excerpt 9. Steady state Availability for the Case (ii) with PM, from [42]

The value computed by El-Damcese, Salem, and Temraz is absolutely WRONG (more than 100% error!!!!)

PM is dangerous when the failure rates are constant, as any intelligent student knows..............

The authors, El-Damcese, Salem, and Temraz, do not know the basics of Probability Theory: IF T is the RV "time to failure" and T' the RV (life-time) for the PM, the RV $(Y|x)=\min[T'=x, T]$ has the mean $E[(Y|x)]$; integrating with the pdf g(x) we have the mean E[Y]=Mean Up Time, well known to any intelligent student in Engineering,

$$E[Y]=\int_0^\infty E[Y\mid x]g(x)dx=\int_0^\infty\int_0^x R(r)dr\,g(x)dx$$

If the RVs are *Exponential*, $T\sim Exp(\lambda)$ and $T'\sim Exp(\lambda')$, then the Mean Up Time is $E[Y]=1/(\lambda+\lambda')$. NO NEED of Semi-Markov Processes! IF there no PM the MUT=$1/\lambda$.

The authors, El-Damcese, Salem, and Temraz, makes big errors also for the CASE (i), where the distributions are all of the Weibull type (with shape parameter=2), as in excerpt 10

$$F_1(t)=1-e^{-\beta_1 t^2/2},F_2(t)=1-e^{-\beta_2 t^2/2},$$

$$G_1(t)=1-e^{-\beta_3 t^2/2},G_2(t)=1-e^{-\beta_4 t^2/2}$$

$$H_A(t)=1-e^{-\beta_5 t^2/2},H_B(t)=1-e^{-\beta_6 t^2/2}$$

$$K_A(t)=1-e^{-\beta_7 t^2/2},K_B(t)=1-e^{-\beta_8 t^2/2}$$

β_1	β_2	β_3	β_4	β_5	β_6	β_7	β_8
0.01	0.015	0.02	0.018	0.025	0.03	0.026	0.034

Excerpt 10. Case (i) with PM, from [42]

The authors, El-Damcese, Salem, and Temraz, show their reliability ignorance when the use the Stochastic Semi-Markov Processes; they say:

The purpose of this paper is to analyze a series-parallel system by using semi-Markov process.

Excerpt 11. Parallel-series system with PM, from [42]

They do not know that, modelling the system with the use of the Stochastic Semi-Markov Processes, one assumes that the *system IS RENEWED at any entrance in any state*; THEREFORE the Researcher using the Semi-Markov Processes has the same problem as described in the figure 5 for a single unit A, and general failure and repair distributions: the downtimes for failures and for PM add together! [see figure 5 and the excerpt 2, with the silly figure 0]

Now the 3 integral equations are the following (where $b_{ij}(s)ds$ are the transition probabilities from the state i to the state j, in the interval s¯¯s+ds. R(t) is the probability that there is no transition out of the state 0 (up-state), both for failure and PM, in the interval 0¯¯t.)

$$A_0(t) = R(t) + \int_0^t b_{01}(s)A_1(t-s)ds$$
$$+ \int_0^t b_{02}(s)A_2(t-s)ds$$

$$A_2(t) = \int_0^t b_{10}(r)A_0(t-r)dr$$

$$A_2(t) = \int_0^t b_{20}(r)A_0(t-r)dr$$

Letting η_A be the characteristic parameter of the unit A for failures, δ_A be the characteristic parameter of the unit A for repairs, η'_A be the characteristic parameter of the unit A for PM, δ'_A be the characteristic parameter of the unit A for restoring due to PM, the Steady State Availability for the unit A is [according to excerpt 10]

$$A_{SS,\ single\ unit} = 1/[1+(1/\eta\delta)^2+(1/\eta'\delta')^2]$$

It is clear that IF $\eta' \to\infty$ (NO Preventive Maintenance) THEN A_{SS} is better, for a single unit; the same is for $\delta'\to\infty$ (0 time for PM=immediate PM!).

For a parallel system of two units A and B, *assuming* a repair crew for A and another repair crew for B, we have

$$A_{SS}=1/[1+(1/\eta_A\delta_A)^2+(1/\eta'_A\delta'_A)^2]+$$
$$+1/[1+(1/\eta_B\delta_B)^2+(1/\eta'_b\delta'_B)^2] - 1/\{[1+(1/\eta_A\delta_A)^2+(1/\eta'_A\delta'_A)^2][1+(1/\eta_B\delta_B)^2+(1/\eta'_b\delta'_B)^2]\}$$

El-Damcese, Salem, and Temraz for this case find the steady state availability [see excerpt 2, with the silly figure 0].

$$A = 0.91688$$

Excerpt 12. Steady state Availability for the Case (i) with PM, from [42]

The value computed by El-Damcese, Salem, and Temraz is absolutely WRONG (more than 100% error!!!!)

PM is dangerous when the system is modelled by a Semi-Markov Process [the *system IS RENEWED at any entrance in any state*], as any intelligent student knows… We can repeat what we said before (see, between excerpts 9 and 10) «The authors, El-Damcese, Salem, and Temraz, do not know the basics of Probability Theory: ... E[Y]=Mean Up Time, well known to any intelligent student in Engineering,… NO NEED of Semi-Markov Processes!»

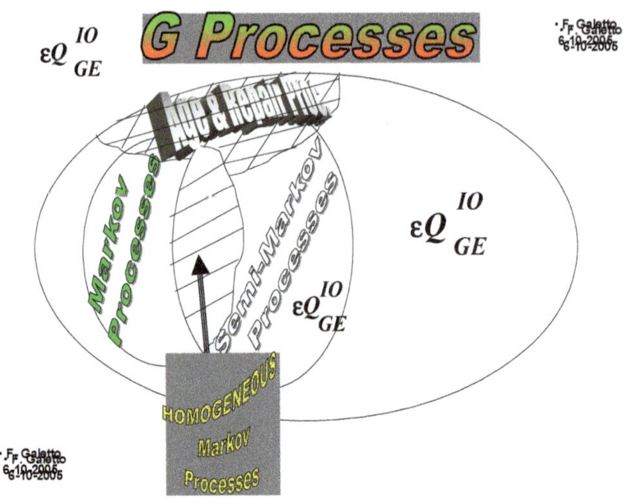

Figure 6. *G-Processes for correct analysis of systems.*

To find the correct solution the authors should have had to use the G-Processes (figure 6), that model also the Age&Repair Processes: IF one wants to make the preventive maintenance PM effective and advantageous he MUST renew the unit with the PM, leaving all the other units Old as they are (BAO=Bad As Old)!

Now we see another case about Maintenance [54], a thesis at Worcester Polytechnic Institute; it is the proof that also some professors do not know the subject they have to analyse:

From a systems or components perspective, failure rate is defined as the frequency at which that component fails and is symbolized by the Greek letter λ, Lambda. The failure rate is function that is time dependent. Specifically,

$$\lambda = \frac{\text{number of failures per unit time}}{\text{number of components exposed to failure}}$$

The reliability rate as a function of time is defined as the exponential of a negative integral of λ(t) where time is measured from o to t. Hence, mathematically, it is the exponential part of the equation and can also be written as:

$$R(t) = e(-\lambda t)$$

Excerpt 13. Wrong statements from [54]

1st error: failure rate h(t) is NOT a frequency, neither a pdf, nor a conditional pdf;

2nd error: failure rate h(t) is NOT estimated by the formula given in the excerpt 13; estimation is a serious matter, and suitable statistical methods are needed;

3rd error: as we said before, putting H(t), the integral from 0 to t of h(x), it is known that [17] the Reliability is R(t)=exp[-H(t)], and, obviously, R(t)≠exp[-h(t)t], (except for the case h(x)=λ=constant). SINCE J. Martinez, said "the failure rate is a function that is time dependent" he CANNOT write R(t)=exp[-λ(t)t]!

A good professor should have found those errors…!

J. Martinez, (2008) and his professors are not alone: see the book [48] M. Lazzaroni, L. Cristaldi, L. Peretto, P. Rinaldi, M. Catelani, (2003), *"Reliability Engineering"* [Springer]. The 5 professors do the same!

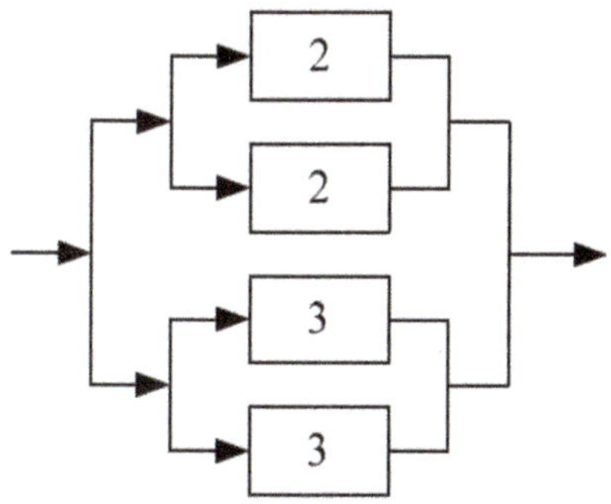

Excerpt 14. A double parallel system from [48]

Those authors indicate as $\lambda_P(t)$ the failure rate of each of the two parallels, 2_2 and 3_3; they then write the reliability $R_{P23}(t)$ of the double parallel as, in the following excerpt 15

$$R_{P23}(t) = e^{-\lambda_P(t)t} + e^{-\lambda_P(t)t} - e^{-\lambda_P(t)t}e^{-\lambda_P(t)t} = 2e^{-\lambda_P(t)t} - e^{-2\lambda_P(t)t}$$

$$MTTF_{23} = \int_0^{+\infty} R_{P23}(t)dt = \int_0^{+\infty}\left(2e^{-\lambda_P(t)t} - e^{-2\lambda_P(t)t}\right)dt =$$

$$= 2\int_0^{+\infty} e^{-\lambda_P(t)t}dt - \int_0^{+\infty} e^{-2\lambda_P(t)t}dt$$

Excerpt 15. Reliability of the double parallel system from [48]

NOTICE: they, being incompetent, used the product $\lambda_P(t)t$ as though it were H(t) of each of the two parallels, 2_2 and 3_3; any intelligent student in Engineering knows that $H_P(t) \neq \lambda_P(t)t$]! Letting T_A, T_B the RVs "time to the failure", the RV $T=\max(T_A, T_B)$ does not comply with excerpt 15; this is another way to see that excerpt 15 is wrong!.

The 5 professors were informed of the problem… NO reaction…. IF they will be Peer-Reviewers, which errors will they be able to find?

It is not surprising that the thesis [35], C. Casciano (L. Peretto referee), *Thesis on the Taguchi Method*, Bologna University 2014, is full of mistakes. The student and the professor (L. Peretto referee) were informed of the problem… NO reaction….

4. Conclusion

We analyzed some very few cases, taken from some published documents found on the web: Montgomery, Rade, M. A. El-Damcese [paper 41], M. A. El-Damcese, A. N. Salem, and N. S. Temraz [paper 42] (and other from books [from 44 to 49, M. Xie, Y-S Dai, K-L Poh, (2004), T. Nakagawa, (2005), H. Pham, (2003), H. Wang, H. Pham, (2006), M. Lazzaroni, L. Cristaldi, L. Peretto, P. Rinaldi, M. Catelani, (2003), MONTGOMERY D.C. (2006)] and theses [35, 54]!):

«*Reliability Equivalence Analysis of a Parallel-Series System Subject to Degradation Facility.* Science Journal of Applied Mathematics and Statistics. Vol. 3, No. 3, 2015, pp. 160-164. doi: 10.11648/j.sjams.20150303.19»

«*Semi-Markov Model of a Series-Parallel System Subject to Preventive Maintenance*", J. Stat. Appl. Pro. 2, No. 3, 307-318 (2013)»

See also all the other cases in the references, about Design Of Experiments.

My students were able to find the right solutions because they had the Sound Theory [17]! Montgomery, Rade, M. A. El-Damcese, A. N. Salem, and N. S. Temraz did not have it.

Citing Rade, El-Damcese improves the indexes of Rade! Citing Rade, El-Damcese, Wang, Pham, Xie, Peretto, Montgomery, Fausto Galetto, WHO found them WRONG, improves the indexes of Rade, El-Damcese, Wang, Pham, Xie, Peretto, Montgomery! WHERE is the Quality?

The problem of ignorance is so huge [1-6,12-16,19-23,29,31-38, 44-54] that a profound change of mind (metanoia, Deming) [5,6] is NEEDED.

See all the figures (mostly figures 12, 13, 14, 15).

The following statements of great scientists and managers are important for any person who wants to make QUALITY Decisions on QUALITY matters.

We think that the YOUNG Researchers MUST be ALERT if they want to LEARN: THEY MUST know the THEORY!

The author Galetto always invited people to be intellectually honest in teaching and taking decisions: THEORY is fundamental in both cases. [see the F. Galetto documents, in the references, in the RG database, and in his books]

From above we see that Fausto Galetto taking into account the following statements by great people, as always did, could provide a sensible advice for any Researcher, in any university, and any Manager, in any Company.

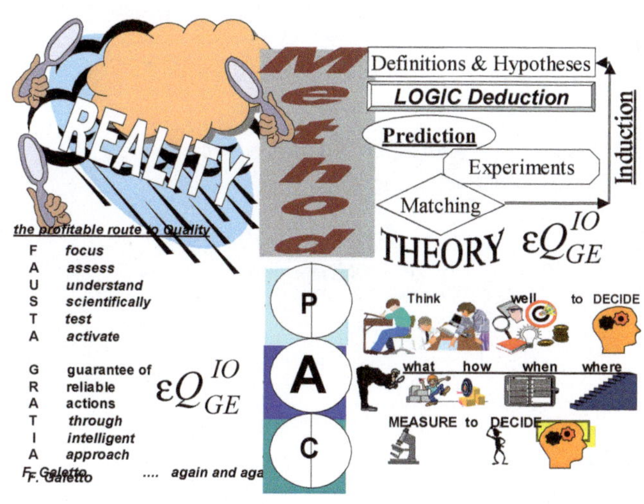

Figure 7. *FAUSTA GRATIA for Quality in order to avoid the Disquality.*

W. E. DEMING "It is a hazard to copy". "It is necessary to understand the theory of what one wishes to do or to make." "Without theory, experience has no meaning." "A figure without a theory tells nothing". <<<The result is that hundreds of people are learning what is wrong. I make this statement on the basis of experience, seeing every day the devastating effects of incompetent teaching and faulty applications.>>>

M. GELL-MANN "In my university studies …, in most of the cases, it seemed that students were asked simply to regurgitate at the exams what they had swallowed during the courses.". Some of those students later could have become researchers and then professors, writing "A_scientific" papers and books … For these last, another statement of the Nobel Prize M. Gell-Mann is relevant: <<<<<"Once that such a misunderstanding has taken place in the publication, it tends to become perpetual, because the various authors simply copy one each other.".>>>>>, similar to "Imitatores, servum pecus" [Horatius, 18 B.C.] and "Gravior et validior est decem virorum bonorum sententia quam totius multitudinis imperitiae" [Cicero].

P. B. CROSBY Paraphrasing P. B. CROSBY one could say "Professors may or may not realize what has to be done to achieve quality. Or worse, they may feel, mistakenly, that they do understand what has to be done. Those types can cause the most harm."

What do have in common Crosby, Deming and Gell-Mann statements? The fact that professors and students betray an important characteristic of human beings: rationality [the "Adult state" of E. Berne]

A. EINSTEIN "Only two things are infinite: the Universe and the Stupidity of people; and I'm not sure about the former".

GALILEO GALILEI Before EINSTEIN, GALILEO GALILEI had said [in the Saggiatore] something similar "Infinite is the mob of fools".

The scientific community as a whole must judge [κρινω] the work of its members by the objectivity and the rigor with which that work has been conducted; in this way the scientific method should prevail. Any professor and any Statistical Consultant should know Probability Theory and Statistics!

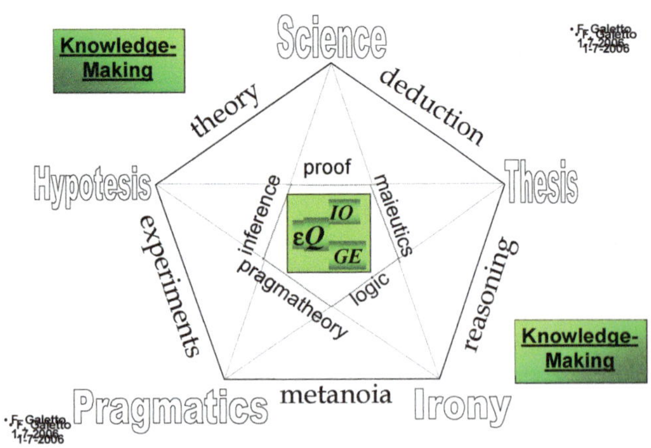

Figure 8. *Quality Tools and Quality Methods: avoid the Disquality.*

I always was used to say to my students: «««««IF a guy suggests books and papers written by incompetents he is TWICE incompetent, because he does not recognize wrong ideas and suggests to read wrong ideas»»»»». Unfortunately several Professors do not practice the two important methods used here, the Logic and the Scientific Theory (Mathematics, Probability, Statistics, Physics,…). See the references…

Please see well the figures 7, 8, 9 and 10, and see IF …

Researchers shall use their intelligence in order to make knowledge for the improvement of people and their life.

Researchers MUST not cheat people and act according to the figures 7 and 8.

Any Intellectually hOnest person that loves QUALITY and hates DISquality will Focus on the problems [potential and/or actual], Assess their importance (money, impact, consequences, risks, …), Understand all the previous items SCIENTIFICALLY and SCIENTIFICALLY Test for finding the causes; when a solution is found anybody will Activate to implement the solution, in order to Guaranty that Reliable Actions (preventive and corrective) are taken Through an Intelligent Approach (approach that uses intelligence, ingenuity and science, avoiding misdeeds). [figure 7]

Eric Berne [32] devised the Transactional Analysis "Theory" [that actually is not a theory in the scientific sense] with the 3 EGO_States: Parent, Adult, Child.

The Parent ego_state is a set of thoughts, feelings, and behaviours that are learned or "borrowed" from our parents or other caretakers. Two parts are comprised: the Nurturing Parent ego_state soft, loving, and permission giving, and Prejudiced Parent, the part of our personality that contains the prejudged thoughts, feelings, and beliefs that we learned from our parents.

The Adult ego_state is our data processing centre. It is the part of our personality that formulate hypotheses to be verified by experiments, uses LOGIC and SCIENCE, invents METHODS to test ideas and to process data accurately, that sees, hears, thinks, and can come up with solutions to problems [potential and/or actual] based on the facts and not solely on our pre-judged thoughts or childlike emotions: it denounces misdeeds. You can see its capacities on the right hand of the figure 7. Qualitatis FAUSTA GRATIA is related to the Adult ego_state.

Figure 9. *The epsilon-Quality to avoid the Disquality.*

The Child ego_state is the part of our personality that is the seat of emotions, thoughts, and feelings and all of the feeling state "memories" that we have of ourselves from childhood. The Child ego_state can also be divided into two parts: the Free Child ego_substate is the seat of spontaneous feeling and behaviour. It is the side of us that experiences the world in a direct and immediate way. Our Free Child ego_substate can be playful, authentic, expressive, and emotional, and the Adapted

Child ego_substate that is the part of our personality that has learned to comply with the parental messages (from everywhere and everybody) we received growing up; if we are faced with parental messages (from everywhere and everybody) that are restricting, instead of complying with them, we rebel against them.

The Adult ego_state [17,18,29]is embodied in the εQ^{IO}_{GE} *symbol*(the epsilon-Quality, see also figure 9).

Intellectually hOnest people use as much as possible their rationality and Logic, in order not to deceive other people.

Deming, Einstein, Gell-Mann are beacons for the Quality Journey.

If we want to achieve QUALITY, MANAGERS (now students) NEED TO BE EDUCATED ON QUALITY εQ^{IO}_{GE} by Quality Professors, EDUCATED on Quality.

I could, at last, paraphrase ST John "And there are also many other things, the which, if they should be written everyone, I suppose that even the world itself could not contain the books that should be written."[1-54]

Will someone want to see the truth? Only God knows that …

The personal conclusion is left to the Intellectually Honest reader to whom is offered the Quality Tetralogy: Prevent, Experiment, Improve, Plan, SCIENTIFICALLY to avoid disquality, to eliminate disquality, to achieve Quality, to assure Quality, using Intellectual Honesty: we wish them to use correctly the Decision-Making Tetrahedron (fig. 10).

Quality Tetralogy and Decision-Making are much better than ISO 9004:2008 (and 2015, as well) because Quality Tetralogy and Decision-Making Tetrahedron take into account explicitly the need for scientific behavior either of people or of organizations that really want to make Quality. Moreover they show clearly that prevention is very important for Quality and Good Management is strongly related to Good Knowledge for Business Excellence.

Figure 10. *The Decision-Making Tetrahedron.*

Brain is the most important asset: let's not forget it, IF we want that our students (Future Managers or Future Researchers) be better than their professors.

We repeat

YOUNG Researchers MUST be ALERT

if they want to LEARN:

THEY MUST know the THEORY!

««The truth sets you free»»

Professors and researchers WHO DO NOT ARE Intellectually hOnest will not grow students and researchers fond of Quality (see figures 1, 6, 7, 8, 9, 10) and [32].

References

[1] BARONE S, ERTO P, LANZOTTI A (2001), "Beyond robust design methodologies: an elementary example of synergy between statistics and advanced engineering design", SIS Sperimentare per la Qualità, Turin February 2001

[2] BORSELLINO C., LO CASTO S., MARAGIOGLIO G., RUISI V. (1999), "Thermovision temperature mapsevaluation in turningoperation", 3rd AITEM 99, Brescia

[3] CAPELLO E., SEMERARO Q. (1999), "Residual stresses in turning", 3rd AITEM 99, Brescia

[4] CARRINO L., GIULIANO G., POLINI W. (2000), "New method to characterise superplastic materials in comparison with alternative methods", Int. Manufacturing Conference in China, Hong Kong

[5] DEMING W.E. (1986), Out of the crisis, Cambridge Press

[6] DEMING W.E. (1997), The new economics for industry, government, education, Cambridge Press

[7] GALETTO F. (1978), "An application of experimental design in the Automotive field", SIA Congress

[8] GALETTO F. (1984)"Assessment of Product Reliability", World Quality Congress '84, Brighton

[9] GALETTO F. (1986)"Quality/Reliability: How to get results", EOQC (Automotive Section), Madrid

[10] GALETTO F. (1987)"Quality and Reliability, the Iveco way", Mgt Dev. Review by MCE, Brussells

[11] GALETTO F. (1988)"Quality and reliability. A must for industry", ISATA, Montecarlo

[12] GALETTO F. (1989)"Quality of methods for quality is important", EOQC Conference, Vienna

[13] GALETTO F. (1990)"Basic and managerial concerns on Taguchi Methods", ISATA, Florence

[14] GALETTO F., LEVI R. (93)"Planned Experiments: key factors for product Quality", 3rd AMST 93, Udine

[15] GALETTO F. (1993) "DOE. Importanti idee sulla Qualità per i manager", DEINDE, Torino

[16] GALETTO F. (1993) "Which kind of Quality? Of products, of processes, of Management?", 1st AITEM, Ancona

[17] GALETTO F. (1995) Affidabilità, Volume 1: Teoria e Metodi di Calcolo, CLEUP, Padova.

[18] GALETTO F. (1995) Affidabilità, Volume 2: Prove di affidabilità, CLEUP, Padova.

[19] GALETTO F. (1996)"Managerial Issues for Design of Experiments", 4th AMST 96, Udine

[20] GALETTO F. (1997)"We need Quality of Managers", Quality 97 6th Int. Conf., Ostrava, Czeh Republic

[21] GALETTO F. (1998)"Quality Education on Quality for Future Managers", 1st Conference on TQM for Higher Education Institutions, Toulon

[22] GALETTO F. (1999)"GIQA, the Golden Integral Quality Approach: from Management of Quality to Quality of Management", Total Quality Management, Vol. 10, No. 1

[23] GALETTO F. (1999)"Quality Methods for Design of Experiments", 5th AMST 99, Udine

[24] GALETTO F. (1999)"Quality Function Deployment, Some Managerial Concerns", AITEM99, Brescia

[25] GALETTO F., GENTILI E. (1999), "The need of Quality Methods used for Quality",CAPE '99, Durham, UK

[26] GALETTO F., GENTILI E. (1999), "Quality of the Quality Methods", AITEM 99 Conference, Brescia

[27] GALETTO F. (99)"Quality Education on Total Quality Management" 2nd Conf. on TQM for HEI, Verona

[28] GALETTO F., GENTILI E. (2000), "In search of Quality in QFD and Taguchi methods", CAPE

[29] GALETTO F. (2000) Qualità. Alcuni metodi statistici da Manager, CLUT, Torino

[30] MONTGOMERY D.C. (1996), Introduction to Statistical Quality Control, Wiley & Sons (many drawbacks)

[31] PARK S. (1996), Robust Design and Analysis for Quality Engineering, Chapman& Hall, London

[32] WATZLAWITCK P. (1976) La realtà della realtà, Astrolabio, Roma

[33] YIN G.Z., JILLIE D.W. (1987), "Orthogonal Design for Process Optimisation and its Application in Plasma Etching", Solid State Technology, (may 87)

[34] W. Eureka, N. E. Ryan The Customer driven Company: Managerial Perspectives on QFD, ASI Press, 1989

[35] C. Casciano (L. Peretto referee), Thesis on the Taguchi Method, Bologna University 2014

[36] J. Z. Zhang et al., "Surface roughness optimization … using the Taguchi design Method", Journal of Material Processing Technology 184(2007) 233-239

[37] Research Gate, Papers and Questions&Answers

[38] GALETTO F. (2014) "Bibiliometrics: Help or Hoax for Quality?" UJER 2(4), DOI: 10.13189/ujer.2014.020404

[39] GALETTO F. (2014) QualityPedia Project. Volume 1, Chapter 1, Research Gate

[40] GALETTO F. (2014) "Riemann Hypothesis Proved", Academia Arena 2014;6(12):19-22]. (ISSN 1553-992X).

[41] M. A. El-Damcese. "Reliability Equivalence Analysis of a Parallel-Series System Subject to Degradation Facility." *Science Journal of Applied Mathematics and Statistics*. Vol. 3, No. 3, 2015, pp. 160-164. doi: 10.11648/j.sjams.20150303.19

[42] M. A. El-Damcese, A. N. Salem, and N. S. Temraz "Semi-Markov Model of a Series-Parallel System Subject to Preventive Maintenance", J. Stat. Appl. Pro. 2, No. 3, 307-318 (2013)

[43] GALETTO F. (2014) "Hope for the Future: Overcoming the DEEP Ignorance on the CI (Confidence Intervals) and on the DOE (Design of Experiments)". *Science Journal of Applied Mathematics and Statistics*. Vol. 3, No. 3, 2015, pp. 99-123. doi:10.11648/j.sjams.20150303.14 DOE 10.11648. j.sjams.20150303.14

[44] M. Xie, Y-S Dai, K-L Poh, (2004) Computing System Reliability, Kluwer Academic Publishers

[45] T. Nakagawa, (2005) Maintenance Theory of Reliability, Springer

[46] H. Wang, H. Pham, (2006) Reliability and Optimal Maintenance, Springer

[47] H. Pham (2003), Handbook of Reliability Engineering, Springer

[48] M. Lazzaroni, L. Cristaldi, L. Peretto, P. Rinaldi, M. Catelani, (2003), Reliability Engineering, Springer

[49] MONTGOMERY D.C. (2006), Introduction to Statistical Quality Control, 6th edition, Wiley & Sons (many more drawbacks than 1996)

[50] K. Bouacha, M. A. Yallese, S. Khamel, S. Belhadi, Analysis and optimization of hard turning operation using cubic boron nitride tool

[51] D. Jurków, application of design of the experiment(DoE) in simulations of passive low temperature co-fired ceramics (LTCC) coolers

[52] D. Jurków, Application of Design of the Experiment in Preliminary Investigations on the end Milling of Low Temperature Co-fired Ceramics, Int. J. Appl. Ceram. Technol., 10 [4] 671–681 (2013) DOI: 10.1111/ j.1744-7402.2012.02763.x

[53] M. S. Sukumar*, B. V. Sudheer Reddy, P. Venkataramaiah, (2015), Analysis on Multi Responses in Face Milling of Ammc Using Fuzzy-Taguchi Method, Journal of Minerals and Materials Characterization and Engineering, 2015, 3, 255-270 Published Online July 2015 in SciRes. http://www.scirp.org/journal/jmmce

[54] J. Martinez, (2008) Application of reliability-Centered Maintenance in Facility Management, Thesis submitted to the Faculty of Worcester Polytechnic Institute.

Tourist destinations positioning: From indexes to managerial implications

Jean Paul Lemaire[1], Milena Viassone[2, *]

[1]ESCP Europe, Paris, France
[2]Department of Management, University of Turin, Turin, Italy

Email address:
jplemaire@escpeurope.eu (J. P. Lemaire), milena.viassone@unito.it (M. Viassone)

Abstract: Despite the numerous attempts to define Tourist Destination Attractiveness (TDA) and Governance (TDG), there are no identified contributions concerning the analysis of these elements in a systemic way. This paper creates a TDA-TDG matrix able to map destinations on the basis of these dimensions, in order to draw development strategies. Drivers of TDA and TDG are chosen by means of literature and validated by 15 tourism stakeholders. TDA index is got throughout Delphi method while TDG index throughout an adaptation of the SERVPERF questionnaire. The paper results in a mapping of tourist destinations that allows tourist managers to draw paths of development.

Keywords: Tourist Destination, Destination Attractiveness, Destination Governance, Delphi Methodology, Likert Scale, SERVPERF Questionnaire

1. Introduction

In the last decades the study of tourist destinations has been more and more at the centre of international academic debate. In particular the competition in global tourism market is increasing thanks to a large number of emerging destinations putting the traditional ones under pressure to innovate and to enhance their quality in order to remain competitive [1]. Many authors [2, 3] have recognized importance of tourism attractiveness as one of the most important dimensions in tourist destination studies. Anyway, the management of tourist destinations involves a high number of stakeholders who are interconnected among themselves and could be more or less ready to cooperate together. This can cause several problems of coordination that can negatively affect the attractiveness of a destination. For these motivations several researches have been carried out on the way the government manages such issues of public interest and promotes suitable industrial policies [4].

Despite the numerous attempts to define and measure tourist destination attractiveness and governance, there are no identified contributions concerning the analysis of these important elements in a systemic way. This research aims at bridging this gap through the proposal of offering a descriptive and prescriptive framework capable of measuring the level of attractiveness and governance of a tourist destination, allowing to assess how to improve its level. In order to carry out this objective, this paper designs both an index of TDA and of TDG which could be associated in a matrix allowing to position any touristic destination, thus getting a classification of possible tourist destinations on the basis of their position in such a matrix leading, for their respective stakeholders, to improve the ranking of the destinations they administrate.

Taking into account the growing interest for these important topics of touristic competition, the purpose of this paper consists of creating a TDA-TDG matrix able to map tourist destinations on the basis of two variables (governance and attractiveness) in order to suggest possible development strategies to the concerned stakeholders.

- The first step of the research process designs an index of tourist destination attractiveness to be validated by a panel of experts (authorities, tourist operators, tourists, academics), throughout the Delphi method: TDA dimensions/indices will stem from the review of literature, then validated and weighted by the Delphi panel before being segmented by SPSS, in order to create the TDAI (Tourist Destination Attractiveness Index).
- The second step measures the level of governance throughout the TDGI (Tourist Destination Governance Index), upon the basis of a questionnaire –sent to a

sample of stakeholders (governors, tourist managers, organizations, academic, tourists)-, asking them to express their opinion towards the characteristics of governance on the basis of a 5-point Likert Scale. This questionnaire is composed of 16 items and organized according to five dimensions of governance identified through the literature review.

This paper covers successively:

- a review of international literature providing definitions, main theories and characteristics of tourist destination attractiveness and governance;
- a description of the respective methodological approach of TDAI and TDGI and of the design of the research model supported by literature and validated by the selected stakeholders;
- an assessment of the proposed methodology and of the possible consecutive strategies which could be implemented.

2. Literature Review

2.1. The Attractiveness of Tourist Destinations

The concepts of destination competitiveness and attractiveness largely differ because they consider tourist destination from different points of view: attractiveness stems from the tourist perception, while competitiveness is a concern of destination stakeholders [5].

Destination attractiveness would be a mental construct of the potential visitors or, better, a mental image of the destination that is formed on the basis of the image they could have of the local assets accessible at the destination [1].

Before analyzing the drivers affecting tourist destination attractiveness, it is necessary to provide a definition both of destination and of attractiveness. Cracolici and Nijkamp [3] consider destination as "the 'supplier' of spatial tourist services with distinct attractiveness features (or attributes), which have to be managed effectively and efficiently" while attractiveness is referred as "the extent to which the availability, quality and management of local tourist services satisfies the needs of the customer". Formica and Uysal [6] consider destination attractiveness as the relationship between the availability of local assets and their importance as perceived by the tourist. In particular, according to Hu and Ritchie [7] the attractiveness of a destination reflects the feelings, beliefs, and opinions that individuals have about a destination perceived capacity to provide satisfaction in relation to their special vacation needs. Cuccia and Rizzo [8] explored the cultural attractiveness of tourist destinations and evaluate the role of cultural tourism in tourism seasonality. Cracolici and Nijkamp [3] analyze tourist attractiveness at a specific level, which is the regional one, while Viassone [2] analyzes this topic with reference to a particular category of tourist (the young one).

The attractiveness of a tourist destination can be led by several drivers and their measure could be very useful both for assessing attractiveness of tourist segment and for determining the main pulling factors of each considered destination [1].

Several researchers have focused their attention on these factors: for example, Ritchie and Crouch [9] find that tourist destination attractiveness is affected by seven different types of driver, i.e., physiography and climate, culture and history, mix of activities, special events, entertainment, superstructure and market ties. UNWTO [10] identifies five main categories of these: natural tourist resources, cultural and historical heritage in tourism, climate conditions, infrastructure, tourist services and facilities. Cracolici and Nijkamp [3] consider as main drivers of tourist destination attractiveness: natural and cultural resources, amount and quality of accommodation and restaurants, accessibility to transportation systems, all the activities available at the destination (the spectrum of choices for the tourist-consumer), tourist safety and local resident behavior. Jin *et al.* [11] tested dimensions of exhibition destination attractiveness in the Mainland China context from the perspective of exhibitors and find how destination attractiveness is a higher order construct composed of six factors:

cluster effect 1 (host city leadership in the industry), venue facilities,

cluster effect 2 (host city/region as a source of exhibitors), destination leisure environment, destination economic environment and accessibility.

Amelung and Nicholls [12] propose the first known empirical analysis of the potential impact of climate changes on Australia's tourism industry, based on projected shifts in climatic attractiveness for Australia's major tourism destinations over the coming century. They explain how these projected changes affect the flows of tourists into and around Australia, tourism planning, development and management.

In a recent study with particular reference to the young people, Viassone [2] individuates as elements considered in the choice of a tourist destination: safety, accessibility of the place/destination, hygiene, natural variables, cultural variables, accommodations, transport, entertainment and wellness and possibility of organizing congresses.

These contributions leads to a proposal of drivers of tourist destination attractiveness on which, after a process of evaluation, will rely the prescriptive model Tourist Destination Attractiveness/Tourist Destination Governance.

2.2. Governance of Tourist Destinations

The management of tourist destination is not simple because of the dynamics of interests and benefits sought by stakeholders: they create numerous links and interdependencies among themselves; often they do not cooperate and could have different development vision. More and more researchers on tourist destination management have paid attention to the way the government manages public issues and make suitable industrial policies [4].

In 2009, Eagles [13] defined the governance as a process by which organizations decide who take the responsibility to choose and who pays the price.

The concept of governance concerns "how societies are

governed, ruled or "steered", and thus it involves the processes for regulating and mobilizing social action and for producing social order" [14]. This includes hierarchical tiers of formal government, networks of actors beyond government, communities and also markets [15].

Several researchers analyze the topic of tourist destination governance providing a comprehensive definition, describing different types of governance models or key problems of governance [16]. Governance can be characterized either by more diffuse policy networks and interaction with market mechanisms (i.e. what occurs in many advanced capitalist nations) or by a comparatively more hegemonic State (as in China) [17].

Different theories for destination governance have been elaborated like, for example, *local elites holder theory* [18], *property rights theory* [19], explaining why some individuals and organizations are more influential than others, the agency *relationships* problem [20, 21] between principals and agents observed in any type of organization, *transaction cost economics* [22] that explains the level of integration of organizations and institution in some destinations, and, finally, *resource dependence theory* [23]. These concepts and models are used in order to discuss different empirical case studies [24-27]. They refer to three different dimensions to study destination governance: the complexity of the destination, the interplay of public and private organizations and the resource interdependency. Beritelli *et al.* [24] analyze two different pattern of tourism destination governance that give a brief definition of each of these models.

A good explanation of implicit destination governance (multiple relationships relying on interdependencies, communication, trust, consensus, etc.), considered as the reason for the success or failure of collective policies and actions, is provided by Beritelli [28] throughout different dimensions applyied in his social-network analysis of elite individuals. These dimensions are:

- *Network vs. Hierarchy*: according to Beritelli [28], behind the network structure, there is an underlying hierarchy, so that decisions occur neither democratically nor randomly and destination planning and development are manageable upon the basis of the hierarchical behavior: according to Simon [29], the grouping of informal organizations must be hierarchically structured and could be measured; while, referring to different measures of structure, Krackhardt [30] individuates *connectedness* (measures the belonging of actors to a common system), *hierarchy* (measures the extent to which it is possible to speak of an organizational cascade), *graph efficiency* (that assesses the redundancies of connections inside the organization), *least upper boundedness (LUB)* (that measures hierarchy in terms of the direction of the line-in-command) [31, 28].
- *Cooperative vs. non-cooperative behavior*: cooperative behavior in tourist destination communities is a very important condition in order to achieve a sustainable planning and development; this behavior turns out to be worthwhile if there is a payoff based on a strategy maximizing advantages. According to Beritelli [28], this cooperative behavior among actors and stakeholder groups in tourist destinations is an interpersonal business . It requires reciprocal sympathy. For this author, tourist destination communities distinguish themselves over all by autonomous key actors. This opinion is also supported by Tang and Tang [32] who considers that some collaborative actions [33] have been at the origin of governance networks, and that they can be considered as an indispensable support to decision-making and strategy-definition, when adapting to global changes. The premise of a tourist destination management is that, throughout cooperative planning, the effectiveness of the joint interactions among destination stakeholders can be improved to the benefit of individual stakeholders [34].
- *Consensus/involvement vs. non-consensus/non-involvement*: even if there is a large consensus on the fact that community-based tourism planning, with a high level of collaboration involving relevant stakeholders, increases effectiveness in enhancing destination strategies [35, 36]. Generally the latter are formulated by a limited number of people, an elite [37], and they are not always accepted or shared by everybody. Beritelli [28] shows how (1) explicit consensus doesn't relate to implicit consensus; (2) the necessary implicit consensus refers to a collective intelligence that allows mass collaboration and resides in individuals' and groups' perception [38]. According to March and Wilkinson [39] performance of a tourist destination particularly depends on the level of cohesion among the various actors/stakeholders present in the destination. Participation by a diverse range of actors in tourism decision-making can potentially enhance the democratic processes and ownership, widely associated with sustainable development [14].
- *Openness vs. closure* [28]: the existence of a trade-off between openness of a destination elite network and the preservation of the local culture and, thus, implicit governance mechanisms and routines has been pinpointed [40].
- In addition, Nunkoo *et al.* [41] underline how political trust is considered as important as power for good governance of tourism. Their study shows how perceived economic and political performance of institutions, in the one hand, residents' power in tourism and interpersonal trust, in the other, are valuable determinants of political trust in tourism institutions and it finds also an important relationship between public trust and political support for tourism.

3. Methodology

In recent years, the growing interest in tourist destination attractiveness (TDA) and governance (TDG) has had an influence on the study of tourism destinations. Despite the numerous attempts to define tourist destination attractiveness and governance, there are no identified contributions concerning the analysis of these important elements in a systemic way. For this reason this theoretical study tries to provide a descriptive and prescriptive framework in order to classify tourist destination upon the basis of their level of attractiveness and their type of governance.

This could represent a starting point for developing specific strategies for different destinations. The research model developed here, relying on tourist destination attractiveness drivers is based on variables inspired by the literature and validated by 15 selected stakeholders (Authorities, Academics, Tourist firms/organizations, Tourists) by means of semi-structured interviews conducted in December 2013: tourist flows, accessibility to the place/destination, natural elements, climate conditions, cultural attractions, accommodation, recreational attractions, prices level and public investments. These are considered those that strongly affect tourist attractiveness by stakeholders on the base of their experience.

The measure of a tourist destination attractiveness has been obtained by means of the Delphi Method [42, 43] (Dalkey, 1969, Okoli and Pavlovski, 2004), an iterative process that, throughout semi-structured interviews, allows to ask stakeholders of different origin,

- the validation of a theoretical framework on the basis of criteria of relevance, accessibility and transferability [44, 45];
- the weighting of different drivers of the destination attractiveness by distributing 100 scores among these drivers, upon the basis on their importance in the definition of TDA.
- In a second step of the analysis,
- scores assigned to each driver must be shared among different sub-drivers by selected stakeholder
- and then, throughout SPSS, these sub-drivers will be segmented in 4 classes containing the same portion of population. In this way a different score will be assigned to each sub-driver according to whether it belongs to class 1 (the lowest level), 2, 3 ore 4 (the highest level). The sum of scores assigned to different sub-drivers allows to get nine different partial indices reflecting the tourist destination attractiveness with reference to single variables. The sum of these indices results in the TDAI (Tourist Destination Attractiveness Index):

$$TDAI=TFS+AS+NES+CCS+CAS+ACS+RAS+PLS+PIS \quad (1)$$

where

TFS: tourist flows scores
AS: accessibility scores
NES: natural elements scores
CCS: climate conditions scores
CAS: cultural attractions scores
ACS: accommodation scores
RAS: recreational attractions scores
PLS: price level scores
PIS: public investment scores that can assume a low, quite low, discrete, quite high or high level.

At the same way, with respect to the tourist destination governance, most papers focus on single or multiple case studies [24, 25] and involve the institutions/stakeholders point of view [46, 47].

The framework adopted here, describing tourist destination governance, chooses the individual as object of research and an adaptation of the social network analysis as methodology [28, 48]. In this paper is presented the logical development of the state-of-the-art in destination planning and management, as well as the recent research field of "destination governance": in particular are used the dimensions described by Beritelli [28] in his networking analysis and Nunkoo *et al.* [41], but evaluated throughout a Likert Scale that better allows to get an evaluation of the different dimensions of implicit destination governance, both by "ruling" and "ruled" individuals.

In fact, in order to provide a measure of TDG, it has been chosen an adaptation of the SERVPERF questionnaire - created in 1992 by Cronin e Taylor [49] – composed, in this case, only by 16 sentences organized according to the five dimensions affecting destination governance (network vs. hierarchy, cooperative vs. non-cooperative, consensus/involvement vs. non-consensus/non-involvement, opening vs. closure, political trust vs. non-political trust).

In this case, on a 5-points Likert scale (between ‹‹I completely disagree›› and ‹‹I completely agree››) [50], individuals must indicate the level of agreement with reference to the different sentences about TDG. In order to evaluate the TDG in a global way, it will be, first of all, necessary to evaluate the TDG perceived by each single tourist involved in the survey.

This will result in the average Qj of judgments provided by the same to the 16 sentences (Q_{ij}) [51]:

$$TDGI_j = \frac{\sum_{i=1}^{16} TDGI_{ij}}{16} \quad (2)$$

Afterwards, the average of the values of Qj registered for all the users involved must be computed [50]:

$$TDGI = \frac{\sum_{j=1}^{n} TDGI_j}{n} \quad (3)$$

Generally, values higher than 3 indicate a good level of stakeholders' agreement vs. TDG [44]. The statistical analysis of data will be carried out through SPSS 19.0 suite.

After these two steps, we are able to cross the two variables object of our study (TDA and TDG) and, on the basis of values they assume, to classify them in seven different categories.

The position of each destination in the matrix TDA/TDG allows drawing possible future paths of action. No missing data were found.

4. From Tourist Destinations' Attractiveness and Governance Indicators to Indexes

The results of our analysis show how tourist destination

attractiveness is affected by nine drivers:

- tourist flows (constituted by two sub-drivers: GDP per capita and density),
- the real output index of a destination attractiveness;
- accessibility (related to roads, railways and airports) [3];
- natural elements, like number of protected areas, of natural parks, coasts, mountains, lakes, climate conditions (daily duration of sun light, amount of precipitations) [52, 7, 53];
- cultural attractions (i.e. number of museums, of visitors of museums, of churches, of other monuments) [54];
- accommodations (number of hotels and of other kinds of accommodations) [55];
- recreational attractions like restaurants, bar, discos, cinemas [1, 56];
- tourist prices level;
- and public investments.

From the review of literature, also, safety [57] and hygiene [58] have been considered but, during the process of validation, they have been eliminated because the data are not accessible at regional or provincial level and a comparison would be impossible. The final framework of drivers and sub-drivers of tourist destination attractiveness is shown in Table 1.

Table 1. *Framework of tourist destination attractiveness (TDA)*

Drivers	Scores assigned
Tourist flows	18
GDP pro capite	9
Density	9
Accessibility	15
Roads km	5
Railways km	5
airports	5
Natural elements	15
n. of protected areas	3
n. of natural parks	3
Coasts	3
Mountains	3
Lakes	3
Climate conditions	12
Daily duration. of sunshines	6
N. of precipitations	6
Cultural attractions	10
n. of museums	2.5
n. of visitors of museums	2.5
n. of churches	2.5
n. of other monuments	2.5
Accomodation	8
n. of hotel	4
n. of other accomodations	4
Recreational attractions	8
n. of restaurants	2
n. of bar	2
n. of disco	2
n. of cinema	2
Prices level	8
Public investments	6
Total scores	100

Table 2. *Levels of tourist destination attractiveness (TDA)*

Classes	Scores	Level of TDA
1	1-20	Low
2	21-40	Quite low
3	41-60	Discrete
4	61-80	Quite high
5	81-100	High

After this first step, selected stakeholders have distributed 100 scores among different drivers on the basis of their contribution to destination attractiveness, according to their previous experiences.

The highest scores have been attribute to tourist flows (18 scores), accessibility (15 scores) and natural elements (15 scores): it is particular how these elements represent respectively an output driver (tourist flows), an input driver (natural elements) and an element of facilitation to enter in a certain tourist destination (accessibility). Drivers considered as less important are accommodations (8 scores), recreational attractions (8 scores), regional prices levels (8 scores) and investments (6 scores). Scores assigned to drivers are then shared among sub-drivers in equal parts.

The application of this framework to specific tourist destination will allow, throughout SPSS, to segment different sub-drivers in four different classes. It attributes them a different score upon the basis of their class. Successively, summing up the scores of each sub-driver, it will be possible to get the TDAI that can assume a minimum value of 0 and a maximum of 100. TDAI will be classified in five different classes as shown in Table 2.

With respect to Tourist Destination Governance, our framework is based on 6 different variables which are results of previous researches by Beritelli [28] and Nunkoo *et al.* [41]:

- network vs. hierarchy [28-30];
- cooperative vs. non-cooperative behavior [28, 33, 34];
- consensus/involvement vs. non-consensus/non-involvement [36-39, 14];
- openness vs. closure [40];
- political trust [41].

Table 3. *Kind of tourist destination governance (TDG)*

	1	2	3	4	5
Hierarchy (vs Network)					
Strategic decisions are taken by people settled in power positions					
The proposals of people in power positions are submitted in some ways to other actors (firms, tourists, citizens) for the approval					
Strategic decisions are the result of a shared process among all the actors involved but respecting hierarchical roles					
Cooperative (vs not cooperative) behavior					
The different tourist organizations cooperate for common purposes					
The different tourist firms cooperate together					
Supplier and users of tourist services need to collaborate in service definition also if there is a standard to respect					
Supplier and users need to collaborate in					

	1	2	3	4	5
product definition also if the supplier has sufficient capacity					
Consensus (vs not consensus)					
There is a formal consensus in networks of actors with regard to strategic issues					
The choices taken by tourist managers are shared by tourists					
Tourists are involved in strategic decisions of tourist governors					
Openness (vs closure)					
Tourist destination cooperate in specific projects with other destinations					
Tourist destination share tourist services with other destinations					
Tourist destination has created tourist paths including also other destinations					
Political Trust					
Tourist Government is able to deliver effective polices in the eyes of people					
Tourist Governors deserve the trust of individuals because able to offer good performances in the destination					
Tourist Governors deserve the trust of individuals because a good governance is their duty					

In order to allow the evaluation of each dimension and obtain a final level of TDG, every dimensions has been described by a number of 3- 4 sentences (Table 3) that should be evaluated for each specific destination by selected stakeholders throughout a 5-points Likert Scale.

This will allow us to calculate TDGIj and, finally, TDGI, whose value will be included in the range 1 (lowest value) – 5 (highest value). Thus, also in this case, TDG will be structured in 5 different levels as shown in Table 4.

Table 4. *Levels of tourist destination attractiveness (TDA)*

Classes	Level of TDA
0-1	Low
1,1-2	Quite low
2,1-3	Discrete
3,1-4	Quite high
4,1-5	High

Crossing the results obtained throughout the computation of TDAI and TDGI, makes it possible to structure a destination in the matrix TDA-TDG proposed in Table 5.

5. Resulting Outputs for Tourist Destinations: The Positioning Matrix

The matrix proposed (Table 5), adopting a comparable framework to territories positioning proposed by Lemaire [21, 45], associates two different axes (Destination Governance and Attractiveness), the first assuming a value between low and excellent while the second between low and high.

In such a way, the tourist destination could be classified in seven different "boxes"on the basis of its position:

- *Indisputable* [21, 45]*diamond tips,* if it shows both a good or excellent governance and a quite high or high attractiveness: these destinations are those in the best position and they will be the benchmarks for other destinations;
- *Inoperative destinations,* if they are attractive but show a low or quite low governance level: probably they can count on a rich baggage of resources or natural attraction that make them attractive despite their unsatisfying governance;
- *Insistent destinations,* if they are in the opposite position of the previous one: in this case, they can count on a good or excellent governance but they fail to become attractive for the lack of resources or natural attractions or because of an inefficient marketing;
- *Immature destinations,* if they perform bad with reference both to attractiveness and governance: they have only margins for improvement;
- *Promises,* if they show discrete value in one dimension and high or quite high value in the other one: they are in a transition position towards the best one that is diamond tips;
- *"on sunset boulevard" destinations,* if they show discrete value in one dimension and low or quite low value in the other one: they are shifting towards the worst position, i.e. Immature destinations;
- *"in the middle" destinations* are all those destinations showing discrete value for both the dimensions: for these destination the game is open and it will depend on their ability to develop their governance and develop their attractiveness.

Table 5. *Matrix TDA-TDG*

		D.G.		
		Excellent Good	Discrete	Low Quite low
D.A.	High Quite high	Indisputable	Promises	Inoperative destinations
	Discrete	Promises	"in the middle" destination	On sunset boulevard destinations
	Quite low low	Insistent destinations	On sunset boulevard destinations	Immature destinations

This matrix can constitute a very important framework for Authorities, tourist organizations and managers in order to analyze the position of a particular tourist destination and to draw suitable development strategies.

6. Conclusive Remarks towards Implications for Tourist Destination Stakeholders

By integrating ideas from tourism management, governance and attractiveness, this theoretical study proposes a useful framework for tourist managers to outline development plans, starting from the measure of two very important dimensions: tourist destination attractiveness and governance. In fact, despite the numerous attempts to define tourist destination attractiveness and governance, there are no identified contributions concerning the analysis of these important elements in a systemic way. The measure of TDA is very important for the determination of the attractiveness of individual tourism attraction groups and of the main pull factors towards particular destinations [1], while the second measure allows to understand which norms, rules and routines prevail in tourist destination communities, in order to better manage and govern the processes of planning, implementing and controlling for the destination [28]. Results show how each of these two dimensions could be affected by several drivers, each of which contributes, in a different way, in the determination of TDAI [2] and TDAG. The framework proposed in this paper could be very useful as it allows to individuate, following an analysis to decision approach [45] the correct position of a tourist destination and the specific drivers on which is necessary to insist in order to improve its ranking.

Starting from these results, it's possible to draw paths of action, both for TDA and for TDG. In fact the matrix TDA-TDG is also a prescriptive model, capable of driving tourist destination managers towards the identification of the most suitable development strategies for each destination. In particular, *indisputable*, being in the best position, should focus their efforts in the valorization of their current governance and attractiveness in order not to lose this very good position; *inoperative* should develop their governance in order to conserve or develop, in the future, their current attractiveness; for insistent *destinations*, a strategy able to improve the current attractions or to propose innovative solution or a most efficient marketing strategy could be developed in order to move towards *promises* and then towards indisputable. *Immature destinations* have very few possibilities to become attractive destination because they have to rely in some external support (eg. Multigovernmental Institutions) on the development of several drivers of attractiveness and on the dimensions of TDG: of course this process would be very long and complex.

Promises are the closest destinations to *indisputable:* for them, small adjustments and effort in TDA or TDG could be enough to move these destinations to the best position in the matrix. *"On sunset boulevard" destinations* need meaningful improvements, either on some drivers of attractiveness or on some aspects of their governance; because, if this doesn't happen, they will start to become immature destinations. Finally, the least clear position is that of *"in the middle" destinations:* for them the game is open and their success or failure will depend from how they will be able to manage the different drivers of the two dimensions, pushing them toward the best or the worst positions.

Although this work offers important issues and enrich existent literature, there are some limitations which should be taken into account. This paper is only a theoretical study, able to describe a framework for tourist destination but it lacks a practical application. It is possible to apply the TDA-TDG matrix to specific destinations in order to propose important comparison at national and international level as to propose and precise appropriate strategies .

References

[1] D. Krešić, and D. Prebežac, "Index of destination attractiveness as a tool for destination attractiveness assessment", Tourism, Vol. 59, No. 4, 2011, pp. 497–517.

[2] M. Viassone, "On the choice of a mountain tourist destination. The evaluation of drivers by young people", Enlightening Tourism. A Pathmaking Journal, Vol. 2, No. 2, 2012, pp. 26-46.

[3] M.F. Cracolici, P. Nijkamp, "The attractiveness and competitiveness of tourist destinations: A study of Southern Italian regions", Tourism Management, Vol. 30, No. 3, 2008, pp. 336-344.

[4] H. Zhang, "Studies on tourist destination governance from the perspective of institutional economics: Retrospect and prospect", in IPEDR, International Proceedings of Economics Development & Research, Vol. 12, Singapore: IACSIT Press, 2011, pp. 217-221.

[5] S. Vengesayi, "A conceptual model of tourism destination competitiveness and attractiveness", in Anzmac 2003 Conference Proceedings. Adelaide, 2003, pp. 637-647.

[6] S. Formica,and M. Uysal, "Destination attractiveness based on supply and demand evaluations: An analytical framework", Journal of Travel Research, Vol. 44, No. 4, 2006, pp. 418-430

[7] Y. Hu, B.J.R. Ritchie, "Measuring destination attractiveness: A contextual approach››, *Journal of Travel Research*, Vol. 32, N° 2, 1993, pp. 25-34.

[8] T. Cuccia, and I. Izzo, "Heritage and tourism: Theoretical and empirical issues", Tourismos: An International Multidisciplinary Journal of Tourism, Vol. 6, No. 3, 2011, pp. 37-56.

[9] B.J.R. Ritchie, and G.I. Crouch, The Competitive Destination: A Sustainable Tourism Perspective, Wallingford: CABI Publishing, 2005.

[10] UNWTO. Sustainable Tourism Development: Guide for Local Planners, Madrid: UNWTO, 1993.

[11] X. Jin, K. Weber, and T. Bauer, "Dimensions and perceptional differences of exhibition destination attractiveness: The case of China", Journal of Hospitality & Tourism Research, Vol. 37, No. 4, 2012, pp. 447-469.

[12] B. Amelung, S. Nicholls, "Implications of climate change for tourism in Australia", Tourism Management, Vol. 41, 2014, pp. 228-244.

[13] P.F.J. Eagles, "Governance and recreation and tourism partnership in parks and protected areas", Journal of Sustainable Tourism, Vol. 17, No. 2, 2009, pp. 231-248.

[14] B. Bramwell, and B. Lane, "Critical research on the governance of tourism and sustainability", Journal of Sustainable Tourism, Vol. 19, No. 4/5, 2011, pp. 411 421.

[15] C.M. Hall, "A typology of governance and its implications for tourism policy analysis", Journal of Sustainable Tourism, Vol. 19, No. 4/5, 2011, pp. 437–457.

[16] H. Pechlaner, F. Raich, P. Beritelli, "Introduction to the special issue: Destination governance", Tourism Review, Vol. 65, No. 4, 2010, pp. 4-85.

[17] M. Bevir, Key concepts in governance. London: Sage, 2009.

[18] E.R. Freeman, Strategic Management: A Stakeholder Approach to Strategic Management. Boston: Pitman, 1984.

[19] R.H. Coase, "The problem of social cost", The Journal of Law and Economics, Vol. 3, No. 1, 1960, pp. 1-44.

[20] M. Jensen, and W. Meckling, "Theory of the firm: Managerial behavior, agency costs, and capital structure", Journal of Financial Economics, Vol. 3, No. 4, 1976, pp. 305-360.

[21] J.P. Lemaire, "Local authorities and foreign companies: the paradoxical issue of FDI towards fast growing economies" in The Paradoxes of Globalization, E. Milliot, and E.N. Tournois, Eds. Houndmills, Basingstoke, Hampshire: Palgrave Macmillan, 2010.

[22] O.E. Williamson, "Transaction-cost economics: the governance of contractual relations", Journal of Law and Economics, Vol. 22, No. 2, 1979, pp. 233-261.

[23] J. Pfeffer, G.R. Salancik, The External Control Of Organizations: A Resource Dependence Perspective. New York: Harper and Row, 1978.

[24] P. Beritelli, T. Bieger, and C. Laesser, "Destination governance: Using corporate governance theories as a foundation for effective destination management", Journal of Travel Research, Vol. 46, No. 1, 2007, pp. 96-107.

[25] W.C. Buteau-Duitschaever, B. McCutcheon, P.F.J. Eagles, T.D. Glover, M.E. Havitz, "Park visitors' perceptions of governance: A comparison between Ontario and British Columbia provincial parks management models", Tourism Review, Vol. 65, No. 4, 2010, pp. 31-50.

[26] F. Raich, Governance räumlicher wettbewerbseinheiten ein ansatz für die tourismus-destination, Wiesbaden, Dt. Univ.-Verl., 2006.

[27] S. Nordin, and B. Svensson, "Innovative destination governance: the Swedish ski resort of Are", Entrepreneurship and Innovation, Vol. 8, No. 1, 2007, pp. 53-66.

[28] P. Beritelli, "Tourist destination governance through local elites - Looking beyond the stakeholder level", Working paper, St. Gallen: University of St. Gallen Institute for Systemic Management and Public Governance, 2011, pp. 1-43.

[29] H.A. Simon, The Sciences of the Artificial (2nd Ed.), Cambridge, Ma.: MIT Press, 1981.

[30] D. Krackhardt, "Graph theoretical dimensions of informal organizations. Computational organization theory", in Computational Organizational Theory, K. Carley, and M. Prietula, Eds. Hillsdale, NJ: Lawrence Erlbaum Associaties, Inc., 1994, pp. 89-111.

[31] P. Beritelli, "Measuring hierarchy in elite networks of tourist destinations - A look beyond the measures of power and centrality", in Conference Proceedings 42th TTRA Annual International Conference 2011. London, Ontario, 2011, pp. 1-11.

[32] C.P. Tang, and S.Y. Tang, "Democratization and capacity building for environmental governance: managing land subsidence in Taiwan", Environment and Planning A, Vol. 38, No. 6, 2006, pp. 1131–1147.

[33] T. Dedeurwaerdere, "The contribution of network governance to sustainable development: a case study on sustainability impact assessment", 2004. Available from: http://www.iddri.org/Evenements/Seminaires-reguliers/s13_dedeurwaerdere.pdf (Accessed: 14th November 2013).

[34] E. Laws, H. Richins, G. Agrusa, and N. Scott, Tourist Destination Governance. Practice, Theory and Issue, Nosworthy Way, Wallighford, Oxfordshire: Cab International, 2011.

[35] T.B. Jamal, and D. Getz, "Collaboration theory and community tourism planning", Annals of Tourism Research, Vol. 22, No. 1, 1994, pp. 186-204.

[36] Y. Wang, and D.R. Fesenmaier, "Collaborative destination marketing: a case study of Elkhart County, Indiana", Tourism Management, Vol. 28, No. 3, 2007, pp. 863-875.

[37] C. Pforr, "Tourism policy in the making an Australian network study", Annals of Tourism Research, Vol. 33, No. 1, 2006, pp. 87-108.

[38] http://www.amazon.com/Wikinomics-Mass-Collaboration-Changes-Everything/dp/B004J8HXOA (Accessed: 15th November 2013).

[39] R. March, and I. Wilkinson, "Conceptual tools for evaluating tourism partnerships", Tourism Management, Vol. 30, No. 3, 2009, pp. 455 – 462.

[40] P. Beritelli, A. Strobl, and M. Peters, "Community closure and social capital against interlocking directorates: A trade-off for development in tourist destinations", in Conference Proceedings 2011 EURAM 11th Annual Conference. Tallinn, 2011.

[41] R. Nunkoo, R. Haywantee, and D. Gursoy, "Public trust in tourist institutions", Annals of Tourism Research, Vol. 39, No. 3, 2012, pp. 1538–1564

[42] N.C. Dalkey, The Delphi Method: An Experimental Study of Group Opinion, Santa Monica (CA): Rand Corporation, 1969.

[43] C. Okoli, and S.D. Pawlowski, The Delphi method as a research tool: an example, design considerations and applications, Information & Management, Vol. 42, No. 1, 2004, pp. 15-29

[44] M. Viassone, and C. Casalegno, "Does a correlation between provincial and district competitiveness exist? the study of italian areas", World Journal of Social Sciences, Vol. 1, No. 5, 2011, pp. 36-53.

[45] J.-P. Lemaire, Strategies d'Internationalisation. Nouveaux Enjeux d'ouverture des Organization, des Activités Et Des Territoires. Paris : Dunod, 2013.

[46] G. Marzano, and N. Scott, "Power in destination branding", Annals of Tourism Research, Vol. 36, No. 2, 2009, pp. 247-267.

[47] A. Presenza, M. Cipollina, "Analysing tourism stakeholders

networks", Tourism Review, Vol. 65, No. 4, 2010, pp. 17-30.

[48] G. Saxena, "Beyond mistrust and competition-the role of social and personal bonding processes in sustaining livelihoods of rural tourism businesses: A case of the Peak District National Park", International Journal of Tourism Research, Vol. 8, No. 4, 2006, pp. 263-277.

[49] J.J. Cronin, and S.A. Taylor, "Measuring service quality: Are-examination and extension", Journal of Marketing, Vol. 56, No.3, 1992, pp. 55-68.

[50] R. Likert, "A tecnique for the measurement of attitudes", Archives of Psycology, No. 140, 1932.

[51] G. Tardivo, A. Scilla, and M. Viassone, "'Codice QR': una risposta innovativa per la comunicazione e la soddisfazione del cliente››, in Sinergie, Referred Electronic Conference Proceeding of the XXV Convegno annuale di Sinergie ‹‹L'innovazione per la competitività delle imprese››, Verona: Sinergie, 2013, pp. 429-444.

[52] D. Jani, C.I. Jang, Y-H. Hwang, "Differential effects of tourism resources on the attractiveness of destination bundles", International Journal of Tourism Sciences, Vol. 9, No. 1, 2009, pp. 23-36.

[53] S. Shoemaker, "Segmenting the U.S. travel market according to benefits realized", Journal of Travel Research, Vol. 32, No. 3, 1994, pp. 8-21.

[54] OECD, The Impact Of Culture On Tourism. Centre for Entrepreneurship, SMEs and Local Development, 2009.

[55] V. Della Corte, La Gestione dei Sistemi Locali di Offerta Turistica. Padova: Cedam, p.

[56] M. Symons, "Gastronomic authenticity and sense of place", in Proceedings of the 9th Australian Tourism Hospitality Research Conference. Camberra: Council for Australian University Tourism and Hospitality Education, BTR, 1999, pp. 333-340.

[57] Y.K. Mak, Safety First, 2007, Available at http://ttgmice.com/index.php?option=com_content&task=view&id=2677&Itemid=89, (Accessed 13th October).

[58] C.H. Van Heerden, Y. Botha, E. Durieux, "The relationship between atmospherics, services cape and destination attractiveness of a holiday destination", Innovative Marketing, Vol. 5, No. 1, 2009, pp. 55-65.

"Total attractiveness" for consumer in advanced D.D.-B.B. systemic marketing in tourism management

Alberto Marino

Department of Management Science, Economics and Quantitative Methods, University of Bergamo, Bergamo, Italy

Email address:
alberto.marino@unibg.it

Abstract: Part of literature and practice in tourism destination (Management) often consider (in case of weak marketing point of view) a too restrictive interpretation and implementation of (destination) "attractiveness". This is a paradox. Frequently attractiveness in tourist destination management only means natural and intrinsic appeal of a destination, site or locus or similar. In important btoc fields, management and systemic marketing enlarge significance/contents of (complete) "attractiveness" (for the consumer-final client). Also tourist destination management, rarely completely oriented to consumer (person-consumer), must reduce gap in implementation of real comprehensive, entire attractiveness (for consumer in btoc tourism). This paper also indicates how to apply to tourist destination management "complete" and impacting attractiveness, with really systemic marketing proposed by the author and gradually activated by outstanding firms also in Italy. So, this paper that enlarges "attractiveness" (for consumers) word , like occurs in other btoc fields, focalizes new kind of systemic marketing concepts and approaches, to increase impact of really comprehensive destination attractiveness (for consumer-final client) not only using web. Also, this paper with neologisms , emphasizes how enlarged "attractiveness"(for consumers) can ameliorate (in btoc tourism management) multiple systemic "differentiation" by a lot of important (systemic) marketing topics, now including neologisms like: bunch, blend, propositioning, and so on, referring to single or aggregate of single advanced systemic marketing. Looking to unrestricted attractiveness, this paper proposes a shift from "natural" limited attractiveness to a real whole attractiveness, involving so called "persumer" (person-consumer) and it presents a new related concepts and a (called D.D.-B.B.) multi polyhedric systemic marketing approach to ameliorate impact on consumer (in btoc Tourism Management). To catch other opportunities referring to so called "external valorization", (multi-polyhedric) S.A.W.A or "Systemic Articulated Whole Attractiveness", activates polyhedric, strong "mixtures" (including experiential marketing), bunch and blend and other concepts impacting on "Whole Multiple Systemic Differentiation" related to a complete attractiveness. This includes effects of propositioning to positioning not only brand or normal packages in tourism. This paper proposes various possible innovations in words and emphasizes how various new attractiveness (of a specific whole firm) for the consumer-customer depends also on aggregating single (multi-articulated) advanced systemic marketing into D.D. (new articulated and consumer oriented D.O., part of a new DOM) , to get (through B.B.) more and really excellent results by comprehensive, whole differentiation (not only of intrinsic site-destination) also sprung from "new" complete Attractiveness (to the consumer- final client).

Keywords: Attractiveness for the Consumer, "Destinator" (Neologism), Persumer (Neologism), New Innovative Marketing Concepts, Blend, Bunch, D.D.-B.B Systemic Marketing Approach

1. Introduction

Governing Business dynamics[1] is by now compulsory in most services fields and also in the tourism industry much more than in last decades. Various disruptions affect a big part of terms and contents of tourism management and destination management. By the way, the role of marketing in this initial part of third millennium [2] must be further increased, more and more using advanced kind of marketing and primarily new systemic marketing (of the firms and similar organization, in btoc -business to consumer- fields) also to increase effectiveness and efficiency, putting more and more efforts into the creation of real value to the final consumer. In btoc tourism management it is too limitative to assume (in btoc tourism) a generic "consumer orientation" for destination and so on [3]. So, it is not sufficient to conceive attractiveness only and generically linked to a set of intrinsic "attractions " of destination. Furthermore, the same opportunities deriving from web and e-commerce can be caught with enlargement of use of systemic marketing tools not only in the consumer loyalty and perception' perspective[4] but also to ameliorate "external valorization" of (backward, not really consumer oriented) D.O. (Destination Organization).

A lot of current tourism management conceptions and approaches, both from the theoretical and practical point of view, can be largely ameliorated by also entering new specific perspective and treatment that consider correctly and differently also destination concept (and various related words).

Tourism destination management uses words as "attractiveness" more frequently than other kinds of management (in other sectors different from the touristic one), but in too restrictive sense than in a lot of other consumer service and good fields! This is a paradox!

It's better to use not only frequently, but ever exactly also "attractiveness" word in tourism destination management, catching theoretical and practice opportunities derived from new kind of concept and of enriched tourism destination (and not only) interpretation, permitted by a specific and well applied marketing also in tourism destination (and so on) management.

This paper introduces and proposes (for destination and other connected words of tourism management) an enlargement of the too strictly interpreted and practiced destination "attractiveness" concept (like for a lot of related ones), by focusing on new very important systemic marketing configuration to ameliorate tourism destination management at all [4].

The paper proposes here new concepts, various neologisms and new ways to use innovatively, combined, revised and enlarged D.O. – Destination binomial and other words by a really, innovative systemic marketing point of view.

A successful marketing is very important for results in services like tourism and in destination management [5]. In destination management (and partially in tourism management at all), is more difficult to build, to maintain and to increase loyalty. So a lot of important and partially new tools and concepts of marketing must be applied. A lot of traditionally conceived and practiced concepts in tourism (and in destination management strictly related to various "moment of truth" for the consumer - client related [6] [7]), must be revised in a larger and incisive marketing perspective. In services and in the tourism industry a different and increasing competition [8] implies a specific review of words and approaches, with emphasis on new marketing. In destination management large opportunities are catching not only with a good knowledge of social media mechanisms [8]. In addition, consumer-client must be also better profiled and knew [9] [10], to assume a larger and precise consumer view, also in (consumer oriented) destination management [11] .

2. The Application of Real, "Total Attractiveness" in Destination Management and in Tourism with Effective and Specific New Systemic Marketing

In tourism an excessive attention is paid on destination as (not enlarged) "product" (or set of products), too restrictively interpreted, and without full referring to (final) consumer-client at all. It is also necessary to study very well "consumer-customer" perception [12] and determinants of consumer and customer satisfaction [13] with more attention to market segmentation [14], and to consider also in tourism management and destination management a really "consumer centric" implementation as in various btoc sectors [15]. It is yet weak a "customer' value" based management not conforming to a new incisive marketing [16]. It is not sufficient to accept concepts like "multiple score card" or "multiple score", involved in measurement of "attractiveness" in the case of consumer oriented tourism management [17]

In "destination and tourism management" excessive focus is on dominant indirect channels (and btob -business to business- approaches). We normally can find a too low attention to consumer and to btoc. approach, also in the current era of internet, web, social network and e-commerce. Very interesting new opportunities can derive from a real, impacting shift to completely and correctly consumer oriented view, also enlarging attractiveness' attributes including shopping and complementary experiences.

From theoretical and practical points of observation, attractiveness (for consumer), not in limited and restricted version, must be interpreted and practiced as S.A.W.A: "Systemic Articulated Whole Attractiveness" for the consumer .

Real "total attractiveness for consumer" is very different from a generic attractiveness or from attractiveness in strategic tongue, of course. In Tourism Management it is not sufficient to generically consider consumer' satisfaction related to a "multifaceted analysis" [18].

In addition, real "total attractiveness" (for the consumer) cannot be confused with partial and generic appealing of limited tourist product or (restricted) destination offering. Primarily, real "total attractiveness" must be considered from the (able of multiple perception) consumer - final customer point of view and interpreted in relation with specific and very impacting multi–polyhedric "responses" [19] to the consumer (in btoc). The complete set of every relevant (and well perceived) component [20] (able to increase benefit for consumer and -possibly in co-valuing- value for consumer), must be considered and activated [21][22][23].

Not a generic or partial attractiveness [24][25][26] but the (perceived, well evaluated and appreciated by final consumer or final customer) real "total attractiveness" must be considered also in Tourism[27], within the entire (of the single locus or site, land and so on) perspective of systemic marketing configuration, also applied in (well and specifically consumer oriented)tourism management.

Assuming the whole systemic marketing configuration perspective, restricted attractiveness [28][29][30] is substituted by an enlarged, really "total attractiveness" (of destination and so on) referred to the final consumer –customer[31][32].

This SAWA (Systemic and Articulated Whole Attractiveness) for consumer-customer, depends on the power of a lot of total complete differentiations that must referred to new enlarged interpretation and (not generically treated and structured) practice of destination, finally included into a real correct and impacting whole systemic marketing configuration.

"total complete differentiation" and (not only related to enlarged destination itself) SAWA are rarely (and not partially) referred to (and involved into) an effective tourism management for a lot of reasons. Including limited orientation to the final consumer (in btoc) and too restricted conception (like a too restricted good or product in other fields) of destination itself. Frequently in tourism destination (and in tourism field at all), attention is strictly paid to (too dominant) big customer (like wholesaler), called tour operators and similar (all included in over evaluated btob approaches) new kinds of intermediate (customer) firms, able to buy bulky or in big volume (with effects on load factor in accomodation field, and so on).

In addition, normally in (old styled) destination management, involved sender firms or D.O. involved are private and not private simultaneously. We can find (in a lot of Countries like Italy): APT, Communities (like City Government and so on) and other normally not private organizations by one side, and large number of strictly small private and family firms (like in Adriatic part of Italy) by the other side.

Rarely these providers act as effective (Systemic Marketing oriented) real "destinators" (our neologism for "sender" into D.O.) well connected in really incisive, aggressive co-marketing (private, not private and mixed). Consequently, rarely these (normally weak) provider organizations (as new revised and enlarged D.O. related to a incisive DOM-Destination Organization Management) are in position to first of all consider, as very important basic and direct target, specifically the final consumer and "consumer bases", like the core of Management approach supported by (really) systemic marketing.

When btoc is really involved like primary or fundamental focus in destination (and other parts of) tourism management, it is frequently possible to reach increased (not only as sales or gross margin) results by activating articulated, composite, advanced, effective, real and very important concepts and tools of systemic marketing configuration.

This (not exclusive in basic btoc) marketing configuration implies a starting definition (referred to a strong integration of two primary kind of co-valuers) of real competition subjects (single private firm itself, or similar not private like community, city, town, consortium and so on, with partner or not) acting as D.D. (Destinator-Destinatari) related to, at the same time, revised Destination (not confused with normal product or various products itself) : "Destinator" ("Tank" for consumer), and very important "Addressees" ("Destinatari") consumers (that can be also reached by web and so on). Incisive D.D. is different from traditional and normal D.O. "Destinator" (also inspiring and driving revised and enlarged Destination) and related, involved "Addressees" ("Destinatari") act as a new impacting D.D., reinforced by specific systemic marketing tools and transformed in a generator of effective "responses" that continuously can "re-define" and ameliorate a not simple (in too strict sense or not completely consumer oriented) destination. Enlarged (for specific final consumers-customers) effective attractions are activated simultaneously by both related "Destinators" "and "Destinatari" that in co-valuing and through B.B. (Bunch and Blend) launch various integrated sets of incisive attributes (and similar ones) perceived as advantage, benefit and value from involved consumers.

These incisive and important sets of (consumer oriented in a broad sense) "Responses" (referring to enlarged destinations) can power and increase significance and effects of a (very) composite attractiveness (and differentiation) not more by traditional (and only polygonal) destination marketing mixes, but, in the current different era, by putting on composite arena new (not polygonal) aggregates.

Now, very effective addictions (for the consumer-customer) depend on the launch (by D.D.) of revised, enlarged set of various so called polyhedric blend and bunch compositions (to be considered as very different from polygonal mixes!).

In an interesting number of increasing situations, by systemic marketing, impacting D.D. (including "Destinators") can arrange (also for enlarged, enriched destination) a lot of (simultaneous) blend compositions (directly for the final consumers and "consumer bases" in btoc tourism) primarily as:

Blend of (total) propositions (also for destination in large sense) involving every kind of combined attractive components, integrated in various effective case, also in propositioning blend;

Blend of (primary) brands like Crans Montana, or Tuscany, or "Dolomiti Ski" and so on;

Blend of specific (but not already branded), "offerings" (like specific services) and complementary "packages" (of multiple services like: parking, travel, car, ski pass and so on).

In fact, various real and not restricted attractiveness (connected largely to various multiple complete differentiations) can be increased and impact (on value production by the firm or similar subject) by new total differentiations not only referred to (in the strictest sense of the word, and rarely branded) destination, when (single or combined) D.D. and primarily "Destinators" are perfectly and directly connected with "Addressees" ("Destinatari") or in btoc well defined and profiled consumer bases. These are different from not alternative and various "Wholesaler" like tour operator and so on and can be also interested by a lot of well articulated (and polyhedric, multi-shaped) blend (different from normal polygonal mixes or P's and normally with five or similar number of components). In addition and at upper level, D.D. and primarily "Destinators" can ameliorate or increase results by activating and using various aggregations of (normally five or similar) versions of marketing in single bunch ("Grappoli"). Every bunch simultaneously involves for example incisive whole PRM (Persumer Relationship Marketing), ECM (Experience Consumer Marketing), and so on.

In every successful D.D. (and D.D.O. different from not consumer oriented D.O.) and destination situation, various articulated (in set of five) and effective combinations are involved as blend (like proposition an so on) eventually integrated by various single upper bunches ("Grappoli") of marketing versions; both are included into the entire (launched by one or more firm or subject) systemic marketing configuration, with important impact on consumers' behavior and satisfaction.

In effective D.D., both (well structured by real various set of systemic marketing) Blend and Bunch (B.-B.) are able to increase power and impact of "responses " (to consumers) not only of single (in too restrict sense of word) destinations, to be enlarged, differentiated and related like Destinators, with activation of a number of "set" of various, new and innovative concepts and words. Important "Addressees" ("Destinatari") and active "Destinators" (marketing' subjects that interact with "Addressees" in two ways) are related and via B.B increase also effect of one or more (not interpreted with too strict thickness) destination.

Then, real, complete and not reduced attractiveness (for consumer), also in (btoc) tourism (management) by incisive D.D., can be activated (also by B.-B.) as a very articulated and important word. It can be interpreted, increased and enlarged with intensive impact on consumer and on value production, if treated by a real, advanced and complete Systemic Marketing Configuration at all ,applied to mentioned D.D. and related B.B. Enlarged significance and intense impact of attractiveness can be reached with a set of important (new) concept really, correctly and completely understood and applied also to tourism management, and specifically to innovative D.D. (using B.B. as a lot of various set) and to a revised, improved destination (and tourism) management, without mistakes, partiality, or mutilations and so on.

First, also every (potential) destination, in effective systemic marketing configuration, must be simultaneously referred to "Destinator" and to (correctly profiled, targeted and involved also in two-fold approach) "Destinatari" or final consumer. To get increased results, a lot a of various combinations (upper than normal polygonal marketing mixes) can be activated as various polyhedric blend, completed, in largely effective D.D., by bunch ("Grappoli") of various marketing versions (in the same D.D. organization, or firm or enlarged "Destinator" subject) .

Also (well interpreted and enlarged as significance and impact using new systemic marketing' tools) new destinations can be consider linked to D.D., a new kind of enlarged (with real, strong consumer orientation) DOM as (Marketing) "Destinator" involving enlarged Destination of a specific subject (Old Town, Large City, Touristic region, Typical Location and so on) involved. In new innovative and effective D.D., destination can be consider, in a lot of successful cases, differently related with "Destinator" itself and as (strong) real brand, or used and reinforced by a single (or combined) very incisive "Destinator". In large number of specific cases, (single) destination can or could be transformed into an "attractive" (by incisive systemic marketing) proposition or other important blends, to be completed also by various bunches in very incisive "Destinator" and D.D. .

So, new binomial D.D. (and related blend and bunch , both reinforcing brand effects) can be innovatively considered and activated with a right application of systemic marketing (configuration) at all. "Destinator" and "Destinatari" must be exactly and effectively combined in a new D.D. (able to activate blend and bunch) construct, to reach more and more results in consumer oriented (btoc) Destination (and tourism) management, open to innovative systemic marketing

In a number of cases, (real) larger and more impacting attractiveness (for the consumer) of destinations also derives from a (set of) bunch ("Grappoli") including simultaneously various specific (and well composed) versions of marketing. Every primary strong (consumer oriented and Persumer- our neologism meaning Person/Consumer-involving) brunch is a enlarged combination, for example, of exciting (for targeted consumers) various marketing: experiential one, plus relational one, plus inter-active-web one [33][34][35], plus other specific versions of marketing (all included into the whole systemic marketing of a specific D.D. Configuration) activated by one or more (also related in consortium and so on) D.D. organization (well structured also as strong, consumer oriented, "Destinators" involving in co-valuing "Destinatari" and not only Destination, acting as consumer oriented D.D.D.O.) .

A real, full, intensive orientation (also through incisive brand) to final consumer (and similarly to customer-stakeholder) implies D.D.(and D.D.D.O.) and relates simultaneously various intensive, effective B.B. (a lot of eventually Branded Blend and Bunch or B.B.B. sets), including impacting Bunch, in order to (for example in leisure btoc) increase results also by synergic marketing sets of combined wishing , emotional, educational ,entertaining[36] experiential[37] and addictive (perceived) effects with amelioration of consequent (and articulated) value for D.D. (and D.D.O.M ,evolution of DOM) and for final consumer in (btoc) tourism[38].

3. Results and Discussion

This paper presents a new, named dual D.D.-B.B., configuration and approach, useful to get more (by consumer) results through increasing (in term of differentiation) impact also of enlarged (by a really systemic marketing perspective) real (whole, total, complete) attractiveness (for the consumer). Paper specifically proposes a lot of neologisms, concepts and articulated constructs, included into a new Multi-polyhedric (Systemic Marketing) Approach (or MSMA) to increase attractiveness for the consumer and to build a more up graded-up dated destination (btoc and consumer oriented) and tourism management .

Particularly, this paper focuses innovative, relevant (in btoc tourism management) and strictly related D.D. and B.B. double binomial, both with set of various (really and completely consumer oriented) upper, superior and effective multiple-polyhedric combinations of revised, enlarged and impacting concepts like D.D. (and D.D.O.M., important evolution of usual DOM) are effectively involving: impacting (for consumer) "Destinator" and "Destinatari" both transforming (incisively revised, enlarged and really ant totally consumer oriented) "Destination", and both to be treated in a really new systemic marketing configuration' perspective. A real and exact deduction of "overall perception" referred to consumer (and not only to the customer at all), can ameliorated and upgraded not only enlarged impressive Proposition. The whole entirely consumer oriented combination of (eventually sustained also by suppliers in a network) really effective "Destinators" (Organization, and Partners, not only single firm or similar) and "Destinatari" both referring to enlarged (also as systemic marketing concept and total systemic brand) destination, and both as effective binomial, can ameliorate impact and overall benefits for consumer and results for D.D. (and related network as D.D.O) using a lot of various (potentially simultaneously) new (consumer oriented) tools : double B. or B.B.. In other words: Blend and Bunch primarily, eventually combined with brand (in a specific B.B.B. related to D.D.D.)

Interesting results are coming now not only from a lot of experiments and activations involving in specific multidimensional compositions of B.B related to composite D.D. of the Destinator pool, including simultaneously organization (of one or more firms and/or similar ones) and destination with a synergic orientation to consumer (as involved "Destinatari") in a D.D.D enlarged systemic marketing configuration, correctly applied to tourism management and to (enlarged, enriched) destination management. To increase results also a complete, effective activation of a complex, articulated co-valuing is needed and depends on a lot of important components .

It's important that two articulated lots of sets of decisions work effectively. First, at blend and bunch levels (of effective D.D. involving sometimes consumers in a D.D.D. or in enlarge co-valuing) also (really integrated into "Destinator" Pool) revised destination must be conceived and launched not only as brand, supported by various other basic attributes. Destination must be reinforced by and included in various specific consumer bases oriented blend [38].

Effective D.D. (Firm as focus of Destinator pool, destination and partners), can also activate various set of bunch (in other words: various combined marketing versions simultaneously directed to "consumer bases") in addition to mentioned various sets of blends, activated as proposition, propositioning, "offering" and so on, to increase power of impact on targeted (and involved) "consumer bases", not only via web tools. It's now possible to enlarge and reinforce also destination, powered as brand[39] and blend simultaneously. Furthermore, real D.D. (consumer oriented organization as mentioned "pool" including reinforced consumer focused destination) can be activated as a set of various very effective bunch, blend and brand at all.

With this multiple innovating, complete and effective (Systemic Marketing) D.D. (and eventually upgraded D.D.D.) approach, "attractiveness" for consumer, can strongly enriched, more as usual, to largely impact on targeted (and involved eventually in co-valuing) consumer (bases). This real, reinforced "attractiveness" (for the consumer and "consumer bases" as final customer-client) increases differentiation and power of D.D. (the pool and similar ones), by blending and eventually by enlarging effects of one or more bunches of versions of marketing, directly referred to various sets of related consumers and consumer bases. In one or more bunches can be also included PRM or effective consumer relationship marketing, more effective that generic CRM. In addition, mentioned bunch can simultaneously include a really effective web marketing. It can add also a specific intensive and incisive experiential marketing and eventually green-social marketing in a perspective of high level of highly involving systemic marketing [38].

It's interesting to discuss about these important upgrading in management by applying mentioned advanced multiple systemic marketing approach. This approach might be used by an important share of revised destination correctly included in mentioned "Destinator' Pool"(as D.D., eventually working as D.D.D.). We suppose that various problems occur sometimes. Culture, and marketing experience are important and enter into discussion.

A declining part of normal D.O. is still resistant to became rapidly and effectively D.D.O.M including mentioned really and effectively consumer oriented "Destinator' Pool". Perception of risk and too binding efforts are still high in a declining portion of specific situations. For a declining number of traditional D.O. or firms,, a complete btoc D.D.-B.B. approach probably remains too difficult if btob business and approaches are exclusively or primary preferred. For primary part of resisting D.O. it is by now typical to continue to go via (normally dominant) btob and to start with testing of web Marketing activities to final consumer. By now it is finally increasing the portion of D.O. and firms that combine new btoc channel with traditional and dominant indirect channels (btob) to reduce or to avoid perceived complexity (and related costs).The number of unchanging D.O. that prefer to ensure and to get "sure" occupation (and similar) rate (not only in accommodation part of offering and so on) is declining at all.

Incoming private, "pool" and firm, really or sufficiently convinced and open to become real, effective D.D (also using B.B.) can rapidly remove last doubts and initiate a progressive change in btoc to (inspired by systemic marketing configuration) D.D.-B.B. approach. So, in our opinion, the main question is not related to percentage of total sales (of DOM) that can pass through direct channel (not only at web level) versus indirect channels of single (revised) D.O.

4. Conclusions

Progressive and open DOM and D.O. (firm and Pool) can by now accept the new role of "Destinator" (in Pool) and D.D.(involving in D.D.D new enlarged Destination really and totally consumer oriented) and can correctly use B.B.(or B.B.B.), also under the pressure by large btob customer-client, also to reduce dependence by (otherwise) increasing dominance of Indirect Channels . Big (additional) value opportunities can be caught if Brand power [39] and other Differentiation components can be (through B.B. and Branding also) used and increased by "Destinators" (into private Pool primarily). Impressive new Systemic Marketing tools and concepts like Blend and Bunch , in addition to Brand, can rapidly improve the normal strength and experience (of D.O.) to accelerate not only "Destination Equity" increase, also by ameliorating effects of large number of related (and well perceived and appreciated by consumer) attributes of Brands , through new Proposition et cetera.

The evolution and increase of web and e- Commerce in Tourism Management, it is not sufficient , to large part of (small and old styled) btob oriented Destination without (potential) strong presence of consumer centric "Destinator" (and D.D.O).

Like in other fields and sectors, it is important to accelerate (also at not private level), the (too backward) D.O. and DOM Education about new word like D.D. and primary Blend and Bunch , without forgetting that it is important to ameliorate also Brand power through D.D.-B.B. Systemic Marketing multi polyhedric approach . It is necessary to insist on a different powered (for consumer) "Attractiveness" built with a lot of related and specific aggregates not only like new Proposition. We need an implementation conforming to other sectors' primary btoc benchmark, obviously considering specificities of Tourism and Tourism Destination . Not only to reinforce "Brand equity" [40] by revised Proposition and other related concepts D.D-B.B. (and upper D.D.D. –B.B.B.) approach, related concepts and mentioned words and neologisms ,can be activated as unavoidable and urgent or , for prudent "Destinators", as complementary process for the growth[41].

References

[1] G.M. Golinelli, "Viable System Approach (VSA). Governing Business Dynamics". Padova: CEDAM, 2010.

[2] D. Buhalis, "Marketing the competitive destination in the future", Tourism Management, Vol. 21, No. 1, 2000, pp. 97-116.

[3] D. Das Gupta, Tourism Marketing, New Dehli: Dorling Kindersley, 2011.

[4] J. Bowen, and S. Shoemaker, "Loyalty: a strategic commitment", Cornell Hotel and Restaurant and Administration Quarterly, Vol. 39, No. 1, 1998, pp.12-25

[5] C.H. Lovelock, and J. Wirtz, Services Marketing, 7th Edition. Upper Saddle River: Prentice Hall, 2011.

[6] R. Normann, Service Management, 2nd Edition. Chichester, UK: John Wiley & Sons, 1991.

[7] J. Carlzon, Moments of Truth. Cambridge, Ma: Ballinger, 1987.

[8] M.D. Johnson, and A. Gustafsson, Competing in a Service Economy. San Francisco: Jossey-Bass, 2003.

[9] J. Lovett, Social Media Metrics Secrets, Indianapolis: Wiley, 2011.

[10] S .Lee, LAGarrow,JA Higbie,K.P Keskinscak and D.KoushiK, "Do you really know who your customers are?", Journal of Revenue and Pricing Management, Vol 10, No 1, pp.73-86, 2011)

[11] J.M. Riddell, "Adopting a customer view", Journal of Revenue and Pricing Management, Vol. 5, No 2, 2011, pp 167-179.

[12] K.V. Rohlfs, and S.E. Kimes, "Customers' Perceptions of best available hotel rates", Cornell Hotel and Restaurant Administration Quarterly, Vol. 48, No 2, pp. 151-162, 2007.

[13] D.E Severt, and P.D. Rompf, "Consumers' perceptions of fairness and the resultant effect on customer satisfaction, Journal of Hospitality Marketing & Management, Vol. 15, No. 1, 2006, pp.101-121.

[14] D. Shapiro, X. Shi, "Market segmentation: the role of opaque travel agencies", Journal of Economics & Management Strategy, Vol 17, No. 4, 2008, pp. 803-837.

[15] B. Vinod, "The continuing evolution: Customer-centric revenue management", Journal of Revenue and Pricing Management, Vol. 7, No. 1, 2008, pp. 27-39.

[16] C. H. Gearing, and W.W. Swart,"Establishing a measure of touristic attractiveness", Journal of Travel Research, Vol. 12, No. 4, pp 1-8, 1974.

[17] T. von Martens, and A. Hilbert,"Customer-value-based revenue management", Journal of Revenue and Pricing Management, Vol. 10 , No. 1, pp. 87-97, 2011.

[18] J.D. Neal, D. Gursay, "A multifaceted analysis of tourism satisfaction", Journal of Travel Research, Vol. 47, No1, 2008, pp 53-62.

[19] E. Gummesson, Total Relationship Marketing. Oxford: Butterworth-Heinemann-Elsevier, 2002.

[20] F. Pollice, and F. Spagnuolo, "Attrattività e sostenibilità: una lettura congiunta per lo sviluppo turistico locale", Turismo e Psicologia, No. 2, 2009, pp. 57-79.

[21] J.P. Valls, J .Sureda, and G. Valls-Tuñon, "Attractiveness analysis of European tourist cities", Journal of Travel & Tourism Marketing, Vol. 31, No. 2, 2014, pp. 178-194.

[22] N.I. Danko, and H.V Dovhal, "Creation of the tourist cluster as a way of increase of investment attractiveness of a region", Problems of Economy, Vol. 4, No. 2, 2013, pp. 212-218.

[23] S. Formica, and M. Uysal, "Destination attractiveness based on supply and demand evaluations: an analytical framework.", Journal of Travel Research, Vol. 44, No. 4, 2006, pp. 418-430.

[24] S.F. Philipp, and F. Steven, "Racial differences in the perceived attractiveness of tourism destinations, interests, and...", Journal of Leisure Research , Vol. 25, No. 3, 1993, pp. 279- 290.

[25] Y. Hu, S. Ritchie, and J.R. Brent, "Measuring destination attractiveness: A contextual approach.", Journal of Travel Research, Vol. 32, No. 2, 1993, p. 25.

[26] S. Vengesayi, A Conceptual Model of Tourism Destination Competitiveness and Attractiveness, University of South Australia, 2003.

[27] C. E. Gearing, W.W. Swart, and T. Var ,"Establishing a measure of touristic attractiveness", Journal of Travel Research, Vol. 12, No. 4 , 1974, pp. 1-8.

[28] L. Andries van der Ark, and G. Richards, "Attractiveness of cultural activities in European cities: A latent class approach", Tourism Management, Vol. 27, No. 6, 2006, pp 1408–1413.

[29] S. Masson, and R. Petiot, "Can the high speed rail reinforce tourism attractiveness? The case of the high speed rail between Perpignan (France) and Barcelona (Spain)", Technovation, Vol. 29, No. 9, 2009, pp. 611–617.

[30] M.F. Cracolici, and P. Nijkamp, "The attractiveness and competitiveness of tourist destinations: A study of Southern Italian regions", Tourism Management, Vol. 30, No. 3, 2009, pp 336–344.

[31] H.H. Wang, "Traveling attraction analysis and theoretical model", Science, Economy, Society, Vol. 21, No. 4, 2003, pp. 44-47.

[32] Q. Li, G.N. Sun, and Y.F. Han, "matrix analysis of inbound tourism resources and location attraction of 31 provinces of China," Journal of Arid Land Resources and Environment, Vol. 22, No. 5 2009, ,pp. 101-106.

[33] L. Vaughan, and G. Wu, "Links to commercial websites as a source of business information", Scientometrics, Vol. 60, No. 3, 2004, pp.487-496.

[34] R. Baggio, M.A. Corigliano, and V. Tallinucci, "The websites of a tourism destination: a network analysis," In 14th International Conference on Information Technology and Travel & Tourism, Ljubljana, Slovenia, 2007, pp. 279-287.

[35] R. Baggio, N. Scott, and Z. Wang, "What network analysis of the WWW can tell us about the organization of tourism destinations", in 17th Annual Conference of the Council for Australian University Tourism and Hospitality education (CAUTHE), 2007 Sydney, Australia.

[36] L.N. Qi, Y. Zhang, and B.H. Wu, L.L.Song, "Research on the measurement of the impact of a mega-event on the awareness of tourism attractions in host city", Acta Scientiarum Naturalium Universitatis Pekinensis, Vol.45, No. 6, 2007, pp.1061-106.

[37] [37] B.J. Pine, and J.H. Gilmore, "Welcome to the experience economy",Harvard Business Review, Vol. 76, No 4 1998, pp.97-108.

[38] A. Marino, Systemic Marketing in Outstanding Firms in BtoC. Bergamo: Bergamo University Press, 2014.

[39] L.L. Berry, "Cultivating service brand equity", Journal of Academy of Marketing Science, Vol. 28, No. 1, 2000, pp. 128-137.

[40] D.A. AAker, Building Strong Brand. New York: The Free Press, 1996.

[41] T. Levitt, Marketing for Business Growth". NewYork: McGraw, 1987.

The Relationship Between Social Bearing Capacities with Conflict as a Result, in the Perception of the Visiting Historical Sites

Fatemeh Mirzaie[1,*], Ali Akbar Nazari[2], Hamid Zargham Boroujeni[3], Mohammad Taghipour[4]

[1]Tourism Management, Non-profit Institution of Higher Education, ABA, Abyek, Qazvin, Iran
[2]Administrator of Non-profit Institution of Higher Education, ABA, Abyek, Qazvin, Iran
[3]Department of Tourism Management, Allameh Tabatabaie University, Tehran, Iran
[4]Research Assistant of Non-profit Institution of Higher Education, ABA, Abyek, Qazvin, Iran

Email address:
Fatemehmirzaie.ar@gmail.com (F. Mirzaie), dr.aliakbarnazary@yahoo.com (A. A. Nazari), drzargham@ymail.com (H. Z. Boroujeni), mohamad.taghipour@srbiau.ac.ir (M. Taghipour)

Abstract: Sustainable tourism needs to prevent the destruction and degradation of social, cultural and ecological systems in the host society. It is obvious that tourism development and social characteristics is changing. But this (whether positive or negative), and severity of these changes depend on the size and number of tourism activities. Any destinations accept specific level of tourism development that further development leads of the socio-cultural decline or reduce the quality of experience for tourists. On the other hand, tourists are faced with a conflict that already is not expect it And. This time the satisfaction of tourists decreased. The host society has a certain capacity for growth and development of tourism particularly hosting is in the monument with a rich history and ancient values. This requires attention to its own dimensions. In Iran, there are a few studies that examine factors affecting the perceived congestion are by foreign visitors. The aim of this study is to identify the concept of conflict and reaction to foreign visitors comes to this conflict. For this research data in holiday 1394 through questionnaires and interviews were collected by field. The populations of the investigation are foreign tourists visiting the palace complex. Data were analyzed using descriptive statistics inferential. The results of the analysis of 100 questionnaires showed that 5's variable were effective on the perception of foreign tourists: history of visiting, Expected crowding, Tensions and physical contact, behavior of other visitors, the number of other visitor.

Keywords: Conflict, Social Carrying Capacity, Congestion Perceived Quality Views, Niyavaran Palace

1. Introduction

History of the effects of the increased use on quality entertainment experience, return after the Second World War The history of the study on carrying capacity as an entrepreneurial approach in the area outing return in the 1930 .The concept of carrying capacity due to increasing concerns about the negative effects of tourism studies came in tourism. According to this concept , came to a head in the 1960s and 1970s, and that was when the growth of a recreational center in the United States increased concerns about the use of a variety of recreational activities in place. (Getz, 1983)

As we expected, the relationship between usage and environmental conditions were considered. It was assumed that increasing use is causing more environmental impacts. Some effects were measured like soil compaction, destruction of vegetation, amortization of buildings and other related variables. But it soon became clear that there is another dimension of capacity dealing with the social aspects of the experience of visitors (Manning, 1997; Manning et al., 2002). The researchers found that increasing the number of visitors' affect not only environmental resource location, but also the quality of the experience of visitors.

The concept of carrying capacity has many definitions, but all these definitions are two common denominator: First, the biophysical factors that are associated with the integration of resource-based aspects and emphasized on threshold or tolerance levels that after the operation or use higher pressures may impose on natural ecosystems Second, behavioral component that shows the quality of the recreational experience. The importance of quality will be doubled Views. Of course, the tourists before choosing their destination obtain information about it and next choose it. So gathering information led to a mental image of the destination. Conflict in tourism occurs when tourists are faced with a situation that is different from what had been on his mind. . If the saturation of tourism development happened, may be the attractions fail and hurt where tourists want to experience them,. Gradually destination loses the quality and popularity. . For example, one of the most common issues that tourists who want to visit historic sites is a conflict, is the waiting time. Before entering the site Visitors often have thought about the antiquities, historical objects dating back to the set and so on. And have made mental image about that. But on arrival at the sight lines crowded with face with duality, and this duality will be even greater after entering and seeing internal congestion. This duality is called conflict. here Conflict is between the mental image of tourists and tourism products, in reality the difference between actual waiting time waiting time expected by visitors by visitors. Standards determining the capacity in relation to tourist image are the following:

2. Theoretical Foundations of Research

Tourist's social carrying capacity, representing the maximum number of tourists and a variety of activities in one place that they don't make unacceptable experience. Therefore, experience quality management of visitors is one of the functional aspects of social carrying capacity in tourism. Altman says:"conflict occurs when visitors experience some situation and compare them with their perception of what is acceptable (standard) and if they feel crowd, the visit won't be successful (Altman. 2009).

Most in 2005 in his article that said every man to see things and focus directly on the object stare.

If we consider the intersection point of the along of that and the subject, there will be a point that human focus is placed on that. He mentioned to the point purpose because he wanted to say of historical tourist focus on something more than recreation and enjoyment, and it is experience and knowledge with the incentive of information about historical reality, they have chosen their favorite place. Earning new knowledge makes a different situation from just entertainment experience. Host community has a certain capacity for the development of quality tourism. Particularly host is a monument with a rich history and ancient values. This requires attention to all its dimensions.

Conflict is one major source of stress and dissatisfaction accordingly. Tension makes conflict that usually has three categories. Miller considers them in 1959 thus:

1) Conflict pleasant / pleasant: conflict is in the result of two incompatible positions, but pleasant to be created. For example, people who travel to participate in special festivals and see overcrowding, although experiencing causes internal conflict, but they usually can solve this type of conflict, easily. While they pay expeditions, they enjoy, too. They will have more excitement when they see more size of the congestion; they think this event is more important.

2) Conflict unpleasant / unpleasant: struggle creates in the result of already imagination and unpleasant situation. For example, those who suffer serious illness and may have to travel for treatment, they see bustle in different parts of the reception and treatment, so they think it's a very unpleasant situation. Those who fall into this situation, try to find a better solution and often hesitant between some selection. They express Discontent and to others are persecutions, because of them. Unpleasant / unpleasant situations are stressful for most people and difficult to be solved. Because there are many different between their previously thought of what is seen and perceived.

3) Conflict unpleasant / pleasant: there are both features pleasant and unpleasant when happens a in a location. This type of conflict is unpleasant and may be resolve difficultly. For example, people who want to visit all the objects and works in an ancient place see everything with great precision and patience. They may want to improve their information, at the same time want to avoid wasting the time of them and others and visit a museum without fatigue or block routes, and person is in a position that does not satisfy the interests and demands. But he knows the cause of this failure return to external factors such as other visitors, officials, and a small space..... . In fact, it can be said that this is the most complex conflict because the adverse effects of this type of conflict would be more damaging for tourism. As a person with previously thought, has the objectives and pre-determined programs to achieve their goal, but the after attending in the environment, goals failed or are in a position to unacceptable. There are many differences in the perception of the crowd of people and everything that are in the environment and this is an important issue and effective on the conflict. Theorists believe that congestion depends on our understanding of the position. Patterson (1976) believes that congestion can occur when people experience arousal due to the very close vicinity with others. Other researchers confirmed this statement and say that the documents proved that there are something more in a collection that can reduce congestion experience (Vrshl and Astrsvn, 1978) The using of social comparison theory, Baum, Fischer and Salomon (1981) believe that having the right information before the destination, especially about the time of the visit, about situations with high density can reduce stress and Discontent of congestion. When people are constantly exposed to environmental stimuli are identified, adaptation is one of the ways to change the perception of these stimuli (Vlvyl, 1974). For example, a person who has prepared to visit from morning, after attending in a tourist collection and seeing the congestion at the entrance, he waits, in the queue like others. . After entering the collection and encountering congestion and noise during circulation even physical contact and conflict with others, it may appear a loud and Unacceptable noise, at the beginning. But it will be

uniform soon and it will be more mindfulness. So unpleasant environmental factors may be more intense for newcomers and they are more annoying for them. Despite Our ability to adaptation our perceptions with new environments, surely we are not safe from their effects, even after the source is removed Discontent. . We call it "subsequent undesirable effects". In one experiment, the participants were taken to a quiet room. Those already were in a noisy environment, unpredictable and uncontrollable noise; they were underperformed in editing the text (Glass Vsygr, 1972.123). Of course there are other factors that affect people, especially tourists and play an important role in adaptation. It is community's culture. In general Culture contains social factors, individual and situational assessments from density by visitors. The fact is that criteria are different from each of culture to another culture. The definition of privacy is different in various places. For example, German tourists have limits for the presence of strangers. But an Arab tourist he did not define it the same. He could even be at a distance of less than a meter with a group of strangers to sit and have lunch. The different reactions return to education, the environment, education, customs and culture of each country. Because of ethnic and tribal life and group life Arabs accept presence of others easier than those who see culture and their life not this way. Generally, when people feel conflict, total individual satisfaction begins to reduce and final suitability will be negative. This shows that the total number of tourists on the site is more than numbers that can be tolerated, which led to the failure of visitors and dissatisfied in the end. Failure happens when they look for a certain purpose but face with, an obstacle frustrated. For example, traffic is a normal source failure that can affect people's frustration. Of course, most of them are short-term failures and less important but some failures will be of great concern, in the field of tourism. Particularly Feedback of tourist s experience is the best advertisement for inviting more tourists to destination. In fact, a tourist destination stays with tourist's satisfaction and reflects of the satisfaction. This is more important when it sends out of bounds of a country and it happens with consent of the foreign tourists. Thus, the researchers went for knowing further about variables that people exposure them in high density sites. we Often call it "the evaluation index" (Weaver, 2010, p. 14). According to studies, conflict and the subsequent discontent comes from several factors. Generally, when a few people or a few units require the use of certain resources to achieve a shared goal, there will be possibility of conflict especially if it is rare.

It can be concluded that the e historical sites are scarce resources; In addition, factors such as internal control, staff, how to enter and exit, facilities and infrastructure, pricing, tips and brochures are not enough. There are other external factors that effect on the management of the collections and they are usually hidden from view of managers.

3. Research Methodology

The aim of this study is practical, it is a field survey in terms of how survey data collection, the method of data analysis is descriptive. It is cross-sectional in terms of time research. The study population was foreign tourists. In this study, random sampling or available was used and a questionnaire was used as a measurement tool. at the beginning we gave the questionnaire to visitors who agreed to complete it and we asked that they answer questions and return the questionnaire to the researcher after the meeting and before leaving the site. To increase the validity of the questionnaire, it confirmed by professors and experts. Finally, in the period of research, 107 questionnaires were completed, which, 100 questionnaires could be analyzed. The time span of this study was the first to thirteenth April 1394. Vesk and Hebrelyn suggested a relatively simple that shows the perceived congestion of people in the crowded the site. They have to choose one number from 1 to 9 to show amount of crowded that they felt. The range of responses 1 and 2 show that the site was not crowded at all, answers 3 and 4 show a little congestion, 5 to 7 shows that the average congestion and 8 and 9 show overcrowding. . Responding to this range is easy and interpreting is easier and so far in several studies is used to assess the perceived congestion. In this study, the perceived congestion was assessed in 3 point of Site (the entrance, the interior, surrounding areas and external). In addition, tourists answered g affecting variables on conflict and the relationship of these variables with perceived crowding was measured. In order to analyze the data, SPSS software was used. The data were analyzed by using descriptive statistics, t-test for independent samples, analysis of variance (ANOVA) and correlation analysis.

3.1. The Study Area

(Historical-cultural complex)Niyavaran is located in the northern parts of Tehran and is located on the slopes of the Alborz mountain range, near the height of 1800 meters above sea level. This is surrounded with 12 hectares and has a total of appropriate vegetation and green space. This collection has a steep gradient from north to south. Uneven topography due to a variety of location of buildings that multiple variations of green space are to be formed. Since we have to consider this area of tourism and history itself, because it is very sensitive and fragile sites and has great historical value to the development of tourism. From this perspective study results will help the management and planning and the relevant authorities.

3.2. The Results

-Perceived crowding

This chart shows the breakdown of responses to the perceived congestion frequency on the whole 9 options. Average total crowding has provided in a three-point of site. People had to choose from 1 to 9 for showing the crowding. According to the theoretical foundations, Niyavaran will be set in the range of average busy.

Table 1. The breakdown of responses to the perceived congestion frequency.

maximum	minimum	Change rang	variance	standard deviation	face	median	average	Perceived crowding
9	2	2.50	5.35	7.16	5.00	5.00	3.07	Outer space palaces
9	1	5.00	5.00	1.21	1.49	5.00	5.00	Entry routes
9	2	7.00	3.16	6.33	5.49	6.00	6.00	Interior Museum space

This chart shows the breakdown of responses to the perceived frequency crowding on the whole 9 the option shows. Average total congestion has provided in a three-point of site and shows range of 5.5 that it is relatively busy. It mentioned that the average response to perceived crowding was 3.07 in outer space palaces and, as well as 5 and 6 are in entry routes and Interior museum. It can be said from the perspective of visitors there aren't sense of crowded in outside the palace a lot, but perceived congestion have reached saturation point in the other parts of the site.

Factors influencing the perception of conflict of visitors

Repeat Visitors

We see Variable frequency visitors in the sample show that the results have shown 91 people have come for the first time, 9 people had met again.

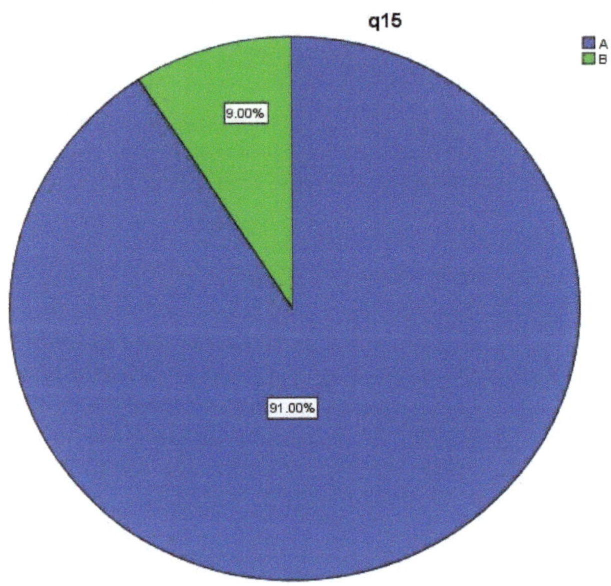

Figure 1. The frequency of visits charts.

Previous visiting experience about the site leads to the formation of expectations about its density and congestion and affects the perception of visitors. Solidarity test results showed that the previous meeting effect on the crowd perceived by respondents. On expression of a more scientific there is significant relationship between perceived congestion of the visit and the previous experience. It is strong and negative relationship. The experience player is. There is less perceived crowd, if people have more experiences. The results of data analysis showed that the majority of respondents were first visited the palace. Perhaps this means that respondents have no idea about the density of the site. . Accordingly, it may be said that those who had visited most of these places it will crowd and therefore less crowd reported.

Table 2. The result of ANOVA to evaluate differences in perceived crowd based on meet experience.

perceived crowd based on meet experience	sum of squares	Degrees of freedom	average of squares	Fisher statistics	A significant number
Between groups	11/104	9	1/234	0/736	0/995
Within groups	157/336	90	1/748		
Total	168/440	99			

3.3. Expect of the Density of Site

Table 3. The expect of congestion frequency chart.

Variable	Abundance	Abundance percent
I expect to see less Size of these people	49	49
I expect to see more than this Size of people	7	7
I expect to see the same Size people	18	18
No previous comment about it	26	26
	100	100

The results of the relationship between people's expectations of density and perceived crowding on proved the findings of the literature and previous research that there was a positive relationship between these two variables. According to the literature, the expectations of people before arriving at the site compared to what's really experience can affect their perception of crowd. As if visitors deal with the number of people more than their expected, perceived crowd will increase. However, the strength of this relationship was very weak.

Table 4. *ANOVA test results for evaluating differences in perceived congestion considering expected congestion.*

perceived crowd based on expected congestion	sum of squares	Degrees of freedom	average of squares	Fisher statistics	A significant number
Between groups	12/702	9	18/323	12/689	0/000
Within groups	89/732	90	1/032		
Total	102/740	99			

It was used the Pearson correlation coefficient to investigate the relation between independent variables (expected congestion) and the dependent variable (perceived crowding). The results at the confidence level of 99% indicates a significant positive relation between these two variables, however the relation is weak.

4. Conclusion

Considering high volume of requests to visit the recreational resources, experience quality management is very important visitors. Perceived crowd, is one of the indicators determine the quality of the recreational experience. Studies have shown that in addition to site density, there are other factors are involved in the perception of crowd. The variables effect the perception of conflict of foreign visitors from Niyavaran collection. Based on the findings, on average, the perception of visitors is moderate crowd. In addition, among variables, the variable's history of visitors and previous expectation of density showed that there is a significant relation between them and perceived crowd. Visitors had visited the site with the more number of their expectations, reported more crowding. . This finding was in a line with previous findings in the literature of this subject. In this respect, the importance of accurate and realistic expectations in the minds of visitors before the site has doubled. Thus, before reaching to destination, realistic expectations have to form in the minds of visitors and consequently faced with a busy site will not be deterioration of the quality of their experience. For this purpose, we have to improve informative websites of Niyavaran and about the peak time of visit, and put some pictures of the site at this time in the site. The findings of this study and similar studies can help managers in identifying the factors that affect the quality of the leisure experience of visitors. They can use the results of the evaluation for management decisions and prevent the degradation of the quality of visitors' experience. Therefore, managers should permanently ensure quality of entertainment experience and to make appropriate solutions.

5. Research Limitations

Because of time limits, this study only happened in one of the peak visiting time, while there are tourists who come to visit the palace in the other peak periods in the spring and summer. In addition, Lake of Knowledge of English by some of the foreign tourists and also not knowing other languages more than English limits for the interview caused some limitations.

References

[1] Altman, Irwin (2009). Environmental and social behavior: privacy, personal space, territory and congestion. Translation A. Namazian. Tehran, Shahid Beheshti University Publications Center.

[2] Jahanbakhsh., Esmaiel. (2002). Simple guide to using SPSS statistical test-use of scientific research: the Institute for Brain Science Scholars - The pillars.

[3] Khaki, Gholam reza (2009). The method of approach to end-letter writing (Fifth Edition). Tehran: reflections.

[4] Darvishsefat, Ali asghar. (2008). Atlas protected areas of Tehran: Tehran University

[5] Delaware, Ali. (2001). Methods in Psychology and Educational Sciences. Tehran: The Institute of editing publishing.

[6] Saroukhani, Bagher. (2006). Research Methods in the Social Sciences, Vol. II: Insights and Techniques. Tehran: Institute for Humanities and Cultural Studies.

[7] Tayebiyan, manouchehr. setoode, ahad, Shayesteh, Kmran (2007) The concepts and methods of quantitative estimation of capacity and offer a practical example based on experience in strategic planning development Abas Abad, Hamedan.

[8] FArhody. Rahmat Allah. Shorcheh Mahmod. (2004) assessment the capacity anahitaa in Kangavar. faslnameh Temple City tourism studies.

[9] Arnberger, A., & Brandenburg, C. (2007). Past On-Site Experience, Crowding Perceptions, an Use Displacement of Visitor Groups to a Peri Urban National Park. Environ Manage, 40, 34.

[10] Velvil, C. L. (1974). "An Investigation of Social Carrying Capacity at Three Open Space Preserves". Master's thesis. San Jose State University.

[11] Fisher Salemon (1981) The Challenge of Tourism Carrying Capacity Assessment: Theory and Practice (pp. 55-99 England: Ashgate.

[12] Patreson (1976). Behavioral Adaptations to Crowdin Disturbance: Evidence from Nature Reserves in Israel". Leisure Sciences, 29, 37–52.

[13] "Visitor Perception of113). Grieser, K. A. (1972) Crowding, Coping, and Social Carryin Capacity: An Exploratory Study in the Mohonk".

[14] Master's thesis, State university of New York, College of Environmental Science and Forestrk Syracuse, New York.

[15] Han, Q., Benedict G.C., D., VanRaaij, W. 14).Getz, H. J. (1983). "Visitors' Strategic Anticipation of Crowding in Scarce Recreational Resources". Journal of Retailing and Consumer Services, 1-8.

[16] Meningh, H. (2002). "Social Carrying Capacity of 15.Tourism Planning at an Alternative Tourism Destination: Crowding, Satisfaction.

24

Managing Openness of the Chinese Economy to Sustain Its Economic Growth

Huiqun Liu

School of Economics, Tianjin University of Commerce, Tianjin, China

Email address:
huiqunliu@tjcu.edu.cn

Abstract: Many studies suggest the positive causal effects of openness on productivity and growth. However, controversies are still prevalent among vast empirical studies on the issue. In this paper, we develop econometric models in the comprehensive framework to shed quantitative light on the implications of a scenario of deeper economic integration in China, where the barriers for trade and foreign direct investment (FDI) are preferentially eliminated. Different versions of the econometric models are specified and numerically implemented. Each provides a framework to experiment the relationship between economic growth and trade, FDI in China. Our findings include: first, both FDI and trade have positive impact on long-term economic growth and no effect on short-term economic fluctuation; second, the interactions between FDI and policy, trade openness and policy have significant impact on economic growth, and with the rapid growth of FDI and trade, their marginal effects on economic growth is reduced; third, the impact of FDI on TFP is positive, and trade openness is also showed positive effect on TFP under the role of FDI. All these findings suggest that openness is becoming an important drive force of China's economic growth. It is necessary for Chinese government to manage openness to sustain its' economic growth.

Keywords: Openness, Foreign Trade, Foreign Direct Investment, Economic Growth, China

1. Introduction

China is a very an interesting and increasingly important case for study of relationship between growth, trade and foreign direct investment (FDI). Since the initiation of economic reforms and trade liberalization from 1978, China has been one of the world's fastest-growing economies and has emerged as a major economic and trade power. Academic researchers have tried alternative explanations for China's miraculous growth. Most of papers found that exports and FDI have a strong and positive effect on economic growth. The results suggest that two development policies adopted in China are useful for other developing and transitional economies: export promotion and adoption of world technology and business practices.

However, the global economic crisis began to impact China's economy in late 2008. After growing by 13% in 2007, China's real GDP slowed to 9.6% in 2008 and to 9.3% in 2011. However, China's trade and inflows of FDI decreased sharply. After growing by 15% in 2007, China's export slowed to 1.3% in 2008 and to -17.7% in 2009. China's inflows of FDI slowed to 3.6% in 2008 and to -1.8% in 2009 (NBSC, 2012). Despite the relatively positive outlook for its economy, China faces a number of difficult challenges that, if not addressed, could undermine its future economic growth and stability. These include over-dependence on exports and fixed investment for growth, and widening income disparities.

Whether this growth performance is sustainable over the next several decades has been also actively debated both inside and outside China. Actually, in recent years, there are two academic debates on openness and economic growth in China. One is whether the ratio of trade to GDP is too high. The ratio in China reaches up 50% in 2011while other developed countries such as USA reach only about 10%. Are we dependent on global market too much? And the other is whether China utilizes FDI too much since China is the world's largest holder of foreign exchange reserves at $3.2 trillion (NBSC, 2012).

Obviously, China can't have a sustainable growth only dependent on foreign markets and FDI. In order to identify the economic growth effect of trade and FDI, in this paper, we develop an econometric model in the comprehensive framework to shed quantitative light on the implications of a scenario of deeper economic integration in China, where the barriers for trade and foreign direct investment are preferentially eliminated. Different versions of the econometric models are specified and numerically implemented. Each provides a framework to experiment the relationship between economic growth and trade, foreign direct investment in China.

This paper is structured as follows. Section 2 reviews the corresponding academic literature. Section 3 presents an overview of China's Economic Development. Section 4 introduces the methodology, data and presents empirical results. Section 5 concludes with policy implications.

2. Literature Review

2.1. Trade and Economic Growth

The idea that international trade fuels economic growth dates back at least to Adam Smith's concept of absolute advantage and David Ricardo's notion of comparative advantage. Numerous theoretical models have been proposed to demonstrate the positive relationship between openness and economic growth. Some of the reasons cited in support of the proposition are: (a) export growth represents an increase in demand for the country's output; (b) exports promote specialization in the production of export products, which in turn may boost the productivity level and the general level of skills and result in a more efficient reallocation of resources; (c) the outward oriented trade policy may also give better access to advanced technologies, learning by doing gains, and better management practices that may result in further efficiency gains; (d) exports may loosen a foreign exchange constraint, which makes it easier to import inputs to meet domestic demand, and so enable output expansion; (e) some authors argue that an outward-oriented strategy of development may provide greater opportunities and rewards for entrepreneurial activity, the key to extended growth. However, openness does not raise economic growth unambiguously. Protection could be a strategy to increase economic growth. They are many arguments for protection such as the infant industry argument, the terms of trade argument and tariff to reduce aggregate unemployment.

Theoretical disagreement on the role of openness is matched by mixed empirical evidence. Many empirical studies have found a positive relationship between openness and economic growth in China. The empirical literature on trade-growth relationships can be classified into two broad strands of studies. One strand used time-series models and assessed mainly the demand-driven effects. Liu et al (1997) used the models of Granger to identify a bi-directional causal relationship between GNP and exports plus imports in China. He found that the bi-directional causation is consistent with China's development strategy of export promotion. Kishor and Deergha (2011) employed the more recent and robust Toda-Yamamoto-Dolado-Lutkephol Augmented vector autoregressive (VAR) technique for testing Granger causality among four time series variables. They focused on the post liberalization period and the results strongly support export-led Growth in China. Imports, however, do not have direct Granger causality towards GDP, but certainly influence it through the indirect channel of influencing Exports and Foreign direct Investment. Qazi Muhammad Adnan Hye (2012) utilized the relative new cointegration method of the autoregressive distributed lag (ARDL) approach to determine the export-led growth, growth-led export, import-led growth, growth-led import and foreign deficit sustainability hypothesis in the case of China, and the direction of long run and short run causal relationship is examined by using modified Granger causality test. The results confirmed the bidirectional long run relationship between the economic growth and exports, economic growth and imports, exports and imports.

The other strand of studies using a cross-section, and more recently panel data, approach examined the productivity and supply-side effects of trade on output and growth, traversing through the accumulation of capital and total factor productivity (TFP) parameter of production technology. Zheng et al (2009) found that reform measures often resulted in one-time level effects on TFP and suggested China needs further institutional reforms to consolidate China's move to a full-fledged market economy. Yao (2006) focused on the effect of exports and FDI on economic performance using a large panel data set encompassing 28 Chinese provinces over the period 1978-2000. Adopting Pedroni's panel unit root test and Arellano and Bond's dynamic panel data estimating technique, he found that both exports and FDI have a strong and positive effect on economic growth. Jiang (2011) investigated the effects of openness on China's regional productivity growth. By using a variety of panel data regression techniques, he showed that the direct growth effect of openness was the main effect while the convergence effect was insignificant. The findings lend strong support to the claim that the opening-up of China promotes the country's economic growth.

2.2. FDI and Economic Growth

It is a general belief among policy makers and academicians that FDI can be a source of valuable technology and know-how in addition to increased capital. Some of the popularly cited potential benefits of FDI are: (a) backward and forward linkages with the rest of the economy; (b) enhanced access to advanced technologies; (c) learning of improved management practices; (d) expansion and diversification of the production capacity of an economy; (e) transfer of best practices in corporate governance and accounting practices; (f) integration of the domestic economy with the global economy and infusion of competition in the domestic economy; and (g) relatively more stability than other forms of international capital flows because of longer-term perspective.

Notwithstanding the strong conceptual case for a positive relationship between economic growth and FDI, the empirical evidence has been mixed. See for example, Blomström and Kokko (1998), Gorg and Greenaway (2004), and Barba-Navaretti and Venables (2006) for surveys of spillover channels and empirical findings. It has been recognized and well documented in the literature that there is possibility of two-way feedbacks between FDI and economic growth along with their long-run and short-run dynamics. John and Xin (2010) presented and assessed of the contribution of inward FDI to China's recent rapid economic growth using a two stage growth accounting approach. They suggested that the sustainability of both China's export and overall economic growth may be questionable if inward FDI plateaus in the future.

Nevertheless, some empirical investigations in the context of the Chinese economy have generally failed to provide any conclusive evidence in support of such two-way feedback effects although long-run cointegrating relation has been found (e.g., Mah, 2005). Liu (2011) used VAR and vector error correction model (VECM) to discern the long-run relations between FDI and economic development in China and found FDI tended to decrease economic growth. Economic development in China seems to be fueled by domestic capital accumulation and employment and FDI inflows do crowd out domestic capitals, and reduce employment growth.

Earlier studies, however, have several limitations in common. First, the period of observation is typically too short to capture the effects of economic reforms and the subsequent boom in trade and FDI during the last 10 years or so. In the present study we show that this factor has significant influence on the results. Second, the econometric techniques employed (even in those studies which take into account the nonstationarity properties) are highly dependent on the results of testing for the cointegration relationships. Third, only bivariate relationship is studied in most of the previous studies, which may involve biases (Love and Chandra, 2005).

In this paper we avoid these methodological problems. We add to the existing literature by (1) using Johansen's (1988) cointegration technique and VAR to test the economic growth effect of openness by using annual time-series log-level data from 1985 to 2010. (2) using two dummy variables to identify the growth effect of trade and FDI policies. (3) taking into account the TFP effect of trade and FDI that allow for further effects on economic development.

3. An Overview of China's Economic Development

Beginning in 1979, China launched several economic reforms. The central government initiated price and ownership incentives for farmers, which enabled them to sell a portion of their crops on the free market. In 1980, the government established four special economic zones along the coast for the purpose of attracting foreign investment, boosting exports, and importing high technology products into China. In 1992 the government sought to decentralize economic policymaking in several sectors, especially trade. Economic control of various enterprises was given to provincial and local governments, which were generally allowed to operate and compete on free market principles, rather than under the direction and guidance of state planning. In addition, citizens were encouraged to start their own businesses. Additional coastal regions and cities were designated as open cities and development zones, which allowed them to experiment with free market reforms and to offer tax and trade incentives to attract foreign investment. In addition, together with a gradual reduction in tariff, removal of non-tarrif barriers and privatization of many state-owned enterprises, China accessed to the World Trade Organization (WTO) in the end of 2001, China state price controls on a wide range of products were gradually eliminated. Trade liberalization was also a major key to China's economic success. Removing trade barriers encouraged greater competition and boosted foreign direct investment flows.

3.1. China's Economic Growth Since Reforms

Since the introduction of economic reforms, China's economy has grown substantially. Figure 1 shows China's Real GDP and Average Annual Growth of GDP from 1980 to 2011. During the reform period, China's average annual real GDP grew by nearly 9.9%; it grew by 14.1% in 2007, but slowed to 9.6% in 2008. Since 1980, economic reforms helped to produce a 36-fold increase in the size of the economy in real terms and a 26-fold increase in real per capita GDP (NBSC, 2012).

China's economy suffered a sharp slow-down as a result of the global financial crisis in the late of 2008, largely due to a decline in foreign demand for Chinese imports and a drop-off in FDI in China.

3.2. An Overview of China's Trade

Economic reforms and trade and investment liberalization have helped transform China into a major trading power. Figure 2 shows China's Values and Share of Merchandise Exports and Imports from 1980 to 2011. Chinese exports rose from $14 billion in 1979 to $ 1899 billion in 2011, while imports over this period grew from $16 billion to $ 1744 billion. China's trade growth has been particularly rapid after accession to WTO. From 2002 to 2011, China's exports grew by 339%, a compound annual growth rate of 23.5%; while imports increased by 283%, a compound annual growth rate of 21.2% (NBSC, 2012).

In 2007, China surpassed the United States as the world's second largest merchandise exporter, after Germany. In 2010, China was the world's the largest and was the second largest importer, after the United. China's trade surplus, which totaled $32 billion in 2004, surged to $155 billion in 2011.

Merchandise trade surpluses, large-scale foreign investment, and large purchases of foreign currencies to maintain its exchange rate with the dollar and other currencies have enabled China to accumulate the world's largest foreign exchange reserves at $3.2 trillion at the end of 2011, making it the world's largest holder of such reserves.

3.3. An Overview of China's FDI Inflows

FDI inflows into China have increased rapidly over the last two decades. Before 1979, FDI was prohibited in China, a restriction which was lifted following the adoption of China's open door policy in 1979, when a new foreign investment law was adopted. In its early stages, FDI was restricted to China's Four Special Economic Zones and limited to equity joint ventures. In 1984, a new forcign investment law was adopted to accelerate FDI growth and a number of preferential policies were used by both central and local governments to attract FDI. A sharp increase occurred after 1992 when China reaffirmed policies of openness and market-oriented reforms introduced earlier.

As Figure 3 indicates, growth in China's inward FDI has been spectacular. In 1985, annual FDI inflows were less than US$2 billion; while in 2011, they were US$105.7 billion, 50 times those of 25 years earlier. Between 1985 and 1991, the annual growth rate of FDI inflows into China was 14%, and annual FDI inflows during this period remained less than US$4.5 billion. FDI inflows increased sharply to US$11 billion in 1992, with growth rates of over 150%.

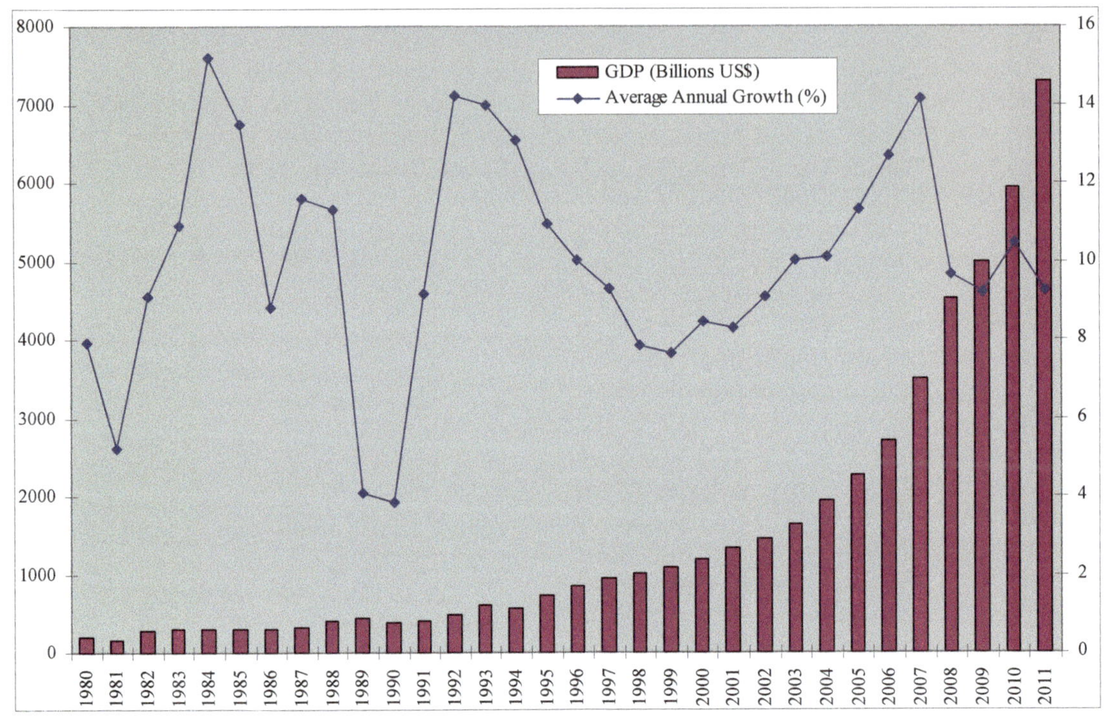

Source: International Monetary Fund, World Economic Outlook Database, April 2012

***Figure 1.** China's Real GDP and Average Annual Growth, 1980-2011.*

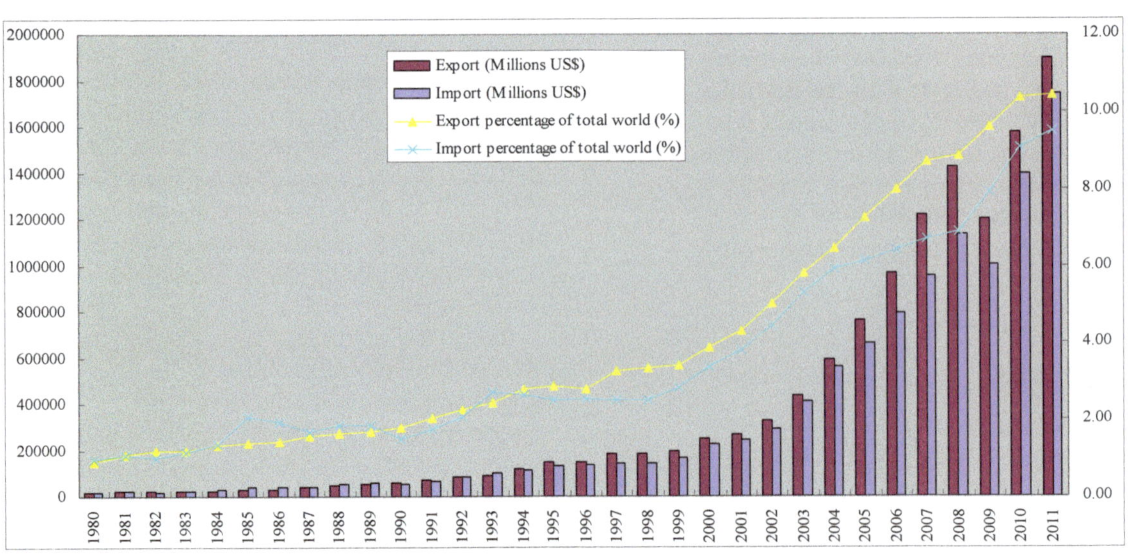

Source: UNCTAD, UNCTAD stat.

***Figure 2.** China's Values and Share of Merchandise Exports and Imports, 1980-2011.*

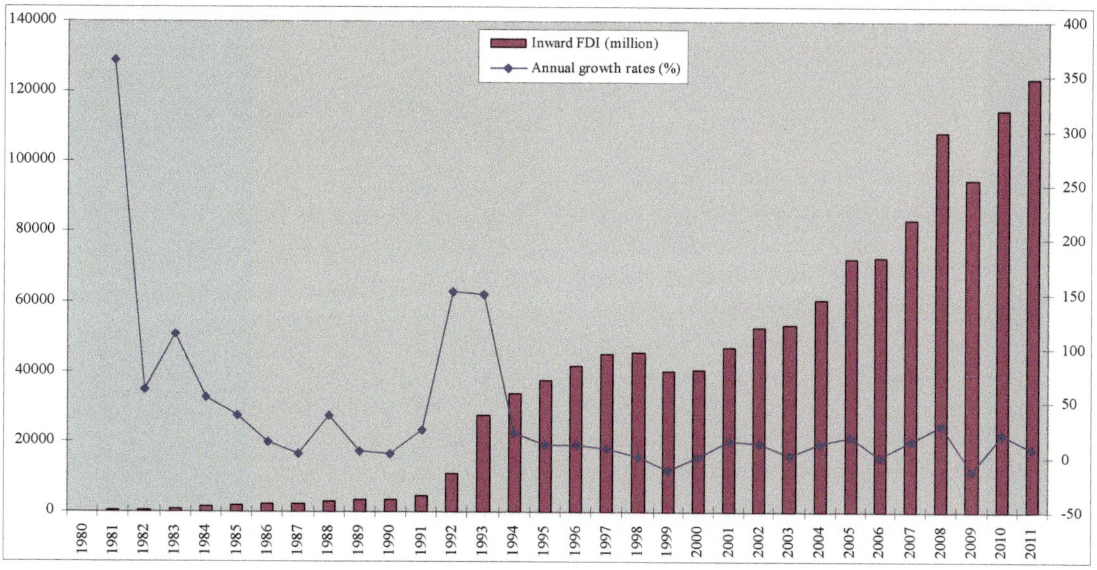

Sources: FDI inflows in billion US$ are from NBSC (2011); growth rates are calculated by authors.

Figure 3. *China's Inward FDI Flows and Their Annual Growth Rates, 1980–2011*

By 1997, China had FDI inflows of US$49 billion. Although the late 1990s saw a small decrease in FDI inflows, the annual growth rate of FDI inflows into China increased again to over 10% after China joined the WTO in 2001. During the three years 2001, 2002 and 2003, world FDI inflows declined sharply by 41%, 13% and 12% respectively, but China registered FDI growth of 15%, 13% and 1.4%. Global FDI inflows increased by only 2% in 2004, while China registered an inward FDI growth rate of 13% (NBSC, 2005). The global economic crisis began to impact China's FDI inflows in late 2008. China's inflows of FDI slowed to 3.6% in 2008 and to -1.8% in 2009. However, it recovered quickly in 2010. China's share of FDI inflows has thus increased sharply in recent years. China is now the world's largest developing country FDI recipient and the world's second largest FDI recipient overall after the US.

China's FDI inflows fall into two broad categories. One is horizontal FDI involving the transfer of production from abroad to China to service the Chinese internal market. The other is vertical FDI which seeks to take advantage of low cost production (and especially low wage rates) for export of products abroad. Most export-oriented FDI inflows originate from other Asia economies, including South Korea, Taiwan, and Hong Kong, and are in the vertical category which seeks to exploit low production costs. FDI flows from North America and Western Europe are more heavily in the horizontal category, which seeks to exploit the Chinese domestic market.

4. Methodology, Variables and Data

4.1. Methodology

Following the framework of Mankiw et al. (1992), we use Cobb-Douglas production function assuming marginal contribution of capital and labor in production. So production function in period t is given below:

$$Y(t) = A(t)K(t)^{\alpha} L(t)^{\beta} \tag{1}$$

Where $\alpha + \beta = 1$, $Y(t)$ is domestic output (GDP), $A(t)$ is technological progress (TFP), K is capital stock and L is employment population. Because of the constant scale return, production function can be written in per capita form:

$$y(t) = A(t)k(t)^{\alpha} \tag{2}$$

Where $y(t)$ is GDP per capita, $k(t)$ is capital stock per capita. We extend production function by assuming openness (FDI and Trade) contributes to economic growth directly. This shows that openness is contributing economic growth by efficient allocation of internal and external resources or attracting foreign direct investment. This leads us to model the empirical equation as follows:

$$y(t) = A(t)k(t)^{\alpha} fdi(t)^{\delta_1} trade(t)^{\delta_2} \tag{3}$$

Where $fdi(t)$ is FDI per capita, $trade(t)$ is Trade per capita. In addition to the direct impact of openness on economic growth, openness may impact on economic growth through TFP. This shows that openness is contributing TFP by shift of technological advancements from developed countries to developing economies. So the empirical equation is given below:

$$A(t) = \phi \cdot rfdi(t)^{\alpha} rtrade(t)^{\beta} \tag{4}$$

Where ϕ is constant term, $rfdi(t)$ is FDI Proportion, $rtrade(t)$ is Trade Proportion, $A(t)$ is TFP. Taking logs in both sides, Equation 3 and Equation 4 can be modeled as follows:

$$\ln y_t = \beta_0 + \beta_1 \ln k_t + \beta_2 \ln fdi_t + \beta_3 \ln trade_t + \mu_t \tag{5}$$

Where $\ln y_t$ is log of GDP per capita, $\ln k_t$ is log of capital stock per capita, $\ln fdi_t$ is log of FDI per capita, $\ln trade_t$ is log of Trade per capita, μ_t is error term assumed to be constant.

$$\ln A_t = \beta_0 + \beta_1 \ln rfdi_t + \beta_2 \ln rtrade_t + \mu_t \quad (6)$$

Where $\ln A_t$ is log of TFP, $\ln rfdi_t$ is log of FDI proportion, $\ln rtrade_t$ is log of international trade proportion, μ_t is error term, which capture the impact of all the unobserved factors.

Based on the general model of the Equation 5 and Equation 6, cointegration regression model and ECM are used to investigate impact of openness on long-term economic growth and short-term economic fluctuation respectively, and a VAR model is estimated to capture dynamic details of the openness impact on economic growth. Furthermore, in order to study how openness impact on economic growth directly or through TFP in detail, we set up linear and non-linear regression with policy and interaction terms, and estimates it by using robust OLS method.

4.2. Variables and Data

Based on the objective of the study and Equation 5&6, a group of variables about openness and economic growth were considered in table 1. The variables used in empirical analysis are shown in table1. To estimate the effect of openness on economic growth, the models were estimated by using data for the period 1985-2010 from "China Statistical Yearbook (2011)" and "comprehensive statistic data and materials on 50 years of new China". In order to eliminate the impact of the price factor, all relevant data is adjusted by different price index based on 1985. For example, GDP is adjusted by GDP deflator Index, capital stock and FDI are adjusted by fixed assets price index, Import and export are adjusted by consumer price index etc.

The variable, capital stock, can be calculated by perpetual inventory method. According to the study of Guo and Jia (2004), the initial capital stock in 1985 is 1244.76 billion RMB and the rate of capital depreciation δ is 5%. Another variable, total factor productivity, can be obtained by formula:

$$\ln(FTP) = \ln(GDP) - \alpha Ln(K) - \beta Ln(L) \quad (7)$$

As to openness, there are several measures to quantify. To measure trade openness, exports per capita (exports divided by employment population) and exports proportion (exports divided by GDP), imports per capita (imports divided by employment population) and imports proportion (imports divided by GDP), trade per capita (sum of exports and imports divided by employment population) and trade proportion (sum of exports and imports divided by GDP) are used. To measure openness in investment market, two indicators are used: FDI per capita (FDI divided by employment population) and FDI proportion (FDI divided by total investment).

Other variables, such as policy variables, are based on the important policy tuning point, and are measured by dummy variable taking value between 0 and 1. Of course, in order to reduce skewness and kurtosia to a normal range, all service variables in empirical analysis were taken logs.

Table 1. *Summery of variables.*

Variables	Name	Definition
Economic growth variables		
Output	Y	Real GDP
Per capita Output	y	Real GDP/ Employment Population
Technological progress variable		
Total Factor Productivity	FTP	$Ln(FTP) = Ln(GDP) - \alpha Ln(K) - \beta Ln(L)$
Capital and labor variables		
Capital Stock	K	$K_t = I_t + (1-\delta)K_{t-1}$
Capital Stock Per capita	k	Capital Stock/ Employment Population
Employment Population	L	Employment Population
Openness variables		
FDI Per capita	FDI	FDI/ Employment Population
Trade Per capita	trade	Imports & Exports/Employment Population
Imports Per capita	import	Imports/ Employment Population
Exports Per capita	export	Exports/ Employment Population
FDI Proportion	rFDI	FDI/Total Investment
Trade Proportion	rtrade	Imports & Exports/GDP
Imports Proportion	rimport	Import/GDP
Exports Proportion	rexport	Export/GDP
Policy variables		
Establishing market economic system	D1	Dummy variable taking value between 0 and 1
Accessing WTO	D2	Dummy variable taking value between 0 and 1

5. Empirical Analysis

Given the important role played by openness in the Chinese economy growth. The main objectives of empirical analysis are as follows: first to examine the effect of Chinese openness on its long-term economic growth or short-term economic fluctuation, and second to examine dynamic effect of the openness impact on economic growth, and third, to examine how openness impacts on economic growth with policy variable in detail, and last, to examine how openness impacts on Economic Growth through total factor productivity with interaction of FDI and trade in detail.

Before empirical analysis, the assumption of constant scale return should be examined. So First we will estimate a log-transformed Cobb-Douglas production function model by OLS:

$$\ln(Y) = -2.75 + 0.73\ln(K) + 0.46\ln(L) \quad (8)$$

t-statistic (20.47)*** (2.34)**

Notes: The 1%, 5% and 10% levels of significance are indicated by ***, ** and * respectively.

Table 2. *Result of constant scale return test*

Null Hypothesis	F-statistic	probability
$\alpha+\beta=1$	2.387	0.1360

The assumption of constant scale return is examined by Wald coefficient restrictions test. Table 2 presents the null hypothesis of constant scale return is accept. This indicates that the constant scale return exists in Chinese economy from 1985-2010. So we can use Cobb-Douglas production function in per capita form.

5.1. Conintegration Analysis and ECM Models

5.1.1. Conintegration Analysis

As the selected variables are all time series data, we need do variables stationary test. In this paper, we use ADF test proposed by Dickey and Fuller (1981) to do unit root test for each variable. Table 3 presents all original variables were not stationary, but variables in the first-order differential were stationary. Therefore, all variables clearly turn out to be ~I(1), they are integrated of order one.

To examine the long-term cointegration relationship among multi-variables, VAR-based multi-variables Johansen cointegration test method is mainly used. So the lag order of VAR should be determined before cointegration analysis. According to the AIC and SC criteria, the final lag order is 2.

Table 4 presents the null hypothesis of cointegration vector is rejected at the 5% significance level. There exists cointegration relationship among these variables. Based on the equation 5, we can get the following cointegration regression equation:

$$\ln(y) = -0.368 + 0.63\ln(k_t) + 0.048\ln(fdi) + 0.064\ln(trade) \quad (9)$$

t-statistic (16.71)*** (4.34)*** (2.15)**

$$\bar{R}^2 = 0.9979$$

Notes: the 1%, 5% and 10% levels of significance are indicated by ***, ** and * respectively.

Table 3. Results of unit root test.

Variable	Data generation process	ADF-statistic	1% Critical Value	5%Critical Value	10% Critical Value
$\ln(y)$	(C, T, 1)	-2.199290	-4.394309	-3.612199	-3.243079
$\Delta\ln(y)$	(C, T, 1)	-2.199290***	-4.394309	-3.612199	-3.243079
$\ln(k)$	(C, T, 5)	-5.230589	-4.498307	-3.6584469	-3.268973
$\Delta\ln(k)$	(C, T, 2)	-4.002130**	-4.440739	-3.632896	-3.254671
$\ln(fdi)$	(C, T, 5)	-3.036018	-4.498307	-3.658446	-3.268973
$\Delta\ln(fdi)$	(C, T, 4)	-4.538906***	-4.498307	-3.658446	-3.268973
$\ln(trade)$	(C, T, 0)	-1.977280	-4.374307	-3.603202	-3.238054
$\Delta\ln(trade)$	(C, T, 0)	-4.023122**	-4.394309	-3.612199	-3.243079

Notes: The 1%, 5% and 10% levels of significance are indicated by ***, ** and * respectively; the data generation process (c, t, n) represents the constant term, time trend, and lag length respectively.

Table 4. Results of Johansen cointegration test.

Hypothesized	Eigenvalue	Trace Statistic	5% Critical Value	probability
r=0 *	0.792358	77.65838	55.24578	0.0002
r≤1*	0.660496	41.50373	35.01090	0.0089
r≤2	0.512142	16.65751	18.39771	0.0862
r≤3	0.006487	0.149694	3.841466	0.6988

Notes: The 5% levels of significance are indicated by *.

The residuals of cointegration regression equation were stationary series by unit root test, and it's value fluctuated around zero, verified the cointegration relationship among the variables is correct.After finding the existence of cointegration between the economic growth and openness, the next task is to explore the long run marginal effects of FDI and trade on economic growth in the case of Chinese. The results documented in equation 8 shows that FDI is positively linked to economic growth and it is statistically significant at 1% significance level. It implies that keeping other things constant, a 0.048% economic growth is stimulated by a 1% growth in FDI. The effect of trade on economic growth is also positive and statistically significant at 5% level. A 0.064% increase in economic growth is due to a rise in 1% in trade keeping all else the same. The coefficient of k shows a positive effect on economic growth. A 1% increase in capitalization raises economic growth by 0.63%. The results show that both FDI and trade have significant impact on economic growth, the impact of trade on economic growth is greater than FDI. This implies that Chinese can attain fruitful effects of openness to sustain economic growth for long span of time by configuring internal and external resource and attracting foreign direct investment. Cointegration regression equation fits very well and eliminating the autocorrelation by using Newey-West HAC Standard Errors & Covariance. Overall, the results of the model estimation are satisfactory.

5.1.2. A Model of ECM

Cointegration regression equation describes the long-term relationship among the variables, and the error correction model describes the short-term relationship among the variables. The error correction model is proposed at first by Sargan (1964) and is further complemented by Hendry-Anderson (1977) and Davidson (1977). According to Granger causality theorem, there must exist the error correction among cointegration variables. So the error correction model can be used to study the impact of openness on short-term economic fluctuation.

$$\begin{aligned}\Delta\mathrm{Log}(y_t) &= -0.016 + 0.787\Delta\mathrm{Log}(k_t) + 0.034\Delta\mathrm{Log}(fdi) \\ &+ 0.038\Delta\mathrm{Log}(trade_t) - 0.571ecm_{t-1}\end{aligned} \quad (10)$$

t-statistic (10.99)*** (1.72) (1.31) (3.20)***

$$\bar{R}^2 = 0.8535$$

Notes: the 1%, 5% and 10% levels of significance are indicated by ***, ** and * respectively.

Equation 10 reveals the results of ECM models with impact of openness on short-term economic fluctuation. The coefficient of FDI and trade is not significant at 10% significance level. This shows that both trade and FDI have no significant effects on short-term economic fluctuations. It implies that openness have no effect on short-term economic fluctuation. The coefficient of ecm is -0.571, which shows that about 57.1% of the gap between actual output and equilibrium output is corrected each year. The effect of capital stock on economic fluctuation is statistically significant at 1% level. This shows other things remain the same, 0.787% economic fluctuation is caused by changing 1% of capital stock. It implies that capital stock has greater impact on both long-term economic growth and economic fluctuation.

5.2. VAR Model with Dynamic Impact of Openness on Economic Growth

Cointegration analysis presents the static characters of impact of openness on economic growth. To capture dynamic details of the openness impact on economic growth. We set up a VAR proposed by Sims (1980) and estimate it for impulse response analysis. According to equation 5, the identification of openness shocks within VAR model can be dealt with, The model includes the main variables through which openness and economic growth interact: log(y), log(k), log(FDI) and log(trade).

Let's focus on the impulse responses of economic growth to FDI and trade shock respectively (shown in figure 4). The response of economic growth to FDI shock is positive, when one S.D innovation is given to FDI in current period, economic growth will increase 0.00461. Thereafter, the intensity of impact is gradually enhanced at first, and then weakened after reaching its peak (0.0302) at sixth period. The response of economic growth to trade shock is positive at fist, when one S.D innovation is given to trade in current period, economic growth will increase 0.0177. Thereafter the intensity of impact presents sinusoidal shape, and becomes negative at the sixth period. Comparing the response of economic growth to FDI and trade shock, we can conclude that the response of economic growth to trade shock is stronger than the FDI shock at first, but Starting from the fourth period, the response of economic growth to FDI shock is stronger than the trade shock, furthermore, FDI shcok has a longer period positive impact on economic growth than trade shock.

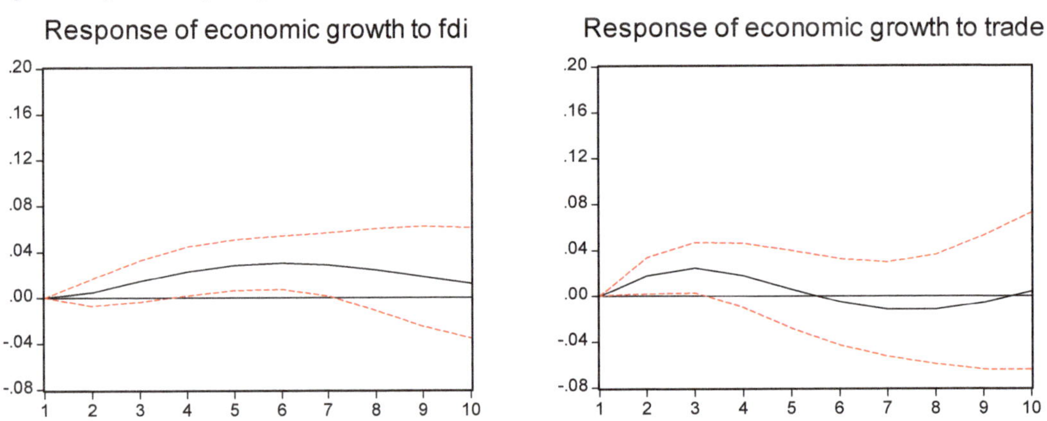

Figure 4. *The Effect of FDI Shock (Left) and Trade Shock (Right) On Economic Growth.*

5.3. Regression by Adding Policy Variables

Although the impact of openness on economic growth is preliminary analyzed, but this is not detailed enough. First, trade can be divided into imports and exports in detail, and second, openness may impact on economic growth through policy interaction.

So we designed four models including FDI model, Trade model, Imports model and Exports model to explain how openness impact on economic growth in detail. In each model, there are three liner regressions: the first is the baseline regression without policy variables, and the second is the regression with policy dummy variable D1, and the third is regression with policy dummy variable D2. In order to improve the robustness of the estimation, the autocorrelation of each model is eliminated by adding AR terms or using Newey-West HAC Standard Errors & Covariance.

Policy dummy variable is based on the important policy turning point. There are two important policy turning point since 1985: one is China established the socialist market economic system in1992, the other is China access to the WTO at the end of 2001. So we can design two policy dummy variable named D1 and D2. The definitions of policy dummy variables are as follows:

$$D_1 = \begin{cases} 0 & 1985-1991 \\ 1 & 1992-2010 \end{cases} \tag{11}$$

$$D_2 = \begin{cases} 0 & 1985-2001 \\ 1 & 2002-2010 \end{cases} \tag{12}$$

Table 5 shows the results of each model. In FDI model, FDI is positively linked to economic growth and it is statistically significant at 1% significance level. It implies that keeping other things constant, a 0.059-0.073% economic growth is stimulated by a 1% growth in FDI. The interaction between D1 and FDI is not significant at any significance level, but the interaction between D2 and FDI is significant at 10% significance level. It implies that China's accession to WTO has greater effect on FDI and hence economic growth, however, establishing socialist market economic system doesn't any matter. The possible reason for this is that China's accession to WTO adds the confidence of foreigner's investors, thereby increases the foreign direct investment, however, due to the distrust of China's market reform, establishing socialist market economic system in China failed to enhance the confidence of foreigner's investors. The coefficient of the interaction terms between D2 and FDI is negative. This implies that with the rapid growth of FDI after China's accession to WTO, although the impact of FDI on economic growth is still positive, but its marginal effect is weakened.

In trade model, imports model and exports model, the impact of trade, import and export on economic growth is positive and it is statistically significant. This shows that the improvement of trade, import and export stimulated economic activity and hence economic growth. Comparing the imports model and exports model, the coefficient of export is larger than import. This implies that the effect of export on economic growth is greater than import. The interaction terms- D1 and trade, D1 and import, D1 and export is significant at 5% significance level, however the interaction terms- D2 and trade, D2 and import, D2 and export is not significant at any significance level. It implies that establishing socialist market economic system has greater effect on trade, import, export and hence economic growth; however, China's accession to WTO doesn't any matter. The possible reason for this is that in 1992 when china starts establishing socialist market economic system, Chinese government carried out a number of reforms involving in exchange rate, foreign trade and financial etc, which promote international trade, however by the end of 2001 when China access to the WTO, these reforms were almost completed, which limited to promote international trade. The coefficient of the interaction terms- D1 and trade, D1 and import, D1 and export- are all negative. This implies that with the rapid growth of trade, import and export after establishing socialist market economic system in China, although the impact of trade, import and export on economic growth is still positive, but their marginal effect is weakened.

5.4. Regression with Impact of Openness on TFP by Adding Interaction Terms

Except the direct impact of openness on economic growth, openness may impact on economic growth through total factor productivity.

***Table 5.** Models of Openness and Economic growth, Includes Policy Variables*

Dependent Variable=lny												
Variables	FDI model			Trade model			Imports model			Exports model		
	(1)	(2)	(3)	(1)	(2)	(3)	(1)	(2)	(3)	(1)	(2)	(3)
Constant	-0.369 (4.52)***	-0.394 (3.60)***	-0.441 (10.06)***	-0.503 (6.68)***	-0.594 (9.46)***	-0.498 (7.04)***	-0.495 (4.61)***	-0.534 (5.78)***	-0.498 (4.48)***	-0.453 (4.85)***	-0.592 (7.51)***	-0.442 (4.58)***
lnk	0.683 (34.99)***	0.685 (32.78)***	0.667 (28.79)***	0.626 (10.36)***	0.663 (15.85)***	0.625 (10.67)***	0.64 (10.78)***	0.656 (14.86)***	0.639 (10.56)***	0.631 (10.69)***	0.678 (17.37)***	0.63 (10.51)***
ln(FDI)	0.073 (3.88)***	0.069 (3.52)***	0.059 (5.53)***	—	—	—	—	—	—	—	—	—
D1×ln(FDI)	—	-0.0019 -0.38	—	—	—	—	—	—	—	—	—	—
D2×ln(FDI)	—	—	-0.0107 (1.84)*	—	—	—	—	—	—	—	—	—
ln(trade)	—	—	—	0.114 (2.30)**	0.085 (2.32)**	0.116 (2.50)**	—	—	—	—	—	—
D1×ln(trade)	—	—	—	—	-0.0281 (2.95)***	—	—	—	—	—	—	—
D2×ln(trade)	—	—	—	—	—	0.0033 -0.15	—	—	—	—	—	—
ln(import)	—	—	—	—	—	—	0.088 (2.25)**	0.086 (2.30)**	0.088 (2.17)**	—	—	—
D1×ln(import)	—	—	—	—	—	—	—	-0.0203 (2.77)**	—	—	—	—
D2×ln(import)	—	—	—	—	—	—	—	—	-0.0028 -0.24	—	—	—
ln(export)	—	—	—	—	—	—	—	—	—	0.104 (2.51)**	0.065 (1.96)*	0.107 (2.58)**
D1×ln(export)	—	—	—	—	—	—	—	—	—	—	-0.0237 (2.97)**	—
D2×ln(export)	—	—	—	—	—	—	—	—	—	—	—	0.0046 -0.26
Adj- R^2	0.9989	0.9989	0.9979	0.9954	0.9985	0.9952	0.9982	0.9986	0.9981	0.9953	0.9984	0.9952

Notes: Numbers in parentheses are t-statistic, the 1%, 5% and 10% levels of significance are indicated by ***, ** and * respectively.

Table 6. Models of Openness and TFP, Includes Interaction Terms.

Dependent variable=ln(TFP)							
variables	Trade & FDI model			Import & FDI model		Export & FDI model	
	(1)	(2)	(3)	(1)	(2)	(1)	(2)
Constant	-0.7744 (23.24)***	-0.8106 (41.51)***	-0.753 (24.19)***	-0.7715 (26.64)***	-0.7483 (28.26)***	-0.7592 (28.90)***	-0.7388 (30.71)***
ln(rtrade)	0.0135 -1.61	0.0037 -0.84	0.0074 -0.91	—	—	—	—
ln(rimport)	—	—	—	0.0158 -1.76	0.00755 -0.87	—	—
ln(rexport)	—	—	—	—	—	0.0115 -1.47	0.0044 -0.58
ln(rtfp)	0.0143 (3.68)***	0.0999 (4.63)***	—	0.0145 (3.79)***	—	0.0141 (3.58)***	—
ln(rtrade)×ln(rFDI)	—	—	0.004 (3.76)***	—	—	—	—
ln(rimport)×ln(rFDI)	—	—	—	—	0.0051 (3.88)***	—	—
ln(rexport)×ln(rFDI)	—	—	—	—	—	—	0.0048 (3.66)***
ln(rFDI)×ln(rFDI)	—	-0.0226 (4.05)***	—	—	—	—	—
Adj-R^2	0.42	0.64	0.43	0.44	0.44	0.41	0.42
F-statisic	4.81***	6.91***	4.95***	5.04***	5.21***	4.63***	4.77***

Notes: Numbers in parentheses are t-statistic, the 1%, 5% and 10% levels of significance are indicated by ***, ** and * respectively.

So we designed three models to explain how openness impact on economic growth through TFP in detail. In Trade & FDI model, considering the non-linear relationship and interaction between variables, there are three regressions: the first is the linear regression without interaction terms, and the second is the non-linear regression by adding FDI square terms, and the third is linear regression with interaction terms. In Imports & FDI model and Exports & FDI model, each model has two linear regressions: the first is the linear regression without interactions, and second is the linear regression with interaction terms. Of course, in order to improve the robustness of the estimation, the autocorrelation of each model is eliminated by adding AR terms or using Newey-West HAC Standard Errors & Covariance.

Table 6 shows the results of each model. In each model, FDI is positively linked to TFP and it is statistically significant at 1% significance level, but trade, import and export is not significant at any significance level. It implies that increase the proportion of FDI in total investment can spur TFP and hence stimulate economic growth, however increase the proportion of trade, import, export in GDP have no effect on TFP. The possible reason for this is that FDI may help China in introducing advanced technology and enhancing skilled labor, which can increase TFP through technology diffusions and spillover effects. In the first linear regression of Trade & FDI model, FDI have a linear positive effect on TFP, but FDI impacting on TFP may be in non-linear way. So we estimated the non-linear regression with FDI square term. According to the results which are shown in the second non-linear regression of Trade & FDI model, we found 9.12% is the appropriate proportion of FDI in total investment. It implies that the reasonable structure of domestic and foreign investment is necessary for china to spur TFP and hence sustain economic growth.

The results of interactions between FDI and indicators of trade openness are also shown in table 6. The coefficient of interactions between trade and FDI, import and FDI, export and FDI are 0.0040, 0.0051 and 0.0048 respectively. This shows that all integrations have positive effect on TFP and it is statistically significant at 1% significance level. It implies that the interaction term between import and FDI has greater impact on TFP. The possible reason for this is that Chinese imports more than 60% share of manufacture items of total imports that help an economy in attracting foreign direct investment which impact on TFP and hence economic growth positively. This implies that China can attain fruitful effects of trade openness to stimulate TFP and hence economic growth by furthering foreign direct investment in the country.

6. Conclusion

Openness promotes economic growth through various channels e.g., achieving efficiency in allocation of internal and external resource due to trade policies; attracting foreign direct investment; enhancing total factor productivity through creating FDI and trade openness integration, to name a few. In line with the theoretical arguments, the present study examines how openness impact on Chinese economic growth and whether openness can sustain Chinese economic growth. Using Cobb–Douglas production function framework of Mankiw et al. (1992), the paper includes economic growth, TFP and four indicators of openness [FDI, exports, imports and trade (exports+imports)], and uses this specification to derive meaningful results, thereby contributes to the literature of openness and economic growth.

According to the results of empirical analysis, we can get

the following findings: first, there exists long run relationship between trade, FDI and economic growth, both FDI and Trade have positive impact on long-term economic growth and no effect on short-term economic fluctuation; and second, although the impact of trade to economic growth is greater than FDI at the beginning, but from the whole period, the impact of FDI to economic growth presents greater interaction strength and length than Trade; and third, Interactions between FDI, trade openness and policy have significant impact on economic growth, and with the rapid growth of FDI and Trade, their marginal effect on economic growth is reduced; and last, the impact of FDI on TFP is positive, and with the interaction of FDI, trade openness also presents positive effect on TFP.

The findings suggest that openness is becoming an important drive force of Chinese economic growth. It is necessary for Chinese government to manage openness to sustain its' economic growth. First, the government should pay more attention on foreign investment market openness, and hence further foreign direct investment which can obtain more fruits in spurring TFP and stimulating economic growth; and second, the government should continue the market-orient reforms and play a more important role in WTO, thereby promoting trade openness and increasing the confidence of foreign investors; and last, the government should control the scale of FDI and trade, and focus on improving the quality and structure of FDI and trade.

The global economic crisis began to impact China's economy through FDI and trade in late 2008. Higher trade dependence and lower proportion of FDI in total investment have brought a number of difficult challenges to Chinese economy. For example, in 2010, the trade dependence has reached more than 50%, while the proportion of the foreign direct investment in total investment is 2.57%, which dramatically deviate from its' reasonable value (9.12%). So under the uncertain international economic situations, improving the quality and structure of FDI and trade may be a better choice for Chinese government.

Appendix

Appendix 1. *China's Average Annual Real GDP Growth, GDP and GDP per capita, 1980-2011.*

Years	Average Annual Growth (%)	GDP (Billions US$)	GDP per capita (Units US$)	Years	Average Annual Growth (%)	GDP (Billions US$)	GDP per capita (Units US$)
1980	7.91	202.46	205.12	1996	10.01	856.08	699.48
1981	5.20	168.37	168.25	1997	9.30	952.65	770.59
1982	9.10	281.28	276.70	1998	7.83	1,019.48	817.15
1983	10.90	301.8	292.99	1999	7.62	1,083.28	861.21
1984	15.20	310.69	297.72	2000	8.43	1,198.48	945.60
1985	13.50	307.02	290.05	2001	8.30	1,324.81	1,038.04
1986	8.80	297.59	276.81	2002	9.08	1,453.83	1,131.80
1987	11.60	323.97	296.41	2003	10.03	1,640.96	1,269.83
1988	11.30	404.15	364.01	2004	10.09	1,931.65	1,486.02
1989	4.10	451.31	400.44	2005	11.31	2,256.92	1,726.05
1990	3.84	390.28	341.35	2006	12.68	2,712.92	2,063.87
1991	9.18	409.17	353.27	2007	14.16	3,494.24	2,644.56
1992	14.24	488.22	416.68	2008	9.64	4,519.95	3,403.53
1993	13.96	613.22	517.41	2009	9.21	4,990.53	3,738.95
1994	13.08	559.22	466.60	2010	10.45	5,930.39	4,421.00
1995	10.93	727.95	601.01	2011	9.24	7,298.15	5,413.57

Source: International Monetary Fund, World Economic Outlook Database, April 2012

Appendix 2. *China's Values and share of merchandise exports and imports, 1980-2011.*

Year	Export (Millions US$)	Percentage of total world (%)	Import (Millions US$)	Percentage of total world (%)	Year	Export (Millions US$)	Percentage of total world (%)	Import (Millions US$)	Percentage of total world (%)
1980	18099	0.89	19941	0.96	1996	151048	2.79	138943	2.53
1981	22007	1.09	22015	1.06	1997	182792	3.27	142189	2.50
1982	22321	1.18	19285	0.99	1998	183712	3.34	140305	2.49
1983	22226	1.20	21390	1.13	1999	194931	3.41	165788	2.83
1984	26139	1.33	27410	1.36	2000	249203	3.87	225024	3.38
1985	27350	1.39	42252	2.08	2001	266098	4.30	243553	3.79
1986	30942	1.44	42904	1.93	2002	325596	5.03	295170	4.43
1987	39437	1.56	43216	1.67	2003	438228	5.79	412760	5.31
1988	47516	1.65	55268	1.86	2004	593326	6.46	561229	5.92
1989	52538	1.70	59140	1.85	2005	761953	7.25	660206	6.11
1990	62091	1.78	53345	1.49	2006	969380	7.99	791797	6.40
1991	71910	2.05	63791	1.76	2007	1217790	8.69	956233	6.70
1992	84940	2.25	80600	2.08	2008	1428660	8.85	1131620	6.86
1993	91744	2.43	103959	2.71	2009	1201790	9.60	1004170	7.91
1994	121006	2.80	115637	2.64	2010	1578270	10.34	1396200	9.05
1995	148780	2.87	132079	2.52	2011	1899180	10.43	1742850	9.48

Source: UNCTAD, UNCTADstat.

Appendix 3. *China's inward and outward foreign direct investment flows, 1980-2011.*

Year	Inward (millions)	Outward (millions)	Year	Inward (millions)	Outward (millions)
1980	57	-	1996	41725.52	2114
1981	265	-	1997	45257.04	2562.49
1982	430	44	1998	45462.75	2633.807
1983	916	93	1999	40318.71	1774.313
1984	1419	134	2000	40714.81	915.777
1985	1956	629	2001	46877.59	6885.398
1986	2243.73	450	2002	52742.86	2518.407
1987	2313.53	645	2003	53504.7	2854.65
1988	3193.68	850	2004	60630	5497.99
1989	3392.57	780	2005	72406	12261.17
1990	3487.11	830	2006	72715	21160
1991	4366.34	913	2007	83521	22468.86
1992	11007.51	4000	2008	108312	52150
1993	27514.95	4400	2009	95000	56530
1994	33766.5	2000	2010	114734	68811
1995	37520.53	2000	2011	123985	65117

Source: UNCTAD, UNCTADstat.

References

[1] Barba-Navaretti, G. and A. J. Venables, 2006, *Multinational Firms in the World Economy*, Princeton University Press.

[2] Blomstrom, M., A. Kokko, 1998, Multinational Corporations and Spillovers. *Journal of Economic Surveys,* Vol.12, pp.247-77.

[3] C.A.Sims, 1980, Microeconomics and Reality, *Econometrical Modeling Economics Series,* Reprinted in C.W.J. Gramger, Ed., Clarendon Press, Oxford, Vol.48, pp.1-48.

[4] Gorg, H., D. Greenaway, 2004, Much Ado about Nothing? Do Domestic Firms Really Benefit from Foreign Direct Investment? *World Bank Research Observer*, Vol.19, No.2, pp.171-97.

[5] Guo Qingwang, Jia Junxue, 2004, Estimating Potential Output and the Output Gap in China, *Economic Research*, Vol.5:31-39 (in Chinese).

[6] Jiang Yanqing, 2011, Understanding openness and productivity growth in China: An empirical study of the Chinese provinces, *China Economic Review*, Vol.22, pp.290–298.

[7] Johansen, S, 1988, Statistical analysis of cointegrating vectors. *Journal of Economic Dynamics and Control,* Vol.12, pp.231-254.

[8] John Whalley, Xian XIN, 2010, China's FDI and non-FDI economies and the sustainability of future high Chinese growth, *China Economic Review,* Vol.21, pp.123-135.

[9] Kishor K. Guru-Gharana, Deergha R. Adhikari, 2011, Econometric Investigation of Relationships among Export, FDI, and Growth in China: an Application of Toda-Yamamoto-Dolado-Lutkephol Granger Causality Test, *Journal of International Business Research,* Vol.10, No.2, pp.31-50.

[10] Liu Liyan, 2011, FDI and Economic Development: Evidence from Mainland China, *Journal of Service Science and Management*, Vol.4, pp.419-427.

[11] LIU Xiaming, Haiyan Song & Peter Romilly, 1997, An empirical investigation of the causal relationship between openness and economic growth in China, *Applied Economics,* Vol.29, pp.1679-1686.

[12] Love, J., R. Chandra, 2005, Testing export-led growth in Bangladesh in a multivariate VAR framework. *Journal of Asian Economics,* Vol.15, pp.1155-1168.

[13] Mah, J.S., 2005, Export Expansion, economic growth and causality in China. *Applied Economic Letters,* Vol.12, pp.105-07.

[14] Mankiw, N.G., Romer, D., Weil, D.N.,1992, A contribution to the empirics of economic growth. *Quarterly Journal of Economics,* Vol.107, pp.407-437.

[15] NBSC, 2012, *China Statistical Yearbook*, China Statistics Press, Beijing.

[16] NBSC, 2005, *China Statistical Yearbook*, China Statistics Press, Beijing.

[17] Qazi Muhammad Adnan Hye, 2012, Exports, imports and economic growth in China: an ARDL analysis, *Journal of Chinese Economic and Foreign Trade Studies*, Vol. 5 No.1, pp. 42-55.

[18] Yao Shujie, 2006, On economic growth, FDI and exports in China, *Applied Economics,* Vol.38, No.3, pp. 339-351.

[19] Zheng Jinghai, Arne Bigstern & Angang Hu, 2009, Can China's Growth be Sustained? A Productivity Perspective, *World Development,* Vol. 37, No. 4, pp. 874-888.

Customer satisfaction in tourist destination: The case of tourism offer in the city of Naples

Valentina Della Corte[*], Mauro Sciarelli, Clelia Cascella, Giovanna Del Gaudio

Department of Economics, Management, Institutions, University of Naples Federico II, Naples, Italy

Email address:
valentina.dellacorte@unina.it (V. D. Corte), mauro.sciarelli@unina.it (M. Sciarelli), clelia.cascella@unina.it (C. Cascella), giovanna.delgaudio@unina.it (G. D. Gaudio)

Abstract: This paper investigates the main elements that can influence customer satisfaction in tourist services, with specific reference to tourism industry. The importance of this topic resides in the fact that tourists' positive experiences of service, products, and other resources provided by tourism destinations can produce customer retention as well as positive word-of-mouth. Indeed, satisfaction with travel experiences contributes to destination loyalty. The degree of tourists' loyalty to a destination is reflected in their intentions to revisit the destination and in their recommendations to others. Thus, information about tourists' loyalty is important to destination marketers and managers in order to sustain destination attractiveness. Although predominant literature has adopted a demand-side perspective, this paper analyses tourist satisfaction according to an overlapping perspective that contemplates both the demand and the offer side where this latter, in the wider meaning, also includes the systemic perspective. More precisely, this paper aims to identify the principle competitive strategies that the variety of stakeholders, cooperating together in a destination, has to implement in order to increase tourist satisfaction and loyalty. Indeed, the point of view of this paper is to understand how destination attributes and services affect the tourist satisfaction. In order to study the link between destination attributes and tourist satisfaction, the paper collects cross-sectional data via questionnaire, from May 2012 to May 2013. The adopted approach allows to individuate the factors that can influence tourist satisfaction, their (positive or negative) direction and their magnitude. This paper uses 14 tourist satisfaction indicators in order to measure the global satisfaction. Furthermore, this study allows to identify the current strengths and weaknesses of the tourist offer. In particular, the study paid attention to the phase of service delivery since it is the time when customer satisfaction is generated. From this study, it comes out that tourist satisfaction depends on a complex process where the role of each actor is fundamental and it must be in tune with all the other ones. Findings show that tourists visiting Naples are not completely satisfied, supporting that Naples has not a clear destination image.

Keywords: Tourist Satisfaction, Destination Attractiveness, Destination Image, Destination Attributes, Tourist Experience

1. Introduction

Customer satisfaction has always been considered an essential objective in all market sectors, because it is assumed that satisfied customers would repurchase the product/service and are more likely to develop product loyalty.

The aim of this paper is to trace an advancement on the topic of customer satisfaction understanding which can effectively be its determinants. This represents the starting point of the research agenda. Indeed, the paper begins by defining the concept of customer satisfaction to after find, through a literature review, the elements generating customer satisfaction. The paper follows a precise choice about the application of the concept of customer satisfaction in the tourist destinations as, this unit of analysis, allows to understand the real complexity of the topic. Indeed, the empirical application helps to precisely comprehend the link between determinants of satisfaction. The paper concludes with a discussion of the main findings.

Customer satisfaction is determined by "overall feelings, or attitudes, a person has about a product after it has been purchased" (Solomon, 2002): it is often found to be at the heart of firms' marketing activities (Machleit and Mantel, 2001), because it helps them achieving their desired strategic objectives. A higher level of consumer satisfaction can increase customer loyalty (Fint et al., 2011; Qi et al., 2012), reduce price elasticity (Fornell et al., 2006), lower transaction costs (Yang and Peterson, 2004), improve the capacity of attracting new customers (Uncles et al., 2013), help developing a strong reputation in the marketplace (Walsh et al., 2009; Rust et al., 1995) and have a direct impact on the customer retention (Rust et al, 1995). Thus, customer satisfaction is considered as an essential indicator of a company's overall performance.

The core concepts within the research stream of customer satisfaction are assumed by the "service quality" (Lazarus, 1991; Kuo et al., 2009; Zhao et al., 2012) and the "value of the product/service", which in turn depends on the price paid for it (De Rust and Oliver, 1994; Nilsson et al., 2001; Morgeson et al., 2011). The higher is the quality in relation to the price paid, the greater is the value perceived by consumers (Ostrowski, O'Brien and Gordon, 1993; Stock, 2011: Blocker and Flint, 2011).

Furthermore, it is important to underline that customer satisfaction is a post consumption evaluation that disappoints, meets or exceeds expectations and is based on the overall experience (Wang and Yang, 2004).

Expectations are defined as "the individual's beliefs about how a product is likely to perform in the future" (Oliver, 1987). The direct effect of expectations can be explained by the Assimilation Theory (Sherif and Hovland 1961): individuals suffer a psychological conflict when they perceive discrepancies between performance and prior beliefs. Subsequently, consumers tend to adjust perception to their expectations in order to minimize or remove that tension (Oliver 1997). Thus, the assimilation effect can be described as a tendency to process new consumption experiences in terms of existing beliefs. Under these circumstances, satisfaction will be led by expectations (Cherry et al., 2003; Frank and Encawa, 2009; Blocker and Flint, 2011). In this perspective, customer satisfaction is defined by customer's post-purchase assessment of service delivered and comparison of customer's expectations and the actual service experience (Spreng and Dröge, 2001; Higgs et al., 2005; Del Bosque et al., 2006). It is important to underline that in the social network era (Brown et al., 2007; Hartley, 2008), this *ex post* stage can also take place in real time. Indeed, social networks allow the customers to post comments about the experienced service/product both in a post consumption phase and in real time. The satisfaction, being an attitudinal measure (Grisseman and Stockburger-Sauer, 2012) and not a temporal one, has not a precise moment in which it can be expressed by the customer. However, these new tools make the process extremely fast, becoming by far more influential for firms' management.

Customer satisfaction is often defined in the marketing literature as a customer's overall evaluation of his or her purchase and consumption experience of a good or service (Hui et al., 2007; Flint et al., 2011; Qi et al., 2012); it is critically important because it reflects subjective customer evaluations, an emotional response associated with the consumption experience (Kumar, 2005; Grewal et al., 2009; Falk et al, 2010). Similarly, Oliver (1989) established that emotions deriving from evaluations will determine the individual's overall response in the consumption process. This cognitive-affective approach is of great value for application in this study since emotional responses are essential components of the destination experiences (Bigné et al 2005; Ryan 1995).

The importance of emotions in the consumer behavior models has increased significantly during the last few years (Loken, 2006). In particular, it should be emphasized that the cognitive system and emotional states play an important role in satisfaction formation. The higher mental processes of understanding and evaluation would be performed by the cognitive system, whereas emotions would be related to the individual's feelings towards the service (Van Dolen et al, 2004). Finally, loyalty or commitment with respect to a brand is conceived as the main consequence of satisfaction (Brady and Robertson, 2001; Selnes 1993; Yu and Dean, 2001).

Based on this discussion, it is clear that customer satisfaction depends on the existence of overlapping elements such as the indicators and the *ex-ante* expectations. This expresses the multifaceted nature of the topic of customer satisfaction.

In recent years, the role of the consumer has changed from a passive purchaser to an active protagonist of the products/service creation (Arussy, 2002; Hetzel, 2002; LaSalle, Britton, 2003; Shaw, Ivans, 2004; Yastrow, 2003). The centrality of the "experience" concept has been reinforced by the technological innovations in the fields of goods purchase and consumption. The consumer wants to be more involved and be on of the main actors in product/service creation.

Concerning this perspective, the experiential approach focuses on the affective and emotional component of the consumption process. The concept of "experience" is strictly connected with the entertainment aspect and implies the consumer participation and interaction during the product/service creation. Building an experience means bring the product/service to life and underline its identity through the sensorial involvement of the consumer (Shaw, Ivens, 2002; Smith, Wheeler, 2002). Pine and Gilmore (2011) define the experience as the main subject of exchange with the consumer: it can be considered as a new type of supply, along with tangible products and intangible services.

The existing literature demonstrates that customer satisfaction can depend on a series of elements that belong to the subjective sphere of the customer and to the objective quality of the product/service experienced. Some works concentrate their attention on the individual components influencing the satisfaction (customer perspective), while others focus on the intrinsic features of the product/service and on the way through which it is delivered (firm perspective). Hence, customer satisfaction is the result of an overlapping perspective. Actually, it is possible to add another perspective to the already existing two. This is the systemic perspective that is verified when it is dealt with complex products such as the tourist product one. Therefore, this paper also adopts the systemic perspective, proposing a design of the paper that adheres to this scheme both in literature background and in the empirical session.

More precisely the objective of the paper is to:

- understand the relationship between the antecedents of customer satisfaction adopting an offer-side perspective;
- comprehend if it exists a systemic perspective in the topic of customer satisfaction of complex product/service and what are the elements that contribute to shape it;
- identify the perception of the customer about the main components of satisfaction, considering so the demand-side perspective

2. Customer Satisfaction in Tourism Industry

In the tourism context the concept of tourist satisfaction is particularly relevant as well as difficult to deal with as the tourist product is "complex" by definition (Smith, 1994). Furthermore, due to the global competition destinations and, more precisely, DMOs (Destination Management Organizations) are facing the competition at global level.

In this scenario destination competitiveness acquires a strategic role (Kozak and Rimmington, 1999) in order to determine the actual and future success of destination itself.

According to some authors (Kozak and Rimmington, 1999) some attributes can contribute to the real destination competitiveness. These attributes refer to the variables that influence the satisfaction or dissatisfaction of tourists during their vacation.

This is the reason why this paper analyzes the issue of tourist satisfaction.

Indeed, it can be easily noticed that the contemporary tourist wants to live a unique experience and is not interested anymore in purchasing a standardized product/service: in order to meet the new needs of the demand, the tourist destinations must give top priority to the achievement of tourist satisfaction.

The literature concerning this subject is limited due to the several aspects defining this issue and the consequent lack of a holistic perspective. This holistic vision should include the cognitive, affective and systemic (Hartman, 1973) constructs of tourist satisfaction and the attributes that characterize the destination.

In other words, tourist satisfaction has to be analyzed according to an overlapping perspective that contemplates both the demand and the offer side where this latter, in the wider meaning, also includes the systemic perspective.

Although predominant literature has adopted a demand-side perspective (Fields 2002; Xia et al., 2009), this paper aims to identify the principle competitive strategies a tourist destination has to implement in order to increase tourist satisfaction and loyalty. Indeed, the point of view of this paper is to understand how destination attributes and services affect the tourist satisfaction.

The previously cited literature illustrates the importance of customer satisfaction and loyalty for the product/service, which is also linked to firm's performance metrics such as higher profitability and repurchase (Kumar and Petersen, 2005; Fornell et al., 2006). Satisfaction reflects "a positive affective state resulting from a customer's cumulative appraisal of its provider relationship" (Lam et al., 2004); customer satisfaction is crucial in all market sectors due to its great impact on future consumer intentions, loyalty and word-of-mouth communications. Its centrality increases in those fields in which the product/service to be delivered is mainly intangible and the principle challenge is the confection of an experience that perfectly matches the consumer's expectations. That is why this paper focuses on customer satisfaction in the tourism market.

The importance of the topic of tourist satisfaction is testified by many academic contributions, whose literary production started in the 1960s (Xia et al., 2009), and by the increasing attention that practitioners have given to this research issue.

Of course numerous scholars have questioned on what tourist satisfaction depends and, hence, have challenged themselves to the research of those elements that could influence the generation of tourist satisfaction.

Within these studies, there is a research stream supporting the vision that the destination image affects the tourist satisfaction (Cooper, Fletcher and Gilbert, 1993; Lee et al, 2002).

Actually, one of the main gaps is that most of works that analyse this bond between destination image and tourist satisfaction do not linger on behavioral consequences of tourists "such as loyalty and positive word-of-mouth" (Veasna et al., 2013) related to the destination. These latters, in a measure, can be the sources of destination image. Indeed, "destination image is defined as an attitudinal concept consisting of the sum of beliefs, ideas and impressions that a tourist holds of a destination" (Hosany et al., 2006). The destination image plays a key role for the choice of the destination, for the consecutive evaluation and for the future intentions to return and recommend it (Bigné et al., 2001; Chen and Tsai, 2007).

The explosion of contributions that conceive destination image as an antecedent of tourist satisfaction represents a clear gap in literature.

This vision, indeed, appears fairly reductive and static since it does not consider that destination image can be influenced by the experience itself (Oliver and Burke, 1999; Rodríguez del Bosque and San Martín, 2008). The modification of destination image, hence, can also be conceived as consequence of satisfaction.

In the light of these observations, this paper is exactly developed on the existence of a clear relationship between tourist satisfaction and destination image.

To better understand this relationship, the article is outlined to first understand what are the items that influence the tourist satisfaction to after capture the destination image shaped in the mind of the tourists.

If tourism literature has mostly focused the attention on tourism satisfaction, this is due to the fact that from it a series of concepts descends such as loyalty (Song et al, 2012) or tourist complaints (Lee *et al.*, 2011).

With reference to the tourism sector, a review of the literature on motivation reveals that people travel because they are "pushed" into making travel decisions by internal, psychological forces, and "pulled" by the external forces of the destination attributes (Crompton, 1979; Dann, 1977; Uysal and Jurowski, 1994). Accordingly, satisfaction with travel experiences, based on these push and pull forces, contributes to destination loyalty. The degree of tourists' loyalty to a destination is reflected in their intentions to revisit the destination and in their recommendations to others (Oppermann, 2000). Thus, information about tourists' loyalty is important to destination marketers and managers.

The complexity of the theme of tourist satisfaction depends on its richness in terms of contents. The satisfaction, in general, is a latent variable (Bagozzi et al, 1981; Fornell et al., 1996; Fonseca, 2009; Kaplan *et al.*, 2007; Song et al, 2012) that, in order to be defined needs to consider what are the antecedents determining it as well as the consequences and the relative relationships among the indicators that are the expression of tourist satisfaction.

Literature on this subject measures the tourist satisfaction in different ways. These differences can depend on the use of various methodologies and indicators.

Since satisfaction derives from a post-purchase analysis (Fornell, 1992; Westbrook and Oliver, 1991), studies have indicated innumerable measures to evaluate travel experience (Bramwell, 1998).

This experience implies an encounter with the service and the relative "judgment" (Bowen and Schouten, 2008) expressed by tourists after their experience that can determine satisfaction or dissatisfaction. The theme is dealt with the perspectives of overall satisfaction (Wan and Chan, 2013).

According to a destination management approach (Xia et al., 2009), destination attributes are of fundamental importance for the valuation of the experience (Alegre and Garau, 2010). The evaluation is also the result between the attributes and the *ex ante* tourist's expectation (Tribe and Snaith, 1998).

Within this theoretical context, several authors (Ekinci and Hosany, 2006; Usakli et al.,2011; Qu et al., 2012) have adopted the concept of destination image: in order to achieve the desired outcomes, the building of a coherent brand image and the way the destination is perceived by actual and potential tourists are considered as the principal factors upon which depends the success of the destination itself (Voase, 2012).

The image could be defined as the "set of values, ideas and impressions a destination is able to stimulate in the minds of the actual and potential tourists" (Della Corte, Micera, 2007). The peculiarity of this vision focuses on the impressions the destination could and must induce both in the potential tourist (induced marketing level), both in the effective visitors (organic marketing level).

During the transmission process of the positive associations, it is important to avoid stereotypes (Kotler et al., 1993) and be able to create and to manage a unique brand image, especially if the destination has a multiple tourist vocation and deals with a variety of different products/services (Della Corte, 2009). The procedure is even more complicated when the destination is characterized by contradictory factors (Ruzzier, de Chernatony, 2013), between which some are able to transmit positive images (such as artistic or natural beauties etc.), some are completely negative (like traffic, criminality, etc.). In addition to this, it is important to underline that the contemporary market is unpredictable and in constant expansion, so it is difficult to build and coordinate an image able to reach the entire target, constituted by both the loyal and the new customers (Ferns and Walls, 2010; Ekinci et al., 2013).

Table 1. *Items of tourist satisfaction*

Item	Literature on tourist satisfaction using these items	6As Model
Easy access through different modes of transportation	Wan and Chan, 2011; 2013; Della Corte, 2013; Kozak and Rimmington 1998; Kozak, 2001; Vetter, 1985	Access
Accommodation	Xia et al, 2009; Hui et al 2007; Ekinci et al., 2003; Kozak, 2001	Accommodation
Quality of streets and road-signs	-	Access
Restaurants' quality and diversity	Xia et al, 2009; Hui et al 2007; Nield et al., 2000	Amenities
Entertainment	Mikulić and Prebežac, 2011; Xia et al, 2009; Wan and Chan, 2013; Coghlan, 2011	Amenities/Ancillary services
Price and value	Yu and Goulden, 2006; Xia et al, 2009; Kozak, 2001	Access, Attractions, Amenities, Ancillary services, Assemblage, Accommodation
On stage information accessibility	Ortega and Rodríguez, 2007	Access
Local transport	Xia et al, 2009; Thompson and Schofield, 2007; Kozak, 2001	Access
Perceived security	Tasci and Boylu, 2010; Weiermair and Fuchs, 1999	Access, Attractions, Amenities, Ancillary services, Assemblage, Accommodation
Disabled friendly infrastructures	Daniels et al., 2005	Access, Attractions, Amenities, Ancillary services, Assemblage, Accommodation
Cleanliness of the city	Xia et al, 2009; Merrilees et al., 2009; Alegre and Garau, 2010	-
Hospitable (local) people	Jenkins, 1999; Kozak, 2001; Yoon and Uysal, 2005)	-
Organization of cultural events	Chhabra et al., 2003; Kim et al., 2010; Kruger et al., 2013	Amenities/Ancillary services
Activities	Bowen and Schouten, 2008; Danaher and Arweiler, 1996; Kozak, 2001	Amenities/Ancillary services

Working on the brand and the image means dealing with the process of connection between induced and organic level: it is important to keep strong the coherence with the reality of the local supply, in order not to cause a "boomerang effect" and a negative word of mouth (Hudson and Ritchie, 2009). In the destination customer satisfaction pyramid (Della Corte, 2000) it is underlined the centrality of the quality of the tourist products and services truly provided in the destination. The organic level marketing, hence, is an essential component of the customer satisfaction and retention (Della Corte, 2009).

3. Methodology

Indeed, scholars use different measures to analyse the effects of attributes on tourist satisfaction. In order to identify the right indicators, this study has proceeded with a systematic review on the works related to tourist satisfaction to understand what items have been taken into account.

Furthermore, this paper conceives these indicators in the light of the scheme of the 6As model (Cooper et al., 1993; Della Corte, 2013), according to which a destination is characterized by the following features: 1. *access*; 2. *attractions*; 3. *accommodation* ; 4. *amenities*; 5. *assemblage* 6. *ancillary services*. Indeed, variables are also grouped according to this scheme.

This review has led to the identification of fourteen indicators, that precisely are:

- *Easy access through different modes of transportation:* several studies (Wan and Chan, 2011; 2013; Della Corte, 2013; Kozak and Rimmington 1998; Kozak, 2001) emphasize the important role of accessibility. The mode of transport used to access the destination contributes in a real way to the overall satisfaction (Vetter, 1985);
- *Accommodation:* extant literature (Xia et al, 2009; Nash et al., 2006) on tourism satisfaction reveals that accommodations are strategic players for both the competitiveness of the destination (Ekinci et al., 2003) and the tourist satisfaction itself.
- *Quality of streets and road-signs:* although this is an underestimate attribute within tourism satisfaction literature, during the phase of fruition the creation of a supportive environment rather than complicated can surely avoid dissatisfaction and complaints. Despite previous literature on the topic, we decide to include this variable in the current study since its can produce dissatisfaction.
- *Restaurants' quality and diversity:* according to some authors (Nield et al., 2000; Kim et al., 2010) the issue of "food service experience" has been understimated within the works studying tourist satisfaction. Since that the consumption of food and beverage in a destination depends on physical, cultural, interpersonal, and status motivations (Fields, 2002), this indicator becomes of extreme importance for the evaluation of satisfaction. In particular the attention in previous studies is stressed on variety, quality and price of food (Hui et al 2007).
- *Entertainment:* some studies find that entertainment has effect on tourist satisfaction (Mikulić and Prebežac, 2011; Xia et al, 2009; Wan and Chan, 2013; Coghlan, 2011). Entertainment per se cannot generate satisfaction but rather its quality, variety and attractiveness (Mikulić and Prebežac, 2011) is able to influence the satisfaction with the destination.
- *Price and value:* the perception of price and value is examined in previous studies as it is considered "one consistent satisfaction attribute" (Yu and Goulden, 2006, p.1338).
- *On stage information accessibility:* during the organic phase the access to local tourist information is of fundamental importance. In the digital age, the information can be delivered through the traditional tourist information center or the most advanced mobile devices. Literature on tourist information has overemphasized the importance of tourist information for destination choice and, hence, at the induced level (Jacobsen and Munar, 2012), underestimating the role of access to information at organic level. The search for information and the relative accuracy and promptness contribute to partial satisfaction. As Ortega and Rodríguez (2007, p. 147) underline that "tourism literature needs more research about information at destinations". This is the reason why this paper takes into account this variable.
- *Local transport:* the availability and perceived quality of local transport at tourist destinations has been established as exercising an influence on visitor experience, overall satisfaction and repeat visitation (Thompson and Schofield, 2007)
- *Perceived security:* safety and security of a destination are seen to have a big impact on the level of satisfaction with a tourist trip (Tasci and Boylu, 2010).
- *Disabled friendly infrastructures:* studies reveal that the combination of barriers affecting travellers with disabilities may operate to decrease their travel satisfaction (Daniels et al., 2005).
- *Hospitable (local) people:* friendliness and hospitality of the locals is one of the principal destination attributes that leads to tourist satisfaction (Jenkins, 1999; Kozak, 2001; Yoon and Uysal, 2005).
- *Organization of cultural events:* the high perception of authenticity of the destination can be pushed by the organization of cultural events, related to heritage, gastronomy, music etc. Studies demonstrate that the organization of cultural events could be a measure of product quality and a determinant of tourism satisfaction (Chhabra et al., 2003; Kim et al., 2010; Kruger et al., 2013).
- *Cleanliness of the city:* various scholars demonstrate that cleanliness and hygiene of the city are one of the main determinants of tourist satisfaction with the destination, while dirtiness is a clear factor of dissatisfaction (Merrilees et al., 2009; Alegre and Garau, 2010).

- *Activities:* the availability of a variety of activity (Bowen and Schouten, 2008; Danaher and Arweiler, 1996; Kozak, 2001) can assure the tourist satisfaction. The paper considers under the voice "activities" all the other activities not previously estimated in the questionnaire.

As viewed, there are many attributes which affect the tourist satisfaction. The complexity of a destination in terms existing factors makes difficult to evaluate the overall satisfaction. This is the reason why we considered the above-identified concepts as items of partial satisfaction since each of them contributes to define the level of satisfaction globally achieved by the tourist. From here the research question at the basis of the paper is: Do these factors singled out of the literature on the topic effectively influence tourist satisfaction?

3.1. Data Collection

The data of this paper was collected in Naples during the period May 2012-May 2013. Naples is a city located in Southern Italy with 2.166.518 presences and 918.485 visitors arrivals per year (Ente Provinciale del Turismo, 2014).

The survey was conducted through an *ad hoc* questionnaire, administrated to a convenience sample during three different periods of time in order to better capture the dynamicity of tourist satisfaction.

The questionnaires was pre-tested in May 2012 and later distributed in December-January and again in May 2013.

Respondents were selected by using convenience criteria, that means be based on the tourists' availability to be interviewed.

The questionnaires have been administered in "collecting areas" (Levy and Lemeshow, 2011) that, in our case, are the INFOPOINTs (i.e. tourist information offices activated by the city of Naples) and some hotels. In particular, for each grading class, the number of selected hotels is proportional to the number of hotels that compose the relative grading (population) class.

We collected cross-sectional data, i.e. data gathered by administering the same questionnaire to different samples composed by tourists characterized by similar features. The principal limitation of this study is our sampling design: we used little and convenient samples, constituted by 120 units in the first wave and 200 units in the second wave: for this reason, our findings cannot be generalized to the entire population. Nevertheless, this paper is aimed at developing a practical brief "guide" that can be used to monitor each satisfaction level over time. Therefore, by using our simple empirical approach it is possible to highlight strengths and weaknesses of the current local offer.

The units that compose our samples, in each wave, have similar features (tab. 2) and this factor facilitates the comparison between the results obtained by using our methodology.

***Table 2.** Descriptive statistics*

	I wave							
	58%							
	Age		Do you are here with		Why do you are here		Professional Status	
Men	Less of 24	9,76	Alone	4,76	Holliday	92,86	Student	17,50
	24 - 44	43,90	With your partner	35,71	Job	2,38	Employee	15,00
	45 - 64	43,90	With your family	57,14	Study	4,76	Self-employed worker	52,50
	More then 64	2,44	With your friends/colleagues	2,38	Other	0,00	Retired	15,00
	42%							
	Age		Do you are here with		Why do you are here		Professional Status	
Women	Less of 24	3,45	Alone	0,00	Holliday	100,00	Student	7,14
	24 - 44	37,93	With your partner	51,72	Job	0,00	Employee	32,14
	45 - 64	41,38	With your family	48,28	Study	0,00	Self-employed worker	39,29
	More then 64	17,24	With your friends/colleagues	0,00	Other	0,00	Retired	21,43

***Table 2.** Continued*

	II wave							
	47%							
	Age		Do you are here with		Why do you are here		Professional Status	
Men	Less of 24	1,64	Alone	10,53	Holliday	89,09	Student	6,56
	24 - 44	37,70	With your partner	56,14	Job	7,27	Employee	22,95
	45 - 64	45,90	With your family	29,82	Study	3,64	Self-employed worker	49,18
	More then 64	14,75	With your friends/colleagues	3,51	Other	0,00	Retired	21,31
	53%							
	Age		Do you are here with		Why do you are here		Professional Status	
Women	Less of 24	11,67	Alone	9,84	Holliday	86,44	Student	17,24
	24 - 44	48,33	With your partner	45,90	Job	8,47	Employee	18,97
	45 - 64	36,67	With your family	39,34	Study	5,08	Self-employed worker	56,90
	More then 64	3,33	With your friends/colleagues	4,92	Other	0,00	Retired	6,90

4. Customers' Satisfaction Analysis

In order to measure the impact of our 14 partial satisfaction indicators, we calculated the *attributable risk*, that is a version of the traditional odd-ratio. The attributable risk expresses the proportion of unsatisfied units (of tourists) attributable to one or more risk factors (i.e. in our case it is imputable to the dissatisfaction connected to the partial satisfaction indicator). Therefore, we can pinpoint all the factors that can influence the tourist experience in Naples and we can also quantify the magnitude of such influence. In other words, the attributable risk index defines the proportion of unsatisfied units that can be removed by eliminating the risk factor (Buzzetti and Mastroiacovo, 2000).

Before calculating this index, we analyzed the internal consistency of our set of partial satisfaction indexes by using the *Cronbach's alpha*. The items' *internal consistency* is a property of scales and concerns empirical indicators of a general concept (Giampaglia, 1990; Corbetta, 1999). Since these indicators are indirect tools useful to reveal a general concept, they imply both casual and systematic errors. By using the *reliability analysis*, and in particular by implementing the *Cronbach's alpha*, we can obtain a measure of reliability level of selected indicators. So, in other words, we can ascertain that selected items constitute a one-dimensional scale, i.e. they are able to reveal the underlying dimension that, in our study, is the global tourist satisfaction (Nunnally, 1978).

When the *alpha* value is higher than 0.75, it confirms the internal consistency of the partial satisfaction indicators (table 3).

Table 3. *Internal consistency (Cronbach α)*

	Alpha	N items
I wave	0.864	14
II wave	0.889	14

By carrying out a descriptive analysis, we can immediately individuate satisfying, unsatisfying and neutral factors.

Among the satisfying factors, we can pinpoint the comfort and the esay access through different modes of transportation, the accommodation, the restaurants' quality and diversity, the price and value, the perceived security, other (not specified by us) activities that are interesting for the tourists interviewed and hospitable local people. Those factors are mainly delivered by local private actors, with the exception of one variable (perceived security), guaranteed by the city of Naples (table 4).

Table 4. *Satisfier factors (I wave)*

	Easy access through different modes of transportation	Accommodation	Restaurants' quality and diversity	Price and value	Perceived security	Other activities	Hospitable (local) people	
unsatisfied	12,50	7,59	7,27	3,33	16,39	26,00	6,15	unsatisfied
uninteresting	25,00	34,18	29,09	15,00	24,59	32,00	3,08	uninteresting
satisfied	62,50	58,23	63,64	81,67	59,02	42,00	90,77	satisfied
	100,00	100,00	100,00	100,00	100,00	100,00	100,00	

Table 5. *Neutral and/or satisfier factors (I wave)*

	Entertainment	On stage information accessibility	Cultural events' organization
unsatisfied	24,24	26,15	26,00
uninteresting	39,39	36,92	34,00
satisfied	36,36	36,92	40,00
	100,00	100,00	100,00

Table 6. *Internal consistency (Cronbach α)*

	Public transportation	Disabled-friendly infrastructures	Quality of streets and road-signs	Cleanliness of the city
unsatisfied	84,06	92,00	38,33	79,37
uninteresting	13,04	2,67	45,00	11,11
satisfied	2,90	5,33	16,67	9,52
	100,00	100,00	100,00	100,00

Other services delivered by the city of Naples (in such cases, in cooperation with local actors) are differently perceived and can be classified as neutral or (quite) satisfying factors (table 5).

Finally, among the dissatisfying factors, we can list the public transportation, disabled-friendly infrastructures, the quality of the streets and road-signs and the cleanliness of the city. All those factors are guaranteed by the city of Naples (table 6).

In order to appreciate the magnitude of each indicator on global satisfaction, we can calculate the *attributable risk (RA)*.

Then, for example, the first index (related to easy access through different modes of transportation) is equal to 0,20. It means that we could diminish the number of unsatisfied customers (-20%) if we improve the comfort and the frequency of access through different modes of transportation. Therefore, the bigger is the value of attributable risk, the greater is the impact of each occurring indicator. So, according to findings showed in table 6, it is clear that some variables, such as amusement (0,05) and perceived security

(0,08) are neutral (Cadotte and Turgeon; 1988), i.e. they do not have an appreciable influence on the global customer satisfaction. Viceversa, other factors, such as the hospitality of the locals (0,40) or the cleanliness of the city (0,30) have a significant impact on global tourist satisfaction.

By carrying out the same type of analysis on the data of the II wave, we obtained diverse results. In this case, on the base of the gathered data, it is possible to pinpoint different satisfying, neutral and dissatisfying factors.

In particular, among satisfying factors, we can list again the accommodation, catering/restaurants/etc., the price/quality ratio, hospitable local people and other (not specified by us) activities that are interesting for the tourists interviewed. Differently from the results showed above, between the satisfying factors, there are also amusement, availability of touristic information and the quality of streets and road-signs (table 8), that, in the previous period, was considered a dissatisfying factor.

Table 7. *Attributable risk (I wave).*

Item	I wave
	RA
Easy access through different modes of transportation	0,20
Quality of streets and road-signs	0,07
Accommodation	0,27
Restaurants' quality and diversity	0,10
Entertainment	0,05
Price and value	0,23
On stage information accessibility	0,11
Public transportation	0,17
Perceived security	0,08
Disabled-friendly infrastructures	0,17
Cleanliness of the city	0,30
Other (not specified by the questionnaire) activities that are interesting for tourists interviewed	0,30
Hospitable (local) people.	0,40
Organization of cultural events	0,17

Table 8. *Satisfaiers factors (II wave)*

	Accommodation	Restaurants' quality and diversity	Entertainment	Price and value
unsatisfied	5,94	2,68	5,94	5,94
uninteresting	17,82	10,71	17,82	17,82
satisfied	76,24	86,61	76,24	76,24
	100	100	100	100
	Quality of streets and road-signs	On stage information accessibility	Hospitable (local) people	Other activities
unsatisfied	5,94	14,95	5,56	8,06
uninteresting	17,82	26,17	16,67	33,87
satisfied	76,24	58,88	77,78	58,06
	100,00	100,00	100,00	100,00

Table 9. *Internal consistency (Cronbach α) Neutral/satisfier factors (II wave)*

	Easy access through different modes of transportation	Cultural events' organization
unsatisfied	5,95	12,77
uninteresting	36,90	37,23
satisfied	57,14	50,00
	100	100

Also the neutral/satisfying factors are different: in this mixed class, there are now easy access through different modes of transportation and organization of cultural events (table 9).

Finally, like in the first case, all the services delivered by the city of Naples are listed among dissatisfying factors (table 10).

Table 10. *Dissatisfiers factors (II wave)*

	Public transportation	Perceived security	Disabled - friendly infrastructures	Cleanliness of the city
unsatisfied	33,33	38,83	37,50	56,19
uninteresting	23,53	23,30	43,06	24,76
satisfied	43,14	37,86	19,44	19,05
	100	100	100	100

In addition to this, in order to appreciate the magnitude of each indicator on the global satisfaction, we calculated the attributable risk (table 11).

Table 11. *Internal consistency (Cronbach α)*

Item	I wave
	RA
Easy access through different modes of transportation	0,06
Quality of streets and road-signs	0,13
Accommodation	0,27
Restaurants' quality and diversity	0,31
Entertainment	0,30
Price and value	0,21
On stage information accessibility	0,19
Public transportation	0,20
Perceived security	0,22
Disabled-friendly infrastructures	0,08
Cleanliness of the city	0,11
Other (not specified by the questionnaire) activities that are interesting for tourists interviewed	0,30
Hospitable (local) people.	0,32
Organization of cultural events	0,23

5. Conclusions and Hints for the Future

This study investigated the effects of some destination attributes on the generation of customer satisfaction.

According to a great deal of scientific literature, tourist satisfaction can influence some behaviours such as customer retention as well as word-of-mouth or word-of-mouse processes.

The empirical section of this paper proposed a demand analysis based on data collected via questionnaire in order to reveal the global tourist satisfaction, measured by using partial satisfaction indexes. In particular, the study analysed: 1. services provided by city (i.e. public transportation and perceived security, etc.), 2. services offered by local firms (i.e., hotel, restaurants, night clubs, etc.); and 3. other services, provided by Public Administration and local firms, such as cultural events (Cooper, Fletcher, Gilbert, Wanhill, 1993; Della Corte, 2009). The focus of our investigation was a city in the South of Italy, Naples.

The findings of this research support that Naples has not a clear destination image. Consequently, if we consider this latter assertion, it is possible to state that tourists visiting Naples are not completely satisfied. More precisely, Naples is denoted by a very conflicting image: on one side, it is associated to excellent food tradition and to natural and artistic beauties but, on the other side, it is perceived as a dirty place and characterized by criminality and disorganization. Moreover, the magnitude of Neapolitan cultural, historical and traditional heritage is under-dimensioned in tourists' perceptions.

From this study, it comes out that tourist satisfaction depends on a complex process where the role of each actor is fundamental and it must be in tune with all the other ones.

According to these results, it is clear that the correct individuation of the main factors that can generate customer satisfaction is fundamental to orient future strategic actions. Furthermore, the longitudinal analysis showed that it is more than ever necessary the realization of orchestration strategies, enacted by both local public and private actors to remove negative factors (or to reduce their impact) and to amplify the effects of positive factors influencing tourist satisfaction.

Thus, from a theoretical point of view, the paper presents a focus on customer satisfaction with specific reference to service industries. These are peculiar since the service is evaluated in the same time of its provision, thus making it very difficult and challenging for firms to propose adequate offers to an increasingly needful demand. Both methods and tools are proposed. Besides, these results are very useful for decision makers since they drive the process of managing tourism offer connected with tourist image, in an experience-based view. The limitations regard the fact that the empirical analysis was carried out just in a specific area and should be extended to other destinations for further comparisons.

References

[1] J. Alegre, J. Garau, "Tourist satisfaction and dissatisfaction," in Annals of Tourism Research, vol. 1, 2010, pp. 52-73.

[2] L. Arussy, "The experience! How to wow your customers and create a passionate workplace," San Francisco: CMP Books, 2002.

[3] M. Augustyn, S. K. Ho, "Service quality and tourism," in Journal of Travel Research vol. 37, 1998, pp. 71-75.

[4] R. P. Bagozzi, "Evaluating structural equation models with unobservable variables and measurement error: a comment," in Journal of Marketing Research, 1981, pp.375-381.

[5] J. E. Bigné, L. Andreu, J. Gnoth, "The theme park experience: An analysis of pleasure, arousal and satisfaction," in Tourism Management, vol. 26, 2005, pp. 833-844.

[6] J. E. Bigne, M. I. Sanchez, J. Sanchez, "Tourism image, evaluation variables and after purchase behaviour: inter-relationship," in Tourism management, vol. 22, 2001, pp. 607-616.

[7] D. J. Flint, C. P. Blocker, P. J. Boutin Jr, "Customer value anticipation, customer satisfaction and loyalty: An empirical examination," in Industrial Marketing Management, vol. 40, 2011, pp. 219-230.

[8] D. Bowen, A. F. Schouten, "Tourist satisfaction and beyond: tourist migrants in Mallorca," in International Journal of Tourism Research, vol. 10, 2008, pp. 141-153.

[9] M. K. Brady, C. J. Robertson, "Searching for a consensus on the antecedent role of service quality and satisfaction: an exploratory cross-national study," in Journal of Business Research, vol. 51, 2001, pp. 53-60.

[10] B. Bramwell, "User satisfaction and product development in urban tourism," in Tourism Management, vol. 19, 1998, pp. 35-47.

[11] J. Brown, A. J. Broderick, N. Lee, "Word of mouth communication within online communities: Conceptualizing the online social network," in Journal of interactive marketing, vol. 21, 2007, pp. 2-20.

[12] E. R. Cadotte, N. Turgeon, "Key factors in guest satisfaction," in Cornell Hotel and Restaurant Administration Quarterly, vol. 28, 1998, pp. 45-51.

[13] C. F. Chen, D. Tsai, "How destination image and evaluative factors affect behavioral intentions?," in Tourism management, vol. 28, 2007, pp. 1115-1122.

[14] B. Cherry, L. D. Ordóñez, S. W. Gilliland, "Grade expectations: The effects of expectations on fairness and satisfaction perceptions," in Journal of Behavioral Decision Making, vol. 16, 2003, pp. 375-395.

[15] D. Chhabra, R. Healy, E. Sills, "Staged authenticity and heritage tourism," in Annals of tourism research, vol. 30, 2003, pp. 702-719.

[16] A. Coghlan, "Linking natural resource management to tourist satisfaction: a study of Australi''s Great Barrier reef," in Journal of Sustainable Tourism, vol. 20, 2011, pp. 41-58.

[17] C. Cooper, J. Fletcher, D. Gilbert, S. Wanhill, "Tourism principles and practice," London: Addison Wesley Longman, 1993.

[18] P. Corbetta, " Metodologia e tecniche della ricerca sociale," Bologna: Il Mulino, 1999.

[19] J. L. Crompton, "Motivations for Pleasure Vacation," in Annals of Tourism Research, vol. 6, 1979, pp. 408-424.

[20] P. J. Danaher, N. Arweiler, "Customer Satisfaction in the Tourist Industry. A Case Study of Visitors to New Zealand," in Journal of Travel Research, v. 35, 1996, pp. 89-93.

[21] M. J. Daniels, E. B. Drogin Rodgers, B. P. Wiggins, "<<Travel Tales>>: an interpretive analysis of constraints and negotiations to pleasure travel as experienced by persons with physical disabilities," in Tourism Management, v. 26, 2005, pp. 919-930.

[22] G. Dann, G., "Anomie, ego-enhancement and tourism," in Annals of tourism research, vol. 4, 1977, pp. 184-194.

[23] R. T. Rust, R. W. Oliver, "The death of advertising," in Journal of Advertising, v. 23, 1994, pp. 71-77.

[24] I. R. Del Bosque, H. S. Martín, "Tourist satisfaction a cognitive-affective model," in Annals of Tourism Research, v. 35, 2008, pp. 551-573.

[25] V. Della Corte, "Imprese e sistemi turistici: il management. II Edizione,", Milano: Egea, 2013.

[26] V. Della Corte, "Imprese e Sistemi Turistici: il Management," Milano: Egea, 2009.

[27] V. Della Corte, R. Micera, "Il caso della Penisola Sorrentina," in S. Sciarelli, "Il management dei sistemi turistici locali: strategie e strumenti per la governance," Torino: Giappichelli, 2007.

[28] S. Hosany, Y. Ekinci, M. Uysal, "Destination image and destination personality: An application of branding theories to tourism places," in Journal of Business Research, v. 59, 2006, pp. 638-642.

[29] Y. Ekinci, P. Prokopaki, C. Cobanoglu, "Service quality in Cretan accommodations: marketing strategies for the UK holiday market," in International Journal of Hospitality Management, v. 22, 2003, pp. 47-66.

[30] Y. Ekinci, E. Sirakaya-Turk, S. Preciado, "Symbolic consumption of tourism destination brands," in Journal of Business Research, v. 66, 2013, pp. 711-718.

[31] T. Falk, M. Hammerschmidt, J. J. Schepers, "The service quality-satisfaction link revisited: exploring asymmetries and dynamics," in Journal of the Academy of Marketing Science, v. 38, 2010, pp. 288-302.

[32] B. H. Ferns, A. Walls, "Enduring travel involvement, destination brand equity, and travelers' visit intentions: A structural model analysis," in Journal of Destination Marketing & Management, v. 1, 2012, pp. 27-35.

[33] K. Fields, "Demand for the gastronomy tourism product: motivational factors," in Tourism and gastronomy, 2002, pp. 36-50.

[34] D. J. Flint, C. P. Blocker, P. J. Boutin Jr, P. J., "Customer value anticipation, customer satisfaction and loyalty: An empirical examination", Industrial Marketing Management, v. 40, 2011, pp. 219-230.

[35] J. R. Fonseca, "Customer satisfaction study via a latent segment model," in Journal of Retailing and Consumer Services, v. 16, 2009, pp. 352-359.

[36] C. Fornell, "A national customer satisfaction barometer: the Swedish experience," in Journal of Marketing, v. 56, 1992, pp. 6-21.

[37] C. Fornell, S. Mithas, F. V. Morgeson III, F. V., M. S. Krishnan, "Customer satisfaction and stock prices: high returns, low risk," in Journal of Marketing, v. 70, 2006, pp. 3-14.

[38] B. Frank, T. Enkawa, "Economic influences on perceived value, quality expectations and customer satisfaction," in International Journal of Consumer Studies, v. 33, 2009, pp. 72-82.

[39] G. Giampaglia, "Lo scaling unidimensionale nella ricerca sociale," Napoli: Liguori, 1990.

[40] D. Grewal, M. Levy, V. Kumar, "Customer experience management in retailing: an organizing framework," in Journal of Retailing, v. 85, 2009, pp. 1-14.

[41] U. S. Grissemann, N. E. Stokburger-Sauer, "Customer co-creation of travel services: The role of company support and customer satisfaction with the co-creation performance," in Tourism Management, v. 33, 2012, pp. 1483-1492.

[42] J. Hartley, K. McWilliam, J. Burgess, J. Banks, "The uses of multimedia: Three digital literacy case studies," in Media International Australia, Incorporating Culture & Policy, n. 128, 2008, pp. 59-72.

[43] R. S. Hartman, "The Hartman Value Profile (HVP): Manual of interpretation, research concepts," Southern Illinois: Muskegon, 1973.

[44] P. Hetzel, "Planète conso: Marketing expérientiel et nouveaux univers de consummation," Paris: Editions d'Organisation, 2002.

[45] B. Higgs, M. J. Polonsky, M. Hollick, "Measuring expectations. Forecast vs. ideal expectations. Does it really matter?," in Journal of Retailing and Consumer Services, v. 12, 2005, pp. 49–64.

[46] S. Hosany, Y. Ekinci, M. Uysal, "Destination image and destination personality: An application of branding theories to tourism places," in Journal of Business Research, v. 59, 2006, pp. 638-642.

[47] J. R. Ritchie, S. Hudson, "Understanding and meeting the challenges of consumer/tourist experience research," in International Journal of Tourism Research, v. 11, 2009, pp. 111-126.

[48] T. K. Hui, D. Wan, A. Ho, "Tourists' satisfaction, recommendation and revisiting Singapore," in Tourism management, v. 28, 2007, pp. 965-975.

[49] J. K. S. Jacobsen, A. M. Munar, "Tourist information search and destination choice in a digital age," in Tourism Management Perspectives, v. 1, 2012, pp. 39-47.

[50] O. H. Jenkins, "Understanding and measuring tourist destination images," in International Journal of Tourism Research, v. 1, 1999, pp. 1-15.

[51] A. M. Kaplan, D. Schoder, M. Haenlein, "Factors influencing the adoption of mass customization: The impact of base category consumption frequency and need satisfaction," in Journal of product innovation management, v. 24, 2007, pp. 101-116.

[52] J. H. Kim, J. S. Chen, "The effects of situational and personal characteristics on consumer complaint behavior in restaurant services," in Journal of Travel & Tourism Marketing, v. 27, 2010, pp. 96-112.

[53] P. Kotler, D. H. Haider, I. Rein, "Marketing Places: Attracting Investment, Industry, and Tourism to Cities, States and Nation," New York: The Free Press, 1993.

[54] M. Kozak, M. Rimmington, "Benchmarking: destination attractiveness and small hospitality business performance," in International Journal of Contemporary Hospitality Management, v. 10, 1998, pp. 184-188.

[55] M. Kozak, M. Rimmington. "Measuring tourist destination competitiveness: conceptual considerations and empirical findings", in International Journal of Hospitality Management, 1999, v.18, pp. 273-283.

[56] M. Kozak, "Repeaters' behaviour at two distinct destination," in Annals of Tourism Research, v. 28, 2001, pp. 784-807.

[57] S. Kruger, C. Rootenberg, C., S. Ellis, "Examining the influence of the wine festival experience on tourists' quality of life," in Social indicators research, v. 111, 2013, pp. 435-452.

[58] V. Kumar, V., J. A. Petersen, "Using a customer-level marketing strategy to enhance firm performance: a review of theoretical and empirical evidence," in Journal of the Academy of Marketing Science, v. 33, 2005, pp. 504-519.

[59] W. Reinartz, J. S. Thomas, V. Kumar, "Balancing acquisition and retention resources to maximize customer profitability," in Journal of Marketing, v. 69, 2005, pp. 63-79.

[60] Y. F. Kuo, C. M. Wu, W. J. Deng, "The relationships among service quality, perceived value, customer satisfaction, and post-purchase intention in mobile value-added services," in Computers in human behavior, v. 25, 2009, pp. 887-896.

[61] S. Y. Lam, V. Shankar, M. K. Erramilli, B. Murthy, "Customer value, satisfaction, loyalty, and switching costs: an illustration from a business-to-business service context," in Journal of the Academy of Marketing Science, v. 32, 2004, pp. 293-311.

[62] D. LaSalle, T. Britton, "Priceless: Turning ordinary products into extraordinary experiences," Harvard: Harvard Business Press, 2003.

[63] R. S. Lazarus, "*Emotion and adaptation,*" Oxford: Oxford University Press, 1991.

[64] G. Lee, J. T. O'Leary, G. S. Hong, "Visiting propensity predicted by destination image: German long-haul pleasure travelers to the US," in International Journal of Hospitality & Tourism Administration, v. 3, 2002, pp. 63-92.

[65] S. Lee, S. Jeon, D. Kim, "The impact of tour quality and tourist satisfaction on tourist loyalty: The case of Chinese tourists in Korea," in Tourism Management, v. 32, 2011, pp. 1115-1124.

[66] B. Loken, B., "Consumer psychology: categorization, inferences, affect, and persuasion," in Annual Review of Psychology, v. 57, 2006, pp. 453-485.

[67] K. A. Machleit, S. P. Mantel, "Emotional response and shopping satisfaction: moderating effects of shopper attributions," in Journal of Business Research, v. 54, 2001, pp. 97-106.

[68] B. Merrilees, D. Miller, C. Herington, "Antecedents of residents' city brand attitudes," in Journal of Business Research, v. 62, 2009, pp. 362-367.

[69] J. Mikulić, D. Prebežac, Evaluating hotel animation programs at Mediterranean sun-and-sea resorts: An impact-asymmetry analysis," in Tourism Management, v. *32*, 2011, pp. 688-696.

[70] F. V. Morgeson III, S. Mithas, T. L. Keiningham, L. Aksoy, "An investigation of the cross-national determinants of customer satisfaction," in Journal of the Academy of Marketing Science, v. 39, 2011, pp.198-215.

[71] R. Nash, M. Thyne, S. Davies, "An investigation into customer satisfaction levels in the budget accommodation sector in Scotland: a case study of backpacker tourists and the Scottish Youth Hostels Association," in Tourism Management, v. 27, 2006, pp. 525-532.

[72] K. Nield, M. Kozak, G. LeGrys, "The role of food service in tourist satisfaction," in International Journal of Hospitality Management, v. 19, 2000, pp. 375-384.

[73] L. Nilsson, M. D. Johnson, A. Gustafsson, "The impact of quality practices on customer satisfaction and business results: product versus service organizations," in Journal of Quality Management, v. 6, 2001, pp. 5-27.

[74] J. C. Nunnally, "*Psychometric Theory*", New York: McGraw-Hill, 1978.

[75] R. L. Oliver, R. S. Winer, "A framework for the formation and structure of consumer expectations: review and propositions," in Journal of Economic Psychology, v. 8, 1987, pp. 469-499.

[76] R. L. Oliver, R. R. Burke, "Expectation Processes in Satisfaction Formation A Field Study," in Journal of Service Research, v. 1, 1999, pp. 196-214.

[77] R. L. Oliver, J. E. Swan, "Consumer perceptions of interpersonal equity and satisfaction in transactions: A field survey approach," in Journal of Marketing, v. 53, 1989, pp. 21-35.

[78] M. Oppermann, "Tourism destination loyalty", Journal of Travel Research, v. 39, 2000, pp. 78-84.

[79] E. Ortega, B. Rodriguez, "Information at tourism destinations. Importance and cross-cultural differences between international and domestic tourists," in Journal of Business Research, v. 60, 2007, pp.146-152.

[80] P. L. Ostrowski, T. V. O'Brien, G. L. Gordon, "Service quality and customer loyalty in the commercial airline industry," in Journal of Travel Research, v. 32, 1993, pp. 16-24.

[81] B. J. Pine, J. H. Gilmore, "*The experience economy,*" Harvard, Harvard Business Press, 2011.

[82] A. Postma, K. A. Jenkins, "Improving the Tourist's Experience: Quality Management applied to Tourist Destinations," in E.P. Murphy Eds., New York: Quality Management in Urban Tourism, Wiley, 1997.

[83] J. Y. Qi, J. P. Zhou, W. J. Chen, Q. X. Qu, "Are customer satisfaction and customer loyalty drivers of customer lifetime value in mobile data services: a comparative cross-country study," in Information Technology and Management, v. 13, 2012, pp. 281-296.

[84] I. R. Del Bosque, H. S. Martín, "Tourist satisfaction a cognitive-affective model," in Annals of Tourism Research, v. 35, 2008, pp. 551-573.

[85] E. L. Dunn Ross, S. E. Iso-Ahola, "Sightseeing tourists' motivation and satisfaction," in Annals of tourism research, v. 18, 1991, pp. 226-237.

[86] R. T. Rust, A. J. Zahorik, T. L. Keiningham, "Return on quality (ROQ): Making service quality financially accountable," in Journal of Marketing , v. 59, 1995, p. 58-70.

[87] M. Konecnik Ruzzier, L. De Chernatony, "Developing and applying a place brand identity model: the case of Slovenia," in Journal of Business Research, v. 66, 2013, pp. 45-52.

[88] B. Trauer, B., C. Ryan, "Destination image, romance and place experience—an application of intimacy theory in tourism," in Tourism Management, v. 26, 2005, pp. 481-491.

[89] F. Selnes, "Antecedents and consequences of trust and satisfaction in buyer-seller relationships," in European Journal of Marketing, v. 32, 1998, pp. 305-322.

[90] C. Shaw, J. Ivens, "Building Great Customer Experiences," London: Prentice-Hall, 2005.

[91] C Shaw, J. Ivens, "Building Great Customer Experiences", Basingstoke: PalgraveMacmillan, 2002.

[92] M. Sherif, C. I. Hovland, "Social judgment: Assimilation and contrast effects in communication and attitude change", Oxford: Yale Univer. Press, 1961.

[93] S. L. Smith, "The tourism product," in Annals of Tourism Research, v. 21, 1998, pp. 582-595.

[94] S. Smith, J. Wheeler, "Managing the customer experience: Turning customers into advocates," Edinburgh Gate: Pearson Education, 2002.

[95] M R. Solomon, "Consumer behavior," Singapore: Prentice-Hall, 1992.

[96] H. Song, R. van der Veen, G. Li, J. L. Chen, "The Hong Kong Tourist Satisfaction Index," in Annals of Tourism Research, v. 39, 2012, pp. 459-479.

[97] R. A. Spreng, C. Dröge, "The impact on satisfaction of managing attribute expectations: should performance claims be understated or overstated?," in Journal of Retailing and Consumer Services, v. 8, 2001, pp. 261-274.

[98] R. M. Stock, "How does product program innovativeness affect customer satisfaction? A comparison of goods and services," in Journal of the Academy of Marketing Science, v. 39, 2011, pp. 813-827.

[99] A. D. Tasci, Y. Boylu, "Cultural comparison of tourists' safety perception in relation to trip satisfaction," in International Journal of Tourism Research, v. 12, 2010, pp. 179-192.

[100] K. Thompson, P. Schofield, "An investigation of the relationship between public transport performance and destination satisfaction", Journal of Transport Geography, v. 15, 2007, pp. 136-144.

[101] J. Tribe, J., T. Snaith, "From SERVQUAL to HOLSAT: holiday satisfaction in Varadero, Cuba," in Tourism Management, v. 19, 1998, pp. 25-34.

[102] M. D. Uncles, R. East, W. Lomax, "Good customers: The value of customers by mode of acquisition," in Australasian Marketing Journal, v. 21, 2013, pp. 119-125.

[103] A. Usakli, S. Baloglu, "Brand personality of tourist destinations: An application of self-congruity theory," in Tourism Management, v. 32, 2011, pp. 114-127.

[104] M. Uysal, C. Jurowski, "Testing the push and pull factors," in Annals of Tourism Research, v. 21, 1994, pp. 844-846.

[105] W. Van Dolen, K. De Ruyter, J. Lemmink, (2004), "An empirical assessment of the influence of customer emotions and contact employee performance on encounter and relationship satisfaction," in Journal of Business Research, v. 57, 2004, pp. 437-444.

[106] S. Veasna, W. Wu, C. Huang, "The impact of destination source credibility on destination satisfaction: The mediating effects of destination attachment and destination image," in Tourism Management, v. 36, 2013, pp. 511-526.

[107] F. Vetter, "Critères de definition du tourisme des grandes métropoles," in F. Vetter (Ed.), Big City Tourism, Berlin: Dietrich Reimer Verlag, 1985.

[108] R. Voase, "Recognition, reputation and response: Some critical thoughts on destinations and brand," in Journal of Destination Marketing & Management, v. 1, 2012, pp. 78-83.

[109] G. Walsh, V. W. Mitchell, P. R. Jackson, S. E. Beatty, "Examining the antecedents and consequences of corporate reputation: a customer perspective," in British Journal of Management, v. 20, 2009, pp. 187-203.

[110] Y. K. P. Wan, S. H. J. Chan, "Factors that Affect the Levels of Tourists' Satisfaction and Loyalty towards Food Festivals: a Case Study of Macau," in International Journal of Tourism Research, v. 15, 2013, pp. 226-240.

[111] Y. Wang, H. P. Lo, Y. Yang, "An integrated framework for service quality, customer value, satisfaction: evidence from China's telecommunication industry," in Information Systems Frontiers, v. 6, 2004, pp. 325-340.

[112] R. A. Westbrook, R. L. Oliver, "The dimensionality of consumption emotion patterns and consumer satisfaction," in Journal of consumer research, v. 18, 1991, pp. 84-91.

[113] W. Xia, Z. Jie, G. Chaolin, Z. Feng, "Examining Antecedents and Consequences of Tourist Satisfaction: A Structural Modeling Approach," in Tsinghua Science and Technology, v. 14, 2009, pp. 397-406.

[114] Z. Yang, R. T. Peterson, "Customer perceived value, satisfaction, and loyalty: the role of switching costs," in Psychology & Marketing, v. 21, 2004, pp. 799-822.

[115] S. Yastrow, "Brand Harmony: Achieving Dynamic Results by Orchestrating Your Customer's Total Experience," New York: SelectBooks, Inc., 2003.

[116] Y. Yoon, M. Uysal, "An examination of the effects of motivation and satisfaction on destination loyalty: a structural model," in Tourism management, v. 26, 2005, pp. 45-56.

[117] Y. T. Yu, A. Dean, "The contribution of emotional satisfaction to consumer loyalty," in International journal of service industry Management, v. 12, 2001, pp. 234-250.

[118] L. Yu, L., M. Goulden, "A comparative analysis of international tourists' satisfaction in Mongolia," in Tourism Management, vol. 27, 2006, pp. 1331-1342.

[119] L. Zhao, Y. Lu, L. Zhang, P. Y. Chau, "Assessing the effects of service quality and justice on customer satisfaction and the continuance intention of mobile value-added services: An empirical test of a multidimensional model," in Decision Support Systems, v. 52, pp. 645-656.

Permissions

All chapters in this book were first published in JIM, by Science Publishing Group; hereby published with permission under the Creative Commons Attribution License or equivalent. Every chapter published in this book has been scrutinized by our experts. Their significance has been extensively debated. The topics covered herein carry significant findings which will fuel the growth of the discipline. They may even be implemented as practical applications or may be referred to as a beginning point for another development.

The contributors of this book come from diverse backgrounds, making this book a truly international effort. This book will bring forth new frontiers with its revolutionizing research information and detailed analysis of the nascent developments around the world.

We would like to thank all the contributing authors for lending their expertise to make the book truly unique. They have played a crucial role in the development of this book. Without their invaluable contributions this book wouldn't have been possible. They have made vital efforts to compile up to date information on the varied aspects of this subject to make this book a valuable addition to the collection of many professionals and students.

This book was conceptualized with the vision of imparting up-to-date information and advanced data in this field. To ensure the same, a matchless editorial board was set up. Every individual on the board went through rigorous rounds of assessment to prove their worth. After which they invested a large part of their time researching and compiling the most relevant data for our readers.

The editorial board has been involved in producing this book since its inception. They have spent rigorous hours researching and exploring the diverse topics which have resulted in the successful publishing of this book. They have passed on their knowledge of decades through this book. To expedite this challenging task, the publisher supported the team at every step. A small team of assistant editors was also appointed to further simplify the editing procedure and attain best results for the readers.

Apart from the editorial board, the designing team has also invested a significant amount of their time in understanding the subject and creating the most relevant covers. They scrutinized every image to scout for the most suitable representation of the subject and create an appropriate cover for the book.

The publishing team has been an ardent support to the editorial, designing and production team. Their endless efforts to recruit the best for this project, has resulted in the accomplishment of this book. They are a veteran in the field of academics and their pool of knowledge is as vast as their experience in printing. Their expertise and guidance has proved useful at every step. Their uncompromising quality standards have made this book an exceptional effort. Their encouragement from time to time has been an inspiration for everyone.

The publisher and the editorial board hope that this book will prove to be a valuable piece of knowledge for researchers, students, practitioners and scholars across the globe.

List of Contributors

Christos Zilidis
Department of Medical Laboratories, Technological University (TEI) of Thessaly, Larissa, Greece

Catherine Kastanioti
Department of Businesses' and Organizations' Administration, Technological University (TEI) of Peloponnese, Kalamata, Greece

Nikos Polyzos
Department of Social Administration and Political Sciences, Democritus University of Thrace (DUTH), Komotini, Greece

John Yfantopoulos
Department of Political Sciences and Public Administration, National (Capodestrian) University of Athens (EKPA), Athens, Greece

Joseph Yensu, Edmond Oppong-Peprah, Elizabeth Dwomo-Fokuo, Francis Boadu and Anthony Kusi
Institute of Entrepreneurship and Enterprise Development, Kumasi Polytechnic, Kumasi, Ghana

Adela Mariana Vadastreanu
National Institute of Research and Development for Isotopic and Molecular Technologies, Cluj Napoca, Technical University of Cluj Napoca, Romania

Adrian Bot
National Institute of Research and Development for Isotopic and Molecular Technologies, Cluj Napoca, Romania

Dorin Maier and Andreea Maier
Technical University of Cluj Napoca, Romania and University of Economic Studies, Bucharest, Romania

Afrin Rifat
Department of Accounting and Finance, School of Business and Economics, North South University, Dhaka, Bangladesh

Giuseppe Tardivo
Department of Management, University of Turin, Turin, Italy

Zeynep Topaloglu
Department of Banking and Finance, Bursa Orhangazi University, Bursa, Turkey

Nwosa Philip Ifeakachukwu
Department of Economics, Accounting and Finance College of Management Sciences, Bells University of Technology, Ota, Ogun State

Jun Dong, Huijuan Huo*
School of Economics and Management, North China Electric Power University, Beijing, China

Gabriele Santoro
Department of Management, University of Turin, Turin, Italy

Milena Viassone
Department of Management, University of Turin, Turin, Italy

Martin Grimmer
Tasmanian School of Business and Economics, University of Tasmania, Hobart, Australia

Carlo Felice Maggi
Dept. of Management, University of Turin, Turin, Italy

Michela Avataneo
Graduate in "Economia e Direzione Delle Imprese", University of Turin, Turin, Italy

Filippo Monge
Department of Economia e Statistica "Cognetti de Martis", University of Turin, Turin, Italy

Daniele Cattaneo and Angela Scilla
Department of Management, University of Turin, Turin, Italy

Md. Nazirul Islam Sarker
School of Business, Bangladesh Open University, Gazipur, Bangladesh

Md. Harun Or Rashid
Department of Management, University of Dhaka, Dhaka, Bangladesh

Grace Melissa Akenga, Margaret Akinyi Olang and Nebat Mugenda Galo
Department of Business Administration, Chuka University, Chuka, Kenya

Fredrick Omondi Ogonda
Master of Business Administration Graduate, School of Business, Kenyatta University, Nairobi City, Kenya

Bula Hannah Orwa, Wambua Philip Peter and Muli Vika Jedida
Human Resource Management, Department of Business Administration, School of Business, Kenyatta University, Nairobi City, Kenya

Fausto Galetto
Industrial Quality Management, Politecnico Di Torino, Turin, Italy

Jean Paul Lemaire
ESCP Europe, Paris, France

Milena Viassone
Department of Management, University of Turin, Turin, Italy

Alberto Marino
Department of Management Science, Economics and Quantitative Methods, University of Bergamo, Bergamo, Italy

Fatemeh Mirzaie
Tourism Management, Non-profit Institution of Higher Education, ABA, Abyek, Qazvin, Iran

Ali Akbar Nazari
Administrator of Non-profit Institution of Higher Education, ABA, Abyek, Qazvin, Iran

Hamid Zargham Boroujeni
Department of Tourism Management, Allameh Tabatabaie University, Tehran, Iran

Mohammad Taghipour
Research Assistant of Non-profit Institution of Higher Education, ABA, Abyek, Qazvin, Iran

Huiqun Liu
School of Economics, Tianjin University of Commerce, Tianjin, China

Valentina Della Corte, Mauro Sciarelli, Clelia Cascella and Giovanna Del Gaudio
Department of Economics, Management, Institutions, University of Naples Federico II, Naples, Italy

Index